NORTHERN
CALIFORNIA
Road Trips

WITHDRAWN

STUART THORNTON & KAYLA ANDERSON

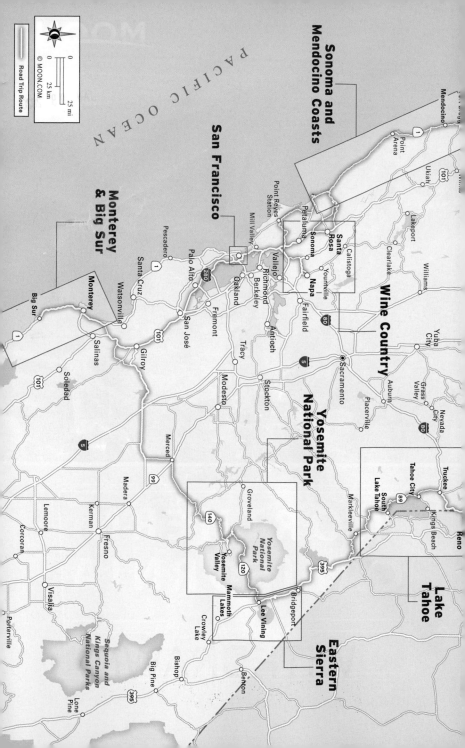

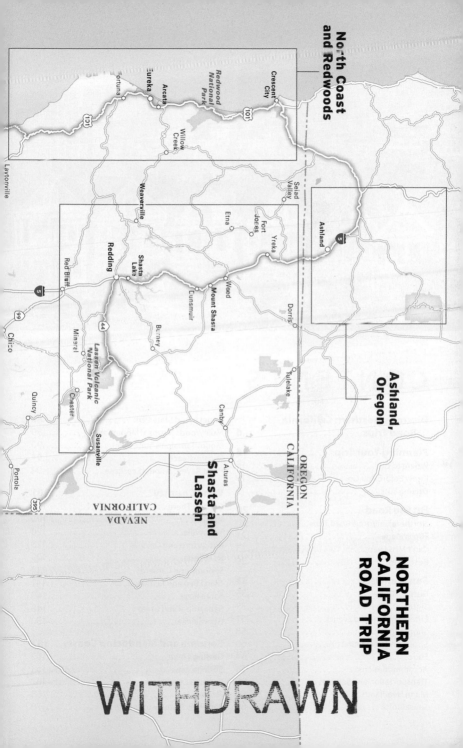

NORTHERN
CALIFORNIA
ROAD TRIP

WITHDRAWN

CONTENTS

DISCOVER
Northern California Road Trips

In Northern California, humankind takes a backseat to nature. This is a region dominated by skyscraping redwood trees, forest-cloaked mountains, driftwood-decorated beaches, snow-frosted peaks, naturally occurring hot springs, and lakes as blue as the sky above. Here, adjectives like "largest," "biggest," "deepest," "tallest," and "highest" frequently precede beaches and bays and falls and forests. This is California at its wildest, its most elemental, its purest.

Less developed, and less visited, than the southern part of the state, Northern California is where you can experience hours alone on a mountain peak or time in the depths of a silent redwood forest. From cosmopolitan San Francisco, roads wind north through the famous Wine Country, where the hillsides are braided with grapevines. Along the coast, the trees become taller and the crowds become smaller. The California coast bleeds inland into Southern Oregon and the foodie-friendly town of Ashland before bending south into the majesty of Northern California's inland mountain ranges. The sparkling blue waters of Tahoe, the snowcapped volcanic peaks of Mounts Shasta and Lassen, the high Sierra of Yosemite, and the low desert valleys lie to the east.

The northern coast and the Sierra Nevada are dotted with distinct communities like Mendocino, Arcata, and Trinidad on the coast, Mount Shasta city and Ashland, Oregon inland, and Bishop in the Eastern Sierra, offering an opportunity for exploration off the beaten path. Taste the fruits of this less developed land, from grass-fed Humboldt beef to Tomales Bay oysters to Napa wines and small craft breweries.

Wherever the road takes you, you'll return home with tales of the wild and rugged land to the north.

10 TOP EXPERIENCES

1 **Wander Along the Beach:** Windy, rocky, and elemental, northern beaches expose the power of the sea along a majestic coastline (pages 167 and 182).

2 **Feast on Seafood:** The fish and shellfish of the Northern California coast are some of the freshest and tastiest food you'll find (page 254).

3 **Hike Amid Redwoods:** Crane your neck at the skyscraping redwoods in the Redwood State and National Parks (page 243).

4 **Circle the Rim Drive:** Circumnavigate the rim of a sunken caldera in Oregon's Crater Lake National Park (page 284).

5 **Explore a Volcanic Landscape:** Boardwalk paths lead past boiling mud pots and steaming streams in Lassen Volcanic National Park (page 349).

<<<

^
^
^
6 **Paddle Tahoe's Waters:** Kayak the lake's cobalt-blue waters to the granite rocks on Fannette Island, perched in the middle of Emerald Bay (page 381).

^
^
^

7 **Taste Local Wine and Craft Beer:** Some of the world's best wines and craft beers are produced in Napa and Sonoma (page 111) and in Humboldt County on the North Coast (page 235).

8 **Admire Fall Foliage:** Walk through Lundy Canyon in the Eastern Sierra as the quaking aspens turn from leafy green to brilliant gold (page 445).

9 **Cross the High Sierra:** Yosemite's Tioga Pass Road passes through an alpine landscape, with stops at Tuolumne Meadows (page 501).

10 **Cruise the Big Sur Coast Highway:** This twisty, two-lane highway follows one of the world's most dramatic coastlines (page 557).

PLANNING YOUR TRIP

Where to Go

San Francisco

Located on a hilly peninsula between San Francisco Bay and the Pacific Ocean, San Francisco is one of the most beautiful cities in the world. Add in a renowned **food scene, world-class museums,** a healthy **arts culture,** and iconic attractions like the **Golden Gate Bridge** and **Alcatraz Island** for a mandatory stop on any serious road trip.

Wine Country

For oenophiles, no trip to Northern California is complete without an excursion to the state's renowned Wine Country. Though the main draw is sampling wines at their source, **Napa** and **Sonoma Valleys** offer multiple ways to spoil yourself, including spas, fine hotels, revered restaurants, and understated natural beauty.

Sonoma and Mendocino

For deserted beaches, towering redwoods, and scenic coastal towns, cruise north along the Sonoma and Mendocino coasts. Explore Russian history at **Fort Ross** on the grassy bluffs of the **Sonoma Coast,** and fall in love with **Mendocino**'s small-town charm and nearby wineries.

North Coast and Redwoods

Of all the natural wonders California has to offer, the one that seems to inspire the purest and most unmitigated awe is the **coast redwood.** The two best places to experience extensive wild groves of these gargantuan treasures are **Jedediah Smith Redwoods State Park** and **Prairie Creek Redwoods State Park,** north of **Arcata** and **Eureka.**

Ashland and Crater Lake

Dipping into **Southern Oregon,** take a detour to drive up to picturesque Crater Lake and take in views from all angles along the Rim Drive. Drive back down to **Ashland** and enjoy the eccentric culture and dining near Lithia Park and live performances during the Oregon Shakespeare Festival.

Shasta and Lassen

The **Volcanic Legacy Scenic Byway** connects the dormant Mount Shasta and Mount Lassen, acting as route markers between the north and the east, as well as playgrounds for outdoor adventure enthusiasts. For powerful cascading waterfalls, stop by the McArthur-Burney Falls to admire the gushing falls.

Lake Tahoe

Lake Tahoe acts as a reprieve from the smoldering heat of the summer. The refreshingly crisp and blue water attracts boaters, **stand-up paddleboarders,** and boat cruises on the **MS** Dixie II or Tahoe Gal. Marvel at this natural environment from the viewpoint at Emerald Bay or the jutting big granite boulders on the **East Shore.** The dozen or so **ski resorts** also make it a popular destination in winter.

Eastern Sierra

The drive south through the **high desert** offers spectacular views, especially when the surrounding mountains are snowcapped. The saline Mono Lake is a sight to see, with hundreds of migrating birds and jagged tufa towers. Bodie State Historic Park is a preserved ghost town from the old mining days. Farther south, Mammoth Mountain is a big draw for skiers and snowboarders in winter and hikers in summer.

Yosemite

Yosemite National Park showcases the stunning Sierra Nevada at its rugged best. Wander amid **sequoia groves, granite**

Clockwise from top left: San Francisco's Palace of Fine Arts; Monterey Bay; Yosemite Valley.

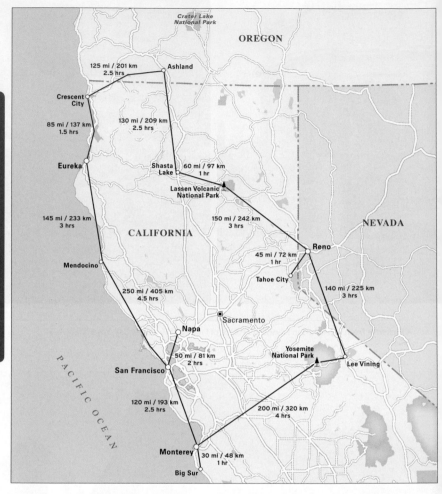

peaks, and mountain lakes to national treasures like Half Dome and El Capitan.

Monterey and Big Sur

Stunning coastal views will fill your windshield as you drive along a stretch of the Pacific Coast Highway. Seaside sights include the Monterey Bay Aquarium before the winding roadway hits its peak passing through the mountains of Big Sur, dramatically perched above the ocean.

Know Before You Go

High Season

Northern California's best feature is its all-season appeal. That said, this trip is best in the **summer** and **early fall**, when most roads will be open. Be aware that summer brings the most visitors, which will not only add to the crowds at attractions along the way, but also add to the traffic on the highways. Summer crowds are more prevalent in San Francisco, Yosemite National Park, Monterey, and Big Sur, while the North Coast gets fewer visitors than other coastal regions. Plan a little extra time to get from place to place anyway.

The easiest places to **fly** into are **San Francisco, Sacramento,** and **Reno, Nevada.** If you're flying into San Francisco, you can avoid some of the hassle of San Francisco International Airport (SFO) by flying into nearby **Oakland** or **San Jose.**

Advance Reservations

Book **hotels** and **rental cars** in advance for the best rates and availability, especially in the summer, which is high season for travel.

High-season travelers should also plan ahead for the **big-name attractions.** If you have your heart set on visiting **Alcatraz** in San Francisco or the **Hearst Castle** in San Simeon, purchase tickets at least two weeks in advance. Reservations are essential at **campgrounds** in Yosemite and along Big Sur. If you plan to stay at the historic **Majestic Yosemite Hotel** or dine in its restaurant, make reservations as far in advance as possible.

What to Pack

Bring **layered clothing.** Summer fog is likely along the California coast, and is pretty much guaranteed in San Francisco, making the air damp and chilly. No matter what, use **sunscreen;** that cold fog doesn't stop the rays from burning unwary beachcombers.

Coming to the United States from abroad? You'll need your **passport** and possibly a **visa.**

Driving Tips

San Francisco, **Sacramento**, and the section of US-101 passing through Santa Rosa suffer from serious **traffic congestion.** Avoid driving in or through these areas during rush hour traffic, typically weekdays 7am-9am and 4pm-6pm, though serious congestion can occur at other times. Of course, special events can create traffic jams on weekends. To view current traffic conditions in the San Francisco Bay Area, visit www.511.org.

Because it's located in the high-altitude Sierra Nevada, **access to Yosemite** is dependent on the weather and the seasons. Two of the most traveled roads in the park, **Tioga Road** and **Glacier Point Road,** are typically **closed November-early June.** In recent years, **forest fires** have occurred in the park and surrounding areas, limiting access in the summer and fall as well. Check for road conditions and closures online at www.nps.gov/yose.

Fires and landslides can also impede a drive along the **Pacific Coast Highway,** especially through **Big Sur.** Visit the **Caltrans website** (www.dot.ca.gov) for highway conditions throughout California.

Cell phone reception is limited or nonexistent in large sections of Yosemite and along the Pacific Coast Highway through Big Sur.

HIT THE ROAD

Northern California Road Trips

Explore Northern California on this 21-day route or break the trip up into multiple getaways that can be combined for one or more road trips. For detailed driving directions for each leg of this road trip, see **Getting There** at the beginning of each chapter. All mileage and driving times are approximate.

San Francisco and Wine Country
DAYS 1-2: SAN FRANCISCO
It's easy to fill two days with fun in San Francisco. On the first day, visit the foodie-friendly **Ferry Building,** then walk down the **Embarcadero** to the ferry that will take you out to **Alcatraz.** For dinner, indulge in Vietnamese fare at **The Slanted Door** or the old-school elegance of **Tadich Grill.**

On your second day, head west to **Golden Gate Park,** where you can explore the art of the **de Young Museum** or the animals at the **California Academy of Sciences.** Visit the **Japanese Tea Garden** for tea and a snack before leaving the park. Spend the afternoon at the **San Francisco Museum of Modern Art** before dining at its touted on-site restaurant **In Situ.**

Rest your head at the tech-savvy **Hotel Zetta,** homey **Golden Gate Hotel,** or **Hotel G** with its three dining and drinking establishments. For more suggestions on how to spend your time in San Francisco, see page 38.

DAY 3: SAN FRANCISCO TO WINE COUNTRY
40 mi/65 km, 1 hr
About 40 miles (64 km) north of San Francisco is the Wine Country of Sonoma, where fine food and wine are served alongside some of the state's most interesting history. Our journey north begins with a drive on US-101 over San Francisco's iconic **Golden Gate Bridge** to the charming little city of **Sonoma.** Upon arrival, explore the historic buildings of **Sonoma State Historic Park,** which includes Mexican-era barracks and the last mission built in California. Make sure to walk over to **Sonoma Plaza** to check out the bronze statue memorializing the **Bear Flag Revolt,** the site of an American rebellion against the Mexican government that established a short-lived independent republic for just 25 days in 1846. Then have lunch at the iconic **the girl & the fig.**

After lunch, drive north on CA-12 to the tiny hamlet of **Glen Ellen.** Fans of the writer Jack London should not miss **Jack London State Park,** a 1,400-acre property that was the author's home in the early 1900s. Hike to **Wolf House,** the haunting stone ruins of London's dream house that burned down in 1913 before he even moved in. Swap stories at the nearby **Valley of the Moon Winery,** itself a historic site where wine has been made since the Civil War era. End the evening with a stay at Glen Ellen's **Gaige House & Ryokan.**

Coastal Cruise
DAY 4: WINE COUNTRY TO JENNER
50 mi/80 km, 1.5 hr
The drive from **Glen Ellen** to Jenner has a few stops that could easily take half a day. Follow CA-12 north along the Valley of the Moon, a scenic wine region on the way to **Santa Rosa,** Northern California's largest city. Beer lovers should stop at the **Russian River Brewing Company** for one of their fabled Pliny the Elder pints and lunch at **The Spinster Sisters.**

Take scenic CA-116 west as it twists and turns alongside the **Russian River** on its way to the coast at **Jenner.** If hunger strikes, make a pit stop in the riverside community of **Guerneville** for a

Top Wineries

one of the Anderson Valley's many vineyards

There are wine-tasting opportunities all over Northern California. Most notable is **Napa Valley** and its world-renowned wineries. **Grgich Hills Winery** (page 126) is the winery that put Napa Valley on the map with a win at the Paris Wine Tasting of 1976. It's still known for its chardonnay. **Mumm** (page 126) produces sparkling wines worth a taste even for wine purists. **Clos Pegase** (page 133) mixes in some culture with its wine, with more than 100 artworks on the grounds, including sculptor Henry Moore's *Mother Earth* and a painting by Francis Bacon.

In nearby **Sonoma County,** taste wine with a side of history or music. **Valley of the Moon Winery** (page 142) in Glen Ellen has been producing wine since the Civil War era, while **Gundlach Bundschu** (page 138) hosts big-time indie rock acts (Angel Olsen, Future Islands, Mac DeMarco) at its on-site amphitheater or inside its redwood barn. **Dr. Wilkinson's Hot Springs Resort** (page 133) has an on-site spa.

The **Anderson Valley Wine Trail** (page 192) is a great place to taste pinot noirs and sparkling wines in a rural atmosphere. Both **Navarro Vineyards** (page 192) and **Toulouse Vineyards** (page 192) are known for their gewürztraminer, an aromatic white wine.

South of the Bay Area, **Carmel-by-the-Sea** has a cluster of wine-tasting rooms in its charming, walkable downtown. Head to **Caraccioli Cellars Tasting Room** (page 547) for a high-end experience of tasting their popular brut and brut rosé. Less upscale is the **Scheid Vineyards Carmel-by-the-Sea Tasting Room** (page 548), where you can sip claret and a cabernet sauvignon-syrah mix in a relaxed atmosphere.

Just inland from Carmel-by-the-Sea, **Carmel Valley** is where the vineyards are located. The unassuming **Carmel Valley Village** has tasting rooms pouring some of the region's best wines. **Boekenoogen Vineyard & Winery** (page 554) has a garden patio, where you can sip their pinot noir, chardonnay, or syrah on sunny days. Nearby, **I Brand & Family Winery** (page 554) produces three different labels at three prices, so it can satisfy wine drinkers with all sorts of incomes.

heavenly biscuit at **Big Bottom Market.** At the coastline, take in the majesty of the Pacific Ocean from one of the many access points in **Sonoma Coast State Park.** End the day with a view of the Russian River and a fine meal at **River's End.** Spend the night in one of the **River's End**'s five rustic cabins or at the more upscale **Timber Cove Resort.**

DAY 5: JENNER TO MENDOCINO
90 mi/145 km, 2.5 hr

The drive along CA-1 up the coast is winding, beautiful, and time consuming, so be sure to take in the many sights on trip from Jenner to Mendocino. Stop at the tiny but unique **Sea Ranch Chapel,** mere feet from the highway, and take a more extended break in **Point Arena.** Snap a photo of the distinctive rocks at **Bowling Ball Beach,** take a hike in the **Point Arena-Stornetta Unit** of the California Coastal National Monument, or get a baked good at **Franny's Cup & Saucer.**

End the day in the community of **Mendocino** with a view of the sunset at **Mendocino Headlands State Park** or a pint at the lively **Patterson's Pub** or at the one-of-a-kind dive bar **Dick's Place.** Spoil yourself with a night at the upscale B&B **Brewery Gulch Inn** or **The Andiron.**

DAY 6: MENDOCINO TO ARCATA
150 mi/240 km, 3.5 hr

Drive north on CA-1 toward **Fort Bragg,** where the road turns inland to connect with US-101. Hop off the highway for a scenic cruise along the redwood-lined **Avenue of the Giants.** Get back on US-101 and head north to **Eureka.** Stop to wander the city's Old Town and waterfront, then have lunch at **Brick & Fire Bistro.**

Continue north on US-101 to charming **Arcata.** Wander through the redwoods of the **Arcata Community Forest** before sundown, then dine at one of the restaurants surrounding the lively **Arcata**

Plaza and follow it with a craft beer at **Redwood Curtain Brewing Company** (the delicious Imperial Golden Ale is recommended). Spend the night at the no-frills **Hotel Arcata.**

DAY 7: ARCATA TO CRESCENT CITY
80 mi/130 km, 2 hr

Start your morning with a tasty crepe from Arcata's **Renata's Creperie and Espresso** before hitting US-101 north on your final day on the coast. North of Arcata, exit to explore the scenic coastal city of **Trinidad.** Have your camera handy for photos of **Trinidad Head** and **Trinidad State Beach.** If you're hungry, a lunch of creative comfort food awaits at **The Lighthouse Grill.**

Continue north on US-101 for 26 miles, turning onto Newton B. Drury Scenic Parkway to explore **Prairie Creek Redwoods State Park.** If you have the energy, drive out Davison Road to **Gold Bluffs Beach,** where Roosevelt elk roam the sands. You can continue the dirt drive to stop and hike the **Fern Canyon Trail,** which passes through a steep canyon draped in bright green ferns.

Return to US-101 and drive 38 miles (61 km) to **Crescent City,** with a beer, a meal, and live music at **SeaQuake Brewing.**

A Weekend in Oregon
DAY 8: CRESCENT CITY TO
ASHLAND, OREGON
125 mi/200 km, 2.5 hr

From Crescent City, take US-199 north to **Cave Junction** and stop for a good deal on an unusually sliced pizza at the **Wild River Brewing and Pizza Company.** Continue north for 30 miles (48 km) through evergreens and burled trees to **Grants Pass.** Visit the famous **Harry & David** country store to try some samples, buy souvenirs, and go on a factory tour. From here, detour east on OR-238 through **Applegate Valley,** stopping by the **Applegate Valley Lavender Farm** or one of the few valley wineries.

Can't-Miss Events

a Chevy Bel Air at Kool April Nites

♦ **Hardly Strictly Bluegrass, San Francisco:** Every October, the best Americana music artists perform for free in Golden Gate Park (page 58).

♦ **Kinetic Grand Championship, Humboldt County:** There's no better celebration of Humboldt County's eclectic individualism than this event held over three days in May (page 222).

♦ **Broadway Under the Stars, Glen Ellen:** Every summer, Jack London State Historic Park hosts four Broadway-inspired musicals in the stone ruins of a former winery (page 143).

♦ **Oregon Shakespeare Festival, Ashland:** This summer festival brings in some of the best actors and dramatists to recreate beloved works by William Shakespeare (page 275).

♦ **Kool April Nites, Redding:** In April, restored classic cars cruise the streets in a celebration of automotive nostalgia (page 334).

♦ **SnowGlobe Festival, South Lake Tahoe:** This annual electronic music festival caters to fans of Burning Man for three days in December (page 387).

♦ **Mammoth Motocross, Mammoth Lakes:** In June, watch the country's top dirt-bike riders race around an artificial track filled with jumps, berms, and varying terrain (page 463).

♦ **Monterey Jazz Festival, Monterey:** Since 1958, the longest-running jazz festival in the world has hosted every major jazz music musician at this September event (page 531).

♦ **Big Sur International Marathon, Big Sur:** Considered the most scenic marathon in the world, this event begins in April in the Big Sur Valley and ends north in Carmel (page 566).

Continue east on OR-238 to **Jacksonville** and explore the old-time buildings of this gold rush era town. Drive 17 miles (27 km) on OR-238 to I-5 and **Ashland**. Have a glass of wine and lamb *sambousek* (fried stuffed pastry) at the **Brickroom**. If it's still light outside, walk through **Lithia Park** and then spend the night at the **Ashland Springs Hotel**.

DAY 9: ASHLAND AND CRATER LAKE

In the morning, get breakfast at the **Breadboard** then drive 75 miles (121 km) northeast to **Crater Lake National Park.** Follow the **Rim Drive** around the lake for incredible views of the geologic wonder. End at the **Rim Village Café** and visitors center, where you can have a chicken teriyaki bowl for lunch. Spend the night camping in the park's **Mazama Campground** or drive to Medford and stay at the **Sovana Inn.**

A Week in the Sierra

DAY 10: ASHLAND TO MOUNT SHASTA
75 mi/120 km, 1.5 hr

Mount Shasta is just on the other side of the Oregon-California border. From Ashland, head south on I-5 for 67 miles (108 km), stopping at the **Hi-Lo Café** in **Weed** for breakfast. Continue south on I-5 to the city of **Mount Shasta** for incredible views of the **massive volcanic peak** covered in snow. Hike the trail on the mountain or head to **Mt. Shasta Bike Park** to enjoy biking the groomed trails.

Several campgrounds line the **Everitt Highway** at the base of Mount Shasta. Or, head back into town to have a reasonably priced meal at the **Black Bear Diner.** Finish your night off at **The Gold Room** for a cocktail before bedding down at the **Inn at Mount Shasta.**

DAY 11: MOUNT SHASTA TO LASSEN
95 mi/150 km, 2 hr

Wake up in Mount Shasta and take CA-89 (the Volcanic Legacy Scenic Byway) 12 miles (19 km) east. Stop in the town of **McCloud** for a refreshing lavender iced tea at **Clearwater Coffee & Kitchen** and consider renting a stand-up paddleboard or a kayak next door at the **McCloud Outdoors & Gear Exchange.** As you drive through the pleasantly sleepy town, say hi to Floyd at **Floyd's Frosty.**

Head southeast on CA-89 for 44 miles (71 km). The scenic two-lane road winds through mountainous terrain and past wild rivers. Stop at **McArthur-Burney Falls Memorial State Park** or do a short hike nearby. Continue 30 miles (48 km) south to the northern entrance of **Lassen Volcanic National Park.** Make a quick stop at the **Loomis Museum** before pressing south to camp at either **Manzanita Lake** or **Summit Lake.**

DAY 12: LASSEN VOLCANIC NATIONAL PARK

Grab a light breakfast at the **Manzanita Lake Camper Store,** then get onto **Manzanita Lake** for a quick paddleboard session. Drive south through the park, taking in the highlights and stopping to hike to the top of **Lassen Peak.** The beauty and the views make the effort worthwhile. Near the south end of the park is **Sulphur Works,** where you can view boiling mud pots right from the road.

Before exiting the park, dip into the **Kohm Yah-mah-nee Visitors Center** and pick up some sundries at **Lassen Café & Gift.** Head east for 12 miles (19 km) on CA-36 to stay at **Mill Creek Resort** or the **St. Bernard Lodge.** Both family-friendly places have small restaurants.

DAY 13: LASSEN TO TAHOE
200 mi/320 km, 3.5 hr

Stop at **Cravings Cafe** in **Chester** for a delectable latte, breakfast, and reading materials. Take CA-36 east for 35 miles (56 km) to **Susanville** where you can fill up on gas and eat at the **Lassen Ale Works at the Pioneer.** Stretch your legs on the **Bizz Johnson Trail** before continuing south on US-395 for 88 miles (142 km) to **Reno, Nevada,** and I-80 back into California.

Clockwise from top left: Yosemite Falls; Mt. Shasta; Prairie Creek Redwoods State Park.

Take I-80 west for 38 miles (61 km) to **Truckee.** Visit the **Donner Memorial State Park,** grab a bite at **Jax at the Tracks,** and do some window shopping. From I-80, take CA-89 south for about 20 miles (32 km) to sleep at the **Pepper Tree Inn** in the heart of **Tahoe City.**

DAY 14: TAHOE

It takes about an hour to drive the 72-mile circumference of Lake Tahoe; you'll want to make a day of it. In Tahoe City, stop to get a coffee at **Tahoe House Bakery & Gourmet.** Head southwest on CA-89 for a scenic drive around the lake. Take a quick hike up **Eagle Rock,** where you can take in panoramic views of the lake. Continue south for another 20 miles (32 km) to **Emerald Bay** and tour the historic **Vikingsholm** mansion.

After taking in the views, drive 20 miles (32 km) south to **South Lake Tahoe** and stop at **Free Bird Café** for a housemade chai tea. In another 5 miles (8 km) you'll pass **Stateline, Nevada,** on the California-Nevada border. Climb aboard the **MS Dixie II** in Zephyr Cove to enjoy the views of the mountain vistas from the water, then drive 22 miles (35 km) north along the **East Shore** through **Cave Rock** and into Incline Village. Have dinner at **Crosby's Tavern & Gaming** and stay the night at the **Tahoe Biltmore** in Crystal Bay or the **Hyatt Regency Lake Tahoe** in **Incline Village.**

DAY 15: TAHOE TO YOSEMITE
125 mi/201 km, 3 hr

Backtrack to Stateline from Incline Village, following Highway 28 south for 12 miles (19 km). Turn left (east) onto US-50 and drive 10 miles (16 km) to US-395 south of Carson City, Nevada. Head south on U.S. 395 for 87 miles (140 km) to **Bridgeport** and stop for a meal at the historic **Bridgeport Inn.** If you have time to spare, detour to **Bodie State Historic Park.** Continue south on US-395 to **Mono Lake** and walk among the tufa towers on the south shore. Buy camping supplies, souvenirs, and firewood at the **Tioga Gas Mart** in **Lee Vining,** then take CA-120 east (summer only) toward the **Tioga Pass Entrance** to **Yosemite.**

DAY 16: YOSEMITE VALLEY

Drive west along Tioga Pass into **Yosemite National Park.** Snap pics of the alpine **Tuolumne Meadows** and stop at **Tenaya Lake** to enjoy the views of the expansive granite rock towering above the crystalline waters. Drive east on Tioga Pass Road to **Crane Flat,** where you'll head south on Big Oak Flat Road into **Yosemite Valley.** Park your car and use the park shuttle to see **Half Dome, El Capitan,** and **Yosemite Falls.** If you want to break a sweat, hike the **Mist Trail,** then refuel at **Degnan's Kitchen.**

If you've made reservations months in advance, then spend the night under the stars at one of the park **campgrounds** or enjoy a night indoors at the classic **Majestic Yosemite Hotel** (make reservations well in advance). If you don't have reservations, try the **Rush Creek Lodge,** 1.5 miles (2 km) west of Yosemite's Big Oak Flat Entrance.

Monterey and Big Sur
DAY 17: YOSEMITE TO MONTEREY
200 mi/320 km, 4.5 hr

It's a long drive across the interior of the state. Plan half a day to reach Monterey from Yosemite Valley. Exit the park via the **Arch Rock Entrance** (CA-140). You'll follow the route west along various stretches of CA-140, CA-59, CA-152, CA-156, and CA-1. Stop for lunch or a snack at **Casa de Fruta** past Pacheco Pass.

Reach **Monterey** in time to watch the sun set over the harbor while eating calamari and sand dabs at **The Sandbar & Grill.** Spend the night in downtown Monterey at the **Portola Hotel & Spa** or opt for a romantic bayside evening at the **Spindrift Inn.**

DAY 18: MONTEREY

Make sure to spend the morning

Clockwise from top left: McWay Falls in Julia Pfeiffer Burns State Park; Point Lobos State Natural Reserve; *Princess Monterey* Whale Watching.

exploring Monterey Bay before the winds come up. Whether you **kayak, stand-up paddleboard, scuba dive,** or head out on a **whale-watching cruise,** being on (or in) the water is the best way to experience this national marine sanctuary. Then further enrich your knowledge of the bay and its unique organisms at the **Monterey Bay Aquarium.**

End the day in downtown Monterey with a beer at **Alvarado Street Brewery & Grill** followed by dinner at **Montrio Bistro.**

DAY 19: MONTEREY TO BIG SUR
35 mi/55 km, 1 hr

Grab a coffee and a pastry at Monterey's **Café Lumiere** before hopping on CA-1 and heading south to explore **Carmel-by-the-Sea** and **Big Sur.** Make sure to detour off the highway for visits to Carmel's scenic **Carmel Beach** and **Point Lobos State Natural Reserve.** Consider having lunch at the unassuming **Carmel Belle.**

Head south on CA-1 along the **Big Sur coast.** Make time to stop at pullouts to take in the view. Take a hike to the beach at **Andrew Molera State Park** or drive to **Pfeiffer Beach** and try to capture the setting sun's light cascading through a keyhole on an offshore rock.

Have an early dinner at the very popular **Nepenthe,** with its stunning coastal views. If there's a long line, drive north to **The Sur House** for an afternoon drink and snack on their ocean-facing deck. Spend the night in a comfy cabin by the river at **Glen Oaks Big Sur** or in a rustic room at the charming **Deetjen's Big Sur Inn,** where you can be amused by reading the guest journals.

DAY 20: BIG SUR

Wherever you stay in Big Sur, start your morning with breakfast at **Deetjen's** restaurant, known for its homey atmosphere and indulgent eggs Benedict. Then drive 5 miles (8 km) south to **Julia Pfeiffer Burns State Park**'s **Partington Cove Trail** for a hike down to a tunnel cut through rock that leads to a small and scenic rocky cove. Following the walk, drive 6 miles (10 km) north to **Henry Miller Memorial Library,** a great bookstore and cultural arts hub to pick up a paperback or sip a coffee on the shaded redwood deck. End the day with a snack and a craft beer at the **Big Sur Taphouse**. If you still have energy, head 2 miles (3 km) north for live music and a nightcap at **Fernwood Tavern.**

Day 21
BIG SUR TO SAN FRANCISCO
150 mi/240 km, 3-3.5 hr

The fastest way back to San Francisco from Big Sur is to take CA-1 50 miles (81 km) north past Monterey and then head east on CA-156 until getting on **US-101 North** for the rest of the drive. Just a half hour longer, traffic willing, is the more scenic **coastal drive** up **CA-1** from Big Sur all the way to San Francisco. Choose what works best for you, but be sure to recall all the amazing sights you saw on your trip while returning to the Bay Area.

Best Hikes

Point Arena Lighthouse

♦ **Kortum Trail, Sonoma Coast State Park:** This easy blufftop trail parallels the Pacific Ocean as it travels through Sonoma Coast State Park, offering opportunities to access the park's beaches and coves (page 167).

♦ **Point Arena Lighthouse, California Coastal National Monument:** This hike begins with views of Point Arena Cove from the bluffs above and levels out to a walk by the sea with views of sea arches (page 178).

♦ **Fern Canyon Trail, Prairie Creek Redwoods State Park:** Walk a mile into a unique, creek-carved canyon decorated with bright green ferns that hang from the canyon walls (page 183).

♦ **Mill Creek Trail, Jedediah Smith Redwoods State Park:** This hike passes by ferns, maples, pines, and, most importantly, some of the biggest coast redwoods in the world (page 249).

♦ **Lithia Park, Ashland:** There is plenty to see and do in this 100-acre park filled with grass, evergreen trees, duck ponds, gardens, and even wild turkeys (page 273).

♦ **Lake Aloha, Desolation Wilderness:** This long hike into the Desolation Wilderness follows the Pacific Crest Trail to a series of alpine lakes that will make you feel like you're in another world (page 383).

♦ **Sacramento River Trail, Redding:** This scenic trail starts at the Sundial Bridge and continues all the way to the Shasta Dam (page 336).

♦ **Subway Cave, Old Station:** This naturally formed lava tube offers road-trippers a quick walk through a dark, somewhat spooky, yet clearly marked tunnel (page 320).

♦ **Lundy Canyon Trail, Hoover Wilderness:** Hike in the Eastern Sierra alongside a lake and through a canyon to visit old mine ruins (page 445).

♦ **Ridge Trail and Panorama Trail Loop, Andrew Molera State Park:** Take in the beauty of the Big Sur coast on this loop trail that includes a detour down to a driftwood-littered beach (page 559).

NORTHERN CALIFORNIA ROAD TRIPS

San
Francisco

San Francisco

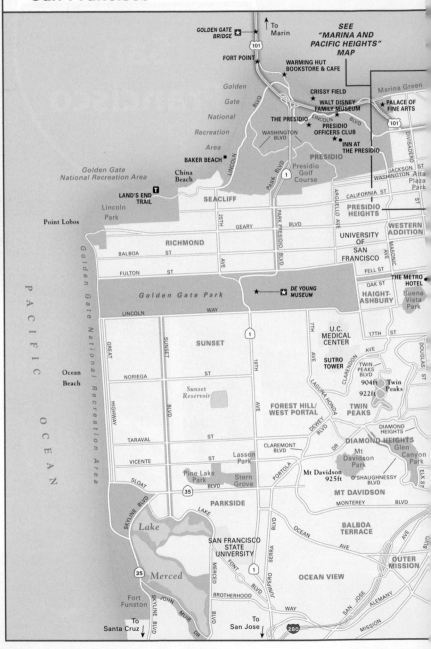

SEE "MARINA AND PACIFIC HEIGHTS" MAP

GOLDEN GATE BRIDGE

To Marin

101

FORT POINT

WARMING HUT
BOOKSTORE & CAFE

Golden

Gate

Marina Green

CRISSY FIELD

WALT DISNEY
FAMILY MUSEUM

PALACE OF
FINE ARTS

National

THE PRESIDIO

LINCOLN

BLVD

101

Recreation

WASHINGTON
BLVD

PRESIDIO
OFFICERS CLUB

INN AT
THE PRESIDIO

DIVISADERO

Area

BAKER BEACH

PRESIDIO

PARK BLVD

Presidio
Golf
Course

JACKSON ST

Alta
Plaza
Park

ST

China
Beach

1

WASHINGTON

ARGUELLO AVE

CALIFORNIA ST

Golden Gate
National Recreation Area

LAND'S END
TRAIL

SEACLIFF

PRESIDIO
HEIGHTS

Point Lobos

Lincoln
Park

25TH

GEARY

PARK
PRESIDIO
BLVD

UNIVERSITY
OF
SAN
FRANCISCO

WESTERN
ADDITION

RICHMOND

BALBOA
ST

AVE

BLVD

MASONIC
AVE

FELL ST

OAK ST

THE METRO
HOTEL

FULTON
ST

Golden Gate Park

DE YOUNG
MUSEUM

HAIGHT-
ASHBURY

Buena
Vista
Park

LINCOLN

WAY

7TH
AVE

17TH
ST

DOUGLAS
ST

PACIFIC

SUNSET

SUNSET

ST

19TH

U.C.
MEDICAL
CENTER

SUTRO
TOWER

CLARENDON

AVE

GREAT

NORIEGA

ST

AVE

LAGUNA HONDA

TWIN
PEAKS
BLVD

904ft

922ft

Twin
Peaks

ST

Ocean
Beach

Golden Gate National Recreation Area

HIGHWAY

Sunset
Reservoir

BLVD

FOREST HILL/
WEST PORTAL

DEWEY
BLVD

TWIN
PEAKS

DIAMOND
HEIGHTS

O C E A N

TARAVAL

ST

CLAREMONT
BLVD

DIAMOND HEIGHTS

Mt
Davidson
Park

Glen
Canyon
Park

ELK ST

VICENTE

ST

Lassen
Park

PORTOLA DR

Mt Davidson
925ft

O'SHAUGHNESSY
BLVD

Pine Lake
Park

Stern
Grove

BLVD

MT DAVIDSON

35

SLOAT

PARKSIDE

LAKE

MONTEREY

BLVD

Lake

SKYLINE BLVD

SAN FRANCISCO
STATE
UNIVERSITY

SERRA

BLVD

OCEAN

BALBOA
TERRACE

AVE

AVE

19TH

Merced

35

MERCED

FONT
BLVD

1

OCEAN VIEW

SAN JOSE
AVE

ALEMANY

OUTER
MISSION

MISSION

Fort
Funston

SKYLINE BLVD

JOHN MUIR DR

BROTHERHOOD

BLVD

WAY

280

To
Santa Cruz

To
San Jose

JUNIPERO

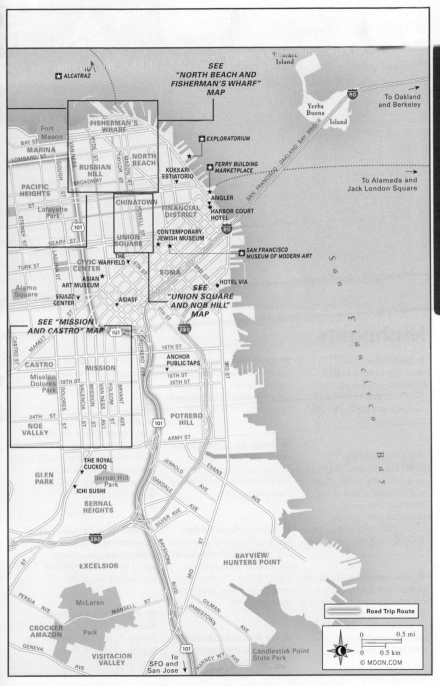

Highlights

★ **Cable Cars:** Get a taste of free-spirited San Francisco—not to mention great views of Alcatraz and the bay—via open-air public transit (page 39).

★ **Ferry Building:** The 1898 Ferry Building has been renovated and reimagined as the foodie mecca of San Francisco. The Tuesday, Thursday, and Saturday farmers market is not to be missed (page 39).

★ **San Francisco Museum of Modern Art:** SFMOMA showcases some of modern art's greatest hits and features the largest space dedicated to photographic art in the country (page 41).

★ **Exploratorium:** The exhibits at this innovative and interactive science museum are meant to be touched, heard, and felt (page 43).

★ **Alcatraz:** Spend the day in prison—at the famous former maximum-security penitentiary in the middle of the bay (page 43).

★ **Golden Gate Bridge:** Nothing beats the view from one of the most famous and fascinating bridges in the country. Pick a fogless day for a stroll or bike across the span (page 46).

★ **de Young Museum:** The de Young is the showpiece of Golden Gate Park. A mixed collection of media and

regions is highlighted by the 360-degree view from the museum's tower (page 49).

★ **Angel Island State Park:** While it once served as a way station for immigrants, today this island offers trails with amazing views of the city, Alcatraz, and the Golden Gate Bridge (page 88).

★ **Muir Woods National Monument:** Trails weave through old-growth red-wood trees in this national monument (page 89).

★ **Point Reyes National Seashore:** This preserved peninsula is known for hiking, beaches, and sheltered bays (page 94).

San Francisco perches restlessly on an uneven spit of land overlooking the bay on one side and the Pacific Ocean on the other.

Visitors come for the great art, world-class music, culinary innovation, and a laid-back club scene. Famed for its diversity, liberalism, and dense fog, the city somehow manages to both embody and defy the stereotypes heaped upon it.

Street-corner protests and leather stores are certainly part of the landscape, but farmers markets and friendly communities also abound. English blends with languages from around the world in an occasionally frustrating, often joyful cacophony. Those who have chosen to live here often refuse to live anyplace else, despite the infamous cost of housing and the occasional violent earthquake. Don't call it "San Fran" or, worse, "Frisco," or you'll be pegged as a tourist. To locals, this is The City, and that's that.

Getting There

Plan to spend at least **two days** in San Francisco, although it's easy to stay longer. Base yourself downtown near Union Square, where you'll have access to public transportation and won't need a car. Don't-miss sights include the foodie-friendly **Ferry Building, Golden Gate Park,** and taking a foggy stroll across the **Golden Gate Bridge.** Make **reservations** in advance for a trip to **Alcatraz** and for any and all **restaurants.**

From Wine Country
45-50 mi/70-80 km, 1.5 hr
The drive from Napa or Sonoma to San Francisco can take a long time depending upon weather and traffic. Avoid driving

the route on Sunday afternoons or on holiday weekends when the traffic flow into the Bay Area will be substantial.

From **Napa,** take CA-121 south for 7 miles (11.5 km) to the junction with CA-12. Continue south on CA-12. In less than 2 miles (3 km), turn east on CA-12 toward I-80. Get onto I-80 West and continue about 30 miles (48 km) south, taking the **Bay Bridge** (toll, $5-7) over into San Francisco.

From **Sonoma,** take CA-12 south for 4 miles (6.4 km). The road ends at a T junction with CA-116 and CA-121. Turn south onto CA-121 and drive 7 miles (11.5 km) to CA-37 West. Continue 8 miles (13 km) west to US-101 South. Take 101 South and drive 25 miles (40 km), crossing over the Golden Gate Bridge (toll, $8) into San Francisco.

From Tahoe
200 mi/320 km, 4 hr
From **Truckee,** take I-80 west for 180 miles (290 km), passing through Sacramento en route to the Bay Area. Near Berkeley, I-80 splits west across the **Bay Bridge** (toll, $5-7) into San Francisco.

The drive from Lake Tahoe into San Francisco can be especially challenging when there's snow and ski traffic. The route follows I-80, a major highway, and it is usually plowed when there is snow. Check road conditions at the Caltrans website (www.dot.ca.gov) before starting the drive.

Stopping in Sacramento
About 10 miles (16 km) north of Sacramento, the aptly named **Pit Stop Bar B-Que** (3515 McClellan Dr., North Highland, 916/344-1771, www.pitstopbarbq.com, 11am-9pm Mon.-Sat., 11am-8pm Sun., $10-18) serves award-winning ribs to hungry motorists.

To get there from I-80 West, take exit 96 and turn west onto Madison Avenue. In 0.7 mile, veer right onto Airbase Drive and continue 0.4 mile to Watt Avenue. Turn right onto Watt Avenue and drive

Best Restaurants

★ **Brenda's French Soul Food:** Start the day with a hearty New Orleans-style breakfast at this Tenderloin eatery (page 64).

★ **Yank Sing:** Sample dim sum from wheeled carts full of dumplings, pot stickers, spring rolls, and more (page 65).

★ **Michael Mina:** A celebrity chef dishes out upscale cuisine, including a Maine lobster pot pie, at his namesake restaurant (page 65).

★ **The Cavalier:** Experience upscale British pub food, like golden fried lamb riblets (page 66).

★ **Tadich Grill:** Open since 1849, this historic restaurant still serves an extensive menu of sensational seafood (page 66).

★ **Tony's Pizza Napoletana:** This North Beach pizzeria employs seven different ovens to cook its unique pies (page 69).

★ **Swan Oyster Depot:** Locals and visitors line up daily for a seafood lunch at this tiny restaurant (page 71).

★ **Jardinière:** Chef Traci Des Jardins combines French and California dining elements at this upscale restaurant (page 71).

★ **Tartine Bakery:** Lines snake out the door all day long, but the fresh baked goods and sandwiches are worth the wait (page 72).

0.3 mile north to McClellan where you will turn right. The Pit Stop is on the left.

From Yosemite
200 mi/320 km, 4 hr

The drive from Yosemite to San Francisco involves lots of time on small highways that frequently pass orchards, farms, and sprawling valley towns. The trip may require navigating heavy traffic in and out of Yosemite National Park (especially on weekends), the annual closure of **Tioga Pass** (**CA-120**), curvy mountain roads, and traffic in the Central Valley and greater Bay Area.

Summer Route

In summer, Yosemite's park roads and the surrounding freeways are open but are also heavily trafficked. From Yosemite, exit the park via the **Big Oak Flat Entrance** and drive 90 miles (145 km) west on CA-120 West toward Manteca. (Stay on CA-120 West when it merges with CA-49 and CA-108.) Near Manteca, CA-120 merges onto I-5. Take I-5 South for about 2 miles (3 km), then take I-205 West for 14 miles (22.5 km) to I-580 West. In about 45 miles (72 km), I-580 merges with I-80 West onto the **Bay Bridge** (toll $5-7) and into San Francisco.

Winter Route

If traveling from Yosemite September-May, your surest access is **CA-140** and the **Arch Rock Entrance.** From this entrance, follow **CA-140 West** for 80 miles (129 km) to Merced. In Merced, merge onto **CA-99 North** and drive 60 miles (97 km) toward Manteca. At Manteca, merge onto **CA-120 West** and continue the summer route to I-5, I-205, I-580, and I-80 into San Francisco.

Many Yosemite park roads are closed

Best Accommodations

★ **Golden Gate Hotel:** This bed-and-breakfast-like hotel has nice, moderately priced rooms in a narrow building near Union Square (page 74).

★ **Phoenix Hotel:** The Phoenix is popular with touring rock bands, but you don't have to be a rock star to enjoy this casual hotel's expansive pool deck (page 75).

★ **Hotel G:** This hotel comes on like an unassuming cool kid that impresses with understated style (page 75).

★ **Hotel Zetta:** This SoMa neighborhood hotel embraces the region's tech-savvy side: Each room comes equipped with a gaggle of gadgets (page 76).

★ **Harbor Court Hotel:** You can't beat this location—a block from the Ferry Building, with a nighttime view of the Bay Bridge lights (page 78).

★ **Marina Motel:** This moderately priced motel in the Marina District has something most accommodations in the city don't: individual parking garages for guests (page 78).

★ **The Metro Hotel:** This family-owned hotel near Haight Ashbury has clean, comfy rooms and some of the better rates within the city (page 79).

---

in winter. **Tioga Pass** and **CA-120**—the east-west access through the park—are closed from the end of September until May or June. In addition, CA-120 west and north through the park and to San Francisco can also be closed due to snow. Chains can be required on park roads at any time.

From Monterey
170 mi /275 km, 3-4 hr

From Monterey, take CA-1 for 14 miles (22.5 km) north. Exit onto **CA-156 East,** which connects with US-101 North in 6.5 miles (10.5 km). Continue north on **US-101** for 97 miles (156 km) through San Jose and into San Francisco.

Air, Train, or Bus

It's easy to fly into the San Francisco Bay Area. There are three major airports. Among them, you should be able to find a flight that fits your schedule. **San Francisco International Airport** (SFO, www.flysfo.com) is 13 miles (21 km) south. **Oakland Airport** (OAK, www. oaklandairport.com) is 11 miles (17.5

km) east of the city but requires crossing the bay, via either the Bay Bridge or public transit. **Mineta San José Airport** (SJC, www.flysanjose.com) is the farthest away, roughly 47 miles (76 km) to the south. These last two airports are less than an hour away by car, with car rentals available. Some San Francisco hotels offer complimentary airport shuttles as well.

Several public and private transportation options can get you into San Francisco. **Bay Area Rapid Transit** (BART, www.bart.gov) connects directly with SFO's international terminal; an airport shuttle connects Oakland airport to the nearest station. **Caltrain** (www.caltrain. com, tickets $3.75-13.75) is a good option from San Jose; an airport shuttle connects to the train station. **Millbrae Station** is where the BART and Caltrain systems connect; it's designed to transfer from one line to the other.

Amtrak (www.amtrak.com) does not run directly into San Francisco, but you can ride to the San Jose, Oakland, or Emeryville stations, then take a connecting bus to San Francisco. **Greyhound**

Two Days in San Francisco

Alcatraz

Day 1

Start your day at the **Ferry Building.** Graze from the many vendors, including **Blue Bottle Café, Cowgirl Creamery,** and **Acme Bread Company,** then walk two blocks to **Yank Sing** for a dim sum lunch. Catch the Muni F line (Steuart St. and Market St., $2) to Jefferson Street and take a stroll along **Fisherman's Wharf.** Stop into the **Musée Mécanique** to play a few coin-operated antique arcade games. Near Pier 39, catch the ferry to **Alcatraz**—be sure to buy your tickets well in advance. Alcatraz will fill your mind with amazing stories from the legendary island prison.

After you escape from Alcatraz, take the N Judah line ($2) to 9th Avenue and Irving Street, then follow 9th Avenue north into **Golden Gate Park,** where you can delve into art at the fabulous **de Young Museum** or into science at the **California Academy of Sciences.** Stroll the scenic **Japanese Tea Garden** and get a snack at the Tea House.

Catch a cab to North Beach and **Tony's Pizza Napoletana** to get some real sustenance directly from one of its seven pizza ovens. Now you are ready to see some live music at the **Great American Music Hall.**

Day 2

Fortify yourself for a day of sightseeing with a hearty breakfast at **Brenda's French Soul Food,** then drive or take a cab out to the **Lands End Trail,** where you can investigate the ruins of the former Sutro Baths and get views of the city's rocky coastline. Then head back to **Crissy Field** for views of the **Golden Gate Bridge.**

Walk to the adjacent Marina District for oysters at **Swan Oyster Depot** or sushi at **Ace Wasabi's.** Venture back downtown to wander the streets of **Chinatown** and adjacent **North Beach.** Browse through **City Lights,** the legendary Beat Generation bookstore. Wind down with a cocktail at **Vesuvio,** a colorful bar and former Beat writer hangout located next door.

Head to the bustling Mission District, stopping first for a drink at the rooftop bar **El Techo de Lolinda** or **Trick Dog.** Then enjoy dinner at **Tartine Manufactory** or **ICHI Sushi.**

(200 Folsom St., 415/495-1569, www.greyhound.com, 5:15am-1am daily) offers bus service to San Francisco from all over the country.

Sights

Union Square and Downtown
★ Cable Cars
Perhaps the most recognizable symbol of San Francisco is the **cable car** (www.sfcablecar.com), originally conceived by Andrew Smith Hallidie as a safer alternative for traveling the steep, often slick hills of San Francisco. The cable cars ran as regular mass transit from 1873 into the 1940s, when buses and electric streetcars began to dominate the landscape. Dedicated citizens, especially "Cable Car Lady" Friedel Klussmann, saved the cable car system from extinction, and the cable cars have become a rolling national landmark.

Today you can ride the cable cars from one tourist destination to another for $7 per ride. A full day "passport" **ticket** ($22, also grants access to streetcars and buses) is totally worth it if you want to run around the city all day. Cable car routes can take you up Nob Hill from the Financial District, or from Union Square along Powell Street, through Chinatown, and out to Fisherman's Wharf. Take a seat, or grab one of the exterior poles and hang on! Cable cars have open-air seating only, making for a chilly ride on foggy days.

The cars get stuffed to capacity with tourists on weekends and with local commuters at rush hours. Expect to wait an hour or more for a ride from any of the turnaround points on a weekend or holiday. But a ride on a cable car from Union Square down to the Wharf is more than worth the wait. The views from the hills down to the bay inspire wonder even in lifetime residents. To learn a bit more, make a stop at the **Cable Car Museum** (1201 Mason St., 415/474-1887, www.

cablecarmuseum.org, 10am-6pm daily Apr.-Oct., 10am-5pm daily Nov.-Mar., free), the home and nerve center of the entire fleet. Here a sweet little museum depicts the life and times of the cable cars while an elevated platform overlooks the engines, winding wheels, and thick steel cable that keeps the cars humming. You can even glimpse the 1873 tunnels that snake beneath the city.

Grace Cathedral
Local icon **Grace Cathedral** (1100 California St., 415/749-6300, www.gracecathedral.org, 7am-6pm Thurs., 8am-6pm Fri.-Wed., 8am-4pm holidays) is many things to many people. The French Gothic-style edifice, completed in 1964, attracts architecture and Beaux-Arts lovers by the thousands with its facade, stained glass, and furnishings. The labyrinths—replicas of the Chartres Cathedral labyrinth in France—appeal to meditative walkers seeking spiritual solace. Concerts featuring world music, sacred music, and modern classical ensembles draw audiences from around the Bay Area and farther afield.

The 1.5-hour **Grace Cathedral Grand Tour** (415/749-6316, www.gracecathedral.org, $25) includes a walk up 94 steps to the top of the cathedral's South Tower. Download the GraceGuide app for information about the structure's architecture, history, and art.

★ Ferry Building
Restored to its former glory, the 1898 **San Francisco Ferry Building** (1 Ferry Bldg., 415/983-8030, www.ferrybuildingmarketplace.com, 10am-7pm Mon.-Fri., 8am-6pm Sat., 11am-5pm Sun., check with businesses for individual hours) stands at the edge of the bay, its 230-foot-tall clock tower serving as a beacon to both land and water traffic. Photos and interpretive plaques just inside the main lobby describe its history. Free **walking tours** (www.sfcityguides.org) of the building are offered one day a week.

Union Square and Nob Hill

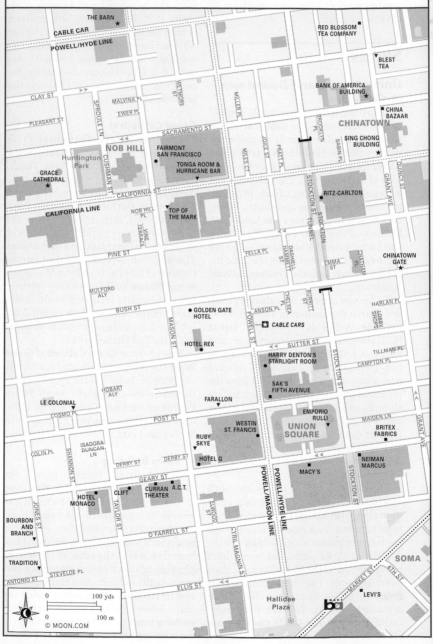

THE BARN ★

CABLE CAR
POWELL/HYDE LINE

RED BLOSSOM
TEA COMPANY ■

BLEST
TEA ■

CLAY ST

MALVINA PL

WETMORE

BANK OF AMERICA
BUILDING ■

CHINA
BAZAAR ■

PLEASANT ST

EWER PL

SPROULE LN

CHINATOWN

SACRAMENTO ST

SING CHONG
BUILDING ★

BROOKLYN PL

NOB HILL

FAIRMONT
SAN FRANCISCO ●

TONGA ROOM &
HURRICANE BAR ▼

Huntington
Park

GRACE
CATHEDRAL ★

CUSHMAN ST

MILES CT

JOICE ST

PRATT PL

SABIN PL

RITZ-CARLTON ●

STOCKTON ST TUNNEL

QUINCY ST

GRANT AVE

CALIFORNIA ST

CALIFORNIA LINE

NOB HILL PL

VINE TERRACE

TOP OF
THE MARK ■

PINE ST

FELLA PL

DASHIELL HAMMETT ST

EMMA ST

CHATHAM

CHINATOWN
GATE ★

MULFORD
ALY

BUSH ST

GOLDEN GATE
HOTEL ●

MASON ST

ANSON PL

CHELSEA PL

BURRITT ST

POWELL ST

HARLAN PL

LOBBY
SHOPS

CABLE CARS ✪

HOTEL REX ●

SUTTER ST

STOCKTON ST

TILLMAN PL

CAMPTON PL

HARRY DENTON'S
STARLIGHT ROOM ●

HOBART
ALY

LE COLONIAL ●

COSMO PL

FARALLON ▼

SAK'S
FIFTH AVENUE

POST ST

WESTIN
ST. FRANCIS

EMPORIO
RULLI ▼

UNION
SQUARE

MAIDEN LN

BRITEX
FABRICS ■

GRANT AVE

ISADORA
DUNCAN
LN

RUBY
SKYE ●

HOTEL G ●

DERBY ST

MACY'S ■

NEIMAN
MARCUS ■

COLIN PL

SHANNON ST

GEARY ST

CLIFT ●

CURRAN
THEATER ■

A.C.T. ■

STOCKTON ST

HOTEL
MONACO ●

TAYLOR ST

ELWOOD ST

BOURBON
AND
BRANCH ▼

JONES ST

O'FARRELL ST

CYRIL MAGNIN ST

POWELL/HYDE LINE

POWELL/MASON LINE

SOMA

TRADITION ●

STEVELOE PL

ANTONIO ST

ELLIS ST

Hallidae
Plaza

MARKET ST

4TH ST

LEVI'S ■

ba

0   100 yds

0   100 m

© MOON.COM

Inside, it's all about the food. Permanent shops provide top-tier artisanal food and drink, with local favorites like Cowgirl Creamery, Blue Bottle Café, and Acme Bread Company, while a few quick-and-easy restaurants offer reasonable meals. The famous **Ferry Plaza Farmers Market** (415/291-3276, www.cuesa.org/markets, 10am-2pm Tues. and Thurs., 8am-2pm Sat.) draws crowds shopping for produce out front.

On the water side of the Ferry Building, boats come and go from Sausalito, Tiburon, Larkspur, Vallejo, and Alameda each day. Check with **San Francisco Bay Ferry** (http://sanfranciscobayferry.com) for information about service, times, and fares.

★ San Francisco Museum of Modern Art

After a massive three-year renovation, the **San Francisco Museum of Modern Art** (SFMOMA, 151 3rd St., 415/357-4000, www.sfmoma.org, 10am-5pm Fri.-Tues., 10am-9pm Thurs., 10am-8pm Sat. summer, 10am-9pm Thurs., 10am-5pm Fri.-Tues. winter, adults $25, seniors $22, youth 19-24 $19, children under 18 free) reopened in 2016 with three times as much gallery space. Modern classics on display include major works by Roy Lichtenstein, Georgia O'Keeffe, Jackson Pollock, and Andy Warhol. The third-floor Pritzker Center for Photography is the largest space dedicated to photographic art in the country. Enjoy views of the building's stunning design by walking across the fifth floor's Oculus Bridge, or get a breath of fresh air on the third-floor sculpture terrace.

Contemporary Jewish Museum

The local favorite **Contemporary Jewish Museum** (736 Mission St., 415/655-7800, www.thecjm.org, 11am-5pm Thurs.-Tues., adults $14, seniors and students $12, children 18 and under free) curates superb temporary exhibits on pop culture. Recent subjects include filmmaker Stanley Kubrick, Bay Area music promoter Bill Graham, and singer Amy Winehouse. The museum's sleek building is part historic power station and part blue steel structure that spells out the Hebrew word *chai*, meaning life.

Chinatown

The massive Chinese migration to California began almost as soon as the news of easy gold in the mountain streams made it to East Asia. And despite rampant prejudice, the Chinese not only stayed, but persevered and eventually prospered. Many never made it to the gold fields, preferring instead to remain in bustling San Francisco to open shops and begin the business of commerce in their new home. They carved out a thriving community at the border of **Portsmouth Square,** then center of the young city, which became known as Chinatown. Along with much of San Francisco, the neighborhood was destroyed in the 1906 earthquake and fire.

Today visitors see the post-1906 visitor-friendly Chinatown that was built after the quake, particularly if they enter through the **Chinatown Gate** (Grant Ave. and Bush St.) at the edge of Union Square. In this historic neighborhood, beautiful Asian architecture mixes with more mundane blocky city buildings to create a unique skyline. Small alleyways wend between the touristy commercial corridors, creating an intimate atmosphere.

North Beach and Fisherman's Wharf

North Beach has long served as the Little Italy of San Francisco, a fact still reflected in the restaurants in the neighborhood. North Beach truly made its mark in the 1950s when it was, for a brief time, home to many writers in the Beat Generation, including Jack Kerouac, Gary Snyder, and Allen Ginsberg.

Coit Tower

Built in 1933 as a monument to

North Beach and Fisherman's Wharf

benefactor Lillie Hitchcock Coit's beloved firefighters, **Coit Tower** (1 Telegraph Hill Blvd., 415/249-0995, http://sfrecpark.org, 10am-6pm daily Apr.-Oct., 10am-5pm daily Nov.-Mar., free) has beautified the city just as Coit intended. Inside the art deco tower, the walls are covered in the restored frescos painted in 1934 depicting city and California life during the Great Depression. For a fee (adults $9, seniors and youth $6, children 5-11 $2, children under 5 free), you can ride the elevator to the top, where on a clear day, you can see the whole city and bay. Part

of what makes Coit Tower special is the walk up to it. Rather than contributing to the acute congestion in the area, consider taking public transit to the area and walking up Telegraph Hill Boulevard through Pioneer Park to the tower, and descend down either the Filbert or Greenwich steps toward the Embarcadero. It's long and steep, but there's no other way to see the lovely little cottages and gardens of the beautiful and quaint Telegraph Hill.

Lombard Street

You've no doubt seen it in movies:

Lombard Street (Lombard St., one-way from Hyde St. to Leavenworth St.), otherwise known as "the crookedest street in the world." The section of the street that visitors flock to spans only one block, from Hyde Street at the top to Leavenworth Street at the bottom. However, the line of cars waiting their turn to drive bumper-to-bumper can be just as legendary as its 27 percent grade. Bypass the car and take the hill by foot. The unobstructed vistas of San Francisco Bay, Alcatraz Island, Fisherman's Wharf, Coit Tower, and the city are reason enough to add this walk to your itinerary, as are the brick steps, manicured hydrangeas, and tony residences that line the roadway. To avoid traffic jams, drive the road in the early morning or at night during the summer.

★ Exploratorium

Lauded both as "one of the world's most important science museums" and "a mad scientist's penny arcade," the **Exploratorium** (Pier 15, 415/528-4444, www.exploratorium.edu, 10am-5pm Tues.-Wed. and Fri.-Sun., 10am-5pm and 6pm-10pm Thurs., $30 adults, $25 seniors and youth 13-17, $20 children 4-12, children under 3 free) houses 150 playful exhibits on physics, motion, perception, and the senses that utilize its stunning location. Make a reservation ($15) to walk blindly (and bravely) into the Tactile Dome, a lightless space where you can "see" your way only by reaching out and touching the environment around you. Exploratorium "After Dark" targets adults 18 and over (6pm-10pm Thurs., $20). Its location between the Ferry Building and Fisherman's Wharf makes a crowd-free trip impossible, especially on the weekends.

★ Alcatraz

Going to **Alcatraz** (415/561-4900, www.nps.gov/alcatraz), one of the most famous landmarks in the city, feels a bit like going to purgatory; this military fortress-turned-maximum-security prison, nicknamed "The Rock," has little warmth or welcome on its craggy, forbidding shores. While it still belonged to the military, the fortress became a prison in the 19th century to house Civil War prisoners. The isolation of the island in the bay, the frigid waters, and the nasty currents surrounding Alcatraz made it a perfect spot to keep prisoners contained, with little hope of escape and near-certain death if the attempt were ever made. In 1934, after the military closed down its prison and handed the island over to the Department of Justice, construction began to turn Alcatraz into a new style of prison ready to house a new style of prisoner: Depression-era gangsters. A few of the honored guests of this maximum-security penitentiary were Al Capone, George "Machine Gun" Kelly, and Robert Stroud, "the Birdman of Alcatraz." The prison closed in 1963, and in 1964 and 1969 occupations were staged by Indians of All Tribes, an exercise that eventually led to the privilege of self-determination for North America's original inhabitants.

Visit the island on tours offered by **Alcatraz Cruises** (Pier 33, 415/981-7625, www.alcatrazcruises.com, adults $38, seniors $36, children $24, times and prices vary), departing from Pier 33. Options include the **Day Tour, Night Tour, Behind the Scenes Tour,** and the **Alcatraz and Angel Island Tour.** Tours typically sell out, especially on weekends, so reserve tickets at least two weeks in advance.

Fisherman's Wharf

Welcome to **Fisherman's Wharf** (Beach St. from Powell St. to Van Ness Ave., backs onto Bay St., www.visitfishermanswharf.org), the tourist mecca of San Francisco! While warehouses, stacks of crab pots, and a fleet of fishing vessels let you know this is still a working wharf, it is also where visitors come and snap photos. Reachable by the Muni F line and the Hyde-Powell cable car, the Wharf sprawls

along the waterfront and inland several blocks.

Be prepared to push through a sea of humanity to buy souvenirs, eat seafood, and enjoy fun pieces of San Francisco's heritage, like the **Musée Mécanique** (Pier 45, Fishermen's Wharf, 415/346-2000, www.museemechaniquesf.com, 10am-8pm daily, free), a strange collection of over 300 working coin-operated machines from the 1800s to today. Machines include a 3-D picture show of San Francisco after the catastrophic 1906 earthquake and fire, along with more modern favorites like Ms. Pac-Man.

Ghirardelli Square

Ghirardelli Square (900 North Point St., www.ghirardellisq.com, 11am-9pm daily), pronounced "GEAR-ah-DEL-ee," began its life as a chocolate factory in 1852 but has since reinvented itself as an upscale shopping, dining, and living compound. The **Ghirardelli Chocolate Manufactory** (900 North Point St., 415/474-3938, www.ghirardellisq.com, 9am-11pm Sun.-Thurs., 9am-midnight Fri.-Sat.) anchors the corner of the square. Here you can browse the rambling shop and pick up truffles, wafers, candies, and sauces for all your friends back home. Finally, get in line at the ice cream counter to order a hot fudge sundae. Once you've finished gorging on chocolate, wander out into the square to enjoy more shopping and an unbelievably swank condo complex overlooking the bay.

San Francisco Maritime National Historical Park

The real gem of the Wharf is the **San Francisco Maritime National Historical Park** (415/561-7000, www.nps.gov/safr), which spreads from the base of Van Ness to Pier 45. At the **visitors center** (499 Jefferson St., 415/447-5000, 9:30am-5pm

From top to bottom: San Francisco cable car; the Ferry Building; the Palace of Fine Arts.

daily), not only will rangers help you make the most of your visit, but you can also get lost in the labyrinthine museum that houses an immense Fresnel lighthouse lens and engaging displays that recount San Francisco's history. For $15, you can climb aboard the historic ships at permanent dock across the street at the **Hyde Street Pier.** The shiniest jewel of the collection is the 1886 square-rigged *Balclutha*, a three-masted schooner that recalls times gone by, complete with excellent historical exhibits below deck. There are also several steamboats, including the workhorse ferry paddle wheeler *Eureka* and a cool old steam tugboat called the *Eppleton Hall*. Farther down, at Pier 45, World War II buffs can feel the claustrophobia of the submarine **USS Pampanito** (415/775-1943, www. maritime.org, 9am-6pm Sun.-Thurs., 9am-8pm Fri.-Sat., adults $20, seniors $12, children 6-12 $10, children under 6 free) or the expansiveness of the Liberty ship **SS Jeremiah O'Brien** (415/544-0100, www.ssjeremiahobrien.org, 9am-4pm daily, adults $20, seniors $12, children 5-12 $10, children under 4 free).

The 1939 art deco **Aquatic Bathhouse Building** (900 Beach St., 415/561-7100, www.nps.gov/safr, 10am-4pm daily, adults $5, children free), built in 1939, houses the Maritime Museum, where you can see rotating exhibits alongside its brilliant WPA murals.

Marina and Pacific Heights

The Marina and Pacific Heights are wealthy neighborhoods, with a couple of yacht harbors, plenty of open space, great dining, and shopping that only gets better as you go up the hill.

Palace of Fine Arts

The **Palace of Fine Arts** (3301 Lyon St.) was originally meant to be nothing but a temporary structure—part of the Panama-Pacific International Exposition in 1915. But the lovely building designed by Bernard Maybeck won the hearts of

San Franciscans, and a fund was started to preserve the palace beyond the exposition. Through the first half of the 20th century, efforts could not keep it from crumbling, but in the 1960s and 1970s, serious rebuilding work took place, and today the Palace of Fine Arts stands proud, strong, and beautiful. It houses the **Palace of Fine Arts Theatre** (415/563-6504, www.palaceoffinearts.org), which hosts events nearly every day, from beauty pageants to conferences to children's musical theater performances.

The Presidio

It seems strange to think of progressive, peace-loving San Francisco as a town with a long military history, yet it is nowhere more evident than at **The Presidio** (Montgomery St. and Lincoln Blvd., 415/561-4323, www.nps.gov/prsf, visitors center 10am-5pm daily, trails dawn-dusk daily, free). This sweeping stretch of land running along the San Francisco Headlands down to the Golden Gate Bridge has been a military installation since 1776, when the Spanish created their El Presidio del San Francisco fort on the site. In 1846, the U.S. Army took over the site (peacefully), and in 1848 the American Presidio military installation formally opened. The Presidio had a role in every Pacific-related war from the Civil War through Desert Storm. It was abandoned by the military and became a national park in 1994.

To orient yourself among the more than 800 buildings that make up the Presidio, start at the **William Penn Mott Jr. Presidio Visitor Center** (Bldg. 210, Lincoln Blvd., 415/561-4323, 10am-5pm daily), where exhibits include a model of the grounds. You can also explore the pioneering aviation area **Crissy Field** (www.parksconservancy.org), Civil War-era fortifications at **Fort Point National Historic Site** (end of Marine Dr., 415/504-2334, www.nps.gov/fopo, 10am-5pm Thurs.-Mon. summer, 10am-5pm Fri.-Sun. winter), and the **Walt Disney Family**

Marina and Pacific Heights

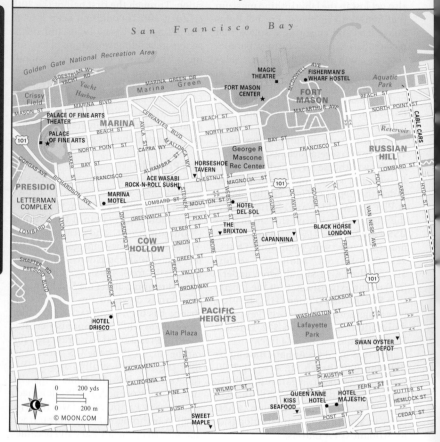

Museum (104 Montgomery St., 415/345-6800, www.waltdisney.org, 10am-6pm Wed.-Mon., adults $25, seniors and students $20, children 6-17 $15), founded by Disney's daughter to examine the animator's life and work. Other highlights include art installations by Andy Goldsworthy, who works with natural materials. The most renowned is *Spire*, a sculpture that rises 90 feet into the air, utilizing 35 cypress tree trunks.

★ Golden Gate Bridge

People come from the world over to see and walk the **Golden Gate Bridge** (US-101/CA-1 at Lincoln Blvd., 415/921-5858, www.goldengatebridge.com, southbound cars $8, pedestrians free). A marvel of human engineering constructed in 1936 and 1937, the suspension bridge spans the narrow "gate" from which the Pacific Ocean enters the San Francisco Bay. Pedestrians are allowed on the **east sidewalk** (5am-9pm daily mid-Mar.-Oct., 5am-6:30pm daily Nov.-mid-Mar.). On a clear day, the whole bay, Marin Headlands, and city skyline are visible. Cyclists are allowed on both sidewalks (check the website for times), but as the scenery is stunning, be aware of pedestrians and cyclists not keeping their eyes on where they are going. A vehicle **toll** (www.bayareafastrak.org) is charged by license plate recognition.

The Golden Gate National Parks Conservancy has quit offering its Golden Gate Bridge Tours, but the nonprofit **City Guides** (415/557-4266, www.sfcityguides.org) leads bridge walks twice a week. Check the website for days and times.

Civic Center and Hayes Valley

The Civic Center functions as the heart of San Francisco. Not only is the seat of government here, but so are venerable high-culture institutions: the War Memorial Opera House and Davies Symphony Hall, home of the world-famous San Francisco Symphony. As the Civic Center melts into Hayes Valley, you'll find fabulous hotels and restaurants serving both the city's politicos and the well-heeled.

City Hall

Look at San Francisco's **City Hall** (1 Dr. Carlton B. Goodlett Pl., 415/554-6079, www.sfgov.org, 8am-8pm Mon.-Fri., free) and you'll think you've somehow been transported to Europe. The stately Beaux-Arts building with the gilded dome is the pride of the city and houses the mayor's office and much of the city's government. Enjoy walking through the parklike square in front of City Hall (though this area can get a bit sketchy after dark). Inside you'll find a combination of historical grandeur and modern accessibility and convenience as you tour the Arthur Brown Jr.-designed edifice.

Asian Art Museum

Across from City Hall is the **Asian Art Museum** (200 Larkin St., 415/581-3500, www.asianart.org, 10am-5pm Tues.-Wed. and Fri.-Sun., 10am-9pm Thurs. mid-Feb.-Aug., 10am-5pm Tues.-Sun. Sept.-mid-Feb., adults $25, seniors and students $20, children 12 and under free), with enormous Ionic columns. Inside you'll have an amazing window into the Asian cultures that have shaped and defined San Francisco and the Bay Area. The second and third floors of this intense museum are packed with great art from all across Asia, including a Chinese gilded Buddha dating from AD 338. The breadth and diversity of Asian culture may stagger you; the museum's displays come from Japan and Vietnam, Buddhist Tibet, and ancient China. Special exhibitions cost extra—check the website to see what will be displayed on the ground-floor galleries when you're in town. The curators regularly rotate items from the permanent collection, so you'll probably encounter new beauty every time you visit.

Alamo Square

At this area's far western edge sits **Alamo Square** (Hayes St. and Steiner St., 415/218-0259, https://sfrecpark.org, 5am-midnight daily), possibly the most photographed neighborhood in San Francisco. Among its stately Victorians are the famous **"painted ladies,"** a row of brilliantly painted and immaculately maintained homes. From the adjacent Alamo Square Park, the ladies provide a picturesque foreground for views of the Civic Center and downtown.

Mission and Castro

Castro is the heart of gay San Francisco, complete with nightlife, festivals, and LGBT community activism. With its mix of Latino immigrants, working artists, and hipsters, the Mission is a neighborhood bursting at the seams with idiosyncratic energy. Changing from block to block, the zone manages to be blue-collar, edgy, and gentrified all at once. While the heart of the neighborhood is still Latin American, with delicious burritos and *pupusas* around every corner, it is also the go-to neighborhood for the tech economy, with luxury condos, pricey

Mission and Castro

boutiques, and international restaurants in a city famous for its food.

Mission Dolores

Mission Dolores (3321 16th St., 415/621-8203, www.missiondolores.org, 9:30am-4:30pm Sun.-Fri., 9am-4pm Sat., adults $7, seniors and students $5), formally named Mission San Francisco de Asís, was founded in 1776. Today the mission is the oldest intact building in the city, having survived the 1906 earthquake and fire, the 1989 Loma Prieta quake, and more than 200 years of use. You can attend Roman Catholic services here each Saturday, or you can visit the Old Mission Museum and the basilica, which house artifacts from the Native Americans and Spanish of the 18th century. The beauty and grandeur of the mission recall the heyday of the Spanish empire in California, as important to the history of the state as it is today.

Golden Gate Park and the Haight

The neighborhood surrounding the intersection of Haight and Ashbury Streets (known locally as "the Haight") is best known for the wave of countercultural energy that broke out in the 1960s. Haight Street terminates at the entrance to San Francisco's gem—Golden Gate Park.

Golden Gate Park

Dominating the western half of San Francisco, **Golden Gate Park** (main entrance on Stanyan St. at Fell St., McLaren Lodge Visitors Center at John F. Kennedy Dr., 415/831-2700, https://goldengatepark. com or http://sfrecpark.org, 5am-midnight daily) is one of the city's most enduring treasures. Its 1,000-plus acres include lakes, forests, formal gardens, windmills, museums, a buffalo pasture, and plenty of activities. Enjoy free concerts in the summer, hike in near solitude in the winter, or spend a day wandering and exploring scores of sights.

★ de Young Museum

The **de Young Museum** (50 Hagiwara Tea Garden Dr., 415/750-3600, http:// deyoung.famsf.org, 9:30am-5:15pm Tues.-Thurs. and Sat.-Sun., 9:30am-8:30pm Fri. summer, 9:30am-5:15pm Tues.-Sun. winter, adults $15, seniors $12, students $6, children 17 and under free) is staggering in its size and breadth: You'll see everything from pre-Columbian art to 17th-century ladies' gowns. View paintings, sculpture, textiles, ceramics, "contemporary crafts" from all over the world, and rotating exhibits that range from King Tut to the exquisite Jean Paul Gaultier collection. Competing with all of that is the building itself.

The museum's modern exterior is wrapped in perforated copper, while the interior incorporates pockets of manicured gardens. Poking out of the park's canopy is a twisted tower that offers a spectacular 360-degree view of the city and the bay. Entrance to the tower, lily pond, and art garden is free. Surrounded by sphinxes and draping wisteria, you can enjoy an art-filled picnic lunch.

California Academy of Sciences

A triumph of the sustainable scientific principles it exhibits, the **California Academy of Sciences** (55 Music Concourse Dr., 415/379-8000, www. calacademy.org, 9:30am-5pm Mon.-Sat., 11am-5pm Sun., adults $40, seniors, students, and children 12-17 $35, children 4-11 $30) drips with ecological perfection. From the grass-covered roof to the underground **aquarium,** visitors can explore every part of the universe. Wander through a steamy endangered **rainforest** contained inside a giant glass bubble, or travel through an all-digital outer space in the high-tech **planetarium.** More studious nature lovers can spend days examining every inch of the **Natural History Museum,** including favorite exhibits like the 87-foot-long blue whale skeleton. The Academy of Sciences takes pains to make itself kid-friendly, with interactive exhibits, thousands of live animals, and endless opportunities for learning. On **Thursday nights** (6pm-10pm, $15), the academy is an adults-only zone, where DJs play music and the café serves cocktails by some of the city's most renowned mixologists.

Japanese Tea Garden

The **Japanese Tea Garden** (75 Hagiwara Tea Garden Dr., 415/752-4227, http:// japaneseteagardensf.com, 9am-6pm daily Mar.-Oct., 9am-4:45pm daily Nov.-Feb., adults $8, seniors and children 12-17 $6, children 5-11 $2, children under 5 free) is a haven of peace and tranquility that's a local favorite within the park, particularly in the spring. The planting and design of the garden began in 1894 for the California Exposition. Today the flourishing garden displays a wealth of beautiful flora, including stunning examples of rare Chinese and Japanese plants, some quite old. As you stroll along the paths, you'll come upon sculptures, bridges, ponds, and even traditional *tsukubai* (a tea ceremony sink). Take one of the docent-led tours and conclude your visit

with tea and a fortune cookie at the Tea House. Free admission is available on Monday, Wednesday, and Friday before 10am.

San Francisco Botanical Garden

Take a bucolic walk in the middle of Golden Gate Park by visiting the **San Francisco Botanical Garden** (1199 9th Ave. at Lincoln Way, 415/661-1316, www.sfbg.org, 7:30am-6pm daily mid-Mar.-Sept., 7:30am-5pm daily Oct.-Nov., 7:30am-4pm daily Nov.-Jan., 7:30am-5pm daily Feb.-mid-Mar., adults $9, students and seniors $6, children 5-11 $3, children under 3 free). The 55-acre gardens are home to more than 8,000 species of plants from around the world and include a California Natives garden and a shady redwood forest. Fountains, ponds, meadows, and lawns are interwoven with the flowers and trees to create a peaceful, serene setting in the middle of the crowded city.

Conservatory of Flowers

For a trip to San Francisco's Victorian past, step inside the steamy **Conservatory of Flowers** (100 John F. Kennedy Dr., 415/831-2090, www.conservatoryofflowers.org, 10am-4:30pm Tues.-Sun., adults $9, students and seniors $6, children 5-11 $3, children under 5 free). Built in 1878, the striking wood and glass greenhouse is home to more than 1,700 plant species that spill out of containers, twine around rainforest trees, climb trellises reaching the roof, and rim deep ponds where eight-foot lily pads float serenely on still waters. Surrounded by the exotic flora illuminated only by natural light, it's easy to transport yourself to the heyday of colonialism when the study of botany was in its first bloom. Plus, it's one of the best places to explore on a rainy day. Strollers

From top to bottom: Japanese Tea Garden; Golden Gate Bridge; the de Young Museum

are not permitted inside; wheelchairs and power chairs are allowed.

Legion of Honor

A beautiful museum in a town filled with beauty, the **Legion of Honor** (100 34th Ave. at Clement St., 415/750-3600, http://legionofhonor.famsf.org, 9:30am-5:15pm Tues.-Sun., adults $15, seniors $12, students $6, children 17 and under free) sits on its lonely promontory in Lincoln Park, overlooking the Golden Gate. A gift to the city from philanthropist Alma Spreckels in 1924, this French Beaux-Arts-style building was built to honor the memory of California soldiers who died in World War I. From its beginning, the Legion of Honor was a museum dedicated to bringing European art to the population of San Francisco. Today visitors can view gorgeous collections of European paintings, sculpture, decorative arts, ancient artifacts from around the Mediterranean, thousands of paper drawings by great artists, and much more. Special exhibitions come from the Legion's own collections and museums of the world.

Entertainment and Events

San Francisco isn't a see-and-be-seen kind of town. You'll find gay clubs, vintage dance clubs, Goth clubs, and the occasional underground burner rave, mixed in with neighborhood watering holes.

Several bus services can ferry your party from club to club. Many of these offer VIP entrance to clubs and will stop wherever you want to go. **Think Escape** (800/823-7249, www.thinkescape.com) has buses and limos with drivers and guides to get you to the hottest spots with ease.

Nightlife
Union Square and Nob Hill

These ritzy areas are better known for their shopping than their nightlife, but a few bars hang in there, plying weary shoppers with good drinks. Most tend toward the upscale. Some inhabit upper floors of the major hotels, like the **Tonga Room & Hurricane Bar** (950 Mason St., 415/772-5278, www.fairmont.com, www.tongaroom.com, 5pm-11:30pm Wed.-Thurs. and Sun., 5pm-12:30am Fri.-Sat.), where an over-the-top tiki theme adds a whimsical touch to the stately Fairmont Hotel on Nob Hill. Enjoy the tropical atmosphere with a fruity rum drink topped with a classic paper umbrella. Be prepared for the bar's virtual tropical storms that roll in every once in a while.

Part live-music venue, part elegant bar, **Top of the Mark** (InterContinental Mark Hopkins, 999 California St., 415/392-3434, www.intercontinentalmarkhopkins.com, 4:30pm-11:30pm Mon.-Thurs., 4:30pm-12:30am Fri. Sat., 10am-1pm and 4:30pm-11:30pm Sun.) has something for every discerning taste in nighttime entertainment. Since World War II, the views at the top of the InterContinental Mark Hopkins Hotel have drawn visitors to see the city lights. Live bands play almost every night of the week, and there's a champagne brunch on Sunday mornings. The dress code is business casual or better and is enforced, so leave the jeans in your room. Have a top-shelf martini, and let your toes tap along.

Harry Denton's Starlight Room (450 Powell St., 21st Fl., 415/395-8595, www.starlightroomsf.com, 6pm-midnight Tues.-Thurs., 5pm-2am Fri.-Sat., Sun. drag shows 11:30am) brings the flamboyant side of San Francisco downtown. Enjoy a cocktail in the early evening or a nightcap and dessert after the theater in this truly old-school nightclub. Dress in your best to match the glitzy red-and-gold decor and mirrors. Whoop it up at the "Sunday's a Drag" shows. Reservations are recommended.

South of the Union Square area in the sketchy Tenderloin neighborhood, brave souls can find a gem: **The Royale** (800 Post St., 415/441-4099, www.theroyalesf. com, 4pm-midnight Sun.-Wed., 4pm-2am Thurs.-Sat.) isn't a typical watering hole by any city's standards, but its intense focus on art fits perfectly with the endlessly eclectic ethos of San Francisco. Local artists exhibit their work in Café Royale on a monthly basis, and a wide range of entertainment is available, from DJs and live jazz to movie nights.

Financial District and SoMa

All those high-powered business suit-clad executive types working in the Financial District need places to drink too. One of these is the **Royal Exchange** (301 Sacramento St., 415/956-1710, http:// royalexchange.com, 11am-11pm Mon.-Fri.). This classic pub-style bar has a green-painted exterior, big windows overlooking the street, and a long, narrow barroom. The Royal Exchange serves a full lunch and dinner menu, a small wine list, and a full complement of top-shelf spirits. But most of all, the Exchange serves beer. With 73 taps pouring out 32 different types of beer, the only problem will be choosing one. This watering hole is open to the public only on weekdays; on weekends it hosts private parties.

In SoMa (South of Market), upscale wine bars have become an evening institution. Among the trendiest you'll find is **District** (216 Townsend St., 415/896-2120, www.districtsf.com, 4pm-close Mon.-Fri., 5pm-close Sat., 11am-2:30pm Sun.). A perfect example of its kind, District features bare brick walls, simple wooden furniture, and a big U-shaped bar at the center of the room with wine glasses hanging above it. While you can get a cocktail or even a beer, the point of coming to District is to sip the finest wines from California, Europe, and beyond. With more than 40 wines available by the glass each night, it's easy to find a favorite, or enjoy a flight of three similar wines to compare. While you can't quite get a full dinner at District, you will find

a lovely lounge menu filled with small portions of delicacies to enhance your tasting experience (and perhaps soak up some of the alcohol).

Secret passwords, a hidden library, and an art deco vibe make **Bourbon & Branch** (505 Jones St., 415/346-1735, www.bourbonandbranch.com, 6pm-2am daily, reservations suggested) a must for lovers of the brown stuff. Tucked behind a nameless brown door, this resurrected 1920s-era speakeasy evokes its Prohibition-era past with passwords and secret passages. A business-class elite sips rare bourbon and scotch in dark secluded booths, while those without reservations step into the hidden library.

The **Rickhouse** (246 Kearney St., 415/398-2827, www.rickhousebar. com, 4pm-2am Mon., 3pm-2am Tues.-Fri., 6pm-2am Sat.) feels like a country shack plopped down in the midst of the Financial District. The artisanal cocktail bar draws in the city's plentiful young urban hipsters. It's dimly lit, the

walls and floors are wood, and stacks of barrels and old bottles line the mantle. There's also live music on Saturday and Monday nights.

Anchor Steam beer was first brewed in San Francisco back in 1896. **Anchor Public Taps** (495 De Haro St., 415/863-8350, www.anchorbrewing.com, noon-9pm Mon.-Wed., noon-10pm Thurs.-Sat., noon-8pm Sun.) is where you can sip that classic brew, as well as the unique beers of The Portero Project, which are brewed specifically for the public taps. The indoor beer garden hosts beer education events, game nights, and food trucks.

It's dark, it's dank, and it's very Goth. The **Cat Club** (1190 Folsom St., 415/703-8965, www.sfcatclub.com, 9pm-3am Tues.-Sun., cover charge) gets pretty energetic on 1980s dance nights, and it's still a great place to go for their Wednesday Bondage-A-Go-Go nights. Each of the two rooms has its own DJ, which somehow works perfectly even though they're only a wall apart from each other. Check the website to find the right party night for you, and expect the crowd to heat up after 11pm.

Monarch (101 6th St., 415/284-9774, www.monarchsf.com, 5:30pm-2am Tues. and Thurs., 5:30pm-midnight Wed., 5:30pm-2:30am Fri., 9am-2:30am Sat., 9am-2am Sun.) aims to be a one-stop after-dark venue. Upstairs is a Victorian-inspired cocktail lounge, while the downstairs club hosts international and local DJs. You might also catch offbeat performers like acrobats twirling from the ceilings.

AsiaSF (201 9th St., 415/255-2742, www.asiasf.com, 7:15pm-11pm Sun. and Wed.-Thurs., 7:15pm-2am Fri., 5pm-2am Sat., cover charge) is famous for its transgender performers and servers, "The Ladies of AsiaSF." Weekend reservations for dinner and a show include free admission to the dance floor downstairs.

North Beach
Jack Kerouac loved **Vesuvio** (255

Vesuvio

Columbus Ave., 415/362-3370, www. vesuvio.com, 8am-2am Mon.-Fri., 6am-2am Sat.-Sun.), which is why it's probably North Beach's most famous saloon. This cozy, bilevel hideout is an easy place to spend the afternoon with a pint of Anchor Steam. Its eclectic decor includes tables decorated with tarot cards.

Almost across the street from Vesuvio is one of the oldest and most celebrated bars in the city. **Tosca Cafe** (242 Columbus Ave., 415/986-9651, http://toscacafesf.com, 5:30pm-midnight Sun.-Thurs., 5:30pm-1am Fri.-Sat.) has an unpretentious yet glam 1940s style. Hunter S. Thompson once tended bar here when the owner was at the dentist. The jukebox plays grand opera to the patrons clustered in the big red booths. Locals love the lack of trendiness, the classic cocktails, the occasional star sightings, and the chicken marsala.

Dress up for a night out at **15 Romolo** (15 Romolo Pl., 415/398-1359, www.15romolo.com, 5pm-2am Mon.-Fri., 11:30am-2am Sat.-Sun.). You'll have to hike up the steep little alley (Fresno St. crosses Romolo Pl., which can be hard to find) to this hotel bar. You'll love the creative cocktails, edgy jukebox music, and often mellow crowd. The bar is smallish and can get crowded on the weekend, so come on a weeknight if you prefer a quiet drink.

Known for its colorful clientele and cluttered decor, **Specs** (12 William Saroyan Pl., 415/421-4112, 4pm-2am daily, cash only) is a dive bar located in a North Beach alley. Its full name is the Specs' Twelve Adler Museum Café.

Marina

Marina and Pacific Heights denizens enjoy a good glass of vino. The **Bacchus Wine Bar** (1954 Hyde St., 415/928-2633, www.bacchussf.com, 5:30pm-11pm daily) is a tiny local watering hole that offers an array of wines, sake cocktails, and craft beers.

The Marina District's Chestnut Street

is known for its high-end restaurants and swanky clientele. The **Horseshoe Tavern** (2024 Chestnut St., 415/346-1430, 10am-2am daily) is a place for people to let their hair down, shoot pool, and drink without pretension.

Get to really know your fellow beer drinkers at the tiny **Black Horse London Pub** (1514 Union St., 415/928-2414, www. blackhorselondon.com, 5pm-midnight Mon.-Thurs., 2pm-midnight Fri.-Sun., cash only), which can accommodate just nine people. Bottles of beer are served from a claw-foot bathtub located behind the bar.

Hayes Valley

Hayes Valley bleeds into Lower Haight (Haight St. between Divisadero St. and Octavia Blvd.) and supplies most of the neighborhood bars. For proof that the independent spirit of the Haight lives on despite encroaching commercialism, stop in and have a drink at the **Toronado** (547 Haight St., 415/863-2276, www.toronado. com, 11:30am-2am daily), a grimy cathedral to superb beer. This dimly lit haven with a metal- and punk rock-heavy jukebox maintains one of the finest beer selections in the nation, with a changing roster of several dozen microbrews on tap, including Russian River Brewing Company's Pliny the Elder, one of the most sought after beers in the state.

If you'd rather drink a cocktail than a beer, head over to **Smuggler's Cove** (650 Gough St., 415/869-1900, http://smugglerscovesf.com, 5pm-1:15am daily). The drink menu includes 70 cocktails and an impressive number of rare rums.

Mission

Trick Dog (3010 20th St., 415/471-2999, www.trickdogbar.com, 3pm-2am daily) is shaking up the city's cocktail scene. A new bar menu is unveiled every six months and features 12 creative cocktails. The menus are as playful as the drinks, presented as dog calendars, catalogs of paint swatch samples, and airline brochures. A small food menu includes thrice-cooked fries, Scotch eggs, and a standout kale salad.

Expect to hear some old-school vinyl from a lo-fi record player in the dimly lit **Royal Cuckoo** (3202 Mission St., 415/550-8667, http://royalcuckoo.com, 4pm-2am Mon.-Thurs., 3pm-2am Fri.-Sat., 3pm-midnight Sun.). There's also live music played on a vintage Hammond B3 organ Wednesday-Sunday. The cocktail list includes variations on the classics, including a sour old-fashioned.

Excellent draft beers, tasty barbecue plates, and a motorcycle-inclined crowd give **Zeitgeist** (199 Valencia St., 415/255-7505, 9am-2am daily) a punk-rock edge. This Mission favorite, though, endears itself to all sorts, thanks to its spacious outdoor beer garden, 40 beers on tap, and popular Bloody Marys.

Get a sweeping view of the city with superb South American cocktails at **El Techo de Lolinda** (2516 Mission St., 415/550-6970, http://eltechosf.com, 4pm-10:30pm Mon.-Thurs., 4pm-12:30am Fri., 11am-12:30am Sat., 11am-10:30pm Sun.), a rooftop bar associated with the Argentinean steak house Lolinda. The bar serves pitchers of margaritas and features agave- and rum-based drinks. The small food menu includes superb snacks like empanadas, ceviche, and a variety of skewers.

The Haight

Haight Street crowds head out in droves to the **Alembic** (1725 Haight St., 415/666-0822, www.alembicbar.com, 4pm-midnight Tues.-Wed., 4pm-2am Thurs.-Fri., 11am-2am Sat., 11am-midnight Sun.) for artisanal cocktails laced with American spirits. On par with the whiskey and bourbon menu is the cuisine.

Hobson's Choice (1601 Haight St., 415/621-5859, www.hobsonschoice.com, noon-2am daily) claims the largest selection of rums in the country. Try your rum in everything from a Brazilian caipirinha to a Cuban mojito, or in one of Hobson's famous rum punches.

Featured in an episode of Anthony Bourdain's travel show *No Reservations*, **Aub Zam Zam** (1633 Haight St., 415/861-2545, 3pm-2am Mon.-Fri., 1pm-2am Sat.-Sun.) is an old-school bar with an Arabian feel. Zam Zam doesn't take credit cards, but it does have an Arabian mural behind the U-shaped bar, where an interesting mix of locals and visitors congregate for the cheap drinks.

Located at the west end of Golden Gate Park, the **Beach Chalet Brewery** (1000 Great Hwy., 415/386-8439, www.beachchalet.com, 11am-9pm Mon.-Thurs., 11am-10pm Fri., 10am-10pm Sat., 10am-9pm Sun.) is an attractive brewpub and restaurant directly across the street from Ocean Beach. Sip a pale ale while watching the sunset, and check out the historical murals downstairs.

Gay and Lesbian

San Francisco's gay nightlife has earned a worldwide rep for both the quantity and quality of options. In fact, the gay club scene totally outdoes the straight club scene for frolicsome, fabulous fun. While the city's queer nightlife caters more to gay men than to lesbians, there's plenty of space available for partiers of all persuasions. For a more comprehensive list of San Francisco's queer bars and clubs, visit http://sanfrancisco.gaycities.com/bars.

You'll have no trouble finding a gay bar in the Castro. One of the best is called simply **Q Bar** (456 Castro St., 415/864-2877, www.qbarsf.com, 4pm-2am daily). Just look for the red neon Bar sign set in steel out front. Inside, expect to find the fabulous red decor known as "retroglam," delicious top-shelf cocktails, and thrumming beats spun by popular DJs almost every night of the week. Unlike many Castro establishments, the Q Bar caters to pretty much everybody: gay men, gay women, and gay-friendly straight folks. You'll find a coat check and adequate restroom facilities, and the strength of the drinks will make you want to take off your jacket and stay awhile.

Looking for a stylin' gay bar turned club, Castro style? Head for **Badlands** (4121 18th St., 415/626-9320, www.sfbadlands.com, 3pm-2am Mon.-Thurs. and Sat., 2pm-2am Fri. and Sun.). This Castro icon was once an old-school bar with pool tables on the floor and license plates on the walls. Now you'll find an always-crowded dance floor, au courant peppy pop music, ever-changing video screens, gay men out for a good time, and straight women who count themselves as regulars at this friendly establishment, which attracts a youngish but mixed-age crowd. The dance floor gets packed and hot, especially on weekend nights. There's a coat check on the bottom level.

The Lookout (3600 16th St., 415/431-0306, www.lookoutsf.com, 3:30pm-2am Mon.-Fri., 12:30pm-2am Sat.-Sun., cover charge) gets its name and much of its rep from its balcony overlooking the iconic Castro neighborhood. Get up there for some primo people-watching as you sip your industrial-strength alcoholic concoctions and nibble on surprisingly edible bar snacks and pizza (kitchen hours 3:30pm-2am Mon. and Wed.-Fri., 3pm-11pm Sat., 3pm-10pm Sun.). Special events come with a cover charge.

Yes, there's a Western-themed gay bar in San Francisco. **The Cinch Saloon** (1723 Polk St., 415/776-4162, 9am-2am Mon.-Fri., 8am-2am Sat.-Sun.) has a laid-back (no pun intended), friendly, male-oriented vibe that's all but lost in the once gay, now gentrified Polk Street hood. Expect fewer females and strong drinks to go with the unpretentious decor and atmosphere.

Live Music
In the late 1960s, **The Fillmore** (1805 Geary Blvd., tickets 800/745-3000, 415/346-3000, www.thefillmore.com, prices vary) became legendary for performances by rock acts like the Grateful Dead, Jefferson Airplane, and Carlos Santana. These days, all sorts of national touring acts stop by, sometimes for multiple nights. The Fillmore is also known for its distinctive poster art: Attendees to certain sold-out shows are given commemorative posters.

With its marble columns and ornate balconies, the **Great American Music Hall** (859 O'Farrell St., 415/885-0750, www.slimspresents.com, prices vary) has hosted live entertainment since 1907. It is also one of the nicest places to see a nationally touring act in the city, with bragging rights for shows by Arcade Fire and the legendary Patti Smith.

The beautiful **Warfield** (982 Market St., 415/345-0900, www.thewarfield.com) books all sorts of acts, from John Prine to the Wu-Tang Clan. Choose from limited table seating on the lowest level (mostly by reservation), reserved seats in the balconies, or open standing in the orchestra below the stage.

The **Boom Boom Room** (1601 Fillmore St., 415/673-8040, www.boomboomroom.com, 4pm-2am Sun. and Tues.-Thurs., 4pm-3am Fri.-Sat.) has kept it real in the Fillmore for more than two decades. Today you'll find the latest in a legacy of live blues, boogie, groove, soul, and funk music in this fun, divey joint.

On the other side of town, **Biscuits & Blues** (401 Mason St., 415/292-2583, www.biscuitsandblues.com, 6pm-11pm Wed.-Thurs., 5:30pm-11:30pm Fri., 5pm-11pm Sat., 5:30pm-10:30pm Sun.) is a local musicians' favorite. Headliners have included Joe Louis Walker, Jimmy Thackery, and Jim Kimo. Dinner is served nightly and features a surprisingly varied and upscale menu.

Bringing jazz to the high culture of Hayes Valley is **SFJazz Center** (201 Franklin St., 866/920-5299, http://sfjazz.org, hours vary Tues.-Sun.), a stunning 35,000-square-foot space with state-of-the-art acoustics. It's designed to feel like a small club, thanks to steep seating that brings the large audience close to the performers and has drawn major acts such as Herbie Hancock and the Afro-Cuban All Stars.

Comedy

Cobb's Comedy Club (915 Columbus Ave., 415/928-4320, www.cobbscomedy. com, shows 7:30pm, 8pm, 9:45pm, 10:15pm Thurs.-Sun., cover varies, two-drink minimum) has played host to star comedians, such as Sarah Silverman and Margaret Cho, since 1982. The 425-seat venue offers a full dinner menu and a bar to slake your thirst. Be sure to check your show's start time—some comics don't follow the usual Cobb's schedule.

The Arts
Theater

San Francisco may not be known as a big theater town, but it does boast a number of small and large theaters. A great way to grab last-minute theater tickets (or for music or dance shows) is to walk right up to **Union Square TIX** (Union Square, 415/433-7827, www.tixbayarea.com, 8am-4pm Sun.-Thurs., 8am-5pm Fri.-Sat.) for same-day, half-price, no-refund tickets to all kinds of shows across the city. TIX also sells half-price tickets to same-day shows online—check the website at 11am daily for up-to-date deals. If you really, really need to see a major musical while you're in San Francisco, check out the three venues where big Broadway productions land when they come to town: the Orpheum and Golden Gate Theatres (www.shnsf.com), and the Curran Theatre (www.sfcurran.com).

Just up from Union Square, the traditional San Francisco theater district continues to entertain crowds. The **American Conservatory Theater** (A.C.T., 415 Geary St., 415/749-2228, www.act-sf.org, shows Tues.-Sun., prices vary) puts on a season filled with big-name, big-budget productions, such as high-production-value musicals, American classics by the likes of Sam Shepard and Somerset Maugham,

and intriguing new works. They perform plays in **The Geary Theater** (405 Geary St.), a venue near Union Square that was nearly destroyed by the 1989 Loma Prieta earthquake, and at the more intimate **The Strand Theater** (1127 Market St.).

The **Curran Theatre** (445 Geary St., 415/358-1220, https://sfcurran.com, prices vary), next door to A.C.T., has a state-of-the-art stage for classic, high-budget musicals, such as *Les Misérables*, *Phantom of the Opera*, and *Chicago*. Expect to pay a premium for tickets to these productions, which can sometimes run for months or even years. Check the schedule for current shows.

Classical Music and Opera

Right around the Civic Center, culture takes a turn for the upscale. This is the neighborhood where the ultra-rich and not-so-rich classics lovers come to enjoy a night out. Acoustically renovated in 1992, **Davies Symphony Hall** (201 Van Ness Ave., 415/864-6000, www. sfsymphony.org) is home to Michael Tilson Thomas's world-renowned **San Francisco Symphony.** Loyal patrons flock to performances that range from the classic to the avant-garde. Whether you want to hear Mozart and Mahler or classic rock blended with major symphony orchestra, the San Francisco Symphony does it.

The **War Memorial Opera House** (401 Van Ness Ave., 415/621-6600, www. sfwmpac.org), a Beaux-Arts-style building designed by Coit Tower and City Hall architect Arthur Brown Jr., houses the **San Francisco Opera** (415/864-3330, http://sfopera.com) and **San Francisco Ballet** (415/865-2000, www.sfballet.org). Tours are available (415/552-8338, 10am-2pm Mon., $5-7).

Cinema

The **Castro Theatre** (429 Castro St., 415/621-6120, www.castrotheatre.com, $9-12) is a grand movie palace from the 1920s that has enchanted San Francisco audiences for almost a century. The

Castro Theatre hosts everything from revival double features (from black-and-white through 1980s classics) to musical movie sing-alongs, live shows, and even the occasional book signing. The Castro also screens current releases and documentaries about queer life in San Francisco and beyond. Once inside, be sure to admire the lavish interior decor. If you get to your seat early, you're likely to be rewarded with a performance of the Mighty Wurlitzer pipe organ before the show.

Festivals and Events

San Francisco is host to numerous events year-round. Following are some of the biggest that are worth planning a trip around.

During the **Chinese New Year Parade** (Chinatown, 415/982-3000, www.chineseparade.com, Feb.), Chinatown celebrates the Lunar New Year with a parade of costumed dancers, floats, and firecrackers.

Join rowdy, costumed revelers for **Bay to Breakers** (Embarcadero to Great Highway, www.baytobreakers.com, May), a 12K run/walk/stumble across the city through Golden Gate Park to a massive street party at Ocean Beach.

One of the year's biggest parades is the **San Francisco LGBT Pride Parade and Celebration** (Market St., www.sfpride.org, June). Hundreds of thousands of people of all orientations take to the streets for this quintessentially San Franciscan party-cum-social justice movement.

Golden Gate Park is host to two wildly popular summer music festivals. **Outside Lands** (www.sfoutsidelands.com, Aug.) is a three-day music festival that floods the park with revelers, food trucks, and hundreds of bands. Headliners have included Radiohead, LCD Soundsystem, Kanye West, Metallica, Neil Young, Janet Jackson, and Elton John. The park barely recovers in time for **Hardly Strictly Bluegrass** (www.hardlystrictlybluegrass.

com, late Sept. or early Oct.), a free music festival celebrating a wide variety of bluegrass sounds, from Lucinda Williams and Emmylou Harris to Ween and Yo La Tengo.

Shopping

Union Square

For the biggest variety of department stores and high-end international designers, plus a few select boutiques, locals and visitors alike flock to **Union Square** (bounded by Geary St., Stockton St., Post St., and Powell St.). The shopping area includes more than just the square proper: More designer and brand-name stores cluster for several blocks in all directions.

The big guys anchor Union Square. **Macy's** (170 O'Farrell St., 415/397-3333, www.macys.com, 10am-9pm Mon.-Sat., 11am-7pm Sun.) has two immense locations, one for women's clothing and another for the men's store and housewares. **Neiman Marcus** (150 Stockton St., 415/362-3900, www.neimanmarcus.com, 10am-7pm Mon.-Wed. and Fri.-Sat., 10am-8pm Thurs., noon-6pm Sun.) is a favorite among high-budget shoppers, and **Saks Fifth Avenue** (384 Post St., 415/986-4300, www.saksfifthavenue.com, 10am-7pm Mon.-Wed., 10am-8pm Thurs.-Sat., noon-7pm Sun.) adds a touch of New York style to funky-but-wealthy San Francisco.

Levi's (815 Market St., 415/501-0100, www.levi.com, 9am-9pm Mon.-Sat., 10am-8pm Sun.) may be a household name, but this three-floor fashion emporium offers incredible customization services while featuring new music and emerging art. Levi's got its start outfitting gold miners in 1849, so it's literally a San Francisco tradition.

The bones of fashion can be found at **Britex Fabrics** (117 Post St., 415/392-2910, www.britexfabrics.com, 10am-6pm Mon.-Sat.), which draws designers, quilters, DIYers, and costume geeks from all over the Bay Area to its legendary monument to fabric. If you're into any sort of textile crafting, a visit to Britex has the qualities of a religious experience. All four floors are crammed floor to ceiling with bolts of fabric, swaths of lace, and rolls of ribbon. From $1-per-yard grosgrain ribbons to $95-per-yard French silk jacquard and $125-per-yard Italian wool coating, Britex has it all.

North Beach

One of the most famous independent bookshops in a city known for its literary bent is **City Lights** (261 Columbus Ave., 415/362-8193, www.citylights.com, 10am-midnight daily). It opened in 1953 as an all-paperback bookstore with a decidedly Beat aesthetic, focused on selling modern literary fiction and progressive political tomes. As the Beats flocked to San Francisco and to City Lights, the shop put on another hat—that of publisher. Allen Ginsberg's *Howl* was published by the erstwhile independent, which never looked back. Today City Lights continues to sell and publish the best of cutting-edge fiction and nonfiction.

Marina and Pacific Heights

The shopping is good in the tony Marina and its elegant neighbor Pacific Heights. **Chestnut and Union Streets** cater to the Marina's young and affluent residents with plenty of clothing boutiques and makeup outlets. Make a stop at **Books Inc.** (2251 Chestnut St., 415/931-3633, www.booksinc.net, 9am-10pm Mon.-Sat., 9am-9pm Sun.), one of the best bookstores in the city. You'll find everything from fiction to travel, as well as a great selection of magazines. **Fillmore Street** is the other major shopping corridor. It's funkier than its younger neighbors in the Marina, probably because of its proximity to Japantown and the Fillmore.

Hayes Valley

In Hayes Valley, adjacent to the Civic Center, shopping goes uptown, but the unique scent of counterculture creativity still permeates. This is a fun neighborhood to get your stroll on, checking out the art galleries and peeking into the boutiques for clothing and upscale housewares, and then stopping at one of the lovely cafés for a restorative bite to eat.

Ver Unica (437B Hayes St. and 526 Hayes St., 415/621-6259, 11am-7pm Mon.-Thurs., 10am-7pm Fri.-Sat., noon-6pm Sun.) is a vintage boutique that attracts locals and celebrities with high-quality men's and women's clothing and accessories dating from the 1920s to the 1980s, along with a small selection of new apparel by up-and-coming designers.

Paolo Iantorno's boutique **Paolo Shoes** (524 Hayes St., 415/552-4580, http://paoloshoes.com, 11am-7pm Mon.-Sat., 11am-6pm Sun.) showcases his collection of handcrafted shoes, for which all leather and textiles are conscientiously selected and then inspected to ensure top quality.

You can hardly walk 10 feet without passing a sweet shop selling macarons. The original is **Miette** (449 Octavia St., 415/626-6221, www.miette.com, 11am-7pm daily), a cheery European-inspired candy shop, sister store to the Ferry Plaza bakery (Shop 10, 415/837-0300, 9am-7pm Mon.-Fri., 8am-7pm Sat., 10am-6pm Sun.). From double-salted licorice to handmade English toffee, the quality confections include imports from England, Italy, and France.

Mission

In a city known for its quirky style, the Mission was the last neighborhood with a funky, easy-on-the-wallet shopping district. Sadly, the days are gone when you could buy cool vintage clothes by the pound, but **Valencia Street** is still the most vibrant and diverse neighborhood for shoppers in the city.

Author Dave Eggers's tongue-in-cheek storefront at **826 Valencia** (826 Valencia St., 415/642-5905, www.826valencia.

org, 9:30am-6pm Mon.-Fri.) doubles as a pirate supply shop and youth literacy center. While you'll find plenty of pirate booty, you'll also find a good stock of literary magazines and books. Almost next door, **Paxton Gate** (824 Valencia St., 415/824-1872, www.paxtongate.com, 11am-7pm Sun.-Wed., 11am-8pm Thurs.-Sat.) takes the typical gift shop to a new level with taxidermy. This quirky spot is surprisingly cheery, with garden supplies, books, and candles filling the cases in addition to the fossilized creatures.

Haight-Ashbury

The **Haight-Ashbury shopping district** isn't what it used to be, but if you're willing to poke around a bit, you can still find a few bargains in the remaining thrift shops. One relic of the 1960s counterculture still thrives on the Haight: head shops.

Music has always been a part of the Haight. To this day you'll find homeless folks pounding out rhythms on *doumbeks* and congas on the sidewalks and on Hippy Hill in the park. Located in an old bowling alley, **Amoeba Music** (1855 Haight St., 415/831-1200, www.amoeba. com, 11am-8pm daily) is a larger-than-life record store that promotes every type of music imaginable. Amoeba's staff, many of whom are musicians themselves, are among the most knowledgeable in the business.

Award-winning **The Booksmith** (1644 Haight St., 415/863-8688, www. booksmith.com, 10am-10pm Mon.-Sat., 10am-8pm Sun.) boasts a helpful and informed staff, a fabulous magazine collection, and Northern California's preeminent calendar of readings by internationally renowned authors.

Originally a vaudeville theater, the capacious **Wasteland** (1660 Haight St., 415/863-3150, www.shopwasteland.com, 11am-8pm Mon.-Sat., 11am-7pm Sun.) has a traffic-stopping art nouveau facade, a distinctive assortment of vintage hippie and rock-star threads, and a glamour-punk staff.

Sports and Recreation

Beaches
Ocean Beach

San Francisco boasts of being a city that has everything, and it certainly comes close. This massive urban wonderland even claims several genuine sand beaches within its city limits. No doubt the biggest and most famous of these is **Ocean Beach** (Great Hwy., parking at Sloat Blvd., Golden Gate Park, and the Cliff House, 415/561-3003, www.parksconservancy. org). This 4-mile stretch of sand forms the breakwater for the Pacific Ocean along the whole west side of the city. Because it's so large, you're likely to find a spot to sit down and maybe even a parking place along the beach, except perhaps on that rarest of occasions in San Francisco—a sunny, warm day. Don't go out for an ocean swim at Ocean Beach: Extremely dangerous rip currents cause fatalities every year.

It may be hard to believe that you can surf in San Francisco, but Ocean Beach has a series of beach breaks that are good in the fall and monstrous in the winter. It's not for beginners, and even accomplished surfers can find it difficult to paddle out. Five blocks from the beach, **Aqua Surf Shop** (3847 Judah St., 415/242-9283, www.aquasurfshop.com, 10am-5:30pm Sun.-Tues., 10am-7pm Wed.-Sat., surfboard rentals $25-35 per day, wetsuits $15 per day) rents shortboards, longboards, and the very necessary 4/3 wetsuit.

Aquatic Park

The beach at **Aquatic Park** (Beach St. and Hyde St., www.nps.gov/safr) sits at the west end of the Fisherman's Wharf tourist area. This makes Aquatic Park incredibly convenient for visitors who want to grab a picnic on the Wharf to enjoy down on the beach. It was built in the late 1930s as a bathhouse catering to wealthy San Franciscans, and today, swimming remains one of Aquatic Park's main attractions: Triathletes and hardcore swimmers brave the frigid waters to swim for miles in the protected cove. More sedate visitors can find a seat and enjoy a cup of coffee, a newspaper, and some people-watching.

Baker Beach

Baker Beach (Golden Gate Point and the Presidio, 415/561-3003, www. parksconservancy.org) is best known for its scenery, and that doesn't just mean the lovely views of the Golden Gate Bridge. Baker is San Francisco's own clothing-optional (that is, nude) beach. But don't worry, plenty of the denizens of Baker Beach wear clothes while flying kites, playing volleyball and Frisbee, and even just strolling on the beach. Because Baker is much smaller than Ocean Beach, it gets crowded in the summer. Whether you choose to sunbathe nude or not, don't try to swim here. The currents get seriously strong and dangerous because it's so close to the Golden Gate.

Parks

Golden Gate Park

The largest park in San Francisco is **Golden Gate Park** (main entrance at Stanyan St. and Fell St., McLaren Lodge Visitors Center at John F. Kennedy Dr., 415/831-2700, www.golden-gate-park. com). In addition to housing popular sights like the **Academy of Sciences,** the **de Young,** and the **Japanese Tea Garden,** Golden Gate Park is San Francisco's unofficial playground. There are three botanical gardens, a **children's playground** (Martin Luther King Jr. Dr. and Bowling Green Dr.), tennis courts, and a golf course. **Stow Lake** (415/386-2531, http://stowlakeboathouse.com, 10am-6pm daily, $22-38 per hour) offers paddleboats for rent, and the park even has its own bison paddock. Weekends find the park filled with locals inline skating, biking,

hiking, and even Lindy Hopping. John F. Kennedy Drive east of Transverse Drive is closed to motorists every Saturday April-September and Sunday year-round for pedestrian-friendly fun.

Crissy Field

Crissy Field (Marina Blvd. and Baker St., 415/561-4700, www.parksconservancy. org), with its beaches, restored wetlands, and wide promenade, is the playground of the **Presidio** (415/561-4323, www.nps.gov/prsf, free). It's part of the Golden Gate National Recreation Area and is dedicated to environmental education. At the **Crissy Field Center** (1199 E. Beach, 415/561-7690, 8:30am-4:30pm daily) you'll find a list of classes, seminars, and fun hands-on activities for all ages. Many of these include walks out into the marsh and the Presidio.

Lands End

The **Lands End Trail** (Merrie Way, 415/561-4700, www.nps.gov/goga) is part of the Golden Gate National Recreation Area. Rising above rugged cliffs and beaches, Lands End (3 mi/4.8 km roundtrip, 1.5 hours, easy) feels wild, but the trail from the visitors center to Eagle's Point near the Legion of Honor is perfect for any hiking enthusiast. For a longer adventure, there are plenty of auxiliary trails to explore that lead down to little beaches. Be sure to look out for the remains of three shipwrecks on the rocks of Point Lobos at low tide. Grab a cup of hot chocolate at the stunning **Lands End Lookout visitors center** (680 Point Lobos Ave., 415/426-5240, www. parksconservancy.org, 9am-5pm daily) when your hike is finished.

Mission Dolores Park

If you're looking for a park where the most strenuous activity is people-watching, then head to **Mission Dolores Park** (Dolores St. and 19th St., 415/554-9521, http://sfrecpark.org, 6am-10pm daily). Usually called Dolores Park, it's

Twin Peaks

San Francisco from Twin Peaks

Twin Peaks rises up from the center of San Francisco and is the second-highest point in the city. Twin Peaks divides the city between north and south, catching the fog bank that rolls in from the Golden Gate and providing a habitat for lots of wild birds and insects, including the endangered Mission blue butterfly.

While you barely need to get out of your car to enjoy the stunning 360-degree views of the city from the peaks, the best way to enjoy the view is to take a hike. To scale the less-traveled **South Peak,** start at the pullout on the road below the parking lot. You'll climb a steep set of stairs up to the top of the South Peak in less than 0.2 mile. Stop and marvel at human industry: the communications tower that's the massive eyesore just over the peak. Carefully cross the road to access the red-rock stairway up to the **North Peak.** It's only 0.25 mile, but as with the South Peak, those stairs seem to go straight up! It's worth it when you look out across the Golden Gate to Mount Tamalpais in the north and Mount Diablo in the east.

If you're seeking an amazing view along with your exercise, head to Twin Peaks on a sunny day. If the fog is in, as so often happens in the summertime, you'll have trouble seeing 5 feet in front of you. Don't expect a verdant paradise—the grass doesn't stay green long in the spring, so most visitors get to see the dried-out brush that characterizes much of the Bay Area in the summer and fall.

Getting There

Drive west up **Market Street** (eventually turning into **Portola Drive**) and turn right onto **Twin Peaks Boulevard** and past the parade of tour buses to the parking lot past the North Peak. Parking is free, and Twin Peaks is open year-round.

a favorite of Castro and Mission District denizens. Bring a beach blanket to sprawl on the lawn and a picnic lunch supplied by one of the excellent nearby eateries. On weekends, music festivals and cultural events often spring up at Dolores Park.

Biking

In other places, bicycling is a sport or a mode of transportation. In San Francisco, bicycling is a religion. Some might say that the high church of this religion is the **San Francisco Bike Coalition** (415/431-2453, www.sfbike.org). In addition to providing workshops and hosting events, the Bike Coalition is an excellent resource for anyone who wants to cycle through the city. Check out its website for tips, maps, and rules of the road.

Newcomers to biking in the city may want to start off gently, with a guided tour that avoids areas with dangerous traffic. **Blazing Saddles** (2715 Hyde St., 415/202-8888, www.blazingsaddles. com, $8/hour, $32/day) rents bikes and offers tips on where to go. There are five locations, most in the Fisherman's Wharf area. If you prefer the safety of a group, take the guided tour (10am, 1pm, and 4pm daily, 3 hours, adult $55, child $35, reservations required) through San Francisco and across the Golden Gate Bridge into Marin County. One of the most popular treks is the easy and flat 9-mile (14.5-km) ride across the **Golden Gate Bridge** and back. This is a great way to see the bridge and the bay for the first time, and it takes only an hour or two to complete. Another option is to ride across the bridge and into the town of Sausalito (8 mi/13 km) or Tiburon (16 mi/26 km), enjoy an afternoon and dinner, and then ride the ferry back into the city (bikes are allowed on board).

Other easy and low-stress options are the paved paths of **Golden Gate Park** (main entrance at Stanyan St. and Fell St., McLaren Lodge Visitors Center at John F. Kennedy Dr., 415/831-2700, www.golden-gate-park.com) and the **Presidio** (Montgomery St. and Lincoln Blvd., 415/561-4323, www.nps.gov/ prsf). A bike makes a perfect mode of transportation to explore the various museums and attractions of these two large parks, and you can spend all day and never have to worry about finding parking. At the entrance of Golden Gate Park, **Golden Gate Tours & Bike Rentals** (1816 Haight St., 415/922-4537, www. goldengateparkbikerental.com, 9:30am-6:30pm daily, $8-15 per hour, $30-60 per day) has a kiosk. **Golden Gate Park Bike and Skate** (3038 Fulton St., 415/668-1117, http://goldengateparkbikeandskate.

com, summer 10am-6pm Mon.-Fri., 10am-7pm Sat.-Sun., winter 10am-5pm Mon.-Fri., 10am-6pm Sat. Sun., $5-15 per hour, $25-75 per day) is just north of the park on Fulton near the de Young Museum.

Whale-Watching

With day-trip access to the marine sanctuary off the Farallon Islands, whale-watching is a year-round activity in San Francisco. **San Francisco Whale Tours** (Pier 39, Dock B, 415/706-7364, www. sanfranciscowhaletours.com, tours daily, $45-99) offers six-hour trips out to the Farallons almost every Saturday and Sunday, with almost-guaranteed whale sightings on each trip. Shorter whale-watching trips along the coastline run on weekdays, and 90-minute quickie trips out to see slightly smaller local wildlife, including elephant seals and sea lions, also go out daily. Children ages 3-15 are welcome on boat tours (for reduced rates), and kids often love the chance to spot whales, sea lions, and pelicans. Children under age three are not permitted for safety reasons.

Spectator Sports

Lovers of the big leagues will find fun in San Francisco. Major League Baseball's **San Francisco Giants** (www.mlb.com/ giants), winners of the 2010, 2012, and 2014 World Series, play at **Oracle Park** (24 Willie Mays Plaza, 3rd St. and King St., 415/972-2000). Come out to enjoy the game, the food, and the views at San Francisco's ballpark. Giants games take place on weekdays and weekends, both day and night. It's not hard to snag last-minute tickets to a regular-season game. Check out the gourmet restaurants that ring the stadium; it wouldn't be San Francisco without top-tier cuisine.

The National Football League's **San Francisco 49ers** (www.49ers.com) left behind their longtime home at Candlestick Park in 2014 and now play at **Levi's Stadium** (4900 Marie P. DeBartolo Way,

Go Wild on the Farallon Islands

On one of those rare clear San Francisco days, you might catch a glimpse of something far offshore in the distance. It's not a pirate ship or an ocean-based optical illusion. It's the **Farallon Islands,** a series of jagged islets and rocks 28 miles (45 km) west of the Golden Gate Bridge.

At certain times, humans have attempted to make a living on these harsh rocky outcroppings. In the 1800s, Russians hunted the Farallons' marine mammals for their pelts and blubber. Following the gold rush, two rival companies harvested murre eggs on the Farallons to feed nearby San Francisco's growing population.

Now the islands have literally gone to the birds. The islands have been set aside as a national wildlife refuge, allowing the region's bird populations to flourish. The Farallons are home to the largest colony of western gulls in the world and have half the world's ashy storm petrels.

But this wild archipelago is also known for its robust population of great white sharks that circle the islands looking for seal and sea lion snacks. The exploits of a group of great white shark researchers on the island were detailed in Susan Carey's gripping 2005 book *The Devil's Teeth.*

Nature lovers who want to see the Farallons' wildlife up close can book an all-day boat trip through **San Francisco Whale Tours** (415/706-7364, www. sanfranciscowhaletours.com) or **SF Bay Whale Watching** (415/331-6267, www. sfbaywhalewatching.com). Don't fall overboard.

at Tasman Ave., 415/464-9377, www. levisstadium.com) in Santa Clara, 45 minutes south of the city.

Food

From near and far, people come to San Francisco to eat. Some of the greatest culinary innovations in the world come out of the kitchens in the city. The only problem is to narrow down the choices for dinner tonight.

Union Square and Nob Hill
Breakfast
Even on a weekday morning, there will be a line out the door of ★ **Brenda's French Soul Food** (652 Polk St., 415/345-8100, http://frenchsoulfood.com, 8am-3pm Mon.-Tues., 8am-10pm Wed.-Sat., 8am-8pm Sun., $12-17). People come in droves to this Tenderloin eatery for its delectable and filling New Orleans-style breakfasts. Unique offerings include crawfish beignets, an Andouille sausage omelet, and beef cutlet and grits. Entrées like chicken étouffée and red beans and rice top the dinner menu.

Bakeries and Cafés
Blue Bottle Café (66 Mint Plaza, 415/495-3394, www.bluebottlecoffee.net, 7am-7pm daily, $5-10), a popular local chain with multiple locations around the city, takes its equipment seriously. Whether you care about the big copper thing that made your mocha or not, you can get a good cup of joe and a small if somewhat pretentious meal at the Mint Plaza, which is Blue Bottle's only café with a full food program. It is in a building made famous by Dashiell Hammett's pulp fiction classic *The Maltese Falcon*. Expect a line.

California Cuisine
Make reservations in advance if you want to dine at San Francisco legend **Farallon** (450 Post St., 415/956-6969, www.farallonrestaurant.com, 5:30pm-9:30pm Mon.-Thurs., 5:30pm-10pm Fri.-Sat., 5:30pm-9pm Sun., $39-69). Dark, cave-like rooms are decorated in an under-the-sea theme complete with

the unique Jellyfish Bar. The cuisine, on the other hand, is out of this world. Chef Mark Franz has made Farallon a 20-year fad that just keeps gaining ground. The major culinary theme, seafood, dominates the pricey-but-worth-it menu.

Chinese

It may not be in Chinatown, but the dim sum at ★ **Yank Sing** (101 Spear St., 415/781-1111, www.yanksing.com, 11am-3pm Mon.-Fri., 10am-4pm Sat.-Sun., $4-11) is second to none. They even won a prestigious James Beard Award in 2009. The family owns and operates both this restaurant and its sister location (49 Stevenson St., 415/541-4949), and now the third generation is training to take over. Expect traditional steamed pork buns, shrimp dumplings, and egg custard tarts. Note that it's open for lunch only.

French

Tucked away in a tiny alley that looks like it might have been transported from Saint-Michel in Paris, **Café Claude** (7 Claude Ln., 415/392-3505, www.cafeclaude.com, 11:30am-10pm Mon.-Sat., 5:30pm-10pm Sun., $23-31) serves classic brasserie cuisine to French expatriates and Americans alike. Much French is spoken here, but the simple food tastes fantastic in any language. Café Claude is open for lunch through dinner (dinner only on Sun.), serving an attractive post-lunch menu for weary shoppers looking for sustenance at 3 or 4pm. In the evening it can get crowded, but reservations aren't strictly necessary if you're willing to order a classic French cocktail or a glass of wine and enjoy the bustling atmosphere and live music (on weekends) for a few minutes.

Thai

Located in the Parc 55 Wyndham Hotel, **Kin Khao** (55 Cyril Magnin St., 415/362-7456, http://kinkhao.com, 11:30am-2pm and 5:30pm-10pm Sun.-Thurs., 11:30am-2pm and 5:30pm-11pm Fri.-Sat., $10-25)

offers cuisine far beyond peanut sauces, with dishes like caramelized pork belly, vegetables in a sour curry broth, and green curry with rabbit meatballs. The curries are made from scratch, and the seafood is never frozen.

Just outside of the Union Square area, **Lers Ros Thai** (730 Larkin St., 415/931-6917, http://lersros.com, 11am-midnight daily, $9-18) is a great place to expand your knowledge of Thai cuisine. Daily specials might include stir-fried alligator or venison, while specialties include shredded green papaya salads, garlic quail, and stir-fried pork belly. Bring a handkerchief to mop up the sweat caused by these spicy dishes! Other locations are in Hayes Valley (307 Hayes St., 415/874-9661, 11am-11pm daily) and the Mission District (3189 16th St., 415/923-8978, 11:30am-10pm Sun.-Thurs., 11:30am-11pm Fri.-Sat.).

Financial District and SoMa
Bakeries and Cafés

One of the Ferry Building mainstays, the **Acme Bread Company** (1 Ferry Plaza, Ste. 15, 415/288-2978, http://acmebread.com, 7am-7:30pm Mon.-Fri., 8am-7pm Sat.-Sun.) remains true to its name. You can buy bread here, but not sandwiches, croissants, or pastries. All the bread that Acme sells is made with fresh organic ingredients in traditional style; the baguettes are traditionally French, so they start to go stale after only 4-6 hours. Eat fast!

The motto of **Café Venue** (67 5th St., 415/546-1144, www.cafevenue.com, 7am-3pm Mon.-Fri., 7am-1pm Sat., $6-10) is "real food, fast and fresh." This simple strategy is clearly working: On weekdays, you can expect a long line of local workers grabbing a salad or a sandwich for lunch. The warm chicken pesto sandwich is a highlight.

California Cuisine

★ **Michael Mina** (252 California St., 415/397-9222, www.michaelmina.net,

11:30am-2pm and 6pm-9pm Mon.-Thurs., 11:30am-2pm and 5:30pm-10pm Fri., 5:30pm-10pm Sat., 5:30pm-9pm Sun., $195) finds the celebrity chef using Japanese ingredients and French influences to create bold California entrées. This sleek, upscale restaurant with attentive service is where Mina showcases his signature dishes, including his ahi tuna tartare. With the only dinner options available being the six-course menu, expect to spend some money.

Gastropub

★ **The Cavalier** (360 Jessie St., 415/321-6000, http://thecavaliersf.com, 7am-10pm Mon.-Wed., 7am-11pm Thurs.-Fri., 10am-11pm Sat., 10am-9pm Sun., $16-34) serves a California take on upscale British pub food. The restaurant is decorated like a British hunting lodge, with mounted game heads on the walls. A stuffed fox named Floyd reclines on a bookcase in the back. As for the food, it is inventive, tasty, sometimes rich, and surprisingly well priced. The golden-fried lamb scrumpets are worth the trip, while other entrées include classics like fish-and-chips.

International

Located in the San Francisco Museum of Modern Art, the Michelin-starred **In Situ** (151 3rd St., 415/941-6050, http://insitu.sfmoma.org, 11am-3:30pm Mon., 11am-3:30pm and 5pm-9pm Thurs.-Sat., 11am-3:30pm and 5pm-8pm Sun., $12-28) is almost an art piece unto itself. The concept behind the dining room and lounge: Chef Corey Lee recreates popular dishes from fine restaurants around the world. The à la carte menu of mostly small plates features the stories of the chefs behind the creations, immersing diners in their creative process. Reservations for the dining room are recommended, but if you can't get in, opt for the 29-seat lounge.

Italian

For fine Italian-influenced cuisine, make a reservation at **Quince** (470 Pacific Ave., 415/775-8500, www.quincerestaurant.com, 5:30pm-9:30pm Mon.-Thurs., 5pm-9:30pm Fri.-Sat., $210-250). Chef-owner Michael Tusk blends culinary aesthetics to create his own unique style of cuisine. There are three options: the single extended tasting menu, the abbreviated seasonal tasting menu, or ordering à la carte from the salon menu.

Japanese

Forget your notions of the plain-Jane sushi bar; **Ozumo** (161 Steuart St., 415/882-1333, www.ozumosanfrancisco.com, 11am-2pm and 5:30pm-10:30pm Mon.-Thurs., 11am-2pm and 5:30pm-11pm Fri., 5:30pm-11pm Sat., 5:30pm-10pm Sun., $28-46) takes Japanese cuisine upscale, San Francisco-style. Order some classic *nigiri*, tempura-battered dishes, or a big chunk of meat off the traditional *robata* grill. High-quality sake lines the shelves above the bar and along the walls. Non-imbibers can choose from a selection of premium teas. If you're a night owl, enjoy a late dinner on weekends and drinks in the lounge nightly.

Seafood

It's easy to see why the ★ **Tadich Grill** (240 California St., 415/391-1849, www.tadichgrill.com, 11am-9:30pm Mon.-Fri., 11:30am-9:30pm Sat., $15-38), claiming to be the oldest restaurant in the city, has been around since 1849. Sit at the long wooden bar, which stretches from the front door back to the kitchen, and enjoy the attentive service by the white-jacketed waitstaff. The food is classic and hearty, and the seafood-heavy menu has 75 entrées, including a dozen daily specials. One of the standouts is the restaurant's delectable seafood cioppino, which might just be the best version of this Italian-American stew out there.

Esquire Magazine has proclaimed **Angler** (132 The Embarcadero, 415/872-9442, www.anglerrestaurants.com,

11:30am-2pm and 5pm-10pm Thurs., 11:30am-2pm and 5pm-11pm Fri.-Sat., 5pm 10pm Sun. Wed., $20 48) to be one of the country's best new restaurants (2018). This latest creation from the chef behind the triple Michelin-starred Saison features an à la carte menu focused on local seafood—oysters, urchins, octopus, abalone—and cooked on a wood fire. The restaurant has fun touches like a 1980s music playlist and a giant taxidermy bear.

Steak
Alexander's Steakhouse (448 Brannan St., 415/495-1111, www. alexanderssteakhouse.com, 5:30pm-9pm Sun.-Thurs., 5:30pm-10pm Fri.-Sat., $21-148) describes itself as "where East meets beef." It's true: The presentation at Alexander's looks like something you'd see on *Iron Chef*, and the prices of the Wagyu beef look like the monthly payment on a small Japanese car. This white-tablecloth steak house is the antithesis of a bargain, but the food, including the steaks, is more imaginative than most, and the elegant dining experience will make you feel special as your wallet quietly bleeds out.

Vietnamese
Probably the single most famous Asian restaurant in a city filled with eateries of all types is **The Slanted Door** (1 Ferry Plaza, Ste. 3, 415/861-8032, www. slanteddoor.com, 11am-10pm Mon.-Sat., 11:30am-10pm Sun., $11-45). Owner Charles Phan, more than 20 family members, and the rest of his staff pride themselves on welcoming service and top-quality food. Organic local ingredients get used in both traditional and innovative Vietnamese cuisine, creating a unique dining experience. Even experienced foodies remark that they've never had green papaya salad, glass noodles, or shaking beef like this before. The light afternoon-tea menu (2:30pm-4:30pm daily) can be the perfect pick-me-up for weary travelers who need some

sustenance to get them through the long afternoon until dinner, and Vietnamese coffee is the ultimate Southeast Asian caffeine experience.

Farmers Markets
While farmers markets litter the landscape in just about every California town, the **Ferry Plaza Farmers Market** (1 Ferry Plaza, 415/291-3276, www. ferrybuildingmarketplace.com, 10am-2pm Tues. and Thurs., 8am-2pm Sat.) is special. At the granddaddy of Bay Area farmers markets, you'll find a wonderful array of produce, cooked foods, and even locally raised meats and locally caught seafood. Expect to see the freshest fruits and veggies from local growers, grass-fed beef from Marin County, and seasonal seafood pulled from the Pacific beyond the Golden Gate. Granted, you'll pay for the privilege of purchasing from this market—if you're seeking bargain produce, you'll better served at one of the weekly suburban farmers markets. Even locals flock downtown to the Ferry Building on Saturday mornings, especially in the summer, when the variety of California's agricultural bounty becomes staggering.

Chinatown
Chinese Banquets
Banquet restaurants offer tasty meat, seafood, and veggie dishes along with rice, soups, and appetizers, all served family-style. Tables are often round, with a lazy Susan in the middle to facilitate the passing of communal serving bowls around the table. In the city, most banquet Chinese restaurants have at least a few dishes that will feel familiar to the American palate, and menus often have English translations.

The **R&G Lounge** (631 Kearny St., 415/982-7877, www.rnglounge.com, 11am-9:30pm Sun.-Thurs., 11am-10pm Fri.-Sat., $12-40, reservations suggested) takes traditional Chinese American cuisine to the next level. The menu is divided

by colors that represent the five elements, according to Chinese tradition and folklore. In addition to old favorites like moo shu pork, chow mein, and lemon chicken, you'll find spicy Szechuan and Mongolian dishes and an array of house specialties. Salt-and-pepper Dungeness crab, served whole on a plate, is the R&G signature dish, though many of the other seafood dishes are just as special. Expect your seafood to be fresh since it comes right out of the tank in the dining room. California-cuisine mores have made their way into the R&G Lounge in the form of some innovative dishes and haute cuisine presentations. This is a great place to enjoy Chinatown cuisine in an American-friendly setting.

Dim Sum

The Chinese culinary tradition of dim sum is translated as "touch the heart," meaning "order to your heart's content" in Cantonese. In practical terms, it's a light meal composed of small bites of a wide range of dishes. Americans tend to eat dim sum at lunchtime, though it can just as easily be dinner or even Sunday brunch. In a proper dim sum restaurant, you do not order anything or see a menu. Instead, you sip your oolong and sit back as servers push loaded steam trays out of the kitchen one after the other. Servers and trays make their way around the tables; you pick out what you'd like to try as it passes, and enough of that dish for everyone at your table is placed before you.

One of the many great dim sum places in Chinatown is the **Great Eastern** (649 Jackson St., 415/986-2500, www. greateasternrestaurant.net, 10am-11pm Mon.-Fri., 9am-11pm Sat.-Sun., $15-25), which serves its dim sum menu 10am-2:30pm daily. It's not a standard dim sum place; instead of the steam carts, you'll get a menu and a list. You must

From top to bottom: Farmers Market at the Ferry Building; dim sum in Chinatown; Tony's Pizza Napoletana.

write down everything you want on your list and hand it to your waiter, and your choices will be brought out to you, so family style is undoubtedly the way to go here. Make reservations or you may wait 30-60 minutes for a table. This restaurant jams up fast, right from the moment it opens, especially on weekends. The good news is that most of the folks crowding into Great Eastern are locals. You know what that means.

Ordering dim sum at **Delicious Dim Sum** (752 Jackson St., 415/781-0721, 7am-6pm Thurs.-Tues., $3) may pose challenges. The signs are not in English, and they don't take credit cards. Also, there is only one table inside so you'll probably be getting your dim sum to go. The inexpensive dim sum, with popular pork buns and shrimp and cilantro dumplings, among other options, is worth rising to the challenge.

North Beach and Fisherman's Wharf
Breakfast
Smack-dab in the middle of North Beach, **Mama's on Washington Square** (1701 Stockton St., 415/362-6421, www.mamas-sf.com, 8am-3pm Tues.-Sun., $8-10) is perched right across from the green lawn of Washington Square. In business since 1951, this institution is the perfect place to fuel up on gourmet omelets, freshly baked breads that include a delectable cinnamon brioche, and daily specials like crab Benedict before a day of sightseeing. Arrive early, or be prepared to wait . . . and wait.

Bakeries and Cafés
Widely recognized as the first espresso coffeehouse on the West Coast, family-owned **Caffé Trieste** (601 Vallejo St., 415/392-6739, http://coffee.caffetrieste.com, 6:30am-11pm daily, cash only) first opened its doors in 1956. It became a hangout for Beat writers in the 1950s and 1960s and was where Francis Ford Coppola penned the screenplay for his classic film *The Godfather* in the 1970s. Sip a cappuccino, munch on Italian pastries, and enjoy frequent concerts at this treasured North Beach institution. There are now four locations, from Berkeley to Monterey.

Serving some of the most famous sourdough in the city, the **Boudin Bakery & Café** (Pier 39, Space 5-Q, 415/421-0185, www.boudinbakery.com, 9am-8pm daily, $6-8) is a Pier 39 institution. Grab a loaf of bread to take with you, or order in one of the Boudin classics. Nothing draws tourists like the fragrant clam chowder in a bread bowl, but if you prefer, you can try another soup, a signature sandwich, or even a fresh salad. For a more upscale dining experience with the same great breads, try **Bistro Boudin** (160 Jefferson St., 415/351-5561, 11:30am-10pm daily, $13-38).

California Cuisine
San Francisco culinary celebrity Gary Danko has a number of restaurants, but the finest is the one that bears his name. **Gary Danko** (800 North Point St., 415/749-2060, www.garydanko.com, 5:30pm-10pm daily, prix fixe $92-134) offers the best of Danko's California cuisine, from the signature horseradish-crusted salmon medallions to the array of delectable fowl dishes. The herbs and veggies come from Danko's own farm in Napa. Choose 3-5 courses. Make reservations in advance to get a table, and dress up for your sojourn in the elegant white-tablecloth dining room.

Italian
North Beach is San Francisco's own version of Little Italy. Poke around and find one of the local favorite mom-and-pop pizza joints, or try a bigger, more upscale Italian eatery.

Want a genuine world-champion pizza while you're in town? Tony Gemignani, winner of 11 World Pizza Champion awards, can hook you up. ★ **Tony's Pizza Napoletana** (1570

Stockton St., 415/835-9888, www.tonyspizzanapoletana.com, noon-10pm Mon., noon-11pm Wed.-Sun., $15-30) has seven different pizza ovens that cook by wood, coal, gas, or electric power. You can get a classic American pie loaded with pepperoni, a California-style pie with quail eggs and chorizo, or a Sicilian pizza smothered in meat and garlic. The chef's special Neapolitan-style pizza margherita is a simple-sounding pizza made to perfection. The wood-fired atmosphere of this temple to the pie includes marble-topped tables, dark woods, and white linen napkins stuck into old tomato cans. The long full bar dominates the front dining room, so grab a fancy bottle of wine or a cocktail to go with that champion pizza. For a slice to go, head next door to **Tony's Coal-Fired Pizza and Slice House** (1556 Stockton St., 415/835-9888, http://tonyscoalfired.com, 11:30am-8pm Tues., 11:30am-11pm Wed.-Sun., 11:30am-10pm Mon., $3-6).

Trattoria Contadina (1800 Mason St., 415/982-5728, www.trattoriacontadina.com, 5pm-9pm Mon.-Thurs., 5pm-9:30pm Fri., 4pm-9:30pm Sat.-Sun., $18-35) presents mouthwatering Italian fare in a fun, eclectic dining room. Dozens of framed photos line the walls, and fresh ingredients stock the kitchen in this San Francisco take on the classic Italian trattoria. Menu items include veal, spaghetti, and gnocchi. Kids are welcome, and vegetarians will find good meatless choices on the menu.

Greek
In the Greek fishing village of Kokkari, wild game and seafood hold a special place in the local mythology. At **Kokkari Estiatorio** (200 Jackson St., 415/981-0983, www.kokkari.com, 11:30am-2:30pm and 5:30pm-10pm Mon.-Thurs., 11:30am-2:30pm and 5:30pm-11pm Fri., 5pm-11pm Sat., 5pm-10pm Sun., $22-49), patrons enjoy Mediterranean delicacies made with fresh California ingredients amid rustic elegance, feasting on such classic dishes as crispy zucchini cakes, moussaka, and grilled lamb chops.

Steak
A New York stage actress wanted a classic steak house in San Francisco, and so **Harris' Restaurant** (2100 Van Ness Ave., 415/673-1888, www.harrisrestaurant.com, 5:30pm-close Mon.-Fri., 5pm-close Sat.-Sun., $49-198) came to be. The fare runs to traditional steaks and prime rib as well as upscale features, with a Wagyu beef and surf-and-turf featuring a whole Maine lobster. Music lovers can catch live jazz in the lounge most evenings.

Marina and Pacific Heights
Breakfast
Sweet Maple (2101 Sutter St., 415/655-9169, www.sweetmaplesf.com, 8am-2:30pm Mon.-Fri., 8am-3pm Sat.-Sun., $11-22) takes breakfast to the next level. The varied menu takes eggs in new directions with morning pizzas, egg tacos, and creations including a Wagyu sliders Benedict. Wash it down with a morning cocktail. It's all served in an airy space with orchids and hanging lamps.

American
The Brixton (2140 Union St., 415/409-1114, www.brixtonsf.com, 11:30am-10pm daily, entrées $13-23) might have rock posters on the wall and loud music blaring overhead, but that doesn't mean you shouldn't try the food. The dinner menu goes late into the night and includes items like half a chicken and a tasty burger. The appetizer menu, including a chorizo clam dish and a crab cake plate, is worth grazing, and the "Tacos of the Day" can sate smaller appetites.

Japanese
With rolls named after rock acts U2 and Ozzy, it's no surprise that **Ace Wasabi's** (3339 Steiner St., 415/567-4903, www.acewasabisf.com, 5:30pm-10pm Mon.-Wed., 5:30pm-10:30pm Thurs., 5:30pm-11pm Fri.-Sat., 5pm-10pm Sun., $6-18 per

item) advertises itself as a "rock 'n' roll sushi" joint. Some of the fish is flown in from Tokyo's Tsukiji Fish Market, and the menu includes unusual offerings like tuna tostadas.

If you're in Pacific Heights, give **Kiss Seafood** (1700 Laguna St., 415/474-2866, http://kissseafoodsf.com, 5:30pm-9:30pm Wed.-Sat., $38-78) a try. This tiny restaurant (12 seats total) boasts some of the freshest fish in town, which is no mean feat in San Francisco. The lone chef prepares all the fish himself, possibly due to the tiny size of the place. If you're up for sashimi, you'll be in raw-fish heaven. Round off your meal with a glass of chilled premium sake. Reservations are a good idea.

Seafood
Anytime you come to the tiny ★ **Swan Oyster Depot** (1517 Polk St., 415/673-1101, 10:30am-5:30pm Mon.-Sat., $10-25, cash only), there will be a line out the door. With limited stools at a long marble bar, Swan, which opened in 1912, is an old-school seafood place that serves fresh seafood salads, seafood cocktails, and clam chowder, the only hot item on the menu. The seafood is so fresh that you pass it resting on ice while waiting for your barstool.

Steak
The Marina is a great place to find a big thick steak. One famed San Francisco steak house, **Boboquivari's** (1450 Lombard St., 415/441-8880, www.boboquivaris.com, 5pm-10pm Sun.-Thurs., 5pm-11pm Fri.-Sat., $23-150) prides itself on its dry-aged beef and fresh seafood. In season, enjoy whole Dungeness crab. But most of all, enjoy "The Steak," thickly cut and simply prepared to enhance the flavor of the beef. The 49-ounce porterhouse costs a pretty penny: $150.

Civic Center and Hayes Valley
California Cuisine
Housed in a former bank, **Nopa** (560 Divisadero St., 415/864-8643, http://nopasf.com, 6pm-midnight Sun.-Thurs., 6pm-1am Fri.-Sat., $16-32) brings together the neighborhood that the restaurant is named after (North of the Panhandle) with a whimsical mural by a local artist, a communal table, and a crowd as diverse as the surrounding area. A creative and inexpensive menu offers soul-satisfying dishes and keeps tables full into the wee hours. The cocktails are legendary.

State Bird Provisions (1529 Fillmore St., 415/795-1272, http://statebirdsf.com, 5:30pm-10pm Sun.-Thurs., 5:30pm-11pm Fri.-Sat., $14-22) burst onto the San Francisco dining scene in a big way, winning two James Beard Awards (Best New Restaurant in the Whole of the USA in 2013 and the Best Chef in the West in 2015). Part of the unique menu is devoted to "Pancakes and Toast," with items like a beef tongue and horseradish buckwheat pancake. Of course, they also serve the state bird (quail) with provisions.

French
★ **Jardinière** (300 Grove St., 415/861-5555, www.jardiniere.com, 5pm-close daily, $25-95) was the first restaurant opened by local celebrity chef Traci Des Jardins. The bar and dining room blend into one another and feature stunning art deco decor. The ever-changing menu is a masterpiece of French California cuisine, and Des Jardins has long supported the sustainable restaurant movement. Eating at Jardinière is not only a treat for the senses, it is also a way to support the best of trends in San Francisco restaurants. Make reservations if you're trying to catch dinner before a show.

Absinthe (398 Hayes St., 415/551-1590, www.absinthe.com, 11:30am-11pm Mon.-Wed., 11:30am-midnight Thurs.-Fri., 11am-midnight Sat., 11am-10pm Sun., $15-37) takes its name from the notorious "green fairy" drink made of liquor and wormwood. Absinthe indeed does serve absinthe, including locally made St. George Spirits Absinthe Verte. It also serves upscale French bistro fare, including what may be the best french fries in the city. The French theme carries on into the decor as well, so expect the look of a Parisian brasserie or perhaps a café in Nice, with retro-modern furniture and classic prints on the walls. The bar is open until 2am on Thursday, Friday, and Saturday, so if you want drinks or dessert after a show at the War Memorial Opera House or Davies Symphony Hall, just walk around the corner.

German

Suppenküche (525 Laguna St., 415/252-9289, www.suppenkuche.com, 5pm-10pm Mon.-Sat., 10am-2:30pm and 5pm-10pm Sun., $12.50-20) brings a taste of Bavaria to the Bay Area. The beer list is a great place to start, since you can enjoy a wealth of classic German brews on tap and in bottles, plus a few Belgians thrown in for variety. For dinner, expect German classics with a focus on Bavarian cuisine. Spaetzle, pork, sausage—you name it, they've got it, and it will harden your arteries right up. They now serve a Sunday brunch that's almost as heavy as its dinners. Suppenküche also has a **Biergarten** (424 Octavia St., 415/252-9289, http://biergartensf.com, 3pm-9pm Mon.-Sat., 1pm-7pm Sun.), two blocks away.

Mission and Castro
Bakeries and Cafés

A line snakes into the ★ **Tartine Bakery** (600 Guerrero St., 415/487-2600, www.tartinebakery.com, 8am-7pm Mon., 7:30am-7pm Tues.-Wed., 7:30am-8pm Thurs.-Fri., 8am-8pm Sat.-Sun.) almost all day long. You might think that there's an impromptu rock show or a book signing by a prominent author, but the eatery's baked goods, breads, and sandwiches are the stars. A slab of the transcendent quiche made with crème

fraîche, Niman Ranch smoked ham, and organic produce is an inspired way to start the day, especially if you are planning on burning some serious calories. Meanwhile, there is nothing quite like a piece of Passion Fruit Lime Bavarian Rectangle, a cake that somehow manages to be both rich in flavor and light as air. The latest endeavor is **Tartine Manufactory** (595 Alabama St., 415/757-0007, 8am-10pm daily), a big industrial building with a bread-baking operation, a coffee bar, a bar, and a café serving breakfast, lunch, and dinner.

You can also satisfy your sweet tooth at **Bi-Rite Creamery & Bakeshop** (3692 18th St., 415/626-5600, http://biritecreamery.com, 11am-10pm daily). The ice cream is made by hand with organic milk, cream, and eggs; inventive flavors include honey lavender, salted caramel, and white chocolate raspberry swirl. Pick up a scoop to enjoy at nearby Mission Dolores Park.

Latin American

Argentina is known for tango, wine, and beef. The latter is done superbly at ★ **Lolinda** (2518 Mission St., 415/550-6970, http://lolindasf.com, 5:30pm-midnight Fri.-Sat., 5:30pm-11pm Sun.-Thurs., $14-78). The six-ounce skirt steak has a big flavor for its modest size, while the "Gaucho," a 26-ounce bone-in rib eye, is the largest and priciest cut. All meat is cooked on a wood-fired *asador* (grill). The menu makes room for ceviche, empanadas, and grilled skewers. It's all served in a lit space decorated with a bull mural and a trio of mounted bull heads above the open kitchen.

Italian

Sometimes even the most dedicated culinary explorer needs a break from the endless fancy food of San Francisco. When the time is right for a plain ol' pizza, head for **Little Star Pizza** (400 Valencia St., 415/551-7827, www.littlestarpizza.com, noon-10pm Sun.-Thurs., noon-11pm Fri.-Sat., $12-23). A jewel of the

Mission District, this pizzeria specializes in Chicago-style deep-dish pies, but also serves thin-crust pizzas for devotees of the New York style. Once you've found the all-black building and taken a seat inside the casual eatery, grab a beer or a cocktail from the bar if you have to wait for a table. Pick one of Little Star's specialty pizzas, or create your own variation from the toppings they offer. Can't get enough of Little Star? They've got a second location in the city (846 Divisadero St., 415/441-1118).

Delfina (3621 18th St., 415/552-4055, www.delfinasf.com, 5pm-10pm Mon.-Thurs., 5:30pm-11pm Fri.-Sat., 5pm-10pm Sun., $10-32) gives Italian cuisine a hearty California twist. From the antipasti to the entrées, the dishes speak of local farms and ranches, fresh seasonal produce, and the best Italian-American taste that money can buy. With both a charming, warm indoor dining room and an outdoor garden patio, there's plenty of seating at this lovely restaurant.

Korean
Owned and operated by three brothers, **Namu Gaji** (499 Dolores St., 415/431-6268, www.namusf.com, 5:30pm-10pm Tues., 11:30am-3pm and 5:30pm-10pm Wed.-Thurs., 11:30am-3pm and 5:30pm-10:30pm Fri., 10:30am-4pm and 5pm-10:30pm Sat., 10:30am-4pm and 5pm-10pm Sun., $13-21) presents a new take on Korean food. One standout dish is the *okonomiyaki*, a pan-fried entrée made with kimchi and oysters. The adventurous can try beef tongue, while the less courageous might opt for salmon or a burger.

Seafood
For great seafood in a lower-key atmosphere, locals eschew the tourist traps on the Wharf and head for the **Anchor Oyster Bar** (579 Castro St., 415/431-3990, www.anchoroysterbar.com, 11:30am-10pm Mon.-Sat., 4pm-9:30pm Sun., $14-39) in the Castro. The raw bar features

different ways to have oysters, including an oyster *soju* (Korean liquor) shot. The dining room serves seafood, including local favorite Dungeness crab. Service is friendly, as befits a neighborhood spot, and it sees fewer large crowds. This doesn't diminish its quality, and it makes for a great spot to get a delicious meal before heading out to the local clubs for a late night out.

Sushi
ICHI Sushi (3369 Mission St., 415/525-4750, http://ichisushi.com, 5:30pm-9:30pm Sun.-Thurs., 5:30pm-10:30pm Fri.-Sat., $5-15) started out as a Bernal Heights food stall and has since evolved into a sleek restaurant with an emphasis on sustainable sashimi.

Thai
Farmhouse Thai (710 Florida St., 415/814-2920, www.farmhousethai.com, 11am-2:30pm and 5pm-10pm Mon.-Thurs., 11am-2:30pm and 5pm-10:30pm Fri., noon-10:30pm Sat., noon-10pm Sun., $15-29) bursts with color. Employees at this vibrant and hip Thai restaurant wear bright flower-print shirts as they deliver attractive dishes in bold colors, such as the blue jasmine rice. Thai staples fill the menu, including street food (fried rice, pad thai), curries, soups, and noodles. The atmosphere is fun, while the food is a creative take on classic Thai cuisine.

Golden Gate Park and the Haight
California Cuisine
One of the most famous restaurant locations on the San Francisco coast is the **Cliff House.** The high-end eatery inhabiting the famed facade is **Sutro's** (1090 Point Lobos Ave., 415/386-3330, www.cliffhouse.com, 11:30am-9:30pm Mon.-Sat., 11am-9:30pm Sun., $25-39). The appetizers and entrées are mainly seafood in somewhat snooty preparations. Although the cuisine is expensive and fancy, in all honesty it's not the best in the

city. What *is* amazing are the views from the floor-to-ceiling windows out over the vast expanse of the Pacific Ocean. These views make Sutro's a perfect spot to enjoy a romantic dinner while watching the sun set over the sea.

The Cliff House also houses the more casual **Bistro** (1090 Point Lobos Ave., 415/386-3330, www.cliffhouse.com, 9am-3:30pm and 4:15pm-9:30pm Mon.-Sat., 8:30am-3:30pm and 4:15pm-9:30pm Sun., $15-30).

Japanese

Sushi restaurants are immensely popular in these residential neighborhoods. **Koo** (408 Irving St., 415/731-7077, www.sushikoo.com, 5:30pm-10pm Tues.-Thurs., 5:30pm-10:30pm Fri.-Sat., 5pm-9:30pm Sun., $30-50) is a favorite in the Sunset. While sushi purists are happy with the selection of *nigiri* and sashimi, lovers of fusion and experimentation will enjoy the small plates and unusual rolls created to delight diners. Complementing the Japanese cuisine is a small but scrumptious list of premium sakes. Only the cheap stuff is served hot, as high-quality sake is always chilled.

Thai

Dining in the Haight? Check out the flavorful dishes at **Siam Lotus Thai Cuisine** (1705 Haight St., 415/933-8031, https://siamlotussf.com, noon-4pm and 5pm-9pm Mon. and Thurs., 5pm-9pm Wed., noon-4pm and 5pm-9:30pm Fri., noon-9:30pm Sat., noon-9pm Sun., $7-13). You'll find a rainbow of curries, pad thai, and all sorts of Thai meat, poultry, and vegetarian dishes. Look to the lunch specials for bargains, and to the Thai iced tea for a lunchtime pick-me-up. Locals enjoy the casually romantic ambiance, and visitors make special trips down to the Haight just to dine here.

Vietnamese

Thanh Long (4101 Judah St., 415/665-1146, http://thanhlongsf.com, 5pm-close Tues.-Sun., $30-50) was the first family-owned Vietnamese restaurant in San Francisco. Since the early 1970s, Thanh Long has been serving one of the best preparations of local Dungeness crab in the city: roasted crab with garlic noodles. This isn't a $5 pho joint, so expect white tablecloths and higher prices at this stately small restaurant in the outer Sunset neighborhood. Fans include actors Harrison Ford and Danny Glover.

Accommodations

Both the cheapest and the most expensive places tend to be in Union Square and downtown. Cheaper digs can be had in the neighborhoods surrounding Fisherman's Wharf. You'll find the most character in small boutique hotels, but plenty of big chain hotels have at least one location in town. Valet parking and overnight garage parking can be expensive. Check to see if your hotel has a "parking package" that includes this expense.

Union Square and Nob Hill

In and around Union Square and Nob Hill, you'll find approximately a zillion hotels. As a rule, those closest to the top of the Hill or to Union Square proper are the most expensive. For a one- or two-block walk away from the center, you get more personality and a genuine San Francisco experience for less money and less prestige. There are few inexpensive options in these areas. Hostels are located to the southwest, closer to the gritty Tenderloin neighborhood, where safety becomes an issue after dark.

$150-250

One of the best deals in town is at the ★ **Golden Gate Hotel** (775 Bush St., 415/392-3702, www.goldengatehotel.com, $180-280), centrally located between Union Square and the top of Nob Hill. This narrow yellow building has 25 rooms decorated with antiques, giving it a bed-and-breakfast feel. The cheapest option is a room with a shared bath down the hall, though there are rooms with their own baths. The Golden Gate serves a fine continental breakfast with fresh croissants.

Despite its location in the seedier Tenderloin neighborhood—or perhaps because of it—the ★ **Phoenix Hotel** (601 Eddy St., 415/776-1380, www.phoenixsf. com, $190-300) has serious rock-and-roll cred. A former motor lodge, the Phoenix has hosted a who's who of rock music, including the Red Hot Chili Peppers, Debbie Harry, and Sublime. When a Kurt Cobain letter was found mocking his wedding vows to Courtney Love, it was written on Phoenix letterhead. The main draw is the large deck with an inlaid, heated pool that has a mosaic on the bottom. Palm trees rising overhead make the Phoenix feels like it's a beachside oasis rather than sited in a gritty urban neighborhood. At night, the sounds of the surrounding Tenderloin remind you of the hotel's true location, but most guests don't come here to catch up on their sleep.

Over $250
★ **Hotel G** (386 Geary St., 415/986-2000, 877/828-4478, www.hotelgsanfrancisco. com, $279-499) comes on like an unassuming cool kid that impresses with understated style. The rooms in this boutique hotel are all simple, clean, and serene with accoutrements like smart TVs, Nespresso coffee makers, Tivoli clock radios, and comfy beds with denim headboards (a nod to Levi's San Francisco roots). The lower-level rooms have bathrooms with subway-tiled floors and showers, while the upper-floor bathrooms utilize marble flooring and shower walls. Choose a room on the 8th floor if you enjoy rooms with high ceilings. There are three drinking and dining establishments within the building. Best of all, your room will feel like a homey apartment or studio even though the hotel is just a block from bustling Union Square.

Certain names just mean luxury in the hotel world. The **Fairmont San Francisco** (950 Mason St., 415/772-5000, www. fairmont.com, 550-700) is among the best of these. With a rich history, above-and-beyond service, and spectacular views, the Fairmont makes any stay in the city memorable. While on-site, head downstairs for a Mai Tai at the Tonga Room & Hurricane Bar.

The **Ritz-Carlton** (600 Stockton St., 415/296-7465, www.ritzcarlton.com, $500-700) provides patrons with ultimate pampering. From the high-thread-count sheets to the five-star dining room and the full-service spa, guests at the Ritz all but drown in sumptuous amenities. Even the "standard" guest rooms are exceptional, but if you've got the bread, spring for the Club Floors, where they'll include a personal concierge, and possibly the kitchen sink if you ask for it.

Financial District and SoMa
Top business execs make it their, well, business to stay near the towering offices of the Financial District, down by the water on the Embarcadero, or in SoMa. Thus, most of the lodgings in these areas cater to the expense-account set. The big-name chain hotels run expensive; book one if you're traveling on an unlimited company credit card. Otherwise, look for smaller boutique and indie accommodations that won't tear your wallet to bits.

Over $250
For something small but upscale, check out **Hotel Griffon** (155 Steuart St., 415/495-2100, www.hotelgriffon.com, $230-300), a boutique business hotel with a prime vacation locale on the Embarcadero, just feet from the Ferry Building. The Griffon offers business and leisure packages to suit any traveler's needs. Although they're pricey, the best guest rooms have views of the Bay Bridge and Treasure Island.

The **Hotel Triton** (342 Grant Ave., 415/394-0500, www.hoteltriton.com, $299-349) reopened in 2019 after a $6 million renovation. The rooms are no longer decorated with text from Jack Kerouac's *On the Road*; instead, they now feature bold colors and lots of natural light. The Wi-Fi has been upgraded as well.

★ **Hotel Zetta** (55 5th St., 415/543-8555, 888/720-7004, www.viceroryhotelgroup.com/en/zetta, $300-400) embraces San Francisco's reputation as a technology hub. The ultra-modern rooms are equipped with a gaggle of gadgets, including a G-Link station for mobile devices and a device that streams content from your smartphone onto the large flat-screen TVs. There are also espresso machines and a large butcher-block desk for those who need to get work done. The hotel's common rooms are more playful, with shuffleboard, a pool table, and an oversize game of Jenga. Recycled art throughout the building includes chandeliers made of old eyeglasses, located in the lobby. The upscale on-site restaurant **The Cavalier** features British-meets-California cuisine.

Hotel Vitale (8 Mission St., 888/890-8688 or 415/278-3700, www.jdvhotels.com, $300-450) professes to restore guests' vitality with its lovely guest rooms and exclusive spa, complete with rooftop hot soaking tubs and a yoga studio. Many of the good-size guest rooms also have private deep soaking tubs. The Vitale's **Americano Restaurant** serves Italian fare.

The modern minimalism of ★ **Hotel VIA** (138 King St., 415/200-4977, www.hotelviasf.com, $300-450) is sleek yet functional and comfortable. Rooms come with rain showerheads in the elegantly tiled bathrooms and electronic tablets that guests can use to request services, play music, or browse *The New York Times*. Enjoy views of the downtown skyline, the bay, and the Bay Bridge from the **Rooftop at VIA,** a rooftop bar and lounge open to overnight guests. It's across the

The Phoenix Hotel

street from Oracle Park, so you can soak up the excitement of a Giants game some nights.

North Beach and Fisherman's Wharf

Perhaps it's odd, but the tourist mecca of San Francisco is not a district of a zillion hotels. Most of the major hostelries sit down nearer to Union Square. But you can stay near the Wharf or in North Beach if you choose; you'll find plenty of chain motels here, plus a few select boutique hotels in all price ranges.

Under $150

The unexpected **Fisherman's Wharf Hostel** (Fort Mason, Bldg. 240, 415/771-7277, www.sfhostels.com/fishermans-wharf, dorm $44-60, private room $120-175) sits in bucolic Fort Mason, far from the problems that plague other SF hostels but within walking distance of frenetic downtown. The best amenities (aside from the free parking, free

continental breakfast, and no curfews or chores) are the sweeping lawns, mature trees, and the views of Alcatraz and the bay.

The **San Remo Hotel** (2237 Mason St., 800/352-7366, www.sanremohotel.com, $124-264) is one of the best bargains in the city. The blocky old yellow building has been around since just after the 1906 earthquake, offering inexpensive guest rooms to budget-minded travelers. One of the reasons for the rock bottom pricing is the baths: You don't get your own. Four shared baths with shower facilities located in the hallways are available to guests day and night. The guest rooms boast the simplest of furnishings and decorations as well as clean, white-painted walls and ceilings. Some rooms have their own sinks, all have either double beds or two twin beds, and none have telephones or TVs, so this might not be the best choice of lodgings for large media-addicted families. Couples on a romantic vacation can rent the Penthouse, a lovely room for two with lots of windows and a rooftop terrace boasting views of North Beach and the bay.

$150-250

Hotel Bohème (444 Columbus Ave., 415/433-9111, www.hotelboheme.com, $194-320) offers comfort, history, and culture at a pleasantly low price for San Francisco. Guest rooms are small but comfortable, Wi-Fi is free, and the spirit of the 1950s bohemian Beats lives on. The warmly colored and gently lit guest rooms are particularly welcoming to solo travelers and couples, with their retro brass beds covered by postmodern geometric spreads. All guest rooms have private baths, and the double-queen room can sleep up to four people for an additional charge.

Over $250

For a luxurious stay in the city, save up for a room at **The Argonaut** (495 Jefferson St., 800/790-1415, www.argonauthotel.com,

$364-849). With stunning bay views from its prime Fisherman's Wharf location, in-room spa services, and a yoga channel, The Argonaut is all San Francisco. The rooms feature exposed brick walls and nautical-inspired decor. Guest rooms range from cozy standards to upscale suites with separate bedrooms and whirlpool tubs. The San Francisco Maritime National Historical Park's visitors center and interactive museum is located in the same building as The Argonaut.

Located on a quiet section of the Embarcadero, the ★ **Harbor Court Hotel** (165 Steuart St., 415/882-1300, www.harborcourthotel.com, $450-600) is housed in an attractive brick building a block from the Ferry Building. Spring for a harbor-view room to watch the ships pass by during the day and the pulsing lights of the Bay Bridge after dark. Modern touches include iPod docks and flat-screen TVs. Guests can get a day pass to the adjacent Embarcadero YMCA, which has a gym, a spa, and a swimming pool.

Marina and Pacific Heights

These areas are close enough to Fisherman's Wharf to walk there for dinner, and the lodgings are far more affordable than downtown digs.

$150-250

Staying at the ★ **Marina Motel** (2576 Lombard St., 415/921-9406 or 800/346-6118, www.marinamotel.com, $209-349) feels like you have your own apartment in the fancy Marina District. This European-style motor lodge features rooms above little garages where you can park your car. More than half the rooms have small kitchens with a stove, fridge, microwave, and dishes for taking a break from eating out. Though the Marina Motel was built in the 1930s, the rooms are updated with modern amenities, including sometimes-working Wi-Fi and TVs with cable. With major attractions like the Exploratorium and the Palace of Fine Arts within walking distance, this reasonably priced motel is a great place to hunker down for a few days and see the nearby sights. Reserve a room away from Lombard Street if you are a light sleeper.

Pack the car and bring the kids to the **Hotel del Sol** (3100 Webster St., 415/921-5520, 877/433-5765, www.jdvhotels.com, $200-350). This unique hotel-motel embraces its origins as a 1950s motor lodge, with the guest rooms decorated in bright, bold colors with whimsical accents, a heated courtyard pool, palm trees, hammocks, and parking for $30 a night, which is a deal in this city. The Marina locale offers trendy cafés, restaurants, bars, and shopping within walking distance, as well as access to major attractions.

The exterior and interior amenities of the **Hotel Majestic** (1500 Sutter St., 415/441-1100, www.thehotelmajestic.org, $200-300) evoke the grandeur of early 20th-century San Francisco. It is said that one of the former hotel owner's daughters haunts the Edwardian-style 1902 building, which boasts antique furnishings and decorative items from England and France. Cozy guest rooms, junior suites, and one-bedroom suites are available. The on-site **Cafe Majestic** serves breakfast and dinner, with a focus on local, healthful ingredients.

The stately **Queen Anne Hotel** (1590 Sutter St., 800/227-3970, www.queenanne.com, $200-700) brings the elegance of downtown San Francisco out to Pacific Heights. Sumptuous fabrics and rich colors in the guest rooms and common areas add to the feeling of decadence and luxury in this boutique hotel. Small, moderate guest rooms offer attractive accommodations on a budget, while superior rooms and suites are more upscale. Continental breakfast is included, as are high-end services such as courtesy car service in the morning and afternoon tea and sherry.

Over $250

Tucked in with the money-laden mansions of Pacific Heights, **Hotel Drisco** (2901 Pacific Ave., 800/634-7277, www.hoteldrisco.com, $400-500) offers elegance to discerning visitors. Away from the frenzied pace and noise of downtown, at the Drisco you get quiet, comfy guest rooms with overstuffed furniture, breakfast with a latte, and a glass of wine in the evening. Families and larger parties can look into the hotel's suite with two bedrooms and two baths. They also have a morning car service to downtown on weekdays.

The aptly named **Inn at the Presidio** (42 Moraga Ave., 415/800-7356, www.innatthepresidio.com, $295-550) is just minutes from the heart of the city, but its location in the Presidio's green space makes it feel a world away. The inn offers immediate access to the national park's hiking trails and cultural attractions along with panoramic views of the bay and Alcatraz in the distance. Most of the rooms are within a former housing unit for bachelor officers. While the inn is modernized, it nods to its past with military decorations on the lobby's walls. Continental breakfast is served in the former mess hall. Suites are spacious for the city, including a bedroom with an adjoining room, a pullout sofa, and a gas fireplace. The nearby four-bedroom **Funston House** is available for large groups.

Civic Center and Hayes Valley

You'll find a few reasonably priced accommodations and classic inns in the Civic Center and Hayes Valley areas.

Under $150

Take a step back into an older San Francisco at the **Chateau Tivoli** (1057 Steiner St., 800/228-1647, www.chateautivoli.com, $150-300). The over-the-top colorful exterior matches perfectly with the American Renaissance interior decor. Each unique guest room and suite showcases an exquisite style

evocative of the Victorian era. Some furnishings come from the estates of the Vanderbilts and J. Paul Getty. Most guest rooms have private baths, although the two least expensive share a bath.

Golden Gate Park and the Haight

Accommodations around Golden Gate Park are surprisingly reasonable. Leaning toward Victorian and Edwardian inns, most lodgings are in the middle price range for well above average guest rooms and services. However, getting downtown from the quiet residential spots can be a trek; ask at your inn about car services, cabs, and the nearest bus lines.

Out on the ocean side of the park, motor inns of varying quality cluster on the Great Highway. They've got the advantages of more space, low rates, and free parking, but they range from drab all the way down to seedy; choose carefully.

Under $150

Just west of the Haight-Ashbury neighborhood, ★ **The Metro Hotel** (319 Divisadero St., 415/861-5364, www.metrohotelsf.com, $118-244) is one of the best priced lodging options in the city. It's a huge plus that the rooms in this wonderful three-story building are also clean and comfy. Some units have bay windows that bulge out over the bustling Divisadero Street below, but don't worry; street noise is near nonexistent due to triple-paned windows. Enjoy the tranquil courtyard garden out back or pepper the friendly, 24-hour-staffed front desk with questions. The only real negative here for discerning budget travelers is the lack of designated parking.

$150-250

To say the **Seal Rock Inn** (545 Point Lobos Ave., 888/732-5762, www.sealrockinn.com, $160-202) is near Golden Gate Park pushes even the fluid San Francisco neighborhood boundaries. In fact, this pretty place perches near the tip of Lands End, only a short walk from the Pacific Ocean. All guest rooms at the Seal Rock Inn have ocean views, private baths, free parking, and free Wi-Fi. With longer stays in mind, the Seal Rock offers rooms with kitchenettes (two-day minimum stay to use the kitchen part of the room; weird but true). You can call and ask for a fireplace room that faces the Seal Rocks, so you can stay warm and toasty while training your binoculars on a popular mating spot for local sea lions. The restaurant downstairs serves breakfast and lunch; on Sunday you'll be competing with brunch-loving locals for a table.

Transportation and Services

Air

San Francisco International Airport (SFO, 800/435-9736, www.flysfo.com) is actually about 12 miles (19.5 km) south of the city center, near the town of Millbrae. You can easily get a taxi, Lyft, Uber, or other ground transportation into the heart of the city from the airport. BART is available from SFO's international terminal, but Caltrain is only accessible via a BART connection from SFO. Some San Francisco hotels offer complimentary shuttles from the airport as well. You can also rent a car here.

As one of the 30 busiest airports in the world, SFO has long check-in and security lines much of the time and dreadful overcrowding on major travel holidays. Plan to arrive at the airport two hours prior to departure for domestic flights and three hours prior to an international flight.

All the major **car rental** agencies have a presence at the airport. In addition, most reputable hotels can offer or recommend a car rental. Rates tend to run $50-100 per day and $200-550 per week (including taxes and fees), with discounts for weekly and longer rentals.

Train and Bus

Amtrak does not run directly into San Francisco. You can ride the train into the San Jose, Oakland, or Emeryville station and then take a connecting bus into San Francisco.

Greyhound (200 Folsom St., 415/495-1569, www.greyhound.com, 5:15am-1am daily) offers bus service to San Francisco from all over the country.

Car

The **Bay Bridge** (toll $5-7) links I-80 to San Francisco from the east, and the **Golden Gate Bridge** (toll $8) connects CA-1 from the north. From the south, US-101 and I-280 snake up the peninsula and into the city. Be sure to get a detailed map and good directions to drive into San Francisco—the freeway interchanges, especially surrounding the east side of the Bay Bridge, can be confusing, and the traffic congestion is legendary. For traffic updates and route planning, visit **511.org** (www.511.org).

If you have your car with you, try to get a room at a hotel with a parking lot and either free parking or a parking package for the length of your stay.

Parking

Parking a car in San Francisco can easily cost $50 per day or more. Most downtown and Union Square hotels do not include free parking with your room. Expect to pay $35-65 per night for parking, which may not include in-and-out privileges.

Street parking meters cost up to $2 per hour, often go late into the night, and charge during the weekends. At least many now take credit cards. Unmetered street parking spots are as rare as unicorns and often require residential permits for stays longer than two hours during the day. Lots and garages fill up quickly, especially during special events.

Public Transportation
Muni
The **Muni** transit system (www.sfmta. com, adults $3.00, youth and seniors $1.25, children under 4 free) can get you where you want to go as long as time isn't a concern. Bus and train tickets can be purchased from any Muni driver; underground trains have ticket machines at the entrance. Exact change is required, except on the cable cars, where drivers can make change for up to $20. See the website for a route map, tickets, and schedules.

BART
Bay Area Rapid Transit, or **BART** (www. bart.gov, fees vary), is the Bay Area's late-coming answer to major metropolitan underground railways like Chicago's L trains and New York's subway system. Sadly, there's only one arterial line through the city. However, service directly from San Francisco Airport into the city runs daily, as does service to Oakland Airport, the cities of Oakland and Berkeley, and many other East Bay destinations. BART connects to the Caltrain system and San Francisco Airport in Millbrae. See the website for route maps, schedules (BART usually runs on time), and fare information.

To buy tickets, use the vending machines found in every BART station. If you plan to ride more than once, you can add money to a single ticket and then keep that ticket and reuse it for each ride.

Caltrain
This traditional commuter rail line runs along the peninsula into Silicon Valley, from San Francisco to San Jose, with limited continuing service to Gilroy. **Caltrain** (www.caltrain.com, one-way $3.75-15) Baby Bullet trains can get you from San Jose to San Francisco in an hour during commuting hours. Extra trains are often added for San Francisco Giants, San Francisco 49ers, and San Jose Sharks games.

You must purchase a ticket in advance at the vending machines found in all stations. The main Caltrain station in San Francisco is at the corner of 4th and King Streets, within walking distance of Oracle Park and Moscone Center.

Taxis and Ride Shares
Ride-sharing drivers abound in the Bay Area. Download the apps for **Lyft** (www. lyft.com) and **Uber** (www.uber.com) on your smartphone and secure a ride. You'll find some taxis scooting around all the major tourist areas of the city. If you have trouble hailing a cab, try **City Wide Dispatch** (415/920-0700, www. citywidetransit.com).

Tours
San Francisco City Guides (415/557-4266, www.sfcityguides.org, free) is a team of enthusiastic San Francisco tour guides who want to show you more about their beloved city. Opt to learn about San Francisco sights like Fort Mason and Fisherman's Wharf, or choose a walk where you'll hear about the locales used by famed director Alfred Hitchcock in his films, including *Vertigo*. Visit the website for a complete schedule of the current month's offerings.

One of the most popular walking tour companies in the city is **Foot** (415/793-5378, www.foottours.com, prices vary). Foot was founded by stand-up comedian Robert Mac and hires comics to act as guides for its many different tours around San Francisco. The two-hour "San Francisco in a Nutshell" tour offers a funny look at the basics of city landmarks and history, and the three-hour "Whole Shebang" is a comprehensive if speedy look at Chinatown, Nob Hill, and North Beach. For visitors who are back for the second or third time, check out the more in-depth neighborhood tours that take in Chinatown, the Castro, or the Haight. You can even hit "Full Exposure," a look at the rise of 18-and-up entertainment in North Beach or "Take Me to the

Castro," a history of gay culture in the Bay Area. Tour departure points vary, so check the website for more information about your specific tour and about packages of more than one tour in a day or two.

For an inside look at the culinary delights of Chinatown, sign up for a spot on **"I Can't Believe I Ate My Way Through Chinatown"** (650/355-9657, www.wokwiz.com, $95 pp). This three-hour bonanza will take you first for a classic Chinese breakfast, then out into the streets of Chinatown for a narrated tour around Chinatown's food markets, apothecaries, and tea shops. You'll finish up with lunch at one of chef Shirley's favorite hole-in-the-wall dim sum places. For folks who just want the tour and lunch, or the tour alone, check out the standard "Wok Wiz Daily Tour" ($55 pp with lunch, $35 pp).

The **Chinatown Ghost Tour** (888/440-7976, www.sfchinatownghosttours.com, 7:30pm-9pm Fri.-Sat., adults $48) delves into the neighborhood's mysticism and rich history. The whole thing burned down more than a century ago, and it was rebuilt in exactly the same spot, complete with countless narrow alleyways. This tour will take you into these alleys after the sun sets, when the spirits are said to appear on the streets. You'll start out at Utopia Cafe (139 Waverly Pl.) and follow your loquacious guide along the avenues and side streets of Chinatown. As you stroll, your guide will tell you the stories of the neighborhood spirits, spooks, and ancestors. The curious get to learn about the deities worshipped by devout Chinese to this day, along with the folklore that permeates what was until recently a closed and secretive culture. Then you head into a former gambling den where a magician will attempt to conjure the soul of a long-dead gambler.

Information and Services

The high-tech, state-of-the-art **Moscone Visitor Information Center** (749 Howard St., 415/391-2000, www.sftravel.com, 9am-5pm Mon.-Fri., 9am-3pm Sat.-Sun.) can help with many travel needs including city tours, attraction tickets, and public transit passes.

The **San Francisco Police Department** (766 Vallejo St., 415/315-2400, http://sanfranciscopolice.org) is headquartered in Chinatown, on Vallejo Street between Powell and Stockton Streets. For life-threatening emergencies or to report a crime in progress, dial 911.

San Francisco boasts a large number of full-service hospitals. The **UCSF Medical Center at Mount Zion** (1600 Divisadero St., 415/567-6600, www.ucsfhealth.org) is renowned for its research and advances in cancer treatments and other important medical breakthroughs. The main hospital is at the corner of Divisadero and Geary Streets. Right downtown, **St. Francis Memorial Hospital** (900 Hyde St., 855/992-9873, www.dignityhealth.org), at the corner of Hyde and Bush Streets, has an emergency department.

Marin Headlands

The Marin Headlands lie north of San Francisco at the north end of the Golden Gate Bridge. The land encompasses a wide swath of virgin wilderness, former military structures, and a historic lighthouse.

Getting There

Fort Baker and the Marin Headlands are just north of the Golden Gate Bridge on CA-1 and US-101. To get to the headlands from San Francisco, take the Alexander Avenue exit, the second exit after you cross the bridge. From the north, Alexander Avenue is the last Sausalito exit. If the visitors center is the first stop on your itinerary, turn left onto Bunker Road and go through the one-way tunnel. If you want to hit Fort Barry and the Bonita Lighthouse first, follow Alexander Avenue right and travel under the highway to Conzelman Road, which leads up the hill along the edge of the headlands. Keep in mind that many of the roads are very narrow and become one-way in places.

Sights
Vista Point

Vista Point (north end of Golden Gate Bridge) offers views from the Marin Headlands toward San Francisco. If you dream of walking across the **Golden Gate Bridge** (877/229-8655, http://goldengate.org, gates 5am-6:30pm daily Nov.-Apr., 5am-9pm daily Apr.-Oct.), bring a warm coat: The wind can really whip across the span. The bridge is 1.7 miles (2.7 km) long, so a round-trip walk will turn into a 3.4-mile (5.5 km) excursion. Bikes are allowed daily 24 hours, though after 9pm they must be buzzed through a gate.

Vista Point is the first exit after crossing the Golden Gate Bridge. Note that this small parking lot fills early.

Marin Headlands Visitors Center

Start your exploration at the **Marin Headlands Visitors Center** (Fort Barry, Field Rd. and Bunker Rd., Building 948, 415/331-1540, www.nps.gov/goga, 9:30am-4:30pm Wed.-Mon.), in the old chapel at Fort Barry. Ask park rangers for the lowdown on the best trails, beaches, and campgrounds.

Point Bonita Lighthouse

The **Point Bonita Lighthouse** (415/331-1540, www.nps.gov/goga, 12:30pm-3:30pm daily, free) has been protecting the headlands for over 150 years and remains an active light station to this day. You need some dedication to visit Point Bonita, since it's only open a few days each week and there's no direct access by car. A 0.5-mile trail with steep sections leads from the trailhead on Field Road. Along the way, you'll pass through a hand-cut tunnel chiseled from the hard rock by the original builders of the lighthouse, and then you'll cross the dramatic suspension bridge that leads to the building. Point Bonita was the third lighthouse built on the West Coast and was the last staffed lighthouse in California. Today, the squat hexagonal building shelters automatic lights, horns, and signals.

Marine Mammal Center

The **Marine Mammal Center** (Fort Cronkite, 2000 Bunker Rd., 415/289-7330, www.marinemammalcenter.org, 10am-4pm daily, free) is a hospital for sick and injured seals and sea lions. Educational displays describe more about what the center does. The one-hour docent-led **tours** (adults $10, seniors and ages 5-17 $5, under age 4 free, check website for tours) explain the program in greater depth. Visitors will also get an education on the impact of human activity on marine mammals, and maybe a chance for close encounters with some of the center's patients.

Nike Missile Site

Military history buffs jump at the chance to tour a restored Cold War-era Nike missile base, known in military speak as SF-88. The **Nike Missile Site** (Field Rd. 415/331-1540, www.nps.gov/goga, 12:30-3:30pm Sat.) is the only such restored Nike base in the United States. Volunteers continue the restoration and lead **tours** (first Sat. of the month, free) of the fueling area and the testing and assembly building. You can even take a ride on the missile elevator down into the pits that once stored missiles built to defend the United States from the Soviet Union.

Recreation
Hiking

Numerous trails thread through the Marin Headlands, with unparalleled views of the Golden Gate Bridge and the Pacific Ocean.

From the Marin Headlands Visitors Center parking lot (Field Rd. and Bunker Rd.), the **Lagoon Trail** (1.75 mi/2.8 km round-trip, 1 hour, easy) encircles Rodeo

Lagoon and gives bird-watchers an ea-gle's-eye view of the egrets, pelicans, and other seabirds that call the lagoon home. The trailhead is near the restrooms.

Rodeo Beach draws many visitors on summer weekends—do not expect soli-tude on the beach or the trails, or even in the water. Locals come to surf when the break is going, while beachcombers look for the unique red and green pebbles on the shore. Note that the wind can re-ally howl out here. The Lagoon Trail ac-cesses the beach, but there is also a fairly large parking lot on Bunker Road that is much closer.

At Rodeo Beach is a trailhead for the **Coastal Trail.** To explore some of the bat-tery ruins that pockmark these hills, follow the Coastal Trail (1.5 mi/2.4 km one-way, 1 hour, easy) north to its inter-section with Old Bunker Road Trail and return to Bunker Road near the Marine Mammal Center. Or extend this hike by continuing 2.3 miles (3.7 km) up the Coastal Trail to the summit of Hill 88

and stellar views. Loop this trail by link-ing it with Wolf Ridge Trail to Miwok Trail for a moderate 5.5-mile (8.9-km) round-trip hike.

To reach the trailheads and parking lots, follow Bunker Road west to either Rodeo Beach or the Marin Headlands Visitors Center.

Biking

If you prefer two wheels to two feet, you'll find the road and trail biking in the Marin Headlands both plentiful and spectacular. From the Tennessee Valley Trailhead, there are many multiuse trails designated for bikers as well as hikers. The **Valley Trail** (4 mi/6.4 km round-trip) takes you down the Tennessee Valley and all the way out to Tennessee Beach. A lon-ger ride runs up the **Miwok Trail** (2 mi/3.2 km) northward. Turn southwest onto the **Coyote Ridge Trail** for 0.9 mile, then catch the **Coastal Fire Road** (2 mi/3.2 km) the rest of the way west to Muir Beach. Another fun ride leads from just off

Point Bonita Lighthouse

US-101 at the Rodeo Avenue exit. Park your car on the side of Rodeo Avenue and then bike down the short **Rodeo Avenue Trail,** which ends in a T intersection after 0.7 mile at **Alta Trail.** Take a left, and access to **Bobcat Trail** is a few yards away. Continue on Bobcat Trail for 2.5 miles (4 km) straight through the headlands to the **Miwok Trail** for just 0.5 mile, and you'll find yourself out at Rodeo Beach.

To rent a bicycle, visit San Francisco's **Blazing Saddles** (2715 Hyde St., 415/202-8888, www.blazingsaddles.com, $8-9/hour, $32-78/day).

Camping

Camping here requires advance planning (book sites up to three months in advance). Bring your warm camping gear, even during summer.

The most popular campground is tent-only **Kirby Cove** (Conzelman Rd., 877/444-6777, www.recreation.gov, reservations required Mar.-Nov., $30). Five secluded and shaded campsites provide a beautiful respite. Make your reservations well in advance for summer weekends, as this popular campground fills up fast. To get there, hike the trail from Battery Spencer on Conzelman Road.

The **Bicentennial Campground** (Battery Wallace parking lot, 877/444-6777, www.recreation.gov, reservations required Mar.-Dec., $20) boasts a whopping three campsites easily accessible from the parking lot. Each site can accommodate a maximum of three people, and there's no water available or fires allowed on-site. A nearby picnic area has barbecue grills that campers can use to cook a hot dinner.

The Tennessee Valley trailhead accesses **Hawk Campground** (415/331-1540, reservations required, free), with three primitive sites. Amenities include chemical toilets but no water.

Getting Around

Traffic in this area, particularly in the headlands, can be heavy on beautiful weekend days, so plan to get here early and spend the time when other people are stuck in their cars exploring the area on foot. Another option is to take bus route 76 of the **Muni** (415/701-2311, www.sfmta.com, $2.50 one-way). Making stops throughout downtown San Francisco and the north end of the city, this Sunday-only Muni line crosses the Golden Gate and ventures as far as Rodeo Cove in the headlands. It makes frequent trips, and you can even load bikes on the front.

Sausalito

The affluent town of Sausalito wraps around the north end of San Francisco Bay. The main drag runs along the shore, and the concrete boardwalk is perfect for strolling and biking. A former industrial fishing town, Sausalito still has a few old cannery buildings and plenty of docks, most now lined with pleasure boats. Sausalito has a community of people living on 400 houseboats along its northern end.

Getting There

Sausalito is north of San Francisco just over the Golden Gate Bridge; it is easily accessible by bicycle on side roads or by car on US-101. To get there, take the Alexander Avenue exit and stay right for downtown Sausalito. Once in town, park your car and walk to minimize (and avoid) traffic congestion. Street parking is mostly metered.

Sights
Fort Baker

Fort Baker (435 Murray Circle, 415/331-1540, www.nps.gov/goga, sunrise-sunset daily, free) is a 335-acre former army post established in 1905. Fort Baker is part of the Golden Gate National Recreation Area and is open to visitors. The location, just east of the Golden Gate Bridge, makes it great for city views and a wind-free beach. The fort is the best example of military architecture from the Endicott Period. It includes many elegant homes with large sweeping porches arrayed around the oval parade grounds.

Fort Baker houses the **Cavallo Point Lodge** and two restaurants. The Bay Area Discovery Museum is also nearby, along with the tiny Presidio Yacht Club.

Bay Area Discovery Museum

The **Bay Area Discovery Museum** (557 McReynolds Rd., 415/339-3900, www.baykidsmuseum.org, 9am-4pm Tues.-Fri., 10am-5pm Sat., 9am-5pm Sun., adults and children over 16 $16, seniors and children age 6-11 $14) offers kids of all ages a chance to explore the world they live in. Most of the permanent exhibits are geared toward small children, with lots of interactive components and places to play. Kids can check out easy-to-understand displays that describe the natural world, plus lots of Bay Area-specific exhibits. The Discovery Museum also has a theater and a café.

San Francisco Bay Model

The **San Francisco Bay Model** (2100 Bridgeway, 415/332-3871, www.spn. usace.army.mil, 9am-4pm Tues.-Sat., free) is a scale model of the way the bay works, complete with currents and tides. Scientists and engineering types love to see how the waters of the bay move and work.

Food

Snag a blanket and a seat on the porch to watch the fog roll in over the Golden Gate Bridge at ★ **Farley Bar** (Cavallo Point Lodge, 601 Murray Circle, Fort Baker, 415/339-4751, www.cavallopoint. com, 11:30am-11pm daily, $18-34). The bar boasts one of the most classic and contemporary cocktail menus around. Options from the bar menu include seafood and a burger made from Marin-raised beef.

The excellent **Murray Circle Restaurant** (Cavallo Point Lodge, 601 Murray Circle, Fort Baker, 415/339-4751, www. cavallopoint.com, 7am-11am, 11:30am-2pm, and 5:30pm-9pm Mon.-Fri., 7am-2pm and 5:30pm-9pm Sat.-Sun., $25-60) has a menu based on the best Marin produce, seafood, meat, and dairy. Simple dishes are executed with French technique.

★ **Fish** (350 Harbor Dr., 415/331-3474, www.331fish.com, 11:30am-8:30pm daily, $9-36, cash only) serves sustainable seafood right on the water—they even have a certificate from the California legislature to prove their commitment to sustainability. Their do-gooder status is well-earned with their delicious seafood. The rich Dungeness crab roll is drenched in butter, while the spicy Saigon salmon sandwich explodes with the taste of carrots, jalapenos, and cilantro.

For California-influenced Chinese food, go to **Tommy's Wok Chinese Cuisine** (3001 Bridgeway, 415/332-5818, http://tommyswok.com, 11:30am-3pm and 4pm-9pm Mon.-Thurs., 11:30am-3pm and 4pm-9:30pm Fri.-Sat., 4pm-9pm Sun., $14-22). The menu includes organic free-range chicken, organic tofu, and a heavy emphasis on fresh vegetables—even in the meat dishes.

★ **Avatar's Restaurant** (2656 Bridgeway Blvd., 415/332-8083, www.enjoyavatars.com, 11am-3pm and 5pm-9:30pm Mon.-Sat., $13-19) is a superb Indian fusion restaurant tucked into a strip mall. Upon entering, you might be greeted by the charismatic owner, Ashok Kumar, who will guide you through the menu. The Punjabi enchiladas are a Mexican-Indian hybrid topped with a delicious mole-like sauce made of more than 20 spices. Their signature dish is the pumpkin enchiladas, which are even better with ground turkey. The menu also includes Punjabi pastas, an Indian take on Italian.

Accommodations

Lodging options are fairly limited in the Marin Headlands except for one luxurious lodge. Many luxury-minded travelers stay in Tiburon or Sausalito.

Travelers who want budget accommodations indoors often choose the **HI Marin Headlands Hostel** (Bldg. 941, Fort Barry, 415/331-2777, www.hiusa.org, dorm $34-41, private room $85-129). Surprisingly cozy and romantic, the hostel is sheltered in the turn-of-the-20th-century buildings of Fort Barry. Facilities include a full kitchen, Internet access, laundry, and a rec room.

The ★ **Cavallo Point Lodge** (601 Murray Circle, Fort Baker, 415/339-4700, www.cavallopoint.com $449-1,300) is on the old military installation's grounds. Stay in beautiful historic homes (former officers' residences) that feature elegant early-20th-century woodwork, box-beam ceilings, and wraparound porches. Cavallo Point Lodge also has rooms and suites in two-story, environmentally friendly buildings situated on a hillside. All rooms have luxury amenities including gas fireplaces and large flat-screen TVs; contemporary rooms include stone bathroom floors and deep soaking tubs. The high-end restaurant Murray Circle and Farley Bar are on-site.

The Gables Inn (62 Princess St., 800/966-1554, www.gablesinnsausalito.com, $245-545) opened in 1869 and is the oldest B&B in the area. Each of the 16 rooms is appointed in tasteful earth tones, with white linens and several baths. Although this inn honors its long history, it has also kept up with the times, adding cable TV and Internet access. Genial innkeepers serve a continental breakfast and host a wine and cheese soiree each evening.

With a checkered history dating back to 1915, the **Hotel Sausalito** (16 El Portal, 415/332-0700, www.hotelsausalito.com, $195-375) was a speakeasy, a bordello, and a home for the writers and artists of the Beat Generation. Today, this tiny boutique hotel, with its yellow walls, cozy rooms, and locally built furnishings, evokes the Mediterranean coast.

For a taste of the good life, stay at Sausalito's **Inn Above Tide** (30 El Portal, 415/332-9435 or 800/893-8433, www.innabovetide.com, $415-1,755). The inn sits over the edge of the water looking out at the San Francisco skyline. Most rooms have private decks with sublime views (except when it's foggy) and upscale appointments. The shops, spas, and restaurants of Sausalito are within walking distance.

Getting Around

A great way to get to Sausalito from San Francisco is by ferry. Two companies make the trip daily, which takes up to an hour. The **Blue & Gold Fleet** (415/705-8200, www.blueandgoldfleet.com, adults $12.50, children and seniors $7.50, under age 5 free) makes the trip from Pier 41. Largely serving commuters, the **Golden Gate Ferry** (415/455-2000, http://goldengateferry.org, adults $12.50, children and seniors $6.25, under age 5 free) leaves from the Ferry Building, closer to downtown San Francisco.

Get your visit started with a stop at the **Sausalito Visitors Center** (780 Bridgeway, 415/332-0505, www.sausalito.org, 11:30am-4pm Tues.-Sun.).

★ Angel Island State Park

The long history of **Angel Island** (415/435-1915 or 415/435-5390, www.parks.ca.gov, 8am-sunset daily, admission rates vary) begins with regular visits (though no permanent settlements) by the Coastal Miwok people. During the Civil War the U.S. Army created a fort on the island in anticipation of Confederate attacks from the Pacific. The attacks never came, but the army maintained a base here. Today, many of the 19th-century military buildings remain and can be seen on the **tram tour** (415/897-0715 or 415/435-3392, https://angelisland.com, daily Apr.-Oct., Sat.-Sun. Nov.-Feb., adults $16.50, seniors $15, ages 6-12 $10.50), on foot, or on a docent-led **Segway tour** (415/897-0715 or 415/435-3392, https://angelisland.com, daily, $68).

Getting There

Tiburon is on a peninsula about 8 miles (13 km) north of the Golden Gate Bridge. From San Francisco, take US-101 north to the Tiburon Boulevard exit. Stay to the right and follow the road along the water for nearly 6 miles (9.5 km) until you reach the small downtown area.

Ferries

The harbor at Tiburon is the easiest place to access Angel Island. The private **Angel Island-Tiburon Ferry** (415/435-2131, http://angelislandferry.com, check website for schedule, adults $15, seniors $14, children ages 6-12 $13, ages 3-5 $5, under 3 free, bicycles $1, cash only) can get you out to the island in about 10 minutes and runs several times a day.

You can also take the **Blue & Gold Fleet** (415/705-8200, www.blueandgoldfleet.com, one-way adult $9.75, seniors and ages 5-11 $5.50, under 5 free) to Angel Island from San Francisco's Pier 41. Blue and Gold ferries sail from San Francisco at 9:45am daily; the last ferry back departs at 3:40pm (Mon.-Fri.) or 4:15pm (Sat.-Sun.). Both ferries accommodate bicycles.

Immigration Station

Angel Island's history also has a sobering side. It served as an immigration station for Chinese emigrants from 1910 to 1940, a holding center for prisoners of war during World War II, and a Japanese internment camp. During its time as an immigration checkpoint, Europeans were waved through with little more than a head-lice check, while the Chinese were herded into barracks while government officials scrutinized their papers. After months and sometimes years of waiting, many were shipped back to China. Today, poetry covers the walls of the barracks, expressing the despair of the immigrants who had hoped for a better life and found little more than prison. The **museum** (415/435-5390, 11am-3pm Wed.-Sun., adults $5, ages 6-17 $3, under 6 free) is open to visitors; docent-led **tours** are also available (11am and 12:30pm Wed.-Fri., 11am, 12:30pm, and 1:45pm Sat.-Sun., adults $7, ages 5-11 $5) that show the poetry and the buildings of the camps.

Hiking and Biking

Angel Island is a major destination for both casual and serious hikers. Adventurous trekkers can scale Mount Livermore via either the **North Ridge Trail** or the **Sunset Trail** (4.5 mi/7.2 km round-trip, 2.5 hours, moderate). Stop at the summit's picnic tables and wooden benches for a rest and to soak in the expanse of the bay region and the skyscrapers of San Francisco. For the best experience, make a loop by taking one trail up the mountain and the other back down.

For a long paved-road hike or bike ride, take the **Perimeter Road** (5 mi/8 km, moderate) all the way around the island. **Bike rentals** (415/435-3392, http://angelisland.com, daily, bikes $15/hour, $60/day, electric bikes $25/hour, $90/day) are available at Ayala Cove.

Food

On the island, the **Angel Island Café** (415/435-3392, http://angelislandsf.com, 10am-2pm Mon.-Tues., 10am-3pm Wed.-Fri., 10am-4pm Sat.-Sun. Apr. and Oct., 10am-3pm Mon.-Fri., 11am-4pm Sat.-Sun. May-Sept., $8-14) serves hot sandwiches, wraps, salads, and even a gourmet cheese platter from Cowgirl Creamery. Craving oysters and a beer? Stroll next door to the **Angel Island Cantina** (11:30am-4:30pm Sat.-Sun., $8-14).

On the marina in the gateway city of Tiburon, head to **Sam's Anchor Café** (27 Main St., 415/435-4527, www.samscafe.com, 11am-10pm Mon.-Thurs., 11am-midnight Fri., 9:30am-midnight Sat., 9:30am-10pm Sun., $18-29), which sits on the water with a large glassed-in deck. Sam's specializes in seafood and wine. Catch some rays over oysters on the half shell, fish-and-chips, or a lobster roll. At night, the fare becomes a bit fancier as dining moves indoors amid low lighting. **Servino** (9 Main St., 415/435-2676, www.servino.com, 11:30am-4pm and 5pm-9:30pm Mon.-Thurs., 11:30am-4pm and 5pm-10:30pm, 11:30am-3:30pm and 5pm-10:30pm Sat., 11:30am-3:30pm and 5pm-9:30pm Sun., $18-30) has a huge outdoor patio that offers stunning views of the bay, and the service is warm and friendly. The menu runs to hearty, Americanized Italian dishes. The full bar makes a great place to wait for a table, and Servino hosts live music on Friday nights.

Camping

Camping (800/444-7275 or www.reservecalifornia.com, $30) is available at nine primitive sites that fill up quickly (reserve six months in advance). Each "environmental site" is equipped with food lockers, surprisingly nice outhouses, running water, and a barbecue. You must bring your own charcoal or camp stove, as wood fires are strictly prohibited. The three **Ridge Sites** sit on the southwest side of the island, known to be fairly windy. The six **East Bay** and **Sunrise Sites** face the East Bay. Plan on walking 0.5-1.75 miles (0.8-2.8 km) from the ferry to your campsite.

★ Muir Woods National Monument

Giant coast redwoods are not far outside San Francisco's city limits. Some of the finest examples of these towering trees can be found at **Muir Woods National Monument** (1 Muir Woods Rd., 415/388-2596, www.nps.gov/muwo, 8am-sunset daily, $10). More than 6 miles (9.5 km) of trails wind through the lush forest and cross verdant creeks.

Getting There

Take US-101 north out of San Francisco and over the Golden Gate Bridge. Once on the north side of the bay, take the Stinson Beach/CA-1 exit. On CA-1, also named the Shoreline Highway, follow the road under the freeway and proceed until the road splits at a T junction at the light. Turn left, continuing on Shoreline

Highway for 2.5 miles (4 km). At the intersection with Panoramic Highway, make a sharp right turn and continue climbing uphill. At the junction of Panoramic Highway and Muir Woods Road, turn left and follow the road 1.5 miles (2.4 km) to the Muir Woods parking lots on the right. **Parking** and **shuttle reservations** (800/410-2419, www.gomuirwoods.com, parking $8, shuttle $3) are required in advance. Take the **Muir Woods Shuttle** (www.marintransit.org, adults $2, children and seniors $1) to avoid parking congestion, especially in summer.

Sights and Recreation

Begin your exploration at the **Muir Woods Visitors Center** (1 Muir Woods Rd., 415/388-2595, from 8am daily, closing time varies). In addition to maps, information, and advice about hiking, you'll also find a few amenities. First-time visitors should follow the wheelchair- and stroller-accessible **Main Trail Loop** (1 mi/1.6 km), an easy and flat walk with an accompanying interpretive brochure that identifies and describes the flora and fauna. Serious hikers can continue the loop on the **Hillside Trail** for an elevated view of the valley. Note that the only way to visit the monument is to reserve a parking spot and a seat on the shuttle bus to the park.

Food and Accommodations

One fine Marin lodging is **The Pelican Inn** (10 Pacific Way, Muir Beach, 415/383-6000, www.pelicaninn.com, $253-387). Inside the Tudor structure, the guest room decor continues the historic ambiance, with big-beam construction, canopy beds, and historical portrait prints. The seven mostly small rooms each come with a private bath and full English-style breakfast, but no TVs or phones. (There is free Wi-Fi.)

Enjoy a hearty plate of food at the Pelican Inn's **restaurant** (11:30am-9:30pm daily, $11-42). Dark wood and a long trestle table give the proper old English feeling to the dimly lit dining room. The cuisine brings home the flavors of old England, with dishes like beef Wellington, shepherd's pie, and fish-and-chips. True fans of the British Isles will round off the meal with a pint of Guinness.

Muir Beach

It's just a short drive to lovely **Muir Beach** (415/561-4700, www.nps.gov/goga, sunrise-sunset daily), a haven for both wildlife and beachcombers. Beach fires are allowed in the fire rings March through November. (In summer, the north end of the cove is clothing-optional.)

Muir Beach is directly off CA-1. The most direct route is to take US-101 to the Stinson Beach/CA-1 exit and follow CA-1 (also called Shoreline Highway) for 6.5 miles (10.5 km) to Pacific Way (look for the Pelican Inn). Turn left onto Pacific Way and continue straight to the Muir Beach parking lot. If arriving from Muir Woods, simply continue following Muir Woods Road down to the junction with CA-1 and turn left onto Pacific Way.

Mount Tamalpais State Park

Mount Tamalpais State Park (801 Panoramic Hwy., Mill Valley, 415/388-2070, www.parks.ca.gov, 7am-sunset daily, day-use parking $8) boasts stellar views of the San Francisco Bay Area—from Mount St. Helena in Napa down to San Francisco and across to the East Bay. The Pacific Ocean peeks from around the corner of the western peninsula, and on a clear day you can just make out the foothills of the Sierra Nevada to the east. This park is the Bay Area's backyard, with hiking, biking, and camping opportunities widely appreciated for both their beauty and easy access. Ample parking, interpretive walks, and friendly park rangers make a visit to Mount Tam a hit even for less outdoorsy travelers.

Getting There

Panoramic Highway is a long and winding two-lane road across the Mount Tamalpais area and extending all the way to Stinson Beach. Take CA-1 to the Stinson Beach exit, then follow the fairly good signs up the mountain. Turn right at Panoramic Highway at the top of the hill. Follow the road for 5 miles (8 km) until you reach the Pantoll Ranger Station. To get to the East Peak Visitors Center, take a right on Pantoll Road and then another right on East Ridgecrest Boulevard. To access the park from Stinson Beach, take a right on Panorama Highway at the T intersection with CA-1 just south of town.

Sights and Recreation

The **East Peak Visitors Center** (11am-4pm Sat.-Sun.) at the top of Mount Tam contains a small museum and gift shop as well as a picnic area with tables and restrooms and a small refreshment stand. The on-site staff can assist with hiking tips or guided walks. The **Pantoll Ranger Station** (3801 Panoramic Hwy. at Pantoll Rd., 415/388-2070, summer 8am-6pm daily, winter hours vary), which anchors the western and larger edge of the park, provides hikers with maps and camping information.

Enjoy the views without setting out on the trail at the **Bootjack Picnic Area** (Panoramic Hwy.), which has tables, grills, water, and restrooms. The small parking lot northeast of the Pantoll Ranger Station fills quickly and early in the day.

Mount Tam also provides the perfect setting for the arts. The **Mountain Theater** (E. Ridgecrest Blvd. at Pan Toll Rd.), also known as the Cushing Memorial Amphitheater, was built in

From top to bottom: Angel Island State Park; Muir Woods National Monument; Mount Tamalpais State Park.

the 1930s and still hosts plays amid its outdoor stone seating. Performances and dates vary; contact the **Mountain Play Association** (415/383-1100, www.mountainplay.org, May-June, ticket prices vary) for information and tickets. Arrive early, as both parking and seating fill completely well before the show starts.

Hiking

Mount Tam's hiking areas are divided into three major sections: the East Peak, the Pantoll area, and the Rock Springs area. Each of these regions offers a number of beautiful trails, so you'll want to grab a map from the visitors center or online to get a sense of the mountain and its hikes. For additional hikes, visit the **Friends of Mount Tam** (www.friendsofmttam.org). They have directions for 18 loop hikes.

East Peak

The charming interpretive **Verna Dunshee Trail** (1.5 mi/2 km, 1 hour, easy) offers a short, mostly flat walk along a wheelchair-accessible trail. The views are fabulous, and you can get a leaflet at the visitors center that describes many of the things you'll see along the trail. Follow Verna Dunshee counterclockwise then, back at the visitors center, climb to **Gardner Lookout** for stellar views from the top of Mount Tam's East Peak (elev. 2,571 ft/784 m).

Pantoll

The Pantoll Ranger Station is ground zero for some of the best and most challenging hikes in the park. The **Old Mine Trail** (0.5 mile, 30 min., easy) leads up to the Mountain Theater via the **Easy Grade Trail** (2 mi/3.2 km, 1 hour, easy-moderate). Eager hikers can continue on the **Rock Springs Trail** to West Point Inn and back via **Old Stage Road** for 4.7 more challenging miles (7.6 km, 5 hours).

The **Steep Ravine Trail** (3.8 mi/6.1 km, 2 hours, moderate) descends through lush Webb Creek and gorgeous redwoods

to meet with the Dipsea Trail. To return to the Pantoll parking area, turn left onto Dipsea Trail and climb the demanding steps back to the **Coastal Fire Road.** Turn left again, then right on the Old Mine Trail for an exhilarating 3.8-mile (6.1-km) hike.

The **Dipsea Trail** (7.3 mi/11.7 km round-trip, 5 hours, strenuous) is part of the famous Dipsea Race (second Sun. in June), renowned for both its beauty and its challenging stairs. The trailhead begins in Muir Woods, near the parking lot, and leads through Mount Tam all the way to Stinson Beach. Hikers can pick up the Dipsea on the Old Mine Trail or at its intersection with the Steep Ravine Trail in Mount Tam.

Rock Springs

Rock Springs is conveniently near the Mountain Theater, and a variety of trails radiate from this historical venue. Cross Ridgecrest Boulevard and take the **Mountain Theater Fire Trail** to Mountain Theater. Along the top row of the stone seats, admire the vistas while looking for **Rock Springs Trail** (it's a bit hidden). Once you find it, follow Rock Springs Trail all the way to the historic West Point Inn. The views here are stunning, and you'll see numerous cyclists flying downhill on Old Stage Road below. Cross this road to pick up Nora Trail, following it until it intersects with **Matt Davis Trail.** Turn right to reach the Bootjack day-use area. Follow the **Bootjack Trail** right (north) to return to the Mountain Theater for a 4.6-mile (7.4-km) loop.

Visit waterfalls via the lovely **Cataract Trail** (3 mi/4.8 km, easy-moderate). From the trailhead, follow Cataract Trail for a short bit before heading right on **Bernstein Trail.** Shortly, turn left onto **Simmons Trail** and continue to Barth's Retreat, site of a former camp that is now a small picnic area with restrooms. Turn left on **Mickey O'Brien Trail** (a map is helpful), returning to an intersection with the Cataract Trail. It's worth the short excursion to follow Cataract Trail to the right through the Laurel Dell picnic area and up to Cataract Falls. Enjoy a picnic at Laurel Dell before returning to Cataract Trail to follow it down to the Rock Springs trailhead.

Biking

To bike up to the peak of Mount Tam is a mark of local cyclists' strength and endurance. Rather than driving up to the East Peak or the Mountain Home Inn, sturdy cyclists pedal up the paved road to the **East Peak.** It's a long, hard 2 miles (3 km) one-way, but for an experienced cyclist the challenge and the views make it more than worthwhile. Just take care: This road is open to cars, many of which may not realize that bikers frequent the area.

Food and Accommodations

At **Mountain Home Inn** (810 Panoramic Hwy., 415/381-9000, www.mtnhomeinn. com, $195-345), the innkeepers would prefer that you relax as much as possible. With 10 rooms, many with jetted tubs, wood-burning fireplaces, and private decks, it would be hard to exert yourself. Opt for a massage, slip downstairs for a complimentary breakfast (available daily to guests), or enjoy dinner in the cozy and warmly lit dining room (11:30am-3pm Mon.-Tues., 11:30am-8pm Wed.-Fri., 8am-10:45am and 11:30am-8pm Sat.-Sun., $15-29).

Reaching the **West Point Inn** (100 Old Railroad Grade Fire Rd., Mill Valley, 415/388-9955, www.westpointinn.com, Tues.-Sat., adults $50, children $25) requires hiking 2 miles (3.2 km) on a dirt road to the entrance. The inn, which was built in 1904, has no electricity. It is lit by gaslights and warmed by fires in the large fireplaces in the downstairs lounge and parlor, where guests are encouraged to read, play games, and enjoy each other's company. There are seven rooms upstairs and five rustic cabins nearby. All guests must bring their own linens, flashlights, and food, which can be prepared in the communal kitchen. The inn hosts a **pancake breakfast** (9am-1pm second Sun. of the month July-Oct., adults $10, children $5) that draws local hikers. The wait can be long, but it is a lot of fun.

Camping

With spectacular views of the Pacific Ocean, it's no wonder that the rustic accommodations at ★ **Steep Ravine** (800/444-7275, www.reservecalifornia. com, cabins $100, campsites $25) stay fully booked. On the steep ravine (the name is no exaggeration) there are seven primitive campsites and 10 cabins adjacent to a small cove. Each rustic cabin comes equipped with a small woodstove, a table, a sleeping platform, and a grill; the campsites are also spare, but each has a table, a fire pit, and a food locker. Restrooms and drinking water are nearby. To book either a cabin or a campsite, call at 8am six months before the date you intend to go.

The **Pantoll** and **Bootjack Campgrounds** (Panoramic Hwy., 415/388-2070, www.parks.ca.gov, first-come, first-served, $25) each have 15 sites with drinking water, firewood, and restrooms nearby. The sites are pleasantly removed from the parking lot, which means that once you have gone to the trouble of hauling in all your gear, you will enjoy the quiet of car-free camping.

Stinson Beach

The primary attraction at **Stinson Beach** (415/388-2595, www.nps.gov, 9am-sunset, daily) is the tiny town's namesake: a broad and sandy stretch of coastline with weather that's unusually congenial. Although it's as plagued by fog as anywhere else in the Bay Area, on rare clear days Stinson Beach is the favorite destination for San Franciscans seeking some surf and sunshine.

To get out on the water, swing by **Stinson Beach Surf and Kayak** (3605 CA-1, 415/868-2739, www.stinsonbeachsurfandkayak.com, weekdays by appointment, 9:30am-6pm Sat.-Sun., $20-45 per day), which rents surfboards, kayaks, boogie boards, and stand-up paddleboards. Wetsuits and surf lessons are available.

Getting There

Stinson Beach is an unbelievably beautiful place to get to. First, take the Stinson Beach exit off US-101. Follow the Shoreline Highway (CA-1) as it snakes up the hill past the turnoffs for Tennessee Valley, Muir Woods, and Mount Tamalpais State Park. The road will pass through Green Gulch, where produce is grown for the legendary Greens Restaurant in San Francisco; Muir Beach; and eventually along cliffs high above the Pacific. After about 5 miles (8 km), the highway descends into Stinson Beach. Most of the town is strung along the highway, and signs make it easy to navigate to the beach.

With only one lane in each direction and a couple of intersections with stop signs, traffic backups that stretch for miles are all too common, especially on summer weekends. Your best bet is to drive in on a weekday or in the evening when everyone else is leaving.

Food and Accommodations

The best of the few small restaurants that dot the town of Stinson Beach is the **Sand Dollar Restaurant** (3458 CA-1, 415/868-0434, www.stinsonbeachrestaurant.com, 11:30am-9pm Mon.-Fri., 11am-9pm Sat.-Sun., 3pm-9pm Tues.-Thurs. in summer, $16-34). This so-called fish joint actually serves more land-based dishes than seafood.

The Siren Canteen (3201 CA-1, 415/868-1777, www.thesirencanteen.com, 11am-7pm daily summer, 11am-6pm Fri.-Mon. winter, $5-10) is right on the beach next to the lifeguard stand. This casual spot has an outdoor deck and serves tacos, crepes, fish-and-chips, and some recommended carne asada nachos.

The **Sandpiper Motel** (1 Marine Way, 415/868-1632, www.sandpiperstinsonbeach.com, $165-385) has six rooms and five cabins. Choose between motel-style accommodations with comfortable queen beds, private baths, and gas fireplaces or the individual redwood cabins, which offer additional privacy, bed space for families, and full kitchens.

★ Point Reyes National Seashore

The Point Reyes area boasts acres of unspoiled forest and beach country. Cool weather presides even in the summer, but the result is lustrous green foliage and spectacular scenery. **Point Reyes National Seashore** (1 Bear Valley Rd., 415/464-5100, www.nps.gov/pore, dawn-midnight daily) stretches for miles between Tomales Bay and the Pacific, north from Stinson Beach to the tip of the land at the end of the bay. Dedicated hikers can trek from the bay to the ocean, or from the beach to land's end. The protected lands shelter a range of wildlife. In the marshes and lagoons, a wide variety of birds—including three different species of pelicans—make their nests.

Over a thousand elephant seals call these beaches home, while endangered Myrtle's silverspot butterflies can be found in the dunes and grasslands. The pine forests shade shy deer and larger elk.

Ranches and dairy farms still operate inside the park. Grandfathered in at the time the park was created, these sustainable, generations-old family farms give added character and historical depth to Point Reyes. Another remnant of past times is the historic Point Reyes Lighthouse, which is on the cliffs of the Point Reyes Headlands, a point of land that is supposed to be the windiest place on the West Coast and the second-foggiest spot in North America.

The Point Reyes area includes the tiny towns of Olema, Point Reyes Station, and Inverness.

Getting There
Point Reyes is an hour north of San Francisco by car, but getting here can be quite a long drive. From the Golden Gate Bridge, take US-101 north to the Sir Francis Drake Boulevard exit toward San Anselmo. Follow Sir Francis Drake Boulevard west for 20 miles (32 km) to the small town of Olema and CA-1. At the intersection with CA-1, turn right (north) to Point Reyes Station and the Bear Valley Visitors Center.

Visitors Centers
The **Bear Valley Visitors Center** (1 Bear Valley Rd., 415/464-5100; 10am-5pm Mon.-Fri., 9am-5pm Sat.-Sun. Mar.-Nov., 10am-4:30pm Mon.-Fri., 9am-4:30pm Sat.-Sun. Nov.-Feb.) acts as the central visitors center for Point Reyes National Seashore. In addition to its maps, fliers, and interpretive exhibits, you can watch a short video introducing the Point Reyes region. You can also talk to the park rangers, either to ask advice or to obtain beach fire permits and backcountry camping permits. Trail maps are also available.

The **Ken Patrick Visitors Center**

(Drakes Beach, 415/669-1250, 10am-4:30pm Sat.-Sun.) sits right on the beach in a building made of weathered redwood. Its small museum focuses on the maritime history of the region, and it acts as the host area for the annual Sand Sculpture event held on the beach every Labor Day Sunday.

Point Reyes Historic Lighthouse
The jagged, rocky shores of Point Reyes make for great sightseeing but incredibly dangerous maritime navigation. In 1870 the first lighthouse was constructed on the headlands. Its first-order Fresnel lens threw light far enough for ships to see and avoid the treacherous granite cliffs.

The **Point Reyes Historic Lighthouse** (Sir Francis Drake Blvd., 415/669-1534, www.nps.gov/pore, 10am-4:30pm Fri.-Mon.) still stands today on the point past the visitors center, accessed by descending a sometimes treacherous, cold, and windblown flight of more than 300 stairs. It's worth a visit; the Fresnel lens and original machinery all remain in place, and the adjacent equipment building contains foghorns, air compressors, and other safety implements from decades past. Check the website for special events when the light is switched on.

Getting There
The lighthouse is 19 miles (31 km) west of the Bear Valley Visitors Center on Sir Francis Drake Boulevard. Parking can be difficult. To alleviate congestion, the park closes Sir Francis Drake Boulevard at the South Beach Junction on weekends. Visitors to the lighthouse must take a **shuttle** (9:30am-3pm Sat.-Sun. late-Dec.-mid-Apr., adults $7, under 16 free) from Drakes Beach. Tickets are available at the Kenneth C. Patrick Visitors Center.

Tomales Bay State Park
Tomales Bay State Park (1100 Pierce Point Rd., 415/669-1140, www.park.ca.gov, 8am-sunset daily, $8) lies within

the northern Point Reyes area and is home to four popular beaches, all accessible via scenic walks from the parking lots. Trails cross the tiny park, which serves as a popular put-in for kayaks and canoes into Tomales Bay. Kayak rentals are available at **Blue Waters** (12944 Sir Francis Drake Blvd., Inverness, 415/669-2600, www.bwkayak.com, 9am-4pm Sat.-Sun., weekdays by appointment, kayak rentals $70-90/two hours, stand-up paddleboard rental $30/hour). They also lead tours around Tomales Bay.

Getting There
To get there from the Bear Valley Visitors Center, drive 1.7 miles (2.7 km) north on Bear Valley Road. In 5.6 miles (9 km), the road becomes Sir Francis Drake Boulevard. Continue north on Sir Francis Drake Boulevard. In 1.3 miles (2.1 km), turn right onto Pierce Point Road and continue into the park.

Food
Olema
The **Sir and Star** (1000 Sir Francis Drake, Olema, 415/663-1034, http://sirandstar. com, 5pm-9pm Wed.-Sun. summer, 5pm-9pm Fri.-Sat. winter, $15-64) intrigues diners with its taxidermy interior and a menu of locally sourced meals.

Point Reyes Station and Marshall
The **Station House Café** (11180 CA-1, 415/663-1515, www.stationhousecafe. com, 8am-8pm Sun.-Tues. and Thurs., 8am-9pm Fri.-Sat., $15-30) serves food with ingredients that reflect the area's agrarian culture. The California cuisine is top-notch, more comfort food than haute cuisine. The dining room's large multi-paned windows let in tons of light, while bartenders deftly mix cocktails in the full bar. There is also an outside patio.
  Osteria Stellina (11285 CA-1, 415/663-9988, http://osteriastellina.com,

From top to bottom: Stinson Beach; Point Reyes National Seashore; Hog Island Oyster Co.

11:30am-2:30pm and 5pm-9pm daily, $16-30) has plenty of local items on the menu prepared in a rustic yet elegant Mediterranean fashion. There are thin crust pizzas, robust pastas with seafood and organic vegetables, and hearty main dishes of grilled pork chop and braised goat.

Nick's Cove (23240 CA-1, Marshall, 415/663-1033, www.nickscove.com, 11am-8pm Sun.-Thurs., 11am-9pm Fri.-Sat., $30-36) overlooks the bay in an expansive redwood building. The menu accommodates all types of diners, from those who want a light nibble with their Bloody Mary to those eager for a high-end meal. Out back is a long deck and a boathouse, perfect to explore with the little ones.

Located on the banks of Tomales Bay, **The Marshall Store** (19225 CA-1, Marshall, 415/663-1339, https://themarshallstore.com, 10am-4pm Mon. and Wed.-Fri., 10am-5pm Sat.-Sun., $8-25) is a great place to taste the bounty of the region in a casual atmosphere. Order oysters (raw, smoked, barbecued), local Dungeness crab from nearby Bodega Bay, house-smoked meat, or hearty sandwiches.

There is no better place to stock a picnic basket than the **Bovine Bakery** (11315 CA-1, 415/663-9420, www.bovinebakeryptreyes.com, 6:30am-5pm Mon.-Fri., 7am-5pm Sat., 7am-4pm Sun.), where you can pick up a cup of coffee, loaves of bread, cookies, pizza, quiche, and salads.

Around the corner is **Cowgirl Creamery** (80 4th St., 415/663-9335, www.cowgirlcreamery.com, 10am-5pm Wed.-Sun.), which produces the best cheese in the Bay Area. All cheese is made on-site in the French brie style. Tours are available Friday mornings by appointment only.

The **Tomales Bay Oyster Co.** (15479 CA-1, Marshall, 415/663-1243, www.tomalesbayoystercompany.com, noon-5pm Fri., 9am-5pm Sat.-Sun.) is a low-key affair where you can buy a wide selection of oysters, clams, and mussels in an open-air market a few feet from where they are harvested.

Hog Island Oyster Co. (20215 CA-1, 415/663-9218, www.hogislandoysters.com, 9am-5pm daily) has an open-air stand where you can buy and barbecue oysters. Hog Island gets insanely busy on weekends and parking can be tricky. Reserve a table and/or grill (10am-5pm daily) online.

For a drink (and a bit of local color), slip through the swinging doors of the **Old Western Saloon** (11201 CA-1, 415/663-1661, 10am-2am daily). At this crusty old West Marin haunt you'll see ranchers yukking it up with park rangers, patrons young and old, longtime natives, and recent transplants. Live music goes down on Friday and Saturday nights.

Inverness

Vladimir's Czechoslovakian Restaurant (12785 Sir Francis Drake Blvd., 415/669-1021, noon-9pm Wed.-Sun., 5pm-9pm Tues., $17-27, cash only) serves serious Czech food: borscht, rabbit, duck, and all manner of delicious things. Dine on the patio if the weather is nice.

The **Saltwater Oyster Depot** (12781 Sir Francis Drake Blvd., 415/669-1244, www.saltwateroysterdepot.com, 5pm-9pm Mon. and Thurs.-Fri., noon-9pm Sat.-Sun., $29-31) is an oyster bar, a wine shop, and a beloved restaurant serving plenty of oysters and wine along with small plates and seafood entrées.

The **Inverness Park Market Deli** (12301 Sir Francis Drake Blvd., 415/663-1491, https://invernessparkmarket.com, 7am-7pm Mon.-Thurs., 7am-8pm Fri.-Sat., 8am-7pm Sun., $5-13) serves killer breakfast sandwiches and Reubens. They also have a **taproom** (4pm-8pm Mon.-Thurs., 4pm-9pm Fri., 11am-9pm Sat., 11am-8pm Sun., $8-16) that serves quality food (sandwiches, fish tacos, and noodle bowls) and has six beers on tap.

Accommodations

Accommodations are a bit limited. Vacation homes in the area are represented by **Point Reyes Vacation Rentals** (415/663-6113, http://pointreyesvacationrentals.com).

Olema

The **Olema House** (10021 CA-1, 415/663-9000 or 800/404-5634, https://olemahouse.com, $225-675) has luxury lodging in 22 remodeled rooms and two cottages. All rooms have private baths, some with whirlpool tubs, and a couple of suites with special amenities are located away from the main lodge for extra privacy. Attractive gardens with winding brick pathways roll out to Olema Creek. The Due West restaurant and market adjoins the hotel, providing plenty of food and drink options.

Point Reyes Station

Point Reyes Station Inn (11591 CA-1, 415/663-9372, www.pointreyesstationinn.com, $150-225) is a five-room inn with light and airy turn-of-the-20th-century charm. Rooms are decorated in heavy antique furnishings that are lightened by the vaulted ceilings, large windows, and glass doors leading to private porches. All but one have fireplaces and private en suite baths. There is a communal hot tub, and the continental breakfast features eggs from the inn's own chickens and seasonal homegrown fruit.

Lingonberry Farm B&B (12430 CA-1, 415/663-1826, www.lingonberryfarm.com, $180) is outfitted in bright, simple Swedish style. Each of the three rooms is distinctively decorated in blues, yellows, and crisp whites with trim farmstyle furniture and minimalist artwork. All have private baths. Downstairs in the sunny dining area, guests are treated to a breakfast buffet.

The eco-friendly ★ **Point Reyes Hostel** (1390 Limantour Spit Rd., 415/663-8811, www.norcalhostels.org/reyes, dorm beds $35-39, private rooms $105-130) is steps from fantastic hiking and lush natural scenery. Dorm accommodations are spare but comfortable. Pick the affordable dorm rooms or one of four private rooms in a newer building with its own kitchen. Each private room has four beds. These are very popular, so try to book well in advance. The hostel also has a communal kitchen and a nice outdoor space on a brick patio.

Inverness

★ **Manka's Inverness Lodge** (30 Callendar Way, 415/669-1034, www.mankas.com, $225-635) has a woodsy charm that has made it a favorite of Bay Area weekenders. The lodge has four upstairs rooms decked out with deep reading chairs, plush beds with tree-limb posts, and antique fixtures. Four similar rooms are in the annex. Two of the four cabins are perched on Inverness Ridge to make the most of the views. All feature large sitting rooms with stone fireplaces. Some have private hot tubs or luxurious outdoor showers. Two more modern lodgings can be found a few miles from the main compound hanging over the edge of Tomales Bay: The Boat House is akin to a small, lushly appointed loft, with two baths and multiple sleeping spaces. The smaller Boatman's Quarters has lovely views of the bay, a private deck, and a fireplace. The celebrated dining room features a prix fixe multicourse dinner ($58).

Constructed of natural wood with lovely and fanciful flourishes, **Motel Inverness** (12718 Sir Francis Drake Blvd., 415/236-1967 or 866/453-3839, www.motelinverness.com, $150-345) is more like a classic lodge than a typical motel. There are rooms and suites with full kitchens, and all are decorated in light colors with minimal fuss. Inside the main lodge is a grand lounge, where you can play pool on the antique pool table, read in front of the stone fireplace, or sip a glass of wine on the expansive deck.

Camping

The only camping is in the **Point Reyes National Seashore** (877/444-6777, www.recreation.gov, $20-50). All are hike-in sites that require reservations months in advance. Campsites have a pit toilet, a water faucet, a picnic table, a charcoal grill, and a food locker.

Sky Camp is accessed via a 1.4-mile (2.3-km) trail on Limantour Road. The campground includes 11 individual sites and 1 group site. From its location at 1,025 feet elevation (312 m), you'll get great views of the Pacific Ocean and Drakes Bay (if it's not foggy).

Near the end of Limantour Road is the trailhead for **Coast Camp.** The campground is in a quiet valley of coastal scrub and willow trees, 200 yards from the beach. There are 12 individual campsites and 2 group sites. There are two routes to get here: one that is 1.8 miles (2.9 km) up-hill along the Laguna and Firelane Trails, and the longer 2.7-mile (4.3-km) Coast Trail route, which is flat and considerably easier when carrying camping gear.

Wildcat Camp has five individual sites and three group sites. It is set away from the beach on an open bluff-top meadow. From Bear Valley it is a 5.5-mile (8.9-km) hike or an easier but longer 6.7-mile (10.8-km) stroll on the Coast Trail.

Secluded **Glen Camp** is hidden deep within a valley and protected from ocean winds. The campground is a healthy 4.6 miles (7.4 km) from the Bear Valley Trailhead. There are 12 individual sites and no group sites.

**Wine
Country**

Wine Country

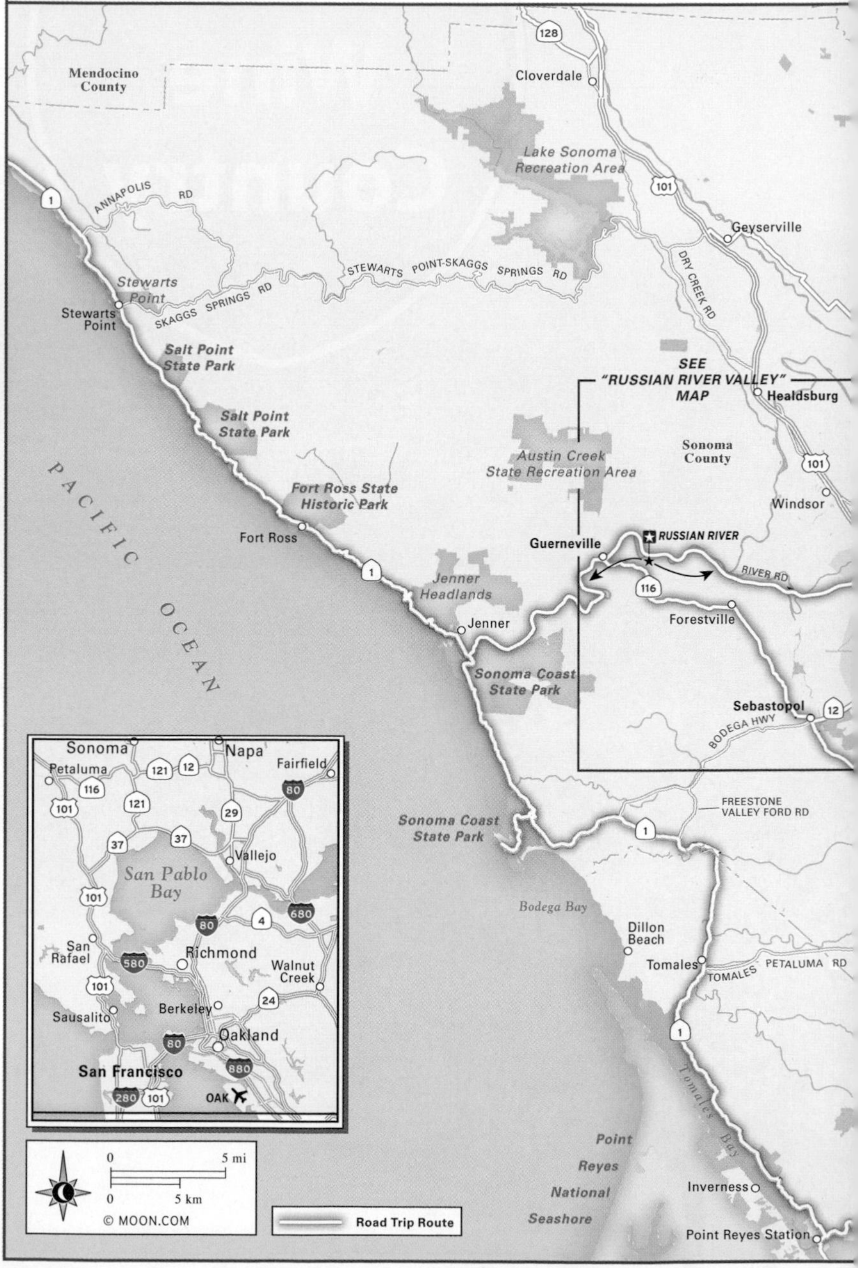

Mendocino County

128
Cloverdale

Lake Sonoma Recreation Area

101

ANNAPOLIS RD
Geyserville

STEWARTS POINT-SKAGGS SPRINGS RD

DRY CREEK RD

Stewarts Point

Stewarts Point

SKAGGS SPRINGS RD

Salt Point State Park

SEE "RUSSIAN RIVER VALLEY" MAP

Salt Point State Park

Austin Creek State Recreation Area

Healdsburg

Sonoma County

101

Windsor

Fort Ross State Historic Park

Fort Ross

RUSSIAN RIVER

Guerneville

116

RIVER RD

Jenner Headlands

Forestville

Jenner

Sonoma Coast State Park

Sebastopol

12

BODEGA HWY

PACIFIC OCEAN

FREESTONE VALLEY FORD RD

Sonoma Coast State Park

1

Bodega Bay

Dillon Beach

Tomales

TOMALES PETALUMA RD

Inset map

Sonoma
Petaluma
121
12
Napa
Fairfield

116
121
80

101
121

37
29

37

Vallejo

San Pablo Bay

101
80
4
680

San Rafael
580
Richmond
Walnut Creek

Berkeley
24

Sausalito
101

Oakland
880

San Francisco

280
101

OAK ✈

0   5 mi
0   5 km
© MOON.COM

Road Trip Route

Point Reyes National Seashore

Tomales Bay

Inverness

Point Reyes Station

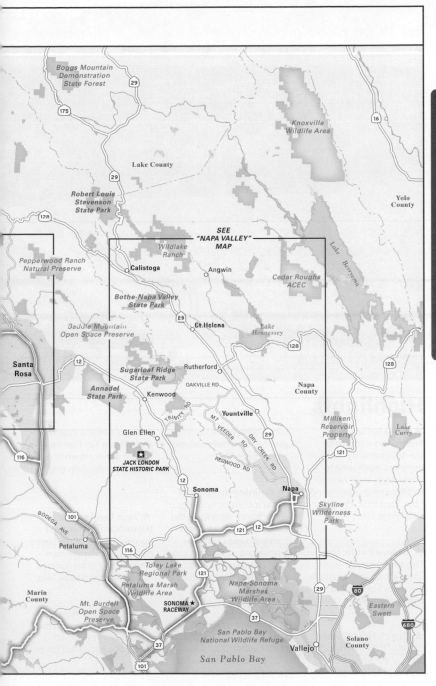

Boggs Mountain
Demonstration
State Forest

29

175

Knoxville
Wildlife Area

16

Lake County

29

Yolo
County

Robert Louis
Stevenson
State Park

29

178

SEE
"NAPA VALLEY"
MAP

Pepperwood Ranch
Natural Preserve

Wildlake
Ranch

Calistoga

Angwin

Cedar Roughs
ACEC

Lake Berryessa

Bothe-Napa Valley
State Park

29

Saddle Mountain
Open Space Preserve

St. Helena

Lake
Hennessey

128

128

Santa
Rosa

12

Sugarloaf Ridge
State Park

Rutherford

Napa
County

Annadel
State Park

Kenwood

OAKVILLE RD

TRINITY RD

Yountville

MT VEEDER RD

DRY CREEK RD

29

Milliken
Reservoir
Property

Lake
Curry

Glen Ellen

REDWOOD RD

121

116

JACK LONDON
STATE HISTORIC PARK

12

Sonoma

Napa

Skyline
Wilderness
Park

101

BODEGA AVE

101

121

12

Petaluma

116

Tolay Lake
Regional Park

121

Petaluma Marsh
Wildlife Area

Napa-Sonoma
Marshes
Wildlife Area

29

80

Marin
County

Mt. Burdell
Open Space
Preserve

SONOMA ★
RACEWAY

San Pablo Bay
National Wildlife Refuge

37

Eastern
Swett

680

37

Vallejo

Solano
County

101

San Pablo Bay

Highlights

★ **Napa Valley Wine Train:** Who wants to be the designated driver when there's so much wine to drink? Enjoy local varietals and food on this train's trip from Napa to St. Helena and back (page 111).

★ **Oxbow Public Market:** This 40,000-square-foot space allows you to sample the valley's best wines, food, and produce (page 114).

★ **Grgich Hills Winery:** Home of the California chardonnay that won the Paris Tasting of 1976, Grgich Hills uses a biodynamic farming process to produce exquisite wines (page 126).

★ **Culinary Institute of America:** Inside buildings of ancient gray stonework, this culinary school comprises cooking classes and demonstrations, a museum, and an exemplary restaurant, all amid forested surroundings (page 131).

★ **Sonoma State Historic Park:** Boasting a handful of unique, historic buildings, this park in downtown Sonoma includes the estate of General Vallejo and Mission San Francisco Solano, the northernmost of California's missions (page 136).

★ **Jack London State Historic Park:** You don't have to be a fan of the famed novelist to enjoy the stunning scenery of his Sonoma Mountain ranch (page 143).

★ **The Russian River:** Swim, canoe, or simply float serenely downriver at this center of summer fun (page 151).

The Wine Country is an in-comparable experience. From the crest of the last hill before you enter the valleys, sunlight paints golden streaks on endless rows of vines that stretch as far as the eye can see.

Trellises run along both sides of every road, tempting visitors to question the unpicked weeds beneath the vines, the rosebushes capping each row, and the strange, motionless fans standing guard high above. A heady aroma of earth and grapes permeates the area. Welcome to the Napa and Sonoma Valleys.

The area's beautiful grapevines are renowned worldwide for producing top-quality vintages and economical table wines. But foodies also know the area as a center for stellar cuisine. Yountville, a tiny, upscale town in the middle of Napa Valley, is the favorite haven of celebrity chef Thomas Keller. The food served at his French Laundry restaurant is legendary, as are the prices. Keller's influence helped to usher in a culinary renaissance, and today the lush flavors of local, sustainable produce are available throughout the region.

Sonoma Valley has long played second fiddle to Napa in terms of viticultural prestige, but the wines coming out of the area are second to none. The Russian River Valley wineries are often friendlier and less crowded than their Napa counterparts, while the wineries in the southern Carneros region are fewer and farther between. Each offers visitors a more personal experience than Napa and the chance to sample unique and amazing varietals. Sonoma County's craggy coastline and natural beauty also provide great recreation opportunities for visitors fonder of the outdoors than the grapes.

The Russian River Valley may be the prettiest part of Wine Country. The Russian River runs through it, providing ample water for forests and meadows. There are wide, calm spots with sandy banks, while rafting, canoeing, and kayaking opportunities abound on the zippier stretches of the river. If you are visiting for the vino, the area called the Russian River Valley actually encompasses several prestigious American Viticultural Areas, including Dry Creek, Alexander Valley, and, of course, Russian River. Wineries are clustered along three main roads: the Gravenstein Highway (CA-116), River Road, and US-101.

Planning Your Time

Napa and Sonoma form the beating heart of California's Wine Country. Many visitors plan a **weekend** in Napa, with subsequent weekend trips to explore Sonoma and the Russian River. If you come during the summer or fall, you'll find a crush in almost every tasting room in the valley; even the smaller boutique labels do big business during the six-month **high season** (May-Oct.).

Getting There

CA-29, which runs through the heart of Napa Valley, gets jammed up around St. Helena and can be very slow on weekends. US-101 slows through Santa Rosa during the weekday rush-hour commute and late in the day on sunny summer weekend afternoons. If you're not up for driving, downtown tasting rooms in the cities of Napa, Sonoma, and Santa Rosa are good alternatives to the slow trek up and down the wine roads.

From San Francisco
To Napa and Sonoma
45-60 mi/70-95 km, 1-2 hr

Sonoma is a one-hour drive north of San Francisco—when there's no traffic. On

Best Restaurants

★ **Bounty Hunter, Napa:** Pair tasty pulled pork, pork ribs, or smoked beef brisket with something off Bounty Hunter's 30-page beverage list at this downtown Napa hot spot (page 116).

★ **Bouchon, Yountville:** Those who can't get into Thomas Keller's other Yountville restaurant can enjoy the acclaimed chef's take on a classic French bistro at Bouchon (page 121).

★ **The Restaurant at Auberge du Soleil, Rutherford:** One of Napa Valley's first fine dining restaurants is still one of its best, and the stellar views of the valley below don't hurt one bit (page 128).

★ **Gatehouse Restaurant at the Culinary Institute of America at Greystone, St. Helena:** Try the food of some of the country's most promising budding chefs (page 132).

★ **the girl & the fig, Sonoma:** Sure, figs might be the MVP in some items at the girl & the fig, including the always-on-the-menu fig and arugula salad, but, there's masterful rustic French food all over the menu (page 139).

★ **LaSalette, Sonoma:** To experience how well Portuguese cuisine works in Wine Country, sample the wood-fired-oven-cooked food of LaSalette, right on Sonoma Plaza (page 139).

★ **The Spinster Sisters, Santa Rosa:** The bohemian Spinster Sisters bistro showcases Sonoma County ingredients at breakfast, lunch, and dinner (page 147).

a summer weekend, however, the drive to Sonoma or Napa can take 2-4 hours.

From San Francisco, take US-101 north over the **Golden Gate Bridge.** In 20 miles (32 km), exit on CA-37 west toward Vallejo and Napa. In 8 miles (13 km), turn north (left) on CA-121 and continue 6.5 miles (10.5 km). Take a slight right on Fremont Drive, then turn north (left) onto CA-12 and drive 3.8 miles (6.1 km) to downtown **Sonoma.** To experience the rest of Sonoma Wine Country, stay north on CA-12 for 10 miles (16 km) to **Glen Ellen** and **Kenwood.**

To reach **Napa,** stay west (instead of north) on CA-12 and continue 9 miles (14.5 km) until reaching a T junction with CA-121. Turn north to enter the Napa Valley. The city of Napa is at the southern end of the Napa Valley. Follow CA-29 north to visit the charming cities of **Yountville** (8.5 mi/13.5 km), **Oakville** (12 mi/19.5 km), **Rutherford** (14 mi/22.5 km), **St. Helena** (18 mi/29 km), and **Calistoga** (26 mi/42 km).

It's also possible to reach Napa via the East Bay by hopping on the **Bay Bridge.** From San Francisco, take US-101/I-80 west to access the Bay Bridge on-ramp. Head east across the Bay Bridge (I-80) and veer left to follow I-80 east. In 11 miles (17.5 km), veer right to take I-80 east toward Sacramento. After crossing the Carquinez Bridge ($6 toll), look for CA-29 near Vallejo. Turn west on CA-29 and drive north. In 12 miles (19.5 km), CA-29 merges with CA-221 and CA-121. Follow either route north to downtown Napa.

To the Russian River
75 mi/120 km, 1.5-2 hr

From San Francisco, take US-101 north over the **Golden Gate Bridge.** Continue

Best Accommodations

★ **Wine Valley Lodge, Napa:** Formerly the place where stars including Elvis and Marilyn Monroe stayed, the Wine Valley Lodge is now one of the better deals in Napa (page 117).

★ **Napa River Inn, Napa:** Sprawled across three buildings on the Napa River, the Napa River Inn offers upscale lodging in downtown Napa (page 118).

★ **Auberge du Soleil, Rutherford:** This luxury hotel is perched on a hillside with some of Wine Country's best views (page 128).

★ **El Bonita Motel, St. Helena:** This moderately priced motel with amenities including a pool, hot tub, and sauna is a great place to save money in super chic St. Helena (page 134).

★ **Gaige House & Ryokan, Glen Ellen:** The Gaige House & Ryokan brings Asian influences to a Wine Country luxury hotel (page 144).

★ **The Astro, Santa Rosa:** Fun, quirky, and moderately priced, The Astro brings the motor lodge into the 2000s (page 147).

GETTING THERE

55 miles (89 km) north on US-101, exiting west on River Road. It is a scenic 16 miles (26 km) west on River Road to reach **Guerneville**. From Guerneville, continue 13 miles (21 km) west on River Road (CA-116) to reach the Pacific Coast at **Jenner**.

From Shasta and Lassen
To Napa and Sonoma
200 mi/320 km, 3 hr

In the Shasta and Lassen region, the gateway town of **Redding** offers a good starting point for this drive to the Wine Country. From Redding, take I-5 south for 127 miles (204 km) past the town of **Williams**. Hop onto I-505 south for 35 miles (56 km) through Winters to meet I-80 in Vacaville.

Continue 30 miles (48 km) south on I-80. Take the exit for CA-12 to drive west, and then north, for 10 miles (16 km). CA-12 merges with CA-12/121 south of Napa. Drive north for 6 miles (9.5 km) to reach downtown **Napa**. To reach Sonoma, follow CA-12 west for 12 miles (19.5 km) and continue north on CA-12 into **Sonoma**.

Stopping in Williams

Williams is midway between Redding and Santa Rosa, so it is a good place for a pit stop. **Granzella's Restaurant & Deli** (451 6th St., 530/473-5496, www.granzellas.com, 6am-9pm daily, $8-10) is a popular deli, restaurant, and sports bar. Try the New Orleans muffuletta, the meatball sandwich, or create your own sandwich.

Cramped and exhausted from hours on the road? A soak in the hot, natural mineral springs at **Wilbur Hot Springs** (3375 Wilbur Springs Rd., 530/473-2306, https://wilburhotsprings.com, 10am-5pm daily, Mon.-Fri. $59, Sat.-Sun. $65) will cure what ails you. It's 23 miles (37 km) west of Williams on CA-20.

To the Russian River
250 mi/400 km, 4 hr

From **Redding,** drive to Sonoma. From **Sonoma,** take CA-12 north for 20 miles (32 km) to **Santa Rosa.** To reach the Russian River from Santa Rosa, take US-101 north for 4.5 miles (7.2 km) and exit onto River Road. It is a scenic 16-mile (26-km) drive west on River Road to

Guerneville. To reach the Pacific Coast at Jenner, continue 13 miles (21 km) west.

Santa Rosa is the largest city in this area. Try to avoid rush hour traffic in the morning (7am-9am) and afternoon (4pm-6pm).

From Lake Tahoe

Access from the Lake Tahoe area can be hampered by inclement weather, snow, and traffic.

To Napa and Sonoma
160-175 mi/260-280 km, 4 hr

From I-80 in Truckee, drive west for 115 miles (185 km) past Sacramento to Davis. From Davis, Continue 30 miles (48 km) south on I-80. Take the exit for CA-12 to drive west, and then north, for 10 miles (16 km). CA-12 merges with CA-12/121 south of Napa. Drive north for 6 miles (9.5 km) to reach downtown Napa.

To reach Sonoma, follow CA-12 west for 12 miles (19.5 km) and continue north on CA-12 into Sonoma.

Stopping in Sacramento

About 10 miles (16 km) north of Sacramento, the aptly named Pit Stop Bar B-Que (3515 McClellan Dr., North Highland, 916/344-1771, www.pitstop-barbq.com, 11am-9pm Mon.-Sat., 11am-8pm Sun., $10-18) serves award-winning ribs to hungry motorists.

To get there from I-80 West, take exit 96 and turn west onto Madison Avenue. In 0.7 mile, veer right onto Airbase Drive and continue 0.4 mile to Watt Avenue. Turn right onto Watt Avenue and drive 0.3 mile north to McClellan, where you will turn right. The Pit Stop is on the left.

To the Russian River
220 mi/355 km, 4-5 hr

From Truckee, follow the directions to Sonoma. From Sonoma, take CA-12 north for 20 miles (32 km) to Santa Rosa. To reach the Russian River from Santa Rosa, take US-101 north for 4.5 miles (7.2 km) and exit onto River Road. It is a scenic, 16-mile (26-km) drive west on River Road to Guerneville. To reach the Pacific Coast at Jenner, continue 13 miles (21 km) west.

Santa Rosa is the largest city in this area. Try to avoid rush hour traffic in the morning (7am-9am) and afternoon (4pm-6pm).

From Yosemite

To Napa and Sonoma
200 mi/320 km, 4-5 hr

The drive from Yosemite Valley to Napa is quite long and subject to traffic congestion. From Yosemite Valley, drive west on CA-120 for 112 miles (180 km) until reaching the town of Manteca. Continue west through town and hop on I-5 north toward Stockton.

Stay on I-5 north for 25 miles (40 km), turning west onto CA-12 north of Stockton. Continue west on CA-12 for 45 miles (72 km). As you pass through the city of Fairfield, veer south onto I-80 for about 3 miles (5 km) before continuing west on CA-12. CA-12 leads about 12 miles (19.5 km) west to a junction with CA-121. Continue north on CA-121 to enter Napa; follow CA-12 west to enter Sonoma.

Stopping in Stockton

Stockton is a three-hour drive from Yosemite Valley and makes for a good place for a pit stop. Flip's Burgers (2503 Waterloo Rd., 209/943-5477, 11am-7pm Tues.-Thurs., 11am-8pm Fri.-Sat., noon-6pm Sun., $5-9) serves a variety of burgers, including one with a fried egg, jalapeno pepper, and bacon on top and drenched in a chipotle sauce.

Whirlow's (1926 Pacific Ave., 209/466-2823, www.whirlows.com, 11am-9:30pm Mon.-Sat., noon-3pm Sun., $7-11) also serves burgers, along with salads and sandwiches.

To the Russian River
245 mi/395 km, 5-6 hr

From Yosemite Valley, follow the directions to **Sonoma.** From Sonoma, take CA-12 north for 20 miles (32 km) to **Santa Rosa.** To reach the Russian River from Santa Rosa, take US-101 north for 4.5 miles (7.2 km) and exit onto River Road. It is a scenic, 16-mile (26-km) drive west on River Road to **Guerneville.** To reach the Pacific Coast at **Jenner,** continue 13 miles (21 km) west.

Santa Rosa is the largest city in this area. Try to avoid rush hour traffic in the morning (7am-9am) and afternoon (4pm-6pm).

Napa

Napa Valley has a blue-collar heart: the city of Napa, many of whose 80,000 residents work in banking, construction, the medical industry, and other businesses that serve the rest of the valley. The Napa River snakes through the heart of downtown, tempering the hot summer weather and providing recreation as well as a healthy dose of natural beauty. It also gives the downtown a historic feel, particularly when among the many 19th-century buildings. The town boasts sparkling new structures with high-end clothiers and cutting-edge restaurants as well as the Oxbow Public Market—a one-of-a-kind culinary treat.

Getting There

To reach CA-29 from San Francisco, take US-101 north across the Golden Gate Bridge to Novato. In Novato, take the exit for CA-37 east to Napa. CA-37 skirts the tip of San Pablo Bay and runs all the way to Vallejo. From Vallejo, take CA-29 (Sonoma Blvd.) north for 7 miles (11.5 km) until you reach downtown Napa. CA-29 will take you as far north as Calistoga.

Connecting to CA-37 in Vallejo is especially easy if you're coming from the East Bay, Lake Tahoe, and Sacramento: It intersects I-80 at the north end of Vallejo at the exit for Six Flags Discovery Kingdom.

Wineries
Robert Sinskey Vineyards

Getting into the foodie act that's sweeping Wine Country, **Robert Sinskey Vineyards** (6320 Silverado Tr., 707/944-9090, www.robertsinskey.com, 10am-4:30pm daily by appointment only, wine-tasting $40, wine/food tastings $70-175) offers a menu of small bites alongside their list of current wines. The appointment-only tastings include a tour of the cave and cellar, and discussions about the art of winemaking. The more intensive Perfect Circle Tour and Chef's Table Tour are also more expensive. With or without the food, the red wines themselves are worth dropping in at this attractive stone-and-wood edifice.

Starmont Winery & Vineyards

Starmont Winery & Vineyards (1451 Stanly Ln., 707/252-8001, www.starmontwinery.com, 10am-5pm daily, $25) purveys moderately priced chardonnays and pinot noirs at an old ranch south of Napa. The tasting room is constructed of wood and concrete, and there's a fire pit outdoors. Break a light sweat on the daily Stanly Ranch Vineyard Tour ($65), which includes a short hike (0.75-1 mile) around the vineyards followed by a barrel tasting.

Outland

Outland (920 Franklin St., Napa, 707/227-1277, https://outlandswine.com, 1pm-7pm Wed.-Mon., tastings $30-35), located in an alley in downtown Napa, offers many choices. Inside the modern white building, visitors can try wines from three different winemakers: Poe (pinots and chardonnays), Farella (Bordeaux varietals), and Forlorn Hope (unusual wines). Choose between four different tasting flights or go all in on a bottle.

Napa Valley

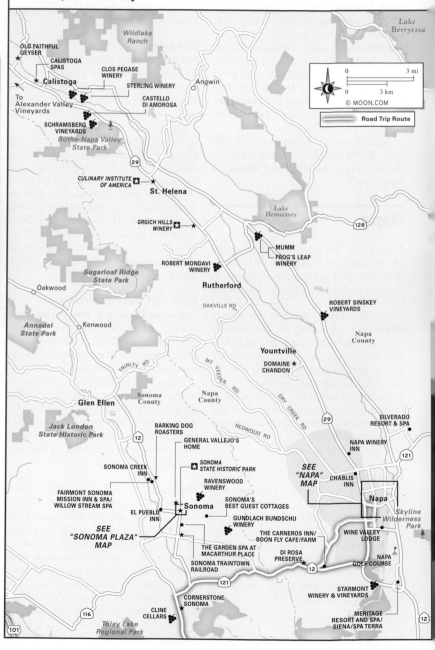

Wildlake Ranch

Lake Berryessa

OLD FAITHFUL GEYSER

CALISTOGA SPAS

★ Calistoga

CLOS PEGASE WINERY

STERLING WINERY

Angwin

CASTELLO DI AMOROSA

To Alexander Valley Vineyards

SCHRAMSBERG VINEYARDS

Bothe-Napa Valley State Park

29

CULINARY INSTITUTE OF AMERICA ★

St. Helena

Lake Hennessey

GRGICH HILLS WINERY ★

128

MUMM
FROG'S LEAP WINERY

ROBERT MONDAVI WINERY

Sugarloaf Ridge State Park

Rutherford

Oakwood

OAKVILLE RD

ROBERT SINSKEY VINEYARDS

Annadel State Park

Kenwood

Napa County

Yountville

DOMAINE ★ CHANDON

Glen Ellen

Sonoma County

Napa County

MT VEEDER RD

DRY CREEK RD

Jack London State Historic Park

12

BARKING DOG ROASTERS

REDWOOD RD

29

SILVERADO RESORT & SPA

GENERAL VALLEJO'S HOME

NAPA WINERY INN

121

SONOMA CREEK INN

SONOMA STATE HISTORIC PARK ★

SEE "NAPA" MAP

CHABLIS INN

FAIRMONT SONOMA MISSION INN & SPA/ WILLOW STREAM SPA

RAVENSWOOD WINERY

Napa

EL PUEBLO INN

★ Sonoma

SONOMA'S BEST GUEST COTTAGES

Skyline Wilderness Park

SEE "SONOMA PLAZA" MAP

GUNDLACH BUNDSCHU WINERY

WINE VALLEY LODGE

THE GARDEN SPA AT MACARTHUR PLACE

THE CARNEROS INN/ BOON FLY CAFE/FARM

NAPA GOLF COURSE

SONOMA TRAINTOWN RAILROAD

DI ROSA PRESERVE

12

121

STARMONT WINERY & VINEYARDS

CORNERSTONE SONOMA

116

CLINE CELLARS

MERITAGE RESORT AND SPA/ SIENA/SPA TERRA

12

101

Tolay Lake Regional Park

0   3 mi
0   3 km
© MOON.COM

Road Trip Route

Two Days in Wine Country

The Napa Valley is less than 100 miles (160 km) north of San Francisco, making it an ever-popular day-trip destination. If you plan to tour Wine Country as a day trip, choose one region to explore. Napa and Sonoma are closest to San Francisco, about a one-hour drive. Traffic on the winding two-lane roads in these regions can easily become clogged with wine-tasting day-trippers, especially on weekends. To avoid the crowds, try to get an early start or visit on a weekday. Note that most wineries close by 4pm, and some are open only by appointment.

One Day in Napa

In downtown Napa, get your bearings at the **Napa General Store** and sample some Napa vintages. Have lunch or just pick up some picnic supplies at **Oxbow Public Market.** Then hop on the **Napa Valley Wine Train** to experience Napa Valley and its wineries without having to drive.

Return to downtown Napa for delicious barbecued meats at **Bounty Hunter** or sleek Japanese food at **Morimoto's.** End your night with a beer or wine nightcap at **Cadet Wine & Beer Bar.**

Overnight: Spend the night at the **Napa Valley Lodge,** an unassuming motel that has hosted the likes of Elvis and Marilyn Monroe, or opt for more luxurious accommodations at the **Napa River Inn.**

One Day in Sonoma

From Napa, CA-121 winds west through the Carneros wine region. Stop off for a bit of bubbly at gorgeous **Domaine Carneros,** where the views and gardens are almost as impressive as the sparkling wines. From CA-121, CA-12 twists north into Sonoma. Stretch your legs in Sonoma Plaza and explore the charming downtown area. Stop in at the **Mission San Francisco Solano** in **Sonoma State Historic Park** for a bit of history, and then grab lunch at **the girl & the fig,** housed in the historic Sonoma Hotel. Be sure to see the **Bear Flag Revolt statue** in Sonoma Square.

After lunch, drive the 10 miles (16 km) to **Jack London State Historic Park.** Be sure to do the short hike to the haunting **Wolf House ruins.** For more wine-tasting, take CA-12 north to quaint Glen Ellen and stop in at the **Valley of the Moon Winery,** where the landmark winery will enchant with its stone buildings and unusual sangiovese rosé.

From here, it's a 30-minute drive to downtown Santa Rosa, where you can catch US-101 south to San Francisco, a little over an hour away. You may decide to grab a bite before you head back; if so, try **The Spinster Sisters** for menu items loaded with local ingredients or **Russian River Brewing Company** for their fabled Pliny the Elder beer with some pub food.

Overnight: Stay in Santa Rosa at the fun, throwback motor lodge **The Astro,** or head to the **Gaige House & Ryokan** in tiny Glen Ellen for Asian meets Wine Country opulence.

Sights
★ Napa Valley Wine Train

If trying to decide which wineries to visit, which restaurants are worth a stop, and how to avoid weekend traffic sounds exhausting, consider taking the **Napa Valley Wine Train** (1275 McKinstry St., 707/253-2111, www.winetrain.com, $149-332).

The Wine Train offers a relaxing sightseeing experience aboard vintage train cars, where you can sit back and enjoy the food, wine, and views. The train runs from Napa to St. Helena and back, a 36-mile (58-km), three-hour round-trip tour. Tour options include lunch, dinner, half-day wine tours, full-day wine tours, or special event trains. Each package

Best Wineries for Specific Tastes

There are more to some wineries than wine. The following wineries offer something else for specific tastes.

★ **Best for Sparkling Wines:** Sip exclusive sparkling wines at Yountville's **Domaine Chandon** (page 120).

★ **Best for Families:** Kids will enjoy the castle at **Castello di Amarosa,** while their parents will enjoy the wine (page 133).

★ **Best for Film Buffs:** Come to the **Francis Ford Coppola Winery** to sample the filmmaker's wines and visit his on-site movie museum with items from his films, including Don Corleone's desk from *The Godfather* (page 155).

includes seating in a different historic railcar that is named after wine varietals.

Di Rosa Preserve

At the unique **Di Rosa Preserve** (5200 Sonoma Hwy., 707/226-5991, www. dirosaart.org, 10am-4pm Wed.-Sun., adults $18, seniors and students $15, children 17 and under free) you'll see the cutting edge of modern California art. With 217 acres, Di Rosa has ample room for three galleries, an outdoor sculpture meadow, and a lake. Take in the festival of color and creativity in the galleries and sculpture garden, or wander the undeveloped portion of the preserve to soak in the colors and shapes of nature. Docent-led tours come free with admission. Check the website for tour times.

Entertainment and Events

Napa is home to two historic live music venues. The **Uptown Theatre** (1350 3rd St., 707/259-0123, www.uptowntheatrenapa. com), which dates back to 1937, has become one of Wine Country's best music venues. The Uptown even lures Bay Area residents to Napa to see intimate performances by acts including Lyle Lovett and Jake Shimabukuro, along with comedians like Steven Wright and filmmaker Kevin Smith.

The **Napa Valley Opera House** (1030 Main St., 707/226-7322, www.nvoh.org) has been around since 1880 and has

hosted everyone from the writer Jack London to country music legend Willie Nelson. There are two venues. On the first floor, there's **Blue Note Napa** (www. bluenotenapa.com), which brings the vibe of a legendary Greenwich Village jazz club to Wine Country. Upstairs is the **Jam Cellars Ballroom** (www.jamcellarsballroom.com), a larger space for bigger acts. The Opera House also hosts other events, such as screenings for the **Napa Valley Film Festival** (707/226-7500, www. nvff.org, early Nov.). Being Napa, the film fest includes culinary demos and winetastings along with film screenings.

Napa has hosted the multiday **BottleRock** music festival (Napa County Fairgrounds, 575 3rd St., www. bottlerocknapavalley.com, late May) since 2013. The eclectic range of acts has included Bruno Mars, The Killers, and Muse.

The **Cadet Wine & Beer Bar** (930 Franklin St., 707/224-4400, www.cadetbeerandwinebar.com, 6pm-1am Mon.-Thurs., 6pm-2am Fri.-Sat., wine-tastings $20, beer tastings $12) is an inclusive place for all imbibers. Long rotating lists of both beer and wine complement a short menu of paninis and charcuterie. This popular spot also hosts frequent vintner and brewer takeovers.

Shopping

In downtown Napa, the **Historic Napa Mill** (500 Main St., www.historicnapamill.

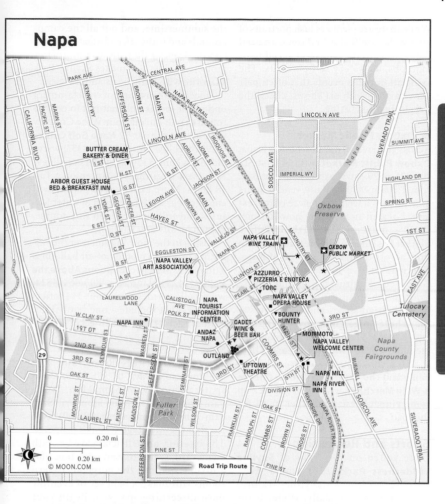

Napa

com) is a lovely shopping and dining center, decorated with rustic touches—weathered redwood, an abundance of trailing vines, and blooming planter boxes and hanging baskets. The historic Napa River Inn is here, as is the **Vintage Sweet Shoppe** (530 Main St., 707/224-2986, http://vintagesweetshoppe.com, 9am-10pm daily), which specializes in chocolate but has enough treats to make anyone's teeth ache. In the same complex, the **Napa General Store** (540 Main St., 707/259-0762, www.napageneralstore.com, 8am-6pm daily) next door offers a

bite to eat, a glass of wine, wine-related knickknacks, and other gifts. The store also sells local artwork, including leather crafts and fiber art, all of which has an arty, ecological bent.

With so much natural beauty in the Napa Valley, is it any wonder that there are so many artists living here? The **Art Association Napa Valley Gallery** (1307 1st St., 707/254-2085, www.artnv.org, 10am-6pm daily) operates a downtown gallery. The space presents pen-and-ink drawings, watercolors, photography, glass jewelry, fiber art, and oil paintings.

While there are plenty of lush portraits of vineyards, you'll also find some unusual subjects—jellyfish, abstract aerial photographs, or watery self-portraits. The association plans events that often pair wine-tasting with art shows; check the website before visiting.

★ Oxbow Public Market

Across the river from downtown Napa, **Oxbow Public Market** (610-644 1st St., 707/226-6529, www.oxbowpublicmarket. com, 7:30am-9:30pm daily, vendor hours may vary) is a well-used piece of real estate. Located next to the now-defunct COPIA museum, the Oxbow Public Market has once again breathed life into this "across the tracks" section of Napa. The market is a food lover's delight. Grab a cup of **Ritual Coffee** and browse through the epicurean wares or get lost in the myriad spices and seasonings at the **Whole Spice Company.** Or indulge with a beer at **Fieldwork** or an organic ice cream at **Three Twins Ice Cream.** There is also a chocolatier, an olive oil company, and the venerable **Oxbow Cheese & Wine Merchant,** where you can pick up some vino, cheese, and other treats for the road.

Sports and Recreation

Once you're on the trails of **Skyline Wilderness Park** (2201 Imola Ave., 707/252-0481, www.skylinepark.org, summer 8am-7pm daily, winter 8am-5pm daily, fall 8am-6pm daily, $5), you may forget you're even in Wine Country. Up at this park, no vineyards encroach on the natural chaparral landscape of Napa's high country. This park includes the Martha Walker Garden—a botanical garden planted with California and Napa native plants in honor of a legendary figure in the local horticultural community. The rest of this 850-acre park is given over to multiple community uses. You'll find campgrounds, hiking trails, horse and bicycle paths, a disc golf course, and more. Be aware that it gets hot here in

the summertime, and not all the campgrounds and trails offer adequate shade to cool off. Even so, the natural beauty of this protected wilderness makes Skyline Park a favorite with both locals and travelers.

Since you're in a land of entertainment options, it seems only natural to enjoy a round of golf during your Wine Country vacation. At the par-72 **Napa Golf Course** (2295 Streblow Dr., 707/255-4333, www. playnapa.com, $32-42), golfers of all levels—even beginners—can enjoy a full 18 holes. More experienced players will enjoy (or curse) the plethora of water features and full-size trees on this course, known locally as a bargain.

Rising in the morning sun over the valley in a brightly colored hot-air balloon is a unique experience. **Balloons Above the Valley** (3425 Solano Ave., 800/464-6824, www.balloonrides.com, $189-344) offers packages that include a one-hour flight with brunch or wine-tasting.

Spas

Spa Terra (Meritage Resort and Spa, 875 Bordeaux Way, 707/251-3000, www. spaterra.com, 9am-6pm Mon.-Wed., 9am-7pm Thurs., 8am-8pm Fri.-Sat., 8am-7pm Sun., massages $140-300) is the jewel of the Meritage Resort's property. The interior, an artificial cave beneath a vineyard, seems like an odd choice for a luxury spa, but the gorgeous cavern rooms will make a believer of even the most discerning spa-goer. Begin your pampering with a warm greeting and a required tour of the public areas from your guide. Show up at least 30 minutes in advance of an appointment—you'll have the run of a tiled hot tub, steam room, and relaxation space both before and after your scheduled treatment. Grab a glass of lemon water, a cool moist cloth for your forehead, and warm out (it's not the least bit chilly in Spa Terra). The menu of treatments includes a full-body scrub using grapeseed extracts, couple's massages in two-person rooms, and an espresso-based facial.

Food
California Cuisine
The Farm (Carneros Inn, 4048 Sonoma Hwy., 707/299-4880, www.farmatthecarnerosinn.com, 5:30pm-10pm Fri.-Sat., 10am-2pm and 5:30pm-9pm Sun., 5:30pm-9pm Mon.-Thurs.; bar/pavilion 4pm-11pm Fri.-Sat., 4pm-10pm Sun.-Thurs., $22-42) serves upscale California cuisine, complete with a chef's tasting menu ($100 pp) and big white plates topped with tiny, artistic piles of food. The food may be a touch pretentious, but it's cooked perfectly, and the chef has put imagination into the dishes. Expect unusual but deft flavor combinations, smaller portions appropriate to the number of courses, and just a touch of molecular gastronomy. The dining room feels comfortable, with cushy banquettes and padded chairs. Servers are friendly and good at their jobs, and can help decipher anything on the menu. Do dress up a little—The Farm has a distinctly upscale vibe. For a more casual experience, ask about the bar menu, with a burger, flatbread, and even a grilled ham and cheese sandwich for considerably less.

Also at the Carneros Inn, the **Boon Fly Café** (4048 Sonoma Hwy., 707/299-4870, www.boonflycafe.com, 7am-9pm daily, $14-22) has classic breakfast dishes and almost down-to-earth salad and sandwich fare. Named after a pioneer settler, Boon Fly features liqueur-spiked coffee and homemade donuts most mornings. Dinners include daily specials and Kobe beef burgers on homemade brioche buns. Eggs are cooked competently, salads are enormous, and the carefully designed down-home dining room is cute. The half-booth banquettes are comfortable to sit in, and lingering over coffee or tea is tolerated.

Torc (1140 Main St., 707/252-3292, www.torcnapa.com, 5pm-9:30pm Wed.-Mon., $25-51) finds international flavors intermingling with American flair. That means items like deviled eggs might be sitting right next to Indian-style sweet potato fritters on the menu. Chef and owner Sean O'Toole has been in the restaurant world for over a decade, at places including San Francisco's Quince and Yountville's Bardessono. The airy, high-ceilinged interior is as unconfined as the globe-trotting menu.

American
When Napa locals need a diner-style breakfast or lunch, they head to the **Butter Cream Bakery & Diner** (2297 Jefferson St., 707/255-6700, www.buttercreambakery.com, diner 5:30am-3pm Mon.-Sat., 5:30am-2:30pm Sun., bakery 5:30am-6pm Mon.-Sat., 5:30am-4pm Sun., $6-11). It's not in the ritzy part of downtown, but the brilliant pink-and-white-striped building is hard to miss. On the diner side, breakfast is served all day; choose between a small table in the fluorescent-lit linoleum dining room or a stool at the old-school counter. Service is indifferent, but you'll get decently cooked eggs, tasty sandwiches, reasonable portions, and best of all, reasonable prices. Over on the bakery side, mouthwatering turnovers, Danishes, and fruit rings make it easy to get a good breakfast on the go. Dessert pastries, cookies, and cakes tempt even dieters.

Italian
The restaurant at the Meritage Inn, **Siena** (875 Bordeaux Way, 707/251-1950, https://meritagecollection.com, 7am-11am, 11:30am-2pm, and 5:30pm-9:30pm Mon.-Thurs., 7am-11am, 11:30am-2pm, and 5:30pm-10pm Fri., 7am-2pm and 5:30pm-10pm Sat., 7am-2pm and 5:30pm-9:30pm Sun., $15-48), doesn't serve typical Wine Country cuisine. The food is mostly Italian, much of it hot, hearty, and welcome after a long day of wine-tasting. Choose from fresh salads, pasta dishes, and big entrées, though if you've been in Napa for a while, you may not be able to resist a pizza or a cheeseburger. The waiter can even suggest the right wine or beer to accompany your burger. Desserts

also tend toward the dense and filling—consider sharing one among your tablemates. The upholstered booths and dim lighting make a romantic dining experience possible, but the vibe in the dining room manages to stay low-key enough to make jeans-clad diners comfortable.

For simple Italian fare, go to **Azzurro** (1260 Main St., 707/255-5552, www. azzurropizzeria.com, 11:30am-9:30pm Sun.-Thurs., 11:30am-10pm Fri.-Sat., $14-17). Veterans of Tra Vigne in St. Helena, Michael and Christina Gyetvan opened Azzurro with the intention of bringing their style of Italian food to downtown Napa. A favorite with locals, this trattoria offers wood-fired pizzas in addition to hearty pasta dishes and big, rustic salads. The warm and modern interior welcomes diners with wood and stone tables and an open kitchen. Wines by the glass are affordable.

Barbecue

Cheese and fruit pair well with wine, but the ★ **Bounty Hunter** (975 1st St., 707/226-3976, www. bountyhunterwinebar.com, 11am-10pm Sun.-Thurs., 11am-midnight Fri.-Sat., $13-35) proves that large slabs of barbecued meats complement local reds just as well. Start by selecting a glass or bottle from the 18-page list, a fine whiskey, or a craft beer. Suggested wine and beer pairings are offered for every menu item. There are classic barbecue sandwiches (pulled pork, smoked brisket), but the truly hungry can go for the Smokin' BBQ Platter: three pounds of delicious barbecued meats piled high on a granite slab. It's served with a caddy containing three house-made sauces. The Bounty Hunter scores extra points for serving food until midnight on weekends.

Japanese

Sake in Wine Country? Not a bad idea,

From top to bottom: the Napa Valley Wine Train; Outland; Napa Mill.

particularly if it's paired with dinner at **Morimoto's** (610 Main St., 707/252-1600, www.morimotonapa.com, 11:30am-2:30pm and 5pm-10pm Sun.-Thurs., 11:30am-2:30pm and 5pm-11pm Fri.-Sat., entrées $22-90, tasting menu $130). Celebrity chef Masaharu Morimoto, who has appeared on the *Iron Chef* TV show, opened this esoteric and sleek Japanese eatery. The elegant interior features steel highlighted by bright yellow accents. The food includes traditional Japanese dishes, all with a unique and modern twist—*gyoza* with bacon cream and duck confit-fried rice are just some of the menu items. There are also non-sequiturs like steak, lobster, and roasted fingerling potatoes. For a full idea of the chef's culinary vision, order the eight-course tasting menu.

Markets

For a bit of this and a bit of that, venture across the Napa River to the ★ **Oxbow Public Market** (610-644 1st St., 707/226-6529, www.oxbowpublicmarket.com, 7:30am-9:30am daily, vendor hours vary). Inside this large, open space you can snack on oysters at the **Hog Island Oyster Co.** or blow your diet at **Kara's Cupcakes.** Hamburgers are just out the side door at **Gott's Roadside,** and around the corner is some of the best charcuterie around in delectable take-out sandwiches at the **Fatted Calf** or pizza by the slice at **The Model Bakery.** The bakery's bacon *levain,* made with hunks of bacon and bacon fat from next door, is irresistible.

Perhaps the most acclaimed of these options is the **Kitchen Door** (707/226-1560, www.kitchendoornapa.com, 11:30am-8pm Mon., 11:30am-9pm Tues.-Fri., 10am-9pm Sat., 10am-8pm Sun., $16-25). Unlike the market's loud and congested interior, the Kitchen Door has an air of calm. The white-tile wood oven, open seating, and large picture windows draw light in for an illuminating meal. Comfort food comes in all stripes, including pizzas and bahn mi sandwiches.

If you've got a taste for tacos, check out

C Casa (707/226-7700, http://myccasa. com, 7:30am-8pm Sun.-Thurs., 7:30am-9pm Fri.-Sat., $5-18) where the taco fillings include everything from fresh Dungeness crab to ground buffalo meat.

Accommodations
Under $150

The pretty, unassuming ★ **Wine Valley Lodge** (200 S. Coombs St., 707/224-7911, 800/696-7911, www.winevalleylodge. com, $119-250) welcomes guests with its redbrick and adobe-tile exterior. Inside, serene rooms feature unobtrusive art, pale yellow walls, and soothing pastel comforters. Rooms are a nice size; choose from a king bed, two queens, or a suite. The units encircle a heated pool deck and small picnic area. The Wine Valley Lodge also boasts a significant past: In the late 1950s and early 1960s, several movies were filmed in Napa, and various A-list stars, including Rock Hudson, Marilyn Monroe, and even Elvis, stayed at the lodge during filming.

$150-250

Outside of town, the **Napa Winery Inn** (1998 Trower Ave., 707/257-7220, www. napawineryinn.com, $219-330) is certainly one of the most affordable options. Standard amenities include complimentary Wi-Fi, and an outdoor pool sweetens the deal. Pricier rooms might boast a fridge, a wet bar, and a kitchenette. The inn also serves a complimentary breakfast and evening wine-tasting.

At the **Chablis Inn** (3360 Solano Ave., 707/257-1944, www.chablisinn.com, $149-289), the rooms include all the usual amenities: a wet bar with a mini fridge, an in-room coffee maker, a TV with cable, and more. Rooms are simply decorated, but the beds are comfortable, the carpets are dark (making it safe to drink just a little bit of red wine in your room), and the address is central to both the attractions of downtown Napa and the famous Highway 29 wine road.

For a unique historic lodging

experience, stay at the **Napa Inn** (1137 Warren St., 800/435-1144, www.napainn. com, $239-399), which comprises two Victorian houses, both painted blue, in historic downtown Napa. You can walk from either to downtown shops and restaurants, and the Wine Train depot is a very short drive away. As bed-and-breakfasts go, the Napa Inn is a big one, with 15 rooms and suites. Elegant fabrics and lush modern textures moderate the floral and carved-wood decor of the Victorian era. The nicest rooms have corner whirlpool tubs and king beds. Breakfast at the Napa Inn is an event, with multiple courses served by candlelight.

Over $250

The ★ **Napa River Inn** (500 Main St., 877/251-8500, www.napariverinn.com, $349-529) has one of the best locations in Napa—right inside the Historic Napa Mill. You can practically fall out of your guest room and hit the General Store, at least one restaurant, several galleries, and the candy store on the way down. Steps away from the center of Napa's bustling downtown, some rooms even afford a view of the Napa River. The interior of this luxury hotel is crammed with high-end antiques and reproductions. Choose from three styles of room decor: Historic Victorian rooms feature canopy beds, floral prints, cushy chairs, and slipper tubs; the nautical rooms, many of which face the river, resemble the inside of a yacht, with wood paneling, porthole-style mirrors, and rope-style accents; and the Wine Country rooms echo the natural wealth of the Napa Valley with floral linens, marble baths, and oak moldings.

The king of Napa lodging is the **Silverado** (1600 Atlas Peak Rd., 707/257-0200, www.silveradoresort.com, $300-800). You'll find the finest in modern amenities and decorations in your room (all guest suites at the Silverado have kitchens and dining rooms), including high-thread-count linens, complimentary Wi-Fi, and a private patio or deck overlooking the grounds. Pale colors with eye-popping jewel-toned accents speak of the best current designers. There's so much to do at the Silverado that you'll find it hard to pry yourself away from the grounds to go wine-tasting. Guests can choose from the immense spa with full fitness and salon services, two 18-hole golf courses, one restaurant, 10 tennis courts, 10 pools, and—believe it or not—more.

The Carneros Inn (4048 Sonoma Hwy., 707/299-4900, www.thecarnerosinn.com, $850-2,900) is an expansive and expensive cottage resort. The immense property, which backs onto countryside, has three restaurants, a spa, two pools, a fitness center, and even a small market. On arrival, follow the signs to the registration area and then keep driving to the lobby at the very top of the resort's hill. The unprepossessing (from the outside) cottages spread out in small clusters for acres, each group surrounding its own garden paths and water features. Inside, the cozy cottages sparkle with white linens, tile floors, and windows overlooking sizable private backyards with decks and comfy chaises. Outdoors, there's a private patio and outdoor shower. But it's the baths that bring Carneros Inn clients back again and again.

The **Meritage Inn** (875 Bordeaux Way, 707/251-1900, www.themeritageresort. com, $200-600) is beside the small Napa Valley airport, convenient to businesspeople and travelers who want easy access to both the Napa Valley and Sonoma-Carneros wine regions. The grounds, common spaces, and rooms have the deep harvest colors and country-elegant style of Tuscany. The lush garden pool is the centerpiece of the property, which also includes a wine-tasting room, a fabulous spa, and a down-to-earth restaurant. The basic shape of the rooms remains true to the Meritage's motel roots, but the

Tuscan-style decor and trimmings make a play for elegance, with comfortable beds, deep soaking tubs in the baths, and posh amenities. Expect a fridge stocked with free water, a coffee maker, and a complimentary bottle of wine.

The prim white exterior of **Arbor Guest House** (1436 G St., 707/252-8144, www.arborguesthouse.com, $249-309) betrays little of the inn's lush Victorian decor. Rich fabric drapes the windows and beds, and polished antiques grace even the smallest corner, while soft lighting and flower-filled vases lend warm touches. There are only five rooms, each distinctively decorated; two offer gas fireplaces and two-person jetted tubs for a romantic stay. Guests are invited to a complimentary hot breakfast in the morning and wine and appetizers in the evening.

Andaz Napa (1450 1st St., 707/687-1234, www.andaz.hyatt.com, $289-700) has 141 modern rooms, all with hardwood floors and marble bathrooms. Upgrade to suites with soaking tubs and dual-sided glass fireplaces. Eat on-site at the **Andaz Farmers Table** or **Mercantile Social.** All guests get complimentary access to the nearby **Exertec Health & Fitness Center** (1500 1st St.).

Information and Services

The **Napa Valley Welcome Center** (600 Main St., 707/251-5895, 855/847-6272, www.napavalley.org, 9am-5pm daily), in the middle of downtown Napa, has complimentary maps, guidebooks, and wine-tasting passes. Chat with a friendly local who can direct you to the favorite wineries and restaurants.

A privately run information outpost, the **Napa Tourist Information Center** (1331 1st St., 707/252-1000, www.napatouristinfo.com, 9:30am-7pm Mon.-Thurs., 9:30am-9pm Fri.-Sat., 9:30am-8pm Sun.) also has wine-tastings, olive oil tastings, a gift shop, and a limousine service.

Getting Around

Napa, in all its bucolic beauty, does not have infrastructure designed for the number of visitors it receives. This is part of its charm—unless you spend your visit sitting in bumper-to-bumper traffic. The best way to experience the valley is to avoid the ever-popular autumn crush and summer weekend afternoons. November and early spring are beautiful seasons to see the valley. But if a summer Saturday spent wine-tasting is impossible to resist, hit the wineries early and stay off the roads from midafternoon to early evening. With great restaurants and seductive spas everywhere, you'll easily be able to pass the extra time.

Car

Considering the number of people that go to Napa, it is not all that easy to get to. Most of the highways in this region are two lanes and frequently go by colloquial names. They are also susceptible to gridlocked traffic thanks to the numerous wine lovers and the occasional race at nearby Infineon Raceway.

CA-29 is the central conduit that runs north into the valley from the city of Napa. It is also known as the Napa-Vallejo Highway between the two cities, and as the St. Helena Highway from Napa to Calistoga, where it becomes Foothill Boulevard.

CA-128 connects the north end of Napa Valley near Rutherford with US-101 in Geyserville. From Geyserville, follow this beautiful two-lane road south to Calistoga, where it joins CA-29.

Coming from **CA-121** in Sonoma, **CA-12** east leads directly to Napa. CA-121 then picks up again at West Imola Avenue and leads east to the **Silverado Trail,** an alternative route north-south in the Napa Valley.

Bus

To avoid the potential headache of driving in Napa, take the **Vine** bus (707/251-2800, www.ridethevine.com, adults

$1.60, children 6-18 $1.10, seniors $0.80), which provides public transportation around Napa Valley, including Napa, Yountville, Oakville, Rutherford, St. Helena, and Calistoga. If you don't want to drive at all, jump aboard the commuter Vine 29 Express, which runs all day Monday-Friday. The Express travels from the El Cerrito BART station in the East Bay and from the Vallejo Ferry Terminal into Napa Valley. Fares are cash-only and require exact change.

Yountville

Named for George Calvert Yount, who planted the first vineyard in Napa Valley, Yountville is the quintessential wine-loving town. There are not even 3,000 residents, but the town has earned wide-spread fame for its epicurean spirit. You'll find a number of prestigious wineries and champagneries, but it is really restaurateur Thomas Keller who put this postage stamp-size town on the map. First came the French Laundry, then Bouchon and the Bouchon Bakery, and eventually Ad Hoc. But it's not just a Keller company town; other notable eateries have opened up and keep pace with the big boy. Still, with so many fantastic dining options, you might wish there was more to do in Yountville to extend your stay in order to accommodate as many meals out as possible.

Getting There

Yountville is on CA-29, just 9 miles (14.5 km) north of Napa. Downtown Yountville is on the east side of the highway, and Washington Street is the main drag, connecting with CA-29 at the south and north ends of town; to reach the heart of Yountville, exit on California Drive in the south and Madison Street in the north. The Yountville Cross Road will take you from the north end of town to the Silverado Trail.

Wineries
Domaine Chandon

One of the premier champagneries in Napa Valley, **Domaine Chandon** (1 California Dr., 888/242-6366, www.chandon.com, 10am-5pm daily, $20-35, tour and tasting $40) boasts lovely gardens, a stream, and an immense estate. Visitors can walk the open paths among the vineyards and enjoy the delights of the tasting room. Check online for an explanation of the different varieties of bubbly.

Hill Family Estate

Right on Washington Street in downtown Yountville, the **Hill Family Estate** (6512 Washington St., 707/944-9580, www.hillfamilyestate.com, 10:30am-6pm daily, tastings $35-45) tasting room and antiques shop offers an elegant tasting and shopping experience. Roam among the pricey French antiques as you sip, or stand at the bar to enjoy the company of the Hill family and a small selection of light, balanced red and white wines. The cabernet sauvignons are not made in the typical heavy-handed Napa style, so even tasters with delicate palates will find them drinkable. The Double Barrel Cab is sold in a box that the younger sons of the family have blasted with buckshot from their grandfather's double-barrel shotgun. Hill Family Estate also offers seasonal **tours** (10:30am Mon.-Sat. June-Sept., $55-65).

Jessup Cellars

In downtown Yountville, the tiny tasting room at **Jessup Cellars** (6740 Washington St., 707/944-5620, www.jessupcellars.com, 10am-6pm daily, $15-30) offers tastes of incredible boutique red wines that you'll have a hard time finding anyplace else. There are no tours here, no picnic grounds or fancy gardens, but you'll find lush, rich zinfandels and deep, smoky cabernets that are more than worth the sometimes-steep price tag. The tasting room boasts a cute little bar, a few shelves with items for purchase, and staff who love their jobs. If you chat them up, you may find yourself tasting rare Jessup vintages that are not on the usual list.

Priest Ranch Winery

There are a few reasons to visit **Priest Ranch Winery** (6490 Washington St., 707/944-8200, www.priestranchwines. com, 11am-7pm Sun.-Thurs., 11am-8pm Fri.-Sat., $25). Priest Ranch's flagship Coach Gun, along with their cabernet sauvignon and sauvignon blanc, are distributed and available—however, some of their wines are only available inside their big, rustic tasting room. The tasting room's late hours make this an ideal last stop on a day of wine-tasting.

Sights

The small **Napa Valley Museum** (55 Presidents Circle, 707/944-0500, www. napavalleymuseum.org, 11am-4pm Wed.-Sun., adults $10, seniors and children under 17 $5) is tucked behind Domaine Chandon on the other side of CA-29 in Yountville. Here, you will find permanent exhibits about the land and people of Napa Valley. Learn about how the region's geological makeup contributes to winemaking, or take in the local art on display.

Sports and Recreation

Biking is a popular way to see the vineyards, forests, and wineries of Napa, allowing visitors to get away from the highways and the endless traffic of the wine roads on two wheels. If you don't know the area, the best way to bike it is to take a tour. **Napa Valley Bike Tours** (6500 Washington St., 707/944-2953, www. napavalleybiketours.com, $124-398) offers standard and custom tours all over the area, from central Napa to Calistoga. You'll get a brand-name bike, a map, a helmet, and an orientation before beginning your trek. Then you'll be off on your chosen tour: a pedal through the vineyards, a half-day or full-day tour that includes both wine-tasting and meals, or a hot-air balloon ride with a full-day bike tour.

Food

The tiny town of Yountville boasts perhaps the biggest reputation for culinary excellence in California—a big deal when you consider the offerings of San Francisco and Los Angeles. The reason for this reputation starts and ends with restaurateur Thomas Keller's indisputably amazing ★ **French Laundry** (6640 Washington St., 707/944-2380, www. thomaskeller.com, 5:30pm-8:45pm Mon.-Thurs., 11am-12:30pm and 5:30pm-8:45pm Fri.-Sun., by reservation only, $325). Once you've obtained that all-important reservation, the fun begins. From the moment you walk in the door of the rambling Victorian, you're treated like royalty. You'll be led to your seat in one of the small dining rooms by one of the many immaculate black and white-clad staff. Even if you're new to this level of dining—and most people are—you'll be made to feel more than welcome. The menu, which changes often, offers two main selections: the regular nine-course tasting menu and the vegetarian nine-course tasting menu. Usually you'll see two options for the fish course and two options for the entrée. The waitstaff can help you identify anything you don't recognize or help make a decision. The sommelier is at your beck and call to assist with a wine list that weighs several pounds. From the start, servers ply you with extras—an *amuse-bouche* here, an extra middle course there—and if you mention that someone else has something on their plate that you'd like to try, it appears in front of you as if by magic. Finally, the desserts come—in four separate courses. A meal can run up to 13 courses and take four hours.

If you can't access the French Laundry, try Thomas Keller's other Yountville option, ★ **Bouchon** (6534 Washington St., 707/944-8037, www.

Reservations for The French Laundry

Most people familiar with the world of high-end food know that the best restaurant in all of California, and possibly all of the United States, is The French Laundry. Thomas Keller's culinary haven in tiny Yountville has earned the hallowed three-star rating from the Michelin Guide every year since 2006. The restaurant sits inside a charming vintage house; its kitchen garden grows right across the street where anyone can walk down the rows of vegetables and herbs.

The French Laundry

Sounds like foodie paradise, right? There's just one problem: getting a table.

The difficulty in getting reservations to the French Laundry is almost as legendary as the French Laundry itself. Rather than expecting to dine at the French Laundry during a planned trip to the Wine Country, savvy travelers expect to plan their whole trip around whatever French Laundry reservation they manage to get.

The bare facts: The French Laundry takes reservations two months in advance. *Precisely* two months. The restaurant accepts reservations by phone, online, and via local concierges. Reservations are accepted for parties of 1-6 individuals. Diners can choose between lunch and dinner seatings that offer the same menu. It's easier to get a table for lunch than it is for dinner. Lunch or dinner takes 2.5-4 hours to consume. Budget $500 *per person* for your meal if you plan to drink wine, and $300-350 if you don't. The meals are priced at $325 per person.

The French Laundry starts taking **phone reservations** at 10am daily. Between 9:30am and 9:45am, program their number on your speed-dial and begin calling. Continue calling again and again until you get an answer. If you get a continuous busy signal past noon, you'll probably need to try again the next day. And maybe the day after that.

Making **reservations online** works much the same way as on the phone, only it's harder. The French Laundry offers only two tables for each service (lunch and dinner) online per day. Go online at OpenTable (www.opentable.com) at about 8:30am and start trying to snag that table. If you're still trying at 9:30am, it's probably already gone.

thomaskeller.com, 10am-midnight Sat.-Sun., 11am-midnight Mon.-Fri., $19-59). Reservations are still strongly recommended, but you should be able to get one just a week in advance. Bouchon's atmosphere and food scream Parisian bistro. Order traditional favorites such as the *croque madame* sandwich or steak frites, or opt for a California-influenced specialty salad or entrée made with local, sustainable ingredients. Keller also has

Ad Hoc (6476 Washington St., 707/944-2487, 5pm-10pm Mon. and Thurs.-Sat., 9am-1:30pm and 5pm-10pm Sun., $55), a casual comfort-food eatery with menu items like fried chicken and barbecue offered in a four-course prix fixe menu.

If you're just looking for a breakfast pastry or a sandwich, walk from Bouchon next door to the **Bouchon Bakery** (6528 Washington St., 707/944-2253, www.bouchonbakery.com, 7am-7pm

Mon.-Fri., 6:30am-7pm Sat.-Sun.). This ultra-high-end bakery supplies both Bouchon and the French Laundry with pastries and breads and operates a retail storefront. Locals and visitors flock to the bakery at breakfast and lunchtime, so expect a line.

There's more to the Yountville dining scene than Thomas Keller. **Ciccio** (6770 Washington St., Yountville, 707/945-1000, www.ciccionapavalley.com, 5pm-9pm Wed.-Sun., $19-32, chef's tasting menu $95 pp) serves Italian food and wood-fired pizzas in an old market building. Many of the ingredients come from Ciccio's own garden. For negroni fans, Ciccio does seven versions of the iconic Italian cocktail.

Situated in the V Market Place, ★ **Bottega** (6525 Washington St., 707/945-1050, www.botteganapavalley. com, 11:30am-3pm and 5pm-9:30pm Tues.-Sun., 5pm-9:30pm Mon., $17-38) is the return to the kitchen for celebrity chef Michael Chiarello. The former host of *Easy Entertaining* on the Food Network has come back to Napa Valley and brought his flair for Italian cuisine. The exposed brick and bare ceiling beams of the dining room pair nicely with such classic dishes as *tagliarini* with veal and porcini *sugo,* duck served with duck liver mousse, and braised short ribs with spaetzle. The prices, particularly the wine list, are fairly reasonable for the area. While the menu changes with the seasons, try to finish your meal with the ricotta *zeppole*—Italian donuts fried to order and topped with praline cream.

Accommodations

If you've come to Napa Valley to dine at the French Laundry or immerse yourself in the food scene, you'll want to stay in Yountville. Several inns are within stumbling distance of the French Laundry, which is convenient for gourmands who want to experience a range of wines with the meal.

$150-250

Thanks to a location next to Bouchon Bakery, you can wake up to mouthwatering smells at the cozy, five-room **Petit Logis Inn** (6527 Yount St., 877/944-2332, www.petitlogis.com, $210-325). Each room is decorated in warm, creamy colors with an occasional wall mural and furnished with a fireplace, a jetted tub, a fridge, and an outdoor sitting area. Low-key and unpretentious, the inn is best described as "the place to come to pretend you live in Yountville." Breakfast is not included, but it can be arranged for an additional fee at a nearby restaurant.

Over $250

The Mediterranean-style **Napa Valley Lodge** (2230 Madison St., 707/944-2468, www.napavalleylodge.com, $400-920) is a stunner with stucco walls and red-tile roofs. Guests are steeped in the luxury that Yountville is known for: Book a spa treatment in your room or out beside the heated pool. Start each day with the complimentary champagne buffet breakfast, or order from the California cuisine room-service menu. Lodging options include the Parkside Terrace rooms, with king beds topped with European-style duvets; the Vineyard Courtyard Terrace rooms, with their own patios; and the luxurious King Junior Suite, with a fireplace, two-person soaking tub, and views of the courtyard.

For a motel with a historic twist, book a room at the **Napa Valley Railway Inn** (6523 Washington St., 707/944-2000, www.napavalleyrailwayinn.com, $275-325). The nine rooms are converted 100-year-old train cars tightly packed together, making a unique type of hotel. The rooms themselves are funky and narrow but carefully decorated in classic style with rich bedspreads. Stop by the Coffee Caboose to start your day with pastries and coffee.

A French-style inn, the **Maison Fleurie** (6529 Yount St., 800/788-0369, www. foursisters.com, $249-379) offers the best of small-inn style for a more reasonable rate. It is in a perfect location for walking to Bouchon, the Bouchon Bakery, and the many other amazing restaurants, boutiques, and tasting rooms in town. The 13 rooms in this "house of flowers" have an attractive but not overwhelming floral decorative theme. The more economical rooms are small but attractive. If you've got the budget to splurge, opt for a room in the Bakery Building, where you'll get a fireplace, a jetted spa tub, a king bed, and a private entrance. Enjoy a full breakfast each morning as well as an afternoon wine reception, fresh cookies, and use of the on-site pool and hot tub.

At **The Cottages of Napa Valley** (1012 Darms Ln., 2 mi/3.2 km south of Yountville, 707/252-7810, www. napacottages.com, $395-575), you'll pay a princely sum to gain a home away from home in the heart of Wine Country. Each cottage has its own king bed, outdoor fireplace, kitchenette, and heated bathroom floor. Every morning the quiet staff drops off a basket of fresh pastries from Bouchon Bakery and a pot of great coffee to greet you upon waking up. Simple yet luxurious country-cottage furnishings feel welcoming and homey, and the staff can help you plan the ultimate Wine Country vacation. They also offer complimentary dinner shuttles into Yountville.

Enjoy the location and luxury of the **Vintage House** (6541 Washington St., 707/944-1112, www.vintagehouse.com, $525-780), where rooms in the elegant hexagonal buildings feature soft sheets, jetted tubs, wood-burning fireplaces, and complimentary bottles of wine. The French Country-meets-Wine Country

decor extends to a private patio or deck overlooking the lush gardens. The dining room serves what might be the best complimentary hotel buffet breakfast in California, with buttery French pastries, fresh fruit, and made-to-order omelets. As it's a sister property of nearby Villagio, Vintage Inn guests can use the Villagio's fitness center, tennis courts, and spa.

Information and Services

Right in the thick of the epicurean madness, the **Yountville Chamber of Commerce** (6484 Washington St., 707/944-0904, http://yountville.com, 10am-5pm daily) also doubles as a visitors center. There are maps available along with always-helpful tips. Swing by to purchase two-for-one tasting coupons for Hill Family Estate, which is just down the street.

Head to Napa's **Queen of the Valley Hospital** (1000 Trancas St., 707/252-4411, www.thequeen.org) for medical emergencies.

Getting Around

To reach Yountville by bus, jump aboard the **Vine** (707/251-2800, www. ridethevine.com, adults $1.60, children $1.10), a commuter bus service that runs from the East Bay north through Calistoga.

Around town, consider taking the **Yountville Trolley** (707/312-1509, www. ridethevine.com, 10am-11pm Mon.-Sat., 10am-7pm Sun., free). The trolley runs on a fixed track from Yountville Park along Washington Street to California Drive, conveniently near Domaine Chandon. It may also be useful for getting back to your hotel after imbibing too much.

Rutherford and Oakville

Driving along on CA-29, you might not even notice the tiny hamlets of Oakville and Rutherford. Neither town has much in the way of a commercial or residential district and both have minuscule populations. Oakville earned a spot on the map in 1903 when the U.S. Department of Agriculture planted an experimental vineyard there. Since then, it has garnered distinction as a unique American Viticultural Area (AVA) known for its Bordeaux-style varietals. Oakville is also home to the outstanding Oakville Grocery, opened in 1881.

Rutherford was named for the 1,000 acres given to Thomas Rutherford by his father-in-law, George Yount. The area now has the distinction of growing some of the best cabernet grapes around. Yountville is also home to Grgich Hills, whose chardonnay crashed the Paris Wine Tasting of 1976. Like Oakville, Rutherford is also its own designated AVA.

Getting There
Oakville is 4 miles (6.4 km) north of Yountville on CA-29; Rutherford is another 2 miles (3.2 km) north. Both can be easy to miss because of their loose organization and rural character. The Silverado Trail runs parallel to CA-29 along this stretch. To reach it from Oakville, take Oakville Road east; in Rutherford, take Rutherford Road (CA-128) east.

Wineries
Beaulieu Vineyards
Since 1900, **Beaulieu Vineyards** (1960 St. Helena Hwy., 707/257-5749, www.bvwines.com, 10am-5pm daily, $30-125) has been known for its cabernet sauvignon, even managing to survive Prohibition. Tastings are in the hexagon-shaped tasting room or the reserve tasting room for high-end, small production wines. Bottles range $10-1,000 each, with wines for all budgets.

Frog's Leap Winery
With so much outrageous winery architecture in the valley, **Frog's Leap Winery** (8815 Conn Creek Rd., Rutherford, 707/963-4704, www.frogsleap.com, 10am-4pm daily, $25-35) is an understated breath of fresh air. Its historic red barn and modest home and vineyard sit among gardens and vines. This big producer is just west of the Silverado Trail in the flats of Napa Valley; it has been a producer since 1981 and a leader in organic wine production and environmental stewardship. Tasting here is relaxing; sample a flight of four wines on the wraparound porch or inside the vineyard house, accompanied by cheese, crackers, and jam. The highly recommended tour (10:30am and 2:30pm Mon.-Fri., $35) also provides a tasting of four wines, and each tasting is enjoyed somewhere different along the tour—the garden, the red barn, or in the vineyard, for example. Tours are by appointment only and last about one hour.

Opus One
Yup, that huge thing on the rise that looks like a missile silo really is a winery. **Opus One** (7900 Hwy. 29, Oakville, 800/292-6787, www.opusonewinery.com, 10am-4pm daily, reservations required, tasting $50, tours $85-140) boasts a reputation as one of the most prestigious, and definitely one of the most expensive, vintners in Napa. The echoing halls inside the facility add to the grandeur of the place, as does the price of a tasting: $50 for a four-ounce pour of a single wine. You're unlikely to find a bottle of Opus One for under $250. If you don't mind the price tag or just can't get enough of the Opus One experience, tours (appointment only) of the estate and its history are also available.

★ Grgich Hills Winery

At **Grgich Hills Winery** (1829 St. Helena Hwy., Rutherford, 707/963-2784, www.grgich.com, daily 9:30am-4:30pm, $25-90), active aging barrels crowd the main building and narrow the path to the tasting room's restrooms. If you're looking for a showy Napa Valley experience, this might not be the best place for you. What you will find at Grgich are some of the best wines in the valley and a biodynamic winemaking operation. Mike Grgich took his California chardonnay to the Paris Wine Tasting of 1976 and entered it in the white burgundy blind-tasting competition. After it won, French winemakers demanded that the contest be held again, and Grgich's chardonnay won a second time. That same year, Robert Mondavi's cabernet sauvignon also took top honors in its category at the same contest.

Visiting Grgich Hills, you'll find plenty of information about biodynamic farming, a process that takes organic practices to the next level. The best wines might be the legendary chardonnay—arguably the best chardonnay made in Napa or anywhere else. But don't ignore the reds, as Grgich offers lovely zinfandels and cabernets. And the Violetta, a dessert wine, is a special treat that's only made in years when the grape conditions are perfect. None of the Grgich wines are cheap, but it's more than worth it when you sip these rare, exquisite vintages.

Mumm

You may have already tasted the sparkling wines produced by **Mumm** (8445 Silverado Trl., Rutherford, 800/686-6272 Mon.-Fri., 707/967-7700 Sat.-Sun., http://mummnapa.com, 10am-6pm daily, $25-45). Even for genuine wine aficionados, it's worth spending an hour or two at Mumm Napa, a friendly and surprisingly down-to-earth winery among the estates on the Silverado Trail. Tastings happen at tables, with menus and service in restaurant fashion. The prices look very Napa Valley, but you'll get more wine

Inglenook

and service for your money. Each pour is three ounces of wine—some of it high-end—and you get three pours per tasting. Nonalcoholic gourmet grape sodas and bottled water are complimentary. Dogs are allowed in the tasting room and get water, gourmet doggie bones, and plenty of petting from the tasting-room staff. Also, there's a 45- to 60-minute **tour** (10am, 11am, 1pm, 3pm daily, $40) that ends in the photography gallery.

Peju

Embodying the ultimate success of the Napa Valley, **Peju** (8466 St. Helena Hwy., Rutherford, 800/446-7358, www.peju. com, 10am-6pm daily, $40-100) is a family winery that has, through hard work, created great wines that have garnered the attention of international magazines and judging bodies. Today, visitors to Peju see gorgeous sycamore trees, hand-pruned by Tony Peju, running up the drive; a fabulous garden tended by Herta Peju; and solar panels on the roof of the elegant winery building. Inside you'll get tastes of an array of aromatic and award-winning red wines—from the lighter Bordeaux-varietal cabernet franc to the many vintages of classic California cabernet sauvignon. A few whites and perhaps a rosé or a port round out Peju's list. Wine-tasting options include a garden tasting, a private reserve tasting, and a wine and cheese pairing.

Inglenook

Wine lovers come to enjoy the grand tasting room and museum at **Inglenook** (1991 St. Helena Hwy., Rutherford, 707/968-1161, www.inglenook.com, 10am-5pm daily, reservations required, tasting $45-125). Check in at the visitors center, which dates to 1879, then head in for a wine-tasting or a bite at the bistro. There's also a boutique for shoppers. Reservations are required for tastings in the large, elegant tasting room, where you'll find a generous bar area with plenty of staff to help you navigate the wine list. The winemakers take their job seriously, and the results can be spectacular. This estate winery also houses the small Centennial Museum, showcasing old Inglenook wines, zoetropes, and magic lanterns.

Rutherford Hill

If you're planning in advance to visit **Rutherford Hill** (200 Rutherford Hill Rd., Rutherford, 707/963-1871, www. rutherfordhill.com, 10am-5pm daily, tasting $20-30), book a spot on the winery-and-cave tour. The winery is pretty standard for a Napa facility, but the caves impress even experienced wine lovers. Dug back into the hillside, Rutherford's caves provide a natural temperature-controlled space in which to age their array of wines, mostly hearty reds. (If you're looking for a place to hold a special dinner or midsize event, Rutherford rents out space in the caves.) Contrary to the myth perpetuated by the movie *Sideways*, Rutherford produces a fine merlot as well as rich cabernet sauvignons and other tasty varietals.

Food

★ The Restaurant at Auberge du Soleil

(707/967-3111, www.aubergedusoleil.com, 7am-11am, 11:30am-2:15pm, and 5:30pm-9:30pm daily, tasting menus $120-165) has a charming Mediterranean-style dining room with sunny yellow tablecloths, a central fireplace, exposed wooden beams, and wall-to-wall picture windows. Executive chef Robert Curry, a legend of the Napa Valley culinary scene, uses the finest local ingredients to create his own take on Mediterranean and California cuisine. Choose one item from each course list on the short but exquisite tasting menu to create a three-course, four-course, or six-course dinner. The adjacent **Bistro & Bar** (11:30am-11pm daily, $20-68) has a bar and small dining area; outside is a deck with fine views of Napa Valley. There's also a list of Napa Valley wines to enjoy while you soak up the view.

A long-standing Wine Country favorite is the **Rutherford Grill** (1180 Rutherford Rd., Rutherford, 707/963-1792, https://rutherfordgrill.com, 11:30am-9:30pm Mon.-Thurs., 11am-10pm Fri.-Sat., 11am-9:30pm Sun., $16-45), which is more casual than many of its Napa Valley peers. Some of the best seats in the house cluster outside the dining room on the wide deck; sheltered by a collection of umbrellas, guests enjoy the pretty gardens with their classic grill fare—cheeseburgers, salads with grilled items, bangers and mash, and a whole array of grilled meats—as well as an extensive and impressive wine list. Perhaps the best part: You can escape from the Rutherford Grill for well under $100 per person.

For a picnic lunch or just a few munchies for the road, stop by the **Oakville Grocery** (7856 St. Helena Hwy., Oakville, 707/944-8802, www.oakvillegrocery.com, 7am-5pm Sun.-Thurs., 7am-6pm Fri.-Sat.) along CA-29. A longtime Napa Valley institution, the Oakville Grocery has a reputation for stocking only the best food, wine, cheese, and other goodies. Browse the tightly packed shelves or order a hot lunch at the center counter; they serve slow-roasted beef and fried chicken sandwiches among other options. To find the building from the northbound highway, look for the large Coca-Cola sign painted on the south side of the building.

Take a break from Wine Country cuisine with local favorite **La Luna Market and Taqueria** (1153 Rutherford Rd., Rutherford, 707/963-3211, www.lalunamarket.com, 7am-7pm Mon.-Fri., 8am-6pm Sat., 8am-5pm Sun., $10), known for its *al pastor* (marinated pork) tacos and breakfast burritos. This Mexican grocery store and taqueria is in a strip mall.

Accommodations

Perched above the valley and off the Silverado Trail, ★ **Auberge du Soleil** (180 Rutherford Hill Rd., St. Helena, 707/963-1211, www.aubergedusoleil.com, $725-5,200) is the ultimate in Wine Country luxury. The compound features multiple wine-tasting and dining options in addition to a pool, a fitness room, a store, and well-kept gardens accented by modern art. The rooms are appointed with Italian sheets, private patios, fireplaces, and TVs in both the living room and the bath. The smallest guest room is 500 square feet, suites can top 1,400 square feet, and the Private Maison is 1,800 square feet. This is the place to stay if you have the cash to focus on the inn's amenities and have less interest in spending your time exploring the area.

For a classic California vibe, book one of the spacious rooms (all start at 400 square feet) at **Rancho Caymus Inn** (1140 Rutherford Rd., Rutherford, 707/200-9300, https://ranchocaymusinn.com, $395-695). Accommodations feature wooden beams and custom-made doors in a Spanish hacienda-style; each offers a furnished deck or patio to take in the Wine Country view. Amenities include a complimentary continental breakfast and wine-tastings (Thurs.-Sat. nights).

St. Helena

There are few Northern California towns as picturesque and well-groomed as St. Helena. Bolstered by the lucrative wine industry, St. Helena has the glossy sheen of a reinvented old California farm town. It is filled with fine eateries and quaint, expensive shops housed in historic buildings and surrounded by block upon block of well-maintained Craftsman homes. The Napa campus of the Culinary Institute of America is a major employer in the area, as is the St. Helena Hospital. CA-29 runs north-south through the center of town, which can give you a quick peek at the sights, but it's not so nice when sitting in traffic on a sunny weekend.

Getting There
St. Helena is on CA-29 in the middle of Napa Valley, 8 miles (13 km) south of Calistoga. To reach the Silverado Trail from St. Helena, take Zinfandel Lane or Pope Street east.

Wineries
Beringer Vineyards
The palatial stone estate buildings of **Beringer Vineyards** (2000 Main St., 707/257-5771, www.beringer.com, 10am-5pm daily, $25-150) belie the reasonably priced Beringer vintages available across the country. Inside, you'll find an array of wines for tasting, many of which are not readily available outside the tasting room. Stroll the beautiful estate gardens, which stretch for acres on prime land next to the highway. You can even go deep with a half-hour cave tour ($30) or the Taste of Beringer Tour ($55), which includes a wine pairing and tasting in the Rhine House kitchen.

Corison
A rarity among Napa Valley's large-scale producers, **Corison** (987 St. Helena Hwy., 707/963-0826, www.corison.com, 10am-5pm daily, by appointment, $55-150) is the genuine article—a tiny single-proprietor winery producing great wines in small quantities. Technically, Corison takes tasters by appointment only, but in truth they've never turned away a drop-in during regular business hours. After turning onto a short gravel driveway, you pass a vintage home to reach the small barn that serves as a tasting room. Open the huge white door and enter the tasting-, barrel-, and stockroom. A tiny bar offers tastings from the 3,000 cases the winery produces each year. Expect the attentive staff to talk in loving and knowledgeable terms about the delicious wines they're pouring. The Library Tasting ($55) highlights current releases, with a few selections from the library. Cabernet sauvignon fans can take their appreciation deeper with the Collector's Vertical Tasting ($150), a flight that showcases four decades of the varietal.

Flora Springs
This winery straddles the line between boutiques and big-deal Napa players. You'll find **Flora Springs** (677 S. St. Helena Hwy., 866/967-8032, www.florasprings.com, 10am-5pm daily, $30-75) on a few menus in upscale restaurants and here in the open, airy tasting room that sweeps in a half circle around the bar, with plenty of windows letting in the Napa sunlight. You'll taste a variety of reds and whites, but the cabernet sauvignons are the standouts here.

Heitz
One of the oldest wineries in the valley, **Heitz** (436 St. Helena Hwy., 707/963-2047, www.heitzcellar.com, 11am-4:30pm daily, $35-75) brings sincere elegance to the glitz and glamour of Napa. The high-ceilinged tasting room is dominated by a stone fireplace with comfy chairs. A

low bar off to the right sets the stage for an array of Napa Valley cabernet sauvignons. To the happy surprise of many, Heitz's cabernets are well balanced and easy to drink, and though costly, they approach affordable by Napa standards. Both the Heritage and Appellation Tastings feature more than one sip of their cabs. Most of the grapes used for these wines are grown right in the Napa Valley. In February, visitors can taste the current release of the Martha's Vineyard Cabernet—a vintage grown in the first wine-designated vineyard in the valley.

Pride Mountain Vineyards

Take advantage of some of Wine Country's scenic drives with a visit to **Pride Mountain Vineyards** (4026 Spring Mountain Rd., 707/963-4949, www.pridewines.com, 10am-3:30pm Wed.-Mon., reservations required, tour and tasting $30-90), at the top of a scenic, winding road 6 miles (9.5 km) from the turnoff on CA-29. In addition to the

wine, the views are the reward for the effort. Wine-tasting is by appointment only, so once you arrive you'll have the pourer's full attention. It's worth it to take the tour, as you'll see the vineyard and the caves and will be able to taste the wine straight out of the barrel. It's a great education in how wine matures with age.

V. Sattui

A boutique winery that doesn't distribute to retailers, **V. Sattui** (1111 White Lane, 707/963-7774, www.vsattui.com, 9am-6pm daily summer, 9am-5pm daily winter, $20-45) won the Best Winery award at the California State Fair in 2006, 2007, and 2012—a mighty feat in a state filled with excellent vintners. V. Sattui produces a wide selection of varietals—everything from light-bodied whites to full-flavored cabernet sauvignons. The dessert Madeira is particularly fine—if it's not on the tasting menu, ask your pourer at the bar if they've got a bottle open, and you might just get lucky.

Culinary Institute of America at Greystone

The big tasting room on CA-29 boasts three spacious bar areas, endless stacks and cases of wine out and ready for purchase, a separate register, and a full deli. The gardens surrounding the facility include picnic tables, and Sattui is a popular lunchtime stop for all-day tasters. There's also a tower (10am-4pm Fri.-Sun., $40) open for weekend tastings. Even the big Sattui tasting room fills up on weekends in high season (May-Oct.).

Sights
★ Culinary Institute of America at Greystone
The premier institute for training professional chefs in the United States has only three campuses: one in upstate New York, one in Texas, and this one, the **Culinary Institute of America at Greystone** (2555 Main St., 707/967-1100, www.ciachef.edu). The campus includes the Gatehouse Restaurant (5:30pm-8pm Tues.-Sat.), the Bakery Café (11am-3pm daily), the Spice Islands Marketplace (10:30am-6pm daily Mar.-Nov.; 11am-5pm Mon.-Thurs., 10:30am-6pm Fri.-Sun. Nov.-Mar.), one-day cooking classes and demos, a food-history museum, and a stunning set of buildings nestled in the forests and vineyards near St. Helena on CA-29. If Napa is the perfect place to introduce newcomers to the world of high-end food and wine, Greystone takes it to the intermediate and advanced levels. Serious foodies and cork dorks should sign up in advance to attend a cooking demo or seminar. Take a few minutes to marvel at the imposing graystone structures of the campus or opt for a **tour** (11:30am Mon.-Fri., 11:30am and 3:15pm Sat.-Sun., $10-25) of the grounds.

Shopping
As you may be able to tell from the traffic in town, downtown St. Helena is hopping. Quaint and historical storefronts line CA-29, housing galleries, clothiers, jewelers, kitchen stores, and, of course, wine shops, many of which offer wine-tasting. Over the years, olive trees have begun spreading across the landscape, which makes perfect sense—Napa Valley has an ideal Mediterranean climate for these trees. The resulting olive oil offers one more thing to taste.

Out of downtown St. Helena's hubbub, the **Napa Valley Olive Oil Manufacturing Co.** (835 Charter Oak Ave., 707/963-4173, www.nvoliveoilmfg.com, 8am-5pm daily) is one of those treasures that travelers feel lucky to find. The tiny, funky old storefront is two blocks off the highway and features a motley collection of plastic-covered picnic tables out front and a faded, hand-lettered sign on the door. Inside, take care not to trip over the uneven floor in the cramped, meandering rooms of the shop. You can't taste the oils and vinegars; you'll just have to go on faith that this Italian-owned and -operated shop sells the best. The tiny store also has fabulous cheeses and freshly baked breads, making it a great stop for picnic supplies. The shop bottles its products on-site. There's also a

storefront (1331 1st St., Napa, 707/265-6866, 8am-5pm daily) in Napa.

Food

A highlight of the St. Helena dining scene is the ★ **Gatehouse Restaurant** (2555 Main St., 707/967-1010, http://ciachef.edu, 5:30pm-8pm Tues.-Sat., $45-55), better known as "the restaurant at the CIA," where the world's top aspiring chefs practice their craft. (CIA's Greystone restaurant is no longer operating.) It's easier to get a reservation here than at French Laundry and Bouchon; with several big dining rooms, the CIA can seat large numbers. From some tables, you can watch your food being prepared in the open kitchen. The ever-changing three- or four-course menu highlights the best of each season, and the wine list features the finest of Napa Valley's vintages; the student chefs plan menus with an eye to wine pairings.

Craving pizza or a low-key meal? **Pizzeria Tra Vigne** (1016 Main St., 707/967-9999, http://pizzeriatravigne.com, 11:30am-9pm Sun.-Thurs., 11:30am-9:30pm Fri.-Sat., $11-25), next door to Tra Vigne, is considerably more relaxed than its renowned sibling. Inside are long tables opposite the open kitchen, where a huge wood-fired oven sits center stage. The famous thin-crust Italian pizzas lure locals many weekend nights; you can also enjoy hearty plates of pasta or heavy Italian salads. Wash it all down with a pitcher of any number of beers on tap. There are also beers by the bottle in addition to a healthy selection of wine. If you're traveling with kids, Pizzeria Tra Vigne is a great place to stop and relax over a meal. There's even a pool table.

Tired of Wine Country fare? The **Himalayan Sherpa Kitchen** (1148 Main St., 707/963-4439, http://himalayansherpakitchen.com, 11:30am-3pm and 5pm-9pm Mon. and Wed.-Fri., 11:30am-9pm Sat.-Sun., $17-26) serves cuisine from the highest region in the world right in downtown St. Helena.

With golden curries, *tikka masala* dishes, and samosas, the menu features the kinds of dishes you'd find in an Indian restaurant. The food is superb, and as in the rest of Napa, there is a selection of fine local wines to sip with your meal.

★ **Gott's Roadside** (933 Main St., 707/963-3486, www.gotts.com, 10am-10pm daily summer, 10am-9pm daily winter, $6-17) was once known as Taylor's Refresher, which explains the wooden sign on CA-29. This classic roadside diner has been around since 1949, but the food has been updated with a modern local-organic sensibility; the burgers, fries, and milk shakes are made with quality ingredients. The Gott brothers, who took over the business in 1999, have added more California-eclectic comfort food like fish tacos, Vietnamese chicken salad, and wines by the glass. They have also earned three James Beard awards for bringing fast food up to the quality of well-respected sit-down restaurants.

Cook Tavern (1304 Main St., 707/963-8082, www.cooktavern.com, 11:30am-9pm Mon.-Thurs., 11:30am-10pm Fri., 10am-10pm Sat., 10am-9pm Sun., $14-22) pairs wine, beer, and craft cocktails with small plates and "not so small" entrées. In addition to pizzas, they serve tacos and burgers.

St. Helena has its own food truck with **Bruschetteria** (by the Clif Family Tasting Room most days, 709 Main St., 707/301-7188, www.cliffamily.com, 11:30am-4pm Tues.-Sun., 11:30am-7:30pm Wed., $11-20). The green truck offers grilled bread with toppings (heirloom tomatoes, seasonal mushrooms, smoked salmon). The porchetta is a favorite, with pork, herbs, onion, aioli, and parmesan.

Accommodations

The charming village of St. Helena is right on CA-29, and its stop signs and traffic signals are often the cause of the endless Wine Country weekend traffic jams. But if you're staying here, you can

Side Trip: Calistoga

Calistoga is the land of great and affordable spas, where soaking is treated more as therapy than beauty treatment. It also has a quirkiness missing from some other Napa Valley towns.

Wineries

Castello di Amorosa (4045 Hwy. 29, 707/967-6272, www.castellodiamorosa.com, 9:30am-6pm daily Mar.-Oct., 9:30am-5pm daily Nov.-Feb., adults $30, youth under 21 $20) produces a number of varietals, such as pinot grigio and muscat, which are overshadowed by their environs. The steep prices for tasting include access to the main floors of the castle. Tours, in addition to barrel-tasting, take visitors to the armory and torture chamber.

Clos Pegase (1060 Dunaweal Ln., 707/942-4981, www.clospegase.com, 10am-5pm daily, tasting $30-45) has more than 100 artworks on its grounds, including sculptor Henry Moore's *Mother Earth* and a painting from Francis Bacon. In the tasting room, you can sample the winery's flagship cabernet sauvignon or their Hommage chardonnay. Clos Pegase also offers tours of its vineyard ($45-60) that include a visit inside the winery's caves.

Schramsberg Vineyards (1400 Schramsberg Rd., 707/942-4558, www.schramsberg.com, visitors center 9am-4:30pm daily, cave tour and tasting times vary, reservations required, $70-125) was founded in 1862 and is considered to be one of the best producers of sparkling wine in California. Tastings include four wines and a tour of the 120-year-old caves.

Sterling Vineyards (1111 Dunaweal Ln., 800/726-6136, www.sterlingvineyards.com, 10am-5pm daily, adults $35, youth under 21 $15) features a gondola ride and an obligatory tasting tour through the estate. The lines can be long on weekends in high season (May-Oct.).

Sights

Old Faithful Geyser (1299 Tubbs Lane, 707/942-6463, www.oldfaithfulgeyser.com, 8:30am-7pm daily Mar.-Sept., 8:30am-6pm daily Oct., 8:30am-5pm daily Nov.-Feb., adults $15, seniors and students $13, children 4-12 $9, under age 4 free) erupts with clockwork regularity: Expect no more than a 40-minute wait to see it erupt 60 feet or higher into the air.

Spas

Dr. Wilkinson's Hot Springs Resort (1507 Lincoln Ave., 707/942-4102, www.drwilkinson.com, 8:30am-3:45pm daily, $79-210) opened in 1952 and offers mud baths, facials, a mineral whirlpool, a sauna, and massage.

At **Calistoga Hot Springs Spa** (1006 Washington St., 707/942-6269, www.calistogaspa.com, 8:30am-4:30pm Tues.-Thurs., 8:30am-9pm Fri.-Mon., $45-252), you can indulge in a mud bath, a mineral bath, or other typical spa treatments. Four outdoor mineral pools are available to the public, guaranteed with a spa reservation.

Indian Springs (1712 Lincoln Ave., 707/942-4913, www.indianspringscalistoga.com, 8:30am-8:30pm daily, mud baths and massages $95-275) is the oldest continuously operating pool and spa facility in the state. It offers mud baths, facials, and a dip in an Olympic-size mineral pool.

Getting There

Calistoga is 8 miles (13 km) north of St. Helena on CA-29. In Calistoga, CA-29 turns east, becoming Lincoln Avenue.

avoid the worst of the traffic and enjoy the wooded central Napa Valley area.

For the best rates in St. Helena, the ★ **El Bonita Motel** (195 Main St./Hwy. 29, 800/541-3284, www.elbonita.com, $150-280) can't be beat. It is within walking distance of the historic downtown and has a 1950s motel charm. The low-slung 48-room hotel wraps about a patio shaded by oak trees, bordered by a clipped lawn, and filled with tables, chairs, and umbrellas. In the center is a pool, a hot tub, and a sauna, which all guests are encouraged to enjoy. The rooms may not match the indulgence of other Napa inns, but they are clean, comfortable, and pet-friendly, with refrigerators and microwave ovens; some even boast kitchenettes.

Information and Services

Pick up maps, information, and discounted wine-tasting vouchers at the **St. Helena Welcome Center** (657 Main St., 707/963-4456, www.sthelena.com, 9am-5pm Mon.-Fri., 10am-4pm Sat.-Sun.). Thankfully, there is parking in back; turn on Vidovich Lane just north of the visitors center.

The **Adventist Health St. Helena Hospital** (10 Woodland Rd., 707/963-9611, www.adventisthealth.org) has a 24-hour emergency room for quick and reliable service.

Getting Around

To avoid the headache of parking and driving around town, hop aboard the **Vine St. Helena Shuttle** (707/963-3007, www.ridethevine.com, 7:45am-6pm Mon.-Thurs., 7:45am-11pm Fri., 10am-11pm Sat., noon-7pm Sun., $1).

Sonoma and Carneros

The Sonoma and Carneros wine regions are in the southeast part of Sonoma Valley. The scenery features oak forests and vineyard-covered open spaces. The terminus of El Camino Real is in the small city of Sonoma, which includes the famed Sonoma Mission Inn, historic sites, and a charming town square with plenty of shopping and great places to grab a bite. Wineries cluster in this region, though not as many as in the Russian River Valley; the tasting rooms still have plenty of traffic, but the crowds can be less vicious than in the ultra-popular Napa and Dry Creek Valleys.

Carneros might be described as the "lost" area of Wine Country. The wineries are a bit more spread out than in the Napa and Russian River Valleys, and fewer visitors cram into the tasting rooms. Some prestigious California names make their homes here, and some small boutique vintners quietly produce amazing varietals you won't find outside their tasting rooms.

Getting There

The town of Sonoma is over the mountains west of the Napa Valley. The main route through the valley is CA-12, also called the Sonoma Highway. To reach Sonoma from Napa, drive south on CA-29 and turn west onto CA-12/121. Turn north on CA-12 to reach downtown Sonoma.

Parking in downtown Sonoma is easy in the off-season and tougher in the high season (May-Oct.). Expect to hunt for a spot during local events, and be prepared to walk several blocks. Most wineries provide ample free parking on their grounds.

Sonoma Wineries

Ravenswood Winery

Ravenswood Winery (18701 Gehricke Rd., 888/669-4679, 707/933-2332, www.ravenswood-wine.com, 10am-4:30pm daily, $25-60) prides itself on making "no wimpy wines." Although owned by a large conglomerate, Ravenswood wines are overseen by the original winemaker, Joel Peterson, who began making California zinfandel in 1976. Zinfandel remains the signature varietal under

Sonoma Plaza

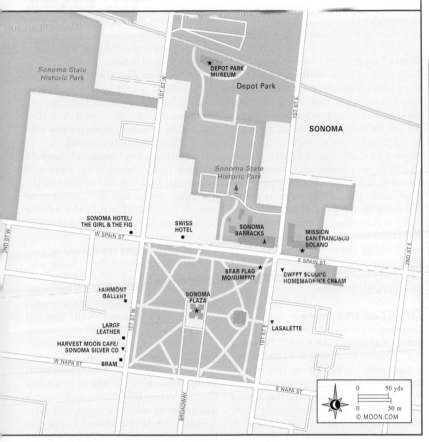

the Ravenswood label, and many of the prized zins come from individual vineyards in Sonoma County. Ravenswood sponsors a race car, hosts a bevy of summer barbecues, and strives to make testers of all types feel at home in the winery. Tours and barrel tastings teach newcomers the process of winemaking, while "blend your own" seminars beckon to serious wine connoisseurs. Ravenswood wines are easy on the pocketbook, ranging $13-50 per bottle.

Carneros Wineries
Domaine Carneros

The Sonoma-Carneros region has perfect conditions for champagne-style grapes, and so the glorious **Domaine Carneros** (1240 Duhig Rd., Napa, 800/716-2788, www.domaine.com, 10am-5:30pm daily, $30-500) makes its estate home here. Visitors rarely fail to be impressed by the grand estate structure, where both the architecture and garden setting are styled like the great châteaux of France. Even more impressive are the finely crafted sparkling wines and a few pinot noirs the winery creates using grapes from the Carneros region. The high-end tasting option allows a couple to taste Domaine Carneros's wines on the balcony of a private chateau with views of the vineyard.

Gloria Ferrer

For a taste of some of the upscale sparkling wines Sonoma can produce, take a long drive through immense estate vineyards to the tasting room at **Gloria Ferrer** (23555 Hwy. 121/Arnold Dr., Sonoma, 707/933-1917, www.gloriaferrer.com, 10am-5pm daily, flights $25-35, glasses $9-25). Ferrer also adheres to the popular format for sparkling wineries—there's no traditional tasting. Visitors order one or more full flutes of sparkling wine, then take a seat at an available table either inside the tasting room or out on the patio overlooking the Sonoma Valley. This style of tasting isn't cheap, but the wines here make the cost worth it for any serious sparkling-wine lover.

Schug Carneros Estate

You might recognize the labels at the **Schug Carneros Estate** (602 Bonneau Rd., Sonoma, 800/966-9365, www.schugwinery.com, 10am-5pm daily, $15). One of the Carneros region's elders, Walter Schug has made wine that has set the tone for California vintages for many years. The estate itself is worth a visit; the Tudor-esque barn sits on the valley floor in the middle of barns and fields of brilliant-yellow flowering mustard, with views of the surrounding mountains all around. Schug's hallmarks are chardonnays and pinot noirs, grapes that grow well in this cooler region, so try the latest releases of both.

They also have a **tasting room** (452 1st St. East, Suite E, 11am-6pm Thurs.-Mon., $15) on Sonoma Plaza.

Sights
★ Sonoma State Historic Park

Sonoma is the site of the short-lived California Republic and the northernmost California mission. To dive into Sonoma's history, spend some time exploring **Sonoma State Historic Park** (707/938-9560, www.parks.ca.gov, 10am-5pm daily, adults $3, children 6-17 $2), a collection of six historic attractions situated around Sonoma Plaza.

The Sonoma Barracks (98 E. Spain St.) were built in 1836 by General Vallejo when California was under Mexican rule. Inside are museum exhibits, a short film that details Sonoma's history, and a replica of a Mexican soldier's room.

The **Mission San Francisco Solano de Sonoma** (114 E. Spain St.) is a low and unpretentious block of buildings without much in the way of decoration or crowds. Established in 1823, this was the last mission in California and the only mission founded by Mexico. Museum-style exhibits depict the life of the missionaries and Native Americans who lived here. Rest on benches by the fountain, observe a moment of silence at the Native American mortuary monument, or check out the cactus "wall" that has been growing here since the mission era. Guided tours are offered Friday through Sunday (11am-3pm).

Located near Sonoma Plaza is **General Vallejo's Home** (3rd St. and W. Spain St.). General Vallejo lived in the state when it was under Spanish, Mexican, and early American rule. Known as Lachryma Montis, the Gothic-style house was the residence of one of early California's most important figures.

Cornerstone Gardens

Take a break from all the history of Sonoma's main attractions with a walk in the **Cornerstone Gardens** (23570 Arnold Dr., 707/933-3010, www.cornerstonesonoma.com, garden 10am-4pm daily, restaurant/shops/tasting rooms 10am-5pm daily, free). This unique installation combines an art gallery with the work of the foremost landscape and garden designers in the world. Stroll the unusual gardens, which range

Bear Flag Revolt

Sonoma has the distinction of being the place where California became an independent republic for 25 days. In 1846, California was still under Mexican rule, though there was a growing concern that the expanding United States might make a play for the western territory. On June 14, 1846, a group of American frontiersmen, under the leadership of William Ide and Ezekiel Merritt, took control of the Mexican outpost of Sonoma, holding retired Mexican general Mariano Vallejo as their captive. They hoisted a flag, decorated with a crudely drawn bear and star, and declared California an independent republic.

The California Republic lasted all of three weeks. On July 7, 1846, Commodore John Sloat of the U.S. Navy raised the American flag in Monterey and claimed all of California as part of the United States. While the rebellion was short lived, the Bear Flag inspired the design of California's state flag with a bear, a star, and the words "California Republic."

the Bear Flag Revolt Monument

Nods to the Bear Flag Revolt still exist in Sonoma. Located on the northeast side of **Sonoma Plaza** is a bronze sculpture installed by the Native Sons of the Golden West to commemorate the rebellion. Mere feet away, in the Sonoma Barracks, is a replica of the original Bear Flag that dates to 1896.

from traditional plantings to postmodern multimedia installations, Finish your excursion with a walk through the surrounding shops and wine-tasting rooms, plus a small-batch distillery and a café.

Depot Park Museum

For more Sonoma history, make a stop at the **Depot Park Museum** (270 1st St. W., 707/938-1762, http://depotparkmuseum. org, 1pm-4pm Sat.-Sun., free) right down the street from the plaza and around the corner from the mission. The museum hosts a small set of exhibits inside a reproduction of the historic Northwestern Pacific Railroad depot—hence the name. Inside are reconstructions of the active depot in the Rand Room, a showcase of the Bear Flag Rebellion, and exhibits on the life of the indigenous Miwok people.

Train Town

Got a train enthusiast in the family? Take them to Sonoma's **Train Town** (20264 Broadway/Hwy. 12, 707/938-3912, www. traintown.com, 10am-5pm daily June-mid-Aug., 10am-5pm Fri.-Sun. Sept.-May, train rides $7.50). Ride the 15-inch scale train through tunnels, over bridges, and into a miniature town complete with a petting zoo. Or opt for a spin on the roller coaster or the Ferris wheel, or a climb up the clock tower for a magnificent view of the park and beyond.

Spas

The most famous spa in the area is the **Willow Stream Spa** (100 Boyes Blvd., 877/289-7354, www.fairmont.com/ sonoma, 8am-6pm Sun.-Thurs., 8am-7pm Fri.-Sat., massages $179-259). A natural mineral hot spring beneath the Sonoma Mission Inn provides warm water for the indoor and outdoor pools and whirlpools. Whether you choose a relaxing massage or a challenging yoga class, arrive at least an hour early to allow time for each step of the ritual. The spa offers an almost bewildering variety of massages, scrubs, wraps, facials, and even more rarified treatments designed to pamper even the most discerning spagoer. The facilities are surrounded by the inn and a gourmet restaurant, both of which draw visitors from around the world.

At the **Garden Spa at MacArthur Place** (29 E. MacArthur St., 707/933-3193, www.macarthurplace.com/spa.php, 9am-8pm daily, massages $135-255), you won't just take in the serene beauty of the inn's lush garden; you will be healed, rejuvenated, and beautified. All of the spa's signature treatments are made from the flowers, herbs, and fruit found in the garden, distilled into such luscious effusions as pomegranate body polish, golden passionflower body wrap, peppermint foot soak, and the red-wine grapeseed bath. The spa also offers a mud-bath soak, a number of different massages, and facial and waxing treatments. Book treatments at least two weeks in advance, as space in this fragrant spa fills up fast.

Entertainment and Events
Live Music
Some of the best concerts happen at **Gundlach Bundschu Winery** (2000 Denmark St., Sonoma, 707/938-5277, www.gunbun.com), a family-owned winery that hosts performances in an outdoor amphitheater and an old redwood barn. Gundlach Bundschu has brought acts like Spiritualized, Angel Olsen, and Parquet Courts to Sonoma. Their annual **Huichica Music Festival** (https://huichica. com, June) pairs great music with wine and food.

Shopping
There's no more pleasant place to stroll, window shop, or browse for an extravagant trinket than in Sonoma. Around its leafy square are famous structures and state parks, little cafés and eateries, and yes, shops. Lots and lots of shops. Many are on the four main streets bordering the square, but most you will have to hunt for in the nooks and crannies inside the remodeled historic buildings and tiny retail alleyways on each block.

Despite the name, **Large Leather** (481 1st St. W., 707/938-1042, www.largeleather.com, 11am-6pm Mon. and Wed.-Thurs., 10am-6pm Fri.-Sun.) is a pint-size store filled with purses, backpacks, belts, wallets, and bracelets. Anything made out of leather can be found here. All items are handcrafted and designed by owners Paul Terwilliger and Jessica Zoutendijk.

A different kind of cooking store, **Bram** (493 1st St. W., 707/678-7411, www.bramcookware.com, 11am-5pm Sun.-Fri., 10am-6pm Sat.) is devoted entirely to clay-pot cooking. Dark shelves are stocked with a beautiful selection of deep skillets, stew pots, rondeaux, open casseroles, tagines, rectangular bakers, brams, and roasters. Shoppers will be astounded by the range and diversity of the clay pots available. If you are at a loss for how to use such a beautiful pot, stacks of cookbooks fill the other side of the shop. The extremely knowledgeable staff are eager to share their experiences and preferences.

For handcrafted artistry with a bit more polish, stroll down to **Sonoma Silver Company** (491 1st St. W., 707/933-0999, www.sonomasilver.com, 11am-6pm daily), a slender shop awash in silver rings, pendants, bracelets, and earrings. Multiple local jewelers sell and showcase their work here, but many of the shiny trinkets are made in-house by the company's resident jeweler of 20 years.

See other local artwork at the **Fairmont Gallery** (447 1st St. W., 707/996-2667, www.fairmontgallery.com, noon-5pm Thurs.-Sun.). Mostly concentrating in oil paintings and other classic brush-on-canvas fine art, the intimate space, set up in an old A-frame house, is a pleasant reprieve from other bustling shops.

Food
Café
If you just need a cup of coffee and maybe a quick pastry, stop in at the **Barking Dog Coffee Roasters** (18133 Sonoma Hwy., 707/939-1905, www.barkingdogcoffee. com, 6:30am-5pm daily). Barking Dog is where locals go to get their morning mochas. Sip a latte or indulge in a scoop of Caffe Classico gelato or a smoothie, take a seat on a comfy old couch, and maybe even enjoy some live music.

California Cuisine
Hot spot **Harvest Moon Café** (487 1st St. W., 707/933-8160, http:// harvestmooncafesonoma.com, 5:30pm-9pm Sun. Mon. and Wed.-Thurs., 5:30pm-9:30pm Fri.-Sat., $24-35) has a beautiful outdoor patio and a seasonal, locally focused menu. The menu of this charmingly casual restaurant changes daily to take advantage of the best ingredients available. The owners previously worked at the Bay Area dining institutions Chez Panisse and BayWolf.

French
A favorite with the local-sustainable-organic food crowd, ★ **the girl & the fig** (110 W. Spain St., 707/938-3634, www. thegirlandthefig.com, 11:30am-10pm Mon.-Thurs., 11am-10pm Fri.-Sat., 10am-10pm Sun., $23-34) is right on Sonoma Plaza. The menu changes often to take advantage of the best local seasonal ingredient—though the delicious fig and arugula salad is always available. For a special treat, order one of the amazing cheese plates or the three-course Bistro Plat du Jour ($42). If you love the sauces and jams, look for the products on-site, at wineries, and at high-end food shops throughout Wine Country.

Portuguese
Locals and travelers agree that traditional Portuguese eatery ★ **LaSalette** (452 1st St. E., 707/938-1927, www. lasaletterestaurant.com, 11:30am-2:30pm and 5pm-9pm daily, $24-36) is the town favorite. It has a simple and charming atmosphere, with a wood-fired oven facing a curving bar. A large outdoor patio is the most popular seating area in summer, although the meandering tile-floored dining room offers plenty of appeal plus a bonus view of the open kitchen. The undisputed star of LaSalette is the food. The Portuguese menu features fresh fish and hearty meat dishes plus good meatless options. Simple yet delectable preparations let the principal ingredients shine. They're happy to accommodate special requests.

Dessert
Need a pick-me-up while strolling around the plaza? **Sweet Scoops Homemade Ice Cream** (408 1st St. E., 707/721-1187, www.sweetscoopsicecream.com, noon-9pm Sun.-Thurs., noon-10pm Fri.-Sat., $3-7) serves delicious flavors like butter brickle, dulce de leche, speckled olive oil, and Chex Mix-a-Lot.

Accommodations
$150-250
For a charming guest room at reasonable rates within the Sonoma town limits, stay at **Sonoma Creek Inn** (239 Boyes Blvd., 888/712-1289, www.sonomacreekinn. com, $159-259). The whimsical, colorful decor and unique art pieces brighten each guest room and each guest's stay. Amenities include cable TV, free wireless Internet access, and a fridge. Some rooms also have private garden patios. A few minutes from downtown Sonoma and convenient to the Carneros wineries, the inn is perfect for travelers who want to spend on wine and dining rather than a motel room.

Right on Sonoma Plaza in the heart of Sonoma, **Sonoma's Best Guest Cottages**

(1190 E. Napa St., 707/933-0340, http://sonomasbestcottages.com, $199-399) offers four cute cottages for a homey stay in the Wine Country. Each cottage has its own style, but all have warm colors and comfy furniture to evoke the relaxation needed for a perfect vacation. All the cottages have fully equipped kitchens that allow you to cook your own fresh food after a visit to the fabulous Sonoma farmers markets. A private patio holds an outdoor fireplace and grill for spending some time outside.

In 1850 one of the first Spanish settlers in the Sonoma area built a home for his family on the town square, and for most of the last century, the **Swiss Hotel** (18 W. Spain St., 707/938-2884, www.swisshotelsonoma.com, $160-280) in the structure has offered beds and meals to travelers. The five rooms are light, bright, and airy, with fresh paint and pretty floral comforters. Downstairs, enjoy a meal at the restaurant or have a drink at the historic bar, and then step outside to take a walk around the historic plaza.

For the price and the character, the **Sonoma Hotel** (110 W. Spain St., 800/468-6016, www.sonomahotel.com, $130-308) can't be beat. Built in 1880, the hotel is one of Sonoma's landmark buildings. The interior is decorated in the fashion of the era, with high wood wainscoting, cream-colored walls, polished antiques, and elegant light fixtures. The rooms, all with private baths except one (a rarity in historic digs), are similarly outfitted in trim Victorian fixtures, and many have sloped ceilings, creating a cozy and intimate atmosphere.

Not nearly as historic but conveniently located just a few blocks from the square is **El Pueblo Inn** (896 W. Napa St., 707/996-3651, www.elpuebloinn.com, $199-379). In true Spanish style, some rooms face a lush central courtyard. The grounds also have a pool and a hot tub that are open 24 hours. Some rooms boast walls of adobe bricks or lounge areas with fireplaces, but many are standard hotel accommodations—clean and modestly decorated. For the price and location, not to mention views of the garden, it's a good deal. The inn also offers a fitness room, complimentary breakfast, and an in-room safe. Another standout is the down comforters.

Over $250

Neither historic nor centrally located, the **Fairmont Sonoma Mission Inn & Spa** (100 Boyes Blvd., 707/938-9000, www.fairmont.com/sonoma, $329-640) has another appeal: luxury. Of course, there is the spa, an 18-hole golf course, and the Michelin-starred restaurant, but the rooms themselves are enough. Your guest room is the kind of place you'll want to return to after a long day of sipping wine or soaking in a mud bath, decorated in smooth Provençal yellows with the occasional brown or red thrown in and featuring four-poster beds with deep mattresses covered in down comforters. Some rooms have fireplaces, while others feature marble bathtubs; many overlook gardens.

Information and Services

Before you begin your Sonoma and Carneros wine-tasting adventure, stop in at the 1st Street **Sonoma Valley Visitors Center** (453 1st St. E., 866/996-1090, www.sonomavalley.com, 9am-5pm Mon.-Sat., 10am-5pm Sun.) or the Arnold Drive location (23570 Arnold Dr., 866/996-1090, 10am-4pm daily). Ask the volunteers for advice on which wineries to visit, and pick up some complimentary tasting passes.

The **Sonoma Valley Hospital** (347 Andrieux St., 707/935-5000, www.svh.com) has a full-service emergency room.

Getting Around

For your public transit needs, use the buses run by **Sonoma County Transit** (SCT, 707/576-7433, 800/345-7433, www.sctransit.com, $1.50-4.80). Several routes serve the Sonoma Valley daily. Use SCT to get from Sonoma Valley to Santa

Raceway Traffic

Think you can safely ignore Sonoma Raceway's schedule because you don't give a darn about auto or bike racing? Not if you're wise in the ways of event traffic. The turn-off to **Sonoma Raceway** lies roughly at the intersection of CA-37 and CA-121. These charming and scenic two-lane roads are great for motoring and sightseeing—unless, of course, you're stuck in bumper-to-bumper race traffic. The absolute worst time to try to drive either of these roads (particularly CA-37 out of Sonoma) is when a major race event has finished. The wretched traffic jams, which truly are more stop than go, can last for hours as people try to exit the racetrack into the unprotected intersection. In the summer, the sweltering heat causes both engines and tempers to overheat, to no good end.

So what can you do?

♦ Check the race schedule (www.racesonoma.com), and avoid the roads in question for at least four hours after the scheduled or estimated end of a big race.

♦ Plot another route to your next destination, or stick around in Sonoma until well after the traffic is likely to have unsnarled. (Give it about six hours post-race.)

♦ Escape via CA-12 east to Napa or west to Santa Rosa. From Santa Rosa, catch US-101 south to Marin or San Francisco or north toward the Russian River. If heading to Napa, pick up CA-37 off of US-101 and then follow it south to I-80. I-80 will take you either south to the East Bay or east into Sacramento and beyond.

Rosa, Guerneville, and other parts of the Russian River Valley as well.

Visitors can take a vineyard tour with **Sonoma Segway** (524 Broadway, 707/938-2080, www.sonomasegway.com, tours $129), which offers a 4.5-hour Segway tour that includes a visit to a local winery, a stop at a local food-based business, and a visit to historic Sonoma. The tour starts with a lesson on the Segway, and when you finish you'll get a complimentary bottle of wine if you're of age. If you'd prefer to explore the Sonoma streets and paths on your own, rent a Segway—rentals are available from two hours and up.

Glen Ellen and Kenwood

North of the town of Sonoma, the valley becomes more and more rural. The next hamlet on CA-12 is Glen Ellen (population 784), which is surrounded by a couple of regional parks and Jack London State Historic Park, named for one of the town's famous residents. The other big name associated with Glen Ellen is Hunter S. Thompson, who lived there for half a year in 1964. Check out Thompson's article on Glen Ellen titled "Nights at the Rustic" if you want an entertaining read on why the writer was sued by a Glen Ellen bar.

Downtown Glen Ellen has a gourmet market, multiple restaurants, a fine French bakery, a popular saloon, and dozens of wineries nearby.

Five miles (8 km) north on CA-12 is the unincorporated community of Kenwood (population 1,028), which is surrounded by wineries and is near Sugarloaf Ridge State Park. The Kenwood area was greatly affected by the 2017 wildfires that swept through the area.

Getting There

Glen Ellen is just off CA-12, about 7 miles (11.5 km) north of Sonoma. Arnold Drive is the main street through town, and it runs all the way south to Sonoma. To reach Glen Ellen from Santa Rosa, take

CA-12 east through Kenwood for 16 miles (26 km).

It is also possible to jump over to Glen Ellen from CA-29 in Oakville. In Oakville, turn west onto Oakville Grade. After 3.2 miles (5.2 km), Oakville Grade becomes Dry Creek Road; the name changes again to Trinity Road in 2.8 miles (4.5 km). Keep to the right onto Trinity Road, and in 3 miles (4.8 km) you'll reach Sonoma Highway (CA-12), where you turn left toward Glen Ellen.

Wineries
Mayo Family Winery
Breaking from the chardonnay-cab-merlot juggernaut of Sonoma, the **Mayo Family Winery** (13101 Arnold Dr., at Hwy. 12, 707/938-9401, www.mayofamilywinery.com, 10:30am-6:30pm daily, tastings $10-15) produces an array of interesting Italian-style varietals. Here you might taste smoky rich Carignane or barbera, enjoy a fruity white viognier, or savor the chianti-based sangiovese. Mayo Family boasts a big presence in the region, with an on-site tasting room and, up north in Kenwood, the prized reserve tasting room (9200 Sonoma Hwy., Kenwood, 10:30am-6:30pm daily, reservations recommended, $50). At the reserve tasting room, your experience includes seven pours of Mayo's best wines, each paired with a small bite of gourmet California cuisine created by chefs on-site.

Valley of the Moon Winery
History mixes with the highest wine-making technology California has to offer at **Valley of the Moon Winery** (777 Madrone Rd., 707/939-4500, www.valleyofthemoonwinery.com, 10am-5pm daily, $20-30). Since the Civil War era, this Sonoma institution has passed through many hands and produced hundreds of wines. The circa-1860s stone

From top to bottom: Jack London State Historic Park; Kenwood's Café Citti; the Glen Ellen Star

buildings house late-model stainless-steel fermentation tanks as well as classic oak barrels. In the tasting room is a small list of boutique wines, from an unusual sangiovese rosé to a classic California cabernet. Valley of the Moon takes pride in its awards, and you'll find that almost every wine you taste has its own list of medals. Check the website for a list of upcoming wine events that show off this great Sonoma landmark at its best.

★ Jack London State Historic Park

Literary travelers come to Sonoma not just for the fine food and abundant wine but for the chance to visit **Jack London State Historic Park** (2400 London Ranch Rd., 707/938-5216, www.jacklondonpark.com, 9am-5pm daily, $10). Famed author Jack London did in fact live and write at this spot in rural Sonoma County at the beginning of the 20th century. He even brought sustainable farming techniques to the land that are now more commonplace throughout Sonoma County and beyond.

There are a handful of worthwhile sites to explore the life of this literary legend. The pretty stone **House of Happy Walls** (10am-5pm daily) holds a small museum. **London's Cottage** (10am-4:30pm daily) is a modest, wooden structure where the author slept and wrote 1,000 words a day.

An easy 1.2-mile (1.9-km) round-trip hike leads from the House of Happy Walls to the **Jack London Grave Site** and the **Wolf House ruins.** These eerie stone ruins are all that remain of London's dream home, which burned down in 1913 one month before London and his wife were to move in. The massive residence was planned as a four-story structure with 26 rooms and nine fireplaces. All that is left are rock fireplaces and moss-covered walls.

The **Ancient Redwood Trail** (3.4 mi/5.5 km round-trip, 3 hours, moderate) starts from London Lake and travels to a first-growth redwood estimated to be 2,000 years old. For a real climb, the **Park Summit Trail** (8 mi/13 km round-trip, 5 hours, strenuous) reaches a vista point with views of Sonoma and Bennett Valleys.

Docents offer tours of the park, which include talks on London's life and history. Check the website for current tours and times.

Entertainment and Events

Jack London State Historic Park brings Big Apple actors to Sonoma every summer for **Broadway Under the Stars** (2400 London Ranch Rd., 707/938-5216, https://transcendencetheatre.org/broadway-under-the-stars), for Broadway-inspired concerts in the stone ruins of an old winery.

The **Jack London Saloon** (13740 Arnold Dr., Glen Ellen, 707/938-8510, www.jacklondonlodge.com, 11:30am-midnight Sun.-Thurs., 11:30am-2am Fri.-Sat.) serves as tiny Glen Ellen's gathering place. The historic building was built in 1905 and housed a grocery store before becoming a saloon in the 1970s. Comedy legends John Belushi, Robin Williams, and The Smothers Brothers spent time here drinking and talking. Today the bar is decorated with posters related to the writer Jack London. Order food at the bar or head out back to the large creekside patio.

Recreation

Mossy waterfalls, hillside grasslands bordered by oaks, exposed rock outcroppings, and even Sonoma Creek's headwaters can be found at **Sugarloaf Ridge State Park** (2605 Adobe Canyon Rd., 707/833-5712, www.sugarloafpark.org, 6am-8pm daily, adults $8, seniors $7), just outside Kenwood. Despite its beauty, Sugarloaf is rarely visited, so if you're seeking solitude in nature, this may be your place. There are plenty of trails to suit your mood and hiking ability; meander down **Creekside Nature Trail** (1 mi/1.6 km, 30 minutes, easy) or take **Canyon Trail** (1.6 mi/2.6 km, 1 hour, easy) to the waterfall, which descends 25 feet through mossy boulders beneath a canopy of redwoods. More athletic hikers can take **Vista Trail Loop** (4.1 mi/6.6 km, 2-3 hours, moderate-difficult) to the Indian Rock outcropping, which has a lovely view of the canyon below. To hike this trail, take Stern Trail to Bald Mountain Trail and turn right. Eventually, take another right on Vista Trail and cross the mountain, taking another right on Grey Pine Trail. Turn right again on Meadow Trail to return to the parking lot.

The crown jewel of the park, however, is Bald Mountain. Although only 2,729 feet (832 m) high, the mountain sports views of nearly all of Wine Country as well as the Golden Gate and Sierra Nevada on clear days. The hike to the summit is not that challenging: **Bald Mountain Loop** (6.6 mi/10.6 km, 5 hours, moderate-difficult) begins at Stern Trail, and eventually you take a right turn onto Bald Mountain Trail and follow it to the top. To descend, turn right on Grey Pine Trail, and then make another right onto Meadow Trail.

While the lower part of the park has a lush, heavy canopy, the upper trails are quite exposed and can get hot in the summer and early fall. Bring sunscreen, a hat, plenty of water, and a map, as the trails can be confusing.

Sugarloaf is also home to the **Robert Ferguson Observatory** (www.rfo.org), which has three telescopes to take in the night skies. From January to November, the observatory hosts monthly star parties. Check the website for upcoming star parties and night-sky classes.

Food

From an unannounced performance by Jim Belushi to a Michelin guide rating, **Glen Ellen Star** (13648 Arnold Dr., Glen Ellen, 707/343-1384, https://glenellenstar.com, 5:30pm-9:30pm Fri.-Sat., 5:30pm-9pm Sun.-Thurs., $23-35)

rides a significant wave of hype. The restaurant's secret weapon—besides *Food & Wine Magazine* favorite chef Ari Weiswasser—is the wood-roast oven. The menu changes frequently but is known for roasted vegetables, tomato cream pie pizza, and the whole fish of the day.

★ **The Fig Café** (13690 Arnold Dr., 707/938-2130, www.thegirlandthefig. com, 5pm-9:30pm Fri.-Sat., 5pm-9pm Sun.-Thurs., $12-24) is the Glen Ellen outpost of Sonoma's the girl & the fig. This cozy, whimsically decorated café serves some of the same menu items as the flagship restaurant—including the outstanding fig and arugula salad with salty prosciutto nuggets and deeply rich and flavorful grilled figs. Comfort food items and three-course dinners ($29) round out the menu. The wine list includes local and European wines made specially for the girl & the fig restaurants. The quality is high, which makes the prices seem fair.

Café Citti (9049 Sonoma Hwy., Kenwood, 707/833-2690, www.cafecitti. com, 11am-3:30pm and 5pm-8:30pm Sun.-Thurs., 11am-3:30pm and 5pm-9pm Fri.-Sat., $8-17) will fill you up with home-style Italian fare before or after wine-tasting. This casual eatery's menu is sprawled over several dry erase boards and includes whole roasted chickens, deli salads, sandwiches, pastas, and pizzas, though the garlicky Caesar salad is one of the standouts. Order at the counter and then sit down for service.

Accommodations

For a bit of Asian-infused relaxation, stay at one of the best-reviewed inns in Wine Country. The ★ **Gaige House & Ryokan** (13540 Arnold Dr., Glen Ellen, 800/234-1425, www.foursisters.com, $279-699) offers comfort and luxury in the rooms and common spaces. Special attention is paid to every detail: Each of the 23 rooms and suites resembles a spread in an interior-design magazine; suites have baths the size of bedrooms and their own tiny garden spaces. Outdoor amenities include a pool and hot tub, while a breakfast buffet is laid out every morning.

Attached to the redbrick Jack London Saloon and the Umbria Glen Ellen Restaurant, the **Jack London Lodge** (13740 Arnold Dr., 707/938-8510, www.jacklondonlodge.com, $135-284) anchors this part of downtown Glen Ellen. The superb location is within walking distance of all Glen Ellen's restaurants. The modern, 22-room lodge has a broad patio, a kidney-shaped pool, and groomed lawns. The rooms are clean and elegant with dark-wood furniture. Vines draping the balcony are a nice touch, as is the hot tub and a creek that runs through the back of the property.

Information and Services
The small town of Glen Ellen does not have a visitors center, so stock up on maps and tips before you leave Sonoma. Some of the local inns and hotels can also provide some information.

Don't expect to find much in the way of wireless Internet access or reliable cell-phone reception.

Santa Rosa

Santa Rosa is the gateway to the Russian River area and the town of Guerneville. Santa Rosa is the biggest city in Wine Country and the largest in the North Bay. Developed at the turn of the 20th century, the older neighborhoods are filled with charming Craftsman-style bungalows, and the downtown area boasts some historical buildings.

Getting There
From US-101, take exit 489 toward downtown Santa Rosa to reach the historical district; downtown is east of the freeway. Wineries are on the west side of town and can be accessed by taking CA-12 west, and also by the US-101 exits for River Road and Guerneville.

Be aware that traffic on this major corridor can get congested, particularly during the morning commute and 3pm-7pm Monday-Friday. It also slows on sunny summer afternoons when people go to cool themselves along the Russian River.

Sights
Charles M. Schulz Museum
Schulz drew the world-famous *Peanuts* comic strip for almost 50 years, and from 1958 until his death in 2000 he lived in Sonoma County. The **Charles M. Schulz Museum** (2301 Hardies Lane, 707/579-4452, www.schulzmuseum.org, 11am-5pm Mon.-Fri., 10am-5pm Sat.-Sun. Memorial Day-Labor Day; 11am-5pm Mon. and Wed.-Fri., 10am-5pm Sat.-Sun. Labor Day-Memorial Day; adults $12, seniors $8, children 4-18 $5, under age 3 free) honors Schulz and the *Peanuts* gang. Inside the 27,000-square-foot building, which looks like it comes from a 4-inch comic strip, is an incredible wealth of multimedia art, original drawings, and changing exhibitions based on Schulz's work. The museum owns most of the original *Peanuts* strips, a large collection of Schulz's personal possessions, and an astonishing array of tribute artwork from other comic-strip artists. The grounds include attractive gardens, the Snoopy Labyrinth, and even the infamous Kite-eating Tree.

Schulz's influence is felt outside the museum property as well. Across the street, visitors can skate at **Snoopy's Home Ice**—Schulz was an avid hockey player. Throughout downtown Santa Rosa, especially in Historic Railroad Square, colorful sculptures depict members of the *Peanuts* gang.

Luther Burbank Home and Gardens
If you love plants and gardening, don't miss the **Luther Burbank Home and Gardens** (204 Santa Rosa Ave., 707/524-5445, www.lutherburbank.org, gardens 8am-dusk daily year-round, free; tours/

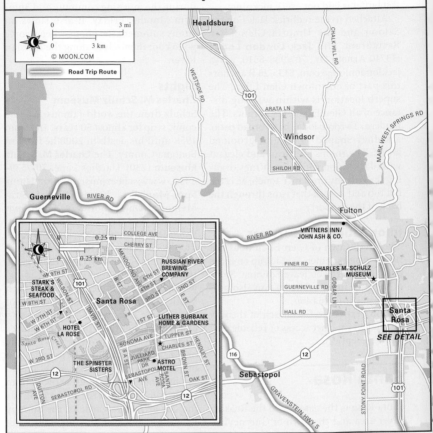

Russian River Valley

museum/gift shop 10am-4pm Tues.-Sat., 11am-3pm Sun. Apr.-Oct., adults $10, seniors and children 12-18 $8.50, children under 12 free). Using hybridization techniques, Luther Burbank created some of the most popular plants grown in California gardens and landscapes today. In the garden's more than one acre of horticulture, which also includes medicinal herbs and showy roses, glimpse the famous Shasta daisy, a hardy pure-white daisy hybrid that now blankets vast areas throughout the state. Check the website for a list of what's in bloom; something is

sure to be showing its finest flowers every month of the year.

Sports and Recreation

Just as in Napa, one of the popular ways to get a great view of the Russian River Valley is from the basket of a hot-air balloon. Granted, you and your hangover must fall out of bed before dawn for this particular treat—so you might want to make this a first-day adventure before you start wine-tasting. **Wine Country Balloons** (meeting site: Kal's Kaffe Mocha, 397 Aviation Blvd., 707/538-7359 or 800/759-5638, www.balloontours.com, adults $235, seniors and children $215) can get you up in the air to start the day high above Wine Country. This big company maintains a whole fleet of balloons that can carry 2-16 passengers. Expect the total time to be 3-4 hours, with 1-1.5 hours in the air.

Food

John Ash & Co. (4350 Barnes Rd., 707/527-7687, www.vintnersinn.com, 5pm-9pm Fri.-Sat., 5pm-8:30pm Sun.-Thurs., $19-48) stands out as one of the best high-end California cuisine restaurants in the region. The large, elegant dining room, done up in Mediterranean style, is part of the Vintners Inn. The food, made with local and sustainable produce, shows off its natural flavors. One way to experience John Ash & Co. is to order the four-course tasting menu ($68). The wine list is something special, with some amazing local vintages that are tough to find outside the Russian River Valley.

Located in a building that dates to 1934, **Stark's Steak & Seafood** (Railroad Square, 521 Adams St., 707/546-5100, www.starkrestaurants.com, 11:30am-9pm Mon.-Thurs., 11:30am-10pm Fri., 3pm-10pm Sat., 5pm-10pm Sun., $11-51) is a classic steak house serving house dry-aged beef and hickory-smoked prime rib. For those on a budget, Stark's fantastic happy hour (3pm-6pm Mon.-Sat.) offers a $3.50 martini with a $6 prime rib sandwich.

Beer connoisseurs from all over come to visit ★ **Russian River Brewing Company** (725 4th St., 707/545-2337, https://russianriverbrewing.com, 11am-midnight daily, $9-28) to taste its highly coveted beers at their source. Russian River's brews have limited distribution, especially outside of the Bay Area, which means it's worth the effort to visit this unassuming brewpub for well-balanced Pliny the Elder, a very drinkable double IPA. (The even more rare Pliny the Younger, a triple IPA, is released on-site

the first Friday of February and is only available for two weeks.) The brewpub serves pub grub including pizzas and wings, but it is the beer that brings people here.

Get a feel for Santa Rosa's creativity at ★ **The Spinster Sisters** (401 South A St., 707/528-7100, http://thespinstersisters.com, 8am-2:30pm Mon., 8am-2:30pm and 4pm-9pm Tues.-Fri., 9am-2:30pm and 5pm-9pm Sat., 9am-2:30pm Sun., $11-31). Located in Santa Rosa's Arts District, this hip eatery showcases the imagination of chef Liza Hinman, who utilizes Sonoma's fresh produce in dishes from scrambles to salads to locally caught seafood. The interior features a large red-wood dining counter and the works of local artists on the walls.

Accommodations

You'll find all the familiar chain motels in Santa Rosa. You'll also see a few charming inns and upper-tier hotels that show off the unique aspects of the city that serves as the transition from the Bay Area to true Northern California.

★ **The Astro** (323 Santa Rosa Ave., 707/200-4655, https://theastro.com, $178-300) brings the classic motor lodge into the new millennium. Midcentury modern pieces offer a nod to the motel's 1963 incarnation, but this artistic motel is no cookie-cutter accommodation. Each room is uniquely decorated with hand-picked art and furniture. The courtyard resembles a small sculpture garden with a giant hunk of redwood from the Russian River a centerpiece. Perks include an enthusiastic staff, local goodies in each room, and morning coffee with pastries in the common room. If you love the decor, you can take it home with you—all of the items in each room are for sale.

At the corner of Historic Railroad Square, **Hotel la Rose** (308 Wilson St., 800/527-6738, www.hotellarose.com, $179-249) exemplifies the luxury-hotel concept as it has evolved over the last century. The stone-clad main building rises high over Railroad Square, with more rooms available in the more modern carriage house just across the street. The hotel, with only 48 rooms, gives an attention to detail and a level of service that are missing in larger motels and hotels. The carriage house offers modern decor and amenities, and each large room and suite feels light and bright. The main building possesses an older style of elegance, with antique furniture and floral wallpaper.

At the north end of Santa Rosa, convenient to the major Russian River wine roads, is the upscale **Vintners Inn** (4350 Barnes Rd., 800/421-2584, http://vintnersinn.com, $295-1,335). The low, attractive red-tile-roof buildings of the inn and the fabulous **John Ash & Co.** restaurant are adjacent to a large stretch of vineyard. Every guest room has a king bed, fluffy down bedding, and a patio or balcony overlooking a cute garden-like courtyard. Many rooms boast fireplaces and spa tubs, and all feature luxurious appointments. Your stay includes access to the inn's outdoor whirlpool tub and the common den, which has a fireplace. The only downside to the Vintners Inn is its regrettable proximity to a local power station; just try to look in the other direction when admiring the view.

Information and Services

As a major city, Santa Rosa has plenty of medical services available. If you need help, try **Santa Rosa Memorial Hospital** (1165 Montgomery Ave., 707/525-5300, www.stjosephhealth.org), which has an emergency room.

Sebastopol and Graton

Low-key and a bit alternative, Sebastopol is undoubtedly the artistic heart of Sonoma County. The relatively modest digs, low cost of living, liberal politics, natural beauty, and small-town vibe have attracted artists that include heavyweights like Jerry

Garcia and Les Claypool of Primus as well as independent painters, sculptors, and ceramists. Downtown Sebastopol contains shops where local artists sell their works, along with bookstores, record stores, and the odd place selling tie-dyed T-shirts. The surrounding farmland was once devoted to orchards, particularly apples, but that has changed over the years; now grapes dominate the Gravensteins. Still, the few remaining orchards give fragrance and beauty to the already scenic country roads, especially during the spring bloom.

Getting There

Sebastopol is west of Santa Rosa, accessed by CA-116 and CA-12. The heart of downtown Sebastopol is at the intersection of Sebastopol Avenue (CA-12) and Main Street (CA-116). Note that Sebastopol Avenue becomes the Bodega Highway once it hits downtown Sebastopol and extends all the way to, you guessed it, Bodega Bay.

To reach Sebastopol from US-101, take either the exit for CA-12 West in Santa Rosa or the exit for CA-116 West at Cotati, 8 miles (13 km) south of Santa Rosa. CA-116 is the most direct route to continue to the Russian River from Sebastopol.

Wineries
Dutton Estate

A small winery along the comparatively undiscovered Gravenstein Highway, **Dutton Estate** (8757 Green Valley Rd., 707/829-9463, http://sebastopolvineyards. com, 10am-4:30pm daily, tasting $15-60) is in the middle of its own vineyards (don't pick the grapes). Tasters enjoy plenty of personal attention from pourers, along with a small list of white and rosé wines, moving into the red pinots and syrahs that do so well in this area. Dutton's syrahs stand out among the offerings, which can include a few extra pours for those who seem genuinely interested in the wines.

Merry Edwards Winery

Merry Edwards was the first woman to earn a degree in enology (winemaking) from the prestigious University of California, Davis, program in 1993. After working as a winemaker for numerous Sonoma vintners and developing her own pinot noir grape clone with the help of the facilities and staff at Davis, Merry finally opened her own winery. The **Merry Edwards Winery** (2959 Gravenstein Hwy., 707/823-7466 or 888/388-9050, www. merryedwards.com, 9:30am-4:30pm daily, free) offers tastings in its two glass-walled tasting rooms. Each member of the tasting staff works with one party of tasters at a time. You'll be led to a table with comfortable chairs set with four glasses ready for four different pinot noirs. There are four samples of the same varietal plus a bonus sauvignon blanc served at the end.

Food

A great break from the endless fancy food is to find a nice ethnic restaurant. In Sebastopol, one of the best is the **Himalayan Tandoori and Curry House** (969 Gravenstein Hwy. S., 707/824-1800, www.himalayan-food.com, 11am-2:30pm and 5pm-9pm Mon.-Sat., $12-19), which serves up Indian food in the Himalayan style. You'll find vegetable curries and meat tandoori, both properly spicy, as well as fresh naan, spicy rice pudding, and all sorts of treats. You'll even get a break from the endless river of wine, since there's plenty of beer on the drinks menu.

The **Underwood Bar and Bistro** (9113 Graton Rd., Graton, 707/823-7023, www. underwoodgraton.com, 11:30am-10pm Tues.-Sat., 5pm-10pm Sun., $16-39) serves upscale cuisine in the tiny town of Graton. Plush red velvet and dark wood tables grace the Underwood's dining room, which is recommended by many locals as the best spot in this wine region to sit down to a serious dinner. With a heavy seafood focus, including raw oysters on the half shell, and top-quality meats and produce, Underwood does in fact exemplify Wine Country cuisine. A whole section of the menu is devoted to cheese. The wine list leans heavily toward small local vintners; ask your server for recommendations. The bar stays open late (10pm-11pm) on Friday-Saturday nights, serving a pared-down but satisfying late-night menu.

Calling the **Willow Wood** (9020 Graton Rd., Graton, 707/823-0233, www. willowwoodgraton.com, 8am-9pm Mon.-Sat., 9am-3pm Sun., $10-25) a deli is somewhat misleading. Sure, they've got a counter, a take-out business, and well-trodden wooden floors. But really, Willow Wood is an upscale California-Italian restaurant for lunch, featuring souped-up versions of traditional deli sandwiches accompanied by pasta and pickled veggies. Diners sit on wooden benches to enjoy the large meals, which can also include giant salads and tureens of fresh soup. The open-faced egg salad hot sandwich with bacon and pesto is a favorite. Weeknight dinners include three-course meals.

Accommodations

In Sebastopol, the best place to stay is the expensive but lovely **Avalon Bed and Breakfast** (11910 Graton Rd., 707/824-0880, www.avalonluxuryinn.com, $239-355). With only three rooms, it offers the ultimate in private and romantic accommodations. All rooms have king beds, hot tubs or access to the garden hot tub, fireplaces, air-conditioning, and many luxurious amenities. Because Avalon was purpose-built as a bed-and-breakfast, each guest room is actually a suite with a private entrance, and there is plenty of space to spread out to enjoy a longer stay. Breakfast is a lovingly prepared organic feast with local produce.

Information and Services

For maps of the area, souvenirs, newspapers, and wine-tasting coupons, swing by the **Sebastopol Chamber of Commerce Visitors Center** (265 S. Main St., 707/823-3032, www.sebastopol.org, 10am-5pm Mon.-Thurs., 9am-5pm Fri., 10am-3pm Sat.).

The new **Sonoma West Medical Center** (501 Petaluma Ave., 707/823-8511, http://sonomawestmedicalcenter.com) has emergency medical care 24 hours a day.

Guerneville

There are only a few wineries in the Guerneville area, but that's OK—people come here to float, canoe, or kayak the gorgeous Russian River that winds through town from Forestville all the way through Monte Rio to the Pacific Ocean at Jenner. In addition to its busy summertime tourist trade, Guerneville is also a very popular gay and lesbian resort area. The rainbow flag flies proudly here, and the friendly community welcomes all.

Getting There

Guerneville is on CA-116, alternately named River Road. In downtown Guerneville, CA-116 is briefly called Main Street. The most direct access is via US-101 north of Santa Rosa; take the River Road/Guerneville exit and follow River Road west for 15 miles (24 km) to downtown Guerneville.

Alternatively, a more scenic and often less crowded route is to take US-101 to CA-116 near Cotati, south of Santa Rosa. Named the Gravenstein Highway for its route through the apple orchards of Sebastopol, CA-116 winds about 22 miles (35 km) through Sebastopol, Graton, and Forestville to emerge onto River Road in Guerneville.

Wineries
Russian River Vineyards
Ironically, **Russian River Vineyards** (5700 Gravenstein Hwy., Forestville, 707/887-3344, www.russianrivervineyards.com, noon-6pm Sun.-Thurs., noon-7pm Fri.-Sat., $20-105) really isn't on the Russian River; it is in the coastal hills of nearby Forestville, which nurture the Sonoma Coast American Viticultural Area vineyards and wineries. The property doesn't look like a typical high-end winery, and the aging wooden buildings seem almost to be falling apart. (Don't worry, the tasting room has recently been shored up.) Sadly, the funky old Victorian house behind the tasting room isn't open for tours—it's part of the private production facility.

Despite the ramshackle look, the friendly staff create a classy, small-winery tasting experience. Russian River Vineyards' small list of red wines features full-bodied, fruity pinot noirs and interesting varietals from the southern reaches of Europe. The charbono tastes especially good.

Korbel Cellars
Champagne grapes like cooler climates, so it makes sense that **Korbel Cellars**

(13250 River Rd., Guerneville, 707/824-7000, www.korbel.com, tasting room 9am-5pm daily Apr.-Oct., 10am-4.30pm daily Nov.-Mar.), the leading producer of California champagne-style sparkling wines, maintains a winery and tasting room on the Sonoma coast. The large, lush estate welcomes visitors with elaborate landscaping and attractive buildings, including a small area serving as a visitors center. **Tours** (11am-3:45pm daily Apr.-Oct., 11am-3pm daily Nov.-Mar.) are available. Sample a wide variety of high-end California champagnes, plus a few boutique still wines. The facility also has a full-service gourmet **deli** (9am-5pm daily Apr.-Oct., 9am-4:30pm daily Nov.-Mar.) and picnic area for tasters who want to stop for lunch. Korbel also sells (but does not sample) brandy on-site.

Recreation
★ The Russian River
Guerneville and its surrounding forest are the center for fun on the river. In summer the water is usually warm and dotted with folks swimming, canoeing, or simply floating tubes serenely downriver amid forested riverbanks and under blue skies.

Burke's Canoe Trips (8600 River Rd., Forestville, 707/887-1222, www.burkescanoetrips.com, Memorial Day-mid-Oct., $75) rents canoes and kayaks on the Russian River. The put-in is at Burke's beach in Forestville; paddlers then canoe downriver 10 miles (16 km) to Guerneville, where a courtesy shuttle picks them up. Burke's also offers overnight campsites for tents, trailers, and RVs.

On the north bank of the river, **Johnson's Beach & Resort** (16215 and 16217 1st St., 707/869-2022, www.Johnsonsbeach.com, daily mid-June-Aug., Sat.-Sun. only in Sept., canoe/kayak rental $50/day, inner tubes $10/day) rents canoes, kayaks, pedal boats, and inner tubes for floating the river. A safe, kid-friendly section of the riverbank

Guerneville's Johnson's Beach

is roped off for small children; parents and beachcombers can rent beach chairs and umbrellas for use on the small beach. The boathouse sells beer and snacks. It's just a couple of blocks from downtown Guerneville.

Navigate the waters of the Russian River with a guided kayaking trip from **Smart Tours** (707/228-5490, www.smart-sonomatours.com, adults $125, children under 15 $60). Tours run 3-4 hours and include lunch.

Armstrong Redwoods

An easy five-minute drive from Guerneville on one mostly straight road, **Armstrong Redwoods State Natural Reserve** (17000 Armstrong Woods Rd., Guerneville, 707/869-2015, www.parks.ca.gov, 8am-60 minutes after sunset daily, $8 per vehicle, $7 senior rate) often gets overlooked, which makes it a bit less crowded than some of the most popular North Coast and Sierra redwood forests. But you can still take a fabulous hike—either a short stroll in the shade of the trees or a multiple-day backcountry adventure. The easiest walk ever to a big tree is the 0.1-mile stagger from the visitors center to the tallest tree in the park, named the Parson Jones Tree. If you saunter another 0.5 mile, you'll reach the Colonel Armstrong Tree, which grows next to the Armstrong Pack Station—your first stop if you're doing heavy-duty hiking. From the Pack Station, another 0.25 mile of moderate hiking leads to the Icicle Tree.

Right next to Armstrong is the **Austin Creek State Recreation Area** (17000 Armstrong Woods Rd., Guerneville, 707/869-9177, www.parks.ca.gov, 8am-60 minutes after sunset daily, $8 per vehicle, $7 senior rate). It's rough going on 2.5 miles (4 km) of steep, narrow, treacherous dirt road to get to the main entrance and parking area; no vehicles over 20 feet long and no trailers of any kind are permitted. But once you're in, some great—and very difficult—hiking awaits you. The eponymous **Austin Creek Trail** (4.7 mi/7.6 km one-way, 3 hours, moderate) leads down from the sunbaked meadows into the cool forest fed by Austin Creek. To avoid monotony on this challenging route, create a loop by taking the turn onto **Gilliam Creek Trail** (4 mi/6.4 km one-way, 2.4 hours, moderate). This way you get to see another of the park's cute little creeks as you walk back to the starting point.

Entertainment and Events
Nightlife

Guerneville wouldn't be a proper gay resort town without at least a couple of good gay bars that create proper nightlife for visitors and locals alike. The most visible and funky-looking of these is the **Rainbow Cattle Company** (16220 Main St., Guerneville, 707/869-0206, www.queersteer.com, noon-2am daily). Mixing the vibes of a down-home country saloon with a happening San Francisco nightspot, the Rainbow has cold drinks and hot men with equal abandon. Think cocktails in Mason jars, wood paneling, and leather nights. This is just the kind of queer bar where you can bring your mom or your straight-but-not-narrow friends, and they'll have just as much fun as you will.

It may not look like much from the road, but the **Stumptown Brewery** (15045 River Rd., 707/869-0705, www.stumptown.com, 11am-midnight Sun.-Thurs., 11am-2am Fri.-Sat.) is the place to hang out on the river. This atypical dive bar holds a pool table, Naugahyde barstools, and a worn wooden bar crowded with locals. Out back are the second bar and an outdoor deck with scattered tables overlooking the river. The brewery makes only a few of the beers sold on tap, but they are all great (especially the Bush Wacker Wheat) and perfect to enjoy by the pitcher. Stumptown also serves a menu of burgers and grilled sandwiches. Opt for the outdoor deck with your pooch on sunny days.

From dancing and swimming to eating

and drinking, the **Rio Nido Roadhouse** (14540 Canyon 2 Rd., Rio Nido, 707/869-0821, www.rionidoroadhouse.com, 11am-10pm Mon.-Fri., 9am-11pm Sat.-Sun.) has you covered. They host live music and have a pool (11:30am-6pm Sun.-Fri., 11:30am-5:30pm Sat. Memorial Day weekend-Labor Day weekend, $8) for when the temperatures climb.

Festivals and Events
Held at Johnson's Beach in Guerneville, the **Russian River Jazz and Blues Festival** (www.russianriverfestivals.com, 707/869-1595, Sept., $55/day) is a two-day affair with jazz one day and blues the next. The main stage has some pretty big acts, including Buddy Guy, War, and Taj Mahal, but there is plenty of music to groove to throughout the festival grounds. In addition to live acts, food vendors showcase regional fare, local artists hawk their wares, and tents serve glass after glass of wine while sunburned devotees splash around in the river. Much more than just a music festival, this event is the last big bash of the summer season; it takes place at the end of September, just before the weather reliably turns cold. If you plan to stay both days, consider camping here. **Johnson's Beach** (707/869-2022) has designated campsites available on a first-come, first-served basis.

If you are in the area in mid-August, you may be able to get tickets for the Stumptown Brewery's annual **Russian River Beer Revival and BBQ Cook Off** (15045 River Rd., 707/869-0705, www.stumptown.com/revival, Sat. noon-6pm mid-Aug.). The event takes place along the river on a grassy field below the restaurant. Enjoy live music, beer tastings from 30 different breweries, and lots and lots of barbecue. Tickets generally go on sale in June and sell out quickly.

Food
Oprah Winfrey has long been a taste-maker, and the icon loves the taste of the biscuits at the **Big Bottom Market** (16228 Main St., 707/604-7295, www.bigbottommarket.com, 8am-5pm Wed.-Mon., $7-13). They do simple butter-and-jam biscuits along with smoked-salmon options. They also have salads and sandwiches, but Oprah recommends the biscuits.

A focal point of downtown Guerneville, **Main Street Station** (16280 Main St., 707/869-0501, www.mainststation.com, 4pm-midnight Mon.-Thurs., 11am-1am Fri.-Sun., $14-25) offers a big menu filled with homey, casual grub. The mainstay is handmade pizza. Grab a quick slice for lunch, or order a whole pie for dinner. In the evenings, locals and visitors order sandwiches and pizza, drink beer, and listen to live entertainment on the small stage. Live folk, jazz, blues, and even comedy happen every single night; this tiny venue gets crowded when a popular act comes to town. Consider making reservations in advance to ensure you'll get a seat.

Light, airy, and open, tiny ★ **Boon Eat + Drink** (16248 Main St., Guerneville, 707/869-0780, www.eatatboon.com, 11am-3pm and 5pm-9pm Sun.-Tues. and Thurs., 11am-3pm and 5pm-10pm Fri.-Sat., $12-24) lures diners to line up on the sidewalk in anticipation of local, organic, and sustainable cuisine served with simple elegance. Lunch usually consists of a simple menu of paninis, small plates, and the grass-fed Boon burger. For dinner, hearty main courses include a flatiron steak with truffle fries. You really can't go wrong here—unless you can't get in.

Accommodations
Because Guerneville is the major resort town for lovers of Russian River recreation, you'll find a few dozen bed-and-breakfasts and cabin resorts in town. Many of these spots are gay-friendly, some with clothing-optional hot tubs.

One of the most popular options for staying in the Russian River area is to rent a house. For recommended rentals, try **Russian River Vacation Homes**

(707/869-9030, 800/997-3317, www.riverhomes.com).

Under $150

The **Creekside Inn & Lodge** (16180 Neeley Rd., 800/776-6586, www.creeksideinn.com, $115-315) is right along the Russian River outside of downtown Guerneville. The river floods fairly regularly, hence the entire resort perches on stilts that provide pretty views as well as dry carpets. Cabins and cottages at the lodge run short on upscale amenities but long on woodsy kitsch. Every cabin has a full kitchen with a fridge, plenty of space, a comfortable bath, and some of the best complimentary coffee you'll ever get in a hotel room. Choose from economical studios, multiple-bedroom family units, and eco-cabins that are designed to have minimal impact on the local environment. The property is large and has a swimming pool, but it does not have good river frontage for swimmers. The owners can offer suggestions for local beaches and make appointments for wine-tasting at their favorite private local wineries.

$150-250

The ★ **Sonoma Orchid Inn** (12850 River Rd., Guerneville, 888/877-4466, www.sonomaorchidinn.com, $149-254) experience is made by its amazing owners. They've created beautiful rooms with elegant linens and furniture, plus just enough tchotchkes to keep things interesting. The best rooms have satellite TV with DVRs, DVD players, microwaves, and small fridges. On the economy end of the spectrum, the rooms are tiny but cute, with private baths and pretty decorations. The owners not only recommend restaurants and spas, they'll make reservations for you. They've got knowledge about the local wineries, hikes, river spots, and just about everything else in the region. Four of the nine rooms are pet-friendly for an added fee.

On the road to Armstrong Redwoods, **Boon Hotel + Spa** (14711 Armstrong Woods Rd., Guerneville, 707/869-2721, www.boonhotels.com, $195-315) is the antithesis of Guerneville's woodsy funkiness. In almost a rebuff to its environs, Boon Hotel + Spa is minimal in the extreme, with white walls devoid of artwork, square armless couches, and beds vast enough to get lost in the fair-trade organic cotton sheets. The slate, chrome, and white palette are offset by bright slashes of red and orange. Many of the 14 rooms have freestanding cast-iron fireplaces, private patios, and fridges. True to its name, amenities include a pool and hot tub (both saltwater, for a little twist) and plenty of facial and massage options to work out the kinks. In the morning, wake up to a continental breakfast with a pressed pot of locally roasted coffee; in the evening, chill out with a cocktail by the pool. There are also three glamping tents ($139) to lightly rough it.

Over $250

The **Farmhouse Inn & Spa** (7871 River Rd., Forestville, 707/887-3300, www.farmhouseinn.com, $545-1,500) is along River Road in the middle of prime wine-tasting country. The yellow-painted farmhouse is the inn's restaurant and contains the two rooms; most of the guest accommodations march up the gently sloped hillside in the form of a row of cottages. The cute little cabins have upscale decor, warm fireplaces, private baths, and precious little space. The most upscale rooms, with jetted tubs and private decks, are in a barn on the property. The pool area and restaurant aren't big either but make up what they lack in size with charm and an adorable outdoor fireplace area.

Getting Around

Sonoma County Transit (707/576-7433, 800/345-7433, http://sctransit.com, adults $3.05, students $2.70, seniors $1.50) runs a Russian River Express bus, route 20, from downtown Santa Rosa to Guerneville.

Side Trip: Healdsburg

The legendary director of iconic movies *Apocalypse Now* and *The Godfather* has his own winery. Sure, the **Francis Ford Coppola Winery** (300 Via Archimedes, Geyserville, 707/857-1400, www.franciscoppolawinery.com, 11am-6pm daily, $12-25) allows you to taste its chardonnays and syrahs, but it also allows film buffs to tour the **Movie Gallery,** which is full of film memorabilia including Coppola's Academy Awards and Don Corleone's desk from *The Godfather.*

Getting to Highway 1

From Guerneville, River Road winds 13 miles (21 km) west to the coast at Jenner, where it meets CA-1. Along the way, stop in the tiny towns of **Monte Rio** and **Duncans Mills,** a former lumber town home to a general store and a handful of shops.

Stopping in Monte Rio

Monte Rio's neon sign welcomes folks to this Russian River community located between Jenner and Guerneville. It's home to the fabled Bohemian Grove, a members-only campground that attracts some of the world's most powerful men each summer.

The biggest beach in the area is **Monte Rio Beach** (20488 Hwy. 116, Monte Rio, 707/865-2487, www.mrrpd.org/monteriobeach.html, daily Memorial Day weekend-Sept.), also known as Big Rocky Beach, where canoe and kayak rentals are available ($40-45/day). Nearby Sandy Beach is good for fly-fishing, while Sandy Beach is dog-friendly.

A worthwhile attraction is the **Rio Theater** (20396 Bohemian Hwy., Monte Rio, 707/520-4075, www.riotheater.com), a movie theater housed in a Quonset hut with an adjacent café (707/865-4190, www.riocafetake2.com).

Sonoma and Mendocino Coasts

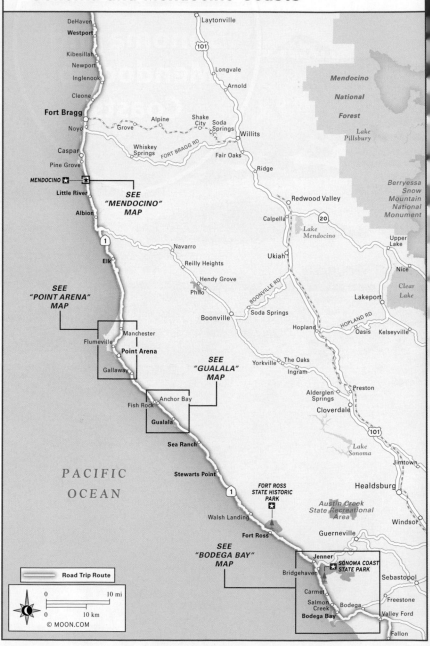

Sonoma and Mendocino Coasts

DeHaven
Westport
Kibesillah
Newport
Inglenook
Cleone
Fort Bragg
Noyo
Grove
Alpine
Shake City
Soda Springs
Whiskey Springs
FORT BRAGG RD
Caspar
Pine Grove
MENDOCINO
Little River
SEE "MENDOCINO" MAP
Albion
Navarro
Elk
Reilly Heights
Hendy Grove
Philo
SEE "POINT ARENA" MAP
Manchester
Flumeville
Point Arena
Gallaway
SEE "GUALALA" MAP
Anchor Bay
Fish Rock
Gualala
Sea Ranch
Stewarts Point

Laytonville
101
Longvale
Arnold
Willits
Fair Oaks
Ridge
Redwood Valley
Calpella
20
Ukiah
Boonville
BOONVILLE RD
Soda Springs
Yorkville
The Oaks
Ingram
Hopland
HOPLAND RD
Oasis
Kelseyville
Alderglen Springs
Preston
Cloverdale
101
Jimtown

Mendocino National Forest
Lake Pillsbury
Berryessa Snow Mountain National Monument
Upper Lake
Nice
Clear Lake
Lakeport

PACIFIC OCEAN

FORT ROSS STATE HISTORIC PARK
Walsh Landing
Fort Ross

Austin Creek State Recreational Area
Lake Sonoma
Healdsburg
Windsor
Guerneville

SEE "BODEGA BAY" MAP
Jenner
Bridgehaven
Carmet
Salmon Creek
Bodega Bay
Bodega

SONOMA COAST STATE PARK
Sebastopol
Freestone
Valley Ford
Fallon

Road Trip Route

0   10 mi
0   10 km
© MOON.COM

Highlights

★ **Sonoma Coast State Park:** There's much to explore here: rocky coves, sandy beaches, iconic rock formations, and the shoreline Kortum Trail (page 167).

★ **Fort Ross State Historic Park:** Wander through the haunting buildings of reconstructed Fort Ross and imagine what it was like here in the early 1800s (page 170).

★ **The Sea Ranch Chapel:** This micro-chapel is decorated with natural elements, from sea urchins to redwoods (page 174).

★ **Bowling Ball Beach:** At low tide, giant boulders appear in neat rows on a Point Arena beach (page 178).

★ **California Coastal National Monument:** The monument's Point Arena-Stornetta Unit is a stunning coastline that showcases sheer cliffs, giant tidepools, and sea arches (page 178).

★ **Mendocino:** Spend an afternoon wandering this arts-filled community on the headlands (page 185).

Best Restaurants

★ **Fishetarian Fish Market, Bodega Bay:** This modest fish market serves treasures from the sea, including superb Baja-style fish tacos (page 166).

★ **River's End, Jenner:** The view of the Russian River chugging toward the Pacific Ocean can't be beat from this cliffside restaurant (page 169).

★ **Stewarts Point Store, Stewarts Point:** This historic store is a market, café, and bakery during the day and a popular speakeasy and pizza parlor on Friday night (page 173).

★ **Trinks Café, Gualala:** A local favorite, Trinks serves sandwiches ideal for a day hike or road trip (page 175).

★ **Franny's Cup & Saucer, Point Arena:** This brightly painted bakery makes its own truffles, pizzas, and other delights (page180).

★ **Circa '62, Little River:** Creative breakfasts draw patrons to this former schoolhouse (page 184).

★ **Café Beaujolais, Mendocino:** Since 1968, Café Beaujolais has been synonymous with coastal Californian French cuisine (page 189).

★ **North Coast Brewing Company, Fort Bragg:** Sample craft brews like Scrimshaw Pilsner and Red Seal Ale at their source in this cozy taproom (page 199).

★ **Piaci Pub & Pizzeria, Fort Bragg:** This micro-pizzeria more than makes up for its small size with tasty pizzas and fine craft beers on tap (page 199).

From Bodega Bay, CA-1 (Hwy. 1) twists and turns north along hairpin curves that will take your breath away.

The Sonoma and Mendocino Coasts (called Mendonoma by some) feature rocky beaches, redwood forests, top-notch cuisine, and a friendly, uncrowded wine region. Along the way, tiny coastal towns—Jenner, Gualala, Point Arena, Mendocino, Fort Bragg—dot the hills and valleys, beckoning travelers with bed-and-breakfasts, organic farms, and relaxing respites from the road. Between the towns are a wealth of coastal access areas where you can take in the striking meeting of land and sea. Inland, Mendocino's hidden wine region offers the rural and

relaxed pace missing from that other famous wine district. Anderson Valley and Hopland can quench your thirst, whether it's for beer at the local microbrewery or wine at one of many tasting rooms.

Days are spent hiking through towering redwood forests or along craggy coastlines. Stop to sample the region's bounty of fresh seafood and produce, organic meat, and locally produced wines and beers. Though just hours from the bustling Bay Area, the Sonoma and Mendocino Coasts are noticeably less crowded even during summer.

The Mendocino Coast is a popular retreat for those who've been introduced to its specific charms. On weekends, Bay Area residents flock north to their favorite hideaways to enjoy windswept beaches, secret coves, and luscious cuisine. This area is ideal for deep-sea

Best Accommodations

★ **Bodega Bay Lodge & Spa, Bodega Bay.** This sprawling resort has everything you need on-site, including comfy rooms, a heated pool, and two restaurants (page 167).

★ **Timber Cove Resort, Jenner:** This chic resort features playful touches like turntables and vinyl records in every room (page 171).

★ **Point Arena Lighthouse, Point Arena:** Spend the night in the renovated quarters of a lighthouse keeper on one of the westernmost spits in California (page 182).

★ **Elk Cove Inn, Elk:** Expect nothing less than luxury, comfort, and hospitality, along with fine views of the Mendocino Coast, at this upscale bed-and-breakfast (page 183).

★ **The Andiron, Little River:** Stay in playfully themed cabins at this fun and quirky property south of Mendocino (page 184).

★ **Heritage House Resort, Little River:** This luxury resort sits on a piece of prime Mendocino Coast real estate (page 184).

★ **Brewery Gulch Inn, Mendocino:** Spoil yourself at this bed-and-breakfast that serves *both* dinner and breakfast (page 191).

★ **Vichy Springs Resort, Ukiah:** The rustic cabins and champagne-like hot springs of Vichy Springs Resort have hosted the likes of Teddy Roosevelt and Mark Twain (page 195).

★ **Surf & Sand Lodge, Fort Bragg:** This moderately priced motel offers luxury coastal views (page 201).

★ **Westport Hotel, Westport:** Relax in one of the six rooms in this 1800s building in a tiny coastal community (page 202).

anglers, wine aficionados, and fans of luxury spas. Art is especially prominent in the culture; from the 1960s onward, aspiring artists have found supportive communities, sales opportunities, and homes in Mendocino County, and a number of small galleries display local artwork.

Planning Your Time

Many Bay Area residents consider **Mendocino** ideal for a weekend getaway or romantic retreat. A **weekend** is about the perfect length of time to spend on the Mendocino Coast or in the Anderson Valley Wine Country.

Summer has average daily temperatures in the mid-60s. Expect rain from November to May. The chances of fog or rain are significantly lower in the **fall,** making it one of the best times to visit. Frequent visitors to the area know this, so many popular hotels book quickly for fall weekends.

Getting There

Driving is the way to get from place to place, unless you're a hard-core backpacker. CA-1 winds along the North Coast from Bodega Bay to above Fort Bragg, where it heads east to connect with US-101 at its northern terminus near Leggett.

If you are heading to Mendocino or a section of the coast north of there, take **US-101,** which is a great deal faster than CA-1, and then take one of the connector roads from US-101 to CA-1. One of the best and most scenic connector roads is **CA-128,** which heads west off US-101 at Cloverdale and passes through the scenic Anderson Valley, with its many wineries, before joining CA-1 just south of the town of Mendocino.

Fill your tank in San Francisco, Santa Rosa, Sebastopol, or Petaluma before heading to the coast. From Bodega Bay north, gas becomes more expensive.

From San Francisco
70 mi/115 km, 1.5-2 hr
From San Francisco, take US-101 north across the **Golden Gate Bridge** and continue north for 40 miles (64 km). Past Petaluma, take exit 479 west for Railroad Avenue. The rest of this drive is 22 miles (35 km) on two-lane back roads.

From Railroad Avenue, turn left onto West Railroad Avenue; this is followed by a right onto Stony Point Road in 1.7 miles (2.7 km). Continue 6.5 miles (10.5 km), then turn left onto Roblar Road. In 5.5 miles (9 km), turn right on Valley Ford Road, which becomes CA-1 in Bodega Bay. Continue 8 miles (13 km) west to **Bodega Bay.**

Mendocino is about 100 miles (160 km) north on CA-1, a drive of 2.5-3 hours.

CA-1 north of Bodega Bay is quite curvy, and driving distances can take longer, especially if you want to take in the coastline and attractions. From Bodega Bay north to **Jenner** is 10 miles (16 km), though the drive will take at least 20 minutes. From Bodega Bay to **Gualala** is a distance of 50 miles (80 km), which can take over an hour to drive.

From Napa and Sonoma
50 mi/80 km, 1.5 hr
From Napa or Sonoma, take CA-12/121 west to CA-116. Follow CA-116 north and then west for 14 miles (22.5 km) until reaching US-101. Head north on US-101 for 7 miles (11.5 km) and take exit 479 west for Railroad Avenue. The rest of this drive is 22 miles (35 km) on two-lane back roads.

From Railroad Avenue, turn left onto West Railroad Avenue; this is followed by a right onto Stony Point Road in 1.7 miles (2.7 km). Continue 6.5 miles (10.5 km), then turn left onto Roblar Road. In 5.5 miles (9 km), turn right on Valley Ford Road, which becomes CA-1 in Bodega Bay. Continue 8 miles (13 km) west to **Bodega Bay.**

Mendocino is about 100 miles (160 km) north on CA-1, a drive of 2.5-3 hours.

From Shasta and Lassen
240 mi/385 km, 4.5 hr
In the Shasta and Lassen region, the gateway town of **Redding** offers the easiest starting point for this drive. From Redding, take I-5 south for 127 miles (204 km) past the town of **Williams.** Hop onto I-505 south for 35 miles (56 km) through Winters to meet I-80 in Vacaville. Continue 30 miles (48 km) south on I-80.

Near **Vallejo,** take CA-37 west along San Pablo Bay for 16 miles. Head north on CA-116 for 14 miles (22.5 km) until reaching US-101. Continue north on US-101 for 7 miles (11.5 km) and take exit 479 west for Railroad Avenue.

The rest of this drive is 22 miles (35 km) on two-lane back roads. From Railroad Avenue, turn left onto West Railroad Avenue; this is followed by a right onto Stony Point Road in 1.7 miles (2.7 km). Continue 6.5 miles (10.5 km), then turn left onto Roblar Road. In 5.5

miles (9 km), turn right on Valley Ford Road, which becomes CA-1 in Bodega Bay. Continue 8 miles (13 km) west to **Bodega Bay.**

Mendocino is about 100 miles (160 km) north on CA-1, a drive of 2.5-3 hours.

Stopping in Williams
Williams is midway between Redding and Santa Rosa, so it is a good place for a pit stop. **Granzella's Restaurant & Deli** (451 6th St., 530/473-5496, www.granzellas.com, 6am-9pm daily, $8-10) is a popular deli, restaurant and sports bar. Try the New Orleans muffuletta, meatball sandwich, or create your own.

From Lake Tahoe
225 mi/360 km, 4 hr
From I-80 in **Truckee,** drive southwest for 157 miles (253 km) past **Sacramento** to Vallejo, then follow the driving directions from Shasta and Lassen. Access from the Lake Tahoe area can be hampered by inclement weather, snow, and traffic.

Stopping in Sacramento
About 10 miles (16 km) north of Sacramento, the aptly named **Pit Stop Bar B-Que** (3515 McClellan Dr., North Highland, 916/344-1771, www.pitstopbarbq.com, 11am-9pm Mon.-Sat., 11am-8pm Sun., $10-18) serves award-winning ribs to hungry motorists.

To get there from I-80 West, take exit 96 and turn west onto Madison Avenue. In 0.7 mile, veer right onto Airbase Drive and continue 0.4 mile to Watt Avenue. Turn right onto Watt Avenue and drive 0.3 mile north to McClellan where you will turn right. The Pit Stop is on the left.

Air
The closest international airport to the region is **San Francisco International Airport** (SFO, www.flysfo.com).

Bodega Bay

Bodega Bay is popular for its coastal views, whale-watching, and seafood—but it's most famous as the filming locale of Alfred Hitchcock's *The Birds.* The town sits on the eastern side of the harbor, while Bodega Head is a peninsula that shields the bay from the ocean. The tiny town with a population of just over 1,000 has kite shops, marinas, and unassuming seafood restaurants. The whole town shuts down around 7pm, even on summer evenings.

Getting There
Bodega Bay is on CA-1 north of Point Reyes National Seashore and west of Petaluma. From the Bay Area, it's a beautiful drive north, but the road's twists and turns require taking it slow. A faster way to get here is to take US-101 north to Petaluma. Take the exit for East Washington Street and follow Bodega Avenue to Valley Ford Road, cutting across to the coast. You'll hit Bodega Bay about 2 miles (3 km) after passing through Valley Ford. The latter route takes about 1.5 hours, with some of the route slow and winding.

Bodega Head
Bodega Bay looks like an open safety pin on maps; **Bodega Head** (3799 Westshore Rd., 707/875-3483, www.parks.ca.gov, sunrise-sunset daily, free) is the thicker side, a knob that protects the bay from the open ocean. A part of Sonoma Coast State Park, it's the best place for a hike that gives you an overview of the area. The **Bodega Head Trail** (1.9 mi/3.1 km, 1 hour, easy) showcases rock arches, sandy coves, and migrating gray whales before hitting the high point and winding back to views of Doran Beach, Bodega Bay, and Bodega Harbor.

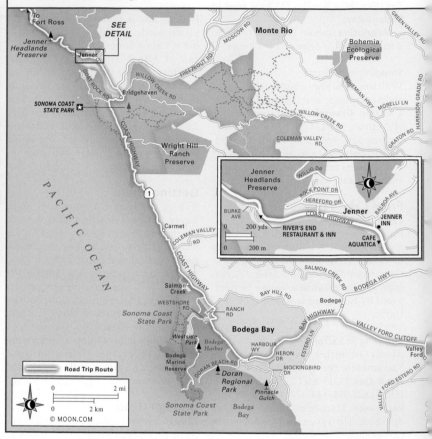

Recreation
Whale-Watching

The best sight you could hope to see is a close-up view of Pacific gray whales migrating home to Alaska with their newborn calves. The whales head past the area January-May on their way from their summer home off Mexico. If you're lucky, you can see them from the shore. **Bodega Head,** a promontory just north of the bay, is a place to get close to the migration route. To get to this prime spot, travel north on CA-1 about 1 mile past the visitors center and turn left onto Eastshore Road; make a right at the stop sign, and then drive 3 miles (4.8 km) to the parking lot.

On weekends from January to Mother's Day, volunteers from **Stewards of the Coast and Redwoods** (707/869-9177, www.stewardscr.org) are available to answer questions. Contact them for organized land-based whale-watching tours or to learn more about their various educational programs.

Many of Bodega Bay's fishing boats offer whale-watching between January and March. Go on a whale-watching trip

Sonoma and Mendocino in Three Days

Day 1

Spend the day exploring the many coastal treasures of **Sonoma Coast State Park** before stopping for lunch—and stunning views—at **River's End.** Walk off lunch at **Jenner Headlands Preserve,** then drive a particularly winding section of CA-1 to explore the fascinating Russian settlement of **Fort Ross State Historic Park.**

At night, stay at **Timber Cove Resort;** relax on your room's deck or by the property's fire pit. Dine at the resort's **Drakes Sonoma Coast Kitchen,** or if it's Friday, drive 12 miles (19.5 km) north to **Stewarts Point Store** for Pizza Night.

Day 2

Drive 20 miles (32 km) north to Gualala for breakfast at **Trinks Café,** then take a short drive to **Bowling Ball Beach;** at low tide, you can watch as the huge boulders in neat little rows are revealed on the rocky shore. Celebrate the natural phenomenon (hopefully!) with baked goods at **Franny's Cup & Saucer** in Point Arena. Spend the afternoon hiking in the Point Arena-Stornetta Unit of the **California Coastal National Monument.** Grab a post-hike beer or wine in Point Arena at **215 Main** and then spend the night in the keeper's quarters at **Point Arena Lighthouse**.

Day 3

It's a one-hour drive from Point Arena to **Mendocino.** Wander around town and take in the unique architecture and the surrounding coastal headlands. Head north to Fort Bragg for lunch at **Piaci Pub & Pizzeria.** Nearby **Glass Beach** provides Instagramworthy photos of colorful sea glass. End the day with a pint at **North Coast Brewing Company.**

---

with **Bodega Bay Sport Fishing** (707/875-3344, www.bodegabaysportfishing.com, $60/half day) on their 60- or 65-foot boat or take a ride with **Miss Anita Fishing Charters** (707/875-3474, www.missanitafishingcharters.com, $100/half day, $200/full day).

Doran Regional Park

When you arrive in Bodega Bay, you'll see a sign pointing left for **Doran Regional Park** (201 Doran Beach Rd., 707/875-3540, http://parks.sonomacounty.ca.gov, 7am-sunset daily, day use $7 per vehicle). It is less than a mile down the road and worth the trip. The wide and level beach has a small boardwalk. You can even swim at Doran Beach; although it's cold, the water is protected from the open ocean waves, so it's much safer than most of the beaches along the coast.

Kayaking and Stand-up Paddleboarding

With a usually calm bay and a protected harbor, Bodega Bay is a great place to kayak or stand-up paddleboard. Stop into the **Bodega Bay Surf Shack** (Pelican Plaza, 1400 Hwy. 1, 707/875-3944, www.bodegabaysurf.com, 10am-6pm Mon.-Fri., 9am-7pm Sat.-Sun. summer, 10am-5pm Mon.-Fri., 9am-6pm Sat.-Sun. winter, kayaks $45/4 hours, SUPs $40/5 hours) to rent your SUP or kayak, then set out in Bodega Bay, Salmon Creek, or the nearby lower portion of the Russian River. They also give private lessons ($165) and group lessons ($119) and rent surfboards ($20/day) and wetsuits ($20/day). Doran Beach has an unintimidating wave for beginners. Just north of town is Salmon Creek, a series of powerful and exposed beach breaks.

Horseback Riding

Long, rugged beaches with few people

mean that the Sonoma Coast is a terrific place to go horseback riding. Just north of town at the 378-acre Chanslor Ranch, **Horse N Around Trail Rides** (2660 N. Hwy. 1, 707/875-3333, www.horsenaroundtrailrides.com, $40-250) offers 30-minute wetlands trail rides and 1.5-hour beach rides. Choose between group rides and slightly pricier private rides.

Shopping

Gourmet au Bay (1412 Bay Flat Rd., 707/875-9875, www.gourmetaubay.com, 11:30am-8pm Thurs.-Mon., 11:30am-7pm Tues.-Wed., $15/tasting) is a shop and tasting bar that offers the chance to taste wines from different vintners: Some are major players in the Napa wine scene, and some are from wineries so small they don't have tasting rooms of their own. You might even get to taste the odd French or Australian wine when you "wine surf," a tasting of three wines poured and presented on a miniature surfboard that you can carry out to a patio with views of Bodega Bay.

Events

The annual **Bodega Seafood, Art, and Wine Festival** (16855 Bodega Hwy., Bodega, 707/824-8717, www.bodegaseafoodfestival.com, Aug.) takes place the last weekend in August, combining all the best elements of the Bodega lifestyle with live music, wine-tastings, and special dinners. The proceeds benefit two worthy organizations: the Bodega Volunteer Fire Department and Stewards of the Coast and Redwoods.

Food

The ★ **Fishetarian Fish Market** (599 Hwy. 1, 707/875-9092, www.fishetarianfishmarket.com, 11am-7pm Fri.-Sun., 11am-6pm Mon.-Thurs., $6-15) nails the Baja-style fish taco with rockfish, a cabbage slaw, and a zingy sauce. They also do Point Reyes oysters and an award-winning clam chowder. Order at the counter above display cases of smoked salmon, oysters, and octopus salad, then dine casually inside or outside at one of the limited tables. Fishetarian has a few well-chosen craft beers on tap along with a fridge filled with bottled beers, sodas, and other cold beverages. Be aware that this place closes early.

A classic and unassuming seafood spot, the **Spud Point Crab Company** (1910 Westshore Rd., 707/875-9472, 9am-5pm daily, $7-11) sits across the street from the boats that bring in its fresh seafood. On weekdays, there can be a line out the door for the clam chowder and the crab sandwich. On crowded days, make a friend and share some space at one of the few picnic tables out front.

Right on the highway, **The Birds Café** (1407 Hwy. 1, 707/875-2900, 11:30am-6pm daily, $8-14) is an easy pit stop when driving through Bodega Bay. Refuel on fried artichoke tacos, fish tacos, and shrimp tacos on a large deck with views of the harbor. The café also serves raw and barbecued oysters from the Hog Island Oyster Company.

Bodega Bay Lodge's **Drakes Sonoma Coast Kitchen** (Bodega Bay Lodge, 103 Hwy. 1, 707/875-3525, https://drakesbodegabay.com, 7:30am-11am and 6pm-9pm daily, $24-51) showcases Sonoma County ingredients including local artisan cheeses and wines produced by area wineries. Adjacent is the less formal **Drakes Fireside Lounge** (11:30am-10pm daily, $14-17), with a small menu and a long list of signature cocktails, wines by the glass, and beer.

One of the best restaurants in the area is ★ **Terrapin Creek Cafe** (1580 Eastshore Dr., 707/875-2700, www.terrapincreekcafe.com, 4:30pm-9pm Thurs.-Mon., $23-32), where they make creative use of the abundance of fresh seafood available and cook up tasty pasta, duck, and beef entrées. Their efforts have been awarded with a prestigious Michelin star.

Accommodations and Camping

The ★ **Bodega Bay Lodge & Spa** (103 Hwy. 1, 707/875-3525 or 888/875-2250, www.bodegabaylodge.com, $289-679) is on a seven-acre property that sits high enough to overlook the bay and harbor, Doran Beach, the bird-filled marshes, and Bodega Head in the distance. Most rooms have views of the water, while all units in the seven separate buildings have private balconies or terraces. Warm up on a foggy day in the heated pool, sauna, or oversized infinity soaking tub. There's a fitness center and spa in the same facility. Dine at the lodge's upscale **Drakes Sonoma Coast Kitchen** (7:30am-11am and 6pm-9pm daily, $24-51) or the casual **Drakes Fireside Lounge** (11:30am-10pm daily, $14-17).

The **Inn at the Tides** (800 Hwy. 1, 707/875-2751, www.innatthetides.com, $260-400) has 86 rooms with fine amenities, including a full breakfast and use of a heated swimming pool, whirlpool spa, sauna, and exercise room.

Doran Regional Park (201 Doran Beach Rd., 707/565-2267, http://sonomacountycamping.org, $32-35) has 120 campsites for tents, trailers, and RVs. Amenities include restrooms with coin-operated showers.

★ Sonoma Coast State Park

TOP EXPERIENCE

Sonoma Coast State Park (707/875-3483, www.parks.ca.gov, sunrise-sunset daily, $8) has it all for coast lovers: broad sandy beaches, cramped coves, wildflower-strewn headlands, rocky tidepools, natural arches, and imposing rocks offshore. The park's boundaries extend south from Bodega Head to the Vista Trailhead, north of Jenner. Although the beaches are lovely, it is not advisable to swim here. If you do go down to the water, bring your binoculars and camera. The cliffs, crags, inlets, whitecaps, mini-islands, and rock outcroppings are fascinating in any weather, and their looks change with the shifting tides and fog.

Getting There

From Bodega Bay, continue 7 miles (11.5 km) north on CA-1 to access Sonoma Coast State Park.

Sights

Located at the park's south end, **Salmon Creek Beach** (2.5 mi/4 km north of Bodega Bay) is a long, sandy beach with a lagoon. From the North Salmon Creek Parking Lot, take the staircase down to the driftwood-decorated beach. This is a popular spot with anglers, beachcombers, and surfers.

Continuing north, **Duncan's Landing** (5 mi/8 km north of Bodega Bay) is a flat-topped promontory with parking, picnic tables, and sweeping ocean views. The section of coastline to the north is **Wright's Beach** (6 mi/9.5 km north of Bodega Bay), a stunning stretch of sand and sea that is home to a small campground and one end of the coastside **Kortum Trail.**

Steep stairs lead from the parking lot to **Shell Beach** (7.5 mi/12 km north of Bodega Bay), a rocky area with tidepools and coves. Located close to the mouth of the Russian River, **Goat Rock** (10.5 mi/17 km north of Bodega Bay) is known for its sandy beach and harbor seal colony.

Recreation

Hiking

The best way to experience the Sonoma coastline is with a walk along the **Kortum Trail** (3.5 mi/5.6 km one-way, 1.5 hours, easy). The hike atop coastal bluffs parallels the crashing Pacific, with several side paths down to the striking beaches and coves. The path is alternately compacted soil, a raised boardwalk over a marshy section, and a footpath, all allowing for an easy stroll. Pick up the trail from the parking lots at Wright's Beach, Shell Beach, and Goat Rock.

More challenging is the **Pomo Canyon Trail** (6.5 mi/10.5 km round-trip, 4 hours, moderate). The trail winds up coastal hills to panoramic views of the Russian River, Jenner, and the rugged coastline. The route follows an ancient route of the native Pomo and Miwok through oaks, redwoods, and grasslands and is known as a great wildflower hike in spring. The trail starts from Shell Beach parking lot.

Surfing

The most popular surf break on the Sonoma Coast is **Salmon Creek Beach** (2.5 mi/4 km north of Bodega Bay), which has significant current and reliable waves. Rent a board or wetsuit at **Bodega Bay Surf Shack** (Pelican Plaza, 1400 Hwy. 1, 707/875-3944, www.bodegabaysurf.com, 10am-6pm Mon.-Fri., 9am-7pm Sat.-Sun. summer, 10am-5pm Mon.-Fri., 9am-6pm Sat.-Sun. winter, surfboard rentals $20/day, wetsuits $20/day). They also have a free 24-hour surf report (707/875-3944).

Camping

Sonoma Coast State Park has two campgrounds. **Bodega Dunes Campground** (2485 Hwy. 1, 1 mi/1.6 km north of Bodega Bay, 800/444-7275, www.reserve-california.com, $35/vehicle, $5/hike/bike) is the bigger of the two with 99 sites. Amenities include hot showers, fire pits, and picnic tables.

★ **Wright's Beach Campground** (7095 Hwy. 1, 6 mi/9.5 km north of Bodega Bay 800/444-7275, www.reservecalifornia.com, $35-45) is in a slightly wooded spot below a coastal bluff and adjacent to Wright's Beach. All 27 sites offer nothing more than a few steps to the beach, though premium campsites (1-10) look right out onto the ocean. Bathrooms have running water, but if you want a shower you'll have to head to Bodega Dunes Campground (5 mi/8 km south). The Kortum Trail starts from the bluff above the campground.

Jenner

Jenner is on CA-1 at the mouth of the Russian River. It's a beautiful spot for a quiet honeymoon or a paddle in a kayak. **Goat Rock State Beach** (Goat Rock Rd., 707/875-3483, www.parks.ca.gov, $8 per vehicle) is at the mouth of the Russian River inside Sonoma Coast State Park. A colony of harbor seals breed and frolic here, and you may also see gray whales, sea otters, elephant seals, and a variety of sea life. Pets are not allowed, and swimming is prohibited.

Getting There

The drive from Bodega Bay is a scenic 10 miles (16 km) north on CA-1 that takes about 20 minutes.

Jenner Headlands Preserve

With panoramic views of the snaking Russian River, the table-topped Goat Rock, and the rocky Sonoma Coast, the 5,630-acre **Jenner Headlands Preserve** (CA-1, 2 mi/3.2 km north of Jenner, 909/797-8507, www.wildlandsconservancy.org, 8am-sunset daily, free) is a great place to hike. Run by the Wildlands Conservancy, the preserve is a well-maintained property with a parking lot, interpretive plaques, picnic areas, and restrooms. The property has 14 miles of trails through redwood forests, coastal prairie, chaparral, oak woodlands, and Douglas fir.

Hiking

The most challenging hike is the **Sea to Sky Trail** (15 mi/24 km round-trip, 8-10 hours, strenuous), which starts at the preserve parking lot and climbs to 2,204-foot (672-m) Pole Mountain. An easier hike is the **Raptor Ridge-Sea to Sky Trail Loop** (4 mi/6.4 km round-trip, 2 hours, moderate). The trail climbs to a bird's-eye view (pun intended) of the coast, including Point Reyes and Bodega Head in the distance. The trail is a narrow path that

switchbacks and follows a four-wheel-drive road, passing through cattle-grazing areas. A mile in is a fine place for a picnic with tables near a barn. At 0.25 mile, a spur trail leads to **Hawk Hill,** which offers views of raptors as they swirl in the thermals. The descent to the bottom section of the trail is a continuous view of scenic ocean vistas.

Visitors short on time should climb the 0.5-mile **Sea to Sky Trail** from the parking lot. At the top, a mounted telescope sits on a rock foundation and allows hikers to zoom in on the coastal features and wildlife below.

Food and Accommodations

★ **River's End** (11048 Hwy. 1, 707/865-2484, www.ilovesunsets.com, 11:30am-8:30pm Fri.-Tues., $20-55, chef's tasting menu $74) began humbly enough in the 1920s as an angler's retreat and hangout. Today, it is the essential place to dine in Jenner thanks to its views and food. The restaurant sources food locally, including seafood from offshore. Sit on the outdoor deck or at a table by the window inside and enjoy the beauty of the Russian River pooled before the sea. Though prices are high, it's worth it for a window seat at sunset.

Mere feet from the restaurant, the five rustic **River's End cabins** ($239-279) were initially built for anglers who had imbibed too much. (Three of the units date to 1927.) Cabins eschew modern conveniences (including TVs) for private decks with views of the river and sea.

You can't miss **Café Aquatica**'s turquoise sign (10439 Hwy. 1, 707/865-2251, 8am-5pm daily, $7-10). The coffee shop housed inside the quirky structure serves handcrafted organic coffee and vegetarian fare (tempeh BLT, roasted Portobello sandwich), as well as fresh local Dungeness crab rolls, with hippie-ish cheer. The wooden deck out back is a

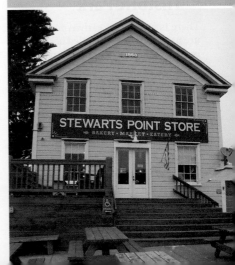

From top to bottom: Café Aquatica; River's End; Stewarts Point Store.

great place to sip coffee while watching the river slowly flow. Catch a music act on Saturday afternoons.

The **Jenner Inn** (10400 Hwy. 1, 707/865-2377, www.jennerinn.com, $159-550) has quite a history. In 1948, a fire burned down the original hotel, the iconic "Jenner By the Sea." It was rebuilt by Swedish shipbuilders and then served time as a post office, tavern, and fish house. The inn has since expanded into a variety of quiet, beautifully furnished buildings that include a former mill cabin mere steps from the river. Some rooms have hot tubs and private decks. Breakfast is included.

Information and Services

It's worth pulling over at the **Sonoma Coast Jenner Visitor Center** (10439 Hwy. 1, Jenner, 707/865-9757, www.stewardscr.org, 11am-3pm Mon.-Fri., 10am-4pm Sat.-Sun.) for the public bathrooms and views of the Russian River. Perched on a dock over the river, the visitors center has information about the coast up to Mendocino and the inland Russian River area, as well as a one-page guide to local hikes.

★ Fort Ross State Historic Park

There is no historic early American figure named Ross who settled here: "Ross" is short for "Russian," and this park commemorates the history of Russian settlement on the North Coast. In the 19th century Russians came to the wilds of Alaska and worked with native Alaskans to develop a robust fur trade, harvesting seals, otters, sea lions, and land mammals for their pelts. The enterprise required sea travel as the hunters chased the animals as far as California. Eventually, a group of fur hunters and traders came ashore on what is now the Sonoma Coast in 1812 and developed a fortified

outpost that became known as Fort Ross State Historic Park. The area gradually became not only a thriving Russian American settlement but also a center for agriculture and shipbuilding and the site of California's first windmills.

Getting There

The drive from Jenner to Fort Ross is 12 miles (19.5 km), but it may feel a lot farther due to the very curvy nature of this section of CA-1. Gates on either end of the two-lane road signal that this portion of CA-1 closes from time to time due to mudslides. Take your time, and you'll be rewarded with a straighter roadway in Fort Ross.

Sights

Learn more about **Fort Ross State Historic Park** (19005 Hwy. 1, Jenner, 707/847-3286, www.fortross.org, 10am-4:30pm Fri.-Mon. Nov.-Mar., 10am-4:30pm daily Apr.-Oct., parking $8) at the park's large visitors center (hours and days vary),

which provides a 15-minute film and a roomful of exhibits.

The reconstructed fort buildings are ringed by an impressive wooden wall to show how the settlers lived. At one time, the fort was home to 59 buildings, but today the only original building remaining is the Rotchev House, built in 1836 for the fort's last administrator. Its creaking boards, cold drafts, and low light give visitors a feel for it was like living here in the 1800s. The other buildings, including the large bunkhouse, a chapel, and the two cannon-filled blockhouses, were rebuilt using much of the original lumber. A visit to the whole fort and the dark, comma-shaped beach beyond entails a long but level walk; wear comfortable shoes and bring water. Tours of the **Call Ranch House,** a historic building from the park's ranching era, are offered the first weekend of every month (1pm-4pm).

Food and Accommodations

The 93-foot-high obelisk above ★ **Timber Cove Resort** (21780 Hwy. 1, Jenner, 707/847-3231, www.timbercoveresort. com, $225-900) rises like a beacon, promising serenity and luxury on the rugged Sonoma Coast. The rustic yet chic resort is perched on 30 park-like acres with hiking trails tracing the clifftops above the crashing sea. The rooms fit the environment with wood furnishings, a turntable (and three albums), and balconies that take in the sky-scattered night sky. The A-frame great room is part lobby, part bar, and part lounge, with a three-story stone fireplace and antler chandeliers. There are also foosball, pool, and Ping-Pong tables, while an outside fire pit draws a crowd most evenings. This is a worthwhile and rejuvenating stop on any Sonoma Coast trip.

Timber Cove Resort's **Coast Kitchen** (21780 Hwy. 1, Jenner, 707/847-3231, www.coastkitchensonoma.com, 8am-11am and noon-9:30pm daily, $26-46)

Fort Ross State Historic Park

is a farm-to-table, and sea-to-table, restaurant. The menu stars local products, from mushrooms to seafood to duck, while half of the wine list is devoted solely to Sonoma and Napa wines. The upscale dining room has a rustic rock wall with windows out to the coast. Dine on the outside patio or opt to eat in the adjacent lounge.

Salt Point State Park

Stretching for miles along the Sonoma coastline, **Salt Point State Park** (25050 Hwy. 1, Jenner, 707/847-3221, www.parks. ca.gov, sunrise-sunset daily, $8 per vehicle) provides easy access from US-101 to more than a dozen sandy state beaches. You don't have to stop at the visitors center to enjoy this park and its many beaches—just follow the signs along the highway to the turnoffs and parking lots.

If you're looking to scuba dive or free dive, head for **Gerstle Cove,** accessible from the visitors center just south of Salt Point proper. The cove was designated one of California's first underwater parks, and divers who can deal with the chilly water have a wonderful time exploring the diverse undersea wildlife.

Getting There

It takes just 15 minutes to make the drive from Fort Ross State Historic Park to Salt Point State Park on CA-1. The 8-mile (13-km) leg is dominated by coastal views and the 93-foot-tall (28-m) peace obelisk on the Timber Cove Resort property. In case you are wondering, the quirky monument was made by artist Benjamino Bufano out of concrete, tile, redwood, and lead.

Kruse Rhododendron State Reserve

For a genteel experience, head east off CA-1 to the **Kruse Rhododendron State Reserve** (Hwy. 1 near milepost 43, 707/847-3221, www.parks.ca.gov, sunrise-sunset daily, free), where you can meander along the **Chinese Gulf Trail** in the spring, admiring the profusion of pink rhododendron flowers blooming beneath the second-growth redwood forest. If you prefer a picnic, you'll find tables at many of the beaches—though it can be quite windy in the summer.

Hiking

Salt Point State Park has miles of trails just begging to be hiked. For constant coastal views, take the **Salt Point Trail to Stump Beach** (3 mi/4.8 km roundtrip, 1.5 hours, easy), which starts from the Gerstle Cove parking lot. Stop to observe the tafoni, honeycomb-like sections of sandstone, on the shoreline.

The **Pygmy Forest Trail** (3.8 mi/6.1 km round-trip, 2 hours, moderate) visits a strange natural phenomenon: a forest of miniature pine, cypress, and redwood trees, their dwarfed height due to the soil. Start on the **Central Trail** and then, after 1.5 miles (2.4 km), turn left on the **North Trail.** Make another left at the **Water Tank Trail** before getting back on the Central Trail to complete your journey. The trailhead is by the ranger station.

Camping

Salt Point State Park (25050 Hwy. 1, 800/444-7275, www.reservecalifornia. com, $25-35) has scenic **Gerstle Cove Campground** on the west side of the highway and **Woodside Campground** on the eastern side.

Stewarts Point

Situated halfway between Salt Point State Park and The Sea Ranch is the blink-and-you-miss-it hamlet of Stewarts Point. Most of the land in the area is owned by the Richardson family. In 1876, Herbert Archer Richardson came to the coast from New Hampshire with a wife and pocket change. Richardson became a timber baron, shipping redwood out of the area via a fleet of nine sailboats.

The best reason to pull over at this bend in the road today is for the Stewarts Point General Store, a thriving roadside stop that was built in 1868.

Getting There

Stewarts Point is 7 miles (11.5 km) north of Salt Point State Park on CA-1. The store is on the left side of the road and will appear quickly; be ready to slow down.

Stewarts Point Store

Stroll around the historic ★ **Stewarts Point Store** (32000 Hwy. 1, Stewarts Point, 707/785-2011, 7:30am-6pm Mon., Wed.-Thurs., and Sat., 7:30am-5pm Sun.) to take in the artifacts (old coffee cans, a baby buggy from 1888, a 160-year-old wheelbarrow now filled with taffy) as well as curated offerings like cold craft beer and local wines.

The building is home to a bakery, a café, and a market run by the Two Fish Baking Company (https://twofishbaking.com). It's known for its breakfast burritos, sandwiches, sticky buns, and baguettes. They also have the "Twofish Tiny Tap Room," featuring two craft beers on tap.

For a truly special experience, plan to visit on **Friday** (4:30pm-8:30pm, $17-24), when the upstairs of the store, a former

From top to bottom: Salt Point State Park; Bufano's obelisk at Timber Cove Resort; The Sea Ranch Chapel.

dance hall, becomes a pizza parlor and speakeasy. The pizza is superb, with a crust as good as it gets, and the house-made cocktails from the old wooden bar are delicious. It seems like everyone within a 20-mile radius comes here, dining at communal tables set under string lights in the barn-like structure. It's an event that will fill you up with great food, conversation, and community.

The Sea Ranch

The last few miles of the Sonoma Coast before entering Mendocino County are the property of The Sea Ranch, a private coastal community known for its distinctive buildings with wood siding and shingles. One of its structures, Condominium 1, won the American Institute of Architects Gold Medal in 1991 and is now on the National Register of Historic Places.

The community's hard-won coastal access points make The Sea Ranch a good place to stop for a short beach stroll. There is public access to six beaches. One of the best is **Black Point Beach** (35050 Hwy. 1, 707/785-2377, www. searanchsales.com/access-trails-beaches, 6am-sunset daily summer, 8am-sunset daily winter, free), a 0.5-mile trail to a 0.25-mile-long beach that offers a reliable break for surfers and a place to take in wildflowers during the spring.

Many vacation rentals are scattered throughout Sea Ranch; some are right by the coast. Rental options include **Sea Ranch Vacation Homes** (707/884-4235, https://searanchrentals.com) and **Ocean View Properties** (707/884-3538, https:// stayinsearanch.com).

Getting There

It is an easy 12-mile (19.5-km) drive on CA-1 from Salt Point State Park north to The Sea Ranch (stopping at the Stewarts Point General Store).

★ The Sea Ranch Chapel

Looking from the outside like a wooden stingray with a plume on top, **The Sea Ranch Chapel** (mile marker 55.66, Hwy. 1 at Bosun's Reach, www. thesearanchchapel.org, sunrise-sunset daily) is one of the smallest and most creatively designed places of worship that you'll ever see. Designed by architect James Hubble, this tiny building's beautiful interior has polished redwood benches, three stained-glass windows, and a stone floor with an inserted mosaic, and there are local seashells and sea urchins embedded throughout the structure.

Annapolis Winery

You'll find a pleasant coastal climate and a short list of classic California wines at **Annapolis Winery** (26055 Soda Springs Rd., Annapolis, 707/886-5460, www. annapoliswinery.com, noon-5pm daily, tasting fee $5). At this small, family-owned winery 7 miles (11.5 km) east of Sea Ranch, you can taste pinot, cabernet, zinfandel, and port, depending on what they've made this year and what's in stock. Take a glass outside to enjoy the views from the estate vineyards out over the forested mountains.

Sea Ranch Golf Links

With its front nine holes perched above the Pacific, the **Sea Ranch Golf Links** (42000 Hwy. 1, 707/785-2468, www. searanchgolf.com, $57-67) are like the legendary golf courses at Pebble Beach except without the crowds. Designed by Robert Muir Graves, the course also allows you to putt past redwood trees.

Gualala

With a population of 585, Gualala (wa-LA-la) feels like a metropolis along the CA-1 corridor in this region. (It has two gas stations *and* two supermarkets.) Named for the Pomo Indian word "water coming down," Gualala is where the Gualala River flows into the sea.

Since 1961, the **Art in the Redwoods Festival** (46501 Gualala Rd., 707/884-1138, www.gualalaarts.org, mid-Aug.) and its parent organization, Gualala Arts, have been going strong. Taking place over the course of a long weekend in mid-August, the festival features gallery exhibitions, special dinners, a champagne preview, bell ringers, a quilt raffle, and awards for the artists.

Getting There

Gualala is 6 miles (9.5 km) north of The Sea Ranch and 60 miles (97 km) south of Fort Bragg on CA-1.

Gualala Point Regional Park

Gualala Point Regional Park (42401 CA-1, 707/785-2377, https://parks.sonomacounty.ca.gov, 6am-sunset daily summer, 8am-sunset daily winter, $7) is across the Gualala River and is a great place to take in the area's natural features. The park's hiking trails include an ADA-accessible path from the visitors center to the beach, where piles of driftwood sit scattered about like jacks. The park's **Bluff Top Trail** (3 mi/4.8 km one-way, 1.5 hours, moderate) connects Gualala Point to Sea Ranch and its beach access.

A wholly unique feature of the park is its *serge* (pronounced "sayr-gay"), ceremonial hitching posts of the indigenous Sakha people that were built as symbols of their connection to the earth. The large wooden poles were constructed in 2014 by Siberian wood carvers and decorated with carved horse heads. (It is believed that 16 Sakha people resided at nearby Fort Ross in the early 1800s.)

Shopping

Four-Eyed Frog (Cypress Village, 39130 Ocean Dr., 707/884-1333, www.foureyedfrog.com, 10am-6pm Mon.-Sat., 11am-5pm Sun.) is a community-owned bookstore with new hardcovers, some used titles, and a section of books about Sonoma and Mendocino. The friendly staff will offer you free coffee while you browse.

Food

★ **Trinks Café** (39140 CA-1, 707/884-1713, http://trinkscafe.com, 7am-4pm Mon.-Tues. and Sat., 7am-4pm and 5pm-8pm Wed.-Fri., 8am-4pm Sun., $5-14) is a local favorite that serves breakfast and lunch along with occasional dinners (Wed.-Fri.). Located in a small shopping center (behind the sign for Seacliff Lodging), the café does a brisk business and is led by graduates of the California Culinary Academy. Order one of their popular breakfast sandwiches, a BLT, or other menu items at the counter.

The **Gualala Hotel** (39301 CA-1, 707/884-3471, 11am-2pm and 5pm-9pm Thurs.-Mon., 4pm-9pm Tues., $10-15) first opened in 1903 and has had quite a history. Lumberjacks used to stay here for just $9 a month, and there's a rumor that it serviced the logging industry as a brothel. It has hosted dignitaries like author Jack London, Chief Justice Earl Warren, and actor Fred MacMurray. Its latest incarnation is a popular pub with 12 beers on tap, local wine, and cocktails. The menu includes fresh fish from Point Arena and build-your-own burgers. Entertainment includes lively locals, live music, and a game room with pool and shuffleboard.

MendoViné (39145 S. Hwy. 1, 707/896-2650, www.mendovinelounge.com, 6:30pm-9:30pm Thurs.-Sat. summer, 6pm-9pm Thurs.-Sun. winter, $9-12) is a wine lounge with a curated selection of local reds and whites. They also do small plates with an international flair, served to the sounds of the occasional jazz band.

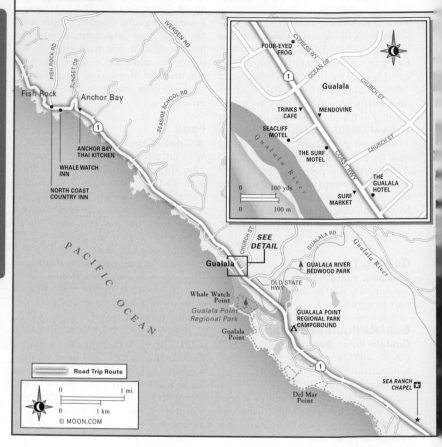

North in the community of Anchor Bay, **Anchor Bay Thai Kitchen** (35517 CA-1, Anchor Bay, 707/884-4141, http://anchorbaythai.com, noon-3pm and 5pm-9pm Tues.-Sun., $12-21) adds local flavor to traditional Thai. Locally caught salmon often appear in special entrées. The Thai beer Singha is on the drink menu, as are many local craft beers and wines.

The ★ **Surf Market** (39250 S. Hwy. 1, 707/884-4184, www.surfsuper.com, 7:30am-8pm Sat.-Wed., 7:30am-9pm Thurs.-Fri. summer, 7:30am-8pm daily winter) is the best supermarket south of Mendocino. This clean, upscale market has local produce, a deli with made-to-order sandwiches, a butcher shop with house-made sausages, a good wine selection, and a coffee stand as well as aisles of gourmet food items. They also grill tritip, chicken, and baby-back ribs on Friday and Saturday.

The Gualala **farmers market** (47950 Center St., 707/884-3726, www.sonomacounty.com, 9:30am-12:30pm Sat. May-Oct.) is at the Gualala Community Center.

Accommodations

When it comes to food and lodging in Gualala, you're not going to hear so many of those Sonoma and Mendocino County adjectives (luxurious, elegant, pricey), but you will find choices.

Within walking distance of Gualala's restaurants, **The Surf Motel** (39170 Hwy. 1, 707/884-3571 or 888/451-7873, www.surfinngualala.com, $149-350) is a good option for the budget-conscious. A few of the more expensive rooms have ocean views, but a full hot breakfast, flat-screen TVs with DVD players, gas fireplace heaters, and wireless Internet access are included for all guests. A little patio out back overlooks the beach and has some chairs, barbecue grills, and a fire pit. The Surf Motel is one of the two places in town to access the Bluff Trail.

In downtown Gualala, the **Seacliff Motel** (39140 Hwy. 1, 800/400-5053, 707/884-1213, www.seacliffmotel.com, $165-205) sits perched on a bluff with views of the river and beach. Each of the 16 units has a private deck, whirlpool spa, and gas fireplace to up the romance level. Guests are greeted with sparkling cider and chocolates upon arrival. Trinks Café is mere feet away.

The **Whale Watch Inn** (35100 Hwy. 1, 800/942-5342, www.whalewatchinn.com, $200-300) specializes in romance. Each of its 18 individually decorated, luxuriously appointed rooms has an ocean view and a wood-burning stove; most also have whirlpool tubs. Some hot tubs are on outdoor decks with views of the Pacific. Every morning, a hot breakfast is delivered to your room. Explore the beach below via a staircase on the grounds.

North of Gualala, the **North Coast Country Inn** (34591 S. Hwy. 1, 707/884-4537, www.northcoastcountryinn.com, $220-255) was once part of a coastal sheep ranch. Six rooms are outfitted with antique furnishings and fireplaces; three also have kitchenettes. Mornings begin with a hot breakfast buffet.

Camping

Two nearby parks provide good camping options: **Gualala River Redwood Park** (46001 Gualala Rd., 707/884-3533, www.gualalapark.com, May-Oct., day use $5 pp, sites $47-54) and **Gualala Point Regional Park** (42401 Hwy. 1, 707/565-2267, http://parks.sonomacounty.ca.gov, day use $7, sites $44), 1 mile (1.6 km) south of the town of Gualala. Both places offer access to redwoods, the ocean, and the river.

Point Arena

A small coastal town south of its namesake point, Point Arena might be one of the North Coast's best secrets. The town's Main Street is CA-1, which has a couple of bars, restaurants, markets, and the Arena Theater. One mile from the downtown section is the scenic Point Arena Cove, which has a small fishing pier with rocky beaches on either side. The cove feels like the town's true center, a meeting place where fisherfolk take in the conditions of the ocean. Just north of Point Arena Cove is the California Coastal National Monument Point Arena-Stornetta Unit, a stunning coastal park.

Getting There

Point Arena is 10 miles (16 km) north of Gualala on CA-1, and about 120 miles (195 km) north of San Francisco.

Point Arena Lighthouse

Although its magnificent Fresnel lens no longer turns through the night, the **Point Arena Lighthouse** (45500 Lighthouse Rd., 707/882-2809 or 877/725-4448, www. pointarenalighthouse.com, 10am-4:30pm daily summer, 10am-3:30pm daily winter, adults $7.50, children $1) remains a Coast Guard light and fog station. But what makes this beacon special is its history. When the 1906 earthquake hit San Francisco, it jolted the land all the way up the coast, severely damaging the Point

Arena Lighthouse. When the structure was rebuilt two years later, engineers devised an aboveground foundation that gives the lighthouse both its distinctive shape and additional structural stability.

The lighthouse's extensive interpretive museum, which is housed in the fog station beyond the gift shop, includes the lighthouse's Fresnel lens. Docent-led **tours** climb 145 steep steps to the top of the lighthouse and are well worth the trip, both for the views of the lighthouse from the top and for the fascinating story of its destruction and rebirth through the 1906 earthquake as told by the knowledgeable staff. Catch your breath by taking in the surrounding coastline from Manchester State Beach to the north to the California Coastal National Monument Point Arena-Stornetta Unit to the south.

B. Bryan Preserve

Antelope, zebras, and giraffes wander around the 110-acre **B. Bryan Preserve** (130 Riverside Dr., 707/882-2297, http://bbryanpreserve.com, tours 9:30am and 4pm daily summer, 9:30am and 3:30pm daily winter, adults $35, children under 11 $20). Take a one-hour tour of the preserve or spend a night in one of three lodging options on-site ($215-235).

★ California Coastal National Monument

The 1,655-acre **Point Arena-Stornetta Unit** of the **California Coastal National Monument** (Point Arena Cove north to Manchester State Park, 707/468-4000, www.blm.gov, sunrise-sunset daily) is like a greatest-hits compilation of the California coast: vertigo-inducing cliffs, far-ranging ocean views, sea arches, rocky points, and tidepools.

The area can be explored by miles of trails including the superb **hike** that starts from behind the Point Arena City Hall and continues 3.5 miles (5.6 km) to Lighthouse Road. Walk another 0.5 mile on the road to visit the **Point Arena Lighthouse.** Parking is available at Point

Arena City Hall and at the pullouts along Lighthouse Road. For a trail map, visit www.mendocinolandtrust.org.

★ Bowling Ball Beach

Bowling Ball Beach (Schooner Gulch State Beach, Schooner Gulch Rd. and Hwy. 1, 3 mi/4.8 km south of Point Arena, 707/937-5804, www.parks.ca.gov) is one of the many quirky natural treasures of the North Coast. At low tide, the blanket of seawater pulls away to reveal a nifty natural phenomenon: an impressively straight line of nearly spherical boulders the size of tractor tires. Long divots in the exposed rocky shelf below hold the stones in place. The geologic oddity is the result of several natural occurrences: concretions, tilted outcrops of strata, and wave erosion. Together they make for an awe-inspiring sight and a photo that is sure to be the envy of others. Be sure to consult a tide chart for the best time to visit.

Getting There

Schooner Gulch State Beach is 10 miles (16 km) north of Gualala and 3 miles (4.8 km) south of Point Arena on CA-1. To get there, cross over Schooner Gulch Bridge and look for a dirt pullout on the west side of the highway. (Face your vehicle to the south to avoid a ticket.)

Two trails lead to two different beaches from the parking area. The southern trail leads to **Schooner Gulch Beach,** a wide, sandy expanse with rocky headlands and a stream flowing into the sea. The northern trail leads to **Bowling Ball Beach.** The end of the trail is steep and has a rope to help descend. Once on the beach, hike north about 0.25 mile to find the photoworthy sight.

Entertainment and Events

The onetime vaudeville **Arena Theater** (214 Main St., 707/882-3456, www.arenatheater.org) was also a movie palace when it opened in 1929. In the 1990s, the old theater got a facelift that returned it to its art deco glory. Today, you can see

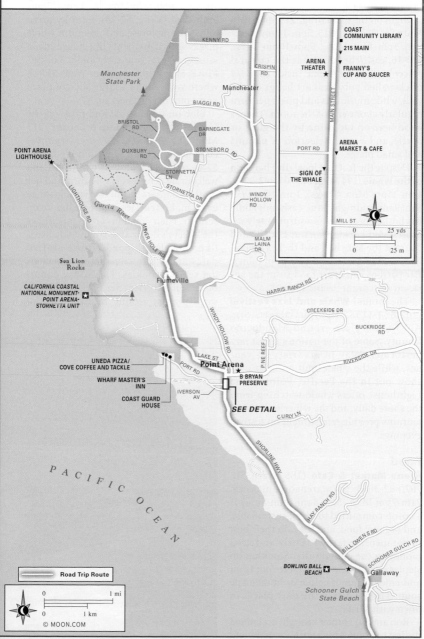

Point Arena

KENNY RD

Manchester State Park

CRISPIN RD

Manchester

BIAGGI RD

BRISTOL RD

BARNEGATE DR

DUXBURY RD

STONEBORO RD

POINT ARENA LIGHTHOUSE

STORNETTA LN

STORNETTA DR

WINDY HOLLOW RD

LIGHTHOUSE RD

Garcia River

MINER HOLE RD

MALM LAINA DR

Sea Lion Rocks

CALIFORNIA COASTAL NATIONAL MONUMENT– POINT ARENA– STORNETTA UNIT

Flumeville

HARRIS RANCH RD

CREEKSIDE DR

BUCKRIDGE RD

WINDY HOLLOW RD

PINE REEF

RIVERSIDE DR

UNEDA PIZZA/ COVE COFFEE AND TACKLE

LAKE ST

Point Arena

B BRYAN PRESERVE

WHARF MASTER'S INN

PORT RD

IVERSON AV

COAST GUARD HOUSE

SEE DETAIL

CURLY LN

SHORLINE HWY

P A C I F I C   O C E A N

HAY RANCH RD

BILL OWENS RD

SCHOONER GULCH RD

BOWLING BALL BEACH

Gallaway

Schooner Gulch State Beach

Road Trip Route

0   1 mi
0   1 km

© MOON.COM

Detail inset

COAST COMMUNITY LIBRARY

215 MAIN

ARENA THEATER ★

FRANNY'S CUP AND SAUCER

MAIN STREET

PORT RD

ARENA MARKET & CAFE

SIGN OF THE WHALE

MILL ST

0   25 yds
0   25 m

recent box-office films, new documentaries, and unusual independent films, or a live musical or theatrical show.

Right on the main drag, **215 Main** (215 Main St., 707/882-3215, 5pm-11pm Wed.-Sat., 5pm-8pm Mon., 5pm-10pm Tues., $10-16, cash/check only) is the cultural epicenter of Point Arena. Inside the cozy brick-walled pub, local art hangs on the wall, while music acts and poets perform regularly at one end of the room. There's good beer on tap, wine by the glass or bottle, and a small selection of paninis and small plates.

Despite the fact that local dive bar **Sign of the Whale** (194 Main St., 707/882-2259, 1pm-11pm Mon.-Thurs., 1pm-1am Fri.-Sat., 9am-midnight Sun., cash only) only has bottled beer, there's a surprisingly sophisticated cocktail menu. Locals hold court at the long bar, and there's a jukebox, arcade game, and two pool tables. Bar patrons can order food from the adjacent restaurant Pacific Plate.

The annual **Whale and Jazz Festival** (707/884-1138, http://gualalaarts.org, Apr.) takes place around Mendocino County. Some of the nation's finest jazz performers play in a variety of venues, while the whales put on their own show out in the Pacific. Point Arena Lighthouse offers whale-watching from the shore daily, and the wineries and restaurants provide refreshment on festival evenings.

Food

Arena Market & Café (185 Main St., 707/882-3663, www.arenaorganics.org, 7am-7pm Mon.-Sat., 8am-6pm Sun.) is a co-op committed to local, sustainable, and organic food, and they do their best to compensate farmers fairly and keep money in the community. Stock up on staples or sit at one of the tables out front and enjoy a cup of coffee or homemade soup. They're one of the only places in town with Wi-Fi.

Rob and Jill Hunter brought acclaimed dining to Point Arena with Pangaea and Uneda Eat. Their latest endeavor is **Uneda Pizza** (Point Arena Cove, 790 Port Rd., 707/882-1960, http://unedaeat.com, 3pm-9pm Wed.-Mon., $7-28), a funky pizza joint serving house and premium whole pizzas with ingredients like house-made sausage. Try to come early for the Lucky 7 Pint & Slice deal (3pm-6pm Wed.-Mon.), where you can get a large slice of pizza and a pint of craft beer for $7.

Blue on the outside and pink on the inside, ★ **Franny's Cup & Saucer** (213 Main St., 707/882-2500, www.frannys-cupandsaucer.com, 8am-4pm Wed.-Sat., $2-6, cash/check only) is whimsical and welcoming. The owners, Franny and her mother, Barbara, do all the baking—they even make truffles and candies from scratch. Their creations are as fanciful as the bakery's decor and can include items like chocolate-dipped truffle-stuffed dates and white chocolate and lavender sea-salt cookies. The Friday donuts often sell out. Heartier options include mini-pizzas, croque monsieurs, and

mind-blowing bacon slippers. It's take-out only, perfect for a picnic.

Slightly north of town, **Rollerville Café** (22900 S. Hwy. 1, 707/882-2077, www.rollervillecafe.com, 8am-2pm Sun.-Thurs., 8am-7pm Fri.-Sat., lunch $8-10, dinner $20-24) is a small, homey place catering to resort guests, locals, and travelers. Dinner may seem a little pricey, but lunch is available all day. Breakfast (order the crab cakes Benedict) is served until 11am.

Cove Coffee and Tackle (790 Port Rd., 707/882-2665, www.covecoffee-ptarena.com, 7am-3pm daily, $3-12) is part coffee shop, part surf shop, part tackle shop. Located by the cove, it attracts locals with coffee and tasty items like Nate's Special, an egg sandwich with pesto, cream cheese, sausage, onion, and Swiss cheese. There's everything from copies of *The New York Times* to surfboards to local art for sale inside.

Accommodations

From 1901 to 1957, the **Coast Guard House** (695 Arena Cove, 707/882-2442 or 800/524-9320, www.coastguard-house.com, $185-295) was a working Coast Guard lifesaving station. Now the main building hosts overnight guests who enjoy views of Point Arena Cove. Four rooms are available, including a suite with two bedrooms. Two detached cottages offer more privacy. The friendly and informative innkeepers serve a hot breakfast in the main house every morning, and restaurants are just a short walk away.

The **Wharf Master's Inn** (785 Port Rd., 707/882-3171 or 800/932-4031, https://wharfmasters.com, $109-500) is built around the historic wharf master's home, a Victorian house dating from 1865. The historic building has three bedrooms and two decks, and can accommodate eight people. Or secure a room in one of the adjacent buildings, where some rooms include soaking tubs. The inn could use a

the Point Arena section of the California Coastal National Monument

touch-up, but the friendly staff and hillside location above Point Arena make this a pleasant place to spend an evening.

For a unique overnight, stay in the old lightkeepers' quarters at ★ **Point Arena Lighthouse** (877/725-4448, 707/882-2809, www.pointarenalighthouse.com, $150-450, cleaning fee, 2-night min. weekends). Located on a spit of land with views of the ocean, this is the real deal. The assistant keepers' homes have three bedrooms, two baths, a kitchen, and a wood-burning fireplace. Rooms or cottages include a free tour of the nearby lighthouse, a small bottle of wine, and chocolates. It makes a great base for exploring the North Coast.

Manchester State Park

TOP EXPERIENCE

Manchester State Park (44500 Kinney Ln., Manchester, 707/882-2463, www.parks.ca.gov, day use free) is a wild place perfect for a long, solitary beach walk. The coast is littered with bleached white driftwood and logs that lie on the dark sand like giant bones amid crashing waves. Even the water offshore is protected as part of the 3,782-acre Point Arena State Marine Reserve. At the southwestern tip of the park is Arena Rock, a nautical hazard known for sinking at least six ships before the construction of the nearby Point Arena Lighthouse to the south. Part of the 1,500 acres of onshore parkland was once a dairy ranch.

Getting There

Manchester State Park is 7 miles (11.5 km) north of the town of Point Arena on CA-1.

Camping

There's a **campground** (Fri.-Sun. late May-early Sept., first-come, first-served, $25) with 41 sites and basic amenities, including fire pits, picnic tables, and pit toilets. Some environmental campsites in the dunes are accessible via a short hike.

Elk

The town of Elk used to be called Greenwood, after the family of Caleb Greenwood, who settled here in about 1850. Details of the story vary, but it is widely believed that Caleb was part of a mission to rescue survivors of the Donner Party after their rough winter near Truckee.

Getting There

The drive from Point Arena north to Elk is 20 miles (32 km) on CA-1.

Greenwood State Beach

From the mid-19th century until the 1920s, the stretch of shore at **Greenwood State Beach** (Hwy. 1, 707/937-5804, www.parks.ca.gov) was a stop for large ships carrying timber to points of sale in San Francisco and sometimes even China. The **visitors center** (10am-4pm Wed.-Sun. Mar.-Nov.) displays photographs and exhibits about Elk's past in the lumber business. It also casts light on the Native American heritage of the area and the natural resources that are still abundant.

A short hike demonstrates what makes this area so special. From the parking lot, follow the trail down toward the ocean. You'll soon come to a fork; to the right is a picnic area. Follow the left fork to another picnic site and then, soon afterward, the beach. Turn left and walk about 0.25 mile to reach Greenwood Creek. Shortly past it is a cliff, at which point you have to turn around and walk back up the hill. Even in the short amount of time it takes to do this walk, you'll experience lush woods, sandy cliffs, and dramatic ocean overlooks. In winter, the walk can be dark and blustery and even more intriguing, although it's a pleasure in any season.

Greenwood State Beach is alongside the town of Elk, 10-15 miles (16-24 km) north of Point Arena and about 17 miles (27 km) south of Mendocino.

Food and Accommodations

With a perfect location in the center of town and across the street from the ocean, **Queenie's Roadhouse Café** (6061 Hwy. 1, 707/877-3285, http://queenies-roadhousecafe.com, 8am-3pm Thurs.-Mon., $9-18) is the place to go for hot food and a friendly atmosphere. Expect to be full for a while after leaving.

The **Beacon Light by the Sea** (7401 S. Hwy. 1, south of Elk, 707/877-3311, 5pm-11pm Fri.-Sat.) is the best bar in the area. Its colorful owner, R. D. Beacon, was born in Elk and has run the Beacon Light since 1971. He claims it's the only place you can get hard liquor for 14 miles in any direction. With 85 different brands of vodka, 20 whiskeys, and 15 tequilas, there's something for every sort of drinker. On clear days, the views stretch all the way to the Point Arena Lighthouse.

Perched on a hillside over stunning Greenwood State Beach, the ★ **Elk Cove Inn** (6300 S. Hwy. 1, 800/275-2967, www.elkcoveinn.com, $195-395) offers luxury accommodations, generous hospitality, and superb views of the Pacific, studded with islands and a scattering of offshore rocks. Check-in comes with a complimentary cocktail or glass of wine and a welcome basket filled with wine, fruit, popcorn, and freshly baked cookies. Choose from rooms in the main house, cozy cabins with an ocean view, or luxurious suites with jetted soaking tubs and private balconies or patios. A private staircase leads down to the beach below. There's also a full-service day spa with a sauna and aromatherapy steam shower. The innkeepers make your stay top notch, from the port wine and chocolates in the rooms to the big morning breakfast buffet of Southern comfort food with a glass of champagne.

Albion and Little River

The tiny towns of Albion and Little River are right along CA-1, with a state park and several plush places to stay.

Getting There

Albion is along CA-1 almost 30 miles (48 km) north of Point Arena and about 8 miles (13 km) south of Mendocino. Little River is about 5 miles (8 km) farther north, also on CA-1.

Van Damme State Park

The centerpiece of **Van Damme State Park** (Hwy. 1, 3 mi/4.8 km south of Mendocino, 707/937-5804, www.parks.ca.gov, 8am-9pm daily, $8) is the **Pygmy Forest,** where you'll see a true biological rarity: mature yet tiny cypress and pine trees perpetually stunted by a combination of always-wet ground and poor soil nutrient conditions. To get there, drive along Airport Road to the trail parking lot (opposite the county airport) and follow the wheelchair-accessible loop trail (0.25 mi, easy). You can also get there by hiking along the **Fern Canyon Trail** (7 mi/11.5 km round-trip, 4 hours, difficult).

Kayak Mendocino launches **Sea Cave Nature Tours** (707/813-7117, www.kayakmendocino.com, 11:30am, 2pm, and sunset, $60 pp) from Van Damme State Park. No previous experience is necessary; the expert guides provide all the equipment you need and teach you how to paddle your way through the sea caves and around the harbor seals.

Food

Ledford House Restaurant (3000 N. Hwy. 1, Albion, 707/937-0282, www.ledfordhouse.com, 5pm-close Wed.-Sun., $19-30) is beautiful even from a distance; you'll see it on the hill as you drive up CA-1. With excellent food and nightly jazz performances, it's one of the true "special occasion" choices in the area. Try to reserve a table for sunset.

A fine restaurant with stunning coast views, the **5200 Restaurant & Lounge** (Heritage House Resort, 5200 N. Hwy. 1, Little River, 707/202-9000, http://heritagehouseresort.com, 7am-10am and 5pm-9pm Mon.-Fri., 7am-11am and 5pm-9pm Sat.-Sun., lounge 4pm-10pm daily, $16-40) has farm-to-fork cuisine for breakfast and dinner. The lounge has a great happy hour (4pm-6pm) in a comfortable setting that includes a fireplace, couches, and board games.

Start the day at ★ **Circa '62** (7051 N. Hwy. 1, Little River, 707/937-5525, www.schoolhousecreek.com, 8am-11am Mon. and Thurs.-Fri., 8am-noon Sat.-Sun., $9-16). Housed within a cozy blue-and-white former schoolhouse on the grounds of the Inn at Schoolhouse Creek, the building oozes charm, from its fireplace to its ocean-facing windows. Yet it's the glorious food that makes this place worthwhile. The creative, oft-changing menu includes steak-and-egg tacos, kimchi pancakes, and a hash-brown waffle drenched in sausage gravy.

Wild Fish (7750 N. Hwy. 1, Little River, 707/937-3055, www.wild-fish.com, 5pm-9pm Sun.-Thurs., 5pm-9:30pm Fri.-Sat., $28-39) utilizes local assets, from organic produce to wild-caught seafood, on an ever-changing menu. The wild king salmon and petrale sole are caught right out of Fort Bragg's Noyo Harbor.

Tucked into a corner of a convenience store, the **Little River Market Grill & Gourmet Deli** (7746 N. Hwy. 1, Little River, 707/937-5133, grill 9am-2:50pm daily, deli 9am-4pm daily, $8) is a local favorite. This better-than-average deli has a wide range of options, including burgers, pulled pork sandwiches, and fish tacos. Vegetarian options include the tasty pesto veggie and avocado sandwich. Grab a sandwich for a picnic on the coast.

Accommodations

There's no place quite like ★ **The Andiron** (6051 N. Hwy. 1, Little River, 707/937-1543, www.theandiron.com, $119-274). The one- and two-room cabins sit in a meadow above CA-1 and are filled with curiosities and kitsch. Every room is different: One has a unique camel-shaped bar, while another has a coin-operated vibrating bed. Most have vintage board games, View-Masters, and an eclectic library of books. Amenities include wooden decks and small flat-screen TVs. A hot tub is available for guests. The fun-loving owners throw happy hour parties every weekend, including "Fondue Fridays," when they also serve local beers and wines.

A longtime lodging destination, the ★ **Heritage House Resort** (5200 Hwy. 1, Little River, 707/202-9000, http://heritagehouseresort.com, $220-420) has a rich history that includes a past as the hideout of bank robber "Baby Face" Nelson and the setting of the 1978 film *Same Time, Next Year*. Perched on stunning cliffs pocked with coves, the numerous buildings spread across 37 acres. The rooms are top tier: Each is enhanced by private decks, rain showers, and wood-burning or gas fireplaces. The units are priced according to proximity to the water and quality of the view. The resort has a full-service spa and restored garden.

The **Albion River Inn** (3790 N. Hwy. 1, Albion, 707/937-1919 or 800/479-7944, www.albionriverinn.com, $136-395) is a gorgeous and serene setting for an away-from-it-all vacation. This cliffside inn is all about romance. A full breakfast is included in the room rates; pets and smoking are not allowed, and there are no TVs.

The **Little River Inn** (7901 N. Hwy. 1, Little River, 707/937-5942 or 888/466-5683, www.littleriverinn.com, $205-379) appeals to coastal vacationers who like a little luxury. It has a nine-hole golf course and two lighted tennis courts. All recreation areas overlook the Pacific, which crashes on the shore just across the highway from the inn. The sprawling white Victorian house and barns hide the expansiveness of the grounds, which also have a great restaurant and a charming sea-themed bar. Relax even more at the in-house Spa at Little River Inn.

Camping

There's camping on the coast at **Van Damme State Park** (Hwy. 1, Little River, 707/937-5804, www.parks.ca.gov, reservations 800/444-7275, www.reservecalifornia.com, $35), 3 miles (4.8 km) south of Mendocino. The appealing campground offers picnic tables, fire rings, and food lockers, as well as restrooms and hot showers. The park's 1,831 acres include beaches as well as forest, so there's lots of natural beauty to enjoy. Reservations are strongly encouraged.

★ Mendocino

Perched on a headland surrounded by the Pacific, Mendocino is one of the most picturesque towns on the California coast. Quaint bed-and-breakfasts, art colonies, and local sustainable dining add to its charm, making it a favorite for romantic weekend getaways.

Once a logging town, Mendocino was reborn as an artist community in the 1950s. One of its most striking buildings is the town's Masonic Hall, dating from 1866 and adorned with a redwood statue of Father Time on its roof. Many New Englanders settled in the region in its early years. With its old water towers and historic buildings, it resembles a New England fishing village—so much so that it played one in the long-running TV series *Murder, She Wrote*. It was also a stand-in for Monterey in the 1955 James Dean film *East of Eden*.

Getting There

From CA-1, the drive north from Elk to Mendocino is 15 miles (24 km).

Sights

Mendocino has a fairly compact downtown area, Mendocino Village, with a concentration of restaurants, shops, and inns just a few blocks from the beach.

Mendocino Art Center

The town of Mendocino has long been an inspiration and a gathering place for artists of many varieties, and the **Mendocino Art Center** (45200 Little Lake St., 707/937-5818 or 800/653-3328, www.mendocinoartcenter.org, 11am-4pm daily, donation) gives these diverse artists a community, provides them with opportunities for teaching and learning, and displays contemporary works. Since 1959, the center has offered artist workshops and retreats. Today it has a flourishing schedule of events and classes, five galleries, and a sculpture garden. You can even drop in and make some art of your own. Supervised open studios in ceramics, jewelry making, watercolor, sculpture, and drawing take place throughout the year (call for specific schedules, $12-15 per session).

Kelley House Museum

The mission of the lovely, stately **Kelley House Museum** (45007 Albion St., 707/937-5791, www.kelleyhousemuseum.org, 11am-3pm Fri.-Mon., free) is to preserve the history of Mendocino for future generations. The permanent exhibits chronicle a notorious local shipwreck and the Native American population, while a collection of photos details the town in present times and 100 years ago. Ask about the town's water-rights issues for a great lesson in the untold history of the Mendocino Coast. On weekends, docents lead two-hour **walking tours** (11am Sat.-Sun., $10) that detail Mendocino's history. Self-guided **audio tours** ($10) are available through the museum (11am-3pm Fri.-Sun.) or research office (1pm-4pm Mon.-Fri.).

Mendocino

California
Coastal
National
Monument

Mendocino
Headlands
State Park

Goat
Island

**SEE
DETAIL**

BLACKBERRY
INN

LARKIN RD

RAVEN LN

FORD ST

PALLETTE DR

HILLS RANCH RD

CLARK ST

BLAIR ST

CAHTO
ST

Hillcrest
Cemetery

Friendship
Park

COVELO ST

LITTLE LAKE RD

PINE ST

PINE ST

KASTEN ST

FORD ST

LANSING ST

HOWARD ST

SCHOOL ST

EVERGREEN ST

Evergreen
Cemetery

JACKSON ST

CRESTWOOD DR

LITTLE LAKE ST

UKIAH ST

CALPELLA ST

KELLY ST

ALBION ST

MAIN ST

Mendocino
Rotary
Park

MAIN ST

Mendocino
Headlands
State Park

Mendocino
Headlands
State Park

Mendocino
Bay

Big River

THE STANFORD INN
BY THE SEA
ECO-RESORT

S. BIG RIVER RD

RAVENS
RESTAURANT

COMPTCHE UKIAH RD

Mendocino
Headlands
State Park

BREWERY GULCH RD

MISS MUFFET DR

BREWERY GULCH
INN

Detail Map:

Hillcrest
Cemetery

COVELO ST

LITTLE LAKE RD

PATTERSON'S
PUB

SCHOOL ST

★ MENDOCINO ART CENTER/
MENDOCINO THEATRE COMPANY

LITTLE LAKE ST

Mendocino
Headlands
State Park

FORD ST

LANSING ST

HOWARD ST

PINE ST

LUNA
TRATTORIA

CAFE
BEAUJOLAIS

GOOD LIFE
CAFE

KASTEN ST

MACCALLUM
HOUSE INN

MENDOCINO
CAFE

BLUE DOOR
INN

SWEETWATER
INN AND SPA

EVERGREEN ST

Evergreen
Cemetery

UKIAH ST

TRILLIUM
CAFE & INN

ALBION ST

★ KELLEY HOUSE
MUSEUM

MAIN ST

FOG EATER
CAFE

DICK'S PLACE

PANACHE
GALLERY

HIGHLIGHT GALLERY

GALLERY BOOKSHOP

0   100 yds

0   100 m

0   0.10 m

0   0.10 km

Road Trip Route

© MOON.COM

Mendocino Headlands State Park

No trip to Mendocino is complete without a walk along the rugged coastline of **Mendocino Headlands State Park** (west of town, 707/937-5804, www.parks. ca.gov, sunrise-sunset daily). A series of trails along the seaside cliffs west of town offer views of the area's sea caves and coves. It's a favorite spot for painters and photographers hoping to capture the majesty of the coast. In winter, the park is a great vantage point for viewing migrating gray whales. In town, the **Historic Ford House** (735 Main St., 707/937-5397, www.mendoparks.org, 11am-4pm daily, free, donations encouraged) doubles as the Mendocino Headlands State Park Visitor Center. A favorite display in the center is a scale model of the town, constructed in 1890.

Point Cabrillo Light Station

Located between Mendocino and Fort Bragg, the beautiful **Point Cabrillo Light Station Historic Park** (45300 Lighthouse Rd., 707/937-6122, http://pointcabrillo. org, park sunrise-sunset daily; light station and museum 11am-4pm daily, $5) has been functioning since the early 1900s. The light station was absorbed into the California State Parks system in 2002 and is currently managed by a volunteer organization, the Point Cabrillo Lightkeepers Association. Take a tour of the famous Fresnel lens, learn about the infamous *Frolic* shipwreck of 1850, and explore the tidepool aquarium. For an overnight stay, rent the **lightkeeper's house** or two cottages on the grounds (800/262-7801, www.mendocinovacations.com, $192-470 per night) for two-night stays.

Entertainment and Events

Nightlife

For a place to hunker down over a pint, head to cozy **Patterson's Pub** (10485 Lansing St., 707/937-4782, www.pattersonspub.com, 10am-midnight daily). This traditional Irish-style pub is in the former rectory of a 19th-century Catholic church. It nods to the 21st century with six plasma TVs that screen current sporting events. Order a simple, filling meal at the tables or at the bar, where you'll find 14 beers on tap, a full-fledged wine list, and liquor imported from around the world.

So where do the locals go for a drink in Mendocino? That would be **Dick's Place** (45070 Main St., 707/937-6010, 11:30am-2am daily, cash only), an old-school bar with a mounted buck head draped in Christmas lights as decor. Dick's is easy to find: Look for the only neon sign on Main Street, in the shape of a martini glass. The bar includes a tiny replica of the establishment and a hallway of murals. Their spicy Bloody Mary is popular.

The Arts

The **Mendocino Theater Company** (45200 Little Lake St., 707/937-4477, www.mendocinotheatre.org, 8pm Thurs.-Sat., 2pm Sun., adults $25, students $12) offers a genuine small-theater experience. Plays are staged in the 75-seat Helen Schoeni Theater for an intimate night of live drama or comedy. The small, weathered old building exudes just the right kind of charm to draw in lovers of quirky community theater. But this little theater company has big goals, and it tends to take on thought-provoking work by contemporary playwrights.

Festivals and Events

For two weekends every March, the Point Cabrillo Light Station is host to the annual **Whale Festival** (707/961-6300, http://mendocinocoast.com, Mar., $5), a chance to get expert guidance as you scan the sea for migrating gray whales headed north for the summer.

In July, musicians descend on the coast for the **Mendocino Music Festival** (707/937-2044, www.mendocinomusic. com, July, prices vary). For 2.5 weeks, live performances are held at venues around the area. There's always chamber music, orchestral concerts, opera, jazz, and bluegrass, and there's usually world music, blues, singer-songwriters, and dance performances. A centerpiece of the festival is the famed big-band concert. In addition to 13 evenings of music, there are three series of daytime concerts: piano, jazz, and village chamber concerts. No series passes are available; all events require separate tickets.

Shopping

The galleries and boutiques of **Mendocino Village** are welcoming and fun, plus the whole downtown area is beautiful. It seems that every shop in the Main Street area has its own garden, and each fills with a riotous cascade of flowers in the summer.

Panache (45120 Main St., 707/937-1234, www.thepanachegallery.com, 10:30am-5pm daily) displays and sells beautiful works of art in all sorts of media—paintings, jewelry, sculpture, and art glass. Much of the artistic focus is inspired by the sea crashing just outside the large multi-room gallery. The wooden furniture and boxes are a special treat: Handmade treasures using rare woods are combined and then sanded and polished to silky-smooth finishes.

If you love fine woodworking and handcrafted furniture, don't miss the **Highlight Gallery** (45094 Main St., 707/937-3132, www.thehighlightgallery. com, 10am-5pm daily). Its roots are in woodwork, which it maintains as a focus, although the gallery also features glasswork, ceramics, painting, and sculpture.

The **Gallery Bookshop** (Main St. and Kasten St., 707/937-2665, www.gallerybookshop.com, 9:30am-6pm Sun.-Thurs., 9:30am-9pm Fri.-Sat.) is a large store with fiction from around the world along with the works of local authors. They host an array of literary events, too.

Sports and Recreation
Hiking
Russian Gulch State Park (Hwy. 1, 2

mi/3.2 km north of Mendocino, 707/937-5804, www.parks.ca.gov, $8) has its own **Fern Canyon Trail** (3 mi/4.8 km roundtrip, 2 hours, moderate), which winds into a second-growth redwood forest filled with lush green ferns. At the four-way junction, turn left to hike another 0.75 mile to the ever-popular waterfall. You'll likely be part of a crowd on summer weekends. Making a right at the four-way junction will take you on a 3-mile (4.8-km) loop, for a total hike of 6 miles (9.7 km) that leads to the top of the attractive little waterfall. If you prefer the shore to the forest, hike west to take in the lovely, wild headlands and see blowholes, grasses, and trawlers out seeking the day's catch. The biggest attraction is the **Devil's Punchbowl,** a collapsed sea cave. There's also a nice beach.

Kayaking and Stand-Up Paddleboarding
The shoreline on the Mendocino Coast is pocked with caves and coves that are ideal for kayaking or stand-up paddling. Some of the best can be accessed in the waters off Van Damme State Park. A short paddle north are some impressive sea caves that adventurous paddlers can pass through. **Kayak Mendocino** (707/813-7117, www.kayakmendocino. com, SUP rentals $25/two hours) has a bus parked by the beach that rents kayaks and SUPs. From there, guides lead SUP and kayak sea cave tours (11:30am and 2pm daily, adults $60, children under 12 $40).

To explore the relatively sedate waters of the Big River estuary, rent an outrigger or a sailing canoe from **Catch a Canoe & Bicycles Too** (Stanford Inn, 1 S. Big River Rd., 707/937-0273, www.catchacanoe. com, 9am-5pm daily, adults $35 pp for 3 hours, children 6-17 $15 pp). Guided **tours** (June-Sept., $65 pp) include an estuary excursion with a naturalist and a ride on an outrigger that utilizes solar energy.

Surfing

Big River is a beach break surf spot just south of the town of Mendocino where the Big River flows into the ocean. It's a place you can check out from CA-1, and on most days, all levels of surfers try their hand at surfing the break. More experienced surfers should try **Smuggler's Cove**, in Mendocino Bay on the south side of Big River. It's a reef break that usually only works during winter swells.

Scuba Diving

A good spot for abalone is **The Blowhole** (end of Main St.), a favorite summer lounging spot for locals. In the water, you'll find abalone and their empty shells; colorful, tiny nudibranchs; and occasionally, overly friendly seals. The kelp beds just offshore attract divers who don't fear cold water and want to check out the complex ecosystem. Abalone is strictly regulated; most species are endangered and can't be harvested. Check with the state Department of Fish and Game (916/445-0411, www.wildlife.ca.gov) for abalone season opening and closing dates, catch limits, licensing information, and the best spots to dive each year.

Spas

Relax on the Mendocino Coast at one of the many nearby spas. The **Sweetwater Spa & Inn** (44840 Main St., 800/300-4140, www.sweetwaterspa.com, 11am-10pm daily summer, 11am-9pm daily winter, $20-30/hour) rents indoor hot tubs and has a range of massage services ($90-154). They also have group tub and sauna rates ($15-20). The rustic buildings and garden setting complete the experience. Appointments are required for massage and private tubs, but walk-ins are welcome to use the communal tub and sauna.

Food

Mendocino has a weekly **farmers market** (Howard St. and Main St., www.mcfarm.org, noon-2pm Fri. May-Oct.), where you can find seasonal produce, flowers, fish, wine, honey, and more.

American

Publications including the *Wall Street Journal* rave about **Trillium Café** (10390 Kasten St., 707/937-3200, http://trilliummendocino.com, 11:30am-2:30pm and 5:30pm-8:30pm Sun.-Thurs., 11:30am-2:30pm and 5:30pm-9pm Fri.-Sat., $22-36). Menu options include locally caught fish and shellfish fettuccine. Dine inside by the fireplace or out on the deck overlooking a garden where many of the restaurant's ingredients grow.

Cafés

The **Goodlife Café & Bakery** (10483 Lansing St., 707/937-0836, www.goodlifecafemendo.com, 8am-4pm daily, $5-13) is a great place for an espresso drink, a freshly made pastry, or a sandwich on delicious, pillowy focaccia. There are lots of gluten-free options as well. The busy café has seating inside and outside.

One of the most appealing and dependable places is the **Mendocino Café** (10451 Lansing St., 707/937-6141, www.mendocinocafe.com, 11am-4pm and 5pm-9pm daily, $16-34). The café has good, simple, well-prepared food, a small children's menu, a wine list, and a beer list. Enjoy a Thai burrito, fresh local rockfish, or a steak in the warm, well-lit dining room. The café is in the gardens of Mendocino Village, and thanks to a heated patio, you can enjoy outdoor dining any time of day.

French

★ **Café Beaujolais** (961 Ukiah St., 707/937-5614, www.cafebeaujolais.com, 5:30pm-9pm Mon.-Tues., 11:30am-2:30pm and 5:30pm-9pm Wed.-Sun., $24-40) is a standout French-California restaurant in an area dense with great upscale cuisine. This charming, out-of-the-way spot is a few blocks from the center of Mendocino Village in an old vine-covered house. Despite the white

tablecloths and crystal, the atmosphere is casual at lunch and only slightly formal at dinner. The giant salads and delectable entrées are made with organic produce, humanely raised meats, and locally caught seafood. The portions are enormous but come half-size by request. The waitstaff are friendly, helpful, and knowledgeable about the menu and wine list. Reservations are available online.

On weekends, the café operates the on-site **Brickery Pizza** (11:30am-3pm Fri.-Sun., $10-16), which serves wood-fired pizzas topped with local ingredients—from house-made sausage to wild-foraged chanterelle mushrooms. Order your pizza to go from the window and enjoy it in the adjacent garden.

Italian

Luna Trattoria (955 Ukiah St., 707/962-3093, www.lunatrattoria.com, 5pm-9pm Tues.-Thurs. and Sun., 5pm-10pm Fri.-Sat., $12-29) is the place for Italian cuisine. The family recipes are from Northern Italy and include a sangiovese wine and cream sauce drenched pasta.

Vegetarian

Vegetarians and carnivores alike rave about **Ravens Restaurant** (Stanford Inn, 44850 Comptche Ukiah Rd., 707/937-5615 or 800/331-8884, www.ravensrestaurant.com, 8am-10:30am and 5:30pm-close daily, $12-27). Inside the lodge, which is surrounded by lush organic gardens, you'll find a big, open dining room. Many of the vegetarian and vegan dishes use produce from the inn's own organic farm. At breakfast, enjoy delicious vegetarian (or vegan, with tofu) scrambles, omelets, and Florentines, complete with homemade bread and English muffins. At dinner, try one of the seasonal vegetarian entrées. The wine list reflects organic, biodynamic, and sustainable-practice wineries.

From top to bottom: Mendocino; Point Cabrillo Light Station; the Brewery Gulch Inn.

The **Fog Eater Café** (45104 N. Main St., 707/397-1806, https://fogeatercafe.com, 3pm-9pm Wed.-Sun., Sun. brunch 10am-2pm, $7-22) serves Southern food with a vegetarian twist. The menu includes grits and red beans and rice along with cauliflower steak. There's also fried-green tomato biscuit sliders and a rotating pie of the day.

Accommodations
$150-250
The warm and welcoming **Blackberry Inn** (44951 Larkin Rd., 707/937-5281 or 800/950-7806, www.blackberryinn.biz, $135-225) is in the hills beyond the center of Mendocino. The inn looks like a town from the Old West. Each of the 16 charmingly decorated rooms has a different storefront outside, including the bank, the saloon, the barbershop, and the land-grant office. Amenities include plush, comfortable bedding cozied up with colonial-style quilts, along with microwaves, fridges, TVs, and free wireless Internet. The manager-hosts are the nicest you'll find anywhere.

Sweetwater Inn & Spa (44840 Main St., 800/300-4140, www.sweetwaterspa.com, $145-305) harks back to the days when Mendocino was a colony of starving artists. A redwood water tower was converted into a guest room, joined by a motley collection of detached cottages that guarantee privacy. Every guest room and cottage has its own style—you'll find a spiral staircase in one of the water towers, a hot tub on a redwood deck in the Garden Cottage, and fireplaces in many of the units. The eclectic decor makes each room different. Thick gardens surround the building complex, and a path leads back to the Garden Spa. The location, just past downtown on Main Street, is perfect for dining, shopping, and art walks. They also run **Sweetwater Vacation Home Rentals** (800/300-4140, http://sweetwatervacationrentals.com, $219-500), which rents apartments and homes in town.

The 1882 **MacCallum House** (45020 Albion St., 800/609-0492, www.maccallumhouse.com, $169-359) is the king of luxury on the Mendocino Coast. The facility includes several properties in addition to the main building in Mendocino Village. Choose from private cottages with hot tubs, suites with jetted tubs, and rooms with opulent antique appointments. There's a two-night minimum on weekends and a three-night minimum for most holidays. Room rates include a cooked-to-order breakfast.

The **Blue Door Inn** (10481 Howard St., 707/937-4892, www.bluedoorinn.com, $169-379) aims to spoil you. Five sleek, modern rooms come with flat-screen TVs and gas fireplaces. The two-course breakfast features homemade pastries and egg dishes delivered to your room.

Over $250
Set amid redwoods, the **Stanford Inn** (44850 Comptche Ukiah Rd., 707/937-5615 or 800/331-8884, www.stanfordinn.com, $370-595) is an upscale forest lodge. The location is convenient to hiking and only a short drive from Mendocino Village and the coast. Rooms have beautiful, honey wood-paneled walls, pretty furniture, and fluffy down comforters. Amenities include a wood-burning fireplace, Internet access, a pool, sauna and hot tub, and free use of mountain bikes. Gardens surrounding the resort are perfect for strolling after a complimentary vegan breakfast at the on-site Ravens Restaurant.

One mile south of the village, the ★ **Brewery Gulch Inn** (9401 Hwy. 1, 800/578-4454, www.brewerygulchinn.com, $385-545) provides a lot of amenities to guests staying in its 11 rooms, including a made-to-order hot breakfast and a light dinner buffet with wine. The rooms are modern and calming, with plush carpets, feather beds, and gas fireplaces; all have ocean views. Downstairs is a wonderful common area with a steel fireplace. Relax with a newspaper, book, or magazine from the extensive collection. There's also a collection of more than 500 DVDs to watch in the comfort of your room. Another option is the Serenity Cottage ($625/three-night minimum), a standalone oceanfront studio.

The beautifully restored 1909 **Point Cabrillo Head Lightkeeper's House** (45300 Lighthouse Rd., 707/937-5033, www.mendocinovacations.com, 2-night minimum, $307-1,163 for 2 nights) sits atop a cliff beside the Pacific, so you can watch for whales, dolphins, and seabirds without leaving the porch. Four bedrooms sleep eight people, with 4.5 baths and a very modern kitchen. Larger groups can rent two of the cottages nearby.

⚑ CA-128: Inland Mendocino Valley

About 60 miles (100 km) east of the coast, Mendocino's interior valley is home to history, art, and wine. The Anderson Valley is the apex of Mendocino's wine region, the tiny town of Hopland also has its share of tasting rooms, and Ukiah is home to several microbreweries. Plan 1.5 hours for the scenic drive.

The interior valleys of Mendocino get hot in the summer. Bring shorts, a swimsuit, and an air-conditioned car if you plan to visit June-September.

Anderson Valley
Wineries and Breweries
The **Anderson Valley Wine Trail** (CA-128) begins in Boonville and continues northwest toward the coast, with most of the wineries clustered between Boonville and Navarro.

A big name in the Anderson Valley, **Scharffenberger Cellars** (8501 Hwy. 128, Philo, 707/895-2957, www.scharffenbergercellars.com, 11am-5pm daily, $3) makes wine in Mendocino. Its tasting room is elegant and child-friendly, decorated with the work of local artists.

A broad-ranging winery with a large

estate vineyard and event center, **Navarro Vineyards** (5601 Hwy. 128, Philo, 707/895-3686 or 800/537-9463, www.navarrowine.com, 8am-6pm daily summer, 8am-5pm daily winter, free) offers a range of tasty wines as well as some interesting specialty products, such as the nonalcoholic verjus.

Roederer Estate sparkling wines (4501 Hwy. 128, Philo, 707/895-2288, www.roedererestate.com, 11am-5pm daily, $10) are some of the best of the state. The large tasting room features a bar with sweeping views of the estate vineyards and huge cases filled with well-deserved awards. Pourers are knowledgeable, and you'll get to taste from magnum bottles—a rarity at any winery. Ask for a taste of Roederer's rarely seen still wines.

Handley Cellars (3151 Hwy. 128, Philo, 800/733-3151, www.handleycellars.com, 10am-6pm daily summer, 10am-5pm daily winter, free) offers a complimentary tasting of handcrafted wines. The intriguing tasting room features folk art from around the world. Books on wine are sold, especially those that focus on women making and drinking wine.

Toulouse Vineyards (8001 Hwy. 128, Philo, 707/895-2828, http://toulousevineyards.com, 11am-5pm daily) is the kind of small operation where the winemaker's dog will greet you upon arrival. Known for pinot noir, they also do a pinot gris and a gewürztraminer.

Anderson Valley Brewing Company (17700 Hwy. 253, Boonville, 707/895-2337, www.avbc.com, 11am-6pm daily) serves up an array of microbrews that change each season and year. The warehouse-size beer hall feels like a wine-tasting room, with a bar, tables, and a good-size gift shop. A beer garden out back is comfortable in spring and fall, and the disc golf course is popular with travelers and locals.

Food
The Buckhorn (14081 Hwy. 128, Boonville, 707/895-3224, www.

thebuckhornboonville.com, 11am-11pm Mon. and Wed.-Thurs., 11am-midnight Fri., 10am-midnight Sat., 10am-11pm Sun., $11-32) has more than 40 local wines and 14 beers on tap, many from nearby Anderson Valley Brewing Company. They also serve big portions of good food including burgers and hot sandwiches, such as a worthwhile French dip.

Touted by glossy magazines like *Food & Wine* and *Travel & Leisure*, **The Bewildered Pig** (1810 Hwy. 128, Philo, 707/895-2088, www.bewilderedpig.com, 5pm-9pm Thurs.-Sun., $24-36, chef's tasting menu $99) is known in foodie circles for its refined yet rustic cuisine. Helmed by Janelle Weaver, a former Napa Valley chef, the menu frequently utilizes pork in the dishes, which is no surprise given the restaurant's name.

Gowan's Oak Tree Farm Stand (6600 Hwy. 128, 2.5 mi/4 km north of Philo, 707/895-3353, www.gowansoaktree. com, 8:30am-6:30pm daily June-Aug., 8:30am-6pm daily Sept.-Oct., 8:30am-5:30pm daily Nov.-May) belongs to the local Gowan's Oak Tree Farm and sells in-season local produce and homemade products made with the same fruits and veggies.

Accommodations

The **Anderson Valley Inn** (8480 Hwy. 128, Philo, 707/895-3325, www.avinn.com, $95-190), between Boonville and Philo, makes the perfect spot from which to divide your time between the Anderson Valley and the Mendocino Coast. Six small rooms are done up in bright colors, homey bedspreads, and attractive appointments. A butterfly-filled garden invites guests to sit out on the porches. Two suites have full kitchens and are perfect for longer stays. The friendly owners welcome children and dogs in the suites and can offer hints about how best to explore the region. This inn often fills quickly on summer weekends, as it's one of the best values in the region. There's a two-night minimum on weekends April-November.

The quaint **Boonville Hotel** (14050 Hwy. 128, 707/895-2210, www.boonvillehotel.com, $165-325) has a rough, weathered exterior that contrasts with the 15 contemporary rooms, each of which is bright and airy and has earth-tone furniture and mismatched decorations. Downstairs are spacious common areas and a huge garden. Amenities include a bookshop and a gift shop, a good-size bar, and a dining room. Book one of the rooms with a balcony, which comes with a hammock, or a guest room with an outdoor bathtub. Child- and pet-friendly rooms are available on request.

Camping

The campgrounds at **Indian Creek County Park** (Hwy. 128 at mile marker 23.48, 707/463-4291, www.co.mendocino. ca.us, $25) are budget-friendly. Eight miles (13 km) northwest of Boonville is **Hendy Woods State Park** (18599 Philo-Greenwood Rd., Philo, 800/444-7275, www.reservecalifornia.com, campsites $40, cabins $55), with woodsy, shaded campsites along with four rustic cabins with wood-burning stoves.

Getting There

CA-128 departs the Mendocino Coast approximately 10 miles (16 km) south of Mendocino. From Mendocino, drive south on CA-1 to the junction with CA-128 and turn east. Follow CA-128 east for 30 miles (48 km) to the town of Boonville.

From Boonville, it's possible to continue east to US-101, which accesses Ukiah (north) and Hopland (south).

Many of the major wine-country touring outfits operate in the Anderson Valley. **Mendo Wine Tours** (707/937-0289 or 800/609-0492, www.maccallumhouse. com/wine-tours, group tours $175 pp, private tours for two $500-800) is a regional specialist that offers a Lincoln Town Car for small groups and a limo for groups of up to 10.

Hopland

This small farming town is on the upper section of the Russian River. The **Solar Living Center** (13771 S. US-101, 707/472-2460, http://solarliving.org, 9am-6:30pm daily) is a "12-acre sustainable living demonstration site," showing, among other things, what life might be like without petroleum. Exhibits include permaculture, an organic garden, and a demonstration of solar-powered water systems. Guided **tours** (707/472-2460, 11am and 3pm Sat.-Sun. Apr.-Oct., $5/person, $10/family) are available.

The on-site **Real Goods** (707/472-2403, https://realgoods.com, 10am-6pm daily) is also a draw for visitors; the completely recycled restrooms are worth a look. If your vehicle happens to run on biodiesel, you can fill your tank here.

The Solar Living Center rents an 89-square-foot house called the **Hobbit House** (https://solarliving.org, $90), a structure made of soil and straw. You can also **camp** (707/472-2456, https://solarliving.org, tents $25, RVs $35), with access to an outdoor kitchen and showers.

Wineries

Hopland's wineries are the perfect place to relax, enjoy sipping each vintage, and chat with the pourer, who just might be the winemaker and owner. Most of the tasting rooms are along US-101, which runs through the center of town.

The star is **Brutocao Cellars** (13500 S. US-101, 800/433-3689, www.brutocaocellars.com, 10am-5pm daily, free), which has vineyards that surround the town. The wide, stone-tiled tasting room and restaurant complex house exceptional wines poured by knowledgeable staff. A sizable gift shop offers gourmet goodies under the Brutocao label, and there are six regulation bocce ball courts. A second tasting room is in the Anderson Valley (7000 Hwy. 128, Philo, 800/661-2103, www.brutocaocellars.com, 10am-5pm daily, free).

Food

The casual **Bluebird Café & Catering Company** (13340 S. US-101, 707/744-1633, 7am-2pm Wed.-Mon., $17-20) does wild game, including bison burgers. The **Hopland Tap House** (13551 S. Hwy. 101, 707/744-1255, http://hoplandtaphouse.com, noon-9pm Wed.-Sat., noon-6pm Sun., $9-14) is located within a historic brick building. The eight craft beers on tap go nicely with the small menu of burgers, hot dogs, paninis, and salads.

Getting There

Hopland is inland on US-101, about 15 miles (24 km) south of Ukiah and 28 miles (45 km) east of the Anderson Valley via CA-253.

Ukiah

Ukiah's low-key, historic downtown has some worthwhile restaurants and shops. The surrounding area is home to organic wineries, the largest Buddhist monastery in the country, and historic mineral springs.

City of 10,000 Buddhas

The **City of 10,000 Buddhas** (4951 Bodhi Way, 707/462-0939, www.cttbusa.org, 8am-6pm daily) is an active Buddhist college and monastery. The showpiece is the temple, which contains 10,000 golden Buddha statues. An extensive gift shop sells souvenirs as well as scholarly texts on Buddhism. For a treat, stop in for lunch at the **Jyun Kang Vegetarian Restaurant** (707/468-7966, 11:30am-3pm Wed.-Mon., $7), which is open to the public.

The monastery asks that guests wear modest clothing and keep their voices down out of respect for the nuns and monks who live here.

Grace Hudson Museum and Sun House

The **Grace Hudson Museum** (431 S. Main St., 707/467-2836, www.gracehudson-museum.org, 10am-4:30pm Wed.-Sat., noon-4:30pm Sun., adults $4, seniors and students $3, family $10) focuses on the life and work of the artist Grace Hudson and her husband, Dr. John Hudson. The museum's permanent collection includes many of Grace's paintings, a number of Pomo baskets, and the works of dozens of other California artists. The 1911 Craftsman-style **Sun House** (docent-guided tours available with museum ticket, noon-3pm Wed.-Sun.) was the Hudsons' home.

Vichy Springs Resort

Established in 1854, **Vichy Springs Resort** (2605 Vichy Springs Rd., 707/462-9515, www.vichysprings.com, 9am-dusk daily, baths $35/2 hours, $70/day) has been patronized by Mark Twain, Jack London, Ulysses S. Grant, Teddy Roosevelt, and former California governor Jerry Brown. The hot springs, mineral-heavy and naturally carbonated, closely resemble the world-famous waters of their namesake at Vichy in France and spill into indoor and outdoor concrete tubs. Services include the baths, a hot pool, and an Olympic-size swimming pool as well as a day spa. The serene 700-acre property also has 12 miles of trails.

Food

Local favorite **Stan's Maple Restaurant** (295 S. State St., 707/462-5221, www.stansmaplecafe.com, 7am-2pm daily, $6-14) serves tasty breakfasts and lunches. Excellent service complements good, American-style food. Shockingly good coffee is a charming final touch.

For a cool, relaxing breather on a hot day, visit one of the three locations of **Schat's Bakery Café** (www.schats.com; 113 W. Perkins St., 707/462-1670, 5:30am-6pm Mon.-Fri., 5:30am-5pm Sat.; 1255A Airport Park Blvd., 707/468-5850, 7am-8pm Mon.-Fri., 7am-7pm Sat., 8am-7pm Sun.; 1000 Hensley Creek Rd., 707/468-3145, 7am-8:15pm Mon.-Thurs., 7am-3pm Fri., $5-12) for a quick, filling

sandwich on freshly baked bread. Enjoy it in the large, airy dining room.

At **Patrona** (130 W. Standley St., 707/462-9181, www.patronarestaurant.com, 11am-9pm daily, $13-29), innovative California cuisine is served in a bistro-casual atmosphere by solicitous servers. The kitchen's attention to detail is impressive. The wine list features Mendocino County vintages, plus a good range of European wines.

Ukiah Brewing Company & Restaurant (102 S. State St., 707/468-5898, http://ukiahbrewing.com, 11am-9pm Sun.-Thurs., 11am-10pm Fri.-Sat., $11-28) has a wide menu that includes pizzas, sandwiches, salads, steak frites, and a chef's tasting menu, but it's the house-blended burgers on brioche buns that shine. Order the burger with bacon jam, white cheddar, and aioli. They also serve Ukiah Brewing Co. beer, which is brewed on-site.

Accommodations

Lodgings in Ukiah tend to be standard chain motels. Out by the airport, the **Fairfield Inn** (1140 Airport Park Blvd., 707/463-3600, www.marriott.com, $209-259) is a good choice, with an indoor pool and spa, a small exercise room, laundry facilities, and a generous complimentary continental breakfast. Rooms are what you'd expect: floral bedspreads, durable, nondescript carpet, and clean baths.

For a peaceful retreat, the best choice is ★ **Vichy Springs Resort** (2605 Vichy Springs Rd., 707/462-9515, www.vichysprings.com, $175-445). Rooms in the genteel and rustic inn and nearby cottages are small but comfortable, with private baths, warm bedspreads, and cool breezes; many have views of the mountains or creek. Two of the cottages date to 1852. Use of the pools and hiking trails is included in the rates, as are Internet access and a buffet breakfast.

Getting There

Ukiah is located on US-101, about 15 miles (24 km) north of Hopland, 22 miles

(35 km) east of Boonville, and 60 miles (97 km) east of the Mendocino Coast.

To reach Ukiah from Boonville, turn east at the junction of CA-128 and CA-253, and continue 22 miles (35 km) to US-101.

Fort Bragg

Fort Bragg is the Mendocino Coast's largest city. With fast-food joints and chain hotels lining CA-1 through town, it lacks the immediate charm of its neighbor to the south. But it does offer some great restaurants, interesting downtown shops, and proximity to coastal landmarks.

Getting There

The drive from Mendocino to Fort Bragg is 10 miles (16 km) north on CA-1 (about 15 minutes). Fort Bragg and Mendocino are so close that they are almost twin cities, though each has a different personality.

Sights
Skunk Train

The California Western Railroad, popularly called the **Skunk Train** (depot at end of Laurel St., 707/964-6371, www.skunktrain.com, 9am-3pm daily), is perfect for rail buffs and traveling families. The brightly painted trains appeal to children, and the historical aspects and scenery call to adults.

There are two rides on these restored steam locomotives. The **Northspur Flyer** (4 hours, adults $84, children 2-12 $42, children under 2 $10) travels 40 miles (64 km) from Fort Bragg through majestic redwood forest to the town of Willits and back. The **Pudding Creek Express** (1 hour, adults $25, children 2-12 $15, children under 2 $10) does a run up to Pudding Creek. Board in either Fort Bragg or Willits and make a round-trip return to your lodgings for the night.

Another option is to take the Skunk Train to **Camp Noyo** (Apr.-Oct., $100-220), a former logging camp on the Noyo River where you can bed down in a campsite or a chalet. Check the train's website for special events like a Halloween pumpkin patch excursion and a special Zombie Train.

The **Mendocino Coast Model Railroad and Navigation Company** (behind the Skunk Train Depot, www.mendorailhistory.org, 10:30am-2:30pm Wed. and Fri.-Mon., adults $5, children $3, Skunk Train ticket-holders free) is an operational train yard that recreates Fort Bragg's logging past in miniature. The large room is full of noise as model trains chug, bells ding, and lumber splashes into water.

Glass Beach

Fascinating **Glass Beach** (Elm St. and Glass Beach Dr.) is strewn with sea glass that has been polished and smoothed by the pounding surf. At the tide line, amber, green, and clear sea glass color the shore. It's against the park rules to

remove the glass, though you can take photos. The trail down to Glass Beach is short but steep and treacherous; wear good walking or hiking shoes.

Triangle Tattoo Museum

The **Triangle Tattoo Museum** (356B N. Main St., 707/964-8814, www.triangletattoo.com, daily noon-6pm, free) displays the implements of tattooing and photos of their results. To enter, walk up a flight of narrow stairs and stare at the walls, which are completely covered with photos of tattoos. All forms of the art are represented, from those done by indigenous people to those done at carnivals and in prisons. In glass cases upstairs are all types of tattooing devices, some antique. More photos grace the walls of the warren of small rooms in a never-ending collage. The street-side rooms house a working tattoo parlor, where intrepid artists and their canvases work late into the evening.

Pacific Star Winery

Pacific Star Winery (33000 N. Hwy. 1, 707/964-1155, www.pacificstarwinery.com, noon-5pm Thurs.-Mon. May-Oct., noon-5pm Thurs.-Sun. Nov.-Apr., tasting $5) makes the most of its location 12 miles (19.5 km) north of Fort Bragg. Barrels of wine are left out in the salt air to age, incorporating a hint of the Pacific into each vintage. Wines are tasty and reasonably priced, and you can bring your own picnic to enjoy on the nearby bluff, which overlooks the ocean.

Mendocino Coast Botanical Gardens

Stretching 47 acres down to the sea, **Mendocino Coast Botanical Gardens** (18220 N. Hwy. 1, 707/964-4352, www.gardenbythesea.org, 9am-5pm daily Mar.-Oct., 9am-4pm daily Nov.-Feb., adults $15, seniors $12, children 6-14 $8, children under 6 free) offer miles of walking through careful plantings and wild landscapes. The star of the gardens

Glass Beach, Fort Bragg

is the rhododendron, with 125 species on the grounds. Children can pick up *Quail Trail: A Child's Guide* and enjoy an exploratory adventure.

Entertainment and Events

The **Gloriana Musical Theatre** (Eagles Hall Theatre, 210 N. Corry St., 707/964-7469, www.gloriana.org) seeks to bring music and theater to young people, so they produce major musicals that appeal to kids, such as *Peter Pan,* while *Into the Woods* and *Chicago* appeal mostly to people past their second decade. Local performers star in the two major shows and numerous one-off performances each year.

The Mendocino Coast hosts a number of art events each year. **Art in the Gardens** (18220 N. Hwy. 1, Fort Bragg, www.gardenbythesea.org, Aug., adults $15-20, children under 16 free) takes place at the Mendocino Coast Botanical Gardens. The gardens are decked out with the finest local artwork, food, and wine, and there is music to entertain the crowds who come to eat and drink, and to view and purchase art.

North Coast Brewing Co.'s **Sequoia Room** (444 N. Main St., 707/964-3400, www.northcoastbrewing.com, Fri.-Sat.) hosts jazz shows featuring national touring acts or the local house band in a cabaret environment. The venue holds a crowd of 60 people.

Shopping

Stop in at the **Glass Beach Museum and Gift Shop** (17801 N. Hwy. 1, 707/357-1585, www.glassbeachjewelry.com, 10am-5pm daily) and you can see a wide array of found treasures; hear stories from Captain Cass, a retired sailor and expert glass scavenger; and buy sea glass set in pendants and rings.

Vintage clothing enthusiasts will love **If the Shoe Fits** (337 N. Franklin St., 707/964-2580, 11am-5:30pm Mon.-Thurs. and Sat., 11am-6pm Fri., 11am-2pm Sun.), an eclectic collection of used clothing and accessories for men and women with well-preserved, interesting pieces in good condition.

The Bookstore and Vinyl Cafe (137 E. Laurel St., 707/964-6559, 10:30am-5pm Mon.-Sat., 11am-4pm Sun.) is a small shop with a well-curated selection of new and used books likely to please discriminating readers. Music lovers can head to the back room, where there is a selection of used records for sale.

Sports and Recreation
Sportfishing

The Mendocino Coast is an ideal location to watch whales do acrobatics, or to try to land the big one (salmon, halibut, rock cod, or tuna). During Dungeness crab season, you can go out on a crab boat, learn to set pots, and catch your own delectable delicacy.

Many charters leave out of Noyo Harbor in Fort Bragg. The *Trek II* (Noyo Harbor, 707/964-4550, www.anchorcharterboats.com, fishing trips $80-125, 2-hour whale-watching $40) offers fishing trips and whale-watching jaunts (Dec.-May). They'll take you rock fishing in summer, crabbing in winter, and chasing after salmon and tuna in season.

The **Noyo Fishing Center** (32440 N. Harbor Dr., Noyo Harbor, 707/964-3000, www.fortbraggfishing.com, half-day fishing trips $100-250, 2-hour whale-watching excursion $35) can take you out for salmon or halibut fishing. They'll help you fish for cod and various deep-sea dwellers in season. The twice-daily trips are an intimate experience, with a maximum of six passengers.

Horseback Riding

What better way to enjoy the rugged cliffs, windy beaches, and quiet forests of the coast than on the back of a horse? **Ricochet Ridge Ranch** (24201 N. US-101, 707/964-9669 or 888/873-5777, www.horse-vacation.com, 9:30am, 11:30am, 1:30pm, and 3:30pm daily, $60) has one-hour beach trail rides departing four times daily. They also offer longer beach and trail rides, sunset beach rides, and full-fledged riding vacations by reservation.

Surfing

Just south of town is **Hare Creek** (southwest of the intersection of CA-1 and CA-20, north end of the Hare Creek Bridge), one of the region's most popular spots. North of town is **Virgin Creek** (1.5 mi/2.4 km north of Fort Bragg on CA-1), another well-known break. The **Lost Surf Shack** (319 N. Franklin St., 707/961-0889, 10am-6pm daily, surfboards $25/day, wetsuits $15/day) in downtown Fort Bragg rents surfboards and wetsuits.

Spas

The **Bamboo Garden Spa** (18300 Old Coast Hwy., 707/962-9396, 1pm-8pm Tues.-Sat., massages $95-190) pampers its guests with a wide array of massage, skin, and beauty treatments.

Food

Fort Bragg hosts a **farmers market** (Franklin St. between Laurel and Pine, www.mcfarm.org, 3pm-6pm Wed. May-Oct., 3pm-5pm Nov.-Apr.) inside the Old Recreation Center Gym that sells wild-caught seafood, free-range beef, and freshly baked bread.

Bakeries and Cafés

Cowlick's Ice Cream (250 N. Main St., 707/962-9271, www.cowlicksicecream.com, 11am-9pm daily) serves delectable handmade ice cream in a variety of flavors. They even serve mushroom ice cream during the fall mushroom season, as well as perennial favorites such as vanilla, chocolate, coffee, and strawberry, and seasonal flavors (banana daiquiri, cinnamon, green tea). Ice cream from this local, family-owned chain is also sold at **Frankie's Ice Cream Parlor** (44951 Ukiah St., Mendocino, 707/937-2436, www.frankiesmendocino.com, 11am-9pm daily) in Mendocino Village; on the

Skunk Train; and at **J. D. Redhouse** (212 S. Main St., Willits, 707/459-1214, 10am-6pm daily).

The **Headlands Coffeehouse** (120 Laurel St., 707/964-1987, www.headlandscoffeehouse.com, 7am-10pm Mon.-Sat., 7am-5pm Sun.) is the place to go for a cup of joe. They have 15 different self-serve roasts of coffee, as well as food ranging from breakfast burritos to paninis. There is free live music in the evenings and free Internet access (but no electrical outlets for customers).

Egghead's (326 N. Main St., 707/964-5005, 7am-2pm daily, $6-19) has been serving an enormous menu of breakfast, lunch, and brunch items to satisfy diners since 1976. The menu includes every imaginable omelet combination, cinnamon raisin toast, burritos, Reuben sandwiches, and "flying-monkey potatoes," derived from the *Wizard of Oz* theme that runs through the place.

American

The ★ **North Coast Brewing Company** (444 N. Main St., 707/964-3400, www.northcoastbrewing.com, 11:30am-9:15pm daily, $15-33) serves seafood, steak, and creative salads, all washed down with a North Coast microbrew. Taste the magic in their Red Seal Ale, Old Rasputin Russian Imperial Stout, and Scrimshaw Pilsner. Sit at the cozy wooden bar in the taproom if you're here for the beer.

Jenny's Giant Burger (940 N. Main St., 707/964-2235, 10:30am-9pm daily, $4-7) has a 1950s hamburger-stand feel. The burgers are fresh and antibiotic-free, with garden burger and veggie sandwich options. Jenny's followers are devoted, so it can get crowded, but there are a few outdoor tables, and you can always get your order to go.

Italian

Small and almost always packed, ★ **Piaci Pub & Pizzeria** (120 W. Redwood Ave., 707/961-1133, www.piacipizza.com, 11am-9:30pm Mon.-Thurs., 11am-10pm

Fri.-Sat., 4pm-9:30pm Sun., $9-26) has an L-shaped bar and just a few tables, so you may share a table with strangers. The 16 delicious pizzas range from traditional pepperoni to creative combinations like pesto, chèvre, pears, prosciutto, and herbs. The Nonnie is a flavorful combination of prosciutto, grilled chicken, mozzarella, herbs, and a garlic sauce on a thin crust. Piaci's has an extensive list of brews, from Belgian-style beers to hearty ales.

Cucina Verona (124 E. Laurel St., 707/964-6844, www.cucinaverona.com, 8am-9pm Mon.-Thurs., 8am-9:30pm Fri.-Sat., 9am-9pm Sun., $12-35) does northern Italian food with touches of Northern California. Menu items run the gamut from butternut squash lasagna to grilled local salmon. Complement your meal with a local wine or beer. Frequent live music provides entertainment.

Mexican

Look for the brightly colored letters on the roof to find **Los Gallitos** (223 N. Franklin St., 707/964-4519, 11am-9pm Fri.-Sat., 10am-8pm Sun., 11am-8:30pm Mon.-Wed., $7-16, cash only). You'll know this is a better-than-average taqueria when the thick, fresh tortilla strips and superb salsa hit your table. Everything on the menu, from burritos to tostadas, is what you'd expect, but the attention to little details like the grilled onions and beans on the tasty carne asada torta make this place special.

Seafood

With the small fishing and crabbing fleet of Fort Bragg's Noyo Harbor, it's natural that lots of seafood restaurants are clustered nearby. One spot known for its fish-and-chips is the **Sea Pal Cove Restaurant** (32390 N. Harbor Dr., 707/964-1300, 11am-11pm Fri.-Sat., 11am-10pm

From top to bottom: Cucina Verona; Headlands Coffeehouse; North Coast Brewing.

Sun.-Thurs., $6-13, cash only). They also have 18 beers on tap.

Thai

Small and unassuming, **Nit's Café** (322 Main St., 707/964-7187, 11am-2pm and 5pm-9pm daily, $14-26, cash only) specializes in Thai and Asian fusion. Noted for its beautiful presentations of both classic and creative dishes, Nit's gets rave reviews. They have a special of the day and a fresh daily catch of the day.

Accommodations
Under $150

A budget option, the **Surf Motel** (1220 S. Main St., 707/964-5361, www.surfmotelfb.com, $95-199) provides a bike-washing station, a fish-cleaning station, an outdoor shower for divers, a garden to stroll through, and an area set aside for horseshoes and barbecues. Your spacious modern guest room comes with breakfast, free wireless Internet access, a microwave, a fridge, and a blow dryer. The two apartments have a kitchen and room for four people.

The stately **Grey Whale Inn** (615 N. Main St., 707/964-0640 or 800/382-7244, www.greywhaleinn.com, $135-190) was once a community hospital. The blocky Craftsman-style building was erected by the Union Lumber Company in 1915. Today, 13 spacious, simple rooms offer views of the water or the city. The lovely, individually decorated rooms feature a private bath and queen or king bed, perhaps covered by an old-fashioned quilt. The inn prides itself on simplicity and friendliness, and its location in downtown Fort Bragg makes visitors feel at home walking to dinner or the beach. It also has a game room with a pool table and foosball.

$150-250

The **Beachcomber Motel** (1111 N. Main St., 707/964-2402, www.thebeachcombermotel.com, $149-309) is just north of town right behind Pudding Creek Beach.

It's one of the most pet-friendly motels along the coast. Not only are there pet-friendly rooms, but there is a dog park and suites with doggie doors that open up to a fenced-in enclosure with a doghouse. Rooms are equipped with private balconies and decks to take in the bluffs and ocean. Some units even have hot tubs. A deck on the northern end of the property has fire pits and barbecue grills. The motel rents beach cruisers for use on the Coastal Trail at adjacent MacKerricher State Park.

Located next door, the ★ **Surf & Sand Lodge** (1131 N. Main St., 707/964-9383, www.surfsandlodge.com, $169-299) is the slightly more upscale sister property of the Beachcomber. Most of the rooms in the six blue buildings have views of the headlands and ocean. Trails, tidepools, crashing waves, and broad beaches are right out front. Every room has a balcony or a porch to take in the view. Or opt for a room with a Jacuzzi spa tub to soak in while looking out at the chilly Pacific.

Over $250

The site of a few hotels over the years (including Casa del Noyo), the **Noyo Harbor Inn** (500 Casa del Noyo, Fort Bragg, 707/961-8000, www.noyoharborinn.com, $285-400) reopened in 2017 after extensive renovations. The property has 15 quiet rooms with views of both the Noyo River and the Pacific Ocean, as well as an on-site restaurant, a tavern, and a patio. Live music acts play during the summer months.

Information and Services

The **Mendocino Coast Chamber of Commerce and Visitors Center** (217 S. Main St., 707/961-6300, www.mendocinocoast.com, 10am-5pm Mon.-Fri., 10am-3pm Sat.) also serves as the Mendocino County film office, which strongly encourages filmmaking in the area. Get the inside story on where to see the filming locations of *Summer of '42,* in which the bluffs of Fort Bragg play the role of Long Island; *East of Eden; Karate Kid III;* and *Humanoids from the Deep.*

The **Mendocino Coast District Hospital** (700 River Dr., at Cypress St., 707/961-1234, www.mcdh.org) has the nearest full-service emergency room.

Getting Around

Fort Bragg has great access to public transportation. The most enjoyable way to get here is to take the **Skunk Train** (707/964-6371, www.skunktrain. com, adults $84, children 2-12 $42, children under 2 $10) from Willits. The **Mendocino Transit Authority** (800/696-4682, http://mendocinotransit.org, $1.50-5.25) has bus lines that pass through Fort Bragg. It also offers **Dial-a-Ride Curb-to-Curb Service** (707/462-3881, 7am-6pm Mon.-Fri., 10am-5pm Sat., adults $6, seniors $3, children under 6 $1.25).

MacKerricher State Park

MacKerricher State Park (Hwy. 1, 707/964-9112, district office 707/937-5804, www.parks.ca.gov, sunrise-10pm daily, day use free) offers the small, duck-filled Cleone Lake, miles of sandy ocean beaches, cliffs and crags, and camping. The main attraction is a gigantic, almost complete skeleton of a whale near the park entrance. If you're lucky, you can also spot live whales and harbor seals frolicking in the ocean. The coast can be rough here, so don't swim or wade unless it's what the locals call a "flat day"—no big waves and undertow. If the kids want to play in the water, take them to **Pudding Creek Beach** in the park, about 2.5 miles (4 km) south of the campground, where they can enjoy the relatively sheltered area under the trestle bridge.

The hike to take is the **Ten Mile Beach Trail** (10 mi/16 km round-trip, 6 hours, moderate), starting at the Laguna Point Parking Area at the north end of Fort Bragg and running 5 miles (8 km) up to the Ten Mile River. Most of this path is fairly level and paved. It's an easy walk, and you can turn around whenever you want. Street bikes and inline skates are also allowed.

Getting There

MacKerricher State Park is 3 miles (4.8 km) north of Fort Bragg on CA-1.

Camping

Campground reservations (800/444-7275, www.reservecalifornia.com, $35) are recommended April 1-October 15, and they're site-specific. In winter, camping is first-come, first-served. The park has 107 sites suitable for tents and RVs (up to 35 feet) in its wooded and pleasant West Pinewood and East Pinewood Campgrounds; there's also a group campground as well as walk-in hike-and-bike sites. Restrooms with flush toilets and hot showers are provided, and each campsite has a fire ring, picnic table, and food storage locker.

Westport

Westport is the last settlement before the wild Lost Coast, with its own patch of ocean, a few essential services, and one lodging gem.

Getting There

Westport is 16 miles (26 km) north of Fort Bragg on CA-1.

Food and Accommodations

The **Old Abalone Pub** (Westport Hotel, 3892 Hwy. 1, 707/964-3688, www.westporthotel.us, 5pm-9pm Thurs.-Sat. Feb.-May, 5pm-9pm Thurs.-Sun. May-Sept., 5pm-9pm Thurs.-Sun. Oct.-Dec., $16-30) serves moderately priced pub meals and gourmet entrées. Thanks to a large mirror over the bar, everyone in the dining room gets an ocean view.

"At last, you've found nowhere" is the motto at the ★ **Westport Hotel**

(3892 Hwy. 1, 707/964-3688, www.west-porthotel.us, $150-250). The marvelous hotel is very private, perfect for a honeymoon spent in luxury and comfort. Each of the six rooms has one bed and a bath with fixtures that blend perfectly into the historic 1890 house. Some rooms have small private balconies that overlook the waves, while all guests have access to the redwood sauna. Fresh scones, fruit, and coffee are delivered to your room in the morning. A full hot breakfast is served in the dining room.

Camping is available 2 miles (3.2 km) north of Westport at **Westport-Union Landing State Beach** (Hwy. 1, 707/937-5804, www.parks.ca.gov, $25), with 86 first-come, first-served sites. There are no showers or other amenities—just the cliffs, the waves, the sunsets, and the views.

North
Coast and
Redwoods

North Coast and Redwoods

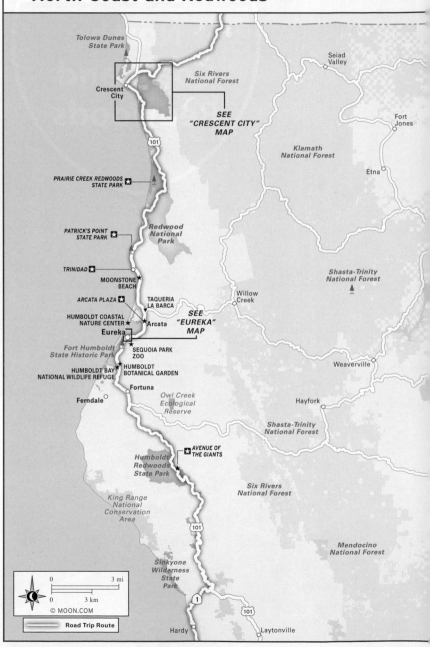

Tolowa Dunes
State Park

Six Rivers
National Forest

Seiad
Valley

Crescent
City

SEE
"CRESCENT CITY"
MAP

Fort
Jones

101

Klamath
National Forest

Etna

PRAIRIE CREEK REDWOODS
STATE PARK

Redwood
National
Park

Shasta-Trinity
National Forest

PATRICK'S POINT
STATE PARK

TRINIDAD

MOONSTONE
BEACH

Willow
Creek

ARCATA PLAZA

TAQUERIA
LA BARCA

HUMBOLDT COASTAL
NATURE CENTER

SEE
"EUREKA"
MAP

Eureka

Arcata

Fort Humboldt
State Historic Park

SEQUOIA PARK
ZOO

HUMBOLDT BAY
NATIONAL WILDLIFE REFUGE

HUMBOLDT
BOTANICAL GARDEN

Weaverville

Fortuna

Ferndale

Owl Creek
Ecological
Reserve

Hayfork

Shasta-Trinity
National Forest

AVENUE OF
THE GIANTS

Humboldt
Redwoods
State Park

Six Rivers
National Forest

King Range
National
Conservation
Area

101

Mendocino
National Forest

Sinkyone
Wilderness
State Park

0   3 mi

0   3 km

© MOON.COM

1

101

Road Trip Route

Hardy

Laytonville

Highlights

★ **Avenue of the Giants:** The towering coast redwoods in Humboldt Redwoods State Park are a true must-see. Simply gaze at the silent giants or head to the nearby Eel River for a quick dip (page 214).

★ **Arcata Plaza:** Arcata is Humboldt County's cultural hub, and its Arcata Plaza is a vibrant, grassy square circled by bars, bookstores, and restaurants (page 233).

★ **Craft Breweries:** The North Coast takes its craft beer seriously, and every significant town has at least one brewpub (page 235).

★ **Trinidad:** This tiny town perched above an idyllic bay is one of the most photogenic coastal communities in the state (page 238).

★ **Patrick's Point State Park:** Patrick's Point is just one square mile in size, but its many worthwhile sights include Wedding Rock over the crashing Pacific Ocean, Agate Beach, and a recreated native Yurok village (page 241).

★ **Prairie Creek Redwoods State Park:** With big trees, a long, lonely beach, and one-of-a-kind

Fern Canyon, this park is worth a stop (page 245).

★ **Jedediah Smith Redwoods State Park:** The park showcases the rugged beauty of the North Coast with its stunning old-growth redwoods (page 248).

★ **Battery Point Lighthouse:** This lighthouse on an island off Crescent City is only accessible at low tide. If you time it right, you can take an insightful tour from the lighthouse keeper (page 252).

The rugged North Coast of California is spectacular, its wild beauty in many places unspoiled and almost desolate.

The cliffs are forbidding, the beaches are rocky and windswept, and the surf thunders in with formidable authority. This is not the California coast of surfer movies, though hardy souls do ride the chilly Pacific waves as far north as Crescent City. Where CA-1 merges with US-101 is the famous Lost Coast, accessed only via steep, narrow roads or by backpacking the famous Lost Coast Trail. This is California at its wildest.

For most travelers, the North Coast means redwood country, and US-101 marks the gateway to those redwoods. The famous, immense coastal sequoias loom along the highway south of the old logging town of Eureka and the hip college outpost of Arcata. A plethora of state and national parks lure travelers with numerous hiking trails, forested campgrounds, kitschy tourist traps, and some of the tallest and oldest trees on the continent; you can pitch a tent in Humboldt Redwoods State Park, cruise the Avenue of the Giants, and gaze in wonder at the primordial Founders Grove. Crescent City, marking the northern terminus of the California Coast, is a seaside town known for fishing, seafood—and for surviving a tsunami.

Planning Your Time

If you're planning a road trip to explore the North Coast in depth and want to make stops in more than one destination, plan to spend a **full week.** Driving is the way to get from place to place, unless you're a hard-core backpacker. CA-1 winds along the North Coast to connect with US-101 at its northern terminus near Leggett. US-101 then heads inland through southern Humboldt County before heading back to the coast at Eureka. North of Eureka, US-101 continues through Arcata, Trinidad, and Crescent City, along with the Redwood National and State Parks.

Along the **Lost Coast,** the most lodging and dining options can be found in Shelter Cove. If you want to explore the Lost Coast Trail, consider hiking it north to south, with the wind at your back. Spend the night in Ferndale or camp at the Mattole Recreation Site, where the trail begins, so that you can get an early start for the first day of backpacking.

If you're exploring the **redwood parks,** consider staying in Arcata or Trinidad, both small towns. The campgrounds at Patrick's Point State Park and Prairie Creek Redwoods State Park are superb places to pitch a tent.

Summer on the North Coast has average daily temperatures in the mid-60s, which is comparable to the temps in Southern California during the winter. Expect rain on the North Coast from November to May. The chances of fog or rain are significantly lower in the **fall,** making it one of the best times to visit. Frequent visitors to the area know this, so many popular hotels book quickly for fall weekends.

Getting There

Most of the major park areas along the North Coast can be accessed via US-101 and US-199. Follow the signs to the smaller roads that lead farther from civilization. To get to the redwood parks from the south, drive up US-101 or the much slower but prettier CA-1. The two roads merge at Leggett, north of Fort Bragg, and continue north as US-101.

Driving times on CA-1 tend to be longer on the North Coast due to the roadway's twists, turns, and many spectacular ocean vistas. On US-101 north of Leggett,

The North Coast and Redwoods in Three Days

Day 1

Begin your morning in Garberville with brunch at the **Benbow Historic Inn** before driving along the **Avenue of the Giants.** Allow time to stop and gaze at the redwoods or hop into the Eel River. Arrive in Eureka and get tickets for a narrated boat cruise around Humboldt Bay on the *Madaket,* a historic vessel with the smallest licensed bar in California. For dinner, head to Eureka's **Brick & Fire Bistro** and order the popular wild mushroom cobbler. That night, stay at the **Carter House Inns** for an upscale Victorian evening or sleep at **Oyster Beach** in a refurbished farm building on a sprawling property located between Humboldt Bay and the Pacific Ocean.

Day 2

Drive north to Arcata for breakfast at **Renata's Creperie** before heading to **Wildberries Marketplace** to pick up supplies for a North Coast adventure. Drive 15 miles (24 km) north to the scenic town of **Trinidad** and its stunning coastline. Hike **Trinidad Head,** walk along **Trinidad State Beach,** or explore the features of nearby **Patrick's Point State Park.** Have a late lunch at **The Lighthouse Grill** or save your appetite for a big dinner at **Larrupin Café.** Camp at nearby **Patrick's Point State Park** or drive a half-hour north to **Elk Meadow Cabins** to wake the next morning near the **Redwood National and State Parks.**

Day 3

Today it's time to experience the serenity and immensity of California's coast redwoods. Pack a lunch with the snacks you bought at Wildberries Marketplace; you'll spend a significant amount of time in **Prairie Creek Redwoods State Park** hiking through redwoods on Cal-Barrel Road or the Cathedral Trees Trail. Then head toward the coast to experience the one-of-a-kind fern walls of **Fern Canyon.** While in the park, keep your eyes peeled for Roosevelt elk. End the day with an hour-long drive north to Crescent City for a craft beer and a good meal at **SeaQuake Brewing.**

GETTING THERE

expect to share the road with logging vehicles. A lot of the roads off US-101 or CA-1 are worthwhile excursions, but expect mountainous terrain.

Note that there are no airports convenient to the north coast, and public transportation is hard to come by. A personal vehicle is required.

From San Francisco
180 mi/290 km, 3-3.5 hr

From San Francisco, take US-101 north over the **Golden Gate Bridge** and continue 180 miles (290 km) north to **Leggett,** which sits at the junction of US-101 and CA-1. From this point north, US-101 becomes the Redwood Highway, dwindling down to a two-lane road in some sections. It's a far cry from the feel of the same highway in the central part of the state.

Stopping in Ukiah

Ukiah is 115 miles (185 km) north of San Francisco and a good place for a pit stop. **Patrona** (130 W. Standley St., 707/462-9181, www.patronarestaurant.com, 11am-9pm daily, $13-29) and the **Ukiah Brewing Company & Restaurant** (102 S. State St., 707/468-5898, http://ukiahbrewing.com, 11am-9pm Sun.-Thurs., 11am-10pm Fri.-Sat., $11-28) are both recommended for food and drinks. A soak at **Vichy Springs Resort** (2605 Vichy Springs Rd., 707/462-9515, www.vichysprings.com, 9am-dusk daily, baths $35/2 hours, $70/day) will loosen up those muscles tense from driving.

Best Restaurants

★ **Benbow Inn, Garberville:** Enjoy California cuisine on an outdoor deck at this historic inn on the Eel River (page 212).

★ **The Chalet House of Omelettes, Eureka:** Omelets are the specialty at this Eureka breakfast institution (page 230).

★ **Samoa Cookhouse, Samoa:** The Samoa Cookhouse offers a cultural experience where visitors dine in a logging camp atmosphere (page 230).

★ **Brick & Fire Bistro, Eureka:** This cozy restaurant cooks its creative Italian food in a brick oven and often utilizes local mushrooms (page 231).

★ **Renata's Creperie and Espresso, Arcata:** These superb organic buckwheat crepes will prepare you for a day of North Coast exploration (page 236).

★ **Wildberries Marketplace, Arcata:** This upscale market has a juice bar, bakery counter, hot food and salad bar, and a café that makes sandwiches and burgers to order (page 238).

★ **Katy's Smokehouse, Trinidad:** Katy's sells locally smoked salmon, smoked oysters, and a salmon jerky that makes a day spent hiking more flavorful (page 239).

★ **Larrupin Café, Trinidad:** A Humboldt institution, this upscale restaurant is known for its mesquite-barbecued meats and popular sauces (page 240).

★ **The Lighthouse Grill, Trinidad:** This eatery serves comfort food made from local ingredients (page 240).

★ **SeaQuake Brewing, Crescent City:** This is the place to go for craft beer and food in Crescent City (page 254).

From Shasta and Lassen
150 mi/240 km, 3 hr
From I-5 in **Redding**, CA-299 shoots 150 miles (240 km) west to meet US-101 on the coast north of **Eureka.**

From Ashland, Oregon
120 mi/195 km, 2.5 hr
From Ashland, Oregon, take I-5 north for 36 miles (58 km) toward **Medford.** Exit onto US-199/Redwood Highway toward Crescent City. Continue south on US-199/Redwood Highway for 80 miles (129 km), hopping onto US-101 South for the last 3.5 miles (5.6 km) into **Crescent City.**
   Leggett is 175 miles (280 km) south on US-101.

Stopping in Cave Junction
Cave Junction is 70 miles (113 km) west of Ashland on US-199. Stop at **Wild River Pizza** (249 N. Redwood Hwy., Cave Junction, 541/592-3556, www.wildriverbrewing.com, 11am-9pm Mon.-Thurs., 11am-10pm Fri.-Sat., noon-9pm Sun., $8-30), the original location of a small chain that serves handcrafted pizzas and their own craft beer. An all-you-can-eat salad and hot food bar (11:30am-2pm Mon.-Fri.) is also available.
   River Valley Restaurant (203 N. Redwood Hwy., Cave Junction, 541/592-4128, www.rivervalleyrestaurant.com, 7am-2:30pm daily, $6-12) is another

Best Accommodations

★ **Benbow Inn, Garberville:** This inn dates to 1926 and perches right on the South Fork of the Eel River (page 213).

★ **Victorian Inn, Ferndale:** This imposing Victorian structure dates from 1890 and is a fine place to spend the evening while exploring historic Ferndale (page 223).

★ **Carter House Inns, Eureka:** A collection of yellow Victorian buildings in downtown Eureka, the Carter House Inns provide luxury and a hot breakfast (page 232).

★ **Oyster Beach, Samoa:** Farmhouses are gussied up with hipster decor and sit across the bay from Eureka on the Samoa Peninsula (page 232).

★ **Best Western Plus Humboldt Bay, Eureka:** This Best Western surprises with a spa area, better-than-average continental breakfast, and an on-site limo that can drive you around Eureka (page 232).

★ **Patrick's Point State Park:** The Agate Beach, Abalone, and Penn Creek campgrounds are the perfect base for exploring this tiny state park (page 242).

★ **Elk Meadow Cabins, Orick:** There's no better place to stay in the Redwood National and State Parks area than at these seven cabins adjacent to Redwood National Park (page 242).

★ **Jedediah Smith Campground, Hiouchi:** Camp under old-growth redwoods on the banks of the Smith River at this state park campground (page 250).

option that serves breakfast omelets, hot lunch sandwiches, and diner fare.

Leggett

As CA-1 heads inland toward Leggett, the ocean views are replaced with redwoods. This part of the road is curvy, winding, and sun-dappled. It's a beautiful drive, so take it slow.

At the junction of CA-1 and US-101, you'll enter Leggett, famed for the local attraction **Chandelier Drive-Thru Tree** (67402 Drive-Thru Tree Rd., 707/925-6464, www.drivethrutree.com, hours and dates vary, $10/car, $5/motorcycle, bike, and walk-in). The tree opening is about 6 feet wide and a little over 6 feet high. Kids will be thrilled. And of course, there's a gift shop.

The Peg House (69501 US-101, 707/925-6444, http://thepeghouse.com, 11am-dusk daily), which was built with pegs instead of nails, gets raves for its burgers, tri-tip, Humboldt Bay oysters, and deli sandwiches. Sometimes there is live music.

Garberville and Redway

Garberville is the first real town in Humboldt County. Just northwest is the slightly larger town of Redway, with a few hundred more residents. Known as the "Gateway to the Avenue of the Giants," both towns are good places to get a meal or fill your tank with gas before heading west to the coast or north to the redwoods.

Getting There

Garberville is 65 miles (105 km) south of Eureka and 200 miles (320 km) north of San Francisco on US-101. From Garberville, take Redwood Drive for 3 miles (4.8 km) to Redway.

Richardson Grove State Park

Richardson Grove State Park (1600 US-101, 707/247-3318, www.parks.ca.gov, daily sunrise-sunset, $8) is the first with old-growth redwoods along US-101. This park has special features, like a tree you can walk through and the ninth-tallest coast redwood. The Eel River flows through the park, offering good fishing as well as camping, swimming, and hiking. The **visitors center** (10am-4pm daily May-Sept., 10am-4pm Fri.-Sun. Oct.-Apr.) in the 1930s Richardson Grove Lodge has cool exhibits and a nature store. Richardson Grove State Park is 7 miles (11.5 km) south of Garberville.

Festivals and Events

The **Mateel Community Center** (59 Rusk Ln., Redway, 707/923-3368, www.mateel. org) brings music, theater, dance, comedy, film, and craft events to southern Humboldt. They also put on local annual events, including the Summer Arts & Music Festival, the Humboldt Hills Hoedown, Winter Arts Faire, and the Reggae on the River Festival.

Food

The restaurant at the ★ **Benbow Inn** (445 Lake Benbow Dr., Garberville, 707/923-2124 or 800/355-3301, www.benbowinn. com, 8am-2pm and 6pm-9:30pm daily, $24-49) serves upscale California cuisine (a vegan menu is available on request) and features an extensive wine list with many regional wineries represented. The white-tablecloth dining room is exquisite, and the expansive outdoor patio overlooking the water is the perfect place to sit as the temperature cools on a summer evening.

An easy place to stop for a pick-me-up, **Flavors Coffeehouse** (767 Redwood Dr., Garberville, 707/923-7717, 7am-7pm daily, $5-11) refuels with a menu of caffeine drinks, sandwiches, paninis, and salads. They serve breakfast all day; a build-your-own-grilled-cheese-sandwich option lets you add ingredients like bacon and roasted bell peppers.

A good breakfast and lunch stop is the **Eel River Café** (801 Redwood Dr., 707/923-3783, 6am-2pm Mon.-Sat., 7am-2pm Sun., $6-12), a diner with black-and-white checkerboard floors and a long counter with red stools. Try the chicken-fried steak with biscuits and gravy. You can't miss the old-school sign towering above the establishment. They must know what they are doing—they've been a local fixture since 1935.

Transport yourself to the Louisiana Bayou courtesy of **Cecil's New Orleans Bistro** (773 Redwood Dr., Garberville, 707/923-7007, https://garbervillebistro. com, 5pm-9pm Tues.-Sat., $24-40). The menu includes crawfish pasta, a rib eye with Cajun butter, and Cajun game hen, but the pecan pie steals the show.

You can enjoy a taste of local Humboldt-roasted coffee at **Signature Coffee** (3455 Redwood Dr., Redway, 707/923-2661, www. signaturecoffeecompany.com, 7am-5pm Mon.-Fri.), which takes pride in its organic products and sustainable practices.

Enjoy a classic roadhouse experience at **The Riverwood Inn** (2828 Ave. of the Giants, Phillipsville, 707/943-3333, https://theriverwoodinn.com, 3pm-midnight daily, $10-20), 6 miles (9.5 km) north of Garberville. This classic tavern was one of the few buildings that survived the Eel River flood of 1964. Come for the tasty Mexican food and stay for the live music Friday and Saturday nights. There are also five hotel rooms upstairs ($80-98).

Ray's Food Place (875 Redwood Dr., 707/923-2279, www.gorays.com, 7am-11pm daily) is a supermarket in Garberville.

Accommodations

The best place to stay is the ★ **Benbow Inn** (445 Lake Benbow Dr., Garberville, 707/923-2124 or 800/355-3301, www.benbowinn.com, $205-475). A swank resort backing onto Lake Benbow, this inn has it all: a gourmet restaurant, a nine-hole golf course, an outdoor swimming pool, and a woodsy atmosphere that blends perfectly with the ancient redwood forest surrounding it. Rooms glow with dark polished woods and jewel-toned carpets. Wide king and comfy queen beds beckon guests tired after a long day of hiking in the redwoods or golfing beside the inn.

Several small motels offer reasonable rooms, and many have outdoor pools. The best of these is the **Best Western Humboldt House Inn** (701 Redwood Dr., Garberville, 707/923-2771, www.bestwestern.com, $179-269). Rooms are clean and comfortable, the pool is sparkling and cool, the breakfast is hot, and the location is convenient to restaurants and shops in Garberville. Most rooms have two queen beds.

Camping

Richardson Grove State Park (1600 US-101, 800/444-7275, www.reservecalifornia.com, camping $35) has 169 campsites in three campground areas surrounded by redwoods and the Elk River. The Huckleberry/Madrone Campground is open year-round, while Oak Flat Campground has sites available the July 4 weekend to Labor Day weekend.

You can park your RV year-round at the 112 sites of the posh **Benbow KOA** (7000 Benbow Dr., Garberville, 707/923-2777, www.benbowrv.com, campsites $46-85, cabins $75-400). Premium sites come with complimentary tea and scones at the nearby Benbow Inn.

Information and Services

The towns in this region can be short on necessary services such as gas stations. Luckily, there are three in Garberville including a **Chevron** (830 Redwood Dr., 707/923-4666), a **Shell** (860 Redwood Dr., 707/923-9144), and **Renner Petroleum** (76 Bear Canyon Dr., 707/923-3380).

The **Humboldt Transit Authority** (https://hta.org) runs the **Humboldt Innercity** bus (adults $4, children and seniors $3.45) from Garberville to Eureka.

Garberville is home to the **Southern Humboldt Community Clinic** (733 Cedar St., 707/923-3921, https://shchd.org, 8:30am-5pm Mon.-Fri.). The nearest hospital with an emergency room is **Redwood Memorial Hospital** (3300 Renner Dr., Fortuna, 707/725-3361, www.stjoehumboldt.org).

Humboldt Redwoods State Park

The largest stand of unlogged redwood trees is in Humboldt, bisected by US-101. A drive along the Avenue of the Giants with a stop at the **Humboldt Redwoods State Park Visitors Center** (Hwy. 254, 707/946-2263, www.parks.ca.gov or www.humboldtredwoods.org, 9am-5pm daily Apr.-Sept., 10am-4pm daily Oct.-Mar., free) and a quick nature walk or picnic can give you a taste of the lovely southern end of the coastal redwoods region.

Getting There

Humboldt Redwoods State Park is 21 miles (34 km) north of Garberville on US-101. The Avenue of the Giants parallels US-101, and there are several marked exits along the highway to reach the scenic redwood drive. The best way to get to Humboldt Redwoods State Park is via US-101. Road signs point to the Avenue of the Giants. Bicycles are not permitted on US-101, but you can ride on the Avenue of the Giants.

★ Avenue of the Giants

The most famous stretch of redwood trees is the **Avenue of the Giants** (www.avenueofthegiants.net), paralleling US-101 and the Eel River for about 33 miles (53 km) between Garberville and Fortuna; look for signs on US-101. Visitors drive this stretch of road and gaze in wonder at the sky-high old-growth redwoods along the way. Campgrounds and hiking trails sprout amid the trees off the road. It's easy to park your car at various points along the way and get out to walk among the giants or down to the nearby Eel River for a cool dip.

The Avenue's highest traffic volume is in July-August, when you can expect bumper-to-bumper traffic along the entire road. That's not necessarily a bad thing: Going slow is the best way to see the sights. But if crowds aren't your thing, visit in spring or fall, or brave the rains of winter to gain a more secluded redwood experience.

To enhance your Avenue of the Giants drive, there's an eight-stop audio tour along the route. Pick up an audio tour card at the visitors center or on either side of the drive.

Recreation
Hiking and Biking

At mile marker 20.5 on the Avenue of the Giants, hop on the **Founder's Grove Nature Loop Trail** (0.6 mile round-trip, 30 min., easy). This sedate, flat nature trail gives a taste of the big old-growth trees in the park. Sadly, the onetime tallest tree in the world, the Dyerville Giant, fell in 1991 at the age of about 1,600. But it's still doing its part in this astounding ecosystem, decomposing before your eyes on the forest floor and feeding new life in the forest.

Right at the visitors center, you can enjoy the **Gould Grove Nature Trail** (0.6 mile one-way, 30 min., easy), a wheelchair-accessible interpretive nature walk with helpful signs describing the denizens of the forest.

For a longer walk, try the lovely **River Trail** (7 mi/11.3 km round-trip, 4 hours, moderate) as it follows the South Fork Eel River. Check with the visitors center to be sure that the summer bridges have been installed before hiking this trail. The trailhead is on Mattole Road (1.1 mi/1.8 km west of Ave. of the Giants).

Hard-core hikers can get their exercise on the **Grasshopper Multiuse Trailhead** (Mattole Rd., 5.1 mi/8.2 km west of Ave. of the Giants), which accesses the **Johnson Camp Trail** (10.5 mi/16.9 km round-trip, 7 hours, difficult) to the abandoned cabins of railroad tie makers. Or pick another fork from the same trailhead to climb more than 3,000 feet (900 m) to **Grasshopper Peak** (13.5 mi/21.7 km, 9 hours, difficult). From the peak, you can see for miles in any direction.

You can bring your street bike to the park and ride the Avenue of the Giants or Mattole Road. A number of the trails around Humboldt Redwoods State Park are designated multiuse, which means that mountain bikers can make the rigorous climbs and then rip their way back down.

Swimming and Kayaking

The **Eel River**'s forks meander through the Humboldt redwoods, creating great opportunities for cooling off on hot summer days. Reliably good spots include **Eagle Point,** near Hidden Valley Campground; **Gould Bar;** and **Garden Club of America Grove.** In addition to the usual precautions for river swimming, a blue-green algae (poisonous if ingested) can bloom August-September, making swimming in certain parts of the river hazardous.

Camping

Humboldt Redwoods State Park (707/946-2263, reservations 800/444-7275, www.reservecalifornia.com, $35) has three developed, car-accessible campgrounds; there are also primitive backcountry campsites ($5). Each developed campground has its own entrance station, and reservations are strongly recommended, as the park is quite popular with weekend campers.

Burlington Campground (707/946-1811, year-round) is adjacent to the visitors center and is a convenient starting point for the marathons and races that traverse the park in May and October. It's shaded and comfortable, engulfed in trees, and has ample restroom facilities and hot showers. **Albee Creek** (Mattole Rd., 5 mi/8 km west of Ave. of the Giants, 707/946-2472, mid-May-mid-Oct.) offers some redwood-shaded sites and others in open meadows. **Hidden Springs Campground** (Ave. of the Giants, 5 mi/8 km south of the visitors center, 707/943-3177, early May-Labor Day) is large and popular. Nearby, a trail leads to a great

Eel River swimming hole. Minimalist campers will enjoy the seclusion of hike-in trail camps at **Johnson Camp** and **Grasshopper Peak.**

Equestrians can make use of the multiuse trails, and the **Cuneo Creek Horse Camp** (old homestead on Mattole Rd., 8 mi/13 km west of Ave. of the Giants, May-mid-Oct., $35) provides a place for riders.

Information and Services

Fill your gas tank in the nearby towns of Piercy, Garberville, Redway, Redcrest, Miranda, and Rio Dell. Markets to stock up on supplies are in Garberville, Redway, Miranda, Phillipsville, Redcrest, Myers Flat, Scotia, and Rio Dell.

The nearest hospital with an emergency room is **Redwood Memorial Hospital** (3300 Renner Dr., Fortuna, 707/725-3361, www.stjoehumboldt.org).

The Lost Coast

The Lost Coast is one of California's last undeveloped coastlines. Encompassing northern Mendocino County and southern Humboldt County, this coast is "lost" because the rugged terrain makes it impractical—some might say impossible—to build a highway here. An arduous trek along its wilderness trails is worthwhile to soak up the raw beauty of its rugged beaches.

Getting There

The main section of the Lost Coast runs from Mattole in the north to Shelter Cove in the south. The best (and most accessible) area of the Lost Coast is the community of Shelter Cove. The drive from Garberville to Shelter Cove is 24 miles (39 km), but the curvy road means the drive takes at least 45 minutes.

To reach Shelter Cove from US-101 North, take the second Garberville exit. After exiting, look for signs for Shelter Cove. Turn west on Briceland Road, which becomes Shelter Cove Road.

Though the drive is just 23 miles (37 km), plan one hour; it's windy and a section of the road narrows to one lane.

Call the **Mendocino County Road Closures hotline** (707/463-4363) to find out whether any roads are temporarily closed.

Sinkyone Wilderness State Park

Encompassing the southern section of the Lost Coast, the **Sinkyone Wilderness State Park** (707/247-3318, www.parks. ca.gov, sunrise-sunset daily, $6) is a wild region of steep coastal mountains and surf-pounded beaches spotted with wildlife, including bears and elk. The Roosevelt elk had disappeared from the region until a herd from Prairie Creek State Park was reintroduced here. With their impressive antlers, the elk bulls usually weigh 700-1,100 pounds and can be quite a sight to see in the wild.

The Sinkyone Wilderness has a 16-mile (26-km) **Lost Coast Trail** that starts at Bear Harbor, south of Needle Rock, and ends at Usal Beach. This trail takes backpackers 2-3 days and has more climbing than the Lost Coast Trail to the north. The rigorous hike is mostly on bluffs above the coastline. It passes through virgin redwood groves and mixed forest with beach access at **Wheeler Beach.**

Needle Rock

The most easily accessible spot in the northern Sinkyone is **Needle Rock,** the former site of a small settlement and the current location of a park visitors center. The area's namesake rock is nearby on a black-sand beach. Visitors can camp at three environmental **campsites** (first-come, first-served, $25), 3 miles (4.8 km) from the visitors center, as well as at an old barn (first-come, first-served, $30) close to the visitors center. Camping is done by self-registration. Needle Rock's visitors center was once a ranch house. Now it is staffed by a volunteer year-round. The visitors center has

the Lost Coast

information on the region's history and various artifacts. You can also purchase maps and firewood.

Getting There
To reach Needle Rock, head off US-101 at the Garberville exit and take Redwood Road to Redway. Drive Briceland Road in Redway until it becomes Mendocino County Road 435. The road dead-ends into the state park. The last 3.5 miles (5.6 km) are unpaved, steep, and narrow.

Usal Beach
At the southern tip of Sinkyone Wilderness State Park, **Usal Beach** is a remote, black-sand beach situated under cliffs bristling with massive trees. It's accessible to adventurous coastal explorers via a steep, unpaved 6-mile (9.5 km) dirt road that is not for the fainthearted or the squeamish. Passenger cars can make the drive until the winter rainy season, when four-wheel drive becomes necessary.

When you reach the beach, you can fish from shore or beachcomb the sandy expanse. Watch sea lions torpedo through the ocean and pelicans splash into the water looking for food. Facilities include 35 primitive drive-in **campsites** (first-come, first-served, $25) with picnic tables, fire pits, and pit toilets. The rangers come here to collect the camping fees on some days, but otherwise you self-register to camp. Be aware that although firearms are not allowed in the park, locals sometimes shoot guns at night here.

Getting There
From Fort Bragg, drive 25 miles (40 km) north on CA-1 to Rockport. Usal Beach is accessible from a dirt road that leaves CA-1 at 3 miles (4.8 km) north of Rockport. Turn left on an unmarked road at mile marker 90.88.

Shelter Cove
Get a taste of the Lost Coast in Shelter Cove, a fishing community with a scattering of restaurants and accommodations and access to the shoreline. Shelter Cove is situated between the King Range Conservation Area and Sinkyone Wilderness State Park. The town has a few restaurant and lodging options and is also home to Black Sand Beach and the Cape Mendocino Lighthouse.

Getting There
To reach Shelter Cove from US-101 North, take the second Garberville exit. After exiting, look for the Shelter Cove signs and turn west on Briceland Road, which becomes Shelter Cove Road. Though the trip on Shelter Cove Road is just 23 miles (37 km), it takes an hour because it's windy and goes down to one lane at one section.

Black Sand Beach
One of the most beautiful and accessible features of the Lost Coast, **Black Sand Beach** (King Range National Conservation Area, www.blm.gov) is

named for its unusually dark sand and stones, which contrast with the deep-blue ocean water and the towering King Range Mountains in the background. The main beach parking lot has interpretive panels about the region as well as bathrooms and a drinking fountain. It's just north of the town of Shelter Cove; to get there, follow Shelter Cove Road and then take a right onto Beach Road, which deadends at Black Sand Beach. The long walk across the dark sands to either Horse Creek or Gitchell Creek is relatively easy. This beach also serves as the south end of the Lost Coast Trail.

Cape Mendocino Lighthouse

At Mal Coombs Park, the 43-foot tower of the **Cape Mendocino Lighthouse** (www.lighthousefriends.com, tours 11am-3pm daily Memorial Day-Labor Day) is quiet and dark. It began life on Cape Mendocino—a 400-foot cliff that marks the westernmost point of California—in 1868. In 1951 the tower was abandoned in favor of a light on a pole, and in 1999 the tower was moved to Shelter Cove, becoming a museum in 2000. When docents are available, you can take a tour of the lighthouse. The original first-order Fresnel lens is now on display in nearby Ferndale.

Hiking

For a great hike, take the **King Crest Trail** (10 mi/16.1 km round-trip, 1 day, strenuous), a mountain hike from the southern Saddle Mountain Trailhead to stunning King Peak and on to the North Slide Peak Trailhead. A good, solid, one-day round-trip hike can be done from either trailhead. To reach Saddle Mountain Trailhead from Shelter Cove, drive up Shelter Cove Road and turn left onto King Peak Road. Bear left on Saddle Mountain Road and turn left on a spur road to the trailhead. Only high-clearance, four-wheel-drive vehicles are recommended.

Accessible from the Saddle Mountain Trailhead, **Buck Creek Trail** (4.5 mi/7 km

one-way, 3-4 hours, strenuous) includes an infamous grade, descending more than 3,000 vertical feet (900 m) on an old logging road to the beach.

An arduous but gorgeous loop trail, the **Hidden Valley-Chinquapin-Lost Coast Loop Trail** (8 mi/12.9 km round-trip, 1-2 days, strenuous) can be done in one day, or in two days with a stop at water-accessible Nick's Camp. Access it by driving out of Shelter Cove and turning right onto Chemise Mountain Road. The trailhead will be less than a mile on your right.

Fishing

The Lost Coast is a natural fishing haven. The harbor at Shelter Cove offers charter services for ocean fishing. Kevin Riley of **Outcast Sportfishing** (Shelter Cove, 707/223-0368, www.outcastsportfish.com, May-Sept., $250 pp/day) can help plan a charter fishing trip chasing whatever is in season. The cost includes gear, tackle, and filleting and packaging your fish at the end of the day, but you must bring your own lunch. The largest kayak fishing event on the west coast is **Gimme Shelter** (www.norcalkayakanglers.com, May).

Surfing

Big Flat is a legendary surf spot about 8 miles (13 km) north of Shelter Cove on the Lost Coast Trail. While the hike in is challenging, hard-core surfers will find it worth the effort. Local surfers are very protective of this break: Even a writer for *National Geographic Adventure* who wrote about the break refused to name it for fear of retaliation. He referred to it as "Ghost Point." Be careful: Big Flat is in the middle of nowhere, and help is a ways off.

Food

The **Delgada Pizza and Bakery** (Inn of the Lost Coast, 205 Wave St., 707/986-7672, https://innofthelostcoast.com, 4pm-9pm daily, $9-30) is the place for

Hiking the Lost Coast

Start: Mattole Beach
End: Black Sand Beach (Shelter Cove)
24 mi/39 km one-way, 3 days

To fully experience one of the country's most remote and rugged coastal areas, back-packers head out on the **Lost Coast Trail.** This 24-mile (39-km) beach hike stretches from the Mattole River south to Shelter Cove's Black Sand Beach. This is a once-in-a-lifetime experience that offers hiking alongside primal, mostly wild coastline, inter-rupted only by the abandoned Punta Gorda Lighthouse and numerous shipwrecks along the shore. Waterfalls feather the coastal bluffs, shorebirds fly above the crashing surf, sea lions congregate at the aptly named Sea Lion Gulch, and migrating whales surface along the horizon. On land, you might encounter deer and bears.

This is a strenuous hike, challenging even for experienced hikers. It demands both preparation and stamina. While scenic, the ocean along the trail is also cold, rough, and unforgiving. Use caution, as multiple people have been swept out to sea.

Planning: You can hike the trail anytime between **spring and fall.** Spring is no-table for blooming wildflowers. Summer is the most crowded. Fall is the least crowded and often has the most pleasant weather. During winter, the trail can be impassable due to massive surf or flooding streams.

Most hikers **begin at the Mattole River** and head south so that you are hik-ing with the wind at your back, rather than in your face. Allow **three days** and **two nights** to complete the trail, hiking around 8 miles (13 km) a day. Be prepared to walk on sand, cobblestones, and boulders. Plan on carrying in everything you'll need (tents, sleeping bags, equipment, food, and water). Carry it all (including any trash) back out to keep the area wild. There are creeks every 1.5-2 miles (2.4-3.2 km) along the trail, but you need to purify the water before drinking it.

This is a wilderness hike, so there are few signs. You'll mostly just be hiking the beach except at a few spots. Two sections of the trail are impassable at high tide: The first is from Sea Lion Gulch to Randall Creek, and the second is from south of Big Flat down to Gitchell Creek. It's critical that you **consult a tide chart** and manage your time to make sure you pass through these areas of the trail during low tide.

Transportation: Parking at the Mattole Trailhead is free. (There have been ve-hicle break-ins, so don't leave valuables in your car.) There's also free parking at Black Sand Beach at the southern end of the trail. The drive between the two trailheads is 1 hour and 45 minutes. Or leave your car in Shelter Cove and contact **Lost Coast Adventures** (707/986-9895, http://lostcoastadventures.com, $85/person) for a ride.

Permits: Hikers need a free backcountry permit that also doubles as a fire permit. Reserve a permit online at www.recreation.gov ($6) or get a permit at a self-service box at the trailheads, at the King Range office (768 Shelter Cove Rd., Whitethorn, 707/986-5400, 8am-4:30pm Mon.-Fri.), or at the Bureau of Land Management (BLM) Arcata Field Office (1695 Heindon Rd., Arcata, 707/825-2300, www.blm.gov, 7:45am-4:30pm Mon.-Fri.).

Bear canisters: Bear canisters ($5) are mandatory for storing food and scented items while on the trail. They can be rented near the Mattole Trailhead from the **Petrolia General Store** (40 Sherman Rd., Petrolia, 707/629-3694). They're also avail-able in Shelter Cove at the BLM Whitethorn Office (768 Shelter Cove Rd., 707/986-5400) or in Arcata at the BLM Arcata Field Office (1695 Heindon Rd., 707/825-2300). **Lost Coast Adventures** rents bear canisters starting at $20.

Camping: The **Mattole Campground** (end of Lighthouse Rd., 707/986-5400, www.blm.gov, $8) has 14 first-come, first-served sites that allow you to camp near the Mattole Trailhead the night before heading out. There are no developed campgrounds or facili-ties along the trail. Dispersed camping is allowed at Cooksie Creek, Randall Creek, Big Creek, Big Flat Creek, Buck Creek, Shipman Creek, and Gitchell Creek.

pizza and pasta. The appropriately named Lost Coast Pizza is a favorite. Bottled beer or wine complements your meal. This is a small place with just one table inside and three tables outside. Next door, go for coffee, breakfast, or a sandwich at the **Fish Tank Espresso Gallery** (205 Wave Dr., 707/986-7850, 7am-2pm Thurs.-Tues., 7am-2pm and 5pm-9pm Fri.-Sat.). They serve sushi Friday and Saturday nights.

Mario's Marina Bar (53 Machi Rd., 707/986-7600, http://mariosofsheltercove. com, noon-11pm Sun.-Thurs., noon-midnight Fri.-Sat.) is the only bar in Shelter Cove.

Accommodations

Shelter Cove offers several nice motels for those who aren't up for roughing it in the wilderness overnight. **The Tides Inn of Shelter Cove** (59 Surf Point, 707/986-7900 or 888/998-4337, www. sheltercovetidesinn.com, $170-220) has standard rooms as well as luxurious suites. The suites come with fireplaces and full kitchens. All rooms face the sea, which is only steps from the inn. The Tides Inn is within walking distance of the airstrip, local shops, and restaurants.

The **Inn of the Lost Coast** (205 Wave Dr., 707/986-7521 or 888/570-9676, www. innofthelostcoast.com, $225-345) has an array of large, airy rooms and suites with stellar views to suit even luxurious tastes. While all rooms take in the coastline, the corner king bedrooms are the most popular.

Camping

There are developed campsites in the King Range National Conservation Area with amenities like restrooms, grills, fire rings, picnic tables, bear boxes, and potable water. For developed camping in Shelter Cove, the **Shelter Cove RV Campground** (492 Machi Rd., Whitethorn, 707/986-7474, RVs $46, tents $36) is just feet away from the airport and has views of the ocean. They have a deli and store (10am-6pm daily) on-site so you don't have to bring all your own food.

Information and Services

There are no medical facilities in Shelter Cove, but emergency services are coordinated through the **Shelter Cove Fire Department** (9126 Shelter Cove Rd., Whitethorn, 707/986-7507, www.sheltercove-ca.gov). The nearest hospital with an emergency room is **Redwood Memorial Hospital** (3300 Renner Dr., Fortuna, 707/725-3361, www. stjoehumboldt.org).

King Range National Conservation Area

The **King Range National Conservation Area** encompasses the northern section of the Lost Coast. Here, King Peak rises more than 4,000 feet (1,200 m) from the sea in less than 3 miles (4.8 km). It's also home to the most popular version of the **Lost Coast Trail:** a 24-mile (39-km) backpacking excursion along the region's wild beaches that begins at the mouth of the Mattole River and traverses beaches right by the ocean to end at Shelter Cove's Black Sand Beach.

Trails in the Kings Range National Conservation Area near Shelter Cove include **Rattlesnake Ridge, Kinsey Ridge, Spanish Ridge,** and **Lightning.** Before heading to the area, try to obtain a copy of Wilderness Press's *California's Lost Coast Recreation Map* (www.wildernesspress. com).

Getting There

Mattole Road, a narrow, mostly paved two-lane road, affords views of remote ranchland, unspoiled forests, and a few short miles of barely accessible cliffs and beaches. It's one of the few paved, drivable routes that allow you to view the Lost Coast from your car (the other is Shelter Cove Road, farther south). In sunny weather, the vistas are spectacular. This road also serves as access to the even smaller tracks out to the trails and campgrounds of the Sinkyone Wilderness. The most common way to get to Mattole Road is from the Victorian village of Ferndale, where you take a right on Ocean Avenue and follow the signs toward the community of Petrolia.

Mattole Beach

At the northern end of the Lost Coast, **Mattole Beach** (end of Lighthouse Rd., 707/986-5400, www.blm.gov) is a broad length of sand that's perfect for an easy, contemplative stroll. It's also popular for picnicking and fishing. Mattole Beach is the northern entry point to the Lost Coast Trail and the start of a shorter, 6-mile (9.7-km) round-trip day hike to the **Punta Gorda Lighthouse.** The lighthouse was built in 1911 after the coast and its rocks caused multiple shipwrecks. It was shut down in 1951 due to high maintenance costs.

To reach Mattole Beach from US-101, take the Garberville, Honeydew, or Ferndale exit. Follow the signs to Petrolia on Mattole Road. Turn off Mattole Road onto Lighthouse Road, which is south of the Mattole River Bridge. Follow Lighthouse Road for 5 miles (8 km) to the beach.

Camping

Developed campsites in the King Range National Conservation Area (no permit required) include amenities like restrooms, grills, fire rings, picnic tables, bear boxes, and potable water. Campgrounds are open year-round. Reservations are not available, but the odds of getting a site are pretty good, given the small number of people who come here, even in high season. Some of the larger BLM camping areas (707/986-5400, www.ca.blm.gov) are **Wailaki** (Chemise Mountain Rd., 13 sites, $8), **Nadelos** (Chemise Mountain Rd., tents only, 8 sites, $8), **Tolkan** (King Peak Rd., 5 RV sites, 4 tent sites, $8), and **Horse Mountain** (King Peak Rd., 9 sites, no water, $5). Trailers and RVs (up to 24 feet) are allowed at most sites except

Nadelos. If you are driving an RV, check road conditions beforehand.

There is a campground at **Mattole Beach** (end of Lighthouse Rd., 707/986-5400, www.blm.gov, $8) with 14 first-come, first-served sites for those who are preparing to hike the Lost Coast Trail.

Ferndale

Ferndale was built in the 19th century by Scandinavian immigrants who came to California to farm. Little has changed since the immigrants constructed their fanciful gingerbread Victorian homes and shops. Many cows still munch grass in the dairy pastures that surround the town.

The main sight in Ferndale is the town itself, which has been designated a historical landmark. Ferndale is all Victorian, all the time: Ask about the building you're in and you'll be told all about its specific architectural style, its construction date, and its original occupants. Main Street's shops, galleries, inns, and restaurants are all set into scrupulously maintained and restored late-19th-century buildings, and even the public restrooms are housed in a small Victorian-esque structure.

Getting There

Ferndale is not directly accessible from US-101; you must get off US-101 at Fernbridge and then follow CA-211 south to Ferndale. Mattole Road leads out of town south toward the Sinkyone Wilderness area, while Centerville Road heads out to the beach. Walking provides the best views and feel of the town.

Sights

The **Ferndale History Museum** (515 Shaw St., 707/786-4466, www.ferndale-museum.org, 11am-4pm Wed.-Sat., 1pm-4pm Sun., adults $2, students free), one block off Main Street, tells the story of the town. Life-size dioramas depict period life in a Victorian home, and antique artifacts bring history to life. Downstairs, the implements of rural coast history vividly display the reality that farmers and artisans faced in the preindustrial era. The museum owns its own seismograph and records the many earthquakes that occur near town.

To cruise farther back into the town's history, wander into the **Ferndale Cemetery** (Bluff St.). Well-tended tombstones and mausoleums wend up the hillside behind the town. Genealogists will love reading the scrupulously maintained epitaphs that tell the human history of the region.

Ferndale locals love that they have their own beach just outside of their quaint village. West of Ferndale, the **Centerville County Park and Beach** (4000 Centerville Rd., 707/445-7651, www.humboldtgov.org, 5am-11:45pm daily, free) stretches for an impressive 9 miles (14.5 km) and is home to a winter congregation of tundra swans. You can drive your four-wheel-drive vehicle on the sand, ride a horse, or build a big beach bonfire at night here.

Entertainment and Events

Ferndale is a quiet town where the sidewalks roll up early, but for visitors who like to be out after 6pm, there are a few options. The **Ferndale Repertory Theater** (447 Main St., 707/786-5483, www.ferndalerep.org, $13-18), the oldest and largest of the North Coast's community theaters, puts on a number of shows each year. Some are suitable for the whole family, like *Mamma Mia!,* while others, including *In the Next Room (Or the Vibrator Play),* feature more adult subject matter.

The Palace (353 Main St., 707/786-4165, 11am-1am Sun.-Thurs., 11am-2am Fri.-Sat.) is the local bar with pool tables, shuffleboard, and a jukebox.

Ferndale has hosted the **Humboldt County Fair** (1250 5th St., 707/786-9511, www.humboldtcountyfair.org, Aug., adults $8, seniors $6, children $5) since

1896. For 10 days, the old-fashioned fair hosts livestock exhibits, horse racing, competitions, a carnival, nightly musical entertainment, and a variety of shows for kids and adults.

Every Memorial Day weekend, moving sculptures race 42 miles (68 km) in three days from Arcata's plaza to Ferndale's Main Street. It's the **Kinetic Grand Championship** (707/786-3443, www.kineticgrandchampionship.com, May).

Shopping

Ferndale's Main Street makes for an idyllic morning stroll. The Victorian storefronts house antiques stores, jewelry shops, clothing boutiques, and art galleries. Ferndale is also a surprisingly good place to buy a hat.

The **Golden Gait Mercantile** (421 Main St., 707/786-4891, www.goldengaitmercantile.com, 10am-5pm Mon.-Sat., noon-4pm Sun.) has it all: antiques, candies, gourmet foodstuffs, clothing, hats, souvenirs, and more. Antiques and collectibles tend to be small and reasonably priced.

Silva's Fine Jewelry (400 Ocean Ave., 707/786-4425 or 888/589-1011, www.silvasjewelry.com, 8am-9pm daily), on the bottom floor of the Victorian Inn, is not a place for the faint of wallet. But the jewels, both contemporary and antique, are classically gorgeous.

The **Blacksmith Shop** (455 Main St., 707/786-4216, www.ferndaleblacksmith.com, 9:30am-5pm daily) displays a striking collection of useful art made by top blacksmiths and glassblowers from around the country. The array of jewelry, furniture, kitchen implements, fireplace tools, and metal defies description.

Food

Tucked into the bottom floor of the Victorian Inn, the **VI Restaurant & Tavern** (400 Ocean Ave., 707/786-4950, https://victorianvillageinn.com, 8am-10:30am, noon-3pm, and 4:30pm-8:30pm Tues.-Sun., 8am-10:30am and 4:30pm-8:30pm

⤷ Side Trip: Grizzly Creek Redwoods State Park

Star Wars fans make the pilgrimage to **Grizzly Creek Redwoods State Park** (16949 Hwy. 36, Carlotta, 707/777-3683, www.parks.ca.gov) to view the setting for one of the film franchise's most popular scenes: the bike chase through the redwoods in *Return of the Jedi*. The exciting segment featured Leia and Luke Skywalker on flying scooters chasing Stormtroopers over ferns and through tight passages between towering trees. The setting is the park's **Cheatham Grove,** a strip of old-growth redwoods in the small park.

The park is 20 miles (32 km) southeast of Eureka on US-101; then head east for 17 miles (27 km) on CA-36. May the Force be with you.

Mon., $12-36) feels like a spruced-up Western saloon. Perch yourself at the bar for casual options like fish-and-chips or sit down at a table for sophisticated dinner entrées like Portuguese paella or cold-water lobster. Sundays are prime rib nights, complete with piano music.

Locals come from as far away as Eureka to dine at the restaurant at the **Hotel Ivanhoe** (315 Main St., 707/786-9000, http://hotel-ivanhoe.com, 5pm-9pm Thurs.-Sun., bar open from 4pm Thurs.-Sun., $16-37), where it's all about the hearty homemade Italian dishes and friendly personal service. A more casual Italian dining experience can be had at the **Ferndale Pizza Co.** (607 Main St., 707/786-4345, 11:30am-9pm Tues.-Thurs., 11:30am-9:30pm Fri.-Sat., noon-9pm Sun., $16-21).

For breakfast, stop in at local favorite **Poppa Joe's** (409 Main St., 707/786-4180, 6am-2pm Mon.-Fri., 6am-noon Sat.-Sun., $5.50-9). The interior is dim and narrow, but the breakfast and lunch offerings are delicious.

Valley Grocery (339 Main St., 707/786-9515, 7am-10pm daily) stocks staples and maintains a deli; it's a perfect last stop on the way out to a beach picnic. Don't forget to drop in at the heavenly candy store **Sweetness and Light** (554 Main St., 707/786-4403 or 800/547-8180, www.sweetnessandlight.com, 10am-5pm Mon.-Fri., 11am-4pm Sat.).

Accommodations

In Ferndale, lodgings tend to be Victorian-style inns, mostly bed-and-breakfasts. Guests of the **Shaw House Inn** (703 Main St., 707/786-9958 or 800/557-7429, www.shawhouse.com, $145-289) must walk a block or two to get to the heart of downtown Ferndale, but the compensation is a spacious garden on the inn's grounds. Huge shade trees and perfectly positioned garden benches make a lovely spot to sit and enjoy the serene beauty. The inn has eight rooms and three common parlor areas. A lush morning breakfast fortifies guests.

The historic ★ **Victorian Inn** (400 Ocean Ave., 707/786-4949 or 888/589-1808, www.victorianvillageinn.com, $139-279) is an imposing structure at the corner that also houses Silva's Fine Jewelry. The inn comprises 13 rooms, all decorated with antique furnishings, luxurious linens, and pretty knickknacks. For a special treat, rent the Ira Russ Suite, a spacious room with a tower alcove that takes in the town below. A full hot breakfast is served downstairs.

In a town full of history, the **Hotel Ivanhoe** (315 Main St., 707/786-9000, www.ivanhoe-hotel.com, $95-145) is the oldest extant hostelry. Plaques on the building's exterior describe its rich legacy. The four rooms are done in rich colors that evoke the Western-Victorian atmosphere of the original hotel.

An inexpensive option is the **Redwood**

Suites (332 Ocean Ave., 707/786-5000 or 888/589-1863, www.redwoodsuites. com, $120-185). Only a block off Main Street, the property has modern rooms that are simple but comfortable. Family suites with full kitchens are available. A stay includes a hot breakfast at the nearby Victorian Inn.

Eureka

The town of Eureka began as a seaward access point to the remote gold mines of the Trinity area. Once settlers realized the value of the redwood trees, the town's logging industry was born.

Visitors can wander the town's five-block-long boardwalk on Humboldt Bay and the charming downtown shopping area, or enjoy the colorful murals and sculptures along the city streets. Outdoors enthusiasts can fish and hike, while history buffs can explore museums, Victorian mansions, and even a working Victorian-era lumber mill.

Getting There

Eureka is on US-101, easily accessed by car from north or south. From Ferndale, drive 20 miles (32 km) north to Eureka. From Garberville, Eureka is 67 miles (108 km) north on US-101.

Sights

For an introduction to Old Town Eureka, take a horse-drawn carriage tour of the historical district with the **Old Town Carriage Co.** (1st St. and F St., 646/591-2058, www.oldtowncarriageco.com, 12:30pm-6:30pm Wed.-Mon., $40-80). The carriage is usually downtown near the gazebo around the small square at 2nd and F Streets. Tours last 25 minutes, 45 minutes, or one hour.

Blue Ox Millworks and Historic Park

Blue Ox Millworks and Historic Park (1 X St., 707/444-3437 or 800/248-4259, www. blueoxmill.com, self-guided tours 9am-5pm Mon.-Fri., 9am-4pm Sat. Apr.-Nov., 9am-5pm Mon.-Fri. Nov.-Apr., adults $12, seniors $11, children $7, children under 6 free, guided tour $12.50 pp) has a working lumber mill, an upscale wood and cabinetry shop, a blacksmith forge, an old-fashioned print shop, a shipbuilding yard, a rose garden, and a historical park. It also has the world's largest collection of human-powered woodworking tools made by the historic Barnes Equipment Company. Today, the rambling buildings are filled with purchased, donated, and rehabbed tools of all kinds. Workshops feature a glassblowing kiln and a darkroom where students can learn nondigital photography methods, making their own photosensitive paper and developing black-and-white and sepia prints.

Visitors to the Blue Ox learn about the real lives and times of craftspeople of the late 1800s and early 1900s as they tour the facilities and examine the equipment. If you ask, you might be allowed to touch and even work a piece of wood of your own. Stop in at the gift shop—a converted lumberjack barracks—to check out the ceramics and woodwork the students have for sale.

Carson Mansion

Gables, turrets, cupolas, and pillars: The **Carson Mansion** (143 M St., www. ingomar.org, closed to the public) has all these architectural flourishes. The elaborate three-story, 18-room Victorian mansion was built by William Carson in 1884 and 1885 after he struck it rich in the lumber business. Almost demolished in the 1940s, it was purchased and renovated by the Ingomar Club, which now uses it for private dinner parties. It's touted as one of the most photographed buildings in the country. The building and grounds are not open to the public, but you can take photos.

Eureka

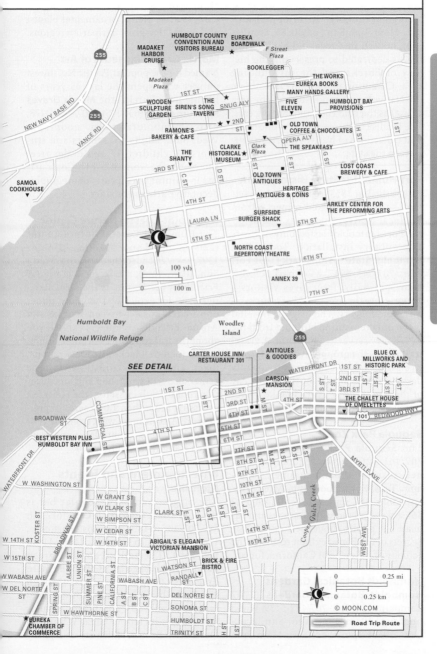

MADAKET HARBOR CRUISE ★

HUMBOLDT COUNTY CONVENTION AND VISITORS BUREAU ★

EUREKA BOARDWALK ★

F Street Plaza

BOOKLEGGER

THE WORKS

EUREKA BOOKS

MANY HANDS GALLERY

Madaket Plaza

1ST ST

WOODEN SCULPTURE GARDEN

THE SIREN'S SONG TAVERN ★

SNUG ALY

FIVE ELEVEN

HUMBOLDT BAY PROVISIONS

2ND ST

OLD TOWN COFFEE & CHOCOLATES

RAMONE'S BAKERY & CAFE

OPERA ALY

Clark Plaza

THE SPEAKEASY

THE SHANTY

CLARKE HISTORICAL MUSEUM ★

3RD ST

C ST

D ST

E ST

F ST

G ST

H ST

1ST

OLD TOWN ANTIQUES

LOST COAST BREWERY & CAFE

4TH ST

HERITAGE ANTIQUES & COINS

LAURA LN

ARKLEY CENTER FOR THE PERFORMING ARTS

SURFSIDE BURGER SHACK

5TH ST

5TH ST

NORTH COAST REPERTORY THEATRE

6TH ST

0   100 yds

0   100 m

ANNEX 39

7TH ST

SAMOA COOKHOUSE ▼

NEW NAVY BASE RD

VANCE RD

255

255

Humboldt Bay National Wildlife Refuge

Woodley Island

255

CARTER HOUSE INN/ RESTAURANT 301

ANTIQUES & GOODIES

BLUE OX MILLWORKS AND HISTORIC PARK

SEE DETAIL

WATERFRONT DR

CARSON MANSION ★

1ST ST

2ND ST

3RD ST

S ST

T ST

U ST

V ST

W ST

X ST

Y ST

1ST ST

H ST

2ND ST

3RD ST

4TH ST

M ST

THE CHALET HOUSE OF OMELETTES

BROADWAY ST

COMMERCIAL ST

4TH ST

5TH ST

6TH ST

101 REDWOOD HWY

BEST WESTERN PLUS HUMBOLDT BAY INN

7TH ST

8TH ST

9TH ST

10TH ST

11TH ST

L ST

M ST

N ST

O ST

P ST

MYRTLE AVE

WATERFRONT DR

W WASHINGTON ST

W GRANT ST

W CLARK ST

W SIMPSON ST

W CEDAR ST

CLARK ST

F ST

G ST

H ST

I ST

J ST

Cooper Gulch Creek

KOSTER ST

BROADWAY ST

W 14TH ST

ALBEE ST

UNION ST

PINE ST

SUMMER ST

CALIFORNIA ST

A ST

B ST

C ST

WABASH AVE

ABIGAIL'S ELEGANT VICTORIAN MANSION ●

WATSON ST

RANDALL ST

BRICK & FIRE BISTRO ▼

WEST AVE

W 14TH ST

W 15TH ST

W WABASH AVE

W DEL NORTE ST

SPRING ST

W HAWTHORNE ST

DEL NORTE ST

SONOMA ST

HUMBOLDT ST

TRINITY ST

J ST

★ EUREKA CHAMBER OF COMMERCE

0   0.25 mi

0   0.25 km

© MOON.COM

Road Trip Route

Clarke Historical Museum

The privately owned **Clarke Historical Museum** (240 E St., 707/443-1947, www.clarkemuseum.org, 10am-6pm Tues.-Sat., 11am-4pm Sun., adults $5, families $10), housed in a regal old bank building, is dedicated to preserving the history of Eureka and the surrounding area. Changing exhibitions illuminate the Native American history of the area as well as the gold rush and logging eras. The Nealis Hall annex displays one of the best collections of Native American artifacts in the state.

Fort Humboldt State Historic Park

Established in 1853 to protect white settlers—particularly gold miners—from the local Native Americans, the original Fort Humboldt lasted only 17 years as a military installation. Today, **Fort Humboldt State Historic Park** (3431 Fort Ave., 707/445-6547, www.parks.ca.gov, 8am-5pm daily, free) gives visitors a glimpse into the lives of 19th-century soldiers and loggers. The original hospital is the only remaining building from the fort; it now serves as a museum. A gravel trail circles the grounds, where interpretive plaques depict the fort's frequently dark history. Come on the third Saturday of the month (May-Sept.) to take a five-minute ride on a steam locomotive.

Sequoia Park Zoo

The **Sequoia Park Zoo** (3414 W St., 707/441-4263, www.sequoiaparkzoo.net, 10am-5pm daily summer, 10am-5pm Tues.-Sun., noon-4pm Mon. winter, adults $10, seniors $7, children 3-12 $6) seeks to preserve local species and educate the public about their needs. The Secrets of the Forest exhibit recreates the ecology of a Northern California forest.

Humboldt Botanical Gardens

Humboldt Botanical Gardens (7707 Tompkins Hill Rd., 707/442-5139, www.hbgf.org, 10am-4pm Wed.-Sun. Apr.-Oct., 10am-2pm Wed.-Sat., 11am-3pm Sun. Nov.-Mar., adults $10, seniors $7, children $5) celebrates the ecosystems of Humboldt County. The 44-acre site includes native plants, ornamental plants, and plants that grow in riparian regions.

Morris Graves Museum of Art

Named for the popular Pacific Northwest painter who spent the last 35 years of his life near Eureka, the **Morris Graves Museum of Art** (636 F St., 707/442-0278, http://humboldtarts.org, noon-5pm Wed.-Sun., adults $5, seniors and students $2, children 17 and under free) showcases the work of North Coast artists in painting, sculpture, photography, decorative art, and folk art.

Humboldt Coastal Nature Center

The **Humboldt Coastal Nature Center** (220 Stamps Lane, Manila, 707/444-1397, www.friendsofthedunes.org, Wed.-Sun. 10am-4pm), run by local nonprofit Friends of the Dunes, is the ideal starting point for exploring the sandy, dune-dominated coast between Eureka and Arcata. Friendly volunteers can tell you about the unique critters in these dunes, which include black-tailed jackrabbits, foxes, and rough-skinned newts. The center also has a gift shop and an education room. Trails crisscross the 118 acres, accessing more than 1,000 acres of public land. A 10-minute walk from the center to the long surf-pounded, windswept beach is highly recommended.

Entertainment and Events
Nightlife

The biggest and most popular bar is the **Lost Coast Brewery & Café** (617 4th St., 707/445-4480, www.lostcoast.com, 11am-10pm Sun.-Thurs., 11am-11pm Fri.-Sat.). The tall cream-and-green building is perched by itself on the main drag, easy to spot as you pass through town. The brewery draws crowds, especially on weekends, and makes popular microbrews including Great White and Downtown Brown, which are on tap. Try the tasty brewpub-style food and a few of the delicious beers. Free **tours** are available at Lost Coast's off site brewery (1600 Sunset Dr., 707/267-9651, www.lostcoast. com).

The Speakeasy (411 Opera Alley, 707/444-2244, 4pm-11pm Mon.-Thurs., 4pm-2am Fri.-Sat., noon-2am Sun.) is the place to go for tasty cocktails. This dark, narrow bar, which sometimes has live music, serves up Southern-style drinks, including a great mint julep.

One of the best dive bars on the North Coast, **The Shanty** (213 3rd St., 707/444-2053, noon-2am Mon.-Sat., 9:30am-2am Sun.) impresses with friendly clientele, a superbly curated jukebox, and a lot of eclectic character. Head outdoors to play table tennis or pool or smoke a cigarette. The extended happy hour (4pm-7pm Mon.-Fri., noon-4pm Sat.-Sun.) offers top-shelf beers and liquors and rock-bottom prices.

The cool, worn-feeling Victorian space at **The Siren's Song Tavern** (325 2nd St., 707/442-8778, www.sirenssongtavern. com, 3pm-10pm Tues.-Thurs., 3pm-midnight Fri.-Sat.) hosts bands that perform on a rug in front of the window. Siren's Song has a superb craft beer list including 18 brews on tap.

The Arts
The **Arkley Center for the Performing Arts** (412 G St., 707/442-1956 or 888/859-8797, www.atlpublishing.com) is the home of the **Eureka Symphony** and **North Coast Dance.** The elegant venue, with its striking mural of musicians and dancers on the back of the building, also hosts rock, country, and jazz acts.

Festivals and Events
Music lovers flock to Eureka each year for a number of big music festivals. One of the biggest is the **Redwood Coast Jazz Festival** (various venues around town,

From top to bottom: the Samoa Peninsula; The Shanty; Humboldt Coastal Nature Center.

707/445-3378, www.rcmfest.org, May). For four days in spring, music lovers can enjoy every style of jazz imaginable, including Dixieland, zydeco, and big band. The festival also features dance lessons and contests.

Experience what Eureka was like during its logging heyday at the **Dolbeer Steam Donkey Days** (Fort Humboldt State Historic Park, 3431 Fort Ave., 707/445-6567, www.parks.ca.gov, Apr.). This two-day event features working logging equipment, train rides, and logging skill competitions.

The **Kinetic Grand Championship** (707/786-3443, http://kineticgrandchampionship.com, Memorial Day weekend) is a pedal-powered moving sculpture race that originates in Arcata and ends in Ferndale. The second day of this event takes place on Eureka's waterfront.

Shopping

Eureka boasts the largest California antiques scene north of the Bay Area. **Annex 39** (610 F St., 707/443-1323, noon-5:30pm Tues.-Sat.) specializes in vintage linens and laundry products and also has a great selection of art deco and midcentury modern pieces. Generalists will love rooting through **Old Town Antiques** (318 F St., 707/442-3235, 10:30am-6pm Mon.-Sat.).

For an afternoon of shopping, head down toward the water to 2nd Street. Most of the buildings are historic, and you might find an unassuming brass plaque describing the famous brothel that once occupied what is now a toy store. Literature lovers have a nice selection of independent bookstores: **Eureka Books** (426 2nd St., 707/444-9593, www.eurekabooksellers.com, 10am-6pm daily) has a big, airy room in which to browse a selection of new and used books. **Booklegger** (402 2nd St., at E St., 707/445-1344, 10am-5:30pm Mon.-Sat., 11am-4pm Sun.) is a small but well-organized new-and-used bookshop that specializes in antique books.

Galleries and gift shops abound. **Many Hands Gallery** (438 2nd St., 707/445-0455, www.manyhandsgallery.net, 10am-9pm Mon.-Sat., 10am-6pm Sun.) represents approximately 100 local artisans and also displays work from national and international artists cooperatives, fair-trade organizations, and commercial importers. You'll find plenty of humor and whimsy, and prices range from 10 cents to $10,000.

The Works (434 2nd St., 707/442-8121, www.theworkseureka.com, 11am-6pm daily) has been providing Humboldt County music fans with vinyl records and CDs since 1971.

Sports and Recreation
Fishing

Eureka is a serious fishing destination. Oodles of both ocean- and river-fishing opportunities are available, and several fishing tournaments are held each year. In California, you must have a valid state fishing license to fish in either the ocean or the rivers. Check with your charter service or guide to be sure they provide a day license with your trip. If they don't, you will have to get your own.

For deep-sea fishing, **Greenwater Fishing Adventures** (707/845-9588, www.eurekafishing.net, fishing trips $190-300) heads out on the 36-foot *Shellback* to catch salmon, rockfish, halibut, and tuna. **Full Throttle Sportfishing** (601 Startare Dr., 707/498-7473, www.fullthrottlesportfishing.com, $210-300) supplies all needed tackle and can take you out to fish for salmon, rockfish, tuna, or halibut. Trips last all day, and most leave at 6:30am. If you're launching your own boat, public launches are the **Samoa Boat Ramp** (New Navy Base Rd., 707/445-7651, www.humboldtgov.org, 5am-11:45pm daily) and the **Fields Landing Boat Ramp** (Railroad Ave., 707/445-7651, www.humboldtgov.org, 5am-midnight daily).

Eureka has good spots for pier fishing. In town, try the K Street Pier, the pier at the east end of Commercial Street, or the pier at the end of Del Norte Street. Farther north, the north jetty (Hwy. 255, across Samoa Bridge) also has a public pier open for fishing.

Bird-Watching

The national, state, and county parks lacing the area are ideal bird-watching havens. The **Humboldt Bay National Wildlife Refuge Complex** (1020 Ranch Rd., Loleta, 707/733-5406, www.fws. gov) encompasses several wildlife-refuge sites where visitors are welcome. At the Salmon Creek Unit, you'll find the **Richard J. Guadagno Headquarters and Visitors Center** (8am-5pm daily), which is an excellent starting place for a number of wildlife walks. To get to the visitors center from US-101, take the exit for Hookton heading north and turn left onto Eel River Drive. Take the first right onto Ranch Road, and you'll find the visitors center parking lot.

Hiking and Biking

There is a vast system of trails in the state and national parks, and the city of Eureka maintains multiuse biking and hiking trails as well. Most familiar is the Old Town Boardwalk, part of the **Waterfront Trail** that comprises disconnected sections along Humboldt Bay. **Sequoia Park Trail** begins at the Sequoia Park Zoo and wends through redwood forests, past a duck pond, and through a meadow. This trail is paved and friendly for strollers and wheelchairs. The unpaved **Elk River Trail** (end of Hilfiker Ln.) stretches for a mile through wild meadows along the coast. **Cooper Gulch Trail** is more a sedate stroll than a strenuous hike, circling the Cooper Gulch park playing fields.

Kayaking, Rafting, and Stand-Up Paddleboarding

The water is cold, but getting out on it in a kayak can be exhilarating. Humboldt State University manages the **Humboldt Bay Aquatic Center** (921 Waterfront Dr., 707/443-4222, www2.humboldt.edu,

office 10am-4pm Mon.-Fri., rentals by appointment, kayaks $26-35, SUPs $26), which rents kayaks and stand-up paddleboards from a location at the Woodsley Island Marina.

River rafters and kayakers have great opportunities for fun on the inland Klamath and Trinity Rivers. **Bigfoot Rafting Company** (Willow Creek, 530/629-2263, www.bigfootrafting.com, adults $89, children $79) leads half-day, full-day, and multiday trips on both rivers as well as on the Cal-Salmon and Smith Rivers. Experts can take inflatable kayaks down the Class IV rapids, while newcomers can find a gentle paddle.

Harbor Cruises

For a great introduction to Eureka and Humboldt Bay, book a tour on the **Madaket** (dock at end of C St., 707/445-1910, www. humboldtbaymaritimemuseum.com, May-Sept.), the oldest continuously operating passenger vessel in the country, with the smallest licensed bar in California. The ferry, built in 1910, offers three tours: a narrated **history cruise** (75 minutes, adults $22, seniors and children 13-17 $18, children 5-12 $12, children under 5 free), a **cocktail cruise** (1 hour, $10), or a **Sunday morning eco cruise** (1.5 hours, adults $26, seniors and children 13-17 $22, children 5-12 $12, children under 5 free). The history cruise follows a scenic 8.5-mile (13.5-km) loop in Humboldt Bay and the adjoining Arcata Bay. Passengers learn about the area's history and the stories behind local landmarks, and visit an egret colony.

Tours

Humboldt County has long been the epicenter of the Emerald Triangle, a region that includes Humboldt, Mendocino, and Trinity Counties and is the largest producer of cannabis in the country. For a closer look at this culture, contact **Humboldt Cannabis Tours** (215 C St., Eureka, 707/839-4640, www.

humcannabis.com). Tour options include the **Cannabis Tour** (4 hours, $89), which includes a visit to four cannabis retail locations. More involved is the **Humboldt Farm Tour** (May-Oct., $159), a full-day excursion that visits a working cannabis farm with a gourmet lunch and a stop at a local dispensary.

Drag Racing

For a down-home American experience, take in a car race at the **Samoa Drag Strip** (New Navy Base Rd., 707/845-5755, www. samoadragstrip.com, May-Sept., adults $10, children under 13 free). The 0.25-mile track is on the Samoa Peninsula. Special nights feature Harley motorcycles or diesel trucks.

Food
Breakfast

One of the older restaurants in downtown Eureka, ★ **The Chalet House of Omelettes** (1935 5th St., 707/442-0333, http://thechaleteureka.com, 7am-3pm daily, $8-11) has been serving delicious omelets in a homey atmosphere since 1975. The build-your-own-omelet (four ingredients and three eggs, $10.25) is a favorite. The Chalet Special Omelet is recommended, filled with bacon, cheese, and avocado slices. Attentive servers fill your cup of coffee to the brim for the duration of your meal. There's another Eureka location (390 Walnut Dr., 707/798-6480, 7am-3pm daily).

Los Bagels (403 2nd St., 707/442-8525, www.losbagels.com, 6:30am-5pm Mon.-Fri., 7am-5pm Sat., 7am-4pm Sun., $2-10) has been fusing Jewish and Mexican foods since 1984. Bagel options include guacamole or chorizo, build-your-own egg scramble, and lunchtime bagel sandwiches. There's also an Arcata location (106 I St., 707/822-3150, 6:30am-5pm Mon.-Fri., 7am-5pm Sat., 7am-3pm Sun.).

Bakeries and Cafés

Ramone's Bakery & Café (209 E St., 707/445-2923, http://ramonesbakery.

com, 7am-6pm Mon.-Fri., 8am-5pm Sat., 8am-4pm Sun.) is a local chain, selling fresh baked goods and candies. Enjoy a fresh cup of coffee roasted in-house with a Danish or scone, or get a whole tart, cake, or loaf of bread to take away.

Old Town Coffee & Chocolates (211 F St., 707/445-8600, http:// oldtowncoffeeeureka.com, 7am-8pm Sun.-Mon., 7am-9pm Tues.-Thurs., 7am-10pm Fri.-Sat.) does more than caffeinate their customers. They also sell chocolate and fudge made on-site, as well as bagels, waffles, wraps, and grilled cheese sandwiches. Many evenings feature live music, open mics, or book readings. They also have a second location (502 Henderson St., 707/442-1522, 6am-5pm Mon.-Fri., 6:30am-5pm Sat., 8am-2pm Sun.).

American

The ★ **Samoa Cookhouse** (511 Vance Rd., Samoa, 707/442-1659, www. samoacookhouse.net, 7am-9pm daily summer, 7am-3pm and 5pm-8pm daily winter, adults $18, children 8-11 $10, children 5-7 $8) is a Eureka institution. Red-checked tablecloths cover long, rough tables to create the atmosphere of a logging-camp dining hall. All-you-can-eat meals are served family-style from huge serving platters. Diners sit on benches and pass the hearty fare down in turn. Think hunks of roast beef, mountains of mashed potatoes, and piles of cooked vegetables for lunch and dinner, or a giant plate of eggs, hash browns, sausage, and toast for breakfast. This is the place to bring your biggest appetite. After dinner, browse the small Historic Logging Museum and gift shop.

Restaurant 301 (301 L St., 800/404-1390, www.carterhouse.com, 5pm-8:30pm daily, $23-47) at the Carter House Inns seems like a big-city spot. The chef creates an ever-changing menu of delectable delicacies, along with tasting menus. Menu options include exotic duck dishes, local seafood preparations, and items from the restaurant's on-site garden. For a treat, try the wine flights suggested with the menus. Restaurant 701 is known for its extensive wine list, with more than 3,400 selections. There's also a five-course tasting menu ($65).

A turquoise floor and jade lighting give **Five Eleven** (511 2nd St., 707/268-3852, 5pm-9pm Tues.-Thurs., 5pm-9:30pm Fri.-Sat., $10-35) a bold, metropolitan feel. The menu changes frequently but usually includes wood-fired meat and seafood. They also serve specialty craft cocktails, a few choice craft beers, and a wide variety of wines at the long stone bar.

The **Surfside Burger Shack** (445 5th St., 707/268-1295, 11am-7pm Sun.-Thurs., 11am-8pm Fri.-Sat., $6-8) is nowhere near the ocean, but it does have surfing decor and darn good burgers made from grass-fed Humboldt cows. The classic cheeseburger hits the spot.

Italian

Mycophiles (mushroom lovers) revere the ★ **Brick & Fire Bistro** (1630 F St., 707/268-8959, www.brickandfirebistro.com, 11:30am-9pm Wed.-Mon. $14-22) for its popular wild mushroom cobbler—shiitake, porcini, crimini, and oyster mushrooms sit in a rich cream sauce under a cheesy cobbler biscuit. Mushrooms also shine on the surprisingly light and tasty chanterelle and winter squash pizza. This creative neighborhood Italian restaurant cooks most items in an artisan brick oven and serves a sensational chopped Caesar salad (with an egg on top), a daily fresh fish of the day, and meat of the day. This intimate bistro might be the best restaurant in Eureka.

Seafood

Sample the products of Humboldt County at **Humboldt Bay Provisions** (205 G St., 707/672-3850, www. humboldtbayprovisions.com, 4pm-9pm

From top to bottom: the *Madaket*; the Samoa Cookhouse; the Special Omelet at The Chalet House of Omelettes.

Mon.-Fri., 1pm-9pm Sat.-Sun., $10-48). Sit at the reclaimed redwood bar, where you can nibble on salmon from nearby Blue Lake and slurp tasty oysters from Humboldt Bay while drinking local brews.

Accommodations
Under $150

The **Bayview Motel** (2844 Fairfield St., 707/442-1673 or 866/725-6813, www.bayviewmotel.com, $130-220) has lovely views of Humboldt Bay from a hilltop location. Spacious rooms are decorated in elegant colors and fabrics. You'll find whirlpool suites, free Wi-Fi, cable TV, wet bars, and coffee makers. If you're traveling with the family, rent a double suite—two rooms with an adjoining door and separate baths. Downtown Eureka is within an easy drive.

The Historic Eagle House dates to 1888 and is home to an Irish pub, a ballroom, a yoga studio, the improbably named Phatsy Kline's Parlor Lounge, and the **Inn at 2nd & C** (139 2nd St., 707/444-3344, www.theinnat2ndandc.com, $119-209). Victorian furnishings and modern touches abound in the 23 rooms. Guests enjoy an afternoon tea and a morning continental breakfast.

$150-250

The ★ **Carter House Inns** (301 L St., 800/404-1390, www.carterhouse.com, $189-589) have a range of accommodations in a cluster of butter-yellow Victorian buildings near the Carson Mansion. The main building has 23 rooms and suites, some with gas fireplaces and soaking tubs. Across the street, a reproduction of a Victorian mansion has six rooms, including a family suite with two bedrooms, while **The Bell Cottage** has three rooms and a full common kitchen. For a splurge, rent **The Carter Cottage,** which has two bathrooms, a deck with a fountain, a soaking tub, and a large den and kitchen area. All guests are treated to a hot breakfast and

an afternoon wine and appetizer hour. Dine at the inn's renowned Restaurant 301.

There's no place along the California coast quite like ★ **Oyster Beach** (865B New Navy Base Rd., 707/834-6555, www.humboldtbaysocialclub.com, $195-295), a set of refurbished buildings on the Samoa Peninsula. The 22-acre property has its own beach on Humboldt Bay and impressive eucalyptus groves. Five units range from The Loft, with reclaimed wood walls, to the Mid-Century Waterfront, mere feet from the bay. Just eight minutes from downtown Eureka, Oyster Beach feels like it's a world away. They also rent three suites and a bunkroom across the street at **Samoa Field** ($150-175).

★ **Best Western Plus Humboldt Bay** (232 W. 5th St., 707/443-2234, www.humboldtbayinn.com, $170-250) is a pleasant surprise. What sets it apart is its Oasis Spa Area, a tropical-themed courtyard with tiki torches, island music, fire pits, and a hot tub grotto that stand in contrast to the industrial neighborhood location. Within the enclosure are a heated pool, 24-hour fitness center, and billiards table. A complimentary continental breakfast is served daily. An unexpected amenity is an on-site limo with a driver who will drive guests to any restaurant in Eureka. The rooms are modern and clean, too.

Information and Services

Bus service in and around Eureka is operated by the **Humboldt Transit Authority** (HTA, https://hta.org, adults $1.70, seniors and children $1.30). The HTA's **Eureka Transit System** (ETS, 707/443-0826, https://hta.org) runs within town limits, and the **Redwood Transit System** (RTS, 707/443-0826, https://hta.org, adults $1.65-5.50, seniors and children $1.40-5) can take you around the area; it runs from Eureka north to Trinidad, south to Scotia, and east to Willow Creek.

Eureka has a small commercial airport, **California Redwood Coast-Humboldt**

North Coast Radio

The community radio stations of the Mendocino and Humboldt Coasts are an accurate reflection of the regions they serve: independent, eclectic, and surprising. Though some of the stations listed carry NPR, they have local programs too. In addition, these media outlets provide information during storms, wildfires, road closures, and other incidents that could affect your travel.

KGUA 88.3FM (http://kgua.org, Gualala): Owned by the nonprofit Native Media Resource Center, KGUA produces local shows including *Peggy's Place*, which covers local stories, and *Pig in a Pen*, which features bluegrass music.

KMUD 88.1FM (www.kmud.org, Eureka and Redway): KMUD calls itself Redwood Community Radio and covers southern Humboldt County from Garberville to Eureka. A handful of programs focus on local affairs, including *The Cannabis Show*.

KHUM 104.7 and 104.3FM (http://khum.com, Eureka and Ferndale): KHUM is a free-form radio station broadcast from Ferndale. They feature local DJs playing music programs, along with original shows like *Humboldt Chronicles* and *Humboldt Bay Watch*.

County Airport (ACV, 3561 Boeing Ave., McKinleyville, 707/839-5401, www.humboldtgov.org), which serves the North Coast region with expensive but convenient flights on United Airlines.

The full-service **St. Joseph Hospital** (2700 Dolbeer St., 707/445-8121, www.stjoehumboldt.org) has an emergency room and an urgent care center.

Arcata

Arcata has a distinctly small-town feel, different from its southern neighbor. The hippie daughter of blue-collar Eureka, Arcata is home to Humboldt State University. Students make up almost half of the city's population, and the town is known for its liberal politics.

Arcata has a lively arts and music scene along with a handful of restaurants that you might expect in a bigger city. It makes a great home base for exploring the wild North Coast.

Getting There

Arcata is 8 miles (13 km) north of Eureka on US-101. It is also a straight shot west from Redding. To reach Arcata from Redding, take CA-299 west for 140 miles (225 km).

Sights
★ Arcata Plaza

The heart of downtown is **Arcata Plaza** (9th St. and G St., 707/822-4500, www.arcatamainstreet.com), which has been the epicenter of town since the 1850s when it was a freight and passenger stop. The park has a couple of palm trees and a grassy lawn where folks hang out. Circling the plaza are independent restaurants, bars, coffee shops, and stores. The plaza hosts many events, from the Saturday farmers market to the start of the annual Kinetic Grand Championship race.

Arcata Community Forest

The first city-owned forest in California, the 2,134-acre **Arcata Community Forest** (east ends of 11th St., 14th St., and California St., 707/822-5951, www.cityofarcata.org, sunrise-sunset daily) has trails winding through second-growth redwoods, open for hiking, mountain biking, and horseback riding. Just east of the city's downtown and behind Humboldt State University, the forest is an ideal place to stroll between the silent giants, many of which are cloaked in moss, and take in stumps the size of compact cars as well as vibrant-green waist-high ferns. The park also has a section with picnic tables and a playground. A trail map is available for download (www.cityofarcata.org).

Entertainment and Events
Nightlife

A strip of dive bars lines the edge of Arcata Plaza on 9th Street. The best of the bunch, **The Alibi** (744 9th St., 707/822-3731, www.thealibi.com, 8am-2am daily), dates to the 1920s. The Alibi serves cheap, well-crafted cocktails with infused liquors, including a wide range of Bloody Marys. It also has an extensive breakfast, lunch, and dinner menu with specialty burgers and entrées.

The North Coast is known for its microbrews, and **Dead Reckoning Tavern** (815 J St., 707/630-5008, 2pm-8pm Sun.-Mon., 2pm-10pm Tues.-Thurs., 2pm-11pm Fri.-Sat.) is a great place to try one. They have 34 rotating beers on tap along with one kombucha tap and a root beer tap for non-imbibers. The tavern's back room has a few arcade games and a small record store to enjoy while sipping suds.

Humboldt Brews (856 10th St., 707/826-2739, www.humboldtbrews.com, 11:30am-10pm daily, open until 2am for live music) serves food and 25 beers on tap. This popular hangout has a pool table and an adjacent room that serves as a concert space for midsize national jam bands, indie acts, and reggae outfits.

Richard's Goat Tavern & Tea Room (401 I St., 707/630-5000, http://richardsgoat.com, 3pm-2am Tues.-Sun., 3pm-midnight Mon.) is an oasis of culture and cocktails blocks away from the plaza's dive bar scene. The liquors are house infused, and there's craft beer on tap. The bar has its own tiny theater dubbed the Miniplex, where art house movies are screened and the occasional live act performs.

Live Music

Music legends like Elvis Costello, John Prine, Melissa Etheridge, The Growlers, and Jake Shimabukuro play at Humboldt State University's **John Van Duzer Theatre** (1 Harpst St., 707/826-4411, www.humboldt.edu). Up-and-coming acts typically perform at **The Depot** (University Center, 1 Harpst St., 707/826-4411) and the **West Gym** (top of Union St.).

Cinema

Dating to 1938, the art deco **Arcata Theatre Lounge** (1036 G St., 707/822-1220, www.arcatatheatre.com) screens movies, hosts concerts, and puts on events like Sci-Fi Night, where they show old science-fiction movies. The theater seats have been replaced by circular tables and chairs, and the full bar serves food as well as drinks.

A few blocks away, the 1914 **Minor Theatre** (1001 H St., 707/822-3456, www.minortheatre.com) is one of the oldest operating movie theaters in the country, showing independent movies as well as Hollywood films. Enjoy your film with food (from empanadas to pizza), draft beer, wine, and beer floats served to your seat.

Festivals and Events

Arcata Plaza is the starting line of the **Kinetic Grand Championship** (707/786-3443, http://kineticgrandchampionship.com, Memorial Day weekend), a three-day, 42-mile (68-km) race featuring human-powered art sculptures that continues to Eureka and Ferndale.

In the plaza is the annual **Arcata Main Street Oyster Festival** (707/822-4500, www.arcatamainstreet.com/oysterfest, June), which celebrates the local Kumamoto oyster with—you guessed it—oysters. This is the largest one-day event in Humboldt County. Live music and microbrews accompany the bivalves.

Sports and Recreation

The 18-hole **Redwood Curtain Disc Golf Course** (accessible from Humboldt State University's Redwood Science Lab, though parking is only available in the lot

★ Craft Breweries

Humboldt County makes great beer. Local craft beer and microbrews are served in restaurants and line the beer aisles of local supermarkets. One way to taste these beers or sample their smaller batches is to visit a North Coast brewery.

If you crave sustainable suds, visit the **Eel River Brewing Company's Taproom & Grill** (1777 Alamar Way, Fortuna, 707/725-2739, http:// eelriverbrewing.com, 11am-11pm daily), where you can sip organic beer made with renewable energy. Drink the Organic IPA or Organic Acai Berry Wheat Ale inside at the taproom's long wooden bar, or head out to the adjacent beer garden. Tours (707/764-1772) of the brewing facilities are in the nearby town of Scotia.

beers on tap at the Mad River Brewing Company Tasting Room

The **Lost Coast Brewery & Café** (617 4th St., Eureka, 707/445-4480, www. lostcoast.com, 11am-10pm Sun.-Thurs., 11am-11pm Fri.-Sat.) feels like a locals' bar and is filled with people even on weeknights. The brewery's Great White and Lost Coast Pale Ale are the most popular brews, but the smooth Downtown Brown is recommended for darker beer fans. Free half-hour tours are at their brewery (1600 Sunset Dr., Eureka, 707/267-9651).

Fifteen miles (24 km) from downtown Arcata, the **Mad River Brewing Company Tasting Room** (101 Taylor Way, Blue Lake, 707/668-4151, www.madriverbrewing.com, 11:30am-9pm Sun.-Thurs., 11:30am-10pm Fri.-Sat.) is a favorite with Humboldt County beer drinkers. Not only do they brew award-winning beers like Steelhead Extra Pale Ale and Jamaica Red Ale, they also have tasty pub food, frequent live music, and an outdoor beer garden on sunny days.

Just outside of Arcata, **Six Rivers Brewery** (1300 Central Ave. McKinleyville, 707/839-7580, www.sixriversbrewery.com, kitchen 4pm-10pm Mon., 11:30am-10pm Tues.-Sun., bar 4pm-11:30pm Mon., 11:30am-11:30pm Tues.-Wed. and Sun., 11:30am-12:30am Thurs.-Sat.) is a fun gathering spot that serves small-batch brews and locally sourced menu items. Sip a popular Macadamia Nut Porter while enjoying weekend live music, trivia night on Sunday, or karaoke on Monday.

A local favorite, the **Redwood Curtain Brewing Company Tasting Room** (550 S. G St., Arcata, 707/826-7222, www.redwoodcurtainbrewing.com, noon-11pm Sun.-Tues., noon-midnight Wed.-Sat.) is in an industrial park a few blocks south of downtown. This unassuming spot is the place to try their Imperial Golden Ale, one of the most drinkable beers in Humboldt County; their award-winning Dusseldorf Altbier; or their creative Cerise Coup, which is aged in a French oak chardonnay barrel and then infused with cherries for six months. Sit at the bar overlooking the brew room or play a game of shuffleboard. They also have a location in Eureka (1595 Myrtle Ave., Suite B, 707/269-7143, noon-11pm Sun.-Tues., noon-midnight Wed.-Sat.).

after 5pm) winds its way through massive redwood trees. On the second hole, the tee is atop a 10-foot-high redwood stump.

For local sports action, get a ticket to see the **Humboldt Crabs** (Arcata Ball Park, F St. and 9th St., 707/840-5665, http://humboldtcrabs.com), the oldest continually active collegiate summer baseball team in the country.

Warm up on the North Coast at the **Finnish Country Sauna and Tubs** (5th St. and J St., 707/822-2228, http://cafemokkaarcata.com, 11am-midnight Fri.-Sat., 11am-11pm Sun.-Thurs., hot tub and sauna rentals $19.50/hour), where you can soak in a private outdoor hot tub or sweat in a red cedar sauna. The garden and facilities are behind the Café Mokka Coffeehouse.

Arcata Marsh and Wildlife Sanctuary

One of Arcata's most popular places to take a hike is in a section of the town's wastewater treatment facility. The **Arcata Marsh Interpretive Center** (569 S. G St., 707/826-2359, www.cityofarcata.org, visitors center 1pm-5pm Mon., 9am-5pm Tues.-Sun., grounds 4am-sunset daily) holds a small museum that explains how the city transformed an industrial wasteland into a 307-acre wildlife sanctuary using Arcata's wastewater. Hike the sanctuary's hiking and biking paths, or try to spot some of the 270 bird species that use the marsh as a migratory stop.

Shopping

Around Arcata Plaza and along H Street are a number of unique stores. Head into **Pacific Paradise** (1087 H St., 707/822-7143, 10am-6pm Mon.-Sat., 10:30am-5:30pm Sun.) to stock up on golf discs, hoodies, tie-dyes, and smoking equipment.

Across the street, the **Tin Can Mailman Used & Rare Books Store** (1000 H St., 707/822-1307, www.tincanbooks.com, 10am-6pm Sun.-Thurs., 10am-7pm Fri.-Sat.) crams together two floors full of used books. For the latest fiction or memoir, head to **Northtown Books** (957 H St., 707/822-2834, www.northtownbooks.com, 10am-7pm Mon.-Thurs. and Sat., 10am-9pm Fri., noon-5pm Sun.), which also has an extensive magazine collection.

Solutions (858 G St., 707/822-6972, 10am-5:30pm Mon.-Sat.) is the place to pick up hemp clothing, organic bedding, and eco-goods.

Pick up some tunes at **Peoples Records** (725 8th St., 707/822-7625, 11am-6pm Mon.-Sat., 11am-4pm Sun.), Humboldt County's largest record store. Located on the edge of Arcata Plaza, Peoples Records sells new and used vinyl albums along with cassettes and CDs.

A few blocks from the plaza, **Holly Yashi** (1300 9th St., 707/822-5132, www.hollyyashi.com, 10am-6pm Mon.-Sat., noon-5pm Sun.) specializes in niobium jewelry. Niobium is a metal that gains streaks of color after being dipped in an electrically charged bath. Watch artists at work crafting the jewelry in the attached studio. Guided tours (11am and 2pm Mon.-Fri.) are available.

Food
Breakfast

★ **Renata's Creperie and Espresso** (1030 G St., 707/825-8783, 8am-3pm Sun.-Thurs., 8am-9pm Fri.-Sat., $4-12) is the best place to start the day. Their organic buckwheat crepes are artfully decorated with drizzled sauces and well-placed garnishes, and deliver on their promising looks with sweet and savory fillings. Expect a wait on weekends. Renata's is open for dinner on Friday and Saturday nights.

The Big Blue Café (846 G St., 707/826-7578, 8am-3pm Sun.-Thurs., 7am-3pm Fri.-Sat., $6-16) is an appropriately colored diner on Arcata Plaza with a menu that skews toward breakfast basics like omelets, French toast, and breakfast burritos. The organic house coffee is flavorful.

Café Brio (8th St. and G St.,

707/822-5922, http://cafebrioarcata.com, 7am-6pm Mon., 7am-9pm Tues.-Fri., 8am-9pm Sat., 8am-4pm Sun., $10-17) serves breakfast, lunch, dinner, and brunch. Dishes freely utilize local mushrooms, from a mushroom *croque madame* to mushroom tacos.

Mexican
Arcata locals swear by **Taqueria La Barca** (5201 Carlson Park Dr., 707/822-6669, 11am-8pm Mon.-Fri., $7-11) for its house-made horchata, chile rellenos, and carnitas.

Seafood
A local institution for more than 30 years, **Tomo Japanese Restaurant** (708 9th St., 707/822-1414, www.tomoarcata.com, 4pm-9pm daily, $10-22) serves sushi rolls and entrées that are as eclectic as its hometown. Get a spicy tofu roll or a unique locally smoked albacore roll. Tomo has a list of sakes, and there's also a full bar. Stop in for happy hour (4pm-5:30pm daily) for $2 pints of beer.

Salt Fish House (761 8th St., 707/630-5300, www.saltfishhouse.com, 11:30am-10pm Tues.-Fri., 4pm-10pm Sat.-Sun., $15-32) serves local sustainable seafood—the cod and chips are a favorite. The weekday happy hour (3pm-5pm Tues.-Fri.) sees fish tacos, raw oysters, grilled oysters, and margaritas at nice prices.

Soup
The North Coast is a great place to settle down and eat a warming bowl of soup. **Japhy's Soup and Noodles** (1563 G St., 707/826-2594, www.japhys.com, 11:30am-8pm Mon.-Fri., $5-10) focuses on Japanese-style noodles (ramen, udon, soba), though there are also Thai-style curries and a Brazilian clam soup.

From top to bottom: Arcata Plaza; the Minor Theatre; the Tin Can Mailman Used & Rare Book Store.

Markets

There's no better market on the North Coast for gourmet food, vegetarian options, and craft beer to go than ★ **Wildberries Marketplace** (747 13th St., 707/822-0095, www.wildberries.com, 6am-midnight daily). They have a café with better-than-average sandwiches, a juice bar, a coffee shop, and a farmers market (3:30pm-6:30pm Tues.). This is a great place to grab supplies for North Coast exploring.

The Arcata Plaza hosts a Saturday **farmers market** (www.humfarm.org, 9am-2pm Sat. Apr.-mid-Nov., 10am-2pm Sat. mid-Nov.-Mar.) that has live music.

Accommodations

Downtown lodging options are limited. The **Hotel Arcata** (708 9th St., 707/826-0217, www.hotelarcata.com, $102-172) has a superb location right on the plaza. The rooms are small, but the bathrooms have claw-foot tubs outfitted with showerheads. The hallways are decorated with framed historical photos of Arcata Plaza and other local landmarks. A stay includes complimentary Wi-Fi and continental breakfast. Secure a free pass to the Arcata Community Pool from the front desk.

The Lady Anne Bed and Breakfast (902 14th St., 707/822-2797, http://ladyanneinn.com, $150-185) has a little more character, with five rooms in an old Victorian built in 1888. All have private bathrooms, and most include gas-burning woodstoves. A music room is decorated with instruments, including a piano, an accordion, and a bass guitar, that guests can play. The Lady Anne serves a full, hot breakfast in the morning.

A few miles from the plaza, the **Best Western Arcata Inn** (4827 Valley West Blvd., 707/826-0313, http://bestwesterncalifornia.com, $101-160) is a well-regarded chain motel in the area. The rooms have satellite TV and Wi-Fi, and there's an indoor/outdoor heated swimming pool and hot tub. Fuel up with a complimentary breakfast.

Information and Services

The **Arcata & Mad River Transit System** (https://hta.org, adults $1.75, seniors and children $1.25) runs a fleet of red-and-yellow buses that travel all over Arcata.

North of downtown, the **Mad River Community Hospital** (3800 Janes Rd., 707/822-3621, http://madriverhospital.com) has an emergency room and urgent care department.

★ Trinidad

With a population of just 360 people, Trinidad is one of the smallest incorporated cities in California; it's also one of the most beautiful. Perched on a bluff over boat-studded Trinidad Bay, Trinidad has a wealth of natural assets, including scenic headlands and wild beaches on either side of town. It also has a long history: The town was named by two Spanish Navy men who came to the area on Trinity Sunday in 1775.

Trinidad is a small city, so don't expect too many services. Most major services can be found in nearby Arcata.

Getting There

Trinidad is 15 miles (24 km) north of Arcata on US-101. The highway on this section is four lanes and well maintained. Take exit 728 off the highway. The **Redwood Transit System** (707/443-0826, https://hta.org, adults $3.50, seniors and children $3.15) has buses that connect from Arcata and Eureka to Trinidad.

Trinidad Head

A rocky promontory north of the bay, the 380-foot-high **Trinidad Head** (end of Edwards St.) affords great views of the area's beaches, bay, and town. A 1-mile loop trail on the headlands goes under canopies of vegetation and then out to a series of clear spots with benches. A large stone cross on the west end of Trinidad Head marks where Spanish seamen initially erected a wooden cross. Below the cross is a small wooden deck where you can glimpse the top of the Trinidad Head Lighthouse. The squat lighthouse on a 175-foot-high cliff was activated in 1871. In 1914, the lighthouse made news when, according to the lighthouse keeper, a huge wave extinguished the light.

Trinidad State Beach

Below the bluffs of Trinidad Head, **Trinidad State Beach** (end of Edwards St., 707/677-3570, www.parks.ca.gov, sunrise-sunset daily, free) runs north for a mile to Elk Head. Spruce-tufted Pewetole Island and a scattering of scenic coastal islets lie offshore. The northern end has caves, an arch, and tidepools. It's a great place for a contemplative walk.

Trinidad Memorial Lighthouse

Trinidad Memorial Lighthouse was built by the Trinidad Civic Club in 1949. It's not an actual lighthouse, but a replica of the one on nearby Trinidad Head. In 2018, the small red-and-white building moved from its longtime location at the end of Trinidad's main drag to a temporary location at the base of Trinidad Head.

Humboldt State University Marine Laboratory

Students come to the **HSU Marine Laboratory** (570 Ewing St., 707/826-3671, www.hsumarinelab.org, 9am-4:30pm Mon.-Fri., 10am-5pm Sat.-Sun., tours by appointment, self-guided tours $1, guided tours $2) to learn about the area's coastal critters. A tour of the lab includes looks at invertebrates from nearby intertidal zones, like sea cucumbers, tube worms, giant green anemones, and red octopi. Visitors can also sign up to explore the area's tidepools with a marine naturalist ($3).

Sports and Recreation
Kayaking

Kayak Trinidad (707/329-0085, https://kayaktrinidad.com) is a recommended outfitter for paddling the waters off Trinidad. They offer the **Trinidad Bay Kayak Tours** (3 hours, 9am daily, $89/person) and tours of nearby **Big Lagoon** (3-4 hours, daily, $69/person).

Sportfishing

Head out to sea with one of two Trinidad-based fishing outfits. Fish for rockfish, salmon, or Dungeness crab with **Trinidad Bay Charters** (707/499-8878, www.trinidadbaycharters.net, $120). Trips leave daily at 6:15am and 12:15pm. **Patricks Point Charters** (707/445-4106, www.patrickspointcharters.com, $120/half day) leaves out of Trinidad Harbor for rockfish, salmon, and Dungeness crab.

Surfing

South of Trinidad are some of Humboldt County's best-known surf spots. **Moonstone Beach** (3 mi/4.8 km south of Trinidad on Scenic Dr.) is a popular surf break where the Little River pours into Trinidad Bay. Up the road a half mile, **Camel Rock** (about 2.3 mi/3.7 km south of Trinidad on Scenic Dr.) has right breaks that peel inside of a distinct, double-humped offshore rock.

Food

For a small community, Trinidad has several worthwhile dining options. Stock up on delicious, locally smoked seafood at ★ **Katy's Smokehouse** (740 Edwards St., 707/677-0151, www.katyssmokehouse.com, 9am-6pm daily summer, 9am-6pm Wed.-Mon. winter, $8-20). There are smoked oysters and salmon jerky, but you can't go wrong with the smoked king salmon. It's not a sit-down restaurant, so you'll need to get your order to go.

The friendly, spunky staff at the **Beachcomber Café** (363 Trinity St., 707/677-0106, http://

trinidadbeachcomber.blogspot.com, 7am-4pm Mon.-Fri., 8am-4pm Sat.-Sun., $5-10) serve coffee, cookies, paninis, and bagels. The café also has free Wi-Fi with purchase.

A diner for these times, ★ **The Lighthouse Grill** (Saunders Plaza, 355 Main St., 707/677-0077, http://trinidadlighthousegrill.com, 11am-8pm daily, $6-13) utilizes fresh, local Humboldt County ingredients in their menu items—from grass-fed beef burgers to locally caught rock cod fish-and-chips. They are known for their mashed potato cones, a scoop of mashed potatoes in a cornmeal cone topped with bacon, cheese, gravy, and a 12-hour roasted beef brisket (if you do the "all the way" version). Great deals on pitchers of Redwood Curtain beers and homemade small-batch ice cream sweeten the deal.

Part art gallery, part gift shop, and part restaurant, the **Trinidad Bay Eatery and Gallery** (607 Parker St., 707/677-3777, https://trinidadeatery.com, 8am-8pm Thurs.-Fri. and Mon., 8am-4pm Tues.-Wed., 7:30am-8pm Sat.-Sun., $11-32) is a popular spot serving breakfast, lunch, and dinner. People rave about their New England-style clam chowder in a bread bowl.

North of Trinidad, the ★ **Larrupin Café** (1658 Patricks Point Dr., 707/677-0230, www.thelarrupin.com, 5pm-9pm daily, $26-50) is probably the most-loved restaurant in the area. They put their legendary mesquite barbecue sauce on everything from tofu kebabs to Creole prawns and are known for their mustard dill and red sauces. Enjoy the heated patio June through September.

Accommodations

The only lodging in Trinidad proper is the **Trinidad Bay Bed & Breakfast** (560 Edwards St., 707/677-0840, www.trinidadbaybnb.com, $325-400), located across the street from a view of Trinidad's coastline and within walking distance of restaurants. Each of the four rooms has

Trinidad Bay Bed & Breakfast

a view of Trinidad Bay; two rooms have private entrances, and all have private bathrooms. A hot three-course breakfast is served.

Between the main section of Trinidad and Patrick's Point State Park, **The Lost Whale Bed & Breakfast Inn** (3452 Patricks Point Dr., 707/677-3425, http://lostwhaleinn.com, $290-345) has five rooms with great views of the Pacific and four with garden views. Two rooms have lofts to accommodate up to four people. There's a private trail to the beach, an oceanview hot tub, and a wood-burning sauna. A seven-course breakfast buffet is served.

The Emerald Forest (753 Patricks Point Dr., 707/677-3554, www.cabinsintheredwoods.com, $179-349) has a variety of rustic cabins for rent. The higher-end cabins have full kitchens and amenities like wood burning stoves. RV and tent campsites are also available ($35-49), although those at nearby Patrick's Point State Park are more spacious.

★ Patrick's Point State Park

Patrick's Point State Park (4150 Patricks Point Dr., 707/677-3570, www.parks.ca.gov, sunrise-sunset daily, day use $8) is a rambling coastal park with beaches, historic landmarks, hiking trails, and campgrounds. It's a fine encapsulation of the North Coast's striking beauty compressed into a tiny park. The climate remains cool year-round, making it perfect for hiking and exploring.

Prominent among the local landmarks is **Patrick's Point,** which can be reached by a brief hike from a convenient parking lot. Adjacent to Patrick's Point in a picturesque cove is **Wedding Rock,** a promontory sticking out into the ocean like an upturned thumb. (People really do hike the narrow trail out to the rock to get married.) Surrounded by the sea on three sides, this has a viewing platform that's a great spot to take in the wild majesty of the North Coast.

The most fascinating area in the park is **Sumeg Village,** a re-creation of a native Yurok village based on an archaeological find east of here. Visitors can crawl through the perfectly round doors into semi-subterranean homes, meeting places, and storage buildings. Check out the native plant garden, a collection of local plants the Yurok people used for food, basketry, and medicine. (The local Yurok people use Sumeg Village as a gathering place; please tread lightly.)

Patrick's Point has a number of accessible beaches. A steep trail leads down to **Agate Beach,** a wide stretch of coarse sand bordered by cliffs shot through with shining quartz veins. The semiprecious stones for which it is named really do appear here.

At the south end of the park is **Palmer's Point Beach.** Take the steep trail at the end of Palmer's Point Road down to a boulder-strewn beach known for tidepool residents including sea stars and sea urchins.

Getting There

Patrick's Point State Park is 25 miles (40 km) north of Eureka and 15 miles (24 km) south of Orick on US-101. It is also 6 miles (9.5 km) north of the town of Trinidad. The scenic route is to take Patricks Point Drive to the park, but you can also take US-101 North and get off on exit 734.

Visitors Center

Get a map and information at the **Patrick's Point State Park Visitors Center** (707/677-1945, 9am-5pm daily summer, 10am-4pm daily winter), immediately to the right of the entry gate. Information about nature walks and campfire programs is posted on the bulletin board.

Hiking

Trails thread through the park, including the **Rim Trail** (4 mi/6.4 km round-trip, 2 hours, moderate), which will take you along the cliffs for a view of the sea and migrating whales (Sept.-Jan., Mar.-June). Tree lovers might prefer the **Octopus Tree Trail** (0.2 mi one-way, easy), which provides a great view of an old-growth Sitka spruce grove.

Camping

★ **Patrick's Point State Park campgrounds** (reservations 800/444-7275, www.reservecalifornia.com, $35) have a total of 124 sites. It can be difficult to determine the difference between **Agate Beach, Abalone,** and **Penn Creek,** so get directions from the park rangers. Most campsites are pleasantly shaded by the groves of trees. All include a picnic table, fire pit, and food storage cupboard, and you'll find running water, restrooms, and showers nearby.

Orick

This small community is named after the native Yurok word for "mouth of the river" due to the hamlet's location near the mouth of Redwood Creek. Though surrounded by the Redwood National and State Parks, the town has few amenities for the many visitors.

A redwood sculpture that once traveled to Washington DC sits unceremoniously on the ground in front of a gas station. The giant redwood stump was carved in the shape of a peanut as a rebuke from the area's loggers to then-president Carter, a peanut farmer. It traveled to the nation's capital with a sign stating: "It may be peanuts to you, but it's jobs to us."

Getting There

Orick is 5.3 miles (9 km) south of Patrick's Point State Park on US-101. The four-lane highway stretches 8 miles (13 km) from Trinidad north to Big Lagoon. After Big Lagoon, the road shrinks to two lanes and becomes curvy for 3 miles (4.8 km). "Elk Passing" signs warn drivers that a massive Roosevelt elk may walk onto the highway anywhere in this section.

Food

EdeBee's Snack Shack (120777 Hwy. 101, Orick, 707/498-0810, 11am-6pm Wed.-Thurs. and Sat., 11am-7pm Fri., 11am-4pm Sun., $8-16) is the best dining option in Orick. This tiny, bright-orange roadside stand serves local elk burgers, Humboldt beef hamburgers, fries, tater tots, and sandwiches. Though this looks like a fast-food joint, everything is cooked to order and can take up to a half hour. Wait for your food on the bright yellow picnic tables out front.

Accommodations

The name ★ **Elk Meadow Cabins** (7 Valley Green Camp Rd., Orick, 866/733-9637, https://elkmeadowcabins.com, $170-300) might evoke a musty collection of rustic hunting cabins, but that is decidedly not the case. These comfortable and nicely appointed units sit on a property bordering Redwood National Park. The one two-bedroom and six three-bedroom "cabins" have everything you need for a comfortable stay: fully equipped kitchens, a living room with a TV stocked with a plethora of channels, a garage, and a washer and dryer unit. There's also a back porch to take in the wonderful scenery and the Roosevelt elk that frequent the grounds. On-site amenities include a Jacuzzi and a fire pit. Redwood Adventures Eco Tours offers wonderful tours of the area. You will not find a more comfortable base for exploring the area's parks.

Redwood National Park

TOP EXPERIENCE

The lands of Redwood National and State Parks (www.nps.gov/redw) meander along the coast and include three state parks—Prairie Creek Redwoods, Del Norte Coast Redwoods, and Jedediah Smith Redwoods. This complex of parkland encompasses most of California's northern redwood forests. The main landmass of Redwood National Park is just south of Prairie Creek State Park along US-101, stretching east from the coast and the highway.

Getting There

The Redwood National and State Parks line US-101 from Prairie Creek Redwoods north to Jedediah Smith near Crescent City. The Thomas H. Kuchel Visitors Center at the south end of the park is 40 miles (64 km) north of Eureka on US-101.

Visitors Center

The **Thomas H. Kuchel Visitors Center** (US-101, west of Orick, 707/465-7765, 9am-5pm daily spring-fall, 9am-4pm daily winter) is a large facility with a ranger station, clean restrooms, and a path to the

From top to bottom: Elk Meadow Cabins; EdeBee's Snack Shack; Prairie Creek Redwoods State Park.

shore. Get advice, maps, backcountry permits, and books. In the summer, rangers run patio talks and coast walks that provide a great introduction to the area for children and adults. Picnic at one of the tables outside the visitors center, or walk a short distance to Redwood Creek.

Redwood Creek Overlook

The 2,000-foot-tall **Redwood Creek Overlook** (Bald Hills Rd.) looks onto the redwood covered hills of Redwood National Park with the Pacific Ocean in the distance. This is a great place to take in the wild majesty of the forests and watershed below. The adjacent hillsides contain 9,000 acres of old-growth redwoods (more than 200 years old) and second-cut redwoods, including the Tall Trees Grove, the Libby Redwood (once thought to be the tallest tree in the world), and the Hyperion Redwood, the world's tallest tree (in an undisclosed location).

Hiking

One of the easiest and most popular trails is the **Lady Bird Johnson Trail** (Bald Hills Rd., 1.4 mi/2.3 km, 1 hour, easy); President Richard Nixon dedicated the grove to Lady Bird Johnson, former First Lady, in 1969. This nearly level loop provides an intimate view of the redwood and fir forests that define this region.

An easy-access trail is **Trillium Falls** (Davison Rd. at Elk Meadow, 2.8 mi/4.5 km, 1.5 hours, easy). The redwood trees along this cool, dark trail are striking, and the small waterfall is a nice treasure in the woods. This little hike is lovely any time of year but best in spring, when the water over the falls is at its peak.

The easy **Lost Man Creek Trail** (east of Elk Meadow, 1 mi/1.6 km off US-101) has it all. The first 0.5 mile is perfect for wheelchair users and families with small children. As the trail rolls along, the grades get steeper and more challenging. Customize the length of this out-and-back trail by turning around at any time. If you reach the Lost Man Creek picnic

grounds, your total round-trip distance is 22 miles (35 km) with more than 3,000 feet (900 m) of elevation gain and several stream crossings.

The more difficult **Redwood Creek Trail** (Bald Hills Rd. spur off US-101) follows Redwood Creek for 8 miles (12.9 km) to the **Tall Trees Grove.** If you have a shuttle car, pick up the **Tall Trees Trail** and walk another 6 miles (9.7 km) for a total of 14 mi (22.5 km) to the **Dolason Prairie Trail,** which takes you back out to Bald Hills Road.

A superb resource for hiking in redwoods, especially on the North Coast, is online at www.redwoodhikes.com.

Camping

There are no designated campgrounds in Redwood National Park, but backcountry camping is permitted in designated locations (free permit required). Secure a permit from either **Hiouchi Information Center** or **Thomas H. Kuchel Visitors Center** in person up to a day before departing on your trip. The **Elam Camp** and the **44 Camp** are both hike-in primitive campgrounds along the Dolason Prairie Trail. The park also allows dispersed, undeveloped tent camping on **Redwood Creek**'s gravel beds with a permit.

Getting Around

The Redwood National and State Parks are difficult to navigate for first-time visitors. Thankfully, **Redwood Adventures Eco Tours** guides (866/733-9637, https://elkmeadowcabins.com, $85-195) utilize local knowledge to unravel the complexities of the park. The charismatic and highly knowledgeable guides, including Justin Legge, take visitors on half-day (3 hours) and full-day (6.5 hours) tours. Options include the popular World's Tallest Tree Tour (an immersion in old-growth redwoods), the Trees to Seas Tour (time in redwoods and by the ocean estuaries), Tidepool Adventure Tour, Fern Canyon Tour, and the Forest Bathing Experience. They also have an Adventure

Shuttle Service for those who want to hike and need a pickup.

★ Prairie Creek Redwoods State Park

In addition to the silent majesty of the redwoods, the 14,000 acres of **Prairie Creek Redwoods State Park** (Newton B. Drury Scenic Pkwy., 25 mi/40 km south of Crescent City, 707/488-2039, www.parks.ca.gov, sunrise-sunset daily, day use $8) offer wild beach, roaming wildlife, and a popular hike through a one-of-a-kind fern-draped canyon.

Getting There

Prairie Creek Redwoods is 50 miles (80 km) north of Eureka and 25 miles (40 km) south of Crescent City on US-101. Newton B. Drury Scenic Parkway traverses the park and can be accessed from US-101.

Visitors Center

The **visitors center** (Newton B. Drury Scenic Pkwy., 707/488-2039, 9am-5pm daily summer, 9am-4pm daily winter) includes a small interpretive museum describing the history of the redwood forests. A tiny bookshop adjoins the museum, well stocked with books describing the history, nature, and culture of the area. Many ranger-led programs originate at the visitors center, and permits are available for backcountry camping.

One of the many reasons to visit is a chance to view a herd of **Roosevelt elk.** This subspecies of elk can stand up to 5 feet high and can weigh close to 1,000 pounds. These big guys usually hang out at—where else?—the Elk Prairie, a stretch of open grassland along the highway, and off the southern end of the Newton B. Drury Scenic Parkway. The best times to see the elk are early morning and around sunset. August to October is the elk mating season, when the calls of the bulls fill the air.

Newton B. Drury Scenic Parkway

A gorgeous scenic road through the redwoods, **Newton B. Drury Scenic Parkway** (off US-101, 5 mi/8 km south of Klamath) features old-growth trees lining the roads, a close-up view of the redwood forest ecosystem, and a grove or trailhead every hundred yards or so. The turnoff is at the **Big Tree Wayside,** where you can walk up to the 304-foot-high (93-m) **Big Tree.** Follow the short, five-minute loop trail to see other giants in the area.

Gold Bluffs Beach

Gold Bluffs Beach (Davison Rd., 3 mi/4.8 km north of Orick off US-101) is truly wild. Lonely waves pound the shore, a spiky grove of Sitka spruce tops the nearby bluffs, and herds of Roosevelt elk frequently roam the wide, salt-and-pepper-colored beach. Prospectors found gold flakes here in 1850, giving the beach its name. But the region was too remote and rugged to maintain a lucrative mining operation. Access Gold Bluffs Beach by taking Davison Road. No trailers are allowed on Davison Road.

Hiking

Perhaps the single most famous hiking trail along the redwood coast is the 1-mile (1.6-km) **Fern Canyon Trail** (Davison Rd.), near Gold Bluffs Beach. The unusual setting was used as a dramatic backdrop in the film *The Lost World: Jurassic Park.* This hike runs through a narrow canyon carved by Home Creek. Five-fingered ferns, sword ferns, and delicate lady ferns cascade down the steep canyon walls. Droplets from seeping water sources keep the plants alive. You can extend this hike into a longer loop (6.5 mi/10.5 km round-trip, 3 hours, moderate): When the trail intersects with James Irvine Trail, bear right and follow that spur. Bear right again onto **Clintonia Trail** and walk to Miners Ridge Trail. Bear right onto Miners Ridge and follow it down to the ocean. Walk 1.5 miles (2.4 km) along Gold Bluffs Beach to complete the loop.

To get to the trailhead, take US-101 for 3 miles (4.8 km) north of the town of Orick. At the Prairie Creek visitors center, turn west onto Davison Road (no trailers allowed) and travel 2 miles (3.2 km). This rough dirt road takes you through the campground and ends at the trailhead in 1.5 miles (2.4 km).

Miners Ridge and James Irvine Loop (12 mi/19.3 km round-trip, 6-7 hours, moderate) starts from the visitors center instead of the Fern Canyon trailhead, avoiding the rough dirt terrain of Davison Road. Start out on James Irvine Trail and bear right when you can, following the trail all the way until it joins Fern Canyon Trail. Turn left when you get to the coast, and walk along Gold Bluffs Beach for 1.5 miles (2.4 km). Then make a left onto the Clintonia Trail and head back toward the visitors center.

Cal-Barrel Road (1.5 mi/2.4 km one-way, 1 hour, easy) is a pet-friendly hike that gently climbs past giant redwood trees and gardens of ferns. The **Rotary Memorial Grove** (also called the Atlas Grove) is an 80-acre grove of redwoods. Find it by hiking Cal-Barrel Road to Foothill Trail and taking the latter 500 feet (150 m) to a granite stone with a Rotary wheel and inscription.

The **Cathedral Trees Trail** (1.4 mi/2.3 km, 1 hour, moderate) showcases several fairy rings (cathedral trees) of giant coast redwoods clustered together. The gentle grade makes it a great walk for families.

The **California Coastal Trail** (www. californiacoastaltrail.info) runs along the park's northern coastline and can be accessed via the **Ossagon Creek Trail** (2 mi/3.2 km round-trip, 1 hour, moderate). It's not long, but the steep grade makes it a tough haul in spots, and the stunning trees along the way make it worth the effort. The trailhead is at the north end of Newton B. Drury Scenic Parkway.

Camping

The **Elk Prairie Campground** (127011 Newton B. Drury Scenic Pkwy., Orick, campground 707/488-2039, reservations 800/444-7275, www.reservecalifornia. com, reservations recommended Memorial Day-Labor Day, vehicles $35, hikers and cyclists $5) has 75 sites for tents or RVs and a full range of comfortable camping amenities, including showers and firewood. Several campsites are wheelchair-accessible (request at reservation). A big campfire area, an easy walk north of the campground, has evening programs put on by rangers and volunteers.

For beach camping, head to **Gold Bluffs Beach Campground** (Davison Rd., 3 mi/4.8 km north of Orick, May-Sept. by reservation, first-come, first-served Oct.-Apr., 800/444-7275, www. reservecalifornia.com, $20-35). There are 26 sites for tents or RVs and 3 environmental sites. Amenities include flush toilets, water, solar showers, and wide ocean views. The surf can be quite dangerous here, so be extremely careful if you go in the water.

Backcountry camping is allowed in two designated camping areas: Ossagon Creek and Miners Ridge (3 sites each, $5). Permits are available at the campground kiosk or the Prairie Creek visitors center (Newton B. Drury Scenic Pkwy., 707/488-2171, 9am-5pm daily).

Klamath

The unincorporated community of Klamath is located where the Klamath River empties into the sea. The waterway is California's second-largest river, and it's prized among anglers for the wild salmon and steelhead that swim in its waters. The Klamath region is also home to the Yurok people, California's largest Native American tribe. Learn more about the Yurok at the **Yurok Country Visitor Center** (101 Klamath Blvd., Klamath,

Trees of Mystery

Generations of kids have enjoyed spotting the gigantic wooden sculptures of Paul Bunyan and his blue ox, Babe, from US-101. The **Trees of Mystery** (15500 US-101 N., 707/482-2251 or 800/638-3389, www.treesofmystery.net, 8am-7pm daily June-Aug., 8:30am-6:30pm daily Sept.-Oct., 9am-5pm daily Nov.-May, adults $18, seniors $14, children 6-12 $9, children under 5 free) is a great place to let the family out for some good cheesy fun. Visitors can enjoy the original Mystery Hike, the SkyTrail gondola ride through the old-growth redwoods, and the palatial gift shop. Perhaps best of all, at the left end of the gift shop is a little-known gem: the **Native American museum.** A large collection of artifacts from both tribes across the country and those indigenous to the redwood forests graces several crowded galleries. The restrooms are large and well maintained, which makes Trees of Mystery a nice rest stop.

707/482-1555, http://visityurokcountry.com).

Klamath Beach

Klamath Beach is a long sandspit south of where the river runs into the ocean. This is a great place to view seals, sea lions, eagles, and migrating whales offshore. To get there, take Klamath Beach Road west from US-101. Park where the road deadends and take the gated road to the beach past the historic Yurok village site.

South of Klamath Beach is a short trail to the **Klamath River Radar Station B-71** (Coastal Dr.), one of the few remaining radar stations in the country. Built in 1942, the stations were designed to resemble farm buildings and used to house radar and anti-aircraft weapons. A sign interprets the empty site, now part of Redwood National Park.

For sweeping views of Klamath Beach, head to the **Klamath River Overlook,** a 650-foot bluff north of the rivermouth. Grab your binoculars to spot gray whales, which feed on the nutrients that pour out of the river into the sea. To reach the overlook, exit on Requa Road off US-101 for 2 miles (3.2 km) north of Klamath. Take Requa Road 2.5 miles (4 km) to the overlook.

Recreation

To better understand the natural beauty of the Klamath River, take a **Klamath River Jet Boat Tour** (17635 US-101, Klamath, 707/482-7775, www.jetboattours.com, 10am, 1pm, 4pm daily mid-May-Sept., adults $47, seniors $42, teens $32, children $27). As you ride upriver from the mouth, your captain details the region's history and wildlife. Look for elk, eagles, and bears on the journey.

Accommodations

The Historic Requa Inn (451 Requa Rd., Klamath, 707/482-1425, www.requainn.com, $119-399) has been serving visitors to the wildly beautiful Klamath area since 1914. Some rooms have river views; a cottage and three-bedroom house are available for larger groups. On-site you'll find a garden with a gazebo, a hot tub, and The Historic Requa Inn Restaurant.

Del Norte Coast Redwoods State Park

Del Norte Coast Redwoods State Park (Mill Creek Campground Rd., off US-101, 707/465-7335, www.parks.ca.gov, $8) encompasses a variety of ecosystems, including miles of wild coastline, second-growth redwood forest, and virgin old-growth forests. One of the largest in this system of parks, Del Norte is a great place to get lost in the backcountry with just your knapsack.

False Klamath Cove (US-101 at Wilson

Creek Bridge), also known as Wilson Beach, is a long gray and sandy beach with lots of driftwood. A rock formation at the southern end is called False Klamath Rock. The outcroppings around the rock are a great place to see tidepool critters at low tide, including sea stars, sea urchins, anemones, and chitons.

Getting There
Del Norte Coast Redwoods State Park is 7 miles (11.5 km) south of Crescent City on US-101. The park entrance is on Hamilton Road, east of US-101. Del Norte has no visitors center, but you can get information from the **Crescent City Information Center** (1111 2nd St., Crescent City, 707/465-7306, 9am-5pm daily spring-fall, 9am-4pm Thurs.-Mon. winter).

Hiking
Several rewarding yet gentle and short excursions start and end in the Mill Creek Campground. The **Trestle Loop Trail** (1 mi/1.6 km round-trip, 30 min., easy) begins across from the campfire center in the campground. Notice the trestles and other artifacts along the way; the loop follows the route of a defunct railroad from the logging era. Another easy stroll is the nearby **Nature Loop Trail** (1 mi/1.6 km round-trip, 30 min., easy), which begins near the campground entrance gate. Interpretive signage teaches you about the varieties of impressive trees you'll pass.

Camping
The **Mill Creek Campground** (US-101, 7 mi/11.5 km south of Crescent City, 800/444-7275, www.reservecalifornia. com, May-Sept., vehicles $35, hikers and cyclists $5) is in an attractive setting along Mill Creek. There are 145 sites for RVs and tents, and facilities include restrooms, fire pits, and a dump station. There are no designated backcountry campsites and backcountry camping is not allowed.

★ Jedediah Smith Redwoods State Park

There's nowhere better to experience the majesty of the North Coast's redwoods than at **Jedediah Smith Redwoods State Park** (1440 US-199, 9 mi/14.5 km east of Crescent City, 707/465-7335 or 707/458-3496, www.parks.ca.gov, sunrise-sunset daily, $8/vehicle). The most popular redwood grove in the park is the **Stout Memorial Grove,** a 44-acre grove of 300-foot-tall redwoods and waist-high sword ferns. These are some of the biggest and oldest trees on the North Coast, somehow spared from the loggers' saws. The quiet grove lacks visitors, since its far-north latitude makes it harder to reach than some of the other big redwood groves in California.

Getting There
Jedediah Smith Redwoods State Park is northeast of Crescent City along the Smith River, next door to the immense Smith River National Recreation Area (US-199 west of Hiouchi). Get to the park by taking US-199 for 9 miles (14.5 km) east of Crescent City.

Visitors Centers
There are two visitors centers, about five minutes apart: **Jedediah Smith Visitors Center** (US-101, Hiouchi, 707/458-3496, 9am-5pm daily summer) and the **Hiouchi Information Center** (US-199, Hiouchi, 707/458-3294, 9am-5pm daily summer, 9am-4pm daily winter). Both offer information and materials about all of the nearby parks.

Recreation
Hiking
The shaded trails at Jedediah make for wonderfully cool summer hiking. Many trails run along the river and the creeks, offering beach access and plenty of lush scenery to enjoy. The short and easy **Simpson Reed Trail** (US-199, 6 mi/9.5

California Coastal Trail

The northern section of the great **California Coastal Trail** (CCT, www. californiacoastaltrail.info) runs right through Del Norte Coast Redwoods State Park. The trail is reasonably well marked; look for signs with the CCT logo. The **"last chance"** section of the California Coastal Trail (Enderts Beach-Damnation Creek, 14 mi/22.5 km, strenuous) makes a challenging day hike. To reach the trailhead, turn west from US-101 onto Enderts Beach Road in Del Norte, 3 miles (4.8 km) south of Crescent City. Drive 2.3 miles (3.7 km) to the end of the road.

The trail follows the historical route of US-101 south to Enderts Beach. You'll walk through fields of wildflowers and groves of trees twisted by the wind and saltwater. Eventually, the trail climbs about 900 feet (300 m) to an overlook with a great view of Enderts Beach. In about 2 miles (3.2 km), the trail enters Del Norte Coast Redwoods State Park, where it meanders through Anson Grove's redwood, fir, and Sitka spruce trees. At 4.5 miles (7.2 km), cross Damnation Creek on a footbridge, and at 6.1 miles (9.8 km), cross the Damnation Creek Trail. (For a longer hike, take the 4-mile (6.4-km) round-trip excursion down to the beach and back.) After 7 miles (11.3 km), a flight of steps leads up to milepost 15.6 on US-101. At this point, you can turn around and return the way you came, making for a gloriously varied day hike of about 14 miles (22.5 km) round-trip.

One alternative is to make this a point-to-point hike, either by dropping a car off at one end to get you back at the end of the day, or by having one group of hikers start at each end of the trail and exchange keys at a central meeting point.

If you've made arrangements for a lift back at the end of the day, continue on to the DeMartin section of the Coastal Trail. From here, descend through a lush grove of ferns and take a bridge over a tributary of Wilson Creek, enjoying views of the rocky coast far below. The wildflowers continue as you enter Redwood National Park and wander through the grasslands of DeMartin Prairie. The southern trailhead (where you pick up your vehicle if you're doing the trail one-way north-south) is at the Wilson Creek Picnic Area on the east side of US-101 at the north end of DeMartin Bridge.

km east of Crescent City) takes you one mile from US-199 down to the banks of the Smith River.

To get a good view of the Smith River, hike the **Hiouchi Trail** (2 mi/3.2 km round-trip, 1 hour, moderate). From the Hiouchi Information Center and campgrounds on US-199, cross the Summer Footbridge and then follow the river north. The Hiouchi Trail then meets the Hatton Loop Trail and leads away from the river and into the forest.

For a longer and more aggressive trek, try the **Mill Creek Trail** (7.5 mi/12.1 km round-trip, 5.5 hours, difficult). Start at the Summer Footbridge (seasonal) and follow the creek down to the unpaved Howland Hill Road. The trail winds through ferns, maples, pines, and stunning redwoods. (Just off the trail is the Grove of the Titans, said to be the home of the world's largest coast redwood.) There's also a pristine swimming hole with a rope swing near the southeast end of the trail.

The **Boy Scout Tree Trail** (5.2 mi/8.4 km round-trip, 3 hours, moderate) is usually quiet, with few hikers, and the gargantuan forest will make you feel truly tiny. From the trailhead on the north side of Howland Hill Road, the dirt path leads 3 miles (5 km) to a fork. Take the left fork to the small, mossy, and very green Fern Falls; the right fork takes you to the eponymous Boy Scout Tree, one of the impressively huge redwoods. The trailhead is located a couple of miles down rugged, unpaved Howland Hill Road. Check at the visitors center to make sure the road to the trailhead is open.

Boating and Swimming

You'll find two boat launches in the park: one at Society Hole and one adjacent to the Summer Footbridge (winter only). Down by the River Beach Trail, you'll find **River Beach** (west of the Hiouchi Information Center), a popular spot for swimming. Swimming is allowed throughout the park, but be very careful—rivers and creeks move unpredictably, and you might not notice deep holes until you're on them.

Fishing

With the Smith River and numerous feeder creeks running through Jed Smith, fishing is a popular activity. Chilly winter fishing draws a surprising number of anglers to vie for king salmon up to 30 pounds and steelhead up to 20 pounds. Seasons for both species run October-February. In the summer, cast into the river to catch cutthroat trout.

Camping

The ★ **Jedediah Smith Campground** (US-199, Hiouchi, 800/444-7275, www.reservecalifornia.com, vehicles $35, hike-in or cycle-in primitive sites $5) is beautifully situated on the banks of Smith River, with most sites near the River Beach Trail. There are 106 RV and tent sites. Facilities include restrooms, fire pits, and coin-operated showers. Reservations (accepted Memorial Day-Labor Day) are advised, especially for summer and holiday weekends.

The park also has four rustic **cabins** (800/444-7275, www.reservecalifornia.com, $100) with bunk beds, heat, and electricity. Jedediah Smith has no designated backcountry campsites; camping outside the developed campgrounds is not allowed.

Crescent City

The northernmost city on the California coast perches on the bay that provides its name. Cool and windswept, Crescent City is a perfect place to put on a parka, stuff your hands deep into your pockets, and wander along a wide, beautiful beach. The small city also has a vibrant surf scene centered on South Beach, which frequently has good waves for longboarders.

Crescent City is also known for surviving tsunamis. In 1964, a tsunami caused by an Alaskan earthquake wiped out 29 city blocks and killed 11 people. It was the most severe tsunami on the U.S. West Coast in modern history. In 2011, a devastating earthquake in Japan resulted in a tsunami that laid waste to the city's harbor.

Getting There

The main routes in and out of town are US-101 and US-199. Both are well maintained but are twisty in spots, so take care, especially at night. From San Francisco, the drive to Crescent City is about 350 miles (565 km). It is 85 miles (137 km) from Eureka north to Crescent City on US-101.

Sights
Point St. George

Wild, lonely, beautiful **Point St. George** (end of Washington Blvd., sunrise-sunset daily) epitomizes the glory of the North Coast. Walk out onto the cliffs to take in the deep blue sea, wild salt- and flower-scented air, and craggy cliffs and beaches. On a clear day, you can see all the way to Oregon. Short, steep trails lead across wild beach prairie land down to broad, flat, nearly deserted beaches. In spring and summer, wildflowers bloom on the cliffs, and swallows nest in the cluster of buildings on the point. On rare and special clear days, you can almost make out the **St. George Reef Lighthouse** alone on its perch far out in the Pacific.

Tolowa Dunes State Park

Sandwiched between the Lake Earl Coastal Lagoon and the Pacific Ocean,

Crescent City

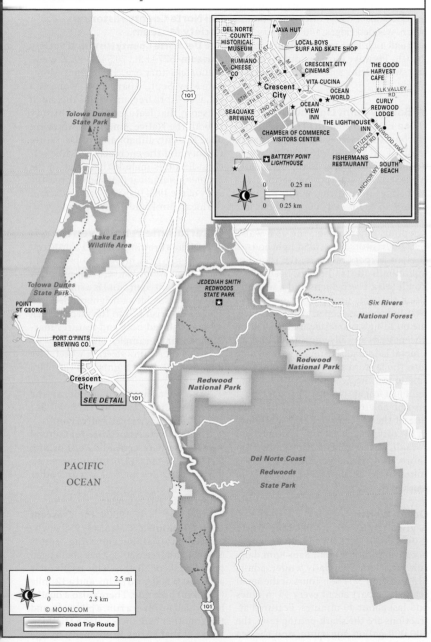

© MOON.COM

Road Trip Route

Tolowa Dunes State Park (1375 Elk Valley Rd., 2 mi/3.2 km north of Crescent City, 707/465-7335, www.parks.ca.gov, sunrise-sunset daily) offers sand dunes, beach, wooded ridges, and wetlands. The nutrient-rich lagoon draws birds on the Pacific Flyway; look for ducks, geese, and swans. Bring a jacket—this park gets windy.

★ Battery Point Lighthouse

On an island just north of Crescent City Harbor, the **Battery Point Lighthouse** (end of A St., 707/464-3089, www. delnortehistory.org, 10am-4pm daily Apr.-Sept., 10am-4pm Sat.-Sun. Oct.-Mar. tides permitting, adults $3, children 8-15 $1) is only accessible at low tide, when a rocky spit littered with tidepools emerges, serving as a walkway for visitors. The 1856 lighthouse's current keepers reside on the island in one-month shifts; they also lead tours. You'll see a Fresnel lens and a working clock that was used by Battery Point's first lighthouse keeper. After you view the building's two residential floors, the docent leads any adventurous visitors up a metal ladder and through a small hole into the lantern room, where you'll be able to feel the heat of the still-working light just feet away. On a clear day, you'll also be able to see the pencil-like outline of the St. George Reef Lighthouse in the distance. St. George is situated on a small, wave-washed rock 7 miles from shore, and its dangerous location resulted in the deaths of four keepers who worked there.

Ocean World

A great family respite is **Ocean World** (304 US-101 S., 707/464-4900, www. oceanworldonline.com, 8am-9pm daily summer, 9am-5pm daily winter, adults $13, children 3-11 $8). Tours of the small sea park depart about every 15 minutes and last about 40 minutes. Featured attractions are the shark-petting tank, the 500,000-gallon aquarium, and the sea lion show. An immense souvenir shop sells gifts with nautical themes.

Del Norte County Historical Society Museum

The **Del Norte County Historical Society Museum** (577 H St., 707/464-3922, www. delnortehistory.org, 10am-4pm Mon.-Sat. May-Sept., 10am-4pm Mon. and Sat. Oct.-Apr., free) maintains this small museum that features the local history of both the Native Americans who were once the only inhabitants of Del Norte County and the encroaching white settlers. Exhibits include the wreck of the *Brother Jonathan* at Point St. George, the story of the 1964 tsunami, and artifacts of the local Yurok and Tolowa people.

Entertainment and Events

Port O'Pints Brewing Co. (1215 Northcrest Dr., 707/460-1154, http://portopints.com, 11am-10pm Mon.-Thurs., 11am-midnight Fri.-Sat., 11am-9pm Sun.) is a small brewpub that resembles a neighborhood bar. There's an Irish feel to the place, which serves Irish red beer and features maritime decor. A sampler platter of brews is served on a ship's steering wheel. Live music on weekend nights gets the place hopping.

Take in a first-run movie at the **Crescent City Cinemas** (375 M St., 707/570-8438, www.catheatres.com).

The **Del Norte Association for Cultural Awareness** (Crescent Elk Auditorium, 994 G St., 707/464-1336, http://dnaca.net) hosts several live musical acts and other performances each year and provides a community arts calendar.

Since the early 1980s, the **Crescent City Triathlon** (707/465-3995, www. crescentcitytriathlon.com, Aug., adults $55-65, children $20-25) has challenged participants of all ages. This triathlon is a 5K run, a 500-yard swim, and a 12-mile (19.5-km) bike ride. There's also a duathlon, which involves a run, a bike ride, and then another run; there's also a triathlon for kids that varies in intensity by age group, making it possible for anyone ages 5-12 to join the fun.

Sports and Recreation
Beaches

The sands of Crescent City are a beachcomber's paradise. **South Beach** (Hwy. 1 between Anchor Way and Sand Mine Rd.), at the south end of town, is long, wide, and flat—perfect for a romantic stroll, as long as you're bundled up. South of town, **Crescent Beach** (Enderts Rd.) is a wide, sandy strip. Down a 0.5-mile dirt trail, **Enderts Beach** (Enderts Rd.) is a superb pocket beach with a creek flowing into the ocean and an onshore rock arch.

No lifeguards patrol these beaches, and swimming here is not for the faint of heart. The water is icy cold, the shores are rocky, and undertow and rip currents are dangerous.

Surfing

Crescent City has a collection of surf breaks. Pioneering big-wave surfer Greg Noll even lives here. Just south of the harbor is the most popular break in town, **South Beach** (Hwy. 1 between Anchor Way and Sand Mine Rd.), with peeling waves perfect for longboarders and beginners. North of town, **Point St. George** (end of Washington Blvd.) has a reef and point break that comes alive during winter.

Local Boys Surf Shop (503 L St., 707/460-6060, www.localboyssurfshop. com, 10am-3pm Sat.-Mon., 10am-6pm Tues.-Fri., surfboard rentals $25-35, wetsuit rentals $20) rents 5- to 9-foot surfboards and offers surfboard repair.

Hiking

Redwood forests nearly meet Crescent City's wide, sandy beaches, making the area a fabulous place to hike. **Tolowa Dunes State Park** (1375 Elk Valley Rd., 2 mi/3.2 km north of Crescent City, 707/465-7335, www.parks.ca.gov, sunrise-sunset daily, free) has miles of trails that wind through forests, across

beaches, and along the shores of Lake Earl. The **Cadra Point Trail** (2 mi/3.2 km round-trip, 1 hour, easy) begins behind the Lake Earl Wildlife Area Information Center and travels through forest, meadows, and wetlands en route to a view of the lagoon from an old homestead site. The **Long Trail** (4 mi/6.4 km round-trip, 2 hours, easy) can be accessed from the end of Sand Hill Road; take the narrow trail right after the gate. The trail meanders through meadows and forests to the top of a dune. At the summit, take the left trail behind the dunes to **Sweetwater Creek Trail**, which leads 1.2 miles (1.9 km) back to the parking area.

Bird-Watching

The diverse climates and habitats nourish a huge variety of avian residents. Right in town, check out **Battery Point Lighthouse Park** and **Point St. George**. For a rare view of an Aleutian goose or a peregrine falcon, journey to **Tolowa Dunes State Park** (1375 Elk Valley Rd., 707/465-7335, www.parks.ca.gov, sunrise-sunset daily, free), specifically the shores of Lake Earl and Kellogg Beach. South of town, **Enderts Beach** is home to another large bird habitat.

Fishing

Anglers on the North Coast can choose between excellent deep-sea fishing and exciting river trips. The Pacific yields ling cod, snapper, and salmon, while the rivers are famous for chinook (king) salmon, steelhead, and cutthroat trout. The **Tally Ho II** (Crescent City Harbor, Citizen Dock R, Slip D29, 707/464-1236, http://tally-ho-sportfishing.com, May-Dec., half day $120 pp) is available for a variety of deep-sea fishing trips.

Horseback Riding

Casual riders can enjoy a guided riding adventure through redwoods or along the ocean with **Crescent Trail Rides** (2002 Moorehead Rd., 707/951-5407, www. crescenttrailrides.com, $70-155).

A great place to ride is **Tolowa Dunes State Park** (1375 Elk Valley Rd., 707/465-7335, www.parks.ca.gov, sunrise-sunset daily, free), which maintains 20 miles (32 km) of trails accessible to horses. Serious equestrians with their own mounts can ride in to a campsite with corrals at the north end of the park off Lower Lake Road.

Food

Seafood is standard fare in Crescent City, but family restaurants and one or two ethnic eateries add some variety. The **Java Hut** (437 US-101 N., 707/465-4439, 5am-10pm daily, $5) is a drive-through and walk-up coffee stand that serves a wide array of coffee drinks. Beware of long lines during the morning hours.

The small, family-owned, award-winning **Rumiano Cheese Co.** (511 9th St., 707/465-1535 or 866/328-2433, www.rumianocheese.com, 9:30am-5pm Mon.-Fri., 9am-3pm Sat. June-Dec., 9am-5pm Mon.-Fri. Jan.-May) has been part of Crescent City since 1921. Come to the tasting room for the cheese and stay for, well, more cheese. The dry jack cheese is a particular favorite.

Enjoy an impressive variety of fresh and healthy food at **The Good Harvest Cafe** (575 US-101 S., 707/465-6028, 7:30am-9pm Mon.-Sat., 8am-9pm Sun., $10-35). It serves the best breakfast in town, with vegetarian options like tofu rancheros and a veggie frittata. Steak entrées are at the pricier end of the dinner menu, which also includes burgers, pasta, vegetarian entrées, and big salads. Kitschy Native American decorations abound.

The chef/owners behind **Vita Cucina** (1270 Front St., Ste. A, 707/464-1076, www.vitacucina.com, 7am-6:30pm Mon.-Fri., $4-15) have upped the city's casual dining cred with bahn mi sandwiches and pulled pork. They also serve pizza (4pm-6:30pm).

Crescent City runs a **farmers market** (Del Norte County Fairgrounds, 421 US-101 N., 707/464-7441, www.delnorte.org, 9am-1:30pm Sat. June-Oct.).

Seafood

★ **SeaQuake Brewing** (400 Front St., 707/465-4444, www.seaquakebrewing.com, 11am-9pm Tues.-Thurs., 11am-10pm Fri.-Sat., $10-19) has revolutionized Crescent City's drinking and dining scene. The giant brewery and restaurant pours tasty brews, including a Citra IPA, enjoyed outside or in one of the cavernous building's two floors. The menu showcases Del Norte County's assets, from fish tacos made with locally caught rock cod, to burgers with local organic beef, to brick-oven pizzas topped with Crescent City's own Rumiano cheese. Live music on Saturday night makes this the city's ideal stop for great beer, local food, and good music.

Fisherman's Restaurant (700 US-101 S., 707/465-3474, 6am-9pm daily, $11-26) is a casual place to grab delicious breakfasts—biscuits and gravy, pancakes, and thick, juicy bacon—and a diverse dinner menu of fresh local seafood.

For seafood at a reasonable price, the best bet is **The Chart Room** (130 Anchor Way, 707/464-5993, https://cccchartroom.com, 7am-8pm Tues.-Sun., $10-23). It's very casual, the food is excellent, and it's right on the ocean.

Accommodations

The aptly named **Curly Redwood Lodge** (701 US-101 S., 707/464-2137, www.curlyredwoodlodge.com, $87-118) is constructed of a single rare curly redwood tree. You'll see the lovely color and grain of the tree in your large, simply decorated room. A 1950s feel pervades this friendly, unpretentious motel even though it offers free Wi-Fi. Some rooms even have antique TVs from the 1950s; others have flat-screens.

The **Lighthouse Inn** (681 US-101 S.,

707/464-3993 or 877/464-3993, http://thelighthouseinncrescentcity.com, $89-146) has an elegant yet whimsical lobby to welcome guests, and the enthusiastic staff can help with restaurant recommendations and sights. Stylish appointments and bold colors grace each guest room. Corner suites with oversize whirlpool tubs make a perfect romantic retreat for couples; standard double rooms are downright cheap.

The "harbor view" inn may be a more apt name for **Ocean View Inn** (270 US-101 S., 707/465-1111 or 855/623-2611, http://oceanviewinncrescentcity.com, $120-165), but the west-facing rooms do overlook a body of water. The lobby is a bit over the top with model sailboat decorations and a large mural of Crescent City's sights, but the rooms are big and worth the price. A complimentary continental breakfast is served in the morning to sweeten the deal. Pay a bit more for a two-room family suite or a room with a Jacuzzi tub and fireplace.

Getting Around

Traffic isn't a big issue in Crescent City, and parking is free and easy to find throughout town. **Redwood Coast Transit** (RCT, 707/464-6400, www.redwoodcoasttransit.org, adults $1.25) handles bus travel in Crescent City. Have exact change handy. Four in-town routes and a coastal bus from Smith River to Arcata provide ample public-transit options. Pick up a schedule at the visitors center (1001 Front St.).

Getting to the Oregon Border

The drive from Crescent City into Oregon is 40 miles (64 km) north on US-101, passing Jedediah Smith Redwoods State Park and the Smith River National Recreation Area. If you get hungry at the start of your drive, the **Hiouchi Cafe** (2095 Hwy. 199, Hiouchi, 707/458-3445, www.hiouchicafe.com, 7am-2pm Sat.-Thurs., 7am-8pm Fri., $6-14) serves breakfast and lunch in a red and white building. It also sells bag lunches for anglers and road-trippers.

Ashland,
Oregon

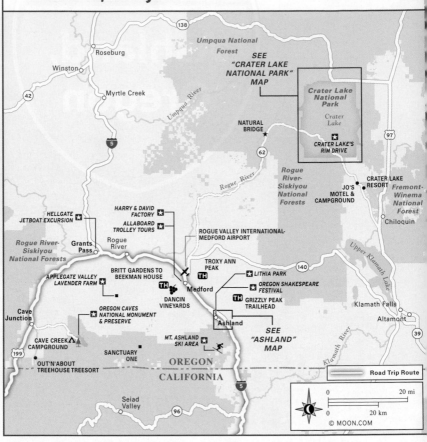

Ashland, Oregon

The change in the landscape from California into Oregon is subtle: dense coniferous forests merge into acres of vineyards with foothills blanketed in green.

The gateway to Oregon is a lush and uncrowded place with rushing rivers and natural geological wonders like Crater Lake. Surrounding the highway, the Rogue River-Siskiyou National Forest gives off an indirect energy that can't be found in any city, gently reminding you to slow down, breathe the fresh air, and admire the scenery.

Attractions here offer a mix of the natural and the urban. Deep underground lie the striking caverns at Oregon Caves National Monument, where tiny spaces and narrow passageways are available via a guided tour. Farther north at Grants Pass, nature takes the form of the rushing

Highlights

★ **Oregon Caves National Monument:** Crawl through cool, naturally formed tunnels via a guided 1.5-hour Discovery Cave Tour (page 262).

★ **Hellgate Jetboat Excursion:** Feel the wind whistle through your hair as you go ripping along the Rogue River through 36 miles of Hellgate Canyon (page 266).

★ **Applegate Valley Lavender Farm:** Make your own fragrant sachet, hand-picked from aromatic purple lavender fields (page 268).

★ **Harry & David Factory Tour:** Bite into a chocolate truffle at the end of the factory tour, where you'll learn how Harry & David preserves, packages, and ships its delicious gourmet gift baskets (page 269).

★ **Allaboard Trolley Tour:** Explore the Rogue Valley vineyards in style on this 1920s-era open-air streetcar (page 270).

★ **Lithia Park:** This 100-acre park features magnificent sculptures, fountains, and wildflowers, and a Japanese garden filled with vibrant maples and shrubs (page 273).

★ **Oregon Shakespeare Festival:** Get caught up in the drama of the Bard by catching a live performance at one of the festival's five live theaters (page 275).

★ **Skiing:** Mt. Ashland's terrain has a variety of slopes to slide down—including atmospheric twilight skiing (page 276).

★ **Crater Lake's Rim Drive:** Take a scenic drive around the rim of this spectacular blue lake (page 284).

Best Restaurants

★ **Northwest Pine Apple, Medford:** Indulge in a buddha bowl, a kale and grain salad, or some scrumptious avocado toast (page 270).

★ **Morning Glory, Ashland:** Start your day right with some Nutella-filled French toast and a spiked coffee drink (page 278).

★ **The Breadboard, Ashland:** This is a popular spot for hung-over college kids to reconvene, especially over the Mountain Man breakfast (page 278).

★ **Brickroom, Ashland:** Somewhat hidden in a second-story building on Main Street, this happening eatery has a hip vibe and offers flavorful locally sourced food and drinks (page 278).

★ **Standing Stone Brewing Company, Ashland:** This trendy bar serves handcrafted brews and dishes filled with ingredients sourced straight from their own garden (page 279).

★ **Ostras Tapas and Bottle Shop, Ashland:** Try unique and savory tapas, best with a bottle of tempranillo (page 279).

★ **Rim Village Café & Gift Shop, Crater Lake:** This cafeteria-style restaurant has basic offerings, but the teriyaki chicken bowl is delicious (page 289).

Rogue River and the artful bear sculptures that pepper this sunny town.

Cruising I-5 east leads through the commuter hub of Medford en route to the Shakespeare-loving town of Ashland, home to Southern Oregon University. Ashland is a foodie-lover's dream, where farm-to-table dining means locally grown and organic ingredients and an overwhelming array of delectable craft spirits and brews. Lodging establishments echo the early 1900s, when the town catered to blue-collar workers who built the railroads and highways that make travel easier today.

North of Ashland, sapphire-blue Crater Lake stuns visitors with its scenic beauty. A day hike or cruise around the caldera's Rim Drive is a must in summer.

Whether you go wine-tasting in the Rogue Valley, raft the white water through Hellgate Canyon, or take in a performance of *Macbeth*, this region offers a bounty of places to see that promise to leave a lasting impression.

Planning Your Time

Spring (Mar.-May) is the best time to visit lush, forest-filled Southern Oregon; festivals like the Oregon Shakespeare Festival are in full swing and the warm weather makes it comfortable to start enjoying the outdoors. This somewhat sleepy region truly wakes in **summer** when outdoor enthusiasts come for hiking, fishing, and water-based activities on the Rogue River. In **autumn,** temperatures start to cool and the crowds at Crater Lake tend to die down. **Winter** brings skiing or snowboarding at Mt. Ashland Ski Area.

Best Accommodations

★ **Out 'n' About Treesort, Cave Junction:** Wooden staircases and swinging bridges lead to rooms at this uniquely designed tree fort (page 265).

★ **Ashland Springs Hotel, Ashland:** This elegant hotel once catered to gold prospectors and has maintained its vintage charm (page 279).

★ **Peerless Hotel, Ashland:** A historic hotel in the railroad district promises lots of character and close access to shops, restaurants, and art galleries (page 280).

★ **Lithia Springs Resort, Ashland:** This health and wellness resort promotes relaxation and rejuvenation via private spring-fed bathtubs in each room (page 280).

★ **RedTail Inn, Ashland:** Stay at a restored farmhouse with features such as an organic garden and a Tesla charging station (page 280).

Getting There

When traveling in Oregon, note that drivers are not permitted to pump their own gas; wait instead for a gas station attendant to assist you.

From the North Coast
125 mi/200 km, 2.5 hr
From Crescent City, drive northeast on US-199 for 40 miles (64 km), crossing the Oregon border. Fill the tank in Crescent City; services farther north are few and far between. At **Cave Junction,** opt for a detour to Oregon Caves National Monument, 30 miles (48 km) east. Or continue 42 miles (68 km) north to Grants Pass, which has a few gas stations. At **Grants Pass,** get on I-5 heading east and drive 30 miles (48 km) to **Medford,** where you'll get a glimpse of the Rogue River. From Medford, it's a straight shot down I-5 for 14 miles (23 km) to **Ashland.**

From Shasta and Lassen
135 mi/220 km, 2.5 hr
From I-5 in **Redding,** head north on I-5 for 15 miles (24 km), where you'll cross the bridge at Shasta Lake. Continue north for 35 miles (56 km), passing Castle Crags State Park, a popular hiking spot. Drive north for 14 miles (23 km) to the city of Mount Shasta, which sits in the shadow of snowcapped 14,179-foot (4,322-m) Mount Shasta. From the city of Mount Shasta, continue north on I-5 for 10 miles (16 km) to Weed. From Weed, it's another 30 miles (48 km) north on I-5, passing the state border between California and Oregon. Stay on I-5 north for 38 miles (61 km) to **Ashland.**

There are gas stations available in Mount Shasta city, Weed, and Yreka along the way.

Air, Train, or Bus
A few major airlines fly into the **Rogue Valley International Medford Airport** (1000 Terminal Pkwy., Medford, OR, 541/772-8068, http://jacksoncountyor. org): **Alaska Airlines** (800/252-7522, www.alaskaair.com), **Delta** (800/221-1212, www.delta.com), **Allegiant** (702/505-8888, www.allegiantair.com), **United** (800/241-6522, www.united.com), and **American Airlines** (800/433-7300, www.aa.com).

Car rentals are available at the airport from: **Avis** (541/772-2632, www.avis.com, 7am-midnight Mon.-Fri., 8am-11pm Sat.-Sun., $55-59), **Budget** (541/773-7023, www.budget.com, 7am-midnight Mon.-Fri., 8am-11pm Sat.-Sun., $49-60), **Hertz** (2300 Biddle Rd., Medford, 541/773-4293,

Ashland in Three Days

Day 1

Crossing the state line into Oregon, stop in Cave Junction to fill the gas tank and grab coffee before taking OR-46 to **Oregon Caves National Monument.** Explore the underground tunnels via the Discovery Cave Tour. Emerge above ground and return to US-199, heading north into **Grants Pass.** Have lunch at **Wild River Brewing and Pizza Company,** then drop your bags off for the night at the **Buona Sera Inn.** In the afternoon, take a scenic detour through the Applegate Valley, returning to Grants Pass for dinner.

Day 2

Wake up in Grants Pass and head east on I-5 to Medford, where you'll stop for breakfast at the **Northwest Pine Apple.** From Medford, take OR-62 north to the Annie Springs Entrance of Crater Lake. Cruise along the Rim Drive, stopping to hike the **Cleetwood Cove Trail** (summer only) down to the lake. Stay the night at **Crater Lake Lodge** or pitch a tent at the **Mazama Campground.** At night, dine at the **Annie Creek Restaurant** (summer only) in Mazama Village.

Day 3

Grab coffee at the **Rim Village Café** and then head to Ashland, returning to Medford via OR-62 southwest before turning east on I-5 to Ashland. Enjoy breakfast in Ashland with French toast or pancakes at **Morning Glory,** then explore **Lithia Park** and walk along Ashland Creek. Stop for lunch at the **Brickroom** before grabbing tickets to a performance at the **Oregon Shakespeare Festival** (Mar.-Oct.). After the curtain closes, pass out at the **Peerless Hotel.**

www.hertz.com, 6:30am-12:30am daily, $57-68), and **National** (1000 Terminal Pkwy. Loop 110, 844/891-0543, www.nationalcar.com, 7am-1am Fri.-Wed., 7am-midnight Thurs., $51-70).

Century Aviation (6775 Arnold Ave., Klamath Falls, OR, 888/833-5911, https://centuryaviation.us) flies a charter service to and from the **Crater Lake Klamath Regional Airport** (6775 Arnold Ave., Klamath Falls, OR, 541/883-5372, www.flykfalls.com).

Amtrak (499 Stadium St., Klamath Falls, OR, 800/872-7245 or 541/884-2822, 7:30am-11am and 8:30pm-10pm daily) Coast Starlight trains travel along the coast with stops in Redding, Klamath Falls, and Portland. From Klamath Falls, hop on an Amtrak thruway bus to reach Ashland in 2-2.5 hours. The stop in Ashland is at Southern Oregon University and has no restrooms, vending machines, or shelter.

Ashland's **Greyhound** bus station

(4882 OR-66, Ashland, 800/231-2222, www.greyhound.com) is convenient to the region. Stations are also located in Redding, California (10 hours, $39-50), and in Medford (30 minutes from Ashland, $12).

Rogue Valley Transportation District (RVTD, 200 S. Front St., Medford, 541/779-2877, www.rvtd.org, 6am-6pm Mon.-Fri., $2 single ride, $6 day pass, $32 20-ride pass) buses ferry passengers to and from Medford, Ashland, and Jacksonville.

★ Oregon Caves National Monument

The story of how the 488 acres of underground tunnels of the **Oregon Caves National Monument** (19000 Caves Hwy., Cave Junction, OR, 541/592-2100, www.nps.gov/orca) came to be is rather fascinating. The "Marble Halls of Oregon," filled with smooth and flowery-looking stalagmites and stalactites, were formed when corrosive rainwater seeped through the forest floor and dissolved the marble rock below, carving out these secret tunnels. Today, these underground caverns feature calcite formations, small spaces, and narrow passageways available to all via a guided tour. When the caves are closed (Nov.-mid-Mar.), you can still explore the lush greenery, valley views, and moss-covered marble features above ground.

Getting There

From Crescent City, head north on US-101 for 4 miles (6.4 km). Turn onto US-199 toward I-5 and Grants Pass. In 49 miles (79 km), cross over the state line into Oregon and enter Cave Junction. Plan two hours to reach Cave Junction, then another hour to reach the Oregon Caves Visitor Center via a curvy, one-lane road.

From Grants Pass, head south on US 199 for 30 miles (48 km) to Cave Junction. Turn left on OR-46 and drive 20 miles (32 km) down the one-lane road to the Oregon Caves Visitor Center.

The road to Oregon Caves can be tricky, and GPS devices often lead people in the wrong direction onto gravel or unpaved roads. The long and winding route climbs to 4,000 feet (1,200 m) in elevation with few shoulders to pull off on. Allow plenty of time for the drive, especially if you've booked a cave tour.

Visiting the Park
Park Passes and Fees

Oregon Caves National Monument is free to enter above ground. Exploring the marble tunnels underground is only possible with a **guided tour** ($10 adults, $7 juniors age 15 and under).

Visitors Centers

The **Oregon Caves Visitor Center** (19000 Caves Hwy., Cave Junction, OR, 541/592-2100, www.recreation.gov, 9:30am-4pm Thurs.-Mon. late Mar.-late May and early Sept.-early Nov., 8:30am-4pm Thurs.-Mon. late May-Aug.) is 20 miles (32 km) down the winding, one-lane road to the cave. Here you'll find restrooms, a bookstore, and a museum with exhibits and an interactive cave experience where visitors can learn about the caves' endemic species, history, and geology.

The **Illinois Valley Visitors Center** (201 Caves Hwy., Cave Junction, 541/592-4076, https://ivcdo.org, 9am-4pm Mon.-Fri. Mar.-late May, 8:30am-6pm daily late May-early Sept., 9am-4pm Mon.-Fri. early Sept.-early Nov.) is near the junction of US-199 and the OR-46 turnoff. Stop here for information and updates on weather and road conditions.

Information and Services

There are two gas stations in Cave Junction; both are on US-199 close to the OR-46/Oregon Caves turnoff. The **76 Gas Station and Car Wash** (112 S. Redwood Hwy., 541/592-6513) is open 24 hours. The **Chevron** (409 Redwood Hwy., 541/592-3080, 7am-7pm daily) includes a vehicle repair shop and tow services. It maintains clean restrooms and facilities. A coffee shop is next door.

Cave Tours

Several different cave tours are offered. Tours are limited to 15 people and tend to fill fast. **Reserve a tour** (877/444-6777, www.recreation.gov, $10 adults, $7 juniors age 15 and under) online in advance. The reservation system opens on March 1 for the upcoming summer season. Spots may be available without a reservation, but be prepared to wait—especially during spring break (late Mar.-early Apr.) and in the peak of summer (July-Aug.). Tours are offered Thursday-Monday early in the season. Tickets may also be purchased at the visitors center.

The **Discovery Cave Tour** (1.5 hours) is the monument's most popular cave tour. Participants crouch through small and narrow holes and climb 500 stone steps

(no handrails) with a chance to explore an underground labyrinth—assuming that you're not afraid of tight, dark places. To ease any claustrophobia, guides point out interesting geological flowstones and features. The moderately strenuous tour ends in a big room 220 feet (67 m) below ground. The pathways are well lit (no flashlights needed), but wearing good walking or hiking shoes is advised. Children must be at least 42 inches (107 cm) tall to enter the caves.

The **Candlelight Cave Tour** (1 hour) is the last tour of the day. Guests carry candlelit lanterns to navigate paths through the cave on this guided tour limited to 12 participants. Children must be age 10 or older.

The **Kids and Family Cave Tour** (1.5 hours) is perfect for kids age 13 or younger (as long as they are 42 in/107 cm tall). A park ranger leads this guided tour through the caves in summer.

For a truly memorable (or terrifying) adventure, take your cave exploration up a notch with the **Off-Trail Caving Tour** (3 hours, times vary June-Aug., $45). During this underground excursion, a guide leads groups of eight people into the deep depths of the Marble Halls. You'll negotiate tight spaces, climb over big boulders, and crawl on your belly Indiana Jones-style using only a headlamp to guide the way. Tour participants must be at least 15 years old, must wear boots with solid ankle support, and should have the physical and mental strength for this tour. Tour times are announced in mid-May.

Hiking

A few aboveground hiking trails loop around the caves. The **Cliff Nature Trail** (1 mi/1.6 km one-way, 1 hour, easy) starts from the visitors center and treks along marble outcroppings and through forest while climbing 371 feet (113 m) to enjoy

From top to bottom: Oregon Caves National Monument; Out 'n' About Treesort; Grants Pass.

views of the surrounding Illinois Valley. (This is the same trail that leads from the cave's exit down to the visitors center.)

The **Big Tree Trail** (3.3 mi/5.3 km round-trip, 3 hours, moderately strenuous) climbs to a 600-year-old Douglas fir before returning to the visitors center. The loop trail starts left of the visitors center and leads through a mixed coniferous forest filled with oak, maples, and pines. Switchbacks steer trekkers past a water tank, the Siskiyou Forest boundary line, and through rocky knolls. After crossing Panther Creek, a platform to the Big Tree comes into view where you can admire its 13-foot (4-m) diameter trunk.

From the Big Tree, the trail drops down through wildflower-filled meadows, eventually coming to the Big Tree-Mt. Elijah Trail Junction. From the junction, turn right to return to the visitors center. This is a nice hike in spring, when the Siskiyou Forest's bright native flowers come into bloom.

Accommodations and Camping

The Oregon Caves Chateau was closed in 2019 due to repairs; it's slated to reopen in 2020. Until then, plan to bring your own food and drinks.

Four miles west of the Oregon Caves Visitor Center, **Cave Creek Campground** (OR-46, mile markers 15-16, 541/592-2100, www.nps.gov/orca, first-come, first-served late May-Sept., $10) has 17 secluded tent sites in a dense coniferous forest. The small sites include a picnic table and fire pit.

Sleep in the trees at the ★ **Out 'n' About Treesort** (300 Page Creek Rd., Cave Junction, 540/592-2208, www.treehouses.com, $150-330), a small, locally run treetop bed-and-breakfast. The tree houses sit 12-47 feet off the ground, which makes getting to your room an adventure. Climb flights of stairs, cross suspension bridges, or shimmy up a ladder and enter via a trap door to reach your bed.

The tallest tree house, the Majestree ($330), has a queen bed in the main room, two single beds in a loft, a kitchenette, and bathroom. The Serendipitree ($150) sits 12 feet above ground and is perfect for couples. Most tree houses sleep 2-4 people. There are no locks on the doors, amenities are sparse, and spaces are small, but the activities (ziplines, horse riding) compensate. Those afraid of heights can opt for the small two-story cabin. Kids love this resort due to its fun swinging bridges, fireman poles, board games, and communal campfire pit.

Grants Pass

You'll smile as you enter Grants Pass, especially after getting a glimpse of the life-size sculptures of bears wearing backpacks (their relatives reside at the Bear Hotel in the winter season). The 218-mile Rogue River runs through Grants Pass, and water-based activities are a draw here, whether white-water rafting, fishing, jet-boat riding, or sitting at a picnic table with the ducks, seagulls, and Canada geese at Riverside Park. An abundance of natural greenery is everywhere, due in part to a practically perfect climate: sunny summers with cool nighttime temperatures and mild rainy winters with occasional snow.

Getting There

From the junction of US-199 and OR-46 near Oregon Caves National Monument, drive 30 miles (48 km) north to Grants Pass.

Sights

BearFest (Evergreen Federal Bank, 969 SE 6th St., 541/479-3351, www.evergreenfederal.bank/bearfest, free) started one summer when a local bank delighted residents by placing 20 life-size bear sculptures around downtown Grants Pass. Everyone loved them and the number of bears kept growing over the years, reaching a total of 182 bears.

Many of the sculptures have since been auctioned off, but those that remain spend the winter hibernating at the **Evergreen Bear Hotel** (2101 NE Spalding Ave.). This warehouse/museum features artwork and sculptures, as well as other community projects. Contact the Evergreen Federal Bank (541/479-3351, www.evergreenfederal.bank, 8am-5pm Mon.-Thurs., 8am-6pm Fri.) to request a free tour.

Recreation

★ Hellgate Jetboat Excursions

One of the most popular activities in Grants Pass is the **Hellgate Jetboat Excursions** tour (966 SW 6th St., 541/479-7204, http://hellgate.com, May-Sept., $46-80/2 hours) along the Rogue River. During the trip, participants speed through 36 miles of Hellgate Canyon, legendary for spectacular scenery and wildlife augmented by the adrenaline rush of these raging waters. The entertaining and informative boat captains point out area wildlife as guests rip through the canyon in a shallow Katanacraft (up to 60 passengers)—sometimes only inches above the river surface. Brunch and dinner tours are also available, as well as an exclusive 75-mile Whitewater Adventure (when conditions permit).

Festivals and Events

The **Back to the Fifties Celebration Car Show** (downtown locations vary, 541/476-7574, https://travelgrantspass.com, last Sat. in July) celebrates the 1950s with classic cars, a concert, a craft fair, and, of course, bears on bikes. Classic car owners cruise down Grants Pass's streets in vintage automobiles while spectators enjoy ice-cream socials, sock hops, and the overall nostalgia.

Summer kicks off with the annual **Boatnik** (Riverside Park, www.boatnik. com, late May), a multiday event featuring a carnival, a beer fest, live music, a pizza-eating contest, and other activities. The highlight of the event is the Tom Rice Memorial White Water Hydroplane Race, whereby folks race tiny jet boats down the Rogue River, from Riverside Park to Carpenters Island and back, as spectators watch from atop Caveman Bridge.

Food

Wild River Brewing and Pizza Company (595 NE E St., Grants Pass, 541/471-7487, www.wildriverbrewing.com, 10am-10pm daily, $6-33) serves handcrafted pizzas and regional beers from Southern Oregon. Pair a Class V wood-fired Deli Delight pizza, full of sausages and veggies (or get those same fixings in a Quarry calzone) with a nut-brown brew.

For a jolt of caffeine, head to **Rogue Roasters** (610 SW 6th St., 541/476-6134, www.rogueroasters.com, 7am-6pm Mon.-Sat., 8am-5pm Sun., $2-5). This local coffee-roasting company has won awards for the best grounds in Oregon. Try the in-house roasted espresso by ordering a Salty Dog or hemp-milk latte with lavender and caramel.

The Haul (121 SW H St., 541/474-4991, www.thehaulgp.com, 11am-10pm Sun. and Wed.-Thurs., 11am-midnight Fri.-Sat., $9-15) is a local brewpub serving wood-fired pizzas, shared appetizers, and sandwiches. Live music is often performed inside the rustic, industrial space.

Accommodations

The **Discovery Inn** (748 SE 7th St., 541/476-7793, www.discoveryinngrantspass.us, $54-89) has 35 basic, clean rooms with a king or two queen beds. A nonheated outdoor pool is on the premises; there's also parking and free Wi-Fi.

The **Knight's Inn Motel** (104 SE 7th St., 541/479-5595, $69-105) is centrally located downtown. The basic rooms feature tall spacious beds, hardwood floors, and air-conditioning. A stay includes free Wi-Fi, a continental breakfast, and plenty of parking. The real highlight is that you can check in anytime.

For a room with a bit more character, check out the **Buona Sera Inn**

(1001 NE 6th St., 541/476-4260, www.
buonaserainn.com, $64). Flowerpots
adorn the exterior; inside, queen beds
feature patterned comforters with brass
or wooden headboards and Victorian sitting chairs. Amenities include free parking, Wi-Fi, and a continental breakfast.
Some rooms are dog-friendly.

After a long day of driving, splurge
with a stay at the **Redwood Hyperion
Suites** (815 NE 6th St., 541/476-0878,
https://redwoodmotel.com, $97-185
rooms, $150-459 suites). The upscale
hotel is carefully designed to blend in
with its resident redwood trees. Standard
rooms are spacious with either one king,
one queen, or two queen beds, a mini
fridge, a microwave, and a wooden desk.
Suites sleep up to six people and include full bathrooms (some with whirl-
pool tubs). Amenities include a hot tub
(year-round), a fitness center, high-speed
Internet, and a free continental breakfast.
An events center is also on-site, with access to workstations and printers.

Information and Services
The **Grants Pass Visitors Center** (1995
NW Vine St., 541/476-7717, https://
travelgrantspass.com, 9am-5pm Mon.-
Fri., 9am-2pm Sat.) has information on
year-round events and outdoor activities
in the area.

⬥ OR-238: Applegate Valley
OR-238 offers a scenic detour en route to
Jacksonville, widely considered one of
Southern Oregon's coolest historic towns.

Getting There
From Grants Pass, follow OR-238 south
out of town for 36 miles (58 km) into
Jacksonville. The Applegate Valley
Lavender Farm appears in about 15 miles
(24 km).

From top to bottom: Grants Pass; Wild River
Brewing and Pizza Company; Applegate Valley
Lavender Farm.

★ Applegate Valley Lavender Farm

Applegate Valley Lavender Farm (15370 Hwy. 238, Grants Pass, 541/291-9229, www.applegatevalleylavenderfarm.com, hours vary in summer, closed in July) is a family-owned farm that started out as a vineyard but soon became known for its heavenly scented lavender blooms. Today, the farm grows 12 different varieties of lavender and keeps ducks, chickens, grass-fed cattle, and a cute Olde English Babydoll dwarf sheep. The farm participates in several regional lavender festivals and runs a U-pick stand in summer.

Apple Valley Wine Trail

The **Applegate Valley Wine Trail** (http://applegatewinetrail.com, 19 stops) visits several wineries within a concentrated area: **Soloro Vineyard** (9110 N. Applegate Rd., 541/862-2693, 1pm-5pm Fri.-Sun. Apr.-Nov.), **Rosella's Vineyard** (184 Missouri Flat Rd., 541/846-6372, https://rosellasvineyard.com, 11am-5pm daily, free tasting with purchase), and **Schultz Wines** (755 Slagle Creek Rd., 541/414-8448, www.schultzwines.com, noon-5pm Fri.-Sat.).

At the center of the wine trail is **Augustino Estate** (16995 N. Applegate Rd., 541/846-1881, http://augustinoestate.com, noon-5pm Sat.-Sun., $10 tasting fee), which specializes in pinot noir and syrah varietals.

Heading east toward Jacksonville, stop at **John Michael Champagne Cellars** (1425 Humbug Creek Rd., 541/846-0810, www.johnmichaelwinery.com, call for hours, $5) to imbibe a little bubbly.

Note that visitors under age 18 are allowed in the tasting rooms.

Sanctuary One

Sanctuary One (13195 Upper Applegate Rd., Jacksonville, 541/899-8627, https://sanctuaryone.org, 90-minute tours 10:30am Fri.-Sat. late Apr.-early Sept., $10) is a 55-acre farm full of happy, rescued animals that live a better quality of life. In summer, volunteers lead tours of the farm, where you'll meet rescued animals like Pepe the alpaca, Travolta the chicken, or Lulu the pig. The sanctuary includes a spacious 35,000-square-foot garden that provides all of the vegetables and food for the animals, as well as the people who manage the property.

Medford

Medford is a well-populated city sandwiched between the Cascade and Siskiyou Ranges. It's a big commuter hub that connects Grants Pass and Ashland along I-5, with travel north to Crater Lake and south into Jacksonville and the Applegate Valley. Medford is also the home of Harry & David's gift basket company. It offers a good midway spot to refuel and relax before continuing on to your next destination.

Getting There

From Grants Pass, take I-5 east for 30 miles (48 km) to Medford. From Ashland, Medford is 13 miles (21 km) west along I-5.

Sights

★ Harry & David Factory Tour

If you've ever bitten into a juicy pear or snacked on fancy nuts from a gift basket courtesy of **Harry & David** (877/322-8000, www.harryanddavid.com, tours 9:15am, 10:30am, 12:30pm, and 1:45pm Mon.-Fri., $5), then you know that nothing beats the quality of their products. For a glimpse at how these delectable treats are made, catch a factory tour and watch how this top-notch culinary team produces, packages, and preserves some of America's favorite snacks, including its popular Royal Riviera pears. Tour tickets are sold at the **Harry & David Country Village** store (1314 Center Dr., 541/864-2278, 9am-7pm Sun.-Thurs., 9am-8pm Fri.-Sat.). Guests then take a bus to visit the Harry & David campus, about a mile away.

Tours lead guests through a bakery and kitchen, where culinary professionals assemble chocolates, caramels, and the signature Moose Munch popcorn. Participants then visit the packing house, where gourmet gift baskets are packaged and shipped. The hour-long tour ends back at the store, where chocolates and treats await.

DANCIN Vineyards

DANCIN Vineyards (4477 S. Stage Rd., Medford, 541/245-1133, https://dancinvineyards.com, noon-7pm Thurs.-Sun., $7-19) is a sprawling neighborhood vineyard situated between Jacksonville, Ashland, and Medford. The two-story tasting room is the perfect place to relax as you sip on a signature chardonnay or pinot noir and take in the views of the Rogue Valley, Mt. McLoughlin, and Table Rocks. The tasting room serves wood-fired pizzas and salads, with

Harry & David Country Village store

recommended wine pairing options. Try the Harlem Shake pizza topped with a locally sourced cream sauce.

★ Allaboard Trolley Tours

A unique ride with **Allaboard Trolley Tours** (541/821-4593, noon-5pm Sat. May Oct., $79) guides visitors through Southern Oregon's wine region aboard a 1920s open-air streetcar. The owner is an Oregon native who shares her passion about history and wine during this five-hour tour. Hop on the two-person padded bench seat and take in the spectacular views of the Rogue and Applegate Valleys, stopping at Red Lily Vineyards and Schmidt Family Vineyards, perhaps enjoying live music at DANCIN, plus wine-tastings and snacks. In December, Allaboard decorates their streetcars with Christmas lights to tour the neighborhoods east of Medford; hot chocolate is served on board.

Entertainment and Events

In spring, Medford and the surrounding area host a few events that appeal to foodies, families, and flower lovers.

The **Oregon Cheese Festival** (Central Point, www.oregoncheesefestival.com, mid-Mar., $11-17) is hosted by the Rogue Creamery and unites cheese producers up and down the coast to share unique creations made with goat, sheep, and cow milk. Admission includes cheese samplings from 100 different vendors and classes with master cheese makers.

The **Oregon Chocolate Festival** (locations vary, Ashland, www.oregonchocolatefestival.com, early Mar.) is where West Coast chocolatiers show off their delectable creations. Attendees indulge in a weekend of cocktail parties and desserts, then burn it all off in a Charlie's Chocolate 5K run.

The annual **Art in Bloom Festival** (downtown Medford, http://art-in-bloom.com, early May, free) celebrates spring with vibrant colors exhibited by local artists and craftspeople. Horticulturists,

painters, photographers, and jewelry makers take over downtown Medford in a showcase of talent at this community-wide event.

Hiking

The **Natural Bridge Loop** (2 mi/3.2 km round-trip, 1 hour, easy) is a great spot to stretch your legs as you drive to Crater Lake. The paved trail meanders along the eastern side of the roaring Rogue River and its energetic waterfalls before approaching one of Southern Oregon's most unique features: a natural land bridge formed by an old lava tube. A green mossy blanket covers the landscape, while busy birds and beavers build habitats in the area. The trailhead is near OR-62, close to Union Creek.

The **Roxy Ann Peak Trail** (4 mi/6.4 km round-trip, 2.5 hours, moderate) is a lovely jaunt to the top of Roxy Ann Peak. The path starts on hard-packed gravel and dirt as it winds through oak trees, meadows, and pines, climbing more than 1,000 feet (300 m) in elevation. At the top, soak in the splendid views of Rogue Valley and Mount Shasta. The dog-friendly trail is accessible from East McAndrews Road, outside of Medford. To get there, turn onto Roxy Ann Drive in Prescott Park.

Food

★ **Northwest Pine Apple** (900 N. Riverside Dr., Medford, https://northwestpineapple.com, 10am-4pm Tues.-Fri., $7-10) is a dream come true for dairy- and gluten-free foodies. Everything on the menu is dairy-free and gluten-free and is made with organic and natural ingredients. Get your fill of their smoothies, acai bowls, and avocado toast.

Situated between Grants Pass and Medford on the Rogue River, **The Teapot on Wheels** (1754 Rogue River Hwy., Gold Hill, 541/855-4343, https://theteapotonwheels.com, 9:30am-3pm Wed.-Sat., $25) is a quaint tearoom and gift shop. Enjoy a classic afternoon tea (2 hours) that includes fruit cups, scones, desserts, and an array of bite-size sandwiches plus endless cups of white, black, or green tea. Seatings are at 9:30am, noon, and 2:30pm; the adjoining gift shop (9am-3pm) sells loose-leaf teas.

Hidden Door Café (1263 N. Riverside Ave., Ste. 4, 541/203-7711, www. hiddendoorcafe.com, 11am-3:30pm daily, $9-11) serves Mediterranean-style falafels, baklava, and gyros in a homey building within the Cobblestone Village. Start with some baba ghanoush followed by a Mongolian chicken salad with tabouli and toasted sesame seeds.

Accommodations and Camping

Valley of the Rogue State Park (off I-5, 13 mi/21 km east of Grants Pass, 800/551-6949 or 541/582-3128, https:// oregonstateparks.org, year-round, $19-53) offers 95 RV spaces with full hookups, 14 tent sites, and 8 yurts on the Rogue River shoreline. The campground has showers, flush toilets, and hiking trails. Pets are welcome in some of the yurts.

Rooms at the **Sovana Inn** (250 E. Barnett Rd., 541/500-8500, http:// sovanainnmedford.us, $65-135) are amazingly comfortable and feature 1-2 queen beds, a flat-screen TV with cable, a desk, a microwave, and free Wi-Fi. Guests have access to an outdoor pool and free parking. Enjoy a complimentary breakfast provided by the friendly staff. Guests receive discounts at local restaurants within walking distance.

Information and Services

The local chamber of commerce is **Travel Medford** (101 E. 8th St., 800/469-6307, www.travelmedford.org, 9am-5pm Mon.-Fri.), which has a wealth of information about events in Medford and all of Rogue Valley. Download a copy of the **Medford Visitor Guide** (www.travelmedford.org) if you plan to spend a significant amount of time in the area.

If you're traveling to Ashland and expect to hit the slopes at Mt. Ashland Ski Area, stop in Medford at the **Rogue Ski Shop** (309 E. Jackson St., 541/772-8047, www.rogueskishop.com, 10am-6pm Mon.-Sat., noon-4pm Sun.) to pick up gear.

Getting Around

Rogue Valley International Medford Airport (1000 Terminal Pkwy., Medford, OR, 541/772-8068, http:// jacksoncountyor.org) is one of Oregon's bigger airports, serviced by five major airlines: **Alaska Airlines** (800/252-7522, www.alaskaair.com), **Delta** (800/221-1212, www.delta.com), **Allegiant** (702/505-8888, www.allegiantair.com), **United** (800/241-6522, www.united.com), and **American Airlines** (800/433-7300, www.aa.com).

Car rental options include: **Avis** (541/772-2632, www.avis.com, 7am-midnight Mon.-Fri., 8am-11pm Sat.-Sun., $55-59), **Budget** (541/773-7023, www.budget.com, 7am-midnight Mon.-Fri., 8am-11pm Sat.-Sun., $49-60), **Hertz** (2300 Biddle Rd., Medford, 541/773-4293, www.hertz.com, 6:30am-12:30am daily, $57-68), and **National** (1000 Terminal Pkwy. Loop 110, 844/891-0543, www. nationalcar.com, 7am-1am Fri.-Wed., 7am-midnight Thurs., $51-70).

❦ OR-238: Jacksonville

On the east side of the Applegate Valley is the lovely National Historic Landmark and town of Jacksonville. The bustling main street is lined with brightly colored Victorian homes and brick buildings housing shops, hotel rooms, and restaurants. Vibrant greenery showcases the native flowers and trees. It's easy to spend several hours on a warm sunny day visiting with the friendly locals who keep the town's legacy alive.

Getting There

Jacksonville is 15 miles (24 km) north of Ashland and 11 miles (17.5 km) west of Medford on OR-238.

Recreation

The **Jacksonville Woodlands Association Trail System** (http://jvwoodlands.org) has 16 miles of trails that include the **Britt Gardens to Beekman House Loop** (4 mi/6.4 km round-trip, 2 hours, easy). The lovely walk along the Sarah Zigler Interpretative Trail leads through the old Rich Gulch Mining District, Chinese Diggings, and groves of oak trees and shrubs, ending at the historic Beekman House and arboretum, filled with native plants and trees such as the bright and colorful Gentner's fritillary and the vibrant red bells.

Food and Accommodations

The **Mustard Seed Café** (130 N. 5th St., 541/899-2977, 7am-2pm Tues.-Sat., $7-10) is a small eatery with a yellow and stone facade. Inside, the smiling staff serves a mean chicken-fried steak, egg scramble, and breakfast items smothered in country gravy.

Cerberus Coffee (310 E. California St., www.cerberuscoffeeco.com, 7am-3pm daily, $3-5) serves crazy-good coffee and tea concoctions on the west side of town. Try their mocha, made with Lillie Belle Farms chocolate (handcrafted in Central Point), or the Odyssey, consisting of blackberry honey syrup, milk, and matcha poured over ice.

The succulent smells emanating from **Las Palmas Mexican Restaurant** (210 E. California St., 541/899-9965, 11am-9pm Sun.-Thurs., 11am-10pm Fri.-Sun., $11-30) will encourage you to dip inside for bountiful bean and rice dishes paired with seasoned shrimp smothered in red sauce or tacos filled with fixings.

Jacksonville Inn (175 E. California St., 541/899-1900, www.jacksonvilleinn.com, $159-199 rooms, $270-465 cottages) offers convenient lodging, dining, and wine-tasting in the center of town. Enjoy a fancy meal of salmon, ahi tuna, or hazelnut chicken paired with a glass of wine and then spend the night in one of eight rooms decorated in authentic antique furnishings. Each room exhibits a distinct personality: the Peter Britt Room features a canopy queen bed, Victorian-style sitting chair, and Jacuzzi tub with modern amenities (flat-screen TV, free Wi-Fi). Be sure to visit the wine shop, which has received accolades from *Wine Spectator* and *GQ Magazine*.

Built in 1928, the **Magnolia Inn** (245 N. 5th St., 541/899-0255, www.magnolia-inn.com, $149-179 summer, $129-149 winter) is a well-maintained mansion in downtown Jacksonville. Each of the nine rooms has a cozy, cottage-like feel and overlooks a veranda, garden, or church. Inside, the rooms feature queen beds and private baths; the Claudette room has two twin beds. This pet-friendly inn is close to everything.

Information and Services

Jacksonville Chamber of Commerce Visitor Center (185 N. Oregon St., 541/899-8118, www.jacksonvilleoregon.com, 10am-3pm daily May-Dec., 10am-2pm Mon.-Sat. Jan.-Apr.) is chock-full of maps and information.

Chevron (945 N. 5th St., 541/899-7761, 24 hours) offers a place to fill up en route to Ashland.

Ashland

Home to about 20,000 people, Ashland's proximity to Crater Lake National Park and the Oregon Shakespeare Festival draws many people to the area for art, culture, and a relaxing green environment. Expansive Lithia Park features amazing gardens that can take a whole day to explore, while the Southern Oregon University caters to a college crowd often found shredding the slopes of Mount Ashland or enjoying a handcrafted brew at Standing Stone Brewing Company.

Ashland's economy relies much on tourism courtesy of the Shakespeare Festival. Locals are happy to share the current lineup and offer recommendations on the best shows to see. With a handful of wine-tasting rooms, natural parks, historical buildings, and the scenic Rogue River, Ashland provides many opportunities to experience something new.

Getting There

Ashland is on I-5 south of Medford and 18 miles (29 km) north of the inland state border between California and Oregon.

★ Lithia Park

Lithia Park (59 Winburn Way, 541/488-5340, www.ashland.or.us, dawn-11:30pm daily, free) is a 100-acre park filled with bridges, gardens, domes, fountains, and sycamores and is also home to the Oregon Shakespeare Festival. A Japanese garden is home to beautiful bonsai bushes and fiery-looking maples. Along Ashland Creek, hiking trails loop through the woods. The park holds a duck pond, a community center, tennis and pickleball courts, a volleyball pit, a playground, a swimming pond, and an ice-skating rink (in winter). Roses brighten the park in the spring months. Make a wish at the base of the beautiful Butler-Perozzi Fountain. Guided nature walks, concerts, and silent discos are held in summer.

Wine-Tasting

The **Dana Campbell Vineyards** (1320 N. Mountain Ave., 541/482-3798, www.danacampbellvineyards.com, 1pm-6pm daily) started by growing malbec, viognier, and tempranillo grapes and has since expanded into sauvignon blanc and mourvedre varietals. The tasting room features an outdoor fire pit and a bocce ball court designed to showcase the beautiful vineyards. From Main Street in Ashland, head north on Lithia Way toward the Standing Stone Brewing Company. Turn right on Oak Street and drive 1.5 miles (2.4 km), crossing I-5. Turn right onto Eagle Mill Road and continue 0.5 mile to North Mountain Avenue. Turn left for Dana Campbell Vineyards.

Belle Fiore Estate & Winery (100 Belle Fiore Ln./955 Dead Indian Rd., 541/552-4900, https://bellefiorewine.com, tasting room: noon-4pm Mon.-Tues., noon-8pm Wed. and Sun., noon-9pm Thurs.-Sat.; tours by appointment: noon and 3pm Fri.-Sun., $55 nonmembers) represents the epitome of luxury. Terraced garden walkways line emerald-green grasses with stunning views of the Rogue Valley. The winery's opulent, over-the-top French architecture resembles a Mediterranean chateau, while inside, dark wood and granite accents complement incredible artwork and painted ceilings. Tastings are on the Wine Pavilion, where you can sit back and take in the scenery of this 55-acre estate. A flight comprises five wines ($15-71) from the estate's 20 options.

Eliana Wines (158 Gaerky Creek Rd., 541/690-4350, www.elianawines.com, noon-5pm Thurs.-Sat. summer) is a boutique winery close to downtown Ashland that is run by a South African couple who used to grow roses before growing wine grapes. The small estate specializes in merlot, cabernet, and a smooth rosé that won gold in the Gold International Rosé Competition.

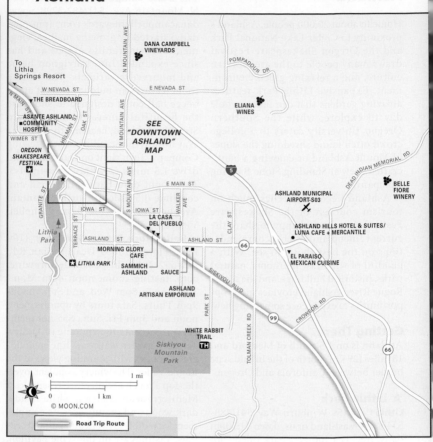

Ashland

To
Lithia
Springs Resort

THE BREADBOARD

ASANTE ASHLAND
COMMUNITY
HOSPITAL

WIMER ST

OREGON
SHAKESPEARE
FESTIVAL

GRANITE ST

Lithia
Park

LITHIA PARK

N MAIN ST

W NEVADA ST

HELMAN ST

OAK ST

TERRACE ST

IOWA ST

ASHLAND ST

MORNING GLORY
CAFE

SAMMICH
ASHLAND

N MOUNTAIN AVE

N MOUNTAIN AVE

DANA CAMPBELL
VINEYARDS

E NEVADA ST

SEE
"DOWNTOWN
ASHLAND"
MAP

S MOUNTAIN AVE

E MAIN ST

S IOWA ST

ASHLAND
ST

LA CASA
DEL PUEBLO

SAUCE

ASHLAND
ARTISAN EMPORIUM

WALKER AVE

POMPADOUR DR

ELIANA
WINES

PARK ST

E MAIN ST

ASHLAND ST

CLAY ST

5

66

SISKIYOU BLVD

WHITE RABBIT
TRAIL TH

Siskiyou
Mountain
Park

TOLMAN CREEK RD

DEAD INDIAN MEMORIAL RD

BELLE
FIORE
WINERY

ASHLAND MUNICIPAL
AIRPORT-S03

ASHLAND HILLS HOTEL & SUITES/
LUNA CAFE + MERCANTILE

EL PARAISO
MEXICAN CUISINE

CROWSON RD

99

66

0   1 mi

0   1 km

© MOON.COM

Road Trip Route

Entertainment and Events
Nightlife
Liquid Assets Wine Bar (96 N. Main St., 541/482-9463, www.liquidassetswinebar. com, 4pm-10pm Mon.-Thurs., 4pm-midnight Fri.-Sat.) serves unique wines, specialty cocktails, and Jones soda or non-alcoholic Bitburger lagers for those who don't drink. Pair it with scrumptious upscale snacks like truffle popcorn ($5) or a hearty entrée.

Alchemy Restaurant and Bar (35 S. 2nd St., 541/488-1115, www.alchemyashland.

com, 4pm-10pm Sun.-Thurs., 4pm-11pm Sat.) serves more than 200 carefully selected liquors that line the shelves from floor to ceiling. Polished wood bar stools and small tables permit intimate conversations over signature cocktails like the Sleeping with the Rancher, made with mezcal, honey, and tobacco bitters, or an L.L. Cool Jess with vodka and pamplemousse (grapefruit). Located next to the Winchester Inn, Alchemy has a hip ambiance and a trendy crowd.

Downtown Ashland

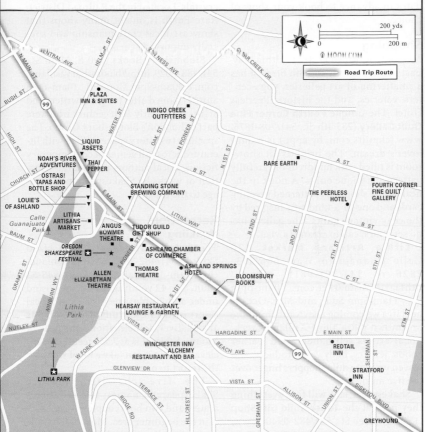

Festivals and Events

★ Oregon Shakespeare Festival

The **Oregon Shakespeare Festival** (800/219-8161, www.osfashland.org, Mar.-Oct., prices vary) was created by Angus Bowmer in 1935. Since its inception, Ashland's theaters have entertained more than 20 million visitors who descend on the town to watch both classic and modern live performances.

The first performance, and a mainstay of the festival, is held at the **Angus Bowmer Theatre** (15 S. Pioneer St., 541/482-2111, www.osfashland.org, $30-90), where

staggered seating ensures that every seat is a good one. Expect anything from a classic Shakespeare play to a live rendition of the Broadway musical *Hairspray*.

The **Thomas Theatre** (15 S. Pioneer St., 541/482-2111, www.osfashland.org, $49-79) is located on the upper east side of Lithia Park and offers mesmerizing, provocative performances. The **Allen Elizabethan Theatre** (15 S. Pioneer St., 541/482-2111, www.osfashland. org, $30-90) hosts the more traditional Bard drama; past performances include *Macbeth* and *All's Well that Ends Well*.

Tickets for the season go on sale the previous November. Secure your travel dates in advance to book your show of choice.

Shopping

Ashland's Railroad District (Lithia Way, East Main, Oak, A, and 8th Streets) has a smattering of art galleries, yoga centers, eateries, and the historic Peerless Hotel. The unique **Fourth Corner Fine Quilt Gallery** (283 4th St., 541/708-1876, www.fcfquilts.com, by appt.) is a quilt lover's dream. The brightly lit showroom is filled with hundreds of carefully patterned antique quilts. A nook in the nearby gift shop sells patterned greeting cards and one-of-a-kind gifts inspired by the cozy vintage quilts. The gallery has no set hours; call to arrange a visit.

Lithia Artisans Market (20 Calle Guanajuato Way, 666/303-2826 or 541/301-9811, https:// lithiaartisansmarket.com, 10am-6pm Sat., 11am-5pm Sun., mid-Mar.-Oct.) is held in a welcoming alleyway behind the downtown plaza along Ashland Creek. Local artists sell handcrafted leather goods, jewelry, body care products, and woven textiles while shoppers linger over the live music.

Shakespeare fans will find everything they need at the **Tudor Guild Gift Shop** (15 S. Pioneer St., 541/482-0940, www. tudorguild.org, 11am-8pm Sun., 11am-4pm Mon., 10am-8pm Tues.-Sat. Mar.-Oct.). Theater lovers will find an array of books, T-shirts, and souvenirs inspired by the Bard.

Ashland's **Artisan Emporium** (1670 Ashland St., 541/708-0577, http:// ashlandartisanemporium.com, 11am-6pm Mon.-Fri., 11am-5pm Sat.-Sun.) is a 17,000-square-foot space filled with creative and collectible items, from hand-poured candles to hemp clothing.

Treasures at **Rare Earth** (340 A St., 541/482-9501, www.rareearthashland. com, 11am-5:30pm Mon.-Sat., noon-4:30pm Sun.) include tapestries, blown glass, and precious stones (turquoise and opal), along with glimmering rocks and crystals. Located in the Railroad District, Rare Earth is one of many shops that showcase local craftsmanship and specially imported items.

Bloomsbury Books (290 E. Main St., 541/488-0029, http://bloomsburyashland. com, 8:30am-9pm Mon.-Fri., 10am-6pm Sun.) is named after the great writers and artists of the early 20th century who were part of London's Bloomsbury Group. The spacious two-story space is filled with literature across all genres of contemporary fiction. Local authors and a large selection of works by Shakespeare pay homage to the town.

Recreation
★ Skiing

The **Mt. Ashland Ski Area** (11 Mt. Ashland Ski Rd., 541/482-2897, www.mtashland. com, 9am-4pm daily Dec.-Apr., $45-52 adult, $35-42 youth ages 7-12, ages 6 and under and 70-plus free) is a small, local resort with 23 trail runs. The resort sits at a relatively low elevation—the peak of Mount Ashland is at 7,533 feet (2,296 m) elevation—so it can take a lot of snow for the resort to open.

The five chairlifts feature Shakespearean names; two are three-seaters and two hold couples. A rope tow is in the beginner area. Most of the trails are intermediate and advanced (the black diamonds could be considered blues). Mt. Ashland also offers **twilight skiing** (3pm-9pm Thurs.-Fri. Jan.-mid-Mar., $25 adults, $19 youth) when conditions permit. The ski area rents ski and snowboard gear ($18-29 all-day ski/snowboard package, $20 ski/snowboard only, $5 helmet or ski poles).

Mt. Ashland is 20 miles (32 km) south of downtown. To get there from Lithia Park, take Siskiyou Boulevard (OR-99) south for 5 miles (8 km), merging onto I-5 South. In 6 miles (9.5 km), take exit 6 toward Mt. Ashland. Head west on Old Highway 99 for a mile.

Rafting

Noah's River Adventures (53 N. Main St., 541/488-2811, http://noahsrafting. com, 8am-8pm daily, $85-155) offers a thrilling experience on the Rogue River in a variety of rafting trips. The standard half-day trip guides a minimum of four people on an exciting (yet safe) 5.5-mile stretch of the tributary, starting with Class I rapids and progressing to Class IV white water. The full-day adventure includes lunch and tacks on an extra 6 miles to the half-day section of the river. Noah's is great for beginners and experts looking for a memorable time on one of Oregon's largest rivers. Note that children must be age 6 or older.

The members of family-run **Indigo Creek Outfitters** (130 A St. #2B, 541/282-4535, https://indigocreekoutfitters.com, 8:30am-5:30pm daily May-Oct., $89-179 adult, $79-169 youth) love to be out on the river as much as possible. Indigo Creek operates half-day, full-day, and multi-day rafting trips on portions of the Scott, Klamath, and Rogue Rivers. Paddle the mixed-level rapids of the Rogue ($99 adults/$89 youth) or float the calmer waters on the Table Rock ($89 adults/$79 youth). Indigo Creek also guides multi-day trips down the Rogue ($995 adults, $945 youth, May-Sept.).

Hiking

The trail to **Grizzly Peak** (Shale City Rd., 4.7 mi/7.6 km round-trip, 3 hours, moderate) follows a well-maintained dirt path carved through avocado-green fields. As you climb uphill, the coniferous forest hits a patch of burned-out trees before subtly reaching the summit. While the peak is not all that spectacular (due to the dense forest), it's still a pretty hike.

To reach the trailhead, take Ashland Street east to I-5. Stay on I-5 for 2 miles (3.2 km). Turn left on Dead Indian Memorial Road and continue 7 miles

From top to bottom: Upper Duck Pond; Lithia Park's Butler-Perozzi Fountain; the Brickroom.

(11.5 km). Turn left onto Shale City Road and drive 3 miles (4.8 km). Turn left at a fork onto 38-3E-9.2 road and follow signage to the Grizzly Peak trailhead.

If anyone in Ashland tells you to "follow the white rabbit," they are referring to the **White Rabbit Trail** (4.5 mi/7.2 km round-trip, 3 hours, moderate). This skinny dirt path leads into the woods (ignore the other *Alice in Wonderland* side trails). Enjoy trekking through the hillside and the peek-a-boo views of the valley and foothills toward the top. Follow switchbacks to descend, resting at one of the picnic benches on the way.

To get there, take Siskiyou Boulevard (OR-99 South) for 2 miles (3.2 km) and turn right on Park Street. Drive 0.5 mile to the trailhead at Siskiyou Mountain Park.

Food
Cafés
★ **Morning Glory** (1149 Siskiyou Blvd., 541/488-8636, 8am-1pm daily, $10-16) lives up to its name with fun, delicious dishes that offer a sure way to start your day. The exterior resembles a neighborhood home, but the interior bustles with activity. Grab a table or a spot at the bar and enjoy an espresso with a seasonal dish like Nutella-filled French toast with walnut and cherry topping.

★ **The Breadboard** (744 N. Main St., 541/488-0295, www.breadboardashland. com, 7am-2pm daily, $8-13) is a popular spot where hungover college students try to regain their senses via generous portions of fried eggs, country potatoes, and stacks of pancakes. This diner is famous for its Mountain Man breakfast, a massive combination of homemade country gravy, sausage and eggs with cheese, a buttermilk biscuit, and home-fried potatoes.

American
Enjoy hearty, picnic-ready portions of burgers, pizzas, and deli sandwiches at the **Luna Café and Mercantile** (2525 Ashland St., 541/482-3372, www. lunacafeashland.com, 8am-9pm Sun.-Thurs., 8am-10pm Fri.-Sat., $11-24), a popular stopping spot. The menu features an equal mix of farm-to-table meat and vegetarian items, including a burger with a quinoa-black bean patty and meatloaf dressed in a barbecue glaze. Indulge in a piece of one of Kali's pies for dessert on the pet-friendly patio overlooking well-manicured grassy areas and the Ashland foothills.

Located on the downtown plaza, **Louie's of Ashland** (41 N. Main St., 541/482-9701, www.louiesofashland. com, 11am-9pm daily, $10-15) serves delectable drinks, desserts, and flavorful organic and gluten-free dishes that will whet anyone's appetite. Indulge in the Oregon blackberry ribs or a Recession burger ($7).

The burgers at **Sammich** (424 Bridge St., 541/708-6055, https:// sammichrestaurants.com, 11am-6pm Mon.-Sat., 11am-4pm Sun., $10-14) are so tall that it's impossible to get the fixings all into your mouth in one bite, but that's half the fun. Whether you get the Melanzane eggplant sandwich or Da Burg dripping in cheese and Sammich sauce, you'll definitely want to eat this over a plate.

You won't find the dishes at **Hearsay** (40 S. 1st St., 541/625-0505, www. hearsayashland.com, 4:30pm-9pm daily, $18-32) anywhere else. Michelin-quality entrées like the Columbia River steelhead encrusted with hazelnuts and the RR Ranch rib eye with Rogue Valley veggies look and taste upscale, but at affordable prices.

★ **Brickroom** (35 N. Main St., 541/708-6030, www.brickroomashland.com, 8am-1am daily, $10-22) is hidden up two flights of stairs above the Juniper Row gift shop. Inside the chic, hip interior, diners feast on minced seasoned lamb and pine nuts in an eggroll or sip the signature Brick Red Blend wine. A small outdoor space faces Ashland's city plaza, or head to the back patio overlooking Ashland Creek.

Any college town will have a few craft breweries and Ashland is no different. ★ **Standing Stone Brewing Company** (101 Oak St., 541/482-2448, www.standingstonebrewing.com, 11am-midnight daily) is a family-owned pub with an appeal to Southern Oregon University students. Inside, tall ceilings and concrete walls surround the brewery tanks. Pair the I Heart Oregon ale, made with locally grown barley, and a lamb burger seasoned with herbs grown from the brewery's very own One Mile Farm. Dine inside at the polished wood tables or out on the lovely outdoor patio.

Mexican
El Paraiso (545 Clover Ln., 541/488-5877, www.mexicanfoodashland.com, 11am-9:30pm Sun.-Thurs., 11am-10pm Fri.-Sat., $10-17) serves traditional Mexican fare with flare. Menu items like albondigas soup, a myriad of burrito options, and chile verde made with a signature tomatillo sauce will fill you up quickly. Try to leave room for a raspberry chimichanga for dessert.

La Casa Del Pueblo (1209 Siskiyou Blvd., 541/482-5092, 10:30am-9:30pm Mon.-Thurs., 10:30am-10:30pm Fri., 11am-10:30pm Sat., 11am-9:30pm Sun., $11-19) is a fun and festive restaurant painted in bright colors that recall Jalisco, Mexico. Choose from 10 different burrito options or opt for a chile relleno and enchilada combination plate that comes with rice and beans.

Spanish
★ **Ostras Tapas & Bottle Shop** (47 N. Main St., 541/708-0528, https://ostrasashland.com, 5pm-9pm Sun.-Thurs., 5pm-10pm Fri.-Sat., $12-22) offers a unique take on the spice and sass of its Spanish specialties. Try tapas with crab, calamari, octopus, or braised pork cheeks. Inside, wine bottles line the walls of the restaurant, antler chandeliers

hang from the wood beam rafters, and a horseshoe-shaped bar faces the flat-screen TV. The staff's festive and friendly attitude matches the hip Spanish vibe.

Vegetarian
Sauce Whole Food Café (1640 Ashland St., 541/482-5863, www.saucewholefoodcafe. com, 11am-9pm daily, $5-16) serves hearty and wholesome meals, many of which are dairy- or gluten-free, in a cozy atmosphere. Try the housemade naan bread or a grain bowl filled with veggies and topped with a special sauce like the Sherpa or the Miso Love You. Many of the desserts are also gluten- or sugar-free.

Accommodations
Ashland's hotels and B&Bs are quaint and rich in history; many are run by friendly, accommodating folks who put their hearts and souls into restoring late 19th and early 20th century homes. Some lodgings have modern features like Tesla charging stations or naturally fed hot spring tubs right in your room.

$100-250
The Lithia Springs Hotel was originally constructed in 1925, built specifically for gold miners traveling to and from Northern California. Today, it's the ★ **Ashland Springs Hotel** (212 E. Main St., 541/488-1700, www.ashlandspringshotel. com, $100 winter, $305 summer), where luxurious guest rooms cater to the Shakespeare Festival crowd. Elegant architecture pairs splendidly with a sunshine-filled lobby and cozy fireplace, while rooms reflect a vintage charm with modern features like flat-screen TVs, Frette linens, and thick monogrammed bathrobes. Most stays include dessert and a bottle of champagne, but other romantic package upgrades are available.

The **Stratford Inn** (555 Siskiyou Blvd., 541/488-2151, https://stratfordinnashland.com, $110-175) was started by a group of friends who relocated to Ashland in order to be closer to the Shakespeare Festival. (One of the original owners still runs it with his children.) The sprawling, modern building has 53 basic rooms, each with a king bed, shower, table, and plush sitting chairs. Luxurious suites include kitchenettes; a few have whirlpool tubs. The inn offers guests shared-use amenities that include an indoor saline pool and spa and an on-site coffee shop. It's close to downtown Ashland.

The **Plaza Inn & Suites at Ashland Creek** (98 Central Ave., 541-488-8900, www.plazainnashland.com, $119-269) is just a stone's throw from the downtown plaza and Ashland Creek. Rooms feature bright-blue carpets and chic window treatments with inviting views of the trees, landscape, and rolling hills outside. A few of the 92 rooms are pet-friendly. There's also a Tesla charging station.

Ashland Hills Hotel & Suites (2525 Ashland St., 541/482-8310, https://ashlandhillshotel.com, $102-179) offers clean and modern accommodations tucked into the foothills. Large rooms hold California king beds (some accented with bright orange headboards) and plush leather sitting chairs. The Champagne Suite ($229-249) has a purple velvet platform bed, a fireplace, and a bathroom with a hot-pink Jacuzzi. The hotel has an outdoor pool, tennis courts, and the attached Luna Café & Mercantile.

★ **Peerless Hotel** (243 4th St., 541/488-1082, https://peerlesshotel.com, $135 winter, $319 summer) is a hip lodging establishment that was built in Ashland's Railroad District in the early 1900s. It still maintains its chic charm, with a brick facade, bright-green doorways, and a vintage Coca-Cola ad painted on the side. The six guest rooms are unique—one features a floor-to-ceiling hand-painted mural of a cobblestone path, while another has a bathroom with twin clawfoot tubs. Stays March-October include a complimentary two-course breakfast.

Spacious gardens, contemporary furnishings, cozy fireplaces, and mineral spring-fed tubs are highlights of ★ **Lithia Springs Resort** (2165 W. Jackson Rd., 800/482-7128, https://lithiaspringsresort.com, $139-229). The 38 suites, studios, and bungalows feature mixed-texture woods, metal, and glass furnishings in soft, soothing colors and accents. Enjoy a complimentary afternoon tea, access to a fitness cottage, or a soak in your personal hot spring-fed bathtub. This is an ideal health and wellness retreat.

Over $250

Located downtown and within walking distance of Lithia Park, the quaint **Winchester Inn** (35 S. 2nd St., 541/488-1113, www.winchesterinn.com, $315 winter, $555 summer) resembles a miniature Winchester mansion. There are nine guest rooms in the main house and eight rooms and suites in the Heritage House. A few cottage suites offer a bit more privacy. Amenities include cozy beds, a garden, and a delicious breakfast (included in stay).

The owners of the Winchester Inn also manage the ★ **RedTail Inn** (550 E. Main St., 541/778-8788, www.redtailinn.com, $315 winter, $555 summer), a historic building with a lot of charm. This eco-boutique offers modern luxuries coupled with a bit of Ashland nostalgia—Ashland City Band coronet player Jesse "Red" McCall once ran the 1890s farmhouse. Rooms feature California king beds covered in soft comforters and private porches or a deck to sit outside. Amenities include an organic garden, Tesla and electric car charging stations, and parking for each of the three suites.

Information and Services

The **Ashland Chamber of Commerce** (110 E. Main St., 541/482-3486, www.ashlandchamber.com, 9am-5pm Mon.-Fri.) has information on upcoming events, outdoor activities, and the Oregon Shakespeare Festival. **Asante Ashland Community Hospital** (280 Maple St., 541/201-4000, www.asante.org) provides urgent and primary care and has a 24-hour emergency room.

Getting Around

Skinner Aviation operates charter and scenic flights out of **Ashland Municipal Airport** (Parker Sumner Field, 403 Dead Indian Memorial Rd., 541/482-7675, www.ashlandairport.com); call for a free quote. **Cascade Shuttle** (3295 Hwy. 66, 541/488-1998 or 888/760-7433, www.cascadeshuttle.com) offers airport shuttle and taxi service from the Rogue Valley to the Ashland Municipal Airport and everywhere in between. The **Rogue Valley Transportation District** (RVTD, 200 S. Front St., Medford, 541/779-2877, www.rvtd.org, 6am-6pm Mon.-Fri., $2 single ride, $6 day pass, $32 20-ride pass) carries passengers to Medford, Ashland, and Jacksonville, passing through its home base at the Front Street Station in Medford.

Crater Lake National Park

Crater Lake was formed thousands of years ago when volcanic Mount Mazama erupted and gigantic columns of ash and pumice escaped the rising magma. The fiery pressure chamber that formed beneath the mountain imploded, forming this impressive caldera. Over time, the caldera filled with rainwater and snow runoff, creating one of the deepest and purest lakes in the United States.

Today, visitors converge on this impressive area to cruise the Rim Drive, stopping at various overlooks to learn more about the national park's features, wildlife, and flora. In summer, an array of hiking trails and trolley and boat tours offer opportunities to explore the park.

The best time to visit is when the winding, one-lane Rim Drive is open (usually June-Oct.), after the snow melts. The park is busiest June-August, when school is out; this is also when the trolley and boat tours are running. Late August-early September is when the Rim Drive is usually open but is less crowded.

Crater Lake typically receives an average of 43 feet of snow in winter. Check the park website for road conditions December-March.

Getting There

From Ashland, take I-5 north for 13 miles (21 km) to Medford. Veer right onto OR-62 East and drive north for about 50 miles (80 km). OR-62 runs along the Rogue River, passing campgrounds, general stores, and fishing spots near the towns of Shady Cove and Prospect. Shady Cove is about half an hour north of Medford, and Prospect is another half hour due east toward Crater Lake. From Prospect, continue 12 miles (19.5 km) north and stay right on OR-62 at the split in Union Creek. From the split in the road, stay on OR-62 for another 17 miles (27 km) to reach the **Annie Springs South Entrance Station** (open year-round) into Crater Lake National Park.

To reach the **North Entrance** (closed in winter), continue straight on OR-230 at the fork and head north for 30 miles (48 km).

Visiting the Park

Late **summer** (Sept. or Oct.) or early June (before the East Rim Drive opens) is a great time to visit if you want to experience Crater Lake when there are fewer crowds. If you come in **high season** (June-Aug.), expect long lines at the entrance stations; the longest wait is usually at the Annie Springs Entrance. Check the Crater Lake **webcam** (www.nps.org/crla) for traffic updates at the entrances and weather conditions. The best time to arrive is in the early morning, right when the park opens, or late afternoon during the week.

Entrances

There are two main entrances to Crater Lake National Park: the Annie Springs

Crater Lake National Park

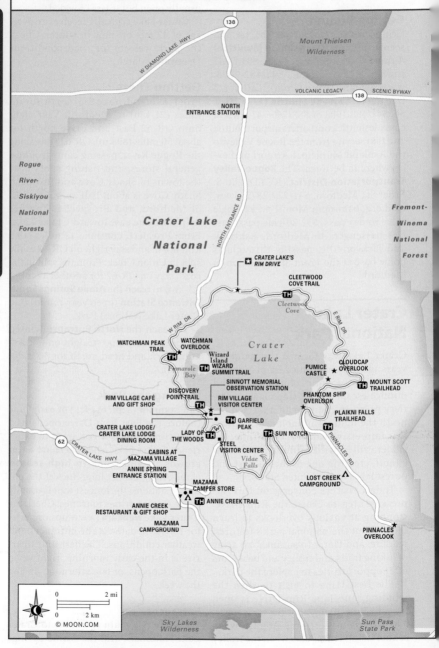

138

W DIAMOND LAKE HWY

VOLCANIC LEGACY   SCENIC BYWAY   138

NORTH
ENTRANCE STATION

Mount Thielsen
Wilderness

Rogue
River-
Siskiyou
National
Forests

Fremont-
Winema
National
Forest

Crater Lake
National
Park

NORTH ENTRANCE RD

CRATER LAKE'S
RIM DRIVE

CLEETWOOD
COVE TRAIL

Cleetwood
Cove

W RIM DR

E RIM DR

Crater
Lake

WATCHMAN PEAK
TRAIL

WATCHMAN
OVERLOOK

Wizard
Island

WIZARD
SUMMIT TRAIL

Pumarole
Bay

PUMICE
CASTLE

CLOUDCAP
OVERLOOK

MOUNT SCOTT
TRAILHEAD

SINNOTT MEMORIAL
OBSERVATION STATION

DISCOVERY
POINT TRAIL

PHANTOM SHIP
OVERLOOK

RIM VILLAGE CAFÉ
AND GIFT SHOP

RIM VILLAGE
VISITOR CENTER

PLAIKNI FALLS
TRAILHEAD

GARFIELD
PEAK

CRATER LAKE LODGE/
CRATER LAKE LODGE
DINING ROOM

LADY OF
THE WOODS

SUN NOTCH

STEEL
VISITOR CENTER

PINNACLES RD

CABINS AT
MAZAMA VILLAGE

Vidae
Falls

ANNIE SPRING
ENTRANCE STATION

MAZAMA
CAMPER STORE

LOST CREEK
CAMPGROUND

62

CRATER LAKE HWY

ANNIE CREEK
RESTAURANT & GIFT SHOP

ANNIE CREEK TRAIL

MAZAMA
CAMPGROUND

PINNACLES
OVERLOOK

0   2 mi

0   2 km

© MOON.COM

Sky Lakes
Wilderness

Sun Pass
State Park

South Entrance Station, accessible from Medford or Klamath Falls, and the North Entrance Station. The **Annie Springs South Entrance Station** (Hwy. 62, year-round) is most efficient for travelers from Ashland and Northern California. Plus it's a beautiful easy drive with views of clusters of pine trees mixed in with flat grassy meadowlands.

The **North Entrance Station** (Hwy. 230, summer only) is ideal for travelers from Northern Oregon. It's also likely to be less crowded than the Annie Springs Entrance. The North Entrance Station is 7 miles (11.5 km) south of Diamond Lake and includes a drive through the Pumice Desert.

Park Passes and Fees

The **entrance fee** is $25 per vehicle ($20 motorcycle, $12 pedestrian/bicycle) mid-May through October. November to May, the entrance fee goes down to $15 per vehicle. The annual National Parks pass ($80) is also accepted.

Visitors Centers

The **Steel Visitor Center** (Rim Village, 9am-5pm daily mid-Apr.-Oct., 10am-4pm daily Nov.-mid-Apr. daily) also serves as the park headquarters. Housed inside a gorgeous stone building, the visitors center is a great place to get detailed information and maps, buy souvenirs, check out the bookstore, watch a 22-minute video about Crater Lake's fiery history, get a backcountry permit, or use the restroom before driving around the lake. Park rangers are available to answer questions and host guided snowshoe treks in the winter.

Perched on the edge of Crater Lake, the **Rim Visitor Center** (541/594-3000, 9:30am-5pm daily late May-Sept.) is a popular spot to get lunch, buy souvenirs, use the ATM, and pick up park maps and information. Many of the summertime ranger-led activities are based from the Rim Visitor Center, including ranger talks, guided sunset hikes to Watchman

Peak, and junior ranger programs. Enjoy one of the first impressive views of Crater Lake from the **Sinnott Memorial Overlook** (9:30am-6:30pm daily July-Aug., 9:30am-5pm daily June and Sept., 10am-4pm daily Oct.), behind the visitors center. To get to the overlook, take a steep walkway down lots of stairs; the stairs are why it is not open in the winter or recommended for people who have limited mobility.

Reservations

For boat tours or overnight accommodations within the park, contact **Aramark** (866/292-6720, www.travelcraterlake.com).

Crater Lake Hospitality manages most activities and amenities. Room reservations at **Crater Lake Lodge** (866/292-6720, www.travelcraterlake.com, mid-May-mid-Oct., $202-269) can be made up to one year in advance and are usually booked several months out. July-September, campers can make reservations online for **Mazama Campground** (866/761-6668, www.travelcraterlake.com, June-late Sept., $21 tents, $31-43 RVs, $5 walk-in); in June, sites are first-come, first-served, depending on weather. The **Cabins at Mazama Village** (866/292-6720, www.travelcraterlake.com, late May-Sept., $160) fill fast; reservations can be made as early as February.

The Crater Lake National Park Service manages the **Lost Creek Campground** (Pinnacles Rd. off East Rim Dr., 541/594-3000, www.nps.gov, July-mid-Oct., $5 first-come, first-served). Since its campsites can be reserved on a first-come, first-served basis, drive through and claim your campsite early in the day to ensure that you have one and then continue your drive around the lake (going counterclockwise). Since there are only 16 sites, they fill up fast. They are weather-dependent since they're on the East Rim Drive.

Crater Lake Hospitality manages the **Crater Lake boat cruises** (866/292-6720, www.travelcraterlake.com, 2-hour lake cruises 9:30am-3:45pm daily summer, $44 adults, $30 children ages 3-12). **Wizard Island cruises** (9:45am and 12:45pm daily summer, $55 adults, $37 ages 3-12) depart at 8:30am and 11:30am daily in the summer ($27 adults, $18 ages 3-12) and tend to fill fast. Half of the reservations are available online in advance; the remaining seats are sold up to 24 hours in advance from kiosks at Crater Lake Lodge or the Annie Creek Gift Shop.

Advance reservations are accepted online for the **Crater Lake Trolley** (445 S. Spring St., 541/882-1896, Klamath Falls, www.craterlaketrolley.net, 10am-3pm daily July-Sept. depending on snowfall, $27 adults, $24 seniors, $17 ages 6-13, ages 5 and under free) or by calling the Klamath Falls headquarters. All trolley tours pick up and depart from the Rim Village.

Information and Services

The *Reflections* visitors guide and park map are handed out at the entrance stations and hold a wealth of information, including services and activities available at the time of your visit. Just past the Annie Springs Entrance Station, the Mazama Village hosts the most amenities, including a gas station (credit card only), showers, and the **Mazama Camper Store** (541/594-2295, www.travelcraterlake.com, 10am-5pm daily late May, 7am-9pm daily mid-June-early Sept., 10am-5pm daily early-mid-Sept.), which sells local snacks, wine, and firewood and has an ATM and a coin-operated laundry. Pacific Crest Trail hikers can pick up their mail here. It's within walking distance of the Mazama campsites and cabins.

Getting Around

The 33-mile (53-km) **Rim Drive** (open May or June; closes at first snowfall) is the primary means of getting around the park. This one-lane road can be congested in July and August and travel can be slow. Without traffic, it takes 2.5-3 hours to circumnavigate around the lake, including stops at overlooks. In the high season of summer, forgo driving the rim yourself and take the trolley instead. You can enjoy the sights and the overlooks without worrying about parking.

The **parking lot** at Rim Village is fairly large, but it tends to fill by late morning or midafternoon. You'll have the best chance of finding parking at Rim Village early in the morning (7am-9am). You can then catch the trolley, which departs at 10am. Your other options are to find a parking spot at the Steel Visitor Center or in Mazama Village.

The **Crater Lake Trolley** (541/882-1896, 445 S. Spring St., Klamath Falls, www.craterlaketrolley.net, 10am-3pm daily July-Sept. weather permitting, $27 adults, $24 seniors, $17 ages 7-13, ages 6 and under free) is based at Rim Village, close to the Annie Springs Entrance Station. Trolleys leave hourly for a two-hour tour around the lake. Make reservations online starting in late May or contact their office in Klamath Falls. The enclosed trolley with shared bench seating stops at overlooks. It is also wheelchair-accessible with weight and size restrictions.

The closest **Amtrak** station (445 S. Spring St., Klamath Falls, http://craterlaketrolley.net, 541/882-1896, www.amtrak.com, $36-176) is in Klamath Falls where the Crater Lake Trolley is also based. Coast Starlight trains stop in Klamath Falls; visitors can then catch the Crater Lake shuttle bus into the park. Buses into Crater Lake depart daily at 9am (July-mid-Oct., $40 adults, $30 kids ages 2-12 and seniors) for the 1.5-hour ride to Rim Village; the return trip departs at 3pm.

TOP EXPERIENCE

★ The Rim Drive

The drive around Crater Lake is spectacular—the crater's deep blue water evokes a sense of calm and a connection to nature. The 33-mile (53-km) **Rim Drive** offers visitors spectacular views of the lake from a variety of unique vantage points. At 7,865 feet (2,397 m) in elevation, this is the highest paved road in Oregon. Outlooks along the road utilize interpretive signs that explain the geology, flora, fauna, and history of the area.

Plan **2-3 hours** for this drive and try to come in **late summer,** when the entire road is open. From late August to early September, you'll beat the crowds and have a chance to access the whole Rim Drive before it closes at first snowfall.

At some points along the Rim Drive (especially on the east side), it can feel like you're driving right to the edge of the caldera (not for the faint of heart if you have a fear of heights).

East Rim

East Rim Drive (summer only) starts at the park headquarters and travels counterclockwise to the North Entrance. Must-see stops include: Vidae Falls, the Phantom Ship Overlook, Cloudcap Overlook, and the Pinnacles Overlook. On the northeastern side is the Cleetwood Cove trailhead, the only access point to the water.

Vidae Falls

Vidae Falls (3.5 mi/5.6 km southeast of park headquarters) is a spectacular sight, with creek-fed water cascading over a series of prominent cliff ledges. The falls are viewable from the road, and there's a small picnic area nearby (this is also the trailhead to Crater Peak). It's particularly beautiful in summer, when bright wildflowers spring up at the base of the falls. The picnic area across the street from the falls is a favorite stop for visitors who want to see one of Crater Lake's water features.

Phantom Ship Overlook

The **Phantom Ship Overlook** (5.4 mi/8.7 km north of Vidae Falls) is your first view of Crater Lake. This 400,000-year old preserved chunk of lava remained engulfed in the millennium-old Mazama volcano. Look closely toward the left of the lake; the Phantom Ship resembles a little sailboat with its tall mast poking out above the water's surface. Acting as an anchor, most of Phantom Ship's solid mass hides beneath the lake's surface— we see only the tip (it looks like a glacier). Depending on the weather and clarity of the lake, it can be easy to miss.

At the Phantom Ship Overlook, look right for a good glimpse at upcoming **Pumice Castle.**

Pinnacles Overlook

South of the Phantom Ship Overlook, turn off East Rim Drive and onto **Pinnacles Road,** which leads to the Lost Creek campground and the eastern edge of the park. At the end of this road lie huge, 100-foot-tall spires called the **Pinnacles,** the product of volcanic gases solidifying volcanic ash into the rock. Follow the easy, 0.8-mile trail along the edge of Pinnacle Valley to spy the spires jetting out on the other side. The leftover pale yellow and gray spikes contrast against the vibrant green pines, making a worthy detour from the lake.

Pumice Castle

Pumice Castle (2.5 mi/4 km northeast of Phantom Ship Overlook) consists of a series of bright orange vertical pumice stones that are named due to their similarity to a castle wall's battlements. They were formed as hot pumice exploded out of Mount Mazama's volcanic vent and became buried as Mazama continued erupting. When the mountain eventually collapsed, these pumice layers were exposed.

Cloudcap Overlook

Cloudcap Overlook (4.6 mi/7.4 km north of Phantom Ship Overlook) offers your first view across the lake to Wizard Island. To get there from Pumice Castle, drive a mile north on East Rim Drive and turn left at a fork in the road to drive through a small canyon. This overlook is off the beaten path, so it's less busy than other overlooks on the Rim Drive.

West Rim

You'll encounter more onlookers on the **West Rim Drive** (open year-round, weather permitting), which accesses the lake's rim from the North Entrance road south to park headquarters. Must-see stops include the Watchman Overlook and the Rim Village, home to a café, gift shop, the Sinnott Memorial Overlook, a visitors center, and the Crater Lake Lodge. The road between the Rim Village and the park headquarters is open year-round (weather permitting).

The following route continues from the North Junction and East Rim Drive.

Watchman Overlook

Watchman Overlook (3 mi/4.8 km southwest of North Junction) is directly across the lake from Cloudcap Overlook (14 mi/22.5 km northeast) and offers the closest view of Wizard Island and Skell Channel, a body of water between Wizard Island and West Rim Drive. From the overlook, gaze down at Fumarole Bay, where boat cruises dock for Wizard Island below. Llao Rock juts out to the left. This is a popular stop on the Rim Drive, with a paved viewpoint, parking, restrooms, picnic tables, and the trailhead for Watchman Peak.

Sinnott Memorial Overlook

Located in the Rim Village, the **Sinnott Memorial Overlook** (behind the Rim Village Gift Shop & Café, 9:30am-5pm daily June and Sept., 9:30am-6:30pm daily late June-Aug., 10am-4pm daily Oct.) is a stone, open-air observation room with 180-degree views of Crater Lake, spanning from Cleetwood Cove and Garfield Peak to Wizard Island. It was built on top of Victor Rock, 900 feet (275 m) above the lake, in the early 1930s,

and its unique stone masonry and round cantilevered wooden roof have withstood decades of strong weather. A short, steep trail leads to the overlook.

Recreation

The park closes to vehicles for two weekends in September, which is when the popular **Ride the Rim** (http://ridetherimoregon.com) is held. Cyclists attempt a strenuous 25-mile (40-km) bike ride around Crater Lake. While it's free to register, a $10 donation is requested.

Boat Tours

A boat tour of Crater Lake is an experience in itself. Don't miss the chance to be on the water, looking up at the rim (rather than down) and enjoying the fresh air and mild temperatures—especially after working up a sweat on the Cleetwood Cove Trail.

Explore the lake from within its crater via a **Crater Lake boat cruise** (866/292-6720, www.travelcraterlake.com, 2 hours, 9:30am-3:45pm daily summer, $44 adults, $30 children ages 3-12), which tours the entire lake and is narrated by park rangers. This tour is great for those who want an in-depth interpretation of Crater Lake's geology.

Wizard Island Tours (5 hours, 9:45am and 12:45pm daily summer, $55 adults, $37 ages 3-12) allows more time to explore Wizard Island, with two hours on the boat and three hours on shore at the island. The **Wizard Island Shuttle** (8:30am and 11:30am daily summer, $28 adults, $18 ages 3-12, children under 2 not allowed) takes travelers from Cleetwood Cove to Wizard Island with no dilly-dallying on the lake.

All boats depart from **Cleetwood Cove,** which is only accessible via the steep **Cleetwood Cove Trail** (1.1. mi/1.8 km one-way, strenuous); on the way back, it's a 700-foot elevation change. (This hike is not recommended for those with physical limitations.)

Tickets for boat tours go on sale 24

hours in advance of the next day and are available for purchase from kiosks in the lobby of the Crater Lake Lodge or the Annie Creek Restaurant and Gift Shop. Boat tours stop running when the crowds die down, which is usually in mid-September.

Hiking
Lady of the Woods
Named after a sculpted woman carved into a rock, the **Lady of the Woods Trail** (0.7 mile round-trip, 30 minutes, easy) appeals to history buffs and those interested in Crater Lake's historical rustic architecture. The interpretive trail starts behind the south side of the Steel Visitor Center and loops around the park headquarters at Mazama Village, winding through the various maintenance buildings constructed over the years.

The actual *Lady of the Woods* sculpture is carved into a rock behind the visitors center. It blends in well; look for a sign that points it out. The lady is thought to have been created by a medical doctor who worked with the road crew building the Rim Drive. When the road construction project was complete, the doctor entered the woods and carved this image of a woman curled over one of the boulders.

The Steel Visitor Center is 4 miles (6.4 km) north of Mazama Village.

Sun Notch
The trailhead for this hike is accessible just past **Vidae Falls** (0.8 mile round-trip, 30 minutes, easy), located in a U-shaped valley that was formed by glaciers as they made their way down Mount Mazama. After a short uphill climb through the meadow and trees, look for stunning views of Phantom Ship from the caldera's rim. The small gravel road is accessible to strong wheelchair users (with assistance) who can manage that first 150-foot climb.

From top to bottom: Steel Visitor Center; Phantom Ship Overlook; Pumice Castle.

The Pinnacles

The Pinnacles hike (0.8 mile round-trip, 30 minutes, easy) is at the end of Pinnacles Road, at the turnoff from the Phantom Ship Overlook. Six miles (9.5 km) down the road is a flat trail that leads along the edge of Pinnacle Valley, where you can see pale gray spires formed out of hot ash, stunningly nestled among the vibrant green of the forest and blue skies.

Plaikni Falls

Although Vidae Falls gets all of the attention (probably due to its accessibility off of the East Rim Drive), **Plaikni Falls** (2 mi/3.2 km round-trip, 1 hour, easy) is deserving of a quick look. This trailhead is 1.2 miles (1.9 km) down Pinnacles Road, past the turnoff to Phantom Ship Overlook. The trail meanders through old-growth forest, delighting summer travelers with striking wildflowers near the cascading waters of Plaikni Falls, which are fed by snowmelt and rainfall. *Plaikni* means "from the high country."

Discovery Point

This path is where prospector John Wesley Hillman found Crater Lake (fortunately his mule stopped at the rim). Today, you can follow in his footsteps along the **Discovery Point Trail** (2 mi/3.2 km round-trip, 1 hour, easy-moderate). From the trailhead at the west side of Rim Village, hike clockwise around the rim of the crater through white pine and evergreen mountain hemlock trees. The trail starts as a paved road but turns to dirt, intersecting the Discovery Point Overlook about 1.5 miles (2.4 km) north of Rim Village.

Fumarole Bay

Fumarole Bay (1.7 mi/2.7 km round-trip, 1 hour, moderate) is a popular place to take a dip on a hot day. To get there, take a boat tour to Wizard Island. After arriving at the island, look for the Fumarole Bay trailhead, clearly marked by the docking area. Be sure to look up along the trail to see the healthy green lichen thriving happily on the trees. Climb the rocky path along the western edge of Wizard Island to a shallow cove where the trail ends. Then jump into the clear blue water to cool off—prepare yourself for a shock as the water can be cold!

Watchman Peak

From the Watchman Overlook parking area, the 420-foot climb to **Watchman Peak** (1.6 mi/2.6 km round-trip, 1 hour, moderate, closed in winter) offers panoramic views of the lake from the fire lookout. The trail itself is clearly marked and isn't all that exciting, but the views—particularly at sunset—are divine. If driving the Rim Drive, start counterclockwise around the lake to end your day here. In summer, park rangers guide free hikes to the top.

Annie Creek

The **Annie Creek Trail** (1.7 mi/2.7 km round-trip, 1.5 hours, moderate) starts behind the Mazama Campground amphitheater in Mazama Village. The trail climbs 200 feet (60 m), winding through a canyon and past a rushing stream. Expect bright wildflowers in spring.

Wizard Summit

The **Wizard Summit Trail** (2.2 mi/3.5 km round-trip, 1.5 hours, moderate, summer only) climbs 760 feet (230 m) to the top of Wizard Island in the heart of the crater. Enjoy views of the lake and take in the lush scenery around you while getting a good workout. Note that the hike requires a boat shuttle to Wizard Island from Cleetwood Cove and thus is only available in summer.

Cleetwood Cove

Steep cliffs lead down to the water's edge (it really does look like a drastic implosion), which means there aren't many access points to the lake itself—only the **Cleetwood Cove Trail** (2.2 mi/3.5 km round-trip, 1.5 hours, difficult), where boat tours launch. The well-maintained path comprises switchbacks that descend 700 feet (215 m) to the boat dock. At the bottom, break up the hike with a boat tour or a swim before making the steep ascent back (the equivalent of walking up a 150-flight staircase).

The trailhead is part of East Rim Drive and is only open in summer. This also tends to be Crater Lake's most popular trail since it's the only access point to the lake. The trailhead is 11 miles (17.5 km) northeast of Rim Village.

Garfield Peak

Located on the south side of the park, the hike to **Garfield Peak** (3.6 mi/5.8 km round-trip, 2-3 hours, strenuous) yields incredible views along the way. From the top of the rim, the rocky 1,010-foot (308-m) climb doesn't seem so bad. The trail features a diverse range of plants and wildlife; you'll see several different species of evergreen trees and wildflowers, with the chance to spy a pika or marmot. The trail ends with a bird's-eye view of Crater Lake and the park.

Mount Scott

Mount Scott (4.4 mi/7.1 km round-trip, 3 hours, strenuous) is the highest point in the park, with an elevation of 8,929 feet (2,722 m) at the peak. From the trailhead, hikers climb a gradual ascent of 1,250 feet (380 m) to the top, where stunning views of the caldera and surrounding scenery await. Plan this hike first thing in the morning to watch the sun rise on the east side, then end your day with a sunset hike to Watchman Peak.

The Mount Scott trailhead is on East Rim Drive near the fork to Cloudcap Overlook. To get there, take the fork left and continue north along East Rim Drive to a picnic area.

Food
Inside the Park

★ **Rim Village Café & Gift Shop** (Rim Village, 866/761-6668, www.

travelcraterlake.com, 10am-4pm daily Jan.-early Mar., 10am-5pm daily Mar.-mid-May and Oct.-early Nov., 10am-6pm daily mid-May-early June and Oct.-early Nov., 9am-8pm daily June-early Sept., $8-11) serves grab-and-go coffee, tea, and sodas, as well as sandwiches and hot rice bowls (for those chilly days). This is a great place to eat before or after driving the Rim Drive. There's plenty of indoor and outdoor seating.

The **Crater Lake Lodge Dining Room** (Rim Village, 541/594-2295, ext. 3217, www.travelcraterlake.com, 7am-10am, 11am-3pm, 5pm-9pm daily mid-May-mid-Oct., reservations recommended, $26-40) is the most upscale dining establishment in the park. This is the place to go for a gourmet meal of steak, pork, or seafood entrées such as seared salmon and rockfish. Soups and salads are also available.

Open in summer only, **Annie Creek Restaurant and Gift Shop** (Mazama Village, 866/761-6668, www.travelcraterlake.com, 8am-10:30am, 11am-4pm, 5pm-8pm daily late May-early June; 7am-10:30am, 11am-4pm, 5pm-9pm daily mid-June-early Sept.; $10-20) serves American classics like meatloaf, pork chops, and burgers, as well as standard breakfast items.

Outside the Park

Jo's Motel and Campground (52851 Hwy. 62, Fort Klamath, 541/381-2234, www.josmotel.com, 9am-7pm daily late May-early Sept., 9am-7pm Sat.-Sun. mid-Sept.-mid-May, $3-8) is an organic deli and grocery store 20 miles (32 km) south of the Annie Springs Entrance. Jo and her staff serve light breakfast items and grilled cheese sandwiches. There's also an espresso bar for that shot or two of caffeine as you drive into the park.

Accommodations and Camping
Inside the Park

Based at Rim Village, **Crater Lake Lodge** (866/292-6720, www.travelcraterlake.

Hiking the PCT

Flowing through the Cascade and Sierra Nevada mountain range is the 2,650-mile (4,265-km) **Pacific Crest Trail.** The full PCT thru-hike starts near the U.S.-Mexico border and takes at least five months to complete at its northern terminus in Canada.

Within Crater Lake, 33 miles (53 km) of the PCT wind through old-growth forest with a few backcountry campsites sprinkled along the way. The park is home to one of the oldest sections of the PCT: the original **Skyline Trail,** which stretches north from Crater Lake National Park to Mount Hood.

From the Annie Springs Entrance, hikers can pick up a backcountry **permit** (or mail) at the Mazama Camper Store. The Crater Lake portion of the PCT begins 6 miles (9.5 km) southwest at the edge of the park, close to OR-62 and the Annie Springs Entrance Station. From here, hikers continue north toward Crater Lake, past the Union Peak trailhead and across the highway. About 0.5 mile north, they will reach the Dutton Creek junction; from here, they can either hike right toward the caldera's rim or continue north on the PCT. The Dutton Creek trail is 2.3 miles farther and a 1,000-foot ascent to Rim Village.

Day-trippers can start at Rim Village and hike north along the edge of the crater for 6 miles (9.5 km) to Grouse Hill and the North Entrance Road, where the trail rejoins the PCT. (This alternative route was developed for PCT hikers who want to see the lake. The established PCT route leads through wilderness along the west side of the park.)

There are also two **drive-to sections** of the PCT: one is on the southwest side of Crater Lake near the Annie Springs Entrance; the other is on the northwest side of the lake by the North Entrance Road.

♦ The southwestern PCT access point is 8 miles (13 km) from Rim Village. Follow Rim Drive south toward the Annie Springs Entrance Station and turn right on OR-62, heading west for 0.8 mile. The PCT is near the Union Peak trailhead.

♦ To explore the northern section of the PCT, drive 6.5 miles (10.5 km) north along West Rim Drive to the junction for the North Entrance Road. Drive north for another 2.6 miles (4.2 km); the PCT crosses the road close to Grouse Hill.

Backcountry campsites line the PCT and include Dutton Creek (close to the Steel Visitor Center and park headquarters), Bybee Creek, and Red Cone Spring. A nice diversion from the PCT is the Lightning Spring backcountry campsite, which is close to the Watchman Overlook and offers incredible views of Crater Lake. The Lightning Spring trailhead is between Trapper and Bybee Creeks on the PCT.

The best time to try the Crater Lake PCT section is in summer after the snow has melted and major access points like West Rim Drive and the North Entrance Road are open.

com, mid-May-mid-Oct., $202-269) is a cozy place to lay your head. The lodge has 71 rooms. Standard lodge rooms include king or queen beds; a few rooms are ADA-accessible. Deluxe Lake View rooms have king or queen beds and upgraded amenities such as oscillating fans and heat. Deluxe rooms face Crater Lake. In the Loft Rooms (which sleep up to four), guests ascend a staircase to reach the king or queen beds. Standard "valley view" rooms on floors 2-4 have the best views of the lake. Amenities include free parking and Wi-Fi; there are no TVs in the rooms and there is no cell coverage. The on-site **Crater Lake Lodge Dining Room** (11am-3pm and 5pm-9pm daily mid-May-mid-Oct.) serves gourmet items created with locally sourced, seasonal ingredients.

After a day of exploring, grab a drink and meet new friends at one of the foyer's two fireplaces. Reservations can be made one year in advance and rooms fill fast.

Much like the Crater Lake Lodge, The Cabins at Mazama Village (www. travelcraterlake.com, 866/292-6720, late May-Sept., $160, reserve online) offer one or two queen beds and a private bathroom with shower; rooms have a fan and a coffee maker, but no televisions, phones, or air-conditioning. The 40 cabins (four rooms in each building) are tucked into the forest yet are close to the Annie Creek Restaurant, gift shop, general store, and gas station.

Located near the Annie Springs Entrance Station off OR-62, the Mazama Campground (Mazama Village, 866/761-6668, www.travelcraterlake.com, June-late Sept., $21 tents, $31-43 RVs) has 214 sites tucked into the pines and located close to the gas station and general store. All sites come equipped with a bear-proof food locker, picnic table, and fire ring. RV rates vary based on electric or full-hookup sites. Facilities include drinking water, flush toilets, showers, and laundry. In June, sites are available first-come, first-served ($5). July-September reservations are accepted, and sites fill by midafternoon.

The tent-only Lost Creek Campground (541/594-3000, www.nps.gov, July-mid-Oct., $5 first-come, first-served) is close to the Pinnacles Overlook off East Rim Drive. The 16 basic sites come with a picnic table and bear-proof food locker and are about 3 miles (5 km) south from the lake's rim. Reservations are not available

and sites fill quickly, especially in July and August; get there early in the morning to claim a spot.

Outside the Park

Established in 1949, Jo's Motel and Campground (52851 Hwy. 62, Fort Klamath, 541/381-2234, www.josmotel. com, $100-185) is south of the Annie Springs Entrance on OR-62. The five rooms feature wood paneling, gas fireplaces, air-conditioning, and flat-screen TVs with free DVDs, but don't expect cable or Wi-Fi. Pets are not allowed in the hotel or at the campsites.

The adjacent campground ($10 adults, $5 kids ages 12 and under) has five tent sites and five RV sites available on a first-come, first-served basis. Sites are set on the Wood River and include picnic tables and shared fire rings. The campground may close in the winter, depending on the weather. GPS and cell services are unreliable here; call for directions or for last-minute bookings. Rooms fill fast in the summer.

Crater Lake Resort (50711 Hwy. 62, Chiloquin, 541/381-2349, http:// craterlakeresort.com, open year-round, $95-160 cabins, $20 tents, $30-35 RVs) is an option for those who don't want to stay in the park. There are about a dozen RV sites and cabins with a few tent sites sprinkled in, all placed right along Fort Creek. Guests have access to a pickleball court, free canoes, Wi-Fi, a camp store, hiking trails, and even a Tesla charging station. The resort is 9 miles (14.5 km) south of the Annie Springs Entrance Station.

**Shasta
and
Lassen**

Shasta and Lassen

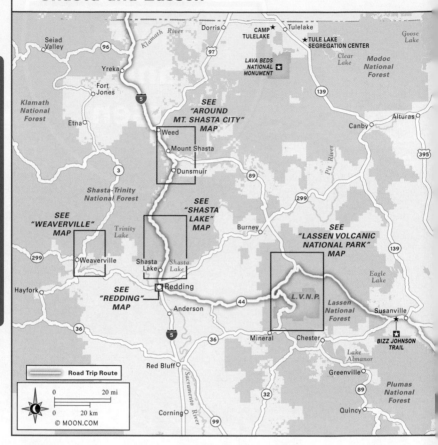

Mount Shasta and Lassen Peak are commanding volcanic mountains that hold a lot of mystery, history, and intrigue waiting to be discovered.

These two geological wonders of Northern California—one active volcano (Mount Lassen) and one possibly active volcano (Mount Shasta) are both over 10,000 feet (3,100 meters) tall and often capped with snow in at least six months out of the year.

Explore natural geological features like the Lake Shasta Caverns and boiling mud pots of Mount Lassen or walk across the Sundial Bridge that connects the Turtle Bay Exploration Park to the Sacramento River Trail as you pass through Redding. There are also campgrounds, state parks, and unique stops along the way.

South of Mount Shasta is the major resort area of Shasta Lake, which attracts boaters and water enthusiasts from far and wide. It is known as a wakeboarding

Highlights

★ **Lava Beds National Monument:** With more than 700 natural caves, famous Native American battle sites, ancient rock art, and 14 thriving species of bats, this strange and amazing place has something to thrill almost anyone (page 301).

★ **Mt. Shasta Ski Park:** Mt. Shasta offers trails for both skiers and cyclists to swoosh down the slopes (page 315).

★ **Lake Shasta Caverns:** A lovely cruise across Shasta Lake is just a prelude to the exploration of these wondrous caverns, filled with natural limestone, marble, and crystal-studded stalactites and stalagmites (page 322).

★ **Boating on Shasta Lake:** When temperatures heat up, visitors flock to Shasta Lake for waterskiing or houseboating in its many coves (page 324).

★ **Sundial Bridge:** This sleek-looking cantilever bridge connects one side of the flowing Sacramento River to the other and acts as a functional sundial (page 332).

★ **Turtle Bay Exploration Park:** This wildlife wonderland is home to native animals like porcupines, barn owls, turtles, and colorful lorikeets (page 333).

★ **Lassen Peak:** Lassen is an active volcano whose last major eruption, in 1914-1915, changed the landscape of the area and altered the shape of the craggy peak itself. The 10,457-foot mountain now offers a rewarding hike to the top or a dramatic view from below (page 352).

★ **Bizz Johnson Trail:** This scenic mountain bike trail stretches for miles across a breathtaking landscape (page 362).

Best Restaurants

★ **Hi-Lo Café, Weed:** This historic diner serves the best chicken burgers and house-made desserts (page 299).

★ **Seven Suns Coffee and Café, Mount Shasta:** This cozy little café is popular with locals, probably due to its delicious breakfast burritos, chocolate chai lattes, and unparalleled views of Mount Shasta (page 303).

★ **Clearwater Coffee & Kitchen, McCloud:** This café serves a refreshing house-made lavender-lemon iced tea that's perfect on a hot summer day (page 317).

★ **Heritage Roasting Co., Shasta Lake:** This popular coffee shop caters to hipsters, foodies, and college students. Try a nitro cold brew or affogato made with ice cream from the Redding-based Taste and See Creamery (page 329).

★ **Jack's Bar & Grill, Redding:** It may not look like much from the outside, but this decades-old establishment serves the best choice-cut steaks and a salad with an impossible-to-replicate French dressing (page 338).

★ **Lassen Ale Works at the Pioneer, Susanville:** After mountain biking at the Susanville Ranch Bike Park or hiking the Bizz Johnson Trail, refuel with a chicken sandwich and a Bizz Johnson Blonde ale (page 362).

mecca due to its miles of channels and glassy coves.

Mount Lassen is classified as an active volcano, and the national park that surrounds it includes many active volcanic features—boiling mud pots, steam vents, and sulfur springs. Both mountains make great vacation destinations; they're beautiful to behold and surrounded by opportunities for recreation and relaxation. Outdoor enthusiasts will find plenty of adventure, whether it's hiking, rock climbing, fishing, or stand-up paddleboarding.

As you drive into this remote area, you'll discover a number of quirky places worthy of a visit. Scan the volcanic landscape of Lava Beds National Monument, scale the cliffs at Castle Crags, and browse kitschy souvenirs in Weed.

Planning Your Time

Shasta and Lassen make a fabulous weekend getaway—particularly if you've got a three-day weekend. Mount Shasta offers fairly easy and reliable year-round access along I-5 with both winter and summer outdoor recreation. The weather on and near Shasta can get extreme; expect winter storms half the year and occasionally brutally high temperatures in the summer months. Check the weather reports so you can pack the right clothes for your trip. If you're planning to climb even part of Mount Shasta, be aware that it's high enough to have its own weather system.

The best time to visit Mount Lassen is mid- to late **summer.** Lassen lies in a remote northeastern part of the state. Due to its high elevation, Lassen can be snowy as late as June, which means that the main road through the park may be closed and unplowed; keep this in mind if planning to camp. August and September are popular times to fish, and if you visit in mid- to late September, it's possible to beat the crowds once the kids are back in school.

Best Accommodations

★ **Stewart Mineral Springs, Weed:** Cabins and rooms dot the ridgeline at this quiet establishment in the woods set above a rushing creek (page 300).

★ **Stoney Brook Inn, McCloud:** A stay here is like visiting grandma, with snow-capped Mt. Shasta watching you from above (page 318).

★ **The Inn at Shasta Lake, Shasta Lake:** Tucked into the Shasta Trinity National Forest, the cottage rooms offer peaceful wildlife-watching opportunities right out your front door (page 330).

★ **Sheraton Redding Hotel at the Sundial Bridge, Redding:** This gorgeous hotel is right next to the Sundial Bridge and Turtle Bay Exploration Park (page 339).

★ **St. Bernard Lodge, Mill Creek:** Even though this historic bed-and-breakfast is right on CA-36, the rooms are quaint and cozy (page 357).

★ **Mill Creek Resort, Mill Creek:** This quaint resort has a campground, cabins, a restaurant, and a playground, all within a few miles of Lassen Volcanic National Park (page 357).

Getting There

From San Francisco
220 mi/354 km, 4 hr

From San Francisco, take US-101 north across the **Bay Bridge.** Stay left to merge onto I-80 East toward Sacramento. Continue for 43 miles (69 km), passing over the **Carquinez Bridge** ($5 toll) to Vacaville. Traffic congestion can be bad around rush hour (7am-10am and 3pm-7pm). Vacaville is a good place to fuel up.

On I-80 East, look for the Winters/Redding exit for I-505 North (exit 56). Drive north on I-505 for 33 miles (53 km) to jump onto I-5. Drive 97 miles (156 km) north on I-5 to Red Bluff where CA-36 leads east to Lassen Volcanic National Park. Continue north on I-5 for 30 miles (48 km) to **Redding,** the gateway hub for this region.

From Redding, CA-44 travels east to the northern entrance of Lassen near Manzanita Lake. I-5 continues north for 60 miles (97 km) to Mount Shasta, where CA-89 east offers side trips to McCloud and Burney Falls.

Stopping in Williams
Williams is midway between Redding and Santa Rosa, so it is a good place for a pit stop. **Granzella's Restaurant & Deli** (451 6th St., 530/473-5496, www.granzellas.com, 6am-9pm daily, $8-10) is a popular deli and restaurant with a sports bar lined with taxidermy. Try the New Orleans muffuletta, the meatball sandwich, or create your own.

From Ashland, Oregon
138 mi/219 km, 2.5-3 hr

From Ashland, take I-5 south for about 18 miles (29 km), crossing the border between Oregon and California. **Redding** is 120 miles (193 km) south on I-5. From Redding, CA-44 leads east to the northern entrance of Lassen Volcanic National Park.

Volcanic Legacy Scenic Byway (CA-89)
From Ashland, take I-5 south for 75 miles (121 km) to the city of Mount Shasta. From Mount Shasta, CA-89 South offers a scenic detour along the Volcanic Legacy Scenic Byway. Stop in the town of **McCloud** for gas and then continue

95 miles (153 km) east on a pretty drive through pine forests. Stop to admire Burney Falls at **McArthur-Burney Falls Memorial State Park** before continuing south where CA-89 crosses CA-299 in Hat Creek.

Continue south on CA-89, stopping in Old Station for camping supplies, then follow signs west toward Lassen Volcanic National Park. (The road turns into CA-44 for a short stretch.) Enter the park at the north entrance near Manzanita Lake. This route is best traveled in summer, when the park road is open.

From Lake Tahoe
195 mi/315 km, 3.5 hr

From Lake Tahoe, follow CA-89 north to I-80 near **Truckee.** Head west on I-80 for 24 miles (39 km). Near Yuba Pass, turn west onto CA-20 and continue 98 miles (158 km) to meet I-5 in Williams. Turn north onto I-5 and drive 70 miles (113 km) north to Red Bluff. Note that **CA-89,** while direct, is more remote, and cell phone reception can be spotty. Both I-80 and CA-20 are subject to closure due to snow; CA-20 in particular is winding and rural, with few services.

Scenic Route (CA-89)

CA-89 wraps around Lake Tahoe and offers a scenic route to the Shasta and Lassen region. From CA-89 near **Kings Beach,** turn right onto CA-267. Continue north on CA-89, crossing I-80. (Look for signs for Prosser Hill OHV Area.) In 30 miles (48 km), you'll reach **Sierraville,** which offers a stop for food and a chance to stretch your legs.

Continue 20 miles (32 km) north on CA-89 through Graeagle, passing the small town of Quincy. In 45 miles (72 km), CA-89 dead-ends into CA-36, where you'll turn west near the town of **Chester.** Continue west on CA-36 for 46 miles (74 km) to reach the south entrance of Lassen Volcanic National Park.

From Sacramento
200 mi/320 km, 3.5 hr

From Sacramento, take I-5 north for 130 miles (210 km) to **Red Bluff.** From here, CA-36 leads east to Lassen Volcanic National Park (take exit 649 for Central Red Bluff). I-5 continues 30 miles (48 km) north to the hub of **Redding,** where CA-44 travels east to the northern entrance of Lassen near Manzanita Lake.

Air, Train, and Bus

The closest airport is the **Redding Municipal Airport** (RDD, 6751 Woodrum Circle, Redding, www.cityofredding. org, 530/224-4320). The **Sacramento International Airport** (SMF, 6900 Airport Blvd., Sacramento, 916/929-5411, https:// sacramento.aero/smf) is another option in the area. Car rentals are available at both airports.

The **Amtrak** Coast Starlight train (800/872-7245, www.amtrak.com, $27-63 one way) departs Sacramento (401 I St.), stopping in Chico (450 Orange St.), Redding (1620 Yuba St.), and Dunsmuir (5750 Sacramento Ave.). It passes through Red Bluff, Shasta Lake, and Mt. Shasta before heading east to Klamath Falls (1600 Oak Ave., Klamath Falls, OR).

Greyhound (800/231-2222, www. greyhound.com, $31-67 one-way) runs buses from Sacramento to Redding and into Oregon. The trip from Redding to Sacramento takes 3-4 hours. Free Wi-Fi is on board.

Shasta and Lassen in Three Days

The Shasta and Lassen area covers a lot of ground. If you only have three days to spare, these are the must-see places.

Day 1

Start your day in Redding with a smoothie or chocolate croissant at **From the Hearth Bakery & Cafe.** Head downtown and walk across the **Sundial Bridge** before playing with the lorikeets at **Turtle Bay Exploration Park.**

From Redding, drive to Lassen Volcanic National Park, stopping in Shingletown for gas. Enter the park at **Manzanita Lake,** where you'll camp for the night. Rent a kayak or stand-up paddleboard to enjoy on the lake until dark. Grab food and snacks at the **Manzanita Lake Camper Store** and make s'mores over the campfire at night.

Day 2

Drive south through the park on CA-89, stopping to touch Hot Rock, hike Lassen Peak, and admire the steaming **Sulphur Works.** Exit the park to the south and then head east on CA-36 to post up for the night at the historic **St. Bernard Lodge.** Take a day trip into Chester for lunch at **Mi Casita** and a little shopping at **B&B Booksellers.** Request dinner in advance so that you can return to St. Bernard Lodge for a cozy meal in their rustic dining room.

Day 3

The St. Bernard Lodge serves an incredible breakfast, so you'll be stuffed once you hit the road east on CA-36. If not, grab coffee in Chester at **Cravings Cafe** or a chai latte at the **Coffee Station** to tide you over until Susanville. Stop in Susanville for lunch and a craft brew at the **Lassen Ale Works at the Pioneer.** Afterward, check out the **Susanville Depot Trailhead Visitors Center and Museum** before stretching your legs on the **Bizz Johnson National Recreation Trail.**

Weed

The town of Weed is a good stopping point for gas, food, souvenirs, or a hotel room. The Hi-Lo Café serves a great breakfast, or enjoy a handcrafted brew at Mount Shasta Brewing Co.

While strolling through Weed, make sure to stop by **The Weed Store** (158 S. Weed Blvd., 530/938-4678, www.weedstore.com 8am-7pm daily) to pick up souvenirs like Weed T-shirts, magnets, shot glasses, keychains, and I Heart Weed lighters.

Getting There

Weed is 10 miles (16 km) north of Mount Shasta city and 66 miles (106 km) south of Ashland, Oregon, on I-5.

Food and Accommodations

Established in 1951, the ★ **Hi-Lo Café** (88 S. Weed Blvd., 530/938-2904, https://hilocafe.com, 6am-10pm daily, $10-18) is a cute family-owned diner in the heart of town. Come for an American-style breakfast, lunch, or dinner, and don't miss the house-made pies, cheesecakes, and cobblers. The burger selection is amazing and the salad bar is well-stocked.

Family-owned **Ellie's Espresso & Bakery** (79 S. Weed Blvd., Ste. 1, 530/938-1041, http://elliesespresso.com, bakery and café 7am-4pm Mon.-Wed., wine bar 5pm-9pm Fri.-Sat., $4-9) serves salads, sandwiches, wraps, and light breakfast items. The house-made breakfast cookies, Russian teacakes, and apple cinnamon twists are favorites of locals and visitors alike.

Mount Shasta Brewing Co. (360 College Ave., 530/938-2394, www.weed-ales.com, noon-8pm daily, $11-26) serves craft beer made with pure Mount Shasta water and named after local features. Choose from the Lemuarian Lager, the Weed Golden Ale, and the Shastafarian Porter. The bistro serves light appetizers, brats, pizzas, and paninis. It's situated next to the College of the Siskiyous.

★ **Stewart Mineral Springs** (4617 Stewart Springs Rd., 530/938-2222, www. stewartmineralsprings.com, $90-140, year-round) is a rustic resort nestled in the woods. Secluded and peaceful, yet close to local attractions, Stewart Mineral Springs offers a variety of accommodations. Four private cabins ($120-140) are perfect for couples; each has a queen bed, full bath, woodstove, and kitchenette with refrigerator and microwave. Campers can choose among tent sites ($40) or one of the five tepees ($50, Apr. 15-Oct. 15 only). Small motel rooms ($90-100), apartments ($100-200) with kitchenettes, and an A-frame house that sleeps up to 12 (from $530) round out the options. There are no phones or TVs on the premises and no Wi-Fi; cell phone coverage is spotty. Overnight guests can enjoy a sundeck and the "last dry-wood sauna in Northern California." Indoor mineral bath tubs are free for guests, with discounted rates for campers (10am-7pm Mon., 10am-6pm Tues.-Sun., 10am-8pm late May-early Sept.). This alcohol-, smoke-, and drug-free environment is known as a place for healing and cleansing.

From top to bottom: Stewart Mineral Springs; Hi-Lo Café; Skull Cave.

✪ ★ Side Trip: Lava Beds National Monument

One of the best places to see the results of volcanic activity is at **Lava Beds National Monument** (1 Indian Well., 530/667-8113, www.nps.gov/labe, visitors center 8am-6pm daily late May-early Sept., 9:30am-4:30pm daily early Sept.-late May, $25). This fascinating 47,000-acre park is delightfully under-visited, no doubt owing to its remote location. With ancient Native American petroglyphs, an unrivaled series of deep and twisting "tube" caves, primordial piles of lava, and an abundance of desert wildlife, it is a mother lode of history, nature, and awe-inspiring sights.

Over the course of about 500,000 years, Medicine Lake Volcano has created an amazing landscape. Among the hiking trails, Modoc battle sites, and scrubby high-desert wilderness are more than 800 caves created by underground lava flows. Some of the caves have been developed for fairly easy access—outfitted with ladders, walkways, and lights—but others remain in their original condition. All are home to whole ecosystems that thrive in the damp darkness.

In summer about 200,000 **bats** live in the park; 2 of the 14 species represented here live in trees, and the other 12 live in caves. In the winter, they will either hibernate or migrate to warmer areas. Park officials monitor where and when bats are likely to be concentrated, and they'll steer you away from those places, mainly for the safety of the bats.

Getting There

Lava Beds National Monument is in the remote northeastern corner of the state about 70 miles (113 km) from Mount Shasta city. To get here from I-5, take US-97 north at Weed. Drive 50 miles (80 km) north, and at the state line just north of Dorris, turn east onto CA-161. Continue 16 miles (26 km) east on CA-161 to Hill Road, then turn right (south) and drive 9 miles (14.5 km) to the park entrance. Plan at least two hours for the drive from Weed. Note that US-97 receives snow at high elevations.

Contact the **visitors center** (530/667-8113) before arrival; they can provide exact directions as GPS is unreliable.

Hiking and Caving

The **visitors center** (530/667-8113, 8am-6pm daily late May-early Sept., 8:30am-5pm daily early Sept.-late May) recommends bringing up to three flashlights per person to explore the caves, as well as caving or bicycle helmets (it's easy to hit your head on the low ceilings of the caves). The visitors center will lend you a large flashlight and sells a simple helmet ($8.15). For the more challenging caves, gloves, knee pads, a cave map, and a compass are also recommended.

The short, paved **Cave Loop Trail** (2.5 mi/3.6 km round-trip, 1.5 hours, easy) outside the visitors center leads past 16 different caves—their cool rocky entrances are fascinating in themselves. Three more caves are accessible via a short hiker-only trail beside the visitors center. The park recommends **Mushpot Cave** as an introductory cave; it's the only one lit with interpretive signs, and it's easily accessible from the visitors center.

After caving Mushpot, visit **Valentine Cave,** formed from a different kind of lava than those on the Cave Loop. The park hosts one-hour guided **tours** through this developed cave, named after the day it was discovered in the early 1930s.

Skull Cave (580 feet) is another popular cave; despite its somewhat creepy name, people like it because it's not as claustrophobic thanks to several large molten rock tubes that form wide spaces. These gaps trap the cold winter air, forming an ice floor that stays frozen all year long.

In addition to the numerous caves, there are 12 hiking trails. One of the best-known trails is **Captain Jack's Stronghold** (1.5 mi/2.4 km round-trip, 1 hour, moderate); the trail's interpretive signage helps explain the contentious history of this area. To get there from Tulelake and Hill Road, turn left after passing through the Lava Beds entrance and drive 3 miles (4.8 km). From the visitors center, take the main park road 12 miles (19.5 km) north.

The wide and easy **Schonchin Butte Trail** (1.4 mi/2.3 km round-trip, 2 hours, moderate) leads to a working fire tower, along with the trail built by the Civilian Conservation Corps between 1939 and 1941. If a ranger is present when you get to the top, you may be able to go up to the fire tower's lookout deck. To get to the Schonchin Butte Trail from the visitors center, turn left onto the main park road and drive 3.2 miles (5.2 km) to the trail sign on the right. From here, it's a 0.5-mile drive on a gravel road to the parking area.

Camping

Lava Beds National Monument features one campground, **Indian Well** (43 sites, first-come, first-served, $10), located close to the visitors center. The campground has ample potable water, modern restrooms with flush toilets (no showers), and an amphitheater; don't expect much shade at the campsites, however. One of the best features for history buffs is the picnic tables, built by hand out of local lava stone by the Civilian Conservation Corps in the 1930s.

Tulelake

Large and lovely **Tule Lake** is visible across the high desert landscape. Although the lake you see today is beautiful, blue, and deep, it is now much smaller. One of the early projects of the U.S. Bureau of Reclamation was to "reclaim" the land beneath Tule Lake and Lower Klamath Lake and make it available for homesteading. What was once underwater, and later homestead land, is now mostly farmland.

Some striking evidence of the lake's original size is viewable from **Petroglyph Point,** a section of Lava Beds National Monument (located east of the lake and separate from the main lava beds area). Walk the **Petroglyph Point Trail** and look for ancient markings on the rock walls high above.

Tule Lake Unit World War II Valor in the Pacific National Monument

From 1942 to 1946, Tule Lake was the home to one of 10 internment camps where Japanese-Americans were held during World War II. In commemoration of the events that went on here and in the other camps, in December 2008 a total of nine sites were made into one national monument, collectively called the **Tule Lake Unit World War II Valor in the Pacific National Monument** (530/260-0537, www.nps.gov/tule). The Tule Lake Unit segregation center remained open after the war ended.

The **visitors center** (1 Indian Well, 530/667-8113) offers free tours of the **Tule Lake Segregation Center** (10am Sat. late May-early Sept.) and **Camp Tulelake** (1pm Sat. late May-early Sept.). Both tours are one hour long and are limited to 20 people. Call (530/260-0537) two weeks in advance to reserve a spot.

Food

Senior Tequila (337 Main St., 530/667-4201, www.senortequilatulelake.com, 11am-8pm Mon.-Sat., 8am-2pm Sun., $9-17) serves authentic Mexican food, including flautas, sopes, and menudo, along with traditional items such as tacos, fajita plates, enchiladas, and burritos.

For Americana, stop in at **Jolly Kone Drive Inn** (223 Main St., 530/667-2622, 6am-6pm Mon.-Sat., 11am-5pm Sun. late Mar.-late Nov., 6am-3pm Mon.-Sat., 11am-3pm Sun. Dec.-Mar., $5-9) for hamburgers, ice cream, biscuits and gravy, and pot roast. The burger patties and buns are made in house, and all veggie items are cut fresh daily.

Getting There

From Weed, take US-97 northeast for 54 miles (87 km), crossing the California-Oregon state line and entering the town of Dorris. Veer right onto CA-161 and head east for 20 miles (32 km), passing through the Lower Klamath National Wildlife Refuge. Turn right onto CA-139 and drive 4 miles (6.4 km) south to the town of Tulelake.

Mount Shasta City

The main street of Mount Shasta city is Mount Shasta Boulevard, and nearly every business in town includes "Shasta" in its name. A plaque outside the **Mount Shasta Police Department** (303 N. Mt. Shasta Blvd., 530/926-7540) proclaims "Mount Shasta—Where Heaven and Earth Meet," and in the town center, near a coin-operated telescope aimed at the mountain, is an inscription of a quote from Joaquin Miller that reads "Lonely as God and white as a winter moon."

The Gold Room (903 S. Mt. Shasta Blvd., 530/926-4125, 11:30am-2am Mon.-Sat., 10am-2pm Sun., cash only) is Mount Shasta's authentic old-time bar with pool tables, dart boards, and vinyl-covered chairs at the bar perfect for settling in. During the day, country and '70s rock music plays on the jukebox for what the bartender describes as her "professional drinkers"; in the evening, the atmosphere changes as the crowd gets younger and the music or karaoke livens things up. Five big-screen TVs show sports so you can stay up to date on the scores while traveling. The Gold Room is cash only, but there's an ATM inside.

Getting There

Mount Shasta is on I-5, 220 miles (335 km) north of Sacramento. From Weed, drive south on I-5 for 10 miles (16 km) to the city of Mount Shasta. Parking in the city is usually easy, except maybe during special events or if streets are sectioned off for the Monday farmers market. The closest major airport is 60 miles (97 km) south in Redding.

Food

Stock up on groceries for camping and picnics at the **Berryvale Grocery** (305 S. Mt. Shasta Blvd., 530/926-1576, www.berryvale.com, store 8am-8pm daily, café 8am-7pm daily). You can pick up high-quality international foods and then enjoy a cup of coffee at the café. With an attractive storefront in the center of town, **Mountain Song Natural Foods** (314 N. Mt. Shasta Blvd., 530/926-3391, 10am-4:30pm Mon.-Sat., noon-3:30pm Sun.) sells healthy food, including local beans from Northbound Coffee Roasters, chocolate bars with an imprint of the mountain, and books. The regular **farmers market** (400 block of N. Mt. Shasta Blvd. between E. Castle St. and E. Alma St., 530/926-6670, www.mtshastafarmersmarket.com, 3:30pm-6pm Mon. mid-May-mid-Oct.) is a treat.

Bakeries and Cafés

★ **Seven Suns Coffee and Café** (1011 S. Mt. Shasta Blvd., 530/926-9701, 6am-4pm daily, $5-12) is a great place to go for breakfast and lunch items such as locally baked goods, burritos, wraps, and salads. They make all sorts of coffee and espresso drinks; the intricate latte designs are sure to cause an instant smile. There's a spacious porch on the south side with umbrella-shaded tables, but the prime spot is the front sidewalk, with two small tables.

The best baked goods in town come from the **Oven Bakery** (214 N. Mt. Shasta Blvd., 530/926-0960, www.theovenbakery.com, 7:30am-noon Mon. and Wed., 7:30am-5pm Tues. and Thurs., 7:30am-noon and 5pm-7pm Fri., 2pm-5pm Sun.), which supplies the local coffee shops and grocery stores with fresh sourdough, rye, wheat, and pumpernickel breads. Visit their storefront, where you can sit down and enjoy a warm scone and

SHASTA AND LASSEN

Vicinity of Mount Shasta City

0 ———— 2 mi
0 ———— 2 km
© MOON.COM

⌇⌇⌇⌇ Road Trip Route

THE WEED STORE/
ELLIE'S ESPRESSO & BAKERY/
HI-LO CAFÉ
Weed

MOUNT SHASTA
BREWING CO.

Mount Shasta▲

Shasta–Trinity

National

Forest

BUNNY FLAT
TRAILHEAD
TH

PANTHER
MEADOWS

MCBRIDE
SPRINGS

BLACK
BUTTE TH

A10

RED FIR
FLAT

MT. SHASTA
FARMERS MARKET

SEE
"MOUNT SHASTA CITY"
MAP

MT. SHASTA BIKE PARK/
MT. SHASTA NORDIC CENTER

★ MT. SHASTA SKI PARK

Mount Shasta

5

MOUNT SHASTA RANCH
BED & BREAKFAST

SISSON-CALLAHAN
NATIONAL RECREATION
TRAIL
TH

MOUNT SHASTA
RESORT

△ FINLANDIA MOTEL
AND LOGE CAMPS

Lake
Siskiyou

LAKE SISKIYOU
TRAIL TH

SACRED MOUNTAIN
SPA

89

Sacramento River

SEE
DETAIL

McCloud

Shasta–Trinity
National
Forest

CASTLE LAKE
△ CAMPGROUND

Shasta Retreat

Dunsmuir

CASTLE CRAGS STATE PARK/
CASTLE CRAGS CAMPGROUND/
CASTLE DOME TRAIL △

5

Castella

McCloud

STONEY
BROOK
INN

AXE & ROSE
PUBLIC HOUSE

W COLOMBERO DR

E COLOMBERO DR

MCCLOUD
HOTEL

DIVISION ST

BROADWAY AVE

CAMPUS WY

W MINNESOTA AVE

MAIN ST

CALIFORNIA ST

QUINCY ST

CLEARWATER
COFFEE & KITCHEN

MCCLOUD
OUTDOORS & GEAR
EXCHANGE

E MINNESOTA AVE

FLOYD'S
FROSTY

0 ——— 100 yds
0 ——— 100 m

89

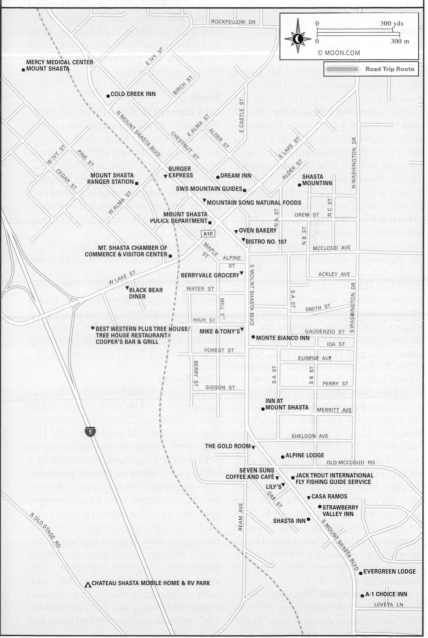

Mount Shasta City

0 | 300 yds
0 | 300 m
© MOON.COM

Road Trip Route

ROCKFELLOW DR

MERCY MEDICAL CENTER
MOUNT SHASTA

E IVY ST

COLD CREEK INN

BIRCH ST

E ALMA ST

E CASTLE ST

CHESTNUT ST

ALDER ST

E LAKE ST

N WASHINGTON DR

N MOUNT SHASTA BLVD

W IVY ST

PINE ST

CEDAR ST

W ALMA ST

MOUNT SHASTA
RANGER STATION

BURGER
EXPRESS

DREAM INN

ALDER ST

SHASTA
MOUNTINN

SWS MOUNTAIN GUIDES

MOUNTAIN SONG NATURAL FOODS

N A ST

OREM ST

N C ST

MOUNT SHASTA
POLICE DEPARTMENT

A10

N B ST

MT. SHASTA CHAMBER OF
COMMERCE & VISITOR CENTER

MAPLE ST

OVEN BAKERY

BISTRO NO. 107

MCCLOUD AVE

W LAKE ST

ALPINE
ST

ACKLEY AVE

BLACK BEAR
DINER

BERRYVALE GROCERY

WATER ST

S MOUNT SHASTA BLVD

S A ST

S WASHINGTON DR

SMITH ST

MILL ST

HIGH ST

S MOUNT SHASTA BLVD

GAUDENZIO ST

BEST WESTERN PLUS TREE HOUSE/
TREE HOUSE RESTAURANT/
COOPER'S BAR & GRILL

MIKE & TONY'S

MONTE BIANCO INN

IDA ST

FOREST ST

BERRY ST

EUGENE AVE

S B ST

PERRY ST

SISSON ST

S A ST

INN AT
MOUNT SHASTA

MERRITT AVE

5

SHELDON AVE

THE GOLD ROOM

ALPINE LODGE

OLD MCCLOUD RD

SEVEN SUNS
COFFEE AND CAFÉ

JACK TROUT INTERNATIONAL
FLY FISHING GUIDE SERVICE

LILY'S

OAK ST

CASA RAMOS

STRAWBERRY
VALLEY INN

SHASTA INN

S MOUNT SHASTA BLVD

REAM AVE

S OLD STAGE RD

EVERGREEN LODGE

CHATEAU SHASTA MOBILE HOME & RV PARK

A-1 CHOICE INN

LOVETA LN

a cup of coffee. The bakery also serves mouthwatering pizzas ($24) on Friday night.

American

As you drive through California, you'll see lots of signs for Black Bear Diners. Since its founding in 1995, it has grown into a chain of more than 120 franchises concentrated in the Western states. The Mount Shasta **Black Bear Diner** (401 W. Lake St., 530/926-4669, www.blackbeardiner.com, 6am-10pm daily, $13-18) was the original Black Bear, and sure enough, it has the feel of a local joint. The food is the usual hearty fare and the staff is helpful and willing to make good recommendations. Plus, it's open late.

Bistro No. 107 (107 Chestnut St., 530/918-5353, www.bistro107.com, 11am-9pm Mon. and Wed.-Sat., noon-9pm Sun. late May-early Sept.; 11am-9pm Mon. and Thurs.-Sat., noon-9pm Sun. mid-Sept.-mid-May, $12-19) is known for gourmet burgers made of imperial Wagyu beef (or the house-made veggie patty) and topped with unique condiments. The melt-in-your-mouth Cabernet burger comes with goat cheese, arugula, grilled onion, bacon, and a cabernet sauce on a brioche bun.

At the north edge of the town center is the retro **Burger Express** (415 N. Mt. Shasta Blvd., 530/926-3950, 11am-6:30pm Mon.-Fri., 11am-5:30pm Sat., noon-4pm Sun., $3-21). With great 1950s-style red stools and tables, a cheerful red-and-white counter, and a checkerboard floor, the place feels up-to-the-minute and delightfully old-fashioned at the same time. It serves basic burgers, chicken baskets, hot dogs, shakes, sundaes, and Hawaiian shaved ice. Eat in or take your food out to the small patio and enjoy the sun and the community. Either way, the eating and the nostalgia are good.

Cooper's Bar & Grill (Best Western Plus Tree House, 111 Morgan Way, 530/926-3101, www.coopersbargrill.com, 11am-10pm Mon.-Thurs., 11am-11pm Fri.,

10am-11pm Sat., 10am-10pm Sun., $12-30) is open for breakfast, lunch, and dinner with a light happy hour menu (3pm-6pm daily) and a dedicated bar menu (3pm-10pm). The burger, beer, and fries special ($14) allows you to fill up quickly. Wine Wednesdays offer half off on bottles of vino.

Mexican

Casa Ramos (1136 S. Mt. Shasta Blvd., 530/926-0250, www.casaramos.net, 11am-9pm Sun.-Thurs., 11am-10pm Fri.-Sat., $16-20) is a local chain serving authentic Mexican cuisine. Choices include steak, chicken, or even cheeseburgers (for picky eaters). Prices are reasonable, portions are ample, and the whole family is welcome.

Italian

Around since 1945, **Mike & Tony's** (501 S. Mount Shasta Blvd., 530/926-4792, www.mikeandtonysms.com, 5pm-9pm Mon. and Thurs., 5pm-10pm Fri.-Sat., 4pm-9pm Sun., $11-28) serves authentic Italian family-style dinners for the weary traveler. Indulge in a house-made pasta, veal, steak, or seafood dinner and warm up with Mike and Tony's minestrone soup.

Fine Dining

At the white-tablecloth end of the dining spectrum is **Lily's** (1013 S. Mt. Shasta Blvd., 530/962-3372, www.lilysrestaurant.com, 8am-2pm and 5pm-8pm daily, $13-30), a lovely cottage house with a spacious patio and dining room, enveloped by a white picket fence out front. Breakfast is a selection of omelets, pancakes, and huevos rancheros, with a smattering of eggs Benedicts. For lunch, opt for a sandwich, salad, pasta, or burger; vegetarian options include grilled eggplant on focaccia and the walnut-garbanzo veggie burger. Dinner entrées charm with skirt steak chimichurri, herb-stuffed trout with Hollandaise sauce, and seasonal vegetables in curry sauce. On Wednesday, Lily's serves a special sushi and bento box menu.

Accommodations
Under $100

One of the first "major" hotels you'll come across is the **Finlandia Motel and Loge Camps** (1621 S. Mt. Shasta Blvd., 530/926-5596, www.logecamps.com, $70-130), which offers simple yet comfortable rooms with a unique Finnish-inspired decor. Options range from a single motel room with a queen bed to a king-bed suite with kitchen. Amenities include an outdoor spa and sauna perfect for relaxing after a hard-core climb up the mountain. The lodge ($175) can sleep up to eight people in three bedrooms and comes with a fully equipped kitchen, a sauna, an outdoor spa, and a wood-burning fireplace crafted out of lava rock. This place is pet-friendly and is close to restaurants and shops on the main street.

Rooms at the **Cold Creek Inn** (724 N. Mt. Shasta Blvd., 530/926-9851, https://coldcreekinn.com, $79-129 winter) feature queen-size beds with pillows and down comforters that you can just sink into, plus complimentary coffee, hot cocoa, and an in-room microwave and mini-fridge. Charge your electronics while watching a movie on the flat-screen TV. Some rooms have mountain views. Pets are welcome and the inn is near the Mt. Shasta Dog Park.

One of the most pleasant inexpensive lodging options is the **Mount Shasta Ranch Bed & Breakfast** (1008 W. A. Barr Rd., 530/926-3870, www.stayinshasta.com, $98-145), offering homey luxury just slightly out of town. The budget-friendly rooms in the Carriage House offer queen beds, kitchens, and shared baths. The separate cottage ($200-230) is the largest option, with two bedrooms that can comfortably sleep up to eight. The four rooms in the main house are spacious and furnished with country-Victorian antiques and tchotchkes; each has its own private bath. All rooms include a full country breakfast.

One of the cheaper motels is the **Evergreen Lodge** (1312 S. Mt. Shasta Blvd., 530/926-2143, $89-159). Rooms include a table and chairs, free Internet service, flat-screen TVs, a microwave, and a mini-fridge. This place doesn't have many amenities; it's just a clean, affordable option to rest your head before hitting the road again.

A bargain spot on the outskirts of the village is the **A-1 Choice Inn** (1340 S. Mt. Shasta Blvd., 530/926-4811, www.mtshastamotel.com, $79-159), with the standard pink-and-green polyester bedspreads and framed reprints of Mount Shasta on the walls. Each room comes with a coffee maker, fridge, and a microwave. There's a small pool and a hot tub beside the highway. With views of the top of Mount Shasta, this place has everything you need as long as you don't need anything fancy.

Heading toward the town center, **Monte Bianco Inn** (504 S. Mt. Shasta Blvd., 530/926-4617, $59-99) is a budget-friendly motel with the same basic amenities but upgraded features like comfortable bedding, a garden, and free Wi-Fi. It shares ownership with **Mike & Tony's,** which is within walking distance to the inn. Guests receive 10 percent off their bill at the popular Italian restaurant.

The cute **Dream Inn** (326 Chestnut St., 530/926-1536 or 877/375-4744, www.dreaminnmtshastacity.com, $80-160) offers bed-and-breakfast accommodations at the base of the magnificent mountain. The four small inexpensive upstairs rooms have shared hallway baths. Downstairs, a bigger white antique bedroom has its own private bath and a view of Mount Eddy out the lace-curtained window. Next door, two large suites share space in a Spanish adobe-style home; each has its own living space, bath, and country-Victorian decor. Rooms at the Dream Inn include a daily full breakfast.

The **Alpine Lodge** (908 S. Mt. Shasta Blvd. 530/926-3145, www.alpinelodgeca.com, $69-159) is on the not-so-fancy end of the spectrum, but it does offer

Internet access and in-room coffee makers. A higher-end option ($159) is the two-bedroom unit with three beds and a kitchenette—great for families.

$100-150

For something more upscale, there's the **Inn at Mount Shasta** (710 S. Mt. Shasta Blvd., 530/918-9292, https://innatmountshasta.com, $79-299). Built in 2000 and renovated in 2018, it's one of the newer facilities in the area. All rooms in the sparkling clean inn come with couches, pull-out sofas, and furniture. The lobby has been refurnished and a fire pit is out back.

To get a sense of what it's like to live in this mountain environment, book a room at the **Shasta MountINN** (203 Birch St., 530/926-1810, www.shastamountinn.com, $150-175). This cute, white farmhouse fits perfectly into its semi-alpine setting. The four rooms ooze country charm and modern comfort with memory-foam mattresses on the beds and a private bath. In the morning, head downstairs for a healthy breakfast and a cup of organic coffee. There are also onsite massage services, a crystal bed, and a barrel-shaped redwood sauna. The retreat's hosts can guide you to other secret spots that make this area one of a kind.

The **Strawberry Valley Inn** (1142 S. Mt. Shasta Blvd., 530/926-2052, http://strawberryvalleyinn.net, $109-238) is an attractive property with a large green lawn and well-kept garden beside the Native Grounds Nursery and Mount Shasta Florist. The inn has an English feel to it, encouraging you to sit among the flowers and have tea before retiring to your charming and smallish-but-lovely room. Continental breakfast is included in the room rates, yet the dining room can get crowded, so try to get there early, and consider taking your breakfast out to the lawn. The Strawberry Valley Inn has a sister property across the street called the **Shasta Inn** (1121 Mt. Shasta Blvd., 530/926-3411, www.shastainn.net,

$99-195). This hotel has a rustic boutique feel with lots of polished wooden decor and modern conveniences, such as a Tesla charging station. It is centrally located in the town center, close to Casa Ramos, art galleries, and day spas. Both properties offer discounted lift tickets to Mt. Shasta Ski Park in winter.

$150-250

In a location and a class by itself is the **Best Western Plus Tree House** (111 Morgan Way, 530/926-3101, www.bestwestern.com, $135-245). Sitting slightly off the main drag near the Mt. Shasta Shopping Center, Mt. Shasta Cinemas, and Black Bear Diner, this is one of Shasta's top lodging options in the area. The Mount Shasta Best Western Plus is a large, full-service hotel with an indoor pool and spa; microwaves, fridges, and pillow-top mattresses in the rooms; wireless Internet access; and a courtyard patio. The on-site **Tree House Restaurant** (www.treehouserestaurantmtshasta.com, 6:30am-10:30am and 5pm-9pm daily, $12-30) serves breakfast and dinner. **Cooper's Bar and Grill** (www.coopersbargrill.com, 11am-10pm Mon.-Thurs., 11am-11pm Fri., 10am-11pm Sat., 10am-10pm Sun., $10-14) serves tacos, burgers, chicken wings, cocktails, wine, and beer.

Off the boulevard are a few more elegant and more expensive places to stay, often with spacious grounds and lots of beautiful scenery. One of the nicest is **Mount Shasta Resort** (1000 Siskiyou Lake Blvd., 530/926-3030, reservations 800/958-3363, https://mountshastaresort.com, $179-359 summer, $129-309 winter). Each room and chalet is different: You can ask for one with a lakeside deck, a fireplace, a jetted tub, two TVs, a kitchenette, or a full kitchen. All rooms come with free wireless Internet access, ironing boards and irons, blow dryers, and other upscale amenities expected. The on-site **Sacred Mountain Spa** (2224 W. A. Barr Rd., 530/926-2331, http://sacredmountainresortspa.com, 10am-6pm daily by appointment, 1-hour massage $95-115) offers massages, facials, makeup, hair, and nail care. You can also play a memorable round of **golf** (530/926-3030, $25-60 walk, $43-78 with cart) on the 18-hole course.

Camping

If the campgrounds on Mount Shasta are full, there are several options on the west side of I-5. The McCloud area also has some developed campgrounds.

Lake Siskiyou Camp Resort (4239 W. A. Barr Rd., 530/926-2618 or 888/926-2618, www.lakesiskiyouresort.com, Apr.-mid-Oct.) is on the shore of glacier-fed Lake Siskiyou, just 3 miles (4.8 km) west of Mount Shasta city. It has 200 tent sites ($32) and 120 RV sites ($38-42) with partial and full hookups as well as trailers and cabins ($98-250) for rent. Plentiful amenities include a beach, boat and equipment rentals, the **Splash Zone** ($8 per hour, $15 per 4 hours, late May-early Sept.), a water park for kids, a **Snack Shack** (10am-6pm daily late May-early Sept.), and the on-site **Lake Sis Grille & Brew** (530/926-1865, 8am-9pm Sun.-Thurs., 8am-10pm Fri.-Sat. late May-early Sept., $20 range).

Castle Lake Campground (Castle Lake Rd., 6 sites, first-come, first-served, May-Nov., free) is about 9 miles (14.5 km) southwest of Mount Shasta city on beautiful Castle Lake. Facilities include picnic tables, fire rings, and vault toilets, but not drinking water. A stay at this campground has a three-night limit.

In addition to Lake Siskiyou Camp Resort, **Chateau Shasta Mobile Home & RV Park** (704 S. Old Stage Rd., 530/926-3279, year-round, $25) offers a great location to park your vehicle and enjoy the area. Some of the spots are a bit crowded and exposed, but they all have great views.

Gumboot Lake (Forest Rd. 26, 6 sites, first-come, first-served, June-Oct. depending on snow, free) is an undeveloped campground about 12 miles (19.5 km) west of Lake Siskiyou Camp Resort.

Accessible by car, this remote place is great for fishing or paddleboarding. Facilities include fire rings and a vault toilet, but no picnic tables or drinking water. A campfire permit is required.

Information and Services

The **Mt. Shasta Chamber of Commerce & Visitor Center** (300 Pine St., 530/926-4865, http://visitmtshasta.com, 9am-4:30pm daily) has information about hotels, restaurants, and local recreation. The staff can provide directions to local destinations.

For wilderness permits and trail advice, head for one of the local ranger stations. The **Mount Shasta Ranger Station** (204 W. Alma St., 530/926-4511, www.shastaavalanche.org, 8am-4:30pm Mon.-Fri.), also called the Mount Shasta Avalanche Center, can supply wilderness and summit passes, park maps, and information about current mountain and weather conditions. A **summit pass** ($25 for three days, $30 for yearly pass) is required when hiking above 10,000 feet (3,000 m) on Mount Shasta, and it allows you to climb to the summit; you can buy one at the ranger station during business hours. A free **wilderness pass** is also necessary. You have the option of self-registering at the trailhead and leaving payment in an envelope as long as you have a check or cash. In person at the ranger station you can use a credit card, too. You can also obtain **California campfire permits** at the ranger station, but you must get them in person, so visit during business hours. The **Shasta Wilderness** requires you to have a permit just to enter, even if you're not spending the night. Those permits are also available here for free, and you can get them inside or from a self-service station out front.

The town of Mount Shasta has a full-service hospital, **Mercy Medical Center Mount Shasta** (914 Pine St., 530/926-6111, www.mercymtshasta.org), with a 24-hour emergency room.

Mount Shasta

Mount Shasta is stunning from every angle at any time of day. Towering over the northern part of the state at 14,162 feet (4,317 m), Mount Shasta is the 49th highest peak in the country, the fifth highest in California, and the second tallest volcano in the Cascade Range. It has a 17-mile perimeter and stands pretty much alone, with no close neighbors near similar stature. In winter, snow covers much of the mountain; in summer glaciers make the mountain appear white and glistening.

Mount Shasta is covered in snow most of the year, which makes it appealing to ice climbers. Recreational skiers and snowboarders go to Mt. Shasta Ski Park for some lift-accessed turns, while families play in the snow at Bunny Flat, accessible at 6,900 feet.

Getting There

From the city of Mount Shasta, the Everitt Memorial Highway leads 15 miles (24 km) northeast to the Panther Meadows campground. From North Mount Shasta Boulevard, take East Lake Street (it turns into North Washington Drive) and stay left for 0.5 mile. The road turns into County Highway A10, which continues 14 miles (22.5 km) to the end of Everitt Memorial Highway.

The main parking lot is at the end of the paved road. Bunny Flat and Old Ski Bowl Trailheads are accessible off Everitt Memorial Highway. Both County Highway A10 and Everitt Memorial Highway are closed in the winter.

Recreation

Hiking

Some of the best hiking in California can be found on and around Mount Shasta. This beautiful region abounds with waterfalls created from fresh snowmelt, pine forests, rivers, streams, and fascinating

Mount Shasta

geology. Informal camping and back-packing (wilderness permits required) can create a wonderful multiday hiking trip. Day hikes offer everything from easy strolls great for kids to strenuous miles that can take you up to small mountain peaks for big views of the whole southern Cascade mountain range.

Gray Butte

If you want to hike on Mount Shasta but don't have the time or the training to go all the way to the top, try a nice day hike to **Gray Butte** (3.4 mi/5.5 km round-trip, 1-3 hours, moderate), an intermediate peak on the south slope of the mountain. The trail runs east across Panther Meadow, facing Mount Shasta's Old Ski Bowl, and into the nearby forest. The meadow is beautiful and full of heather and other wildflowers. At the first fork in the trail (past 0.5 mile), choose the fork to the right. In 1.5 miles, you'll come to a saddle—a good place for views, but there are more to come. From the saddle, bear right again to reach the peak of Gray Butte in less than 0.25 mile. Not only can you see the peak of Mount Shasta, but on a clear day you can see all the way to Castle Crags, Mount Eddy, and even Lassen Peak. Return the same way

To reach the trailhead, take I-5 to the Central Mount Shasta exit. Turn east onto Lake Street, which becomes Everitt Memorial Highway. In 13.5 miles (21.5 km), you'll reach Panther Meadows Campground, which has extensive trail signage and plenty of information about the ecology and wildlife of the area.

Ah-Di-Na Historic Trail

For an unexpected connection to the Hearst family, take a walk along the **Ah-Di-Na Historic Trail** (0.25 mile, 30 minutes, easy). Follow the signs from Squaw Valley Creek Road at the reservoir to this odd little resort area along the McCloud River. The William Randolph Hearst family built a retreat here, and you'll see photos of their property on the interpretive signs marking the short, flat trail.

It's a bit of a drive out to Ah-Di-Na on slow dirt roads. It is possible to get there in a passenger car, but not an RV or towing a trailer; expect the drive to take some time. For more information, visit the **McCloud Ranger Station** (2019 Forest Rd., 530/964-2184) off of CA-89.

Sims Flat Historic Trail

The **Sims Flat Historic Trail** (Sims Rd., 1 mi/1.6 km one-way, 30 minutes, easy) starts at the Sims Flat Campground, 8 miles (13 km) south of Castella and 16 miles (26 km) north of Lakehead. This short out-and-back trail travels along the river past oaks and pines and moss-covered rocks on a partially paved path. Interpretive signs point out the locations of a former lumber mill and conservation camp. Enjoy the up-close views of Mount Shasta, which loom over Sims Flat.

To get there from I-5, take the Sims Road/718 exit and drive east, crossing the Sacramento River. Contact the **Mount**

Shasta Ranger Station (204 W. Alma Rd., 530/926-4511) for information.

Sisson-Callahan National Recreation Trail

On the other end of the hiking spectrum is the **Sisson-Callahan National Recreation Trail** (North Shore Rd., 18 mi/29 km round-trip, 6-9 hours, difficult). From its trailhead near Lake Siskiyou, the trail gains almost 1 mile in elevation, peaking at more than 8,000 feet (2,400 m) at Deadfall Summit before then dropping 1,000 feet (300 m) to Deadfall Lakes. The trail is long, steep, and challenging; many hikers prefer to break this up over two days. A number of campsites line the North Fork of the Sacramento River, welcoming weary backpackers to pitch a tent and rest. The Sisson-Callahan trail links with the Pacific Crest Trail (www.pcta.org) near Deadfall Lakes, so backpackers can keep going if they choose. Be sure to dress in layers; you might start out in the intense summer heat of the lower elevations and end up making snowballs on the summit.

Whether you are hiking just for the day or overnight, check with the **Mount Shasta Ranger Station** (530/926-4511) for updated information on weather and special wilderness regulations.

The trailhead is past Deer Creek Bridge. Take the left fork and park off the road.

Lake Siskiyou Trail

For a hike big on views with not so much climbing, the **Lake Siskiyou Trail** (W. A. Barr Rd., 7 mi/11.3 km, 3-4 hours, easy) is for you. This mostly flat loop circumnavigates the spectacular Lake Siskiyou and offers changing perspectives of the surrounding mountains and shores. Start from any one of several well-marked parking areas; there are four rest stops with pit toilets and helpful signage along the way.

To get there from the city of Mount Shasta, head west on W. A. Barr Road.

A parking area is next to Mount Shasta Resort. Keep going south and you'll pass the Sacred Mountain Spa; there's another parking lot at Box Canyon Dam.

Mount Eddy

The trek up **Mount Eddy** (Forest Rte. 42N17, 10 mi/16 km round-trip, 5-6 hours, difficult) is a long and lovely hike with views of the mountain region into Oregon. This steep trail climbs to the 9,000-foot peak, where you can admire the highlights of the Cascade Range: Mount Shasta, Mount Lassen, the Trinity Alps, and even Mount McLoughlin in Oregon. From the Deadfall Lake trailhead, the early section of the trail is mostly mild climbing. It's the last 0.8 mile that's the hard part—a serious climb along steep exposed switchbacks, guaranteed to give you a workout. The reward is worth it, though: You'll soon be on a truly exceptional mountaintop with views you'll remember for a long time.

If you're not up for such a long day hike, consider an overnight camping trip; the lake makes for a great primitive campground. Bring plenty of water; there's none at the Deadfall Lake trailhead. For more information, contact the Mount Shasta Ranger Station (530/926-4511).

Black Butte

Black Butte (5.2 mi/8.4 km round-trip, 3-4 hours, difficult) is a great half-day adventure for serious hikers. This odd cinder-cone peak stands at 6,325 feet (1,928 m) and resembles a giant cone of black pepper. (The U.S. Forest Service says it's actually made of hornblende andesite.) Although it's only 2.6 miles (4.2 km) to the top, the hike up Black Butte is rocky, steep, and mostly unshaded. You'll gain 1,845 feet (560 m) in elevation within that short distance.

Bring sunscreen, plenty of water, binoculars, and a camera, and leave more time than you think you'll need. Finding the trailhead can be a little confusing as it's located off of Forest Service roads. Though it's only 6 miles (9.5 km) from the town center, it takes at least 20 minutes to get there.

From Mount Shasta Boulevard in the city of Mount Shasta, turn east onto Lake Street, which becomes Everitt Memorial Highway. Drive 3 miles (4.8 km) and look for a small "Black Butte Trail" sign. Turn left onto a gravel road (Forest Rd. 41N18) and follow it as it winds through the forest on narrow, uneven, rocky roads. (Go slow if you value your car's undercarriage and windshield). Stick to the main narrow gravel road all the way to the trailhead.

Climbing

Many climbers come to tackle Shasta's majestic 14,162-foot peak. If you decide to do so, bring your sturdiest hiking boots and your strongest leg muscles; fewer than one-third of the 15,000 intrepid mountaineers who try to conquer Mount Shasta each year actually make it to the top. Though it's only 6 miles (9.7 km) to the peak from Bunny Flat, it's also a 7,000-foot (2,100 m) elevation gain. Shasta's steep and rocky slopes, long-lasting snowfields, year-round icy glaciers, and changing weather all make this one of the most difficult climbs in the country. In addition, the thin air at altitude makes breathing a challenge. It's best to attempt this climb in summer.

For healthy, well-trained, and well-equipped ice climbers, this is paradise. If you're lucky enough to go at the right time with the right people and make it to the top, you'll see Mount Shasta in a way that makes it more spectacular, with views that most never see. The main climbing season is June-August, but do not expect sunny weather and easy footing. Falling ice balls and strong winds can catch climbers off-guard at any time. Some of the dirt roads require a four-wheel-drive vehicle, and weather conditions can severely affect road conditions. Contact the **Mount Shasta Climbing Advisory** (530/926-4511, www.shasta-avalanche.org) for current weather and climbing conditions.

More than a dozen routes lead to the top. The most popular route begins near the **Shasta Alpine Lodge** (www.sierraclubfoundation.org) at Horse Camp and runs along Avalanche Gulch. The quick, hard-core climb through Avalanche Gulch takes you from the base camp up to the top in a single day to really get your heart pumping (beware of altitude sickness). A longer, more leisurely hike means spending two days to make the trek, with an overnight in the wilderness to acclimate to the elevation.

The **Shasta Alpine Lodge** was built in 1923 of local volcanic rock and wood from the surrounding forest. It is owned by the Sierra Club (it is sometimes called the Sierra Club climbers hut) and is at an altitude of 7,900 feet on the mountain's southwest side. This is a great destination for a modest day hike or a good base camp for those heading toward the summit.

Guides and Outfitters

Mountaineering classes are available, and several guides and outfitters provide equipment and even lead trips up the mountain. Private mountain guide **Robin Kohn** (530/926-3250, www.mountshastaguide.com) maintains a comprehensive website with up-to-date information and helpful advice. Contact her for help hiring a guide or arranging trip plans.

Shasta Mountain Guides (530/926-3117, www.shastaguides.com, $550-750 pp) has been taking climbers to the top for decades. Join one of their scheduled group trips along various routes up the mountain or call to arrange a custom expedition. Snowboard and backcountry ski tours ($129-650 pp, min. 2 people) are also available.

SWS Mountain Guides (210 E. Lake St., 888/797-6867, www.swsmtns.com, Apr.-July, $725 pp) leads groups of up to eight people on Mount Shasta. To learn as well as climb, check out the Basic Glacier Expedition Course (June-Sept., 5 days, $1,375). The rigorous training on the use of ice axes and crampons, and what to do if someone falls into a crevasse, may come in handy during the climb to Shasta's summit along a "glaciated north-side route." The company's one-day Ice Ax Clinic (Mar.-July, 6-8 hours, $150) teaches basic snow-climbing techniques. Make a weekend of it by combining this with the Basic Mountaineering Clinic (6-8 hours, $175). All clinics and climbs take place on Mount Shasta.

Alpine Skills International (530/582-9170, www.alpineskills.com, $495-980 pp) provides training and guides for climbers of various skill levels. Founder Bela Vadasz earned a lifetime achievement award from the American Mountain Guides Association and was instrumental in establishing certification programs for mountain guides in the United States. His company takes training as seriously as adventure. Their most challenging course on Mount Shasta is the Glacial Ice Seminar (4 days, July-Aug., $825), which takes place on the Hotlum or Whitney Glaciers near the top of the mountain.

Fishing

Most of the major rivers and feeder streams in the Mount Shasta region are open to fishing. You can tie your fly on and cast into the McCloud, Sacramento, and Trinity Rivers, which carry salmon, steelhead, and trout. Guide services are also available.

Guides and Tours

For fly-fishing or scenic rafting tours, contact **Jack Trout International Fly Fishing Guide Service** (1004 S. Mt. Shasta Blvd., 530/926-4540, www.jacktrout.com, year-round, $375-475 for 2 people). Jack leads trips on the McCloud, Klamath, Upper and Lower Sacramento, Pit, and Trinity Rivers, and all the way to Hat Creek near Lassen. Trips include all gear and a gourmet barbecue lunch complete with wine and homemade strawberry shortcake. Expert fly-fishers can learn to improve their technique, and beginners will always catch something. Check out his blog (www.mtshasta.com), complete with great photos, to help visualize your trip. Bring a California fishing license, available online (www.dfg.ca.gov).

Wild Waters Fly Fishing (1512 Holiday Ln., 877/934-7466, http://wildwaters-flyfishing.com, $500 for 8-9 hours with 1-2 anglers) specializes in scouring the Sacramento, Klamath, Trinity, McCloud, and Rogue Rivers for big, beautiful steelhead. Their full team of expert anglers lead you to the best spots and provide the boat, extra fly-fishing equipment, tackle, and lunch.

SacRiverGuide.com (530/515-5951 or 800/670-4448, www.sacriverguide.com, year-round by appointment only, $175-225 pp/day) takes anglers on fly-fishing drift trips on the Sacramento and Trinity Rivers, where they specialize in catching salmon, trout, striped bass, and steelhead; they'll also guide you on a jet-boat trip on Shasta Lake.

Rafting and Kayaking

When the snow melts off the Cascades, it flows into energetic tributaries, creating classes of rapids ideal for white-water rafting. **Trinity River Rafting** (31021 Hwy. 299 W, Big Flat, 530/623-3033, www.trinityriverrafting.com, guided trips $65-190 per day, kayak rental $45 single, $65 tandem per day) offers flagship runs on the Trinity, as well as runs on the Klamath, Salmon, and Upper Fork Sacramento Rivers. Half-day or full-day trips are available. Guests can choose from a placid Class I-II float suitable for the whole family (Mr. Toad's Wild Ride is the most popular) to a Class IV-V run through Burnt Ranch Gorge for fit, experienced rafters. Trinity also rents rafts and inflatable kayaks for paddlers who want to go on their own.

Bigfoot Rafting Company

(530/629-2263, www.bigfootrafting.com, $69-89) offers day trips on the Trinity and Cal Salmon Rivers, plus multiday rafting campouts ($135 pp/day) on the Trinity and Klamath Rivers. Guides reveal a depth of knowledge of the rivers and natural surroundings and are certified in CPR and Swift Water Rescue. They also provide fabulous meals on the full-day and multiday trips. Bigfoot rents rafts ($70-145, 2-10 people), inflatable kayaks ($45-65), and inner tubes ($10) at Willow Creek.

Winter Sports

Cross-country skiers can get their fix at the **Mount Shasta Nordic Center** (Ski Park Hwy., 530/925-3495, www.mtshastanordic.org, 9am-4pm Thurs.-Sun. winter, $15-20 adults, $15 seniors ages 65-69 and youth ages 8-17, $9 seniors ages 70-plus, children ages 7 and under free). The center has about 16 miles (26 km) of groomed trails for cross-country skiing and ample backcountry to explore off-trail. Snowshoers are allowed on the groomed trails (as long as they stay to the side). Opening dates are determined by snowfall, usually late December through mid-April. Call the hotline (530/925-3494) for conditions and grooming updates. Full winter memberships are available, as are cross country ski equipment and snowshoe rentals. The nonprofit organization hosts school groups, offers lessons, and is involved in winter community events.

★ Mt. Shasta Ski Park

Mt. Shasta Ski Park (Ski Park Hwy., off Hwy. 89, 530/926-8610 or 530/926-8600, www.skipark.com, 9am-4pm daily mid-Dec.-mid-Apr., $59-65 adults, $40-45 seniors and children ages 8-12, $20-25 children ages 7 and under, $15-20 for 3 hours snow tubing) has three chairlifts and one magic carpet lift that access 425

From top to bottom: Black Butte; McCloud; Stoney Brook Inn.

acres of terrain. When there's enough snow, Mt. Shasta keeps half of the mountain open on Friday and Saturday evenings for twilight skiing. The magic carpet, located behind the base lodge, and the Marmot lift are the perfect grades for beginners to learn or get their snow legs. More advanced skiers and snowboarders can head up the Douglas lift to take the mid-mountain Coyote Butte chair to access the terrain park and half-pipe.

Horseback Riding

The wilderness around Mount Shasta is perfect for trail rides or equestrian entertainment. The **Rockin Maddy Ranch** (11921 Cram Gulch Rd., Yreka, 530/340-2100, www.rockinmaddyranch.com, year-round, by reservation only, 1-2 hours $85 pp) is the main hacienda for happy horses. The family-owned operation saddles horses for rides that take in the vistas and surroundings on safe, yet adventurous safe trails. You can even book a pony party for your child, rent a horse-drawn carriage ride, or a hop aboard a hayride led by a team of powerful Percherons. Riders must be at least 12 years old; there's a 225-pound (102-kg) maximum weight limit.

Mountain Biking

In summer, Mt. Shasta Ski Park becomes a mountain bike park with an 18-hole disc golf course and scenic chairlift rides. The **Mt. Shasta Bike Park** (Ski Park Hwy., Hwy. 89, 530/926-8600, www.skipark.com, 10am-4pm Sat.-Sun., lift tickets $32 adults, $16 youth) features several beginner and intermediate mountain biking trails, as well as a nice big skills park with jumps and berms for bikers, which is accessed by the Marmot chair. The Douglas chair transports skilled cyclists to an advanced route, dropping riders off at the top of Douglas peak, which is also where the disc golf course begins.

The bike park **rents** mountain bikes ($40-95), E-mountain bikes ($75-120), and helmets ($10-15). Camping is free in the parking lot on Friday and Saturday nights (no hookups). Campers and mountain bike riders have access to the lodge for bathrooms and food items. A full bar is available in the **Mud Creek Café** (10am-4pm Sat.-Sun.).

Camping

The Shasta-Trinity National Forest (Shasta Ranger Station, 530/926-4511, www.fs.usda.gov, 8am-4:30pm Mon.-Fri.) manages three campgrounds on Mount Shasta. All are popular and fill quickly on summer weekends. Reservations are not accepted; come on weekdays when it's easier to find a space.

McBride Springs (12 sites, first-come, first-served, late May-Oct., $10) is conveniently located on the mountain at 5,000 feet, 5 miles (8 km) from Mount Shasta city. Facilities include drinking water, vault toilets, and picnic tables.

Panther Meadows (Everitt Memorial Hwy., 1.7 mi/2.7 km past Bunny Flat, 15 sites, July-Nov., free) is 14 miles (22.5 km) northeast of Mount Shasta city at an elevation of 7,500 feet (2,285 m) on the slopes of Mount Shasta. Because of the high elevation, it can be cold at night and snowed-in well into summer. Although this is a walk-in campground, it is only 100-500 feet from the parking lot to the campsites. Facilities include picnic tables, fire rings, and vault toilets; bring your own water. This is the most popular campground on Mount Shasta; it has a maximum stay of three nights.

The third campground is **Red Fir Flat** (530/926-4511, $12), a group site (9-35 people) available by reservation. Facilities include picnic tables, fire rings, and vault toilets, but not drinking water.

Dispersed camping is allowed throughout the Shasta-Trinity National Forest. A wilderness permit is required on Mount Shasta itself. Otherwise, anywhere you want to sleep is fair game, though you do need a free campfire permit, available at any ranger station. For permits and information, contact the

Mount Shasta Ranger Station (204 W. Alma St., 530/926-4511, www.fs.usda.gov, 8am-4:30pm Mon.-Fri.).

McCloud

With Mount Shasta looming in the distance, the sleepy town of McCloud is emblematic of the area's friendly people and relaxed pace of life.

Getting There
McCloud is 12 miles (19.5 km) east of the city of Mount Shasta on CA-89.

McCloud Falls
McCloud Falls (McCloud Ranger Station, 530/964-2184, www.shastacascade.com) is a wonderful waterfall on the McCloud River. There are three different falls along this stretch of river. At Lower McCloud Falls, roiling white water pours over a 30-foot rock wall into an aerated river pool below. Middle McCloud Falls resembles a tiny Niagara, a level fall of water that's wider than it is tall. Upper McCloud Falls cascades briefly but powerfully down into a chilly pool that can double as a swimming hole if you're feeling brave.

A trail (3.5 mi/5.6 km round-trip, easy) starts at the lower falls below Fowlers Campground (Fowler Public Camp Rd.) and follows the outer edge of the McCloud River past the middle falls and ending at the upper falls.

To get here, take the McCloud exit from I-5 onto CA-89 east. After about 5 miles (8 km), look for a sign on the left directing you to Fowlers Camp and Lower McCloud Falls. In another mile is the Lower Falls picnic area, where you can park.

Shopping
The McCloud Outdoors & Gear Exchange (209 S. Quincy Ave., 530/316-4327, www.mccloudoutdoors.com, 8am-4pm daily) rents SUPs and kayaks ($40 per day), fishing gear, hunting equipment, and all of the accessories for an outdoor adventure. It's next door to Clearwater Coffee & Kitchen.

Food
Floyd's Frosty (125 Broadway Ave., 530/964-9747, 11am-7pm daily late-May-early Sept., hours vary in winter) is on the main drag in McCloud. Inside this old-school burger shack you'll find incredibly juicy burgers, fries, and refreshing frosties. Try the half-pound Logger, the cheeseburger, or an elk burger if it's available. There's a good chance that Floyd himself will serve you!

For a quick coffee, stop at ★ Clearwater Coffee & Kitchen (207 S. Quincy Ave., 530/316-4327, 8am-4pm daily, $7-12). This inviting establishment offers the perfect amount of caffeine and an energy-fueled meal before heading outdoors on the McCloud River. Enjoy a signature blended or espresso drink, light breakfast item, lunch, or a freshly brewed lavender-lemon iced tea that's to die for.

Located in the "heart" of downtown McCloud, the Axe & Rose Public House (424 Main St., 530/964-2822, 11:30am-8pm Sun.-Tues., 11:30am-10pm Wed., 11:30am-9pm Thurs., 11:30am-11pm Fri.-Sat., $12-18) has a rustic yet modern feel that pays homage to the once-bustling town that catered to the lumber mill and railroad workers. Inside the polished wood interior, diners munch on fish-and-chips or hanger steak amid casual conversation. This former dance hall is still a happening place in McCloud; locals and skiers come here after a day of shredding at Mt. Shasta Ski Park.

Accommodations
Located next to the Axe & Rose Public House, the lovely McCloud Hotel (408 Main St., 530/964-2822, https://mccloudhotel.com, $149-259) was originally built in 1916 to house local mill workers. Today, the hotel still maintains 12 rooms and four suites, some with jetted or two-person copper tubs and dedicated sitting

areas. Guests enjoy access to the surrounding gardens, a free glass of wine (4pm-5pm), and a complimentary full breakfast buffet. The hotel is also close to Mt. Shasta Ski Park.

Adjacent to the McCloud Hotel, the ★ **Stoney Brook Inn** (309 W. Colombero Dr., 530/964-2300, www.stoneybrookinn. com, $70-130) is a lovely country mansion enveloped by inviting brick steps that lead to a spacious porch. Inside, the guest rooms convey an old-timey feel with lace curtains. A stay includes access to an outdoor sauna and hot tub. Stoney Brook is also a short walk from the Axe & Rose Public House.

Little Mount Hoffman Lookout Tower (Hwy. 89, McCloud District Office 530/964-2184, reservations 877/444-6777, www.recreation.gov, June-mid-Oct., $75 per night, $525 per week, max. 4 people) is in the northeast corner of the Shasta-Trinity National Forest near Medicine Lake. This 1920s-era lookout tower was used regularly until 1978 and is sometimes still employed in fire emergencies. Meanwhile, you can rent it for a romantic vacation, writer's retreat, or hiking base camp. The views are outstanding—from the tower's height of more than 7,300 feet (2,225 m), you can see Mount Shasta, Mount Lassen, and Mount McLoughlin.

Camping

The McCloud area has several campgrounds with access to the McCloud River as well as to nearby Mount Shasta. Popular **Fowlers Camp** (39 sites, www. recreation.gov, Apr.-mid-Oct., $15) is at 3,400 feet (1,040 m) elevation on the Upper McCloud River. Facilities include picnic tables, fire rings, vault toilets, and drinking water. Fowlers Camp is 5 miles (8 km) east of McCloud on CA-89.

Cattle Camp (off Hwy. 89, 27 sites, first-come, first-served, May-Nov., $15) is a campground at 3,700 feet (1,130 m) elevation on the Upper McCloud River, making it a popular spot for fishing, swimming, and hiking. Facilities include picnic tables, fire rings, vault toilets, and drinking water. Cattle Camp is 10 miles (16 km) east of McCloud on CA-89.

Ah-Di-Na (off Hwy. 89, 16 sites, first-come, first-served, Apr.-Nov., $10) is a remote campground at 2,300 feet (700 m) elevation on the Lower McCloud River. Facilities include picnic tables and flush toilets; bring your own drinking water. The campground is 10 miles (16 km) south of McCloud; the last 4 miles (6.4 km) are on a rough, dirt road.

For more information about camping in the area, contact the **McCloud Ranger Station** (530/964-2184).

McArthur-Burney Falls Memorial State Park

Often billed as the most beautiful waterfall in California, Burney Falls in **McArthur-Burney Falls Memorial State Park** (24898 Hwy. 89, Burney, 530/335-2777, www.parks.ca.gov, $10) has been

thrilling visitors with its cascading falls for generations. No less a naturalist than Theodore Roosevelt declared these falls one of the wonders of the world. The park is the second oldest in the California State Park system.

Getting There

McArthur-Burney Falls Memorial State Park is 44 miles (71 km) east of McCloud on CA-89 near Burney. To get here from Redding, take CA-299 east for 65 miles (105 km) to Cassel, and then head north on CA-89 for 6 miles (9.5 km).

Burney Falls

Burney Falls flows strong and true year-round and is just as beautiful in September as in April. More good news: You don't have to hike to reach the falls; they're right by the parking lot. Still, it's more than worth your time to get out of your car and take a walk around the wide sheets of water that almost look like a miniature Niagara; it's only a quick walk to the pool at the base of the falls.

For the best views, take the **Burney Falls Loop Trail** (1 mi/1.6 km round-trip, easy) around the 129-foot waterfall. The loop starts at an overlook; the mostly paved single track descends clockwise into the valley toward the base of the falls, crossing an arching wooden bridge.

The park is open year-round, but it's busiest April-October, especially during weekends and holidays when the parking lot fills fast. Due to the varying terrain, wheelchairs are not advised on the loop trail. Parts of the trail may also be closed due to storm damage or fallen trees.

Accommodations and Camping
Inside the Park

The state park **campground** (Hwy. 89, 530/335-2777) has 121 campsites (reservations accepted at 800/444-7275 or www.reservecalifornia.com May-Sept., $35, $8 reservation fee) and 24 cabins (reservations accepted at 530/335-4800

McArthur-Burney Falls Memorial State Park

or www.reservecalifornia.com Apr.-Oct., $105) with propane heaters and platform beds; the cabins do not have plumbing or electricity. A separate facility with showers and bathrooms is close by. The campground is open year-round but closes a large portion of the sites in winter. After the first major snow, only 30 campsites are available for snow camping (first-come, first-served, $30).

Outside the Park

Charm Motel & Suites (37371 Hwy. 299E, Burney, 530/335-3300, www.burneylodging.com, $91-225) provides rooms with comfortable beds and warm lighting, plus plenty of parking right outside your door. Its sister property, **Green Gables** (37371 Hwy. 299E, Burney, 530/335-3300, www.burneylodging.com, $91-235) is named after the green gable-styled porch covering adorning each room. One suite sleeps up to six and features two bedrooms, a dining room, living room, and a bathroom. Both properties are a 10-minute drive from Burney Falls and Lassen Volcanic National Park.

⊕ CA-89 South

Hat Creek

Hat Creek is a sleepy rural area on CA-89 northwest of Manzanita Lake. **Rancheria RV Park & Store** (15565 Black Angus Lane, Hat Creek, 530/335-7418, https://rancheriarvpark.net, 9am-6pm daily) has tent sites ($27-32) and cabins, including one that can sleep up to eight people ($42-142). The on-site **restaurant** (9am-5pm daily late May-early Sept., 11am-4pm, Wed.-Sun. in winter) serves breakfast, lunch, and dinner. Guests have access to coin-operated showers and a laundry room. A general store sells beer, wine, groceries, and camping supplies.

Hereford Ranch RV Park & Campground (17855 Doty Road, Hat Creek, 530/335-7171, www.hatcreekherefordrv.com, 8am-7pm daily Apr.-mid-Oct., 10am-5pm daily winter) is a quaint and quiet place that is all about the outdoors. The ranch has 87 tent and RV sites ($30-45 for 2 people, $2-3 per each additional person, $1 per pet). There's a fully stocked fishing pond on-site ($10 to fish with a 5-catch limit) and a swimming pool.

Old Station

Subway Cave (Hwy. 89, 530/336-5521, www.fs.usda.gov, Apr.-Oct., free) is almost 30 miles (48 km) south of Burney Falls. About 30,000 years ago, molten lava spewed forth and rivers of hot liquid covered Hat Creek Valley. As the top layer hardened, the lava continued to flow until it eventually dried up, leaving this wide-open lava tube called Subway Cave. A short and easy loop hike (0.75 mile) offers a good place to stretch your legs and cool down. This self-guided trail leads to the top of the tube. Then hike down into the dark 1,300-foot abyss using a headlamp or flashlight to navigate cave features with names like Stubtoe Hall, Wind Tunnel, The Sanctum, Lavacircle Lane, and Partial Collapse. It can be a little spooky in the heart of the cave, but there's only one place to end up—a lighted tunnel at the end.

Food and Accommodations

If you're craving a nice hot home-style breakfast where many items on the menu are made from scratch, then check out **JJ's Café** (13385 State Hwy. 44, 530/335-7225, https://jjscafeoldstation.com, 7am-3pm Mon.-Thurs., 7am-8pm Fri.-Sun.).

Across the street, the **Cave Campground** ($16 Apr.-Oct., $10 winter, first-come, first-served) has 45 tent sites and flush toilets, picnic tables, and drinking water on-site.

The **Hat Creek Resort & RV Park** (12533 Hwy. 44, 530/335-7121, http://hatcreekresortrv.com, 9am-5pm daily mid-Apr.-Oct.) offers a range of lodging options. Choose from five tent sites ($25-46), four yurts ($69-149), 11 cottages ($129-224), 10 motel rooms ($69-154), two small cabins ($109-159) that sleep up to four people, and 55 RV sites ($38-73), 12 of which are right on Hat Creek. The Pacific Coast Trail runs behind the resort. An on-site store sells night crawlers and salmon eggs for anglers looking to catch brown, brook, or rainbow trout fed by the Crystal Lake Hatchery.

Information and Services

The **Old Station Visitor Center** (13435 Brians Way, Old Station, 530/335-7517, www.recreation.gov, 8:30am-4pm Thurs.-Mon. late May-early Sept., 8:30am-4pm Sat.-Sun. Sept.-mid-Dec.) has information about the Hat Creek area, plus nice gardens and restrooms that are open late May through mid-December.

Past the CA-89/44 junction is the **Old Station Fill-Up** (13413 State Hwy. 44, 530/335-3152, www.oldstationfillup.com, 7am-7pm daily), which sells gas 24 hours a day. It's also a good place to get fishing licenses, snacks, ice, souvenirs, worms, and tire chains, and the people who work here are super friendly.

Castle Crags State Park

Castle Crags State Park (20022 Castle Creek Rd., Castella, 530/235-2684, www.parks.ca.gov, $8 per vehicle) is one of the greats in California's extensive network of state parks. With 4,350 acres of land, miles of hiking trails, and some very dramatic granite peaks and cliffs, it is a wonderful destination or a convenient place to camp while you enjoy Mount Shasta to the north or Shasta Lake to the south. You can fish and swim in the Sacramento River, rock-climb the spectacular 6,000-foot crags, take a variety of hikes, or just enjoy stunning views of Shasta and other nearby mountains and ranges.

If you don't have much time, you can still have a nice little walk and a great Castle Crags experience. After you enter at the gate, drive through the park following the signs for "Vista Point." A paved walk of no more than 0.25 mile from the Vista Point parking lot leads to a spectacular overlook with views all around. Bring your binoculars and your camera.

Getting There

Castle Crags is easy to find. Take I-5 north toward the city of Mount Shasta and follow signs for the park. From the Bay Area, it's a 170-mile (275-km) trip on I-5 north to exit 724 at Castella. Turn left onto Castle Creek Road, and the park is less than 0.5 mile. If you're coming from the north, the park is just 6 miles (9.5 km) south of Dunsmuir and about 13 miles (21 km) south of the city of Mount Shasta.

Hiking and Climbing

If you can stay longer, drive to the Vista Point parking lot and use it as access to the Crags Trailhead. The **Castle Dome Trail** (5.5 mi/8.9 km round-trip) is strenuous and worth every step. If you're a strong hiker with a brisk pace, it will take about 2 hours on the way up and 1-1.5 hours on the way down. Feel free to go slower, though—it's a steep climb with memorable views all along the way. Pull out your camera for an excuse to take lots of breaks. About 2 miles up the trail is a sign for Indian Springs, a 0.25-mile jaunt off the main trail.

Castle Crags has more than 40 established **rock climbing** routes plus plenty of wide-open formations for explorers who prefer to make their own paths. You'll get to tackle domes, spires, and walls of granite that reach 6,000 feet into the sky. The crags first thrust upward and then broke off and were scrubbed by glaciers into the fascinating climbable formations visible today. Some favorite climbs at Castle Crags are the Cosmic Wall on Mount Hubris, Castle Dome, and Six Toe Crack.

Note that leashed dogs are not allowed on hiking trails.

Camping

The park **campground** (reservations accepted at 800/444-7275, www.

reservecalifornia.com, mid-May-mid-Sept.; first-come, first-served Oct.-Apr.; $25, $8 reservation fee) has 76 sites. The Lower, Upper, and Little Loops are north of I-5 with access to trailheads. The 12 sites in the Riverside loop are situated along the Sacramento River and are shaded by oak and pine trees. Some sites are close to the freeway and can be loud, but others are tucked deep enough in the pines to feel miles away from civilization. Flush toilets, showers, and drinking water are available throughout the campground.

Shasta Lake

Shasta Lake's flat and glassy surface makes it the perfect destination for water sports, fishing, and houseboating. Numerous campgrounds, houseboat rentals, and caverns offer plenty of opportunities to explore and cool off on a hot summer day. Hiking trails and 4WD roads thread through the forested wilderness that surrounds the lake.

Shasta Lake has three main arms, including the McCloud, the Pit River, and the Sacramento. Most marinas, campgrounds, and services are located near the McCloud River Arm or at Jones Valley at the end of the Pit River Arm (accessible via CA-299). It takes a few hours to travel from one end of the lake to the other in a speedboat; folks tend to stick to one section of the lake to spend the day there. At the south end of the lake lies the city of Shasta Lake, with playgrounds, a skate park, baseball fields, and a BMX park.

Getting There

I-5 accesses Shasta Lake in three places. **Lakehead** is a popular fishing spot on the north end of the lake at the Sacramento River Arm. From Castle Crags and Mount Shasta, head south on I-5 for about 20 miles (32 km). About 8.5 miles (13.5 km) south of Lakehead is the exit for the **O'Brien Inlet,** a popular spot for

waterskiing and camping. This is also the exit for Lake Shasta Caverns. Continue 5 miles (8 km) south on I-5, crossing a bridge over the lake, and take exit 680 for **Bridge Bay Resort,** which houses a restaurant, a launch ramp, and houseboat rentals.

The Sacramento Arm runs parallel to I-5 on the west side, accessible near Bridge Bay and up into Lakehead. The Pit River Arm is on the east side, closer to Silverthorn and Jones Valley. The McCloud Arm runs parallel to I-5 on the east side; exit near the O'Brien Inlet and Holiday Harbor.

Sights
★ Lake Shasta Caverns

Find some natural air-conditioning inside the **Lake Shasta Caverns** (20359 Shasta Caverns Rd., Lakehead, 800/795-2283, www.lakeshastacaverns.com, tours 9am-4pm daily late May-early Sept.; 9am-3pm daily Apr.-May and Sept.; 10am, noon, 2pm daily Oct.-Mar., adults $30, children age 3-15 $18), where the cavern interior is a cool 68-72 degrees Fahrenheit. The caves were officially "discovered" in 1878 and later opened to the public as a natural attraction.

Tours and Cruises

Tours (2 hours, every 30 minutes 9am-4pm daily in summer) begin across the lake from the caverns at the Caverns Park and gift shop. When your tour is called, walk down to the boat launch and board a broad flat-bottomed ferry with plenty of bench seats and a canopy. On the quick ride across a narrow section of the lake, the pilot regales you with tales of the caverns. At the dock, board a bus for the staggeringly steep drive 800 feet up to the cavern entrance. The road has some fabulous views over the lake and all the way to Mount Shasta.

At the cave entrance, a tour guide leads you through an artificial tunnel, and then you'll climb stairs into a series of natural limestone and marble caverns. Inside,

Shasta Lake

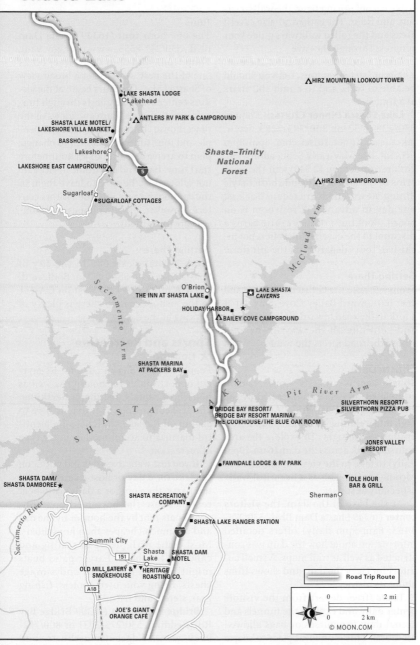

LAKE SHASTA LODGE
Lakehead

△ ANTLERS RV PARK & CAMPGROUND

SHASTA LAKE MOTEL/
LAKESHORE VILLA MARKET

▼ BASSHOLE BREWS

Lakeshore

△ LAKESHORE EAST CAMPGROUND

Sugarloaf ● SUGARLOAF COTTAGES

Shasta–Trinity
National
Forest

△ HIRZ MOUNTAIN LOOKOUT TOWER

△ HIRZ BAY CAMPGROUND

McCloud Arm

O'Brion

THE INN AT SHASTA LAKE ●

HOLIDAY HARBOR ■

□ LAKE SHASTA
CAVERNS
★

△ BAILEY COVE CAMPGROUND

Sacramento Arm

SHASTA MARINA
AT PACKERS BAY ■

S H A S T A   L A K E

Pit River Arm

SILVERTHORN RESORT/
● SILVERTHORN PIZZA PUB

BRIDGE BAY RESORT/
BRIDGE BAY RESORT MARINA/
THE COOKHOUSE/THE BLUE OAK ROOM

JONES VALLEY
■ RESORT

● FAWNDALE LODGE & RV PARK

SHASTA DAM/
SHASTA DAMBOREE ★

▼ IDLE HOUR
BAR & GRILL

Sherman ○

SHASTA RECREATION
COMPANY ■

■ SHASTA LAKE RANGER STATION

Sacramento River

Summit City ○

151

Shasta
Lake ○

SHASTA DAM
MOTEL ●

OLD MILL EATERY &
SMOKEHOUSE ▼

▼ HERITAGE
ROASTING CO.

A18

JOE'S GIANT
ORANGE CAFÉ ▼

Road Trip Route

0   2 mi

0   2 km

© MOON.COM

amazingly delicate formations of stalactites, drapes, pancakes, and ribbons of "cave bacon" spring from the walls, ceiling, and floor. The cathedral-size cavern areas and the railed walkways guide your progress through the cave.

Bring a jacket or sweater for the tour. The tour isn't strenuous, but you should be able to walk and to climb 100 stairs at a time.

Lake Shasta Dinner Cruises (2 hours, 530/238-2752 or 800/795-2283, www.lakeshastadinnercruises.com, 6pm-8pm Fri.-Sat. late May-early Sept., adults $80, children under age 12 $43) tour the main arms of the lake and include buffet-style dining. Reservations are required at least one day in advance. A restroom is on board. Booking a dinner cruise earns a discount to the caverns tour but is not inclusive. Tours depart from the gift store.

Getting There

From I-5, take the O'Brien Inlet exit and veer left toward Bailey Cove. Stay left at a fork in the road toward Holiday Harbor and continue all the way to the end, where the road meets the water.

Shasta Dam

Shasta Dam is a massive concrete dam completed in 1945 and operated by the U.S. Bureau of Reclamation. At 60 stories high and weighing 30 billion pounds, it is an impressive sight. To explore the area yourself, walk across the dam (6am-10pm daily) to take in the views of the lake and Mount Shasta. This is a beautiful walk, especially at sunset.

At the base of the dam, the **visitors center** (16349 Shasta Dam Blvd., 530/275-4463, 8am-5pm daily) offers detailed information about how the dam was constructed as well as trail maps. A small auditorium faces the dam and shows films about its history.

Tours (free) depart from the visitors center daily and explore the tunnels and actual dam (no purses or bags allowed on tours). This is an ideal place to snap a

photo of the three Shastas: Shasta Dam, Shasta Lake, and Mount Shasta.

Tours

The one-hour **tour** (16349 Shasta Dam Blvd., 530/247-8555, www.usbr.gov, 9am, 11am, 1pm, and 3pm daily, free) offers one of the best ways to get a broad view of Shasta Lake. The tours begin at the visitors center and take guests through tunnels into the actual dam and views of the powerhouse. Tours are limited to 40 people and tour times are subject to change; plan to arrive at least half an hour before start time. Bags and electronic devices are not allowed, so be sure to leave them in the car on your way into the visitors centers (however, mobile phones and cameras are permitted).

Getting There

From I-5, take exit 685 in the city of Shasta Lake onto Shasta Dam Boulevard. Drive 6 miles (9.5 km) west on CA-151 to the visitors center. There is plenty of parking at the dam.

Sports and Recreation
★ Boating

People flock to Shasta Lake for its myriad opportunities for boating as well as houseboat rentals, fishing, waterskiing, and wakeboarding. Everyone is here to get out on the lake, and there are plentiful marinas to accommodate every type of recreation.

If you just want to go out and putter on the lake for a day or host a sunset cocktail party, then opt for a daily patio boat rental. These flat-bottomed pontoon-style boats rent by the hour or by the day and are much cheaper than houseboats. Most come with plenty of seating and canopies for shade. Larger patio boats might include barbecues and storage chests. Bring your own coolers, fishing gear, stereo, and friends.

Bridge Bay Resort (10300 Bridge Bay Rd., Redding, 530/275-3021 or 800/752-9669, www.bridgebayhouseboats.com)

rents patio boats ($225 per day) and fishing boats ($100 per day).

Silverthorn Resort (16250 Silverthorn Rd., Redding, 800/332-3044, https://silverthornresort.com) rents patio boats ($230-310 per day); the deluxe boat has a 130-horsepower engine and a hardtop roof perfect for suntanning with a capacity for eight people. Silverthorn also rents aluminum fishing vessels ($75 per day, min. 4 passengers).

Many people bring their own boats to Shasta Lake (or rent one in Redding) rather than paying rent from one of the marinas. Expect to pay a small fee at any public launch ramp. Boaters must have a valid driver's license and proper equipment on board. All drivers of boats over 15 horsepower (that includes personal watercraft) must be age 16 or older. Children ages 12-15 can drive if directly supervised by an adult. All children under age 13 must wear a life jacket at all times when on board a boat. For more information about boating rules, visit www.shastalake.com.

Marinas

Shasta Lake is big and spread out. If you've got a vacation rental or a campsite on or near the lake, choose a marina near your lodgings for convenience, or stock up on groceries in Redding or the city of Mount Shasta before arriving. Most of the marinas in Shasta Lake provide watersport rentals and services.

In some years, boat launch ramps may close if the lake level is too low. (The campgrounds are generally still open.) It costs $12 per day to launch a boat from any of the Shasta Lake ramps; to pay dues, self-register near the information booths.

Shasta Marina at Packers Bay
Shasta Marina at Packers Bay (16814 Packers Bay Rd., Lakehead, 800/959-3359, www.shastalake.net) includes a mooring facility, public launch ramp, and houseboat rentals (mid-June-Nov.).

To get there from I-5 northbound, take the exit for Shasta Caverns and O'Brien Road. Drive under a bridge and then get back on I-5 south to reach the Packers Bay Road (exit 693). Drive southwest on Packers Bay Road for about 2 miles (3.2 km) to the marina.

Holiday Harbor
Holiday Harbor (20061 Shasta Caverns Rd., O'Brien, 530/238-2383 or 800/776-2628, https://lakeshasta.com) rents fishing boats, ski boats, and Sea-Doos. It is one of the only places with patio boats available. Fishing boat rentals run as little as $30 per day (25 horsepower, 4-seaters run $145). Simply designed and functional houseboats rent for an affordable price ($498-1,338 for 2 nights). Holiday Harbor is on the north end of the lake.

Bridge Bay Resort Marina
You can see **Bridge Bay Resort Marina** (10300 Bridge Bay Rd., Redding, 530/275-3021 or 800/752-9669, www.bridgebayhouseboats.com, $75-225 patio boat, $125-300 ski boat, $1,100-3,800 houseboat for 2 nights) from the big bridge on I-5. This huge marina is the largest on the lake, part of a full-scale resort that gets busy in the summer. Bridge Bay Marina has a large rental fleet, which includes small-medium houseboats, closed-bow ski and fishing boats with outboard motors, patio boats, and WaveRunners, most of which can be rented for a couple of hours up to a week. There's good fishing all year around Bridge Bay—anglers regularly tend to hook trout and bass. Fishing boat rentals start at $60 for a half day. Bridge Bay also hosts a couple of bass-fishing tournaments, some of which are televised.

It's $20 per day to launch your own boat, but you get one free launch with any room or rental. You can also moor your boat temporarily. Three docks are available: the **Gas Dock,** where you can also get ice, propane, stand-up paddleboard rentals, and pump-outs of your holding

Houseboating on Shasta Lake

Shasta Lake is "the houseboating capital of the world," and rightfully so—its fingers and coves offer days of lazy floating and relaxation. Most houseboats have sleeping accommodations for 10-18 people. The beds aren't large and private bedrooms are few, so bring a sleeping bag and camp out on the roof under the stars.

Houseboat rentals are available at a few marinas. No special boating knowledge is required to rent a houseboat, though you may be required to provide a valid driver's license. Most marina websites post photos and price lists.

Houseboats.com (833/474-2782, www.houseboats.com) operates out of Jones Valley and Silverthorn at the end of the Pit River arm of Shasta Lake. Their website includes photos and details about the houseboats available, as well as information about what to bring and a pet policy. Wherever you rent, expect to pay anywhere from $1,200 per weekend for a small minimal craft to $9,600 per weekend for a huge luxury boat. Seven-night rates, which include one weekend, are often a bargain at double or less the cost of a single weekend.

You can expect to find a fair amount of luxurious options. Many Shasta houseboats come with upper-deck hot tubs, waterslides, barbecues, satellite TV, and high-end entertainment systems. The **Shasta Marina at Packers Bay** (16814 Packers Bay Rd., Lakehead, 800/959-3359, www.shastalake.net) rents five houseboat types, ranging $1,935-7,500 ($1,935-4,200 Apr.-May and mid-Sept.-Nov., $3,600-7,500 mid-June-Labor Day, 3-night min.). Options include *The Mirage,* a 56-foot-long boat that sleeps 2-14 people and is equipped with three staterooms, two private lofts, a full-range kitchen, a six-person hot tub, a satellite TV, a swim slide, and an outdoor shower. It feels like your own private cruise ship. Renters must be age 25 or older; on Mother's Day and Memorial Day weekends, the minimum age increases to 30. There's a two-pet maximum per houseboat.

Houseboats come with some necessities; most have fully equipped kitchens, basic cleaning supplies, and plenty of toilet paper. Bring pillows, towels, sheets, paper towels, bug spray, sunscreen, inner tubes, flashlights, first-aid kits, food, and drinks. Leave water balloons, fireworks, golf clubs, and guns at home. The rental company can advise a full list of supplies.

Piloting a mammoth houseboat is a bit like driving a big RV on I-5. Take it slow and carefully follow the instructions given by the marina and you'll do fine. Most houseboaters pull their craft into small inlets and moor them for the night. Marina staff can advise how best to maneuver a houseboat safely toward shore in the evening and back out again the next morning.

Many houseboats include equipment for towing smaller watercraft behind them, allowing you to rent a ski boat, personal watercraft, or fishing boat and bring it along with you. Aye, aye, Captain!

tank; the **Load-out Dock,** for houseboat customers of Bridge Bay only; and the **Courtesy Dock,** which is open to the public and located next to the launch ramp. If you pull up and park your boat at the Courtesy Dock, it's just a short walk to a **store** (7am-7pm daily May-Aug.) where you can get groceries, bathing suits, bait and tackle, and souvenirs.

You can also walk to the marina's restaurant, **The CookHouse** (10300 Bridge Bay Rd., Redding, 530/691-7329, https://bridgebayhouseboats.com, 8am-9pm daily, late May-early Sept., $14-29), formerly known as the Tail O' the Whale. This casual establishment serves California-style breakfast, lunch, and dinner; if you're extra hungry, order the chicken-and-waffles entrée, which is served with a side of maple syrup and buffalo hot sauce. The lounge upstairs is **The Blue Oak Room.** The restaurant is attached to a **hotel** that rents rooms and suites that can sleep up to six people ($75-250).

Jones Valley

Situated on the secluded Pit River Arm, **Jones Valley Resort** (22300 Jones Valley Marina Dr., Redding, 530/275-7950 or 833/474-2782, www.houseboats.com, $1,190-7,590 for 3 nights) is one of the few year-round marinas on Shasta Lake. It is also one of the few marinas to sell gas in this part of the lake. Jones Valley Marina includes a floating recreation center with Ping-Pong, shuffleboard, and basketball, plus wheelchair-accessible docks and houseboats. Should you find yourself needing a three-deck houseboat that sleeps 22 people with eight flat-screen TVs, you can rent it here—it's called *The Titan*.

The McCloud Arm and the Squaw Creek Arm adjoin the marina, which is easily accessible from Redding and I-5.

Silverthorn

Tucked into a cove next to Jones Valley, **Silverthorn Resort** (16250 Silverthorn Rd., 800/332-3044, https://silverthorn-resort.com, $1,190-5,290 for 3 nights) has been in operation since 1853. It was named after George Silverthorn and is still going strong. It rents luxury houseboats, Sea-Doos, fishing boats, ski boats, and on-shore cabins ($100-200 per night) and has a fuel dock, grocery store, and pizza parlor and sells apparel for those chilly nights on the lake.

Waterskiing and Wakeboarding

Shasta Lake is an ideal place for watersports; even on crowded weekends, chances are good that you'll find a nice cove to yourself. Many marinas rent recreation equipment for waterskiing and wakeboarding.

Bridge Bay Resort (10300 Bridge Bay Rd., Redding, 530/275-3021 or 800/752-9669, www.bridgebayhouseboats.com) rents wakeboards ($50), ski boats

($125-300), water skis ($50 per day), and stand-up paddleboards ($25 for 2 hours, $70 per day).

Jones Valley Resort (22300 Jones Valley Marina Dr., Redding, 833/474-2782, www.houseboats.com) rents wakeboards, water skis, tubes, kayaks, and SUPs. Their wakeboard boat fleet includes a 21-foot open bow Malibu Wakesetter ($550 per day), a 22-foot Centurion Avalanche ($750 per day), and a Centurion T-5 with a wakeboard tower ($550 per day).

Silverthorn Resort (16250 Silverthorn Rd., Redding, 800/332-3044, https://silverthornresort.com, $550 daily) also rents a few wakeboard boats; each is equipped with a Bimini shade top, stereo, and a tower to get maximum pop off the wake. The wakeboard boats can be rented by the week ($3,300) with a $500 deposit.

Holiday Harbor (20061 Shasta Caverns Rd., O'Brien, 530/238-2383 or 800/776-2628, https://lakeshasta.com) has what they call the "Toy Box," filled with kneeboards, water-skis, Hyperlite wakeboards, and even a hydrofoil SkySki (also called an Air Chair) to tow behind your Ski Nautique or Crownline. Rentals range $20-45, except for the Air Chair ($75 per day).

You can put your own boat in at any number of public launches; if you don't have your own boat, most of the marinas rent speedboats or personal watercraft. Personal watercraft are mostly WaveRunners and the occasional Sea-Doo (get a Sea-Doo if you can; they're better machines), and prices run around $350 per day with full-week rates available at most marinas. Be aware that no matter which marina you work with, these high-performance rental boats aren't anything like operating a vehicle; you'll have to watch how you approach docks and the shoreline and be mindful of the prop and safety regulations. Most marinas require a hefty deposit.

Fun Factory (530/925-1465 or 530/926-5387, Weed, www.funfactoryrentals.com,

$170-650, reservations required) guides boating adventures on a 22-foot professional series Sanger wakeboard boat. They operate on the Shasta, Shastina, Siskiyou, McCloud, Whiskeytown, and Iron Gate Reservoirs. Training and boat safety are included. Water toys run from wakeboards, kneeboards, and tubes to fishing equipment.

Entertainment and Events

The main entertainment in the Shasta Lake area centers primarily on the lake itself. Most people rent a patio boat or a fishing boat and throw their own parties on the water. The major festival at Shasta Lake, the **Shasta Damboree** (City of Shasta Lake, 530/949-2759, www.shastadamboree.org, May), occurs each year in the spring. Referred to as the Boomtown Festival, this small-town celebration has been going since 1956. Activities include spaghetti feeds, a pancake breakfast, a fun run, a car show, an arts-and-crafts fair, and a parade.

One of the best places near Shasta Lake is **Basshole Brews** (formerly The Basshole, 20725 Lakeshore Dr., Lakehead, 530/962-3050, www.bassholebrews.com, 6am-midnight daily, $10-18). The bar and restaurant features a menu of locally sourced and seasonal entrées complemented by craft cocktails made with freshly squeezed fruit and house-made simple syrups. Coffee drinks include beans roasted from Heritage Roasting Co. It's off the northern Sacramento River Arm, west of I-5.

On the Jones Valley and Silverthorn side of the lake, check out the **Idle Hour Bar & Grill** (14961 Bear Mountain Rd., Redding, 530/275-0230, 11am-9pm daily, $4-9), known for ice-cold beer, bacon cheeseburgers, corn dogs, and sandwiches.

From top to bottom: Bridge Bay; Joe's Giant Orange Café; The Inn at Shasta Lake.

Food

The CookHouse (Bridge Bay Resort, 10300 Bridge Bay Rd., Redding, 530/275-3021, https://bridgebayhouseboats.com, 8am-9pm daily late May-early Sept., shorter hours Sept.-May, $14-29) offers casual dining that's perfect for lakeside vacationers. Hearty breakfasts feature Southern and California accents—avocado toast and biscuits and gravy are served along with eggs and pancakes. Lunch offers a nice selection of burgers, salads, and appetizers, such as spicy fried green beans and smoked chicken wings. Dinner runs the full range of options—from surf-and-turf and cedar-plank salmon to prime rib and chicken marsala. Seating is on the porch or inside with views of Shasta Lake through the large windows. Upstairs, **The Blue Oak Room** lounge has its own share of the view.

On the east side of the lake, the best (and only) pizza is at the **Silverthorn Pizza Pub** (Silverthorn Resort, 16250 Silverthorn Rd., Redding, 530/275-1571, www.silverthornresort.com, noon-9pm Thurs.-Mon., $6-29). This casual eatery serves piping-hot pizzas and ice-cold beer, and has a pool table plus a few big-screen TVs to watch the game. A huge deck overlooks the lake and lures people outdoors for cocktails.

In the city of Shasta Lake, you'll find a local place with a little character. The **Old Mill Eatery & Smokehouse** (4132 Shasta Dam Blvd., Shasta Lake, 530/275-0515, 7am-8pm Sun.-Thurs., 7am-9pm Fri.-Sat., $10-40) is noted for its large portions of slow-cooked fare. Breakfast is served all day, burgers are a common lunch item, and prime-rib dinners come with a salad and two sides. Enjoy it all within this friendly hometown atmosphere.

★ **Heritage Roasting Co.** (4302 Shasta Dam Blvd., 530/605-1990, 6am-6pm Mon.-Fri., 8am-6pm Sat., 8am-4pm Sun., $3-5) has a modern, comfortable vibe and is a must-visit on your way to or from the lake. Passionate baristas serve the perfect espresso drinks made with their in-house roasted beans. The house-made chai is amazing (but the Firecracker is pretty spicy). The menu includes biscuits and gravy, a hearty pesto roll topped with Havarti cheese and tomato, and affogatos made with ice cream from Redding-based Taste & See Creamery.

Perfect for breakfast, **Joe's Giant Orange Café** (3104 Cascade Blvd., Shasta Lake, 530/275-9582, 6am-8pm Mon.-Sat., 6am-2:30pm Sun., $13-16) stemmed from a giant orange juice stand built in the 1950s on what used to be old Route 99. Decades later, the giant orange frame still stands and the café that was built around it serves one of the most delicious orange smoothies you'll ever try. Mexican dinner entrées are also served six days a week.

The **Lakeshore Villa Market** (20750 Lakeshore Dr., Lakehead, 530/238-8615, 7am-8pm daily Oct.-mid-May; 7am-9pm Sun.-Thurs.-Sat. late May-early Sept.) is a full-service grocery store that rents movie and sells souvenirs, clothing, and basic camping, fishing, and outdoor recreation supplies. Located at the north end of the lake, the market often stays open until 10pm in summer, as business permits.

Accommodations

If accommodations don't work out for you at Shasta Lake, then Redding (15 mi/24 km south of Bridge Bay Resort on I-5) is your best bet on finding a hotel.

Lakehead's cutest motel is the cozy **Lake Shasta Lodge** (21417 Main St., Lakehead, 530/238-9688, www.lakeshastalodge.com, $72-99 summer, $60-85 winter). The 11 small but adequate rooms come with free wireless Internet access. Amenities include a rec room with a flat-screen TV and pool table, laundry services, and a large parking lot perfect for boats and trailers. It's a cheerful oasis located in a quiet woodsy area that has the advantage of being very close to the lake.

Located on the Sacramento River Arm, the **Sugarloaf Cottages** (19667 Lakeshore Dr., Lakehead, 530/238-2448, http://

shastacabins.com, $1,365-3,080 per week late May-early Sept., $910-1,890 in winter) offer a comfortable resort-like feel with access to the lake. Wood-accented cabins include air-conditioning and free Internet access and include boat moorage. An outdoor swimming pool is within a short walk.

One of Shasta Lake's newest lodging spots is ★ **The Inn at Shasta Lake** (18026 O'Brien Inlet Rd., Lakehead, 530/863-7645, http://theinnatshastalake.com). The 11 rooms and cottages are named after the birds and animals that populate the area and feature modern amenities like gas fireplaces, patios, or balconies. A three-course breakfast is included, as is free Internet access and parking for guests. Some rooms are pet-friendly. Children under age 12 are not permitted. Located in the Shasta-Trinity National Forest, the inn provides quick access to Shasta Lake, Burney Fall, and Lassen.

If your main purpose is to visit Shasta Dam, crash for the night at the **Shasta Dam Motel** (1529 Cascade Blvd., Shasta Lake, 530/275-1065, www.shastadammotel.com, $65-70). Located 4 miles (6.4 km) from the dam, this simple motel may be light on amenities, but it has an outdoor pool and is surrounded by old-growth oak trees. Free Internet access is available. Pets are permitted with advance notice.

Located along I-5, the **Fawndale Lodge & RV Park** (15215 Fawndale Rd., 530/275-8000, $80-120 winter, $100-145 summer) offers comfortable lodge rooms and two-room suites (with kitchen) at bargain prices. Rooms come with a fridge, a microwave, and private bath; suites sleep six and include full kitchens and air-conditioning. Tent campers ($18-21) are welcome, as are RVers ($30, full-hookup). Book a reservation to guarantee a spot. While you can't see the lake from the lodge, the surrounding forest is charming and the premises hold a garden and a swimming pool.

At the north end of the lake, **Shasta Lake Motel** (20714 Lakeshore Dr., Lakehead, 530/238-2545 or 886/355-8189, www.shastalakemotel.com, $55-150) is a favorite for regular visitors. Rooms glow with wood-paneled walls and furniture and are decorated with rustic prints. Amenities include air-conditioning, DirecTV, mini-fridges, and microwaves. As a bonus, twins and double beds come extra-long, so they fit folks over six feet tall. Enjoy the on-site pool or walk to the lakeshore. The motel is close to I-5, but not so near that you'll hear trucks all night.

Bridge Bay Resort (10300 Bridge Bay Rd., Redding, 530/275-3021 or 800/752-9669, www.bridgebayhouseboats.com, $75-250) has one of the best locations in the area: It's close to both I-5 and the center of the lake's arms and it has a full-service marina. Rooms are simple and clean, furnished in green, blue, and white shades that accent the lake. Bridge Bay includes a restaurant and a store for groceries, souvenirs, SUP rentals, bait, and tackle.

Located on the tip of a small peninsula in the Pit River Arm, **Silverthorn Resort** (16250 Silverthorn Rd., Redding, 530/275-1571 or 800/332-3044, www.silverthornresort.com, $99-150 per night, $594-1,194 per week only in summer, 3-day minimum year-round) has the advantage of being right on the water. Accommodations are in simple but attractive cabins with wood-paneled interiors and a lodge-style decor. All cabins include small bedrooms, a full kitchen with a full-size fridge, and phenomenal views; most cabins sleep 4-6 people (the large family cabin can handle 8 people). The resort has a full-service marina and rents houseboats. Book a boat rental when reserving your cabin. A small grocery store and a pizza pub offer easy on-site dining.

Camping

The U.S. Forest Service rents the **Hirz Mountain Lookout Tower** (530/275-8113, reservations at 877/444-6777, www.rec-reation.gov, May-mid-Oct., $75 for up to 4 people). Located in the Shasta-Trinity National Forest, this 20-foot tower is set atop a 3,521-foot peak with phenomenal views of the McCloud Arm of Shasta Lake, Mount Lassen, and Mount Shasta. The tower comes with two twin beds, cabinets, and cleaning supplies. A picnic table is located below and a vault toilet is nearby. There is no drinking water (bring your own) and garbage must be packed out. Bring everything you need for a stay here, including bedding, flashlights, and a campfire permit for operating cooking stoves.

Getting here is a little tricky; four-wheel-drive is best for navigating the steep and mountainous terrain. Take I-5 to Gilman Road (exit 698) and follow Gilman Road for 5 miles (8 km) to Forest Road 35N04 (a dirt road). Turn left onto Forest Road 35N04 and continue 5 steep and rocky miles to a locked gate. Park and walk the last 0.25 mile to the tower.

For more traditional camping, one of the best places is **Hirz Bay Campground** (Gilman Rd., 530/275-1587, www.fs.usda.gov, reservations accepted at 877/444-6777 or www.recreation.gov mid-May-mid-Sept., first-come, first-served mid-Sept.-mid-May, $20-35). This U.S. Forest Service campground has 42 sites with picnic tables, paved parking, and flush toilets. It also offers easy access to the lake via the Hirz Bay boat ramp. Hirz Bay is 20 miles (32 km) northeast of Redding off I-5.

Antlers RV Park & Campground (20682 Antlers Rd., Lakehead, 800/238-3924, www.antlersrvpark.com, 8am-7pm daily late May-early Sept., 8am-4:30pm Mon.-Fri. Sept.-May, $21-35 tents, $30-50 RVs) has 116 tent and RV sites set next to the Sacramento Arm of Shasta Lake. Tent sites sleep up to two people ($6 per guest over age of 5) and pets are welcome ($2 per night up to two). There's a pool, a convenience store, a Wi-Fi hot spot, and hot showers, with a pancake breakfast

on Sunday. Rent a boat slip or watercraft next door at Antlers Resort.

Nestled between the Lakeshore Inn and Sugarloaf Cottages on the upper end of the Sacramento Arm, **Lakeshore East Campground** (Lakeshore Dr., Lakehead, reservations accepted at 877/444-6777 or www.recreation.gov May-Sept., first-come, first-served Sept.-May, $23-46 tents, $65 yurts) has 23 tent sites plus a couple of weatherproofed yurts. Blackberry bushes, pine trees, and oaks provide privacy between sites. Sugar Loaf and Antlers boat ramps are nearby.

Bailey Cove Campground (Shasta Caverns Rd., 877/444-6777, www.recreation.gov, first-come, first-served, open year-round, $23-46) is perfect for anglers, hikers, birders, and water sports enthusiasts. The tiny, protected inlet offers pretty smooth water most of the time and there's a boat launch ramp. This small campground has seven tent and RV sites. The Bailey Cove Trail enters the trees while still hugging the shoreline, where it's common to see ospreys, deer, and maybe a bald eagle. The campground is off I-5. Take exit 695 toward the Shasta Caverns dock and veer right toward the lake.

Information and Services

The **Shasta Recreation Company** (14538 Wonderland Blvd., Shasta Lake, 530/275-8113, www.shastatrinitycamping.com, 8am-4:30pm Mon.-Fri.) is a U.S. Forest Service facility that provides information and can book campgrounds in the Shasta, Trinity, and Lewiston Lake areas.

The **Shasta Lake Ranger Station** (14225 Holiday Rd., 530/275-1589, www.fs.usda.gov, 8am-4:30pm Mon.-Fri. year-round) issues campfire permits and passes into the Trinity Alps Wilderness. For Shasta Wilderness backcountry camping, visit the **Mount Shasta Ranger Station** (204 W. Alma St., 530/926-4511, www.fs.usda.gov, 8am-4:30pm Mon.-Fri.). The nearest major medical facilities are in Redding.

Seasonal Events

Spring

In April, classic car lovers come to Redding for **Kool April Nites,** where they can cruise the strip, admire antique vehicles, and reminisce about the good ol' days.

In May, Shasta Lake hosts the **Shasta Damboree,** a fun community get-together that celebrates Shasta's boom era and recognizes local citizens with parades, a pancake breakfast, and live music.

Summer

The Sacramento River flows through Redding, offering visitors a cool body of water on a hot summer day. In early June, the **Sundial Splash** event celebrates the community of rafters and paddlers with a group float from the Sundial Bridge through downtown Redding.

In early July, Chester celebrates America's independence with fireworks displays over the water at **Lake Almanor**.

Fall

In October, the **Historic Hawes Farm** in Anderson offers a pumpkin patch, corn maze, roller coasters, and loads of family-friendly activities for the Halloween season. Wild turkeys are often seen near the shore of the Sacramento River on the Hawes property. Get in shape for Thanksgiving with a jog in the annual **Redding Turkey Trot,** held on Thanksgiving morning.

Winter

Mt. Shasta Ski Park opens after the snow starts falling, usually in December. Hit the slopes or go tubing, then hang out in the lodge, where you can gaze up at the towering mountain.

Redding

Redding (pop. 90,000) is a large city north of Sacramento that serves as the gateway to the Shasta and Lassen region. Its proximity to the Sacramento River, Shasta Lake, Whiskeytown, and Mount Shasta makes it a great place if you're into the outdoors, plus it has all the amenities you need—gas stations, restaurants, and shopping malls are easily accessible off I-5. Popular sights include the Turtle Bay Exploration Park, the Sundial Bridge, and even an aqua golf driving range.

Getting There

Redding is on I-5 about 160 miles (255 km) north of Sacramento. From Sacramento, simply follow I-5 north.

Sights
★ Sundial Bridge

Designed by sculptor and structural engineer Santiago Calatrava, the **Sundial Bridge** (844 Sundial Bridge Dr., 530/243-8850, www.turtlebay.org/sundial-bridge, open 24 hours, free) was built in 2004 to connect the Turtle Bay Exploration Park to the Sacramento River Trail. At one end of the gorgeous, white, cable-stayed bridge is a 217-foot-tall pylon that acts as a working sundial, visually tracking the time from 11am to 3pm on sunny days. The 700-foot-long bridge is open to pedestrians and bicyclists, who travel its length across the emerald-green glass floor. The bridge also makes for a romantic walk when it's lit at night.

Park at the Turtle Bay Exploration Park to walk across the bridge; there are plazas situated at either end. In summer, the Lions Club puts on the Sundial

Redding

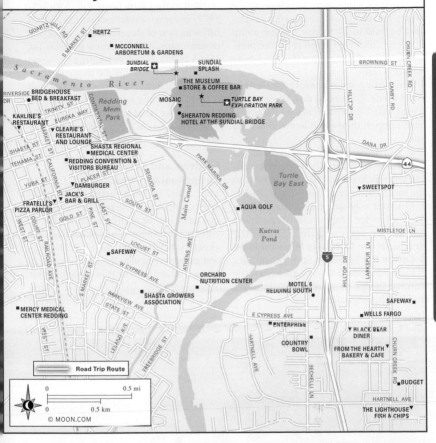

Splash, when people paddle rafts, kayaks, or SUP on the river through downtown Redding. The event begins at a launch ramp close to the bridge. The 6-mile float offers great views of Mount Shasta to the north and Mt. Lassen to the east.

★ Turtle Bay Exploration Park

The **Turtle Bay Exploration Park** complex (844 Sundial Bridge Dr., 530/243-8850, www.turtlebay.org, 9am-5pm daily summer, 9am-4pm Wed.-Fri., 10am-4pm Sat.-Sun. winter, $16 adults, $12 ages 4-15 and seniors) houses 34,000 square feet of fun, including a museum, forestry and wildlife exhibits, and botanical gardens (7am-7pm daily).

Walk across the lovely wooden bridge into **Paul Bunyan's Forest Camp,** which has a playground for kids, an aviary, the Mill Building, a steam engine, animal shows at the Forest Amphitheatre, and a seasonal butterfly exhibit. Say hello to the magpies, barn owl, porcupine, skunk, and the red-tailed hawk eyeing you suspiciously from the Forest Camp exhibits.

The **Parrot Playhouse** (9:30am-4pm Wed.-Fri., 10:30am-4pm Sat.-Sun.

Sept.-Apr.; 9:30am-5pm Mon.-Fri., 10:30am-5pm Sat.-Sun. May-Aug.) is the highlight of Turtle Bay. This interactive aviary is home to colorful lorikeets who aren't afraid to fly to you and eat a cup of nectar from your hand ($1). The playhouse closes 11:45am-1pm daily to let the lorikeets rest.

The turtle pond is home to the western pond turtle. On a good day, these small, friendly dark-green and black turtles will even jump in their pond to swim over to you.

A visit here is a delightful way to spend an afternoon, especially if you're traveling with little ones. The park is next to the south entrance of the Sundial Bridge.

On your way out, grab a Turtle Bliss caramel coffee Frappuccino-type drink and locally made Off the Farm nutrition bar at the **Turtle Bay Museum Store & Coffee Bar** (8:30am-5pm Mon.-Sat., 9:30am-5pm Sun.). Then walk across the Sundial Bridge to access the arboretum and botanical gardens.

Entertainment and Events

Feeling lucky? **Win-River Resort & Casino** (2100 Redding Rancheria Rd., 530/243-3377, www.winrivercasino.com) has a full selection of slot machines, blackjack tables, craps, and an arena popular for MMA fights. If you're looking for some nightlife, this is the place to go. On-site dining options include the CreekSide Pub & Grill, Overtime Lounge, and Elements, plus there's a hotel and RV park for folks who have too much fun and want to stay the night.

Festivals and Events

During **Kool April Nites** (1666 E. Cypress Ave., 530/226-0844, https://koolapril-nites.com, Apr.), classic car enthusiasts show off (or admire) a collection of vintage American vehicles at different locations throughout the city. The biggest gathering is usually at the Saturday "show and shine" event in a parking lot (next to the Civic Auditorium and Viking Skate Country). The Friday evening prior,

Sundial Bridge

classic cars slowly cruise Hilltop Drive in a longstanding tradition, waving to bystanders on the side of the road.

The **Historic Hawes Farm** (21923 Dersch Rd., Anderson, 530/365-8488, www.historichawesfarms.com, Oct.) was started in 1863 by ambitious gold prospector William Hawes, who came here looking for gold but ended up with a lot of land in a town called Anderson instead. Six generations later, the farm remains in the hands of great-great-grandson Greg Hawes. In addition to acres of wheat, walnuts, and vegetables, the farm has a huge pumpkin patch and hosts an intricate corn maze during the month of October. Roller coasters, a goat walk, a dance floor, bumper cars, go-carts, a pumpkin shooter, a cow train, playgrounds, and plenty of other attractions delight families come autumn.

The **Sundial Splash** (840 Sundial Bridge Pkwy., Redding, www.sundialsplash.com, a weekend day in June) kicks off summer with a group float

down the Sacramento River. Floating the river is a longstanding tradition with locals, especially during hot summers. Every year, people bring their rafts, SUPs, kayaks, and blow-up floats to laze under the Sundial Bridge. Floaters travel 6 miles throughout downtown Redding, ending at a river access point on South Bonneyview Drive. There's a SUP and kayak race before the group float.

On Thanksgiving morning, friends and family gather at Caldwell Park (58 Quartz Hill Rd., 530/225-4095) to participate in the annual 5K **Redding Turkey Trot** (late Nov.) fun run.

Recreation

Located near the Sacramento River Trail, **Caldwell Park** (58 Quartz Hill Rd., 530/225-4095, free) is a great place to play basketball, catch a baseball game, or ride the bowls at the skate park. It also accesses a network of paved (and unpaved) paths on the Sacramento River Trail.

For an easy, half-day stroll, follow the **Sundial Bridge** to **Stress Ribbon Bridge** (4.5 mi/7.2 km, 2-4 hours, easy), passing through Caldwell Park and the Diestelhorst Bridge on the north side of the river. It's paved, easy, and flat, which also makes it popular for bicycles. Enjoy great views of the Sacramento River along the way.

Aqua Golf (2275 Park Marina Dr., 530/244-4653, 10am-5pm daily winter, 10am-8pm daily, $7-12) has 20 stalls on a "driving range" that faces out over the Sacramento River. Hit a bucket of balls as far as you can out into the river. Markers in the water indicate how far the ball makes a splash. This activity is fun for the whole family and is a unique way to enjoy the river.

WaterWorks Park (151 N. Boulder Dr., 530/246-9550, www.waterworkspark. com, 10am-6pm daily late May-early Sept., $23-27) is haven on hot 100-degree days. The water park offers fun for kids of all ages. The extreme Avalanche water slide, the Cyclone, and the enclosed pitch-black tube appeal to those with a low fear level. The Lazy Lagoon is mellower, as it slowly carries you past a small waterfall in a tropical atmosphere. After splashing around in the Cowabunga Beach wave pool, relax in a cabana with an ice-cold drink.

Country Bowl (2615 Bechelli Ln., 530/223-1080, www.countrybowl.com, 11am-11pm Mon., 9am-11pm Tues.-Thurs. and Sun., 9am-midnight Fri.-Sat., $4 pp/game, $3 shoes) is a 16-lane bowling alley in the center of town. The owners are friendly and games are fairly cheap.

Sacramento River Trail

Across the Sacramento River from the Turtle Bay Exploration Park, the **Sacramento River Trail** (844 Sundial Bridge Dr., Redding, www.visitredding.com) spans 11-18 miles (18-29 km) from the Sundial Bridge to Shasta Dam. To start, head north across the Sundial Bridge, then turn left to walk through the **McConnell Arboretum & Gardens** (840 Sundial Bridge Dr., 530/243-8850, 9am-5pm daily, free). This garden is lovely in spring when brightly colored irises and clusters of daisies are in full bloom.

Continue west on the Sacramento River Trail to walk across the concrete **Diestelhorst Bridge** (2 mi/3.2 km west of the Sundial Bridge). Built in 1914 to permit vehicles to cross the Sacramento River into Redding, this thruway was in use until 1997, when it was replaced by the Lake Redding Bridge. The wide paved Diestelhorst remains open to pedestrians, cyclists, and skateboarders and parallels a patina-covered train track.

Water Sports

Headwaters Adventure Company (930 Merchant St. #1, 530/223-2411, https://headwatersadventure.com, 10am-5pm Tues.-Sat.) rents single and tandem kayaks for a half day ($30-50), full day ($50-65), or two days ($90-115). They also rent stand-up paddleboards ($50-65/half day).

This outdoor adventure shop also hosts four-hour intro to paddleboarding classes on Whiskeytown Lake ($80-125).

North Country Raft Rental (Sundial Bridge Dr. at Turtle Bay, 530/244-4281, https://raftredding.com, 9am-9pm daily late May-early Sept., $29 for 2 hours, $100 all day) is a popular place to rent gear to float the Sacramento River and also offers affordable guided trips. Paddles, life jackets, and pumps are available to rent; rates include a shuttle service and a safety clinic.

Food

Bakeries and Cafés

From the Hearth Bakery & Cafe (1292 College View Dr., 530/424-2233, www.fthcafe.com, 7am-8pm Mon.-Sat., 7am-6pm Sun., $9-11) sells homemade sourdough bread, chocolate croissants, and other baked goods as well as smoothies, sandwiches, rice bowls, omelets, and even New Orleans Chicory Cold Brew. From the Hearth has other locations (2650 Churn Creek Rd.; 1427 Market St.) with the same hours and yummy menu.

★ **Sweetspot** (1675 Hilltop Dr., 530/226-8086, 9am-9:30pm Sun.-Thurs., 9am-10pm Fri., $5-15) serves eclectic sweet treats that taste as good as they look: the best cupcakes, a gratifying gelato, and melt-in-your-mouth chocolate mousse that comes in travel-friendly Mason jars. There's also a separate room with a beer and wine bar. The shop hosts special ramen noodle nights (Wed.-Sat.) and is an ideal place to throw a party or special event. Who doesn't love celebrating a special occasion in a room full of cupcakes?

American

Bartels Giant Burger (75 Lake Blvd. E., 530/243-7313, www.bartelsgiantburger.com, 10am-8pm Mon.-Wed., 10am-9pm Thurs.-Sat., 11:30am-8pm Sun., $5-7) has been flipping patties in the Redding/Corning area since 1975. The simple menu includes burgers (cooked well-done), hot dogs, milkshakes, and mochas. Dress up your burger with cheese and an Ortega chili (extra fee); pickles and ketchup are available by request. Bartels is one of the hosting locations for Kool April Nites.

Around since 1938, the **Damburger** (1320 Placer St., 530/241-0136, www.damburger.net, 9am-5pm Mon.-Fri., 10am-3pm Sat., 11am-3pm Sun., $4-10) is always pretty busy—probably because it's well known that they serve the best burgers close to a dam site. Along with great burgers, Damburger serves hot dogs, milk shakes, and soft-serve ice cream, as well as vegetarian options. Midweek deals include the Single Dam Deal ($8.50) and the Double Dam Deal ($9.75), which include a burger, small order of fries, and a soft drink.

At the **Black Bear Diner** (2605 Hilltop Dr., 530/221-7600, www.blackbeardiner.com, 6am-10pm Sun.-Thurs., 6am-11pm Fri.-Sat., $13-18) you'll find large portions of classic American dishes, including standard breakfast options, salads, sandwiches, and chicken entrées. This Northern California chain began in the mountains nearby and now has more than 120 locations along the West Coast. Breakfast is served all day, as are the thick, ice-cream milk shakes (try the huckleberry). Service is friendly, but it can get crowded on weekends. To get there, take the Cypress Avenue exit off I-5 and proceed to Hilltop Drive.

Italian
Karline's Restaurant (1100 Center St., 530/244-7663, www.karlinesrestaurant.com, 4pm-9pm Sun.-Thurs., 4pm-10pm Fri.-Sat., $13-33) serves Italian favorites such as osso bucco and pasta, as well as pizzas and cioppino. The roasted-beet salad is perfect for those who want something light yet flavorful.

In the heart of downtown, **Fratelli's**

From top to bottom: Turtle Bay Exploration Park; Historic Hawes Farm; Sweetspot.

Pizza Parlor (1774 California St., 530/244-4121, 11am-10pm Sun.-Thurs., 11am-midnight Fri.-Sat., $21-29) features fabulous pizzas in 14- and 20-inch rounds. Try the Broadway, a thin-crust pizza topped with artichokes, white sauce, garlic, and chicken. There's also a full salad bar, craft beers, a couple of pinball machines, and all-around good vibes.

Steak and Seafood

Fancy restaurants are hard to come by in Redding, but a couple fill the void. After a day outdoors, sometimes you just need a big ol' steak. ★ **Jack's Bar & Grill** (1743 California St., 530/241-9705, www.jacks-grillredding.com, 4pm-10pm Mon.-Sat., $19-45) is a locally owned favorite that has been serving steaks since 1938. The somewhat drab exterior does little to indicate the friendly ambiance and delicious steaks inside. Plates include the New York steak, filet mignon, and deep-fried ocean scallops, all served with garlic bread, soup or salad, and a baked potato or fries. All salad dressings are made in-house; the tossed salad with French dressing is to die for. Jack's also has a full bar that serves beer, wine, and cocktails.

With roomy booths and a slick decor, **Clearie's Restaurant and Lounge** (1325 Eureka Way, 530/241-4535, http://clear-iesrestaurant.com, 11am-9pm Mon.-Thurs., 11am-10pm Fri.-Sat., $18-85) is a throwback to the swanky eateries of the 1950s and '60s. They offer a mix of classic steaks and sweetbreads along with contemporary dishes. A full bar serves strong mixed cocktails. The standard American fare includes steaks, seafood, and chicken entrées as well as specialty dishes such as abalone ($85). The lounge offers affordable menu options with a weekday happy hour (3-6pm) and is open late Friday and Saturday evenings. Try the blackberry lavender or Georgia peach smokin' martini—it is literally served with smoke pouring out of it.

The Lighthouse Fish & Chips (1109 Hartnell Ave., 530/223-9200, http://the-lighthousefishandchips.com, 11am-9pm Sat.-Thurs., 11am-10pm Fri., $8-17) is known for fish-and-chips baskets that hit the spot. They also serve salads, chicken, seafood baskets, and clam chowder in a bread bowl. The Lighthouse Platter ($15) has a bit of everything for seafood lovers, including fish, shrimp, clam strips, and calamari. Plus, they deliver.

Markets

For campers in Lassen, Mount Shasta, or on Shasta Lake, the cheapest grocery options are in Redding. For a good selection, head to one of two **Safeways** (www.safeway.com, 2275 Pine St., 530/247-3030, 6am-midnight daily; 1070 E. Cypress Ave., 530/226-5871, 24 hours daily). To stock up for a multiday houseboat trip, stop at **Costco** (1300 Dana Dr., 530/222-0199, www.costco.com, 10am-8:30pm Mon.-Fri., 9:30am-6pm Sat., 10am-6pm Sun., membership required).

For local meat and produce, go to **Kent's Meats** (8080 Airport Rd., 530/365-4322, www.kentsmeats.com, 6am-10pm daily). Kent's makes the best tri-tip steaks and salsa (it's homemade by Kent's wife, Kathy), plus they are the nicest owners you could ever meet. The store also hosts classic car shows through the year, including the big one held during Kool April Nites.

Orchard Nutrition Center (221 Locust St., 530/244-9141, www.orchardnutrition.com, 7am-9pm daily) sells a huge array of local produce, essential oils, vitamins, tea, local wine, and a wide variety of flour and nuts. In summer, the **Shasta Growers Association** (behind Redding City Hall, 777 Cypress Ave., 530/226-7100, www.shastagrowersassociation.com, Apr.-Sept.) hosts local farmers markets at locations all over Redding; check their website for details on days and locations.

Accommodations
Under $100
The **Motel 6 Redding South** (2385

Bechelli Ln., 530/221-0562, www.motel6. com, $66-75) is one of the best Motel 6's anywhere, with clean, brightly painted rooms, a clean bath, and a comfortable bed for the night. The outdoor pool is totally swimmable. This location is in a better part of town than the other two Motel 6 options in Redding.

One tier up in the hierarchy of chain motels, the **Travelodge by Wyndham** (540 N. Market St., 530/243-5291, reservations 800/525-4055, www.wyndhamhotels. com/travelodge, $80-100) offers a few more amenities for a little more money. Rooms have queen or king beds, cream comforters with decorative bed runners, dark carpets, and plenty of space; some rooms include fridges, and all have free high-speed Wi-Fi. Take a dip in the heated outdoor pool or soak in the indoor whirlpool tub (year-round). A free continental breakfast is included. The hotel is close to Turtle Bay and WaterWorks Park.

$100-150

The **Bridgehouse Bed & Breakfast** (1455 Riverside Dr., 530/247-7177, www.bridgehousebb.com, $119-189) is a lovely little yellow house with a steeply pitched roof set along the Sacramento River. Inside this tranquil haven are four rooms, each named after the main streets in Redding. The California Street room has an incredible view of the Sacramento River. The two largest rooms boast upscale bathtubs (one is made of handcrafted copper; the other has air jets). All rooms come with TVs, spa bathrobes, and lots of amenities. The Bridgehouse offers a quiet retreat for couples; small children are not recommended. There are four additional rooms next door in the **Puente,** owned by the same innkeepers. The Bridgehouse is just a few blocks from historical downtown Redding.

Set on the banks of the Sacramento River, ★ **Gaia Hotel and Spa** (4125 Riverside Pl., 530/365-7077, www.gaiahotelspa.com, $104-165) is a boutique hotel. The spacious rooms are furnished in beige and brown undertones and include deluxe king suites and guest rooms with two queen beds. The eco-friendly establishment is powered by solar panels and has energy-conserving shower heads along with luxurious Gilchrist & Soames bath essentials. Plentiful foliage separates the river from the hotel; request the bungalow room for a peek of the rushing river. The hotel is right off of I-5 between Anderson and Redding.

★ **Sheraton Redding Hotel at the Sundial Bridge** (820 Sundial Bridge Dr., 530/364-2800, www.marriott.com, $150-420) is a beautiful LEED-certified building close to the attractions of downtown Redding. Rooms face the civic center, exploration park, or the swimming pool and feature modern amenities such as a working desk, iPod docks, Netflix, free Wi-Fi, and plentiful USB outlets. There's also a 24-hour fitness center and year-round heated outdoor swimming pool for guest use.

On-site dining is at the **Mosaic** (826 Sundial Bridge Dr., 530/319-3456, www. mosaicredding.com, 6:30am-9:30pm Sun.-Thurs., 6:30am-10:30pm Fri.-Sat., $9-14 breakfast, $10-17 lunch, $22-38 dinner), a high-end restaurant serving California fare with a twist.

The pet-friendly hotel offers guests private entrance into Turtle Bay Exploration Park, with live-animal exhibitions in the lobby (Fri.-Sat. afternoons). It's conveniently located close to Redding's civic center, the Sundial Bridge, and the Turtle Bay Exploration Park. You can park and leave the car without missing out on Redding's popular sights and attractions.

Win-River Resort & Casino (2100 Redding Rancheria Rd., 530/243-3377, www.winrivercasino.com, $139-269) has 84 rooms in a three-story hotel. Rooms feature deluxe king and queen beds with cozy pillow-top mattresses, mini-fridges, and Wi-Fi. On-site dining options include CreekSide Pub & Grill, Overtime Lounge, and Elements. Win-River also has an adjoining RV park with 13 spaces, full hookups, and 24-hour security. The casino is off CA-273 on the south end of Redding.

Information and Services

For visitors planning to camp at Shasta Lake or Mount Lassen, Redding is the last outpost of civilization before trekking to the more remote reaches of the state. The **Redding Convention & Visitors Bureau** (1448 Pine St., 530/225-4100 or 530/365-1800, www.visitredding.com, 8am-5pm Mon.-Fri.) in downtown Redding is a good first stop for maps and information. It's close to CA-299 en route to Whiskeytown Lake and the coast.

The **California Welcome Center** (1699 Hwy. 273, Anderson, 530/365-1180, www. visitredding.com, 9am-5pm Mon.-Fri., 10am-4pm Sat.-Sun.) staffs a friendly front desk that will provide you with maps and information. The convenient location is close to the Shasta Outlets shopping center south of Redding off I-5.

Redding is the best place to find ATMs and a bank branch. **Bank of America** (1300 Hilltop Dr., 530/226-6172, www. bankofamerica.com, 9am-5pm Mon.-Fri., 9am-1pm Sat.) and **Wells Fargo** (830 E. Cypress Ave., 530/221-6835, 9am-6pm Mon.-Sat.) are near I-5 for easy access. There are also branches in downtown Redding.

Redding has the only major medical services available in the Shasta-Lassen region. **Mercy Medical Center Redding** (2175 Rosaline Ave., 530/225-6000, www. redding.mercy.org) has a 24-hour emergency room with a full trauma center. **Shasta Regional Medical Center** (1100 Butte St., 530/244-5400 or 866/800-2987, www.shastaregional.com) has a 24-hour emergency department.

Getting Around

The **Redding Municipal Airport** (RDD, 6751 Woodrum Circle, 530/224-4320, http://ci.redding.ca.us) offers flights on United Express, which runs multiple daily nonstop trips from San Francisco. Flying in and out of the small airport isn't cheap, but ticketing and security lines are short.

Most visitors will need a car to explore farther. Outside of nearby airports, the best opportunities to rent a car are in Redding at **Hertz** (773 N. Market St., 530/241-2257, 7:30am-5:30pm Mon.-Fri.; 6751 Woodrum Circle in the airport, 530/221-4620, www.hertz.com, $650-1,200 per week) and **Budget** (2945 Churn Creek Rd., 530/225-8652; 6751 Woodrum Circle, 530/722-9122, www. budget.com, $225-480 per week). **Avis** (6751 Woodrum Circle, 530/221-2855, www.avis.com, $210-465 per week) has an office at the airport and shares the Churn Creek Road location with Budget. **Enterprise** (225 E. Cypress Ave., 530/223-0700, www.enterprise.com, $224-1055 per week) has a full range of cars in stock and premium SUVs. With advance notice, they can often accommodate special requests for luxury cars and cargo vans.

◆ CA-299

CA-299 leads west from Redding into the rolling hills, with plentiful stops for hidden lakes and mountainous exploration. The route is subject to closures in spring and summer. Check conditions with CalTrans (800/427-7623) before starting the drive.

Whiskeytown

Whiskeytown is a national recreation area comprising 39,000 acres of wilderness for hiking, biking, and water sports. In 2018, the Carr Fire burned 98 percent of the forest in this area and displaced wildlife. The landscape is rejuvenating quickly, providing researchers an opportunity to study the area in order to prevent further wildfires.

Getting There

Whiskeytown is 10 miles (16 km) west of Redding on CA-299. From downtown

Redding, head west on CA-299/Eureka Way for 8 miles (13 km). There are gas stations at the west end of town and it's a good idea to fill up your tank.

In about 7 miles (11.5 km), turn left on J. F. Kennedy Memorial Road to reach the visitors center. A half mile down the road, check out the **Glory Hole Spillway,** a 24-foot-wide opening that diverts water from the Trinity River over to the Sacramento River.

Visitors Center

Exhibits at the **Whiskeytown Visitors Center** (Hwy. 299 and J. F. Kennedy Memorial Dr., 530/246-1225, www.nps.gov/whis, 10am-4pm daily, $10 per vehicle) illuminate the area's history. The visitors center sells fun souvenirs and offers interesting facts about the local wildlife. It's also a good place to get maps, advice, and information about camping, hiking, and tours in the park.

Whiskeytown Lake

Whiskeytown Lake is the centerpiece of this delightfully uncrowded outdoor playground. The lake, formed by the Whiskeytown Dam on Clear Creek, has 36 miles of shoreline and is an underwater haven for fish and scuba divers who plunge beneath the 3,200-acre surface area. The lake is stocked with rainbow and brown trout; largemouth, smallmouth, and spotted bass; and kokanee salmon. Bald eagles nest and breed nearby. Personal watercraft are prohibited on the lake, but almost every other kind of water activity is encouraged—kayak, canoe, swim, sail, water-ski, fish, or paddleboard.

Recreation

About a mile south of the visitors center, **East Beach** (J. F. Kennedy Memorial Dr.) has a modest parking lot with about 30 spaces on the south end of the lake; the lot tends to fill quickly on weekends. Navigate a wooden staircase (with 100 steps) to reach a nice wide and sandy beach with a dedicated swimming area, restrooms, and a few picnic tables.

Starting at the visitors center, the **Shasta Divide Nature Trail** (0.4 mile round-trip, easy) is a walkable loop perched above the lake with an incredible view of the striking blue water and surrounding greenery.

The **Whiskey Creek Group Picnic Area** (Whiskey Creek Rd., 530/242-3412) has a boat launch and ramp with several wide lanes, making it easy to load skis, wakeboards, and fishing boats. A small launch fee is required; pay at the information kiosk in the parking lot. To get there, drive west on CA-299, cross the bridge, and turn right onto Whiskey Creek Road.

Weaverville

Weaverville is listed on the National Register of Historic Places. This sparsely populated area has a smattering of gas stations, restaurants, and local amenities for exploring the nearby Trinity Alps.

Getting There

From Whiskeytown, head west on CA 299 for 35 miles (56 km). Parts of CA-299 may close due to landslides or construction; contact the **California Department of Transportation** (800/427-7623, www.dot.ca.gov) for updated road conditions.

Weaverville Joss House State Historic Park

Weaverville Joss House State Historic Park (Hwy. 299 and Oregon St., 530/623-5284, www.parks.ca.gov, 10am-5pm Thurs.-Sun., adults $4, ages 6-17 $2) has been part of California's state park system since 1956, but the temple it preserves and celebrates has been around much longer. The Temple of the Forest Beneath the Clouds, also known as Joss House, is California's oldest Chinese temple in continual use. A Taoist house of worship, it is now a museum as well. The current building was erected in 1874 as a replacement for a previous incarnation that was lost in a fire. Through displays of

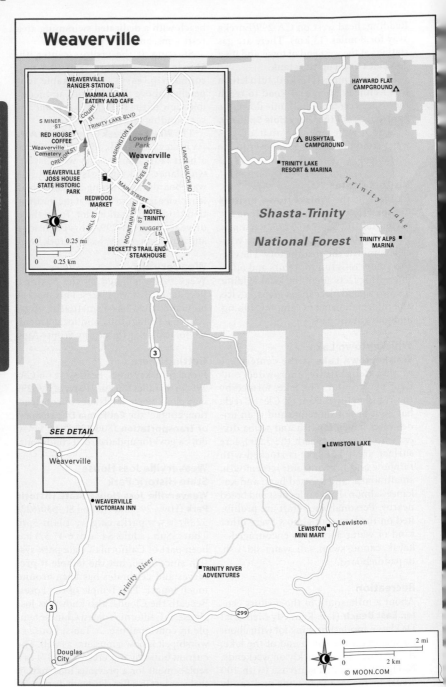

Chinese art, mining tools, and weapons used in the 1854 Tong War, this museum tells some of the Chinese immigrant history in California. Admission includes a tour of the temple (hourly 10am-4pm).

Food

Red House Coffee (86 S. Miner St., 530/623-1635, 6:30am-4:30pm Mon.-Fri., 7:30am-1pm Sat., $4-7) is a cute, locally owned café in a historical 1930s building. They serve simple breakfast and lunch items along with the gamut of coffee beverages, including a few house specialties.

Beckett's Trail End Steakhouse (1324 Nugget Ln., 530/623-2900, noon-3pm and 4:30pm-7pm Mon., 4:30pm-9pm Tues. and Thurs., 11am-3pm and 4:30pm-9pm Wed. and Fri.-Sat. summer, shorter winter hours, $10-30) doesn't let diners go home hungry. The plate-busting portions come with two generous sides, like the sweet potato fries or crunchy onion rings; a big hit is the Black and Blue Steak, which comes slathered in a Cajun rub and bleu cheese.

The **Mamma Llama Eatery & Café** (490 Main St., 530/623-6363, www.mammallama.com, 8am-2pm Mon.-Fri., 9am-2pm Sat., $4-10) has a large breakfast and lunch menu with items made from fresh ingredients. Try the spicy breakfast burrito, spicy egg mountain, the Spicy Benjamin sandwich, or the Yum-Wich, all of which are made with Mamma Llama's secret ingredient—Spicy Ben sauce. Mamma's also serves a large variety of espresso drinks.

Accommodations

The **Weaverville Victorian Inn** (2051 Main St., 530/623-4432, www.weavervillevictorianinn.com, $104-149) offers a comfortable place to rest after the long drive down CA-299. Most of the 64 spacious rooms have at least one queen bed, a TV, and sitting chairs; suites feature a king bed and Jacuzzi tub. Amenities include a free continental breakfast and an outdoor swimming pool. The inn offers a discount to contractors, federal employees, and AAA members.

Rooms at the **Motel Trinity** (1270 Main St., 530/623-2129, www.moteltrinity.com, $75) are a bit dated—expect to find boxy TVs with VHS players—but some rooms have kitchen units, Jacuzzi tubs, and free ice. A heated pool is available to guests in summer, along with coin-operated laundry services and free Wi-Fi.

Information and Services

The U.S. Forest Service maintains **Weaverville Ranger Station** (360 Main St., 530/623-2121, www.fs.usda.gov, 8am-4:30pm Mon.-Fri.), which offers free recreation and boating safety maps for Shasta Lake and Trinity Lake. Come to the office in person. If you arrive after hours, use the self-service center in front of the office to get a campfire permit or a Trinity Alps Wilderness permit.

Fill your gas tank at **Weaverville Gas** (900 Main St., 530/623-2013), **Chevron** (31540 Hwy. 3 and Browns Ranch Rd., 530/623-2515), or the **Redwood Market** (930 Main St., 530/623-1100), which has cheap fuel and decent restrooms.

Trinity Alps

The **Trinity Alps Wilderness** (530/623-2121, www.fs.usda.gov) is one of the five federally designated wilderness areas within the Shasta-Trinity National Forest. At 517,000 acres, it's the second-largest wilderness area in California. The Alps are part of the Klamath Mountain Range; the highest point is Thompson Peak (8,994-9,002 feet).

The Alps encompass various small glaciers and permanent snowfields, including a 15-acre glacier on the north side of Thompson Peak. The forest is noted for its wide variety of conifers: subalpine fir, ponderosa pine, foxtail pine, and the native Brewer spruce are just a few of the trees you'll find. Wildflower enthusiasts will find the rare Trinity penstemon (*Penstemon tracyi*)—almost worth a trip on its own. Given the minimal human impact of this area, birds, fish, and wildlife abound. Visitors are likely to encounter black bears as well as deer, coyotes, and maybe even the Trinity Alps giant salamander, an elusive alligator-size creature that may or may not exist but holds a place in the annals of cryptozoology—our own Loch Ness Monster of the woods.

Getting There

The **Trinity Scenic Byway** (CA-299) stretches from Redding west through Whiskeytown and Weaverville. From Redding, drive 27 miles (43 km) west on CA-299. Turn right (north) on Trinity Dam Boulevard and drive 4.5 miles (7 km) to the town of Lewiston.

Fishing

Trinity and Lewiston Lakes are good places to catch rainbow trout, brown trout, and smallmouth bass. Fishing licenses are required and are available; prices and requirements vary. For information, contact the **California Department of Fish and Game** (601 Locust St., Redding, 530/225-2300, www.dfg.ca.gov, 8am-12:30pm and 1:30pm-4:30pm Mon.-Fri.).

Scott Stratton at **Trinity River Adventures** (361 Ponderosa Pines Rd., Lewiston, 530/623-4179, www.trinity-riveradventures.com, $450-550 per day for 1-3 people, including lunch) takes anglers out on his 16-foot Lowe jet boat on Lewiston Lake, Klamath River, or Trinity River. Trips include a gourmet lunch as well as fly-fishing instruction to catch salmon and steelhead. He'll also take you out on a memorable two-day camping trip ($750 pp) down the river.

Travis Michel from **Sweet Trinity Fishing Guide Service** (Weaverville, 530/623-4695, www.sweet-trinity.com, $350-450 for 1-2 people) always has a smile on his face when he's out fishing, and plenty of people whom he has taken out have come back with big ol' honkin'

chinook. Specializing in the Northern California waterways, Michel is a great guide as well as a friendly and innovative resource for rookie anglers looking to bag their first steelhead, chinook, or salmon on either the Trinity or Lower Sacramento River while also respecting the local ecology.

Versatile **Steve Huber** (866/531-3474, www.stevehuberguideservice.com, $225 pp) takes anglers out on the Trinity River in a drift boat or powerboat, as well as on the Rogue, Oregon, Klamath, and Sacramento Rivers. Huber supplies the gear and assists with fly-fishing, bait casting, or trolling—you name it—his sole purpose is to get you a fish. Stock up on snacks at one of the local grocers before going out.

Lewiston Lake

Located north of the town of Lewiston, **Lewiston Lake** is an artificial reservoir created by a dam on the Trinity River. Lewiston Lake has a surface area of 750

acres and is a popular spot for paddling, fishing, and camping.

In Lewiston, stock up on supplies or fill your gas tank at the **Lewiston Mini Mart** (4789 Trinity Dam Blvd., Lewiston, 530/778-3268, 6:30am-9pm Mon.-Sat., 7am-9pm Sun.).

Trinity Lake

North of Lewiston Lake, clear blue **Trinity Lake** stands out. Formed by Trinity Dam, the lake is one of California's largest reservoirs, with 145 miles of shoreline and a capacity of about 2.5 million acre-feet. This large lake is an aquatic playground, and it's particularly popular with waterskiers, houseboaters, and birdwatchers.

Marinas

The lake has three marinas. **Trinity Alps Marina** (1 Fairview Marina Rd., Lewiston, 530/286-2282, www.trinityalpsmarina.com, 9am-5pm daily May-mid-Oct., $429-657 per night houseboats, $375 daily wakeboard boat, $100 daily fishing boat, $350 party deck boat, $225 pontoon boat). West of the Alps Marina is the **Trinity Lake Resorts & Marina** (530/286-2225 or 800/709-7814, www.trinitylakeresort.com, 8am-6pm daily May-Oct., $560-1,200 per day), which has 56- to 60-foot houseboat rentals (3-day, 2-night min., $2,700-3,861), 16-foot fishing boats ($270 daily), patio pontoon boats ($750 daily), and personal watercraft ($500 daily).

Accommodations and Camping

Trinity Lake Resorts & Marina (530/286-2225 or 800/709-7814, www.trinitylakeresort.com, year-round) has 10 cabins that sleep 4-12 people. Reservations are available on a nightly ($98-335) or weekly basis ($625-2,175).

Located near Trinity Lake, with easy access to the boat dock, is the U.S. Forest Service **Bushytail Campground** (877/444-6777, www.recreation.gov, June-Sept., $22-90), which has 12 large and wooded campsites; 9 have electrical hookups.

Whiskeytown Lake

CA-299

Amenities include flush toilets, drinking water, and showers. It's on CA-3, 16 miles (26 km) north of Weaverville and 0.5 mile from Trinity Lake.

The larger, and popular, **Hayward Flat Campground** (877/444-6777, www.recreation.gov, mid-May-mid-Sept., $20-35) has 98 sites on the shore of Trinity Lake, which makes it a great spot for waterskiing, wakeboarding, and fishing. Amenities include flush toilets, drinking water, and an amphitheater with ranger programs. It's on CA-3, 15 miles north of Weaverville. At Hayward Flat Road, turn right and drive 2 miles (3.2 km) to the campground.

Getting There
Trinity Lake is along CA-3 at the eastern edge of the Trinity Alps, north of Lewiston Lake and west of Shasta Lake.

Hayfork
The small town of Hayfork is 30 miles (48 km) southwest of Weaverville on CA-3. Traveling west on CA-299 from Whiskeytown Lake, look for the turnoff for Hayfork and CA-3 in Douglas City (if you make it to Weaverville then you've gone too far). Douglas City is 24 miles (39 km) north of Hayfork; despite what the name implies, this "city" has a population of only about 700 residents, a few campgrounds, and a market.

If you plan on spending time outdoors here, stop by the **Hayfork Ranger Station** (11 Trinity St., 530/628-5227, www.fs.usda.gov, 8:30am-4pm Mon.-Fri.) for information on wilderness hiking, camping, and exploring the Trinity River's south fork and other parts of the Chanchelula Wilderness. Note that marijuana crops are rampant in this area; ask the ranger for guidance navigating this territory.

Natural Bridge
The incredible **Natural Bridge** (Trinity-Shasta National Forest) has both geological and historical significance. This natural limestone arch spans a 200-foot ravine near Hayfork. Names and dates engraved in the limestone attest to the fact that early pioneers used this as a picnic site. Striking to behold, this limestone phenomenon is worth a side trip—but please be respectful. Water, wind, and other forces alter the bridge's natural formation, but the more gently we treat it, the longer it will be around for others.

This is also the site of the infamous Bridge Gulch Massacre of 1852, in which a conflict between a band of Wintu people and some prominent Weaverville settlers ended with the deaths of most of the Wintu people living in the area. Descendants of the Wintu still consider this a place of cultural significance.

Natural Bridge is about 11 miles (17.5 km) southwest of Hayfork. From Hayfork, follow CA-3 east for 4.5 miles (7.2 km). Turn right onto Wildwood Road, and in another 5 miles (8 km) the road becomes Forest Road 31N19. Natural Bridge is 1.4 miles (2.3 km) south.

Food
Lucky Trail Bistro (91 Trinity St., 530/628-5600, 5pm-9pm Fri.-Sat., 10am-2pm Sun., $10-15) is Hayfork's hidden gem and totally worth a stop if you catch it when it's open. This casual coffee shop serves classic organic dishes, including basic burgers, fries, and salads, plus unique dishes like vegan Jamaican spinach soup and a black-bean and beet quinoa burger.

The main draw of the **Red Bud Woodfired Restaurant** (6861 Hwy. 3, 530/628-4653, 8am-10pm daily, $13-30) is the big stone and concrete dome out back that always has a wood-burning fire going. The restaurant serves breakfast, lunch, and dinner, with burgers, specialty pizzas, and fish-and-chips, Try its famous Spudzilla for a hearty, filling meal. This homey restaurant is a favorite among road-trippers.

Wiley's Supermarket (Main St., 530/628-5646, www.wileysmarket.com,

8am-8pm Mon.-Sat., 10am-7pm Sun.) is known for their delicious steaks, friendly service, and community involvement. Named after Jim Wiley, who opened the original market in 1962, this local favorite is steeped in history and has all of the food you need (especially meat) for the perfect camping or fishing trip.

Accommodations

The **Forest Glen Guard Station** (Hwy. 36, Hayfork, 877/444-6777, www.recreation. gov, mid-Apr.-early Dec., $75) was built in 1916 and is the oldest Forest Service building in the Shasta-Trinity National Forest. The two-story building sleeps up to eight and has an indoor kitchen and bath and a large porch. It's located near the South Fork of the Trinity River, so the nearby swimming and hiking are both excellent.

Timberjack Lodge (250 Big Creek Rd., 530/628-5648, www.timberjacklodge. com, $76-89) is a sleepy 12-room motel that blends in with the large oak trees and greenery that surround it. Rooms are quaint and simple, with flat-screen TVs, mini-fridges, and free Wi-Fi. Some rooms are pet-friendly.

Red Bluff

One hour west of either entrance to Lassen Volcanic National Park, Red Bluff has a quaint and lively Main Street, good shopping, and multiple parks and recreation opportunities for fishing, hiking, and camping.

Getting There

Red Bluff is 130 miles (210 km) north of Sacramento on I-5. From Redding, drive 30 miles (48 km) south on I-5, passing through Anderson and Cottonwood. Red Bluff is also 50 miles (80 km) west of the south entrance to Lassen Volcanic National Park via CA-36 East.

Recreation

Red Bluff Recreation Area

The **Red Bluff Recreation Area** (1000 Sale Ln., 530/527-2813, www.fs.usda.gov) is a flat, grassy area close to the Sacramento River. The visitors center houses the **Sacramento River Discovery Center** (530/527-1196, www.sacramentoriverdiscoverycenter.com, 8am-4pm Tues.-Sat. summer, 9am-3pm Tues.-Sat. winter), a great place to get trail maps for nature hikes in the area, like the **Shasta View Trail** (2 mi/3.2 km round-trip, 1 hour, easy). This mostly flat loop delivers on the views it promises.

Bird-watching is big, and the park is home to great blue herons, great egrets, great horned owls, wood ducks, Anna's hummingbirds, and many other species. Bobcats, western pond turtles, Pacific tree frogs, opossums, woodchucks, and river mammals may also pass through here. Various short nature trails make for easy forays into the best wildlife-viewing spots. The park is also home to a day-use area and a **campground.**

The Red Bluff Recreation Area is 1 mile (1.6 km) south of the CA-36/ Antelope Boulevard exit on I-5.

Fishing

Red Bluff is a favorite fishing spot for seasoned anglers (and duck hunters). Trout, bass, striper, and salmon are the most common species caught in the Sacramento River.

Red Bluff Sporting Goods (501 Madison St., 530/529-3877, 8am-6pm Mon.-Fri., 8am-5pm Sat., 10am-4pm Sun.) has one of the biggest selections of fishing gear and tackle. They're also a great source of information for local guided services.

Guides and Outfitters

River Pursuit Guide Service (Red Bluff, 916/997-2765, www.riverpursuit.com, $200 pp daily, min. 2 people) takes you out on the local tributaries in search of salmon and fighting striper. Guides provide all tackle and bait; anglers are responsible for their own lunch and fishing license. Bring a big ice chest for all of the fish you're going to catch.

Northern California Guide Service (Red Bluff, 530/755-7196, http://norcal-salmonguide.com, $175 pp daily) takes anglers out in search of sturgeon, steelhead, and salmon. The guided trips on aluminum jet boats include all equipment and fish-cleaning services.

Confluence Outfitters (14625 Molluc Dr., Red Bluff, 888/481-1650, www.confluenceoutfitters.com, $375-525 pp) has guides all over Northern California, with trips on the Klamath, Rogue, Trinity, and Lower Sacramento Rivers. Half- and full-day trips are available (full-day trips include lunch). Guides will meet you at your hotel and provide a shuttle back from the trip.

Food

Green Barn Whiskey Kitchen (5 Chestnut Ave., 530/527-3161, 11am-9pm Mon.-Thurs., 11am-10pm Fri.-Sat., $16-40) has been satisfying locals since 1959 with quality steaks at a great price. Kentucky native Bruce Geveden renovated the restaurant with a shiny wood interior, dark leather booths, and rustic furnishings. Upscale menu items include a porterhouse steak, the popular New York steak sandwich, seafood entrées, and a full line of top-shelf whiskey.

Los Mariachis (604 Main St., 530/529-5154, www.redblufflosmariachis.com, 9am-9pm Mon.-Fri., 9am-9:30pm Sat.-Sun., $10-15) serves traditional Mexican fare for breakfast, lunch, and dinner. Order burritos and quesadillas along with authentic fare like *molcajetes* and *parrilladas,* a plate of food that feeds up to three people.

Casa Ramos (2001 Main St., 530/527-2684, www.casaramos.net, 11am-9pm Sun.-Thurs., 11am-10pm Fri.-Sat., $9-20) is a local chain that serves traditional Mexican cuisines in a festive, brightly painted interior. Gorge on heaping portions of meat, beans, and rice or enjoy deep-fried flautas or *borrego*—braised lamb shank served with avocado and beans—along with a top-shelf margarita served by friendly staff.

Accommodations and Camping

Red Bluff offers standard hotel chains such as **Super 8** (30 Gilmore Rd., 530/776-0032, www.super8.com, $90-100) and **Comfort Inn** (90 Sale Ln., 530/529-7060, www.choicehotels.com, $110-145). If you've got your own bed on wheels, the place to park it is the upscale **Durango RV Resort** (100 Lake Ave., 866/770-7001, www.durangorvresorts.com, $56-65), which offers a heated pool, spa services, dog run, tennis, bocce ball courts, a lodge and concession center, and facilities to wash your pup *and* your vehicle. The resort is on the Sacramento River and is surrounded by woods. Due to underground watering, this is not a place for tents.

Within the Red Bluff Recreation Area, **Sycamore Grove Campground** (Sale Ln., 2 mi/3.2 km southeast of Red Bluff, reservations 877/444-6777, www.recreation.gov, year-round, $16-30) offers 30 sites for tents and trailers with up to eight people allowed per site; it also has a large group site that accommodates 16 people. Coin-operated showers are available in the modern restrooms, and a 4-mile (6.4-km) paved hiking trail dips down to the Sacramento River, where chinook, striped bass, salmon, and steelhead fish swim. Some campsites are more private than others; try to reserve one closest to the river.

Information and Services

The **Sacramento River Discovery Center** (1000 Sale Ln., 530/527-1196, www.sacramentoriverdiscoverycenter.com, 9am-3pm Tues.-Sat. winter, 8am-4pm Tues.-Sat. summer) is the go-to spot for information about the river and wildlife in the area.

The **Tehama County Visitors Center**

(250 Antelope Blvd., 530/529-0133, 9am-6pm Mon.-Sat., 10am-5pm Sun.) also offers a lot of information about what to do in the area.

Lassen Volcanic National Park

Lassen Volcanic National Park is one of the oldest national parks in the United States, home to an active volcano with a long-recorded history of eruptions (the last took place 1914-1921). It's a peaceful haven for wildlife and a wonderland for nature aficionados with ample hiking trails, lovely ponds, and several campgrounds that let visitors enjoy the amazing panoramas of Mount Lassen. The park road offers a wonderful drive past the stark slopes and jagged rocks evident of volcanic eruptions. Beyond the boundaries of the national park, national forest lands allow for additional exploration.

Rugged weather and a remote location mean that a visit to Lassen Volcanic National Park is a trip to a largely unspoiled wilderness. Half of the park is only accessible via minimal dirt-road access, but its rugged beauty is perfect for those willing to hike miles into the backcountry.

The best time to visit Lassen is **August** and **early September;** everything is open in the height of the summer, but the trails and campgrounds tend to be more crowded. Winter usually begins in November and continues through May. If planning to visit during the off-season, contact **CalTrans** (800/427-7623) for current road conditions.

Visiting the Park

Lassen Volcanic National Park (530/595-4480, www.nps.gov/lavo, $25 per vehicle, $12 cyclists/pedestrians) is easily accessed from Red Bluff or Redding. There are two park entrances. The **southwest entrance,** near the Kohm Yah-mah-nee Visitors Center, is accessed from CA-36. The **northwest entrance,** near Loomis Plaza, is accessed from CA-44. Both entrances are open year-round (weather permitting); in winter, the park road connecting the two entrances is closed.

Entrances

Redding is closest to the **northwest entrance.** From downtown Redding, drive east on CA-44. In 5 miles (8 km), you'll pass Palo Cedro, which has gas stations, mini-marts, and a full-service grocery store. Continue east on CA-44 for 20 miles (32 km) to Shingletown, which has gas and the Shingletown Store. In about 20 miles (32 km), the two-lane highway reaches Manzanita Lake and the northwest entrance of the park. Plan one hour for the pretty drive.

Red Bluff is closest to the **southwest entrance.** From Red Bluff, exit I-5 and drive east on CA-36 for 43 miles (69 km). Go through the town of Mineral, which has a few campgrounds and accommodations: Battle Creek Campground, Mt. Lassen Camp, and Lassen Mineral Lodge. Continue 4 miles (6.4 km), then turn left onto CA-89 into the park. Note that CA-89 may close in winter due to snow; check road conditions and the weather forecast and fill your gas tank in Red Bluff before heading into the park. Plan one hour for the drive.

Visitors Center

Lassen's year-round visitors center, **Kohm Yah-mah-nee Visitors Center** (530/595-4480, 9am-5pm daily May-Oct., 9am-5pm daily Wed.-Sun. Nov.-Apr.) is a modern and LEED-certified state-of-the-art facility. Inside are interactive exhibits that illuminate local geology and ecology, as well as an auditorium, an amphitheater, a first-aid center, large modern restrooms, and **Lassen Café & Gift** (530/595-3555, 9am-5pm daily late May-mid-Oct., 11am-2pm Sat.-Sun. mid-Oct.-late May), a snack bar and souvenir shop. Outside are short interpretive trails with

Lassen Volcanic National Park

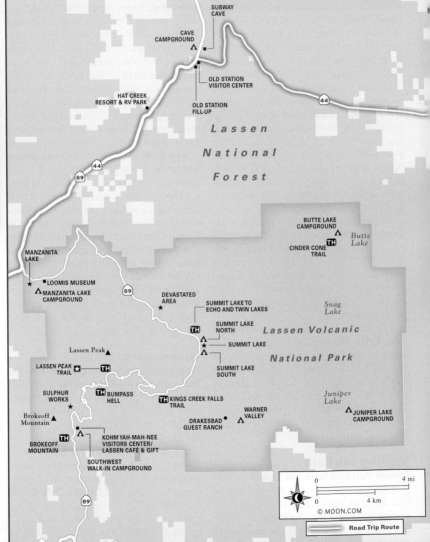

RANCHERIA RV PARK & STORE

89

SUBWAY CAVE

CAVE CAMPGROUND

OLD STATION VISITOR CENTER

OLD STATION FILL-UP

HAT CREEK RESORT & RV PARK

44

44

89

Lassen

National

Forest

89

MANZANITA LAKE

LOOMIS MUSEUM

MANZANITA LAKE CAMPGROUND

89

DEVASTATED AREA

SUMMIT LAKE TO ECHO AND TWIN LAKES

SUMMIT LAKE NORTH

SUMMIT LAKE

Lassen Peak

SUMMIT LAKE SOUTH

BUTTE LAKE CAMPGROUND

CINDER CONE TRAIL

Butte Lake

Snag Lake

Lassen Volcanic

National Park

Juniper Lake

JUNIPER LAKE CAMPGROUND

LASSEN PEAK TRAIL

SULPHUR WORKS

BUMPASS HELL

KINGS CREEK FALLS TRAIL

WARNER VALLEY

Brokeoff Mountain

DRAKESBAD GUEST RANCH

BROKEOFF MOUNTAIN

KOHM YAH-MAH-NEE VISITORS CENTER/ LASSEN CAFÉ & GIFT

SOUTHWEST WALK-IN CAMPGROUND

89

0   4 mi

0   4 km

© MOON.COM

Road Trip Route

paved walkways and informative signage. Strategically placed benches make great spots to enjoy lunch or a snack while you enjoy gorgeous views of the mountains.

The visitors center is near the southwest entrance to the park on CA-89, convenient to the Sulphur Works and to the trailheads for Brokeoff Mountain and Ridge Lakes, and it's accessible when other roads in the park are closed. The name Kohm Yah-mah-nee is from the language of the local Maidu people and means "snow mountain," which was their name for Lassen Peak.

There's a **ranger station** at the northwest entrance (Hwy. 44/89).

Scenic Drive

A paved road runs through the middle of the park, making it easy for summer visitors to enjoy campgrounds, miles of trails, and major attractions like Mount Lassen as well as the park's active volcanic features. In winter, the park road closes and access is limited. Stops are listed north to south from the northwest entrance.

Loomis Museum

At the northwest entrance (CA-89), you'll find the **Loomis Museum** (530/595-6140, 9am-5pm Fri.-Sun. mid-May-mid-June and Oct., 9am-5pm daily mid-June-early Oct., free). Inside this cute stone museum is a wonderful opportunity to learn about the known history of Mount Lassen, focusing heavily on the 1914-1915 eruptions photographed by B. F. Loomis. Prints of those rare and stunning photos have been enlarged and captioned to create these exhibits; the museum was named for the photographer, who later became a major player in the push to make Mount Lassen a national park. This interpretive museum offers a rare chance to see, through photos, the devastation and following stages of regrowth of the ecosystem on the volcanic slopes.

Manzanita Lake

About a mile south of the Loomis Museum is calm and peaceful Manzanita Lake. Sitting at an elevation of 5,875 feet (1,791 m), Manzanita Lake is a popular spot for fishing, boating, hiking, and camping. In summer, the **Manzanita Lake Camper Store** (8am-8pm daily summer, 9am-5pm daily spring and fall) rents kayaks, canoes, stand-up paddleboards, and catarafts (a combo of a catamaran and pontoon). The area also hosts an amphitheater, a small boat launch ramp, showers, a laundromat, a campground, and a choice selection of wood cabins. The 1.8-mile (2.9-km) **Manzanita Lake Loop Trail** winds along the water's edge.

Chaos Jumbles

The broken and decimated area known as **Chaos Jumbles** may seem like another spot that was splashed with rocks and lava during the 1915 eruption of Mount Lassen, but rather than a volcanic eruption, this interesting formation was caused by a massive avalanche about 300 years ago. The results look similar to the regions affected by volcanoes, with devastation of the living ecosystem, displacement of massive rocks, and the general disorder of the landscape. The avalanche that occurred here was so big and came down so fast that it trapped a pocket of air underneath it, adding to the destruction. Now visitors can enjoy a wealth of new life, including a broader-than-average variety of coniferous trees. The newness of the living landscape has allowed a greater variety of competing types of plants to get a foothold.

Hot Rock

This huge boulder was untouchable back when the Loomises explored the eruption zone soon after the 1915 blast. The now-cooled and smooth 300-ton **Hot Rock** is accessible from the Devastated Area interpretive trail.

Devastated Area

The **Devastated Area** is one of the most fascinating geological and ecological sites in California. When Mount Lassen blew its top in 1915 after nearly a year of sporadic eruptions, a tremendous part of the mountain and all the life on its slopes were destroyed. Boiling mud and exploding gases tore off the side of Lassen's peak and killed all the vegetation in the area. A hail of lava rained down, creating brand-new rocks, in sizes from gravel to boulders, across the north side of the mountain.

Today visitors can easily see how a volcano's surface ecosystem recovers after an eruption. First, park at the Devastated Area lot and take a short interpretive walk through a small part of the recently disrupted mountainside. You'll see everything from some of the world's youngest rocks to grasses and shrubs through tall pine trees. Be sure to check out the photos in the Loomis Museum that depict the area during and immediately after the eruption for a great comparison to the spot as it looks now.

The 0.5-mile Devastated Area interpretive walk is flat and wheelchair accessible, with interpretive plaques along the way. Don't pick up any of the red and black volcanic rocks; they are part of the redeveloping ecosystem and necessary to the area's recovery. The trailhead offers ample parking.

Summit Lake

Lassen National Park is dotted with tiny lakes, though many better resemble ponds or puddles. One of the most popular and most easily accessible is **Summit Lake.** The bright and shining small lake attracts many campers to its two forest-shaded campgrounds. An easy walk around the lake lets you see its waters and the plants that proliferate nearby. Find one of the small trails down to the edge of the water to eke out a spot on the minuscule beach with all the other visitors who come to escape the heat. You can swim and fish in Summit Lake, and even take rafts and paddleboards out. No power boats are permitted anywhere in Lassen Volcanic National Park.

★ Lassen Peak

Lassen Peak reaches 10,457 feet (3,187 m) into the sky. Even if you're not up to climbing the trail to the top, it's worth stopping at the trailhead parking lot to enjoy the view. The craggy broken mountain peak is what's left after the most recent eruption—hence the lack of vegetation. The starting elevation for the summit trail is 8,000 feet (2,440 m), which means the Lassen Peak trailhead tends to be cool even in the heat of summer. You may need to break out a windbreaker or light sweater if you plan to explore at length.

The **Lassen Peak Trail** (5 mi/8 km round-trip, 3 hours, difficult) leads to the highest point on Mount Lassen. Hike to the top for a unique vantage point of the whole region.

Bumpass Hell

The best and most varied area of volcanic geothermal activity on Lassen is at a location called **Bumpass Hell** (6 mi/9.5 km from the southwest entrance). The region was named for Kendall Vanhook Bumpass, who, during his explorations, stepped through a thin crust over a boiling mud pot and severely burned his leg, ultimately losing the limb. In fact, the tale of the unfortunate Bumpass illustrates a good point for travelers visiting the mud pots and fumaroles: Stay on the paths! The dangers at Bumpass Hell are real, and if you step off the boardwalks or let your children run wild, you are risking serious injury.

Still, a hike down to Bumpass Hell on the **Bumpass Nature Trail** is fun. As long as you're careful, it's worth the risk. You'll need to walk about 2 miles (3.2 km) from the parking lot and trailhead out to the interesting stuff—boiling mud pots, fumaroles, steaming springs, and pools of steaming boiling water cluster here. Prepare for the strong smell of sulfur, more evidence that this volcano is anything but extinct. Boardwalks are strategically placed through the area and were just redone, creating safer walking paths for visitors.

The spacious parking lot at Bumpass offers stunning views to the east and south, giving you a hint at the scope of the ancient volcano that once stood here. Right at the parking lot you can see a famous "glacial erratic," a boulder carried along by a glacier; this one is about 10 feet high, demonstrating the colossal forces of nature that have been at work in this park over the millennia.

Sulphur Works

For visitors who can't quite manage the trek out to Bumpass Hell, the **Sulphur Works** site offers a peek at the geothermal features of Lassen from the main road. A boardwalk runs along the road, and a parking area is nearby, making it easy for visitors to get out of the car and examine the loud boiling mud pots and small steaming stream. The mud pots both look and sound like a washing machine, sending up steam and occasional bursts of boiling water. Keep hold of your children.

Starting from the Sulphur Works, a 2-mile (3.2-km) round-trip trail leads to the two tiny **Ridge Lakes.** It's a fairly steep climb, but the payoff at the top is a view of two alpine lakes between Brokeoff Mountain (elevation 9,235 ft/2,815 m) and Mount Diller (elevation 9,087 ft/2,770 m). Along the way, you'll walk through beautiful green meadows dotted with bright yellow wildflowers and then into a forest before reaching the lakes.

From top to bottom: Mt. Lassen; Sulphur Works; Lassen Peak trailhead.

Recreation
Hiking

Easy interpretive walks and short day hikes access the most popular sights of Lassen Volcanic National Park. For hikers who want to get away from the more heavily visited areas but still make it back to the car before dark, several moderate-difficult hiking trails offer adventure, challenge, and maybe even a touch of solitude.

Be aware that the lower elevations of Mount Lassen's trails are still more than 7,000 feet (2,135 m) above sea level. If you're planning to do some serious hiking, come a day early to acclimate to the elevation first. Wear sturdy boots, bring extra layers of clothing, carry a flashlight, snacks, and sunscreen, and remember to stay well hydrated.

Lassen Peak Trail

The must-do hike for any serious hiker is **Lassen Peak Trail** (5 mi/8 km round-trip, 3-5 hours, difficult). A large parking lot with chemical-toilet facilities is at the trailhead, and you're likely to see a lot of other cars here. This path not only takes you to the highest point on Mount Lassen, it's also a starkly beautiful, unusual trail that offers long views of the rest of the park and beyond.

The climb to the top is dramatic, challenging, and worth it. It's not actually a long hike—only 5 miles (8 km) round-trip—but the trail gains more than 2,000 vertical feet (600 m) on the way up. The trail is well graded and has many switchbacks, which help manage the steepness. And some good news: Interpretive signs along the way explain some of the fascinating views of volcanic remains, lakes, wildlife, and rock formations and give you a chance to catch your breath.

The recent (by geologic standards) eruption and prevailing weather conditions leave this peak without much plant life, which means nothing blocks your views downward and outward, and the rocky terrain is visually interesting.

Only the last 0.25 mile or so actually involves any scrambling over large rocks; most of the trail is just a steady upward walk. When you get to the top, be sure to turn all the way around to get 360-degree views back down to the newest volcanic landscape, across to the remains of the giant caldera of a huge extinct volcano, and then out west toward the Cascade Range, where you'll see Mount Shasta shining in the distance.

Kings Creek Falls Trail

The **Kings Creek Falls Trail** (Hwy. 89, road marker 32, 3 mi/4.8 km round-trip, 1.5 hours, moderate) starts out easy—you hike through a meadow and downhill to the falls via a stone staircase. Be sure to stop to admire the small cascade and pool and sit down and have a snack to prepare for the 700-foot (215-m) climb back to the trailhead. This is a good hike for fit day-hikers who've already been on the mountain for a few hours.

Summit Lake to Echo and Twin Lakes

It's the length of the trail that runs from **Summit Lake to Echo and Twin Lakes** (east side of Summit Lake, 8 mi/13 km round-trip, 5 hours, moderate-difficult) that makes it challenging. But you can choose how many lakes you want to see if you run short of breath. The elevation gain over the course of this long trail is only 500 feet (150 m) in total—that's nothing compared to some of Lassen's other more strenuous hikes.

A pleasant and sedate 4-mile (7-km) walk is out to **Echo Lake.** It's another 2 miles (3.2 km) to get to **Upper Twin Lake** and **Lower Twin Lake.** You might want to wear a swimsuit under your hiking clothes on hot summer days to cool off in one of the lakes before trekking back to base.

Brokeoff Mountain

For a solid all-day hike with some invigorating uphill stretches, climb **Brokeoff Mountain** (Hwy. 89, road marker 2, 7.4

mi/11.9 km round-trip, 4 hours, difficult). The hike involves a 2,600-foot (790-m) ascent from a mile-high starting point; the thin air and rigorous climb can be difficult for hikers who are not yet acclimated to the altitude. (Brokeoff makes a good second- or third-day Lassen hike, after you've seen the sights and climbed Mount Lassen.) This is one of the prettiest and most serene hikes in the park, with mountain streams and stellar views.

The trailhead is near the Kohm Yah-mah-nee Visitors Center (CA-89) at the southwest entrance to the park, so it can serve as a last big adventure before you head back on the road.

Cinder Cone Trail

For a radical change of scenery, take the **Cinder Cone Trail** (west end of Butte Lake Campground, 4-5 mi/6.4-8 km round-trip, 3 hours, moderate). Be sure to wear your sturdiest ankle-covering hiking boots on this adventure, since the ground on the Cinder Cone is . . . well . . . cinders. Watch your footing so you don't slide down; even cold cinders can cut you up. The trail rises 800 vertical feet (245 m) over 2 miles; to lengthen the hike, walk down the south side of the cone. Geology and photography buffs particularly like this hike, which is accessible by dirt road and shows off some of the more interesting and less-seen volcanic history of Mount Lassen. Allocate at least three hours to do this hike.

Boiling Springs Lake

Enter the park from Warner Valley Road to hike to **Boiling Springs Lake** (Warner Campground parking lot, 3 mi/4.8 km, 1.5 hours, easy-moderate). The walk out and back is reasonably short and nonstrenuous. You'll see bubbling mud pots and can check out the boiling springs from a safe distance. Just be very careful once you reach the geothermal area; unlike Bumpass Hell, this area has no safe boardwalks encircling the mud pots and fumaroles, which can be extremely

dangerous. This might not be a hike for spirited young children, but it's heaven for serious nature lovers. Needless to say, swimming in sulfurous, acidic, 125°F Boiling Springs Lake is a very bad idea.

Backpacking

Some of the most beautiful and interesting remote hiking can be found in Lassen's expansive backcountry. Although you might not be the only backpacker out here, you'll definitely leave the crowds behind. You might even have a pristine lake or mountain stream to yourself.

Check with the ranger station for maps, advice on route planning and trail conditions, suggested equipment, and to obtain any necessary backcountry permits. Once you're in the park, the visitors centers can issue a free wilderness permit for backcountry hiking and camping and provide last-minute trail information.

Boating and Fishing

Many of Lassen's small and midsize lakes allow unpowered boating (canoe, kayak, or stand-up paddleboard) and fishing. Kayak and stand-up paddleboard rentals are available at **Manzanita Lake.** Bring your own to hit the waters at **Summit Lake.** In the eastern part of the park, Juniper, Snag, and Butte Lakes have plenty of space to row or paddle and enjoy the serenity of the water.

Several varieties of trout inhabit the larger Lassen lakes. All you need is a pole, some bait, and a valid California fishing license. Manzanita Lake offers catch-and-release fishing only, but at all the other fishable lakes you're welcome to take a state limit of rainbows and browns. Fishing at several of the campgrounds makes it easy to enjoy the freshest dinner possible.

Fishing licenses are available online (www.wildlife.ca.gov), at the Redding office of the California Department of Fish and Game (601 Locust St., Redding, 530/225-2300, 8am-4:30pm Mon.-Fri.), at

Hat Creek Resort & RV Park (12533 Hwy. 44, Old Station, 530/335-7121, http://hatcreekresortrv.com, 9am-5pm daily mid-Apr.-Oct.), and at the **Old Station Fill-Up** (13413 Hwy. 44, Old Station, 530/335-3152, www.oldstationfillup.com, 7am-7pm daily). A one-day fishing license costs $15.

Food

Mount Lassen offers little in the way of dining options. The best food in the park is at the Kohm Yah-mah-nee Visitors Center, where **Lassen Café & Gift** (Hwy. 89, 530/595-3555, 9am-5pm daily late May-mid-Oct., 11am-2pm Sat.-Sun. mid-Oct.-late May, $8-10) sells burgers, slices of pizza, hot coffee, and ice cream. Hours vary in the winter.

The **Manzanita Lake Camper Store** (9am-5pm daily late spring and early fall, 8am-8pm daily summer) sells gifts, camping supplies, hot food, snacks (including s'mores for campfires), and ice cream.

If you're camping, stock up at one of the small markets in Hat Creek or Old Station.

Accommodations
Inside the Park

Accommodations near Lassen Volcanic National Park are few and far between. Plan to camp in the park, or stay near Hat Creek, Mill Creek, Chester, or Redding and take day trips into the park. For information for Drakesbad, Warner Valley, and Manzanita visit http://lassenlodging.com.

Located near Chester, east of the southwest entrance station, the **Drakesbad Guest Ranch** (Chester Warner Valley Rd., Chester, 866/999-0914, www.drakesbad.com, June-mid-Oct., $159-237) is an all-inclusive ranch that is technically located within the park boundaries. Guests are within easy reach of hiking trails and fishing lakes and streams; the ranch can connect you with local guides for fishing trips. The basic rooms feature wood

Painted Dunes at the Cinder Cone

paneling and well-worn beds topped with comforting quilts; there is no Wi-Fi or TV. Guided trail rides are available through the park on one of the ranch's horses ($40-215). There's even a wonderful pool fed by water from a local hot spring. Rates includes three meals daily; the national park entrance fee is not included.

Outside the Park
Mill Creek

Mill Creek is 9 miles (14.5 km) east of the park's southwest entrance on CA-36/89 and offers two lodging options. Charming ★ **St. Bernard Lodge** (44801 Hwy. 36, Mill Creek, 530/258-3382, www.stbernardlodge.com, $102-110) is a bed-and-breakfast in a cozy historical mansion rich in history. The seven rooms share two bathrooms; rooms are clean with comfortable beds, an in-room sink, and vintage decor. The fancy parlor doubles as the check-in area, complete with a full bar, and is situated next to a dining room where a delicious breakfast is served (grab a piece of the French toast brûlée). Dinner is available by request 24 hours in advance (the owner must source the ingredients). Some guests have claimed paranormal experiences, but all spirits are friendly.

South of CA-36 is a small horseshoe-shaped highway, CA-172, which leads to ★ **Mill Creek Resort** (40271 Hwy. 172, 530/595-4449, www.millcreekresort.net, late May-early Sept., $105-150 2-bedroom cabins, $20 tents, $35 RVs). It's been around since 1936, when William H. Foster built a post office and a general store here (now a restaurant). A few more families came and built summer cabins, and now, decades later, the young couple who run the place are establishing their own legacy. The cabins are nicely spaced; each contains one or two bedrooms, a bathroom, and a kitchenette with views of the great outdoors. The on-site **restaurant** uses organic ingredients and features locally sourced brews. The friendly owners are happy to point you to their favorite hikes in Lassen, a mere 12 miles (19.5 km) away. The meadow behind the restaurant is a great place to play or view wildlife.

Mineral

Lassen Mineral Lodge (Hwy. 36, Mineral, 530/595-4422, www.minerallodge.com, late May-early Nov., $90-115 plus tax) is near the southwest entrance to the park with 20 small motel-style rooms with private baths and few frills; pets are not allowed. The lack of TVs and telephones encourages visitors to enjoy the park and the surrounding landscape. The on-site **Mineral Lodge Restaurant** (8am-8pm daily late May-early Nov., $12-24) has a bar and is open to non-guests. Try the famous Flaming Volcano shot ($6).

Camping
Inside the Park

Lassen has eight campgrounds, four of which are accessible via the paved park road. The remaining four campgrounds offer primitive facilities or are accessible via a short hike. Although the park is open year-round, most campgrounds open in late spring and close September or October. The exception is the campground at the Kohm Yah-mah-nee Visitors Center, where snow camping is available in the winter.

Backcountry camping is permitted. A free wilderness permit is required and is available from the Loomis Museum (530/595-6140, 9am-5pm Fri.-Sun. mid-May-mid-June and Oct., 9am-5pm daily mid-June-early Oct.) and Kohm Yah-mah-nee Visitors Center (530/595-4480, 9am-5pm daily May-Oct., 9am-5pm daily Wed.-Sun. Nov.-Apr.). Self-registration is possible at the Loomis, Butte Lake, Warner Valley Ranch, and Juniper Lake Ranger Stations.

Manzanita Lake

★ **Manzanita Lake** (179 sites, 877/444-6777, www.recreation.gov, $26 May-Oct., $15 first-come, first-served in winter) is the closest campground to the northwest park entrance. This is the largest campground in the park, with both campsites and cabins ($72-97) and a full slate of amenities—flush toilets, potable water, fire rings or pits, picnic tables, an RV dump station, and a 24-hour gas station. It's also the only place in the park with coin-operated showers (quarters required), a laundromat, and camper store. Trailers and campers up to 40 feet are allowed. The cabins come with either one or two bedrooms; bring your own bedding. Flush toilets and showers are outside of the cabins next to the camper store. Advance reservations are recommended.

Summit Lake

Summit Lake lies almost in the middle of the park and has two campgrounds. **Summit Lake North** (46 sites, late June-Sept., $24) and **Summit Lake South** (48 sites, late June Sept., $22) are some of the most popular sites in Lassen. Swimming is a lure for campers, and the banks of Summit Lake are easily accessible from trails and campsites. The campgrounds have pit toilets (in South), flush toilets (in North), fire pits, picnic tables, food lockers, and potable water. Ranger programs are held at the amphitheater. At almost 7,000 feet (2,135 m) elevation, these campgrounds are some of the highest in the park.

Trailers and campers up to 35 feet are allowed. Advance **reservations** (877/444-6777, www.recreation.gov) are recommended. Some sites (Loops A and E) are first-come, first-served.

Southwest Walk-In

Located near the southwest entrance, **Southwest Walk-In Campground** (21 sites for tents only, first-come, first-served, $16 high season, $10 dry camping mid-Oct.) is the only park campground open year-round. These "walk-in" sites are quite close to the overnight parking lot next to the Kohm Yah-mah-nee Visitors Center; it's just a short jaunt on a paved walkway to your site. Flush toilets and drinking water are available at the campground mid-May through mid-October. In winter, the plumbing is turned off and snow camping is allowed. Flush toilets and drinking water are available year-round at the visitors center.

Warner Valley

Warner Valley (17 sites, first-come, first-served, www.lassenlodging.com, June-Oct., $16) is found in the southwest corner of the park. A small gem, this semi-developed campground has vault toilets, drinking water, picnic tables, and fire pits. The Drakesbad Guest Ranch is nearby, as is a section of the Pacific Crest Trail that passes Boiling Springs Lake. Supplies are available in Chester.

To get there, exit the park's southwest entrance and drive 30 miles (48 km) east on CA-36 to Chester. In Chester, turn north on Warner Valley Road and continue north on a gravel road for 17 miles (27 km). Pass the Warner Valley Ranger Station and continue 1 mile (1.6 km) north to the campground. Trailers and RVs are not recommended on the rough road.

Juniper Lake

Juniper Lake (18 sites, first-come, first-served, June-Oct., $12) takes campers off the beaten path. Located on the east side of the park, this small campground sits beside beautiful Juniper Lake and is perfect for tent campers. Facilities include pit toilets, food lockers, fire pits, and picnic tables, but there is no drinking water (bring your own). The campground is at the end of a rough dirt road, so trailers and RVs are not recommended.

Equestrians can reserve a rugged site at the nearby **Juniper Lake Stock Corral** (www.recreation.gov, late June-mid-Oct., $32 per day). Two corrals can hold a total of 8 animals and 4 vehicles with trailers for groups up to 10. There are pit toilets, and non-potable water is available for livestock. Campers must register their animals for backcountry permits and bring their own livestock feed. The campsite and corral are directly behind the Juniper Lake Ranger Station.

Juniper Lake is accessible via a 13-mile (21-km) paved and gravel road. To get there, exit the park from the southwest entrance and drive 30 miles (48 km) east on CA-36 to the town of Chester. (Look for signs to Drakesbad and Juniper Lake.) Turn north onto Feather River Drive and drive 13 miles (21 km) to Juniper Lake. The last 6 miles (9.5 km) are on a rough dirt road.

Butte Lake

Located in the backcountry far from the park road, **Butte Lake** (101 sites, 877/444-6777, www.recreation.gov, June-Oct., $22) shows off the beauty of Lassen to its advantage. Despite a remote location in the northeast corner of the park, this is a fairly well-developed campground, with vault toilets and potable water. Sites have a fire pit, picnic table, and metal food storage locker. Trailers and RVs up to 35 feet are permitted, as long as they can negotiate the dirt road to Butte Lake. Reservations are recommended.

To reach the campground, exit the park from the northwest entrance near Manzanita Lake. Drive 15 miles (24 km) east on CA-44 to Old Station. Stay right (west) on CA-44 and drive 10 miles (16 km) to Butte Lake Road. Continue 6 miles (9.5 km) south on the dirt road to the campground.

Chester

The tiny town of Chester is practically on the shores of Lake Almanor, where camping is popular in summer (especially during Fourth of July weekend). Chester is also convenient to the southwest entrance of Lassen Volcanic National Park, 25 miles (40 km) east.

Getting There

In summer, many people enter Lassen Volcanic National Park at the northwest entrance (Hwy. 44), travel the park road south to hit the sights (Sulphur Works, Hot Rock, and popular trailheads), and then exit via the southwest entrance before continuing on to Chester.

From Lassen's southwest entrance, CA-36 intersects CA-89 to travel 24 miles (39 km) east to the town of Chester. From I-5 in Red Bluff, the 70-mile (113-km) drive east takes about one hour.

From the north, it's possible to reach Chester via CA-44. From Old Station, at the junction of CA-44 and CA-89, drive 18 miles (29 km) east and turn right onto Mooney Road. In another 18 miles (29 km), you'll hit CA-36 in Westwood. Continue west for 17 miles (27 km) to Chester, hugging the shoreline of Lake Almanor. Plan about one hour for the drive.

Lake Almanor

Lake Almanor is a heart-shaped lake situated near Chester, 35 miles (56 km) west of Susanville. The reservoir features 52 miles of shoreline and is a popular destination in summer, with two large coves for fishing, as well as room for waterskiing, wakeboarding, and swimming. It's common to see herons, ospreys, Canada geese, and perhaps even a bald eagle.

A few resorts and campgrounds dot the west side of the lake, and the U.S. Forest Service maintains two paved **boat ramps** at Canyon Dam and West Shore; each is free to launch from. The east shore of the lake has fewer services and amenities.

In early July, Chester celebrates Independence Day with fireworks displays over Lake Almanor. The **4th of July Fireworks Spectacular** (www.lakealmanorarea.com, July 4) is the headline event of a celebration that includes a parade, a rodeo, a pancake breakfast, a craft fair, and a 5K fun run.

Getting There

Lake Almanor is accessed via CA-36, which runs east-west on the north side of the lake. CA-89 runs north-south along the west side of the lake and continues into Lassen Volcanic National Park.

Shopping

Chester has several bookstores and gift shops to peruse. In the historic Stover Landing Commons, **B&B Booksellers** (278 Main St., 530/258-2150, www.bbbsellers.com, 9am-5pm Mon. and Wed.-Sat., 9am-3pm Sun.) sells kitschy gifts and fun souvenirs along with the latest bestsellers. The friendly owners (and their dog, Fergus the Yorkie) are often milling around. Don't miss the local art gallery upstairs. **Cravings Cafe** (7am-2pm Thurs.-Mon.) is also on the premises.

Find the perfect gift at **The Giggling Crow** (131 Main St., 530/258-3010, 10am-4pm Tues.-Sat.), with a wide selection of unique home decor, women's dresses and scarves, and one-of-a-kind jewelry.

Recreation

The **Collins Pine Nature Trail** (500 Main St., 530/258-2111) is a nice spot to stretch your legs. The 1-mile trail loops around a manicured park with a large showcase of aspens, cottonwoods, and Jeffrey pines, including one with an impressive 53-inch-diameter tree trunk.

Lake Almanor West Golf Course (111 Slim Dr., 530/259-4646, Chester, www.lakealmanorwest.org, dawn-dusk summer, $16-30) is a nine-hole golf course with manicured greens and well-kept fairways. Some spots offer great views of Mt. Lassen in the background. **Bailey Creek Golf Course** (433 Durkin Dr., Lake Almanor, 530/259-4218, https://baileycreek.com, dawn-dusk May-Oct., $35-89) is another spot for hitting some balls in a beautiful setting.

Bodfish Bicycles (149 Main St., 530/258-2338, www.bodfishbicycles.com, 10am-5pm Tues.-Sat., noon-4pm Sun.) rents skinny and fat-tired bikes ($28 per day) and sells kayaks and stand-up paddleboards.

Food

Cravings Cafe, Espresso Bar & Bakery (278 Main St., 530/258-2229, www.stoverlanding.com, 7am-2pm Thurs.-Mon., $8-11) is filled with good company, good coffee, and good books (it shares the space with B&B Booksellers). With a variety of espresso drinks and wholesome breakfast items with vegetarian options, you can't go wrong. The breakfast burrito is a local favorite and pairs well with a Thai tea.

The Coffee Station (192 Main St., 530/258-4112, 7am-3pm Mon.-Fri., 7:30am-1pm Sat., $5-7) is an old-time espresso and bakery shop that serves the best dirty chai lattes this side of CA-36. The shop has a drive-through, or go inside and chat with the friendly staff. Settle into a little dining nook across from the counter and take in the funny Chuck Norris phrase-of-the-day (the rumor is that his wife grew up in the area).

Pine Shack Frosty (321 Main St., 530/258-2593, 11am-8pm daily spring-late Sept., $4-18) is a walk-up burger and ice-cream joint that's popular in summer. Come for the frosties, as well as the burgers, broasted chicken, and smoked barbecued ribs.

★ **Mi Casita** (686 Main St., 530/258-1879, 11am-9pm daily, $10-26) serves authentic Mexican food in a colorful interior. If you're hungry, go for a plate of steak or prawns served with beans and rice, and top it off with a strawberry margarita or a sopaipilla dessert. They sometimes have apple, cherry, and peach fried ice cream.

Accommodations and Camping
North Shore Campground (541 Catfish Beach Rd., 530/258-3376, www.northshorecampground.com, May-Oct., $39 tents, $49-59 RVs) is on the shore of Lake Almanor, with 100 sites for tents and RVs and some cabins. Facilities include picnic tables, fire rings, drinking water, restrooms with low-flow flush toilets and showers, and a small store. There's high-speed Internet in a library and a few Wi-Fi access spots. Stand-up paddleboard and kayak rentals ($25 per hour, $80 per day) are available. The campground is 2 miles (3.2 km) east of Chester.

Rocky Point Campground (916/386-5164 or 530/284-1785, http://recreation. pge.com, May-Sept., $25) is at the southwest end of Lake Almanor with 163 sites for tents and RVs. Facilities include picnic tables, fire rings, drinking water, and vault toilets, plus a group site ($142 per night); there are no hookups for RVs. Reservations ($10 fee) are available seasonally, either by phone or online, with a two-night minimum.

The 104 sites at **Almanor Campgrounds** (Almanor Dr. W., 877/444-6777, www. recreation.gov, May-Sept., $15-18) are situated on the west shore of Lake Almanor. They offer great views of Lassen, with access to biking, hiking, and fishing. Facilities include picnic tables, fire rings, drinking water, vault toilets, and a boat ramp. Group sites ($36-100) can accommodate families. The campground is operated by the Almanor Ranger District (530/258-2141, www.fs.fed.us). To get there from Chester, follow CA-36 west and turn left onto CA-89 south. Drive 6 miles (9.5 km) to Almanor Drive West and turn left. You'll reach the South campground in a mile.

Information and Services
The visitors center is at **Stover Landing Commons** (278 Main St., 530/258-2150, www.stoverlanding.com). A lovely creek runs alongside the historic building. Chester has plenty of gas stations; most are on Main Street. Beacon (303 Main St., 530/259-3500) usually has the cheapest gas, but there's also a Shell (314 Main St., 530/258-3597) and a Chevron (225 Main St., 530/258-2717).

Susanville

The small town of Susanville is the seat of Lassen County and a bike-riding mecca thanks to its proximity to the scenic Bizz Johnson National Recreation Trail and the Susanville Ranch Bike Park. The town is located on the Susan River and has two cinemas, a bowling alley, a bookstore, and eating establishments embedded with a certain Old West charm. It's also a good place to fill your gas tank before leaving the area.

Getting There

Susanville is on CA-36, 35 miles (56 km) east of Chester. CA-36 becomes Main Street as it passes through town.

Sights and Recreation

Susanville Ranch Park (Cherry Terr. and Lakewood Way, Lassen County Public Works 530/251-8288, www.susanville-ranchpark.com, free) is a paradise for mountain bike enthusiasts and is a favorite for local runners, walkers, and horseback riders. This 1,100-acre park contains almost half of the 65 miles of trails available in the area, with unparalleled access to meadows, canyons, creeks, and bluffs.

Mountain Biking
★ **Bizz Johnson National Recreation Trail**

Susanville is the main trailhead for the 25.4-mile (40.9-km) **Bizz Johnson National Recreation Trail** (530/257-0456, www.blm.gov), a favorite with hikers and cyclists. The trail begins at the **Susanville Depot Trailhead Visitors Center and Museum** (601 Richmond Rd., 530/257-3252, no set hours, free) and winds along the Susan River, following the Fernley and Lassen branch line of the former Southern Pacific Railroad route to the small community of Westwood. Mountain bikes are best for navigating this dirt and packed gravel path, which ranges from narrow and rocky terrain to wide stretches through railroad tunnels and over wooden bridges. Pick up trail maps at the visitors center, where you can learn more about the trail and surrounding area.

Entertainment

Sierra Theatre and Uptown Cinemas (819 Main St. and 501 Main St., 530/257-7469, www.sierratheatreanduptowncinemas.com, $6-9) show new releases and box office hits on a combined six screens. The Sierra Theatre has two screens and is right across from Lassen Ale Works; Uptown Cinemas is at the edge of town on the way toward Lassen.

Food

After hitting the Bizz Johnson Trail, grab a brew at the ★ **Lassen Ale Works at the Pioneer** (724 Main St., 530/257-7666, www.lassenaleworks.com, 4pm-10pm Mon., 11am-10pm Tues.-Thurs., 11am-11pm Fri.-Sat., $8-27). Housed in an old saloon, this brewpub serves upscale pub grub made from scratch. The fish-and-chips are the most popular item, but the burgers, sandwiches, and rib eye steaks are all good. A full-length bar with 12 beers on tap takes up most of the front room, with cushy private booths and a pool table in the back. Delicious housemade brews include the Bizz Johnson Blonde and the seasonal Bumpass Helles, which pairs nicely with the chicken sandwich.

Its sister property, the **Lassen Ale Works at the Boardroom** (530/257-4443 Johnstonville Rd., 530/257-4443, www.lassenaleworks.com, 3pm-9pm Wed.-Thurs., noon-9pm Fri.-Sun., $13-17) serves Italian thin-crust specialty pizzas, salads, and chicken wings.

The lively **Lassen Steak House** (1700 Main St., 530/257-7220, 5pm-9pm Mon.-Thurs., $15-34) serves carnivore favorites like a flat-iron steak and a porterhouse. The same owner, self-professed workaholic Esther Faustino, also runs **El Tepeyac Grille** (1700 Main

St., 530/257-7220, https://eltepeyac-grille.com, 7am-9pm Sun.-Tues., 7am-10pm Wed.-Sat., $11-22), a Mexican restaurant that shares a space with the steak house.

The **Diamond Mountain Casino Hotel Brewery** (900 Skyline Rd., 877/319-8514 or 530/252-1100, www.diamondmountaincasino.com, 6am-10pm Sun.-Thurs., 6am-2am Fri.-Sat.) serves its locally brewed beers along with breakfast, lunch, and dinner. Weekly specials include fajitas, Indian tacos, spaghetti, and a 14-ounce prime rib on weekends.

Artisan Coffee (464-440 Church St., Janesville, 530/253-3000, 5am-5pm Mon.-Fri., 7am-5pm Sat.-Sun., $5-7) serves espresso drinks and fruit smoothies. Order at the drive-through or go inside to check out the local artwork and handcrafted items. The outdoor seating is a nice place to catch some sun. The baristas are always friendly. The café is conveniently located off US-395 just south of Susanville.

Accommodations

Built in the 1970s, **The River Inn** (1710 Main St., 530/257-6015, http://riverinnsusanville.us, $60-80) is a simple motel with no frills. The location—on Main Street next to several restaurants—is good, the rooms are clean, and the beds don't sag. A continental breakfast is included. This locally owned business is pet-friendly and has a helpful and pleasant staff.

Red Lion Inn & Suites (3015 Riverside Dr., 530/247-3450, www.redlion.com, $100-135) is in a nice neighborhood off Main Street. Rooms are clean with modern furnishings in queen- or king-bed rooms and suites featuring 37-inch flat-screen televisions, ironing boards, and reclining sitting chairs. Guests have access to free Wi-Fi, and there's a swimming pool, a small gym, and Tesla charging stations. It's also pet-friendly.

Built in the early 1900s by Thomas A. Roseberry (who later died climbing Mt. Lassen), the **Roseberry House Bed & Breakfast** (609 North St., 530/257-5675, www.roseberryhouse.com, $140-165) is a must-stay for history buffs. Rooms have kept their antique furnishings and flowery wallpaper but have no telephones. The best part of your stay is the home-cooked breakfast, most of which is made from scratch, including the muffins, cookies, and jams.

Information and Services

Downtown Susanville's Main Street (CA-36) has plenty of gas stations. You'll find the best rates at **Beacon** (1001 Main St., 530/257-7222) and **Alliance** (1850 Main St., 530/251-5330).

Lassen County Public Works (707 Nevada St., 530/251-8288, www.lassencounty.org, 8am-5pm Mon.-Fri.) provides information about the Susanville Ranch Park.

Lake
Tahoe

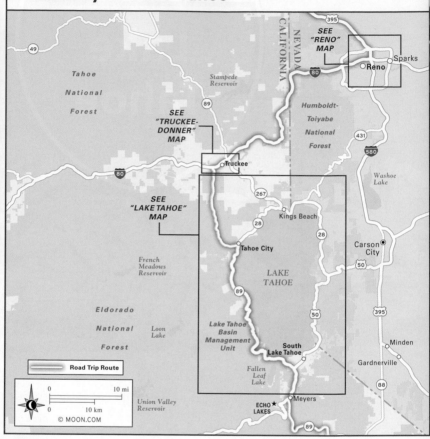

Vicinity of Lake Tahoe

Sitting at an elevation of 6,220 feet (1,895 m) above sea level, Lake Tahoe is a haven for hikers, bikers, boaters, skiers, and snowboarders.

The pristine cobalt lake nestled amid snowcapped mountains and miles of pine trees offers a picturesque scene that's hard to forget. The Nevada state line also runs through Lake Tahoe, so casinos await you the second you cross the border between North Shore and South Lake Tahoe. There are usually two types of visitors who come to Tahoe—ones who want to enjoy the nightlife, sleep in, and then relax on the beach, and the others who get up early and go on a 10-mile (16-km) mountain bike ride or hike before the trails get too crowded.

No matter what you're into, Lake Tahoe is a must-see. Reno, a mere 45-minute drive from Tahoe, also offers plenty of culture, events, and nightlife.

Highlights

★ **Vikingsholm:** Take a fascinating tour of this historic castle-like mansion, which rests on the shores of Emerald Bay (page 374).

★ **Boat Cruises:** Take in the sweeping views of Emerald Bay and the surrounding Sierras while gently gliding through the azure waters of Lake Tahoe (page 379).

★ **Emerald Bay State Park:** This sparkling bay offers some of Tahoe's best hikes, including portions of the Rubicon Trail (page 382).

★ **Ski Resorts:** Tahoe's North Shore offers a variety of terrain and resorts for skiers of all abilities (page 404).

★ **Thunderbird Lodge:** This 19th-century mansion on Tahoe's East Shore contains massive gardens, fountains, a card room, a boat house, and an underground tunnel leading to a former opium den (page 411).

★ **Hot August Nights:** Since 1986, classic car aficionados have been coming to Reno to show off their vintage cars in a week of cruising, drag racing, and fun events (page 433).

Best Restaurants

★ **Free Bird Café, South Lake Tahoe:** Free Bird serves a sweet and spicy chai tea (brewed in-house) to accompany superfood bowls and smoothies (page 389).

★ **Bacchi's Italian Dining, Tahoe City:** Established in 1932, Bacchi's Italian Dining is a family-owned business that has managed to keep Grandma Josephine's story and recipes alive. Indulge in a family-style meal and revel in Tahoe's history (page 409).

★ **Crosby's Tavern & Gaming, Incline Village:** A *Cheers*-like atmosphere makes this the perfect place to indulge in a stuffed avocado or hot wings while watching your favorite team on the screen (page 416).

★ **I.V. Coffee Lab, Incline Village:** This independently owned coffee shop has great decor, comfortable seating, friendly baristas, and espresso drinks served with love (page 416).

★ **Pho 777 Vietnamese Noodle Restaurant, Reno:** For authentic Vietnamese noodle bowls served in big portions, this restaurant in downtown Reno hits the spot (page 434).

Planning Your Time

Lake Tahoe has numerous recreation options accessible year-round. In **winter** (Dec.-Apr.), folks come to Tahoe for the snow. Multiple resorts dot the region; you can see the trails of Diamond Peak, Homewood, and Heavenly from the lake. Ski resorts such as Boreal and Sugar Bowl are right off I-80. Hard-core skiers and snowboarders come to Squaw Valley for the heart-pumping chutes and cliffs off of the KT-22 chairlift.

Summers (June-Aug.) are usually sunny and clear, and thanks to the high elevation around the lake, temperatures never get too hot.

Getting There

While the Tahoe region enjoys 275 days of sunshine annually, winter can start as early as October and temperatures can drop below freezing well into May. June and September are quieter times to come when the weather is still nice. However, there always seems to be at least one snowstorm in June and one in October. It's a good idea to pack an emergency kit in your car if you travel October-May; also bring a snow shovel, chains, blankets, food, and water.

From Shasta and Lassen
185 mi/300 km, 3.5 hr

From **Lassen Volcanic National Park,** take CA-44 east for 14 miles (22.5 km) to **Old Station,** which has a gas station and general store. Continue east on CA-44 for 46 miles (74 km) to Susanville; Main Street/CA-36 connects with US-395, passing several gas stations. Travel south on US-395 for 77 miles (124 km) toward **Reno.** Traffic can be slow through Reno at midweek rush hour.

From Reno, take Mt. Rose Highway (NV-431) southwest for 36 miles (58 km) to **Incline Village** on Lake Tahoe's East Shore. The curvy road climbs quickly in elevation; carry tire chains (Nov.-Apr.) in case of inclement weather. After passing Mt. Rose-Ski Tahoe and the Mount Rose summit, drive through Mt. Rose Meadows as Lake Tahoe comes into view.

Best Accommodations

★ **Camp Richardson, South Lake Tahoe:** This place is a town in itself, with a campground and cabins, a beach and marina, bar and grill, general store, a coffee/ice cream shop, and boat rentals (page 392).

★ **MontBleu Casino, South Lake Tahoe:** Appealing to a young hip crowd out to enjoy some gaming and nightlife, MontBleu has comfortable rooms close to all of the action (page 393).

★ **Granlibakken:** Stay at one of the only "inns" on the West Shore; it's also family friendly (page 400).

★ **Hyatt Regency Lake Tahoe, Incline Village:** With the utmost luxury and convenience, the Hyatt has everything you could want in a Tahoe vacation: rooms with lake and mountain views, a day spa, a classy casino, and lakefront dining (page 417).

★ **Tahoe Biltmore, Crystal Bay:** The historic Tahoe Biltmore has comfortable rooms and cottages located next to a decent casino, across the street from the Crystal Bay Club (page 417).

Stopping in Susanville

On US-395, 11 miles (17.5 km) south of Susanville, is **Artisan Coffee** (464-440 Church St., Janesville, 530/253-3000, 5am-5pm Mon.-Fri., 7am-5pm Sat.-Sun., $5-7) in Janesville. The drive-through offers a good place to stop for a quick espresso and perhaps a souvenir.

From San Francisco
200 mi/320 km, 4 hr

From downtown San Francisco, take I-80 east across the **Bay Bridge** then head north on I-80 for 29 miles (47 km) toward Vallejo. Cross the **Carquinez Bridge** ($5 toll) and continue north for 62 miles (100 km) to **Sacramento,** passing Vacaville on the way (a good place to stop for gas). As you near Sacramento, take US-50 east toward South Lake Tahoe. In 110 miles, US-50 passes the small town of Pollock Pines before entering the curvy, mountainous section of the road. From Pollock Pines, continue 47 miles (76 km) west on US-50 to **South Lake Tahoe.**

Lake Tahoe is a popular getaway destination from San Francisco; traffic congestion can be a nightmare on weekends,

especially when volatile weather hampers I-80. If traveling during these times, bring lots of food, water, and warm clothes. In winter, bring tire chains (and know how to attach them) or drive a four wheel-drive vehicle with snow tires.

From Yosemite
185 mi/300 km, 3.5-4 hr

Lake Tahoe is easily accessible from Yosemite. From the **Big Oak Flat Entrance,** take CA-120 northwest for 58 miles (93 km) toward Copperopolis. In Copperopolis, head north on CA-49 for 65 miles (105 km) to **Placerville,** a good place to refuel. From Placerville, head east on US-50 for 13 miles, passing through Pollock Pines. It's another 47 miles (76 km) northeast on CA-50 to **South Lake Tahoe.**

Summer Option (US-395)

In summer, Yosemite's Tioga Pass Entrance (CA-120) offers access to Lake Tahoe through the Eastern Sierra. From the **Tioga Pass Entrance,** drive 11 miles (17.5 km) east toward **Lee Vining.** At the junction with US-395, veer north and

Lake Tahoe from the East Shore

drive 30 miles (48 km) to **Bridgeport.** If you have enough gas, wait until Gardnerville to fill up your tank (gas is a lot cheaper in Nevada).

From Bridgeport, continue 65 miles (105 km) north on US-395 to Gardnerville and turn west onto curvy Kingsbury Grade/NV-207 and drive 30 miles (48 km) to **South Lake Tahoe.** Or, for a safer route, head north on US-395 for 30 miles (48 km) and take US-50 west toward the lake. Plan 2.5-3 hours to drive this 135-mile (215-km) route.

Air, Train, or Bus
The **Lake Tahoe Airport** (1901 Airport Rd., 530/542-6182, www.cityofslt.us, 7am-4pm Mon.-Fri.) has no commercial flights. The nearest commercial airport is the **Reno-Tahoe International Airport**

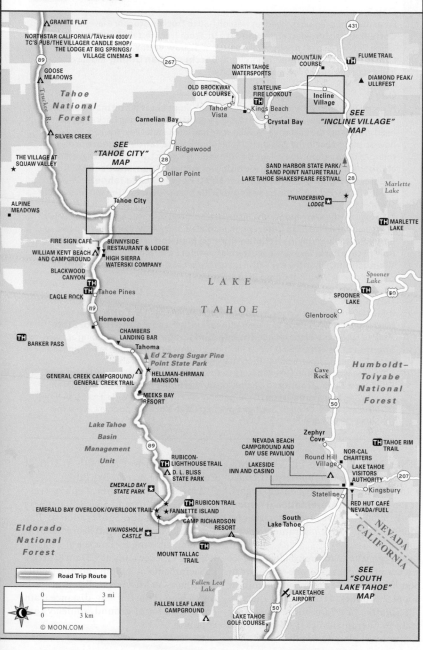

Lake Tahoe

GRANITE FLAT

NORTHSTAR CALIFORNIA/TAVERN 6330'/
TC'S PUB/THE VILLAGER CANDLE SHOP/
THE LODGE AT BIG SPRINGS/
VILLAGE CINEMAS

267

431

MOUNTAIN
COURSE

TH FLUME TRAIL

89

GOOSE
MEADOWS

NORTH TAHOE
WATERSPORTS

OLD BROCKWAY
GOLF COURSE

STATELINE
FIRE LOOKOUT
TH

DIAMOND PEAK/
ULLRFEST

Incline
Village

Tahoe
National
Forest

SILVER CREEK

Tahoe
Vista

Kings Beach

SEE
"INCLINE VILLAGE"
MAP

THE VILLAGE AT
SQUAW VALLEY

Carnelian Bay

Ridgewood

Crystal Bay

SAND HARBOR STATE PARK/
SAND POINT NATURE TRAIL/
LAKE TAHOE SHAKESPEARE FESTIVAL

Marlette
Lake

SEE
"TAHOE CITY"
MAP

28

28

Dollar Point

THUNDERBIRD
LODGE

ALPINE
MEADOWS

Tahoe City

Spooner
Lake

TH MARLETTE
LAKE

FIRE SIGN CAFÉ

SUNNYSIDE
RESTAURANT & LODGE

WILLIAM KENT BEACH
AND CAMPGROUND

HIGH SIERRA
WATERSKI COMPANY

LAKE

BLACKWOOD
CANYON

TH

TAHOE

SPOONER
LAKE

TH

50

EAGLE ROCK

Tahoe Pines

89

Homewood

Glenbrook

TH BARKER PASS

CHAMBERS
LANDING BAR

Tahoma

Ed Z'berg Sugar Pine
Point State Park

Cave
Rock

Humboldt–
Toiyabe
National
Forest

GENERAL CREEK CAMPGROUND/
GENERAL CREEK TRAIL

HELLMAN-EHRMAN
MANSION

MEEKS BAY
RESORT

Lake Tahoe
Basin
Management
Unit

89

RUBICON-
LIGHTHOUSE TRAIL
TH

D. L. BLISS
STATE PARK

50

NEVADA BEACH
CAMPGROUND AND
DAY USE PAVILION

LAKESIDE
INN AND CASINO

Zephyr
Cove

Round Hill
Village

NOR-CAL
CHARTERS

TH TAHOE RIM
TRAIL

LAKE TAHOE
VISITORS
AUTHORITY

207

EMERALD BAY
STATE PARK

RUBICON TRAIL
TH

Stateline

Kingsbury

Eldorado
National
Forest

EMERALD BAY OVERLOOK/OVERLOOK TRAIL

FANNETTE ISLAND

VIKINGSHOLM
CASTLE

CAMP RICHARDSON
RESORT

South
Lake Tahoe

RED HUT CAFÉ
NEVADA/FUEL

NEVADA

CALIFORNIA

MOUNT TALLAC
TRAIL
TH

Fallen Leaf
Lake

SEE
"SOUTH
LAKE TAHOE"
MAP

Road Trip Route

FALLEN LEAF LAKE
CAMPGROUND

LAKE TAHOE
AIRPORT

0   3 mi

0   3 km

LAKE TAHOE
GOLF COURSE

50

© MOON.COM

Lake Tahoe in Three Days

Day 1

Enter the Tahoe region by heading west on I-80 to Truckee. Stop for a lavender latte at **Coffeebar** and breakfast at the **Squeeze In.** From Truckee, take CA-89 south toward Tahoe City, veering off to explore the village at **Squaw Valley,** where you'll ride the tram to High Camp. In the evening, dine at **Bacchi's Italian Dining** and stay the night at the **Pepper Tree Inn** in Tahoe City.

Day 2

Wake up in Tahoe City and drive 15 minutes east, stopping at **Waterman's Landing** for a paddleboarding session. After getting a good workout, jump back in the car and head east across the California-Nevada state line into Crystal Bay. You're in Nevada now, so place a bet in the William Hill sports book at the **Tahoe Biltmore** or play a round of blackjack. Incline Village is a 10-minute drive east, where you'll have lunch at **Crosby's Tavern & Gaming.** Go hiking (or skiing) at **Diamond Peak Ski Resort** and stay the night close to the lake at the **Hyatt Regency Lake Tahoe.** Have a Golden Eagle cocktail in the **Lone Eagle Grille** bar as you watch the sun set over the Sierra.

To explore the West and South Shores instead, head south along CA-89 and enjoy breakfast at the **Fire Sign Café.** Continue south along CA-89, stopping for a hike to **Eagle Rock,** then visit the **Hellman-Ehrman Mansion** at **Ed Z'berg Sugar Pine Point State Park.** Take in the spectacular views of **Emerald Bay** and take a tour of **Vikingsholm.** Finish the day with a cactus burger at the **Burger Lounge.** Either camp or stay in a cabin at **Camp Richardson.**

Day 3

If you stayed in Incline Village, wake up with an espresso at **I.V. Coffee Lab,** then head south on NV-28. Stop to wiggle your toes in the sand at **Sand Harbor State Park** or take a tour of the unique **Thunderbird Lodge.** Consider stopping at **Spooner Lake** at the US-50/NV-28 junction to admire the aspens in fall. From Spooner Lake, follow US-50 south to Stateline and South Lake Tahoe.

If you stayed in South Lake Tahoe, get a Cookie Monster donut from **Glazed and Confuzed Tahoe Donut** and a house-made chai from **Free Bird Café.** Continue your driving loop northeast on US-50, passing into Stateline, Nevada. From Stateline, US-50 heads north through **Zephyr Cove** and **Cave Rock** to Spooner Lake at the US-50/NV-28 junction.

(RNO, 2001 E. Plumb Ln., Reno, NV, 775/328-6400, www.renoairport.com), with more than 130 daily nonstop flights, or the **Sacramento International Airport** (SMF, 6900 Airport Blvd., Sacramento, 916/929-5411, https://sacramento.aero/smf).

You can take an **Amtrak** (800/872-7245, www.amtrak.com, $34 one-way) bus to South Lake Tahoe from Sacramento in about 2.5 hours. From San Francisco, the *Capitol Corridor* route travels by train to Sacramento ($31-94 one-way). Continue via bus to South Lake Tahoe ($34 one-way) to the South Y Transit Center (1000 Emerald Bay Rd.).

Amtrak's California Zephyr (reservations required, $53-97) departs Emeryville in the San Francisco Bay Area daily at 9:10am and Sacramento at 11:09am, arriving in Truckee at 2:38pm. It leaves Truckee daily at 9:37am to arrive in Sacramento at 2:13pm and Emeryville at 4:10pm—at least when all goes according to plan. This is a long-distance train covering a lot of ground, so delays are common.

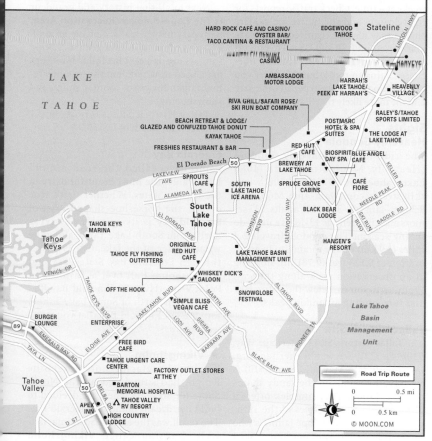

South Lake Tahoe

Map labels: HARD ROCK CAFÉ AND CASINO/ OYSTER BAR/ TACO.CANTINA & RESTAURANT; EDGEWOOD TAHOE; Stateline; CASINO; HARVEYS; AMBASSADOR MOTOR LODGE; HARRAH'S LAKE TAHOE/ PEEK AT HARRAH'S; HEAVENLY VILLAGE; RIVA GRILL/SAFARI ROSE/ SKI RUN BOAT COMPANY; RALEY'S/TAHOE SPORTS LIMITED; BEACH RETREAT & LODGE/ GLAZED AND CONFUZED TAHOE DONUT; POSTMARC HOTEL & SPA SUITES; THE LODGE AT LAKE TAHOE; KAYAK TAHOE; FRESHIES RESTAURANT & BAR; RED HUT CAFÉ; BIOSPIRIT DAY SPA; BLUE ANGEL CAFÉ; El Dorado Beach; 50; BREWERY AT LAKE TAHOE; LAKEVIEW AVE; SPROUTS CAFÉ; SOUTH LAKE TAHOE ICE ARENA; SPRUCE GROVE CABINS; CAFÉ FIORE; ALAMEDA AVE; South Lake Tahoe; BLACK BEAR LODGE; KELLER RD; NEEDLE PEAK RD; EL DORADO AVE; JOHNSON BLVD; GLENWOOD WAY; SKI RUN BLVD; SADDLE RD; TAHOE KEYS MARINA; Tahoe Keys; TAHOE FLY FISHING OUTFITTERS; ORIGINAL RED HUT CAFÉ; LAKE TAHOE BASIN MANAGEMENT UNIT; HANGEN'S RESORT; VENICE DR; WHISKEY DICK'S SALOON; OFF THE HOOK; SNOWGLOBE FESTIVAL; AL TAHOE BLVD; Lake Tahoe Basin Management Unit; TAHOE KEYS BLVD; MARTIN AVE; SIMPLE BLISS VEGAN CAFÉ; LODI AVE; BURGER LOUNGE; ENTERPRISE; EMERALD BAY RD; ELOISE AVE; SIGRA BLVD; BARBARA AVE; PIONEER TR; FREE BIRD CAFÉ; TATA LN; TAHOE URGENT CARE CENTER; FACTORY OUTLET STORES AT THE Y; BLACK BART AVE; Tahoe Valley; 50; MELBA DR; BARTON MEMORIAL HOSPITAL; TAHOE VALLEY RV RESORT; APEX INN; D ST; HIGH COUNTRY LODGE; 89; Road Trip Route; 0 0.5 mi; 0 0.5 km; © MOON.COM; LAKE TAHOE

South Shore and Stateline

Lake Tahoe's South Shore is known more for casinos and nightlife than for outdoor recreation. Heavenly and Kirkwood ski resorts offer terrain for advanced skiers and snowboarders, while the nearby Desolation Wilderness lures serious hikers.

Stateline sits east of South Lake Tahoe on the Nevada side of the lake. This is where you'll find casinos like Harrah's and Harvey's.

Getting There

US-50 provides the quickest access to South Lake Tahoe. From the San Francisco Bay Area, the drive takes about five hours in good weather without traffic; from Sacramento it's about two hours. However, don't expect good weather or light traffic if you plan to drive on a Friday in winter or summer. Everybody else will be on the road with you, significantly slowing down the routes. Be sure to check traffic reports before you hit the road.

In winter, highways may close during

major storms, and smaller roads surrounding the lake can shut down for weeks at a time. Check traffic reports for road closures and alternative routes. Tire chains may also be required. There are many spots on I-80 and US-50 to pull off in order to attach chains. You can purchase chains en route, but the closer you get to Tahoe, the more expensive they are and the more likely they'll be out of stock.

Sights

Heavenly Gondola

The ride up the **Heavenly Gondola** (Heavenly Mountain Resort, 4080 Lake Tahoe Blvd., 775/586-7000, www. skiheavenly.com, 9am-4pm Mon.-Fri., 8:30am-4am Sat.-Sun., $61 adults, $37 seniors and children age 13-18) is a must-do in any season. The gondola travels 2.4 miles (3.9 km) up the mountain to an elevation of 9,123 feet (2,781 m), stopping at an observation deck along the way. From here, you can view the entire lake and surrounding mountain peaks.

Tallac Historic Site

The **Tallac Historic Site** (1 Heritage Way, 530/541-5227, www.tahoeheritage.org, tours daily late May-mid-Sept., $10) is a sprawling estate on the sandy shores of Lake Tahoe. This complex offers a glimpse into the lifestyles of the 19th-century Baldwin and Pope families who made Tahoe their summer home. Start your exploration off at the **Baldwin Museum** (10am-4pm daily late May-mid-Sept., free) and learn about the history of the local Washoe people, the estate preservation, and information about navigating the grounds.

Visitors can tour the interior of the 1894 **Pope House** (11am, 12:30pm, 2pm daily late May-early Sept., reservations recommended, $10 adults, $5 children age 6-12, children 5 and under free). Parents can take advantage of children's activities like the free Make It & Take It Kids Art Projects workshop (ages 4-12, Wed. and Fri. June-Aug.). Kids learn how to make nature journals, wood puzzles, and owls out of pine cones.

Next to all that history and grandeur is the **Pope-Baldwin Recreation Area,** with easy nature trails, a picnic ground, and a beach for swimming and kayaking (rentals available). The Tallac buildings are closed in winter, but the grounds remain open for cross-country skiing and snowshoeing.

Tallac Historic Site is off CA-89, 3.1 miles (5 km) north of US-50.

Emerald Bay

Some have called the road around Lake Tahoe the most beautiful drive in the United States. Whether that's true or not, the horseshoe-shaped inlet of **Emerald Bay** is its epicenter. Driving north from South Lake Tahoe along the western edge of the lake, CA-89 passes through Emerald Bay State Park and Vikingsholm. Pull over at **Inspiration Point Vista** (Hwy. 89/Emerald Bay Rd., 8 mi/13 km north of South Lake Tahoe) for views of Emerald Bay that you won't want to miss.

★ Vikingsholm

Wealthy benefactor Lora Josephine Knight had summered on the North Shore for 16 years when she decided to build her dream home on Emerald Bay. The result was the elegant Scandinavian-style mansion called **Vikingsholm** (Emerald Bay State Park, Hwy. 89, 530/525-7232, http://vikingsholm.com or www.parks.ca.gov, tours 10:30am-3:30pm daily late May-Sept., grounds free, tours $10 adults, $8 ages 7-17). This architectural gem is an intriguing reminder of a world gone by. Built by a Swedish architect in 1929, the castle-like structure is composed of granite boulders and includes towers, hand-cut timbers, and sod roofs green with growing grass. Knight was an environmentalist who tried to keep the grounds pristine; several old-growth cedar trees around the castle and within the courtyard still stand. The interior is furnished with authentic Scandinavian period reproductions, including a Steinway piano.

Visitors are welcome to enjoy the beach, the grounds, and the exterior of Vikingsholm at no charge; entrance to the mansion is only accessible via a ranger-led tour. To access the grounds, take the hard-packed 1-mile (1.6-km) trail from the parking lot at the **Emerald Bay Overlook** (Hwy. 89/Emerald Bay Rd., $10). It's fairly steep, but the amazing views and waterfalls are worth it. You can also reach Vikingsholm via the Rubicon Trail (1.7 mi/2.7 km one-way) from Eagle Point Campground in Emerald Bay State Park (note that the parking spots tend to fill early on summer weekends). Dogs are not allowed on the trail.

D. L. Bliss State Park

D. L. Bliss State Park (Hwy. 89, 530/525-7277, www.parks.ca.gov, late May-mid-Oct., $10) has some of the best views in Tahoe. The 744 acres of land were gifted to the California State Parks by the Bliss family in the late 1920s. Several hiking paths and a campground make this a popular place in summer. Trails include the **Rubicon-Lighthouse Trail** to Rubicon Point's lighthouse, which was built in 1919. Play in the water at the Lester and Calawee Cove Beaches, or trek to the natural rock formation on the Balancing Rock Trail.

The park is 2 miles (3.2 km) north of Emerald Bay State Park.

Sports and Recreation
Ski Resorts

Tahoe has more than a dozen ski resorts; however, the average price of a lift ticket can be prohibitive ($89-160). Heavily discounted rates may be available with some advance planning; or, purchase lift tickets online through Liftopia (www.liftopia.com). Check the websites of ski resorts for special deals. The best time to go is **midweek** (non-holidays), when it's less likely that you'll see long ticket lines.

Heavenly

Heavenly Mountain Resort (4080 Lake Tahoe Blvd., South Lake Tahoe, 775/586-7000, www.skiheavenly.com, 9am-4pm Mon.-Fri., 8:30am-4pm Sat.-Sun. Dec.-Apr., $133-154 adults, $109-126 youth ages 13-18 and seniors 65-plus, $73-85 children ages 5-12) is located in the middle of South Shore, within walking distance to casinos and ski trails. At 10,067 feet (3,068 m), Heavenly offers the highest elevation of any mountain at Tahoe, along with a 500-foot tubing hill, a gravity-powered alpine coaster, and a 5-mile-long ski run.

Skiers can choose from four lodge and village access points to the trails that start at mid-mountain: the gondola at Heavenly Village, the California Lodge at the top of Ski Run Boulevard, and the Boulder/Stagecoach lodges on the Nevada side along Kingsbury Grade (NV-207). Ninety-seven runs snake down the mountain, taking advantage of the more than 3,500 vertical feet (1,050 m). Beginners should start with the gondola to Tamarack Lodge, where most of the green circle runs are. Advanced skiers and expert backcountry enthusiasts will love Killebrew and Mott Canyons, which are steep, filled with snow, and only accessible when the gates are open.

There are also a couple of terrain park choices for beginners. Groove, an easy terrain park, is accessible from the California side via Patsy's chairlift. The High Roller Park has medium-to-advanced features with several lines to choose from. It's on the upper mountain near the Canyon Express.

Heavenly is an intensely popular resort. Parking is a challenge at whichever lodge you choose. Crowding and lines at the lifts, especially at the bottom of the mountain, can get bad on weekends and holidays. On the other hand, once you're out of your car and on the gondola, you'll have access to nearly every service and amenity you need.

Public transportation is

provided by **BlueGo** (530/541-7149, www. tahoetransportation.org, adults $2-5), which picks up at major lodging areas around town and drops skiers off at any of Heavenly's four lodges.

Sierra-at-Tahoe

For a smaller, less-crowded, and cheaper South Shore experience, check out **Sierra-at-Tahoe** (1111 Sierra-at-Tahoe Rd., Twin Bridges, 530/659-7453, www. sierraattahoe.com, 9am-4pm Mon.-Fri., 8:30am-4pm Sat.-Sun. late Nov.-Apr., $105-110 adults, $95-100 youth ages 13-22, $41-45 children ages 5-12, $41-76 seniors). Sierra-at-Tahoe appeals to a freestyle crowd with its fun, challenging terrain parks and half-pipe. It features plenty of long sweeping advanced runs as well as many good intermediate tracks. The Easy Street area is 100 acres of beginner-only terrain. More advanced beginners can enjoy the Sugar 'n' Spice Trail, which runs all the way from the top. Grandview Express quad chairs take skiers to the very top, while the Nob Hill double chair lands midway up the mountain. The Rock Garden and Easy Rider Express lifts handle those looking for easy runs and terrain parks. It's all black-diamond runs on the outer edges of the mountain, and mostly blues and blacks off the West Bowl Express quad or the Puma triple chair. A few beginning and intermediate runs go down the back of the mountain. The Huckleberry Bowl boasts off-piste, advanced backcountry terrain.

The resort has 10 **restaurants.** For incredible views, go to the top of the mountain and eat at the 360 Smokehouse BBQ (10:30am-3pm daily) within the Grandview Lodge. At the Main Lodge, visit The Sierra Pub (10:30am-4:30pm Mon.-Fri., 9am-5pm Sat.-Sun.), Mama's Kitchen (8:30am-4pm daily), Golden Bear Terrace (11am-2:30pm Fri.-Sun.), Java Junction (8am-4:30pm daily), or Aspen Café (11am-2:30pm).

In Solstice Plaza, find Solstice Eatery (10:30am-3:30pm Mon.-Thurs., 10:30am-4:30pm Fri.-Sun.), Corkscrew Bar (11am-4:30pm Mon.-Fri., 9am-4:30pm Sat.-Sun.), and Nacho Mamas (11am-4pm) in hand. In the West Bowl, relax at the Baja Grill (10:30am-3pm daily).

Sierra-at-Tahoe is about 20 miles (32 km) southwest of South Lake Tahoe off US-50 west of Meyers.

Kirkwood

Heavenly's sister resort is **Kirkwood Mountain Resort** (1501 Kirkwood Meadows Dr., Kirkwood, 209/258-6000, www.kirkwood.com, 9am-4pm daily Dec.-Apr., $133-154 adults, $109-126 youth ages 13-18 and seniors 65-plus, $73-85 children ages 5-12), known for its cliffs, cornices, and a few wide-groomed trails for beginners. Kirkwood has four major peaks, all of which are above 9,250 feet (2,800 m), with single- and double-black-diamond bowls, chutes, and trails.

The **Kirkwood Ski & Ride School** (209/258-7754) and **Children's Center** (209/258-7754) are both located near the Timber Creek Base Area, which has most of the easy and intermediate runs. Advanced and expert skiers will want to park at the Mountain Village and take The Wall or Cornice Express to the top.

Kirkwood features terrain parks for intermediate skiers and snowboarders; a skier-snowboarder cross course is available when conditions allow. For a gentler walk in the woods, visit the **Kirkwood Cross Country & Snowshoe Center** (Hwy. 88 before Kirkwood, 209/258-7248, 9am-4pm daily winter, $30 adults, $23 youth and seniors, $14 children, $5 dogs), next to the Kirkwood Inn. You can rent equipment and take lessons before skating off into the 60 kilometers of machine-groomed tracks.

The resort has eight **restaurants.** The Wall Bar & Grill (209/258-7365), The Cornice Pizza (209/258-7225), Monte Wolfe's, and the K-Bar are in the Mountain Village. The General Store is at Red Cliffs Day Lodge. The Kirkwood Inn

& Saloon (209/258-7309) and Snowshoe Thompson's Bar & Grill are at Timber Creek. The Sunrise Grill is on the back side of the mountain.

Those who prefer to stay where they ski should book one of the properties under **Kirkwood Lodging** (844/471-3753, 8am-5pm Mon.-Fri., 8am-4pm Sat., 9am-2pm Sun.), which offers hotel rooms at The Lodge at Kirkwood and The Mountain Club, along with townhomes at Timber Ridge, for $171-561 per night.

Expedition: Kirkwood (reservations 209/258-7360, $504-661) offers private tours, backcountry excursions, and avalanche clinics that run 3-6 hours (up to 5 people). Tours are available by phone only and depend on snow conditions. Bring avalanche beacons, probes, shovels, touring gear, and backpacks, or rent them on-site.

Kirkwood is 35 miles (56 km) south of South Lake Tahoe along CA-89/88, near Carson Pass. Plan one hour for the drive, though it's impossible to get to during a storm.

Cross-Country Skiing and Snowshoeing

Cross-country skiers will find groomed and maintained trails at numerous cross-country centers, easy trails for a glide through the woods, and some serious backcountry adventures.

A **Sno-Park** parking pass (recording 916/324-1222, information 916/324-4442, www.ohv.parks.ca.gov, $5 per day, all-season $25) is required for many forest ski trailheads November-May. You can buy the pass online, order one by mail, or purchase it in person at one of the following South Lake Tahoe vendors: Kyburz Silver Fork Store (13200 Hwy. 50, Kyburz, 530/293-3172, 7am-8pm Mon.-Thurs., 7am-11pm Fri., 7am-10pm Sat.-Sun.), Strawberry Station (17481 Hwy. 50, Twin Bridges, 530/659-0744, 7am-6pm daily), Tahoe Paradise Chevron (2986 Hwy. 50, South Lake Tahoe, 530/577-1127, 6am-11pm daily), Tahoe

Roadrunner (2933 Hwy. 50, South Lake Tahoe, 530/577-6946, 6am-10pm Sun.-Thurs., 6am-11pm Fri.-Sat.), or the Tahoe Bike & Ski Company (3131 Harrison Ave., South Lake Tahoe, 530/600-0267, 9am-5pm Mon.-Thurs., 8am-6pm Fri.-Sun.). The website lists additional vendors. Call ahead to make sure each vendor has passes in stock.

Adventure Mountain (21200 US-50, Echo Summit, 530/659-7217, http://adventuremountaintahoe.com, 10am-4pm Mon.-Fri., 9am-4pm Sat.-Sun., $35 Mon.-Fri., $40 Sat.-Sun.) is a privately operated snow park on Echo Summit with snowshoe trails, groomed sledding runs, and a lodge with fireplace and café. Equipment rentals include two-person sleds ($15 per day), inner tubes ($28 for 2 hours, $40 all day), and helmets ($8/day). It's cash only at the entrance gate, but the lodge does take credit cards.

Those planning overnight ski-camping trips must first get a **wilderness permit** (877/444-6777, www.recreation.gov, $5 pp/1 night, $10 pp/2 or more nights). Permits are sold at the **Lake Tahoe Basin Management Unit Supervisor's Office** (35 College Dr., South Lake Tahoe, 530/543-2600, 8am-4:30pm Mon.-Fri.) and the **Taylor Creek Visitor Center** (Hwy. 89, 3 mi/4.8 km north of the Hwy. 50/89 intersection, 530/543-2674, 8am-4:30pm daily summer). While snow conditions tend to be best in the morning, moonlight skiing is also fun. Ensure conditions are safe and bring a probe, avalanche shovel, and beacon; tell someone where you are going.

Sections of the beautiful **Tahoe Rim Trail** can be ideal for snowshoeing, depending on conditions. The west side of the lake (locally called "the banana belt") tends to get more snow than the east side. The first snowfall usually hits the trail in November; some places will still have snow as late as July. The **Tahoe Rim Trail Association** (128 Market St., Ste. 3E, Stateline, 775/298-4485, www.tahoerimtrail.org) suggests calling for

an updated report on conditions and specific advice on where to go. In winter (Jan.-Mar.), the association offers guided snowshoe hikes and snow camping workshops.

A number of cross-country trails are maintained by the U.S. Forest Service. Some trails offer short single-day excursions, while others lead miles back into the Desolation Wilderness. These trails appeal to hard-core ski-campers who want a multiday adventure. Beginner explorers can have the safest backcountry fun at **Taylor Creek** (Hwy. 89, 530/543-2674, www.fs.usda.gov or www.fs.fed.us), west of Camp Richardson and Tallac Historic Site. The uncongested yet populous area has many flat marked trails that help newcomers get a feel for the forest. Trails for skiers of all levels run along the South and West Shores of Lake Tahoe. For camping in the Desolation Wilderness, the most popular trailhead leads past **Echo Lakes** (US-50 at Echo Lake Rd.) toward **Aloha Lake** and then into the backcountry along the Pacific Crest Trail.

Snowmobiling

Lake Tahoe Adventures (1300 Apache Ave., 530/577-2940 or 800/865-4679, www.laketahoeadventures.com, 8am-5pm daily Nov.-Apr., $150-290) specializes in snowmobile tours for groups and individuals. A shuttle takes riders from the center to the base camp in Hope Valley, where a fleet of Arctic Cat, Polaris, and Ski-Doo snowmobiles are used to explore the high-elevation backcountry. Choose an easy two-hour trail tour to the summit or one of the "ultimate" off-trail tours that go deep into the backcountry. Reservations are required; boots, gloves, and helmets are included (snow suits and goggles are available for rent). The company also offers Jeep and ATV tours.

From top to bottom: Heavenly Gondola; Zephyr Cove Marina; D. L. Bliss State Park.

Tahoe Snowmobiles (55 US-50, Stateline, NV, 530/542-3294, https://tahoesnowmobiles.com, 9am-5pm daily winter, $70 for 30 minutes) has a flat track available to cruise around on some electric sleds. Snowmobiles fit up to two people and include one helmet; drivers must be age 16 and older. The outfitter also rents snow tubes ($40/hour).

The **Zephyr Cove Snowmobile Center** (Zephyr Cove Resort, 760 US-50, 775/589-4906 or 800/238-2463, www.zephyrcove.com, $160-280) offers scenic lake-view tours and adventures through mountainous snowy terrain 9,000 feet (2,700 m) above sea level. A convenient shuttle offers pickups and drop-offs, complimentary for all reserved riders. With a fleet of more than 100 electric snow sleds, Zephyr Cove has several different tour options, including a two-hour Lakeview tour and an Ultimate Experience Tour for experienced riders; both tours include breathtaking views, easy riding on groomed trails, hill climbing, and plenty of stops for pictures.

Sledding and Snow Play

Hansen's Resort (1360 Ski Run Blvd., South Lake Tahoe, 530/544-3361, www.hansensresort.com, 10am-4pm daily mid-Dec.-Mar., $20 pp/hour, cash only) offers more features than many impromptu snow-play spots. With a couple of 400-foot snow tracks, you'll definitely get some thrills slipping down the hill. Hansen's hourly rate includes the use of a saucer or tube. Hours are dependent upon snow conditions and may be reduced if Mother Nature isn't cooperating.

Adventure Mountain Lake Tahoe (21200 US-50, Echo Summit, 530/659-7217, http://adventuremountaintahoe.com, 10am-4pm Mon.-Fri., 9am-4pm Sat.-Sun., $35 Mon.-Fri., $40 Sat.-Sun., $45 holidays) has some of the nicest groomed sledding runs in Tahoe. With 40 acres of sled runs and play areas, plus restrooms and a concession stand that sells hot coffee and new sleds, Adventure

Mountain also intersects with the Pacific Crest Trail and a few other cross-country skiing and snowshoeing trails for those who want a quieter but more labor-intensive day in the snow. Feel free to bring your own sled and tubes. Adventure Mountain is in the South Shore area between Meyers and Sierra-at-Tahoe.

Near Stateline, **Borges Family Sleigh Rides** (4130 Lake Tahoe Blvd., South Lake Tahoe, NV, 775/588-2953, www.sleighride.com, 11am-3pm Nov.-Dec., 11am-4pm Jan.-Feb., 11am-5pm dates vary Mar.-Apr., $50 adults, $20 children ages 2-10) gives sleigh rides that seat 2-20 passengers pulled by lovely blond Belgian draft horses; rides on Sand Harbor are also available. Cuddle under blankets as you listen to stories and songs—bring a thermos of cocoa.

Ice-Skating

As the temperatures start to drop, **Heavenly Village** (1001 Heavenly Village Way, 530/542-4230, www.theshopsatheavenly.com, 10am-8pm daily Nov.-early Apr., $20 adults, $15 children under 13) turns into a winter wonderland. Their outdoor ice-skating rink appeals to kids and newbies, as well as those looking to have fun. As Tahoe attractions go, this is an entertainment bargain since your pass includes skate rental and in-and-out access all day long.

For serious skaters and hockey players, the **South Lake Tahoe Ice Arena** (1176 Rufus Allen Blvd., 530/544-7465, www.tahoearena.co, 11am-7pm daily, $15 adults, $6 children 6 and under) is a year-round center with drop-in hockey, public skating, and a skate school (drop-in lessons $20/half-hour) on an NHL standard-size arena. Admission rates include skate rental.

★ Boat Cruises

Any number of cruises and tours are offered all around Lake Tahoe. To get out on the water, book a cruise with **Lake Tahoe Cruises** (760 Hwy. 50, Zephyr

Cove, 800/238-2463 or 775/589-4906, www.laketahoecruises.com or www.zephyrcove.com). Two big and beautiful boats—a yacht and a paddle-wheeler—cruise the lake on a daily basis, even in winter. The 82-foot *Tahoe Paradise* ($55 adults, $33 children ages 3-11) holds up to 90 passengers and features two stories with a dining room, bar, galley, and a sundeck. The MS *Dixie II* ($55 adults, $33 children ages 3-11) is a replica of a rear paddle-wheeler imported from the Mississippi River. The MS *Dixie II* accommodates up to 500 passengers, making it Tahoe's largest vessel. The 2.5-hour tour departs the Zephyr Cove Marina for Emerald Bay, with options for daytime, dinner, or a private charter cruise.

The *Safari Rose* (900 Ski Run Blvd., 775/588-1881, www.tahoecruises.com, 11am-2pm daily summer, 11am-2pm Sat.-Sun. winter, $95 adults, $49 children 11 and under) takes passengers on a three-hour tour that includes lunch in Emerald Bay. A 2.5-hour sunset champagne cruise ($85 adults) is also available.

Lake Tahoe Bleu Wave (2435 Venice Dr. E., 866/413-0985 or 775/588-9283, www.tahoebleuwave.com, $80-90 adults, $40-45 children 4-12, year-round) operates out of the Tahoe Keys Marina. The yacht has a private lounge, an outdoor party bow, restrooms, and a fireplace inside. The 2.5-hour Emerald Bay lunch and sunset cruises treat guests to views of Emerald Bay, Eagle Waterfall, Vikingsholm, and the Rubicon area year-round. In summer, the Bleu Wave offers Wine Down Wednesdays (June-Sept., $80), a two-hour cruise with cheese, appetizers, and unlimited wine-tasting.

In winter, take the Bleu Wave's floating **ski shuttle** (7am-4pm Sat.-Sun., mid-Dec.-mid-Apr., $188 pp) to Homewood on the West Shore, which includes a continental breakfast. Free pickup is available from some lodging properties in South Lake Tahoe.

Beaches

Nestled between Zephyr Cove and Stateline, **Nevada Beach Campground and Day Use Pavilion** (3 mi/4.8 km north of Stateline, 775/588-5562, www.fs.usda.gov, fee) has several tent sites and a wood-roofed meeting space with 10 picnic tables and barbecue grills. More populated is **El Dorado Beach** (1004 Lakeview Ave., 530/542-6000, www.cityofslt.us), a long sandy shoreline with staggered natural rock seating that makes it a popular place for SUP races and other special events.

Boating, Waterskiing, and Wakeboarding

With miles of open water, a number of docks and marinas, and a lovely shoreline to explore, Lake Tahoe is irresistible to water-skiers, wakeboarders, parasailers, stand-up paddleboarders, and powerboaters. The chilly water can feel refreshing in the middle of July when temperatures start to heat up.

Tahoe Keys Marina (2435 Venice Dr. E., South Lake Tahoe, 530/541-2155, www.tahoekeysmarina.net) is one of the largest marinas. They sell gas, provide launch access, rent boast and slips, and offer sailing lessons.

Tahoe Keys Boat & Charter Rentals (2435 Venice Dr. E., South Lake Tahoe, 530/544-8888, www.tahoesports.com, 10am-6pm daily May-Oct., $462-957 for 4 hours) operates out of the Tahoe Keys Marina. Boat rentals include pontoon boats, Four Winns powerboat cruisers, Reinells, SUPs, and kayaks. Jet Skis, parasailing, and buoy rentals are also available.

The **Ski Run Boat Company** (Ski Run Marina, 900 Ski Run Blvd., South Lake Tahoe, 530/544-0200, www.tahoesports.com) has even more variety. In addition to Jet Skis, pontoon boats, and Reinell powerboats, you can rent canoes, kayaks, stand-up paddleboards, and even a water tricycle.

The marina at **Camp Richardson** (1900 Jameson Beach Rd., South Lake Tahoe,

530/541-1801 or 800/544-1801, www. camprichardson.com, 9am-5pm daily mid-May-mid-June and early Sept.-mid-Oct., 8am-8pm daily mid-June-mid-Sept.) rents kayaks ($30-40/hour), pontoon boats ($642/4 hours, $1,284/day), paddleboards ($35/hour), and Sea-Doos ($130/hour). They also offer a 1.5-hour Rum Runner Emerald Bay Cruise (530/542-6570, 1pm, 3:30pm, 6pm daily late May-mid-Oct., $59 adults, $29 children 12 and under).

Zephyr Cove Marina (750 US-50, Zephyr Cove, NV, 800/238-2463, www. zephyrcove.com) rents a full line of watercraft. For water-skiers and wakeboarders, Zephyr Cove offers a small fleet of 22-44-foot Sea Rays ($169-269/hour) plus skis, boards, and tubes. Personal watercraft riders can rent one of the marina's three-person WaveRunners ($110-155) or go parasailing ($79-199) with professional drivers.

TOP EXPERIENCE

Kayaking

On the beach behind Vikingsholm, **Kayak Tahoe** (Vikingsholm, 530/544-2011, www.kayaktahoe.com, $25-65 single kayak and SUP, $35-85 double kayak) rents stand-up paddleboards and kayaks for a paddle to Fannette Island.

For a guided kayak tour of Emerald Bay, contact **Kayak Tahoe** (Timber Cove Marina, 3411 Lake Tahoe Blvd., South Lake Tahoe, 530/544-2011, www. kayaktahoe.com, 8:30am-2:30pm daily late May-early Sept., $70-95 pp min. 6 people). Trips paddle the perimeter of the bay with a knowledgeable guide, stopping at Vikingsholm and Fannette Island. Kayak Tahoe also hosts sunset tours near Timber Cove (6:30pm-8:30pm daily, $50 pp). Their Upper Truckee River Tours (9am-noon daily, $55 pp) offer a chance to see Tahoe's beautiful flora and fauna. Guests must be at least 12 years old. A $10 parking fee is charged at all locations except Timber Cove Marina. The outfitter also rents kayaks ($25-35/hour, $35-55/2 hours, $65-85/day) and stand-up paddleboards ($25/hour, $35/2 hours, $65/day) at locations at Vikingsholm, Nevada Beach, and Pope Beach, as well as at Timber Cove.

Fishing

Several companies offer charter trips on Lake Tahoe for anglers looking to score mackinaw, rainbow, and brown trout or kokanee salmon. Operating out of the Ski Run Marina (900 Ski Run Blvd. Ste. 101, South Lake Tahoe, 530/541-5448, www. skirunmarina.com) and the Zephyr Cove Marina (760 US-50, Zephyr Cove, NV, 775/586-9338, www.zephyrcove.com), **Tahoe Sport Fishing** (530/541-5448 or 775/586-9338, www.tahoesportfishing. com, $125-135 pp, year-round) offers five-hour fishing trips tailored to suit all styles of lake fishing. The fishing boats have heated cabins and modest restroom facilities, and trips include all the trimmings: bait and tackle, cleaning and bagging services, and nonalcoholic refreshments on board. You are responsible for bringing a valid fishing license ($16), but they do sell them at the marina. Private charters are also offered ($900-965).

Tahoe Fly Fishing Outfitters (2705 Lake Tahoe Blvd., South Lake Tahoe, 530/541-8208, www.tahoeflyfishing. com, $250-600) can take you on an expert-guided fly-fishing or spin-fishing trip on one of the smaller lakes, Walker River, Carson River, Truckee River, or the Indian Creek Reservoir.

At Zephyr Cove book a fishing trip with **Nor-Cal Charters** (195 US-50, Zephyr Cove, 530/318-1981, www. fishingintahoe.com, Apr.-Oct., $120 pp). Nor-Cal Charters supplies the bait, tackle, and equipment. *The Professor,* a 35-foot fishing boat, and a sleek-looking Donzi take anglers out with one of three guides that each have decades of fishing experience. Bring a fishing license.

Hiking

Mount Tallac

The hard-core trek up **Mount Tallac Trail** (10 mi/16 km round-trip, 7-9 hours, difficult) starts easy, with a casual stroll past Floating Island and Cathedral Lakes, and then gets steeper as it ascends the face of the mountain. You'll feel less oxygen as you summit to the 9,735-foot (2,967-m) peak, but the incredible views from the top are worth it. After making it to the top, your reward is a mild descent that is equally beautiful.

The trailhead is near Fallen Leaf Lake (Hwy. 89 at Baldwin Beach, South Lake Tahoe). To access the trail, turn off CA-89 and follow Mount Tallac Road toward the trailhead parking lot.

★ Emerald Bay State Park

Emerald Bay State Park (Hwy. 89, 530/525-7232, www.parks.ca.gov) is a treasure trove of easy and moderate hiking trails. Start with the **Overlook Trail** (0.5 mi one-way, easy), a short trail to a camera-ready spot near the Eagle Point Campground.

The well-known **Rubicon Trail** (1.7 mi/2.7 km one-way, 1 hour, easy) loops around the bay to Vikingsholm and then continues on another 4 miles or so past Vikingsholm. The well-marked trail features undulating terrain, shade, gorgeous views and even a waterfall or two. (There is also a short but steep 0.5-mile trail from the Harvey West parking lot.) The first mile gently slopes downhill, overlooking the lake. The water is so shallow and clear that you can see the lake bottom from the trail. At a bridge, detour left to visit Lower Eagle Falls, or turn right to reach the visitors center in less than a mile. The visitors center sells tickets for a tour of Vikingsholm, or continue another 0.2 mile to explore the grounds on your own. Bring food, water, money for the tour, and a bathing suit to take a dip near the sandy beach beside Vikingsholm.

D. L. Bliss State Park

Hiking trails within D. L. Bliss State Park include the **Rubicon-Lighthouse Trail** to Rubicon Point's lighthouse. You can take a short portion of this trail, from Calawee Cove Beach to the lookout at Rubicon Point, or walk a little farther to see the lighthouse. For a longer adventure, follow the **Rubicon Trail** (1.7 mi/2.7 km one-way) all the way down around the bay, past Vikingsholm, and on to its end point at Upper Eagle Point Campground in Emerald Bay State Park. The complete trail has a total distance of about 4.5 miles (7.2 km) one-way, but the terrain is mostly easy. On the west side of D. L. Bliss is a short (0.5-mile) self-guided **nature trail** to Balancing Rock that nearly anyone can enjoy. Nineteen numbered signs along the way illuminate the history and geology of the area.

Tahoe Rim Trail

If you're in good shape and like a challenge, you will definitely want to experience part of the 165-mile (265-km) **Tahoe Rim Trail** (www.tahoerimtrail.org). This beautiful and varied trail, built between 1984 and 2001, encircles the entire lake through six counties in California and Nevada, one state park, three national forests, and three wilderness areas. About a third of it overlaps the Pacific Crest Trail. You can hike the trail in segments or, if you're up for a little planning, do it in a multiday loop. Casual day-hikers can pick one portion of the trail and tackle it, either doing an out-and-back or using a shuttle service to get back at the end of the day.

The Tahoe Rim Trail is managed and maintained by the nonprofit **Tahoe Rim Trail Association** (TRTA, 128 Market St., Stateline, NV, 775/298-4485, www. tahoerimtrail.org). The TRTA organizes a number of events, including trail maintenance work parties, workshops on backcountry skills, and informative Trail Talks. They're the people to contact if you want to volunteer, become an official member of the 165 Mile Club, or get information about the trail. Note that horseback riding is permitted on the Tahoe Rim Trail, and mountain biking is permitted on certain sections. For details, check the website, which includes regular updates and specifics.

In summer, the TRTA runs several guided "Taste of the TRT" **backpacking trips** (775/298-4491, 4 days/3 nights, $640). Participants hike 38-41 miles. The cost includes food, trip leaders, transportation to and from the trail, and delivery of meals and supplies to key locations. The trips fill up quickly and registration is not guaranteed; apply through the website or contact the trail-use director (775/298-4491, lindseys@tahoerimtrail.org).

Desolation Wilderness

Locals like to say that visiting **Lake Aloha** (5-12.5 mi/8-20 km round-trip, 8 hours, moderately strenuous), located in the Desolation Wilderness at 8,116 feet (2,474 m) in the Sierra Nevada, is like being on the surface of the moon. Blue waters, granite rock, and petrified trees define this area, with occasional snow in the surrounding mountains.

From the trailhead at Lower Echo Lake (Johnson Pass Rd.), the **Echo Lakes Trail** hugs the water as you trek past granite rock while slowly gaining elevation, passing a few homes toward Upper Echo Lake. The hike from Lower Echo Lake to Upper Echo Lake is 2.4 miles (3.9 km), but you can shave off this leg of the journey by taking the boat taxi across Lower Echo Lake.

A **boat taxi** (8:30am-5pm on demand in summer, www.echochalet.com, $14 one-way) drops hikers off at Upper Echo Lake, where the trail continues 1.1 miles, heading west into the backcountry to Tamarack, Lucille, and Margery Lakes. In about a mile, the trail splits; go left to follow the northern shore of Lake in the Woods; stay right to head straight to Lake Aloha.

Lake Aloha is a serene, deep-blue swimming hole dotted with granite. There are some places to enjoy lunch or sunbathe on the rocks. In summer, it's common to see PCT hikers on the trail or stopping for the night along the shoreline. Bring bug spray, as the mosquitoes tend to come out around sunset as you head back the way you came.

Biking

A great place to get out and cycle in summer is **Kirkwood Mountain Resort** (1501 Kirkwood Meadows Dr., off Hwy. 88, www.kirkwood.com, 209/258-7277, early July-early Sept.). When there's no snow, the slopes of this ski resort turn into great mountain biking tracks. On summer weekends, two lifts (10am-4pm Sat.-Sun., $46 adults, $34 ages 13-18, $28 children 5-12) access 22 trails, half of which are within the park. The Red Cliffs Lodge base area (209/258-7240, 9:30am-4:30pm Sat.-Sun. summer) rents high-end mountain bikes ($48-83 adults, $21-28 children, includes gear). Kirkwood also offers several mountain bike clinics through the season.

Experienced mountain bikers looking for an intense workout can take **Mr. Toads Wild Ride/Saxon Creek Trail** (6 mi/9.5 km one-way, 3-5 hours). This rocky and technical downhill trek starts at the base of Heavenly's Stagecoach chairlift on Kingsbury Grade and rips through boulders and forest down to Freel Peak by way of the Tahoe Rim Trail. If you're feeling adventurous, you can go another 54 miles (87 km) all the way to Mount Rose. The **Tahoe Area Mountain Biking Adventure** (TAMBA, https://tamba.org) lists the locals' favorite routes.

Horseback Riding

A few stables offer guided rides. On the west side of the South Shore, find the **Camp Richardson Corral** (4 Emerald Bay Rd., 530/541-3113 or 877/541-3113, www.camprichardsoncorral.com, summer only, $52-94), family-owned and

-operated since 1934. Guests can choose one- or two-hour trail rides to explore the meadows and the forest. Camp Richardson offers one- or two-hour evening rides that end with a country-style meal on the corral's patio or a hay ride ($35 pp) for the whole family. Riders must be at least six years old and weigh less than 225 pounds.

For a gorgeous guided trail ride into the Mokelumne Wilderness, join **Kirkwood Sierra Outfitters** (209/258-7433, www.kirkwoodsierraoutfitters.com, from $175 pp). The outfit specializes in low-volume, customized tours that access a variety of trailheads in the Sierra.

Zephyr Cove Stables (800 US-50, Zephyr Cove, 775/588-5664, www.zephyrcovestable.com, 9am-5pm daily summer, 10am-4pm daily spring and fall, $50-90) offers one- and two-hour rides into the backcountry above the lake. Trips include meals: either a full country breakfast, hamburgers and hot dogs for lunch, or a tri-tip steak and teriyaki chicken for dinner. Riders must be at least seven years old and weigh less than 225 pounds.

Golf

Tahoe Paradise Golf Course (3021 US-50, South Lake Tahoe, 530/577-2121, www.tahoeparadisegc.com, 8am-7pm daily May-Oct., $32-62) is conveniently located on US-50 toward Meyers. This dog-friendly course has pretty mountain views and plenty of lovely pine trees along its 18 holes of moderately undulated terrain. It also has a small pro shop, a practice area, and a modest snack bar. It's best to get there early, as it gets busy by midafternoon.

The **Lake Tahoe Golf Course** (2500 Emerald Bay Rd., South Lake Tahoe, 530/577-0788, www.laketahoegc.com, sunrise-sunset daily spring-fall, 18 holes $59-89) offers a full-service restaurant and bar, cart service on the course, a 25-stall driving range, professional instruction, pro shop, and—the main selling

Lake Aloha

point—gorgeous views. If you want to save a little money, go later for the "super twilight" price (from 4pm, $39) for 18 holes and a cart. The course closes for the season by November.

Spas

The welcoming and soothing **BioSpirit Day Spa** (1116 Ski Run Blvd. #3, South Lake Tahoe, 530/542-4095, www. massagetahoe.com, 9am-2pm Mon., 9am-7pm Tues.-Sat.) is a stand-out in the area. With a full menu of massages, facials, waxing, and wraps, BioSpirit is also one of the few places in the area where you can add a CBD crème to any service. Their eucalyptus steam room will leave you refreshed and rejuvenated. In addition to their regular hours, BioSpirit is usually open on Sunday holiday weekends.

Entertainment and Events
Casinos

Stateline, Nevada, has an abundance of

multistory casinos and nightlife, combined with plenty of shopping and outdoor activities.

MontBleu Resort Casino and Spa

MontBleu Resort Casino and Spa (55 US-50, Stateline, NV, 775/588-3515 or 800/648-3353, www.montbleuresort.com) is the first casino coming from Zephyr Cove. It's common to see a youthful crowd playing pop-culture video game slots, but you'll also find table games of the Vegas variety: craps, roulette, blackjack, and Texas hold 'em. The Zone/Party Pit contains a sports book, a few blackjack tables, and go-go dancers on weekend nights. MontBleu's casino is well-lit, loud, and lively, making it easy to stay and play late into the night. There's also a full-service salon and spa, pool, lingerie shop, cigar store, apparel shop, nightclub, and several restaurants.

For late-night entertainment, **Opal at MontBleu** (10pm-dawn Fri.-Sat., cover $10) is the place to get your dance on with expert mash-up DJs and go-go dancers. Bottle service is available for those who want their own VIP table. Ladies get in for free before midnight on Saturday and enjoy free cocktails on Friday.

Hard Rock Café and Casino

Across the street from MontBleu, the **Hard Rock Café and Casino** (50 US-50, Stateline, 844/588-7625, https://hardrockcasinolaketahoe.com) appeals to a young crowd with a hip music vibe. Along with a William Hill sports book, craps table, pop-culture slots, and accommodating bars, Hard Rock also has a variety of rooms and suites. Downstairs on the casino floor, **Fuel** (844/588-7625, 5am-3pm Sun.-Thurs., 24 hours Fri.-Sat.) offers smoothies, cappuccinos, and frappes. Or consider pulling up a stool at the **Oyster Bar** (844/588-7625 ext. 7678, 11am-midnight daily, $10-30), where you can also get a dozen oysters for $26.

Harrah's Lake Tahoe

Gambling fans should definitely bring their frequent player cards to the casino floor at **Harrah's Lake Tahoe** (15 US-50, Stateline, NV, 800/427-7247, www. caesars.com/harrahs-tahoe), which has all the Vegas gaming favorites—classic craps, rapid roulette, baccarat, blackjack, and Let It Ride poker. The atmosphere is a bit more classic casino, with dim lights in the evening and a warren of slot machines that make it easy to get lost. When you've had enough gaming, check out the live entertainment in the South Shore Room or a big act at the Lake Tahoe Outdoor Arena at Harvey's.

Late-night watering hole **PEEK at Harrah's** (775/586-6705 or 775/339-1803, www.caesars.com/peek, 10:30pm-close Fri.-Sat., cover $5-20) features in-house and guest DJs that play house music, with some hip-hop sprinkled into the mix. Grab a cocktail at the bar, or for additional cost, enjoy table service by the lovely staff in one of the 40 plush VIP booths. Many celebrities have come here to party; ladies and locals get in free before 11pm on Friday.

Harveys Lake Tahoe

Harrah's affiliated casino **Harveys Lake Tahoe** (18 US-50, Stateline, 775/588-6611, www.caesars.com/harveys-tahoe) has all the usual games of chance. Enjoy state-of-the-art video screens while betting on football, NASCAR, and horse races in the sportsbook area. Harveys also boasts a fitness center, a pool, and concerts in the outdoor arena in summer.

For an evening of laughter, get tickets to **The Improv at Harveys** (855/234-7469 or 702/777-2782, www.caesars.com/harveys-tahoe, 9pm Wed.-Sun., $25-30). Five nights a week the funniest up-and-comers in comedy showcase their barrel-of-laughs act at the Cabaret Theater, along with guest appearances by big-name humorists. This is the place where many of today's major comedy

stars honed their acts—come see who'll be famous next.

Dining options include the **Taco Cantina & Restaurant** (775/588-2411, 4pm-9pm Mon.-Thurs., 4pm-9:30pm Fri., noon-9:30pm Sat., noon-9pm Sun., $20), serving fast-casual Mexican food and hosting live music. Get dressed up and head to the 19th floor for the **19 Kitchen & Bar** (775/586-6777, 5:30pm-8:30pm Tues.-Thurs., 5:30pm-9pm Fri.-Sat., $10-52) and a fancier meal.

Lakeside Inn and Casino

Smaller and less flashy, **Lakeside Inn and Casino** (168 US-50, Stateline, NV, 775/588-7777 or 800/624-7980, www.lakesideinn.com) is a local favorite, probably because of its generous slot machines and incredible prime-rib dinners. This inn looks more like a mountain lodge than a high-rise gaming emporium, and it has won votes for Best Casino, Loosest Slots, and Friendliest Casino Employees. The staff is welcoming and the sports book is lively. Increase your chance of winning a Lakeside Lightning progressive jackpot by using your Lakeside player's club card every time you gamble.

Nightlife

The **Brewery at Lake Tahoe** (3542 Lake Tahoe Blvd., South Lake Tahoe, 530/544-2739, www.brewerylaketahoe.com, 11am-10pm daily, $13-26) is a casual, comfortable bar with a menu of local microbrews, including the signature Bad Ass Ale and the popular Washoe Wheat Ale, as well as a selection of seasonal brews. The menu includes pizza, pasta, salads, salmon, burgers, and barbecued ribs. The Brewery is across the street from the lake; the outdoor picnic tables are a great place to sit and enjoy a meal in the beautiful Tahoe landscape.

A happening place, especially for punk rockers, reggae, and rap enthusiasts, is **Whiskey Dick's Saloon** (2660 Lake Tahoe Blvd., South Lake Tahoe, 530/544-3425, noon-2am daily), with a full bar and live bands several times a week. Cover charges range from free to $20, depending on the band. This saloon also has pool tables, shuffleboard, and cornhole.

Festivals and Events

The **Valhalla Boathouse Theatre** (870 Emerald Bay Rd., 530/541-4975, www.valhallatahoe.com) is a cultural space that hosts concerts and live performances in summer. Floor-to-ceiling windows frame a backdrop of stunningly gorgeous Tahoe sunsets. The nearby Grand Hall (located within the historical Heller residence) is a memorable place for special events, especially those exchanging vows in front of the 40-foot-tall stone fireplace.

If you enjoy getting dressed up in 1920s fringe and fine suits, indulge in the living history of the early 20th century at the **Annual Gatsby Festival** (530/544-7383, www.tahoeheritage.org, 2nd weekend in Aug.) at the Tallac Historic Site. Each summer, actors and volunteers dress in period attire and stroll the grounds as 1920s vacationers. The most popular event of this two-day festival is the Gatsby Tea ($65, Sun.), a sumptuous afternoon tea spiced up by entertainment and culminating in a vintage fashion show.

What happens when you pair top-performing DJs, artists, and musicians with an abundance of snow? You get a New Year's to remember during the annual **SnowGlobe Festival** (Lake Tahoe Community College, 1 College Dr., http://snowglobemusicfestival.com, Dec. 29-31, 1:30pm-midnight, $139-400). Dress warmly to dance the final days of the year away in freezing temperatures amid snowcapped mountains surrounding the outdoor stage. Tickets usually go on sale early in the year; buy early to get the best rate.

Celebrities and professional golfers gather at **Edgewood Tahoe** (100 Lake Pkwy., Stateline, 855/358-2350, www.edgewoodtahoe.com, July) for a week full of excitement at the **American Century Celebrity Golf Championship** (http://americancenturychampionship.com, Tues.-Sun. in July, $20-30/day, $70 season pass). Watch athletes, actors, and personalities like Steph Curry, Justin Timberlake, and Tony Romo pair with professionals to claim a piece of the $600,000 cash purse on Tahoe's most famous golf course.

Shopping

At the upscale **Shops at Heavenly Village** (1001 Heavenly Village Way, www.theshopsatheavenly.com) you'll find all the clothing and sports accessories you need, either at the **Patagonia** (530/542-3385, www.patagonia.com, 8am-8pm Mon.-Fri., 8am-9pm Sat.) or **Powder House Ski & Snowboard** (1001 Heavenly Village Way #20, 530/541-6422, https://tahoepowderhouse.com, 7am-10pm daily).

Pick up fun and practical souvenirs at **Sock City** (530/541-1478, https://funsockcity.com, 10am-8pm Mon.-Thurs., 10am-9pm Fri.-Sat., 10am-6pm Sun.) or shop **On Tahoe Time** (530/541-3588, https://ontahoetime.com, 9:30am-8pm Sun.-Thurs., 9:30am-9pm Fri.-Sat.) for cool keepsake ornaments and gifts. At the edge of the village, the outdoor outfitter **The Boardinghouse** (4118 Lake Tahoe Blvd. #8, 530/544-9062, www.heavenlysports.com, 8:30am-8pm Mon.-Thurs., 8:30am-9pm Fri., 8am-9pm Sat., 8am-8pm Sun.) sells recreational gear.

For general items and basic needs, visit **Raley's** (4000 Lake Tahoe Blvd., 530/544-3417, www.raleys.com, 6am-midnight daily), **Ross Dress for Less** (1030 Al Tahoe Blvd., 530/541-5029, www.rossstores.com, 9am-10pm Mon.-Thurs., 8:30am-10:30pm Fri.-Sat., 8:30am-9:30pm Sun.), or the **Factory Outlet Stores at the Y** (2014-2042 Lake Tahoe Blvd., at Hwy. 89 and US-50, South Lake Tahoe). A large variety of athletic equipment, rental gear, and apparel can be found at **Tahoe Sports Limited** (4000 Lake Tahoe Blvd., South Lake Tahoe, 530/542-4006, www.

Wineries of the Sierra Foothills

South of Lake Tahoe is one of the best-known wine regions in the Sierra foothills: The Shenandoah Valley. Wineries near the towns of Plymouth, Coloma, and Fair Play are available for tours and tastings.

Plymouth

At **Story Winery** (10525 Bell Rd., 800/713-6390, www.zin.com, noon-4pm Mon.-Thurs., 11am-5pm Fri.-Sun., free), you can taste the true history of Amador County wines. The house specialty is red zinfandel at this winery, which has vineyards dating back to 1894.

The friendly folks at **Bray Vineyards** (10590 Shenandoah Rd., 209/245-6023, www.brayvineyards.com, 10am-5pm Sat.-Sun., 11am-4pm Sun., $5) pour unique wines made from verdelho, angelica, alicante bouschet, or an intriguing blend of Portuguese grapes.

Montevina (20680 Shenandoah School Rd., 209/245-6942, www.montevina.com, 10am-4:15pm daily, free) prides itself on its zinfandels, but you can also taste whites, reds, blends, and more at this fun tasting room.

At charming **Deaver Vineyards** (12455 Steiner Rd., 209/245-4099, www.deavervineyards.com, 10:30am-5pm daily, $5), you can sip a range of intense layered zins and petite sirahs or try a range of sparkling wine, from pomegranate- to almond-flavored bubbly.

Wilderotter Vineyard (19890 Shenandoah School Rd., 209/245-6016, www.wilderottervineyard.com, 10:30am-5pm daily, $5) is a small charming estate with unique varietals, including vermentino and Roussanne whites.

Placerville and Camino

Visit elegant **Boeger Winery** (1709 Carson Rd., Placerville, 800/655-2634 or 530/622-8094, www.boegerwinery.com, 10am-5pm daily, $5) to taste hearty reds. Better yet, bring a picnic to enjoy in the oak grove.

Tiny **Fenton Herriott Vineyards** (120 Jacquier Court, Placerville, 530/642-2021, www.fentonherriott.com, 11am-5pm daily, free) makes only a few hundred cases of wine each year, specializing in cabernet sauvignon, chardonnay, and gewürztraminer.

Madroña Vineyards (2560 High Hill Rd., Placerville, 530/644-5948, www.madronavineyards.com, tasting room 11am-5pm daily, free, tours by appointment) was among the first local winemakers to produce Rhône and Bordeaux varietals.

Wofford Acres Vineyards (1900 Hidden Valley Ln., Camino, 530/626-6858, www.

tahoesportsltd.com, 8am-8pm daily winter).

Food
Breakfast and Cafés

For a classic American breakfast, it's tough to do better than the **Original Red Hut Café** (2723 Lake Tahoe Blvd., South Lake Tahoe, 530/541-9024, www.redhutcafe.com, 6am-2pm daily, $7-13). This down-home waffle spot serves banana waffles, walnut waffles, bacon waffles, and a waffle with chicken served with it, plus egg dishes and a whole lunch menu. The waffle sandwich is a complete breakfast in itself. Expect to wait for a table or a seat at the counter on weekend mornings, as this spot is very popular. If you can't get in, try the other **Red Hut Café** (3660 Lake Tahoe Blvd., 530/544-1595, 6am-9pm daily). The **Red Hut Café Nevada** (229 Kingsbury Grade, Stateline, NV, 775/588-7488, www.redhutcafe.com, 6am-2pm daily, $6-12) is on Kingsbury Grade/NV-207 en route to Gardnerville.

Perched on the edge of Heavenly Village, **Driftwood Café** (1001 Heavenly Village Way, Ste. 1a, South Lake Tahoe, 530/544-6545, www.driftwoodtahoe.com, 7am-3pm daily, $7-11) serves wholesome and healthy breakfasts that hit the spot. If you need help slowly easing into

wavwines.com, 11am-5pm Thurs.-Sun., free) is a small vineyard at the end of a bumpy country road, but its low-priced high-flavored reds and yummy ciders are worth the drive.

Fair Play

Charles B. Mitchell Vineyards (8221 Stoney Creek Rd., Fair Play, 530/620-3467, http://charlesbmitchell.com, 11am-5pm Wed.-Sun., $10 or free with a wine purchase) pours a wide variety of wines, including sparkling, white, and lush dessert ports.

Skinner Vineyards (8054 Fairplay Rd., Somerset, 530/620-2220, www.skinnervineyards.com, 11am-5pm Thurs.-Mon., $10-15) produces well-balanced Rhône varietals in its Smithereens collection, featuring grapes that exude complex aromas.

Miraflores (2120 Four Springs Trail, Placerville, 530/647-8505, www.mirafloreswinery.com, 10am-5pm daily, $5) produces muscular, focused reds, from small lots of syrah to aged Malbec and tempranillo.

Food and Accommodations

The **Argonaut** (331 Hwy. 49, Coloma, 530/626-7345, http://argonautcafe.com, 8am-4pm daily, $8) serves locally sourced sandwiches, soups, and renowned Temple coffee on a patio with views of the American River. Set in a modest building off Plymouth's main drag, **Taste Restaurant** (9402 Main St., Plymouth, 209/245-3463, http://restauranttaste.com, 5pm-9pm Thurs.-Tues., 11:30am-2pm, Fri.-Sun., $11-39) is stocked with gourmet food paired with a balanced selection of Amador wines. Stay the night at the **Amador Harvest Inn** (12455 Steiner Rd., Plymouth, 800/217-2304, www.amadorharvestinn.com, $150-170), which brings a bit of Napa to the Shenandoah Valley while retaining its down-home feel.

Getting There

Shenandoah Valley is on the way to South Lake Tahoe from Sacramento. The Shenandoah Valley is 47 miles (76 km) southeast of Sacramento; to get there take CA-99/US-50 east toward South Lake Tahoe for 2 miles (3.2 km) and then CA-16/CA-49 north toward Amador County for 37 miles. Plymouth is a detour on CA-49; you'll head north into Fair Play and Somerset before rejoining US-50 in Camino west of Pollock Pines. Drive 58 miles (93 km) west from Camino to South Lake Tahoe. This route is best taken in summer, when potential snowstorms and volatile weather are less likely to impact your trip.

the day in comfort, get the Huevos Del Driftwood paired with a Bloody Mary made with potato vodka.

One of the most pleasant spots for a light breakfast is **Camp Richardson Coffee & Confectionery** (1900 James Beach Rd., www.camprichardson.com, South Lake Tahoe, 530/541-1801, 7am-5pm daily late May-early Sept.). This small friendly spot, right across CA-89 from the main lodge at Camp Richardson, fills a need for good coffee, good pastries, and a no-hassle Internet connection in a somewhat remote area. While technically part of Camp Richardson Resort, the coffee shop is operated by the same people who

run the **Keys Café** (2279 Lake Tahoe Blvd. Ste. 2, South Lake Tahoe, 530/542-3800, 7am-4pm daily), 3 miles (4.8 km) southeast of the resort.

★ **Free Bird Café** (2229 Lake Tahoe Blvd., South Lake Tahoe, 530/578-0001, www.freebirdtahoe.com, 7:30am-2pm daily, $4-8) has made a name for itself thanks to a delicious variety of house-brewed chai. The sweet and spicy tea, made with all-natural ingredients, simmers in a pot for hours and is served fresh daily. Smoothies, espresso drinks, and superfood bowls are also available.

It is absolutely necessary to get a delectable treat at **Glazed and Confuzed**

Tahoe Donut (3447 Lake Tahoe Blvd., Ste. 1, South Lake Tahoe, 530/600-0198, www.glazedandconfuzedtahoedonut. com, 7am-2pm Wed.-Mon., $4-6). These fun and fresh donuts appeal to just about anybody, whether you're a NOFX fan yearning for a Punk in Drublic donut or in town for the Edgewood Celebrity Golf Tournament and craving a Shooter McGavin pastry.

American

Riva Grill (Ski Run Marina, 900 Ski Run Blvd., Ste. 3, South Lake Tahoe, 530/542-2600, www.rivagrill.com, 11:30am-12:30am Sun.-Thurs., 11:30am-1:30am Fri.-Sat., $35-46) is a nice upscale restaurant right on Lake Tahoe. The Riva serves excellent fish tacos, a potent Wet Woody rum punch, and a filet and lobster combo. It may be pricey, but the ambiance is worth it.

Burger Lounge (717 Emerald Bay Rd., South Lake Tahoe, 530/542-2010, www. burgerloungeintahoe.com, 11am-7pm Thurs.-Mon., $5-8) has more than 40 burger selections, all reasonably priced. Try the delicious Desert Delight—a vegan hamburger made with a black bean patty, grilled cactus, and chipotle mayo. Enjoy your burger on the nice outdoor patio with bright yellow umbrellas.

The Loft Tahoe (1021 Heavenly Village Way, 530/523-8024, https://thelofttahoe. com, 4pm-close Sun.-Thurs., 4pm-2am Fri.-Sat., $22-47 show, $11-18) offers dinner and a magic show all in one. Inside its 107-seat theater, guests can watch renowned magicians while also enjoying plates of osso bucco and filet mignon. The American-style tapas have an Italian flare, exhibited in dishes like ricotta gnocchi and butternut squash tortellini. The more adult-oriented Friday night "Magic After Dark" shows are edgy, sexy, and completely unfiltered.

Californian Cuisine

Blue Angel Café (1132 Ski Run Blvd., South Lake Tahoe, 530/544-6544, www.

blueangelcafe.com, 11am-8:30pm Mon.-Thurs., 11am-9pm Fri., 8am-9pm Sat., 8am-7:30pm Sun., $16-26) has a globe-trotting menu with a distinct West Coast flavor. The pizzas are amazing; try the Thai chili chicken with goat cheese and sweet chili sauce with cilantro. For something lighter, opt for the salmon with a miso-ginger glaze served with quinoa and grilled veggies.

At the **Edgewood Tahoe** (100 Lake Pkwy W., Stateline, 775/588-2787, www. edgewoodtahoe.com), dining options include **The Bistro** (888/769-1924, www. edgewoodtahoe.com, 7am-10pm daily, $8-44), a casual breakfast, lunch, and dinner space with an urban mountain contemporary design. The views from the **Edgewood Restaurant** (888/769-1924, www.edgewoodtahoe.com, 5pm-9pm daily, $28-79) aren't bad either. The award-winning **Brooks' Bar & Deck** (888/769-1924, www.edgewoodtahoe. com, 11:30am-9pm Thurs.-Mon., $8-38) is the perfect place to end a round of golf with a $5 draft beer and some Wagyu beef sliders.

Hawaiian

An unassuming local joint with great food and veggie options is **Freshies Restaurant & Bar** (3330 Lake Tahoe Blvd., South Lake Tahoe, 530/542-3630, http:// freshiestahoe.com, 11:30am-9pm daily, $15-25). This small, popular Hawaiian-themed restaurant has been voted the "Best Place for Dinner" and "Best Place for Lunch" by the *Tahoe Daily Tribune*. The main dining room is accessed through a mall, but the best way to experience Freshies is to go to the side entrance and get a rooftop table where you can see the lake.

Italian

If the crowds at Heavenly have you longing for a more intimate evening, book one of the seven tables at **Café Fiore** (1169 Ski Run Blvd., South Lake Tahoe, 530/541-2908, www.cafefiore.com, 5:30pm-10pm daily, $8-43). This tiny bistro serves up-scale Italian fare with a fabulous wine list. The exterior charms with its alpine chalet look while the interior is the definition of a romantic restaurant. Try the eggplant crepes with smoked salmon and drizzled with a sherry cream sauce, or splurge on the *bistecca alla fiorentina* with heaps of filet mignon medallions, pine nuts, basil, and garlic. Café Fiore is convenient to both the Heavenly ski resort and the lakeshore resorts of South Lake Tahoe.

Pizza

If you're hungry and approaching South Lake Tahoe from the west, you can get a decent pizza at **Bob Dog Pizza** (3160 US-50, Meyers, 530/577-2364, www.bobdogpizza.com, 10am-9pm daily, $7-19). Enjoy a Veggie Greek or Hair of the Dog pie outside by the fire pit. Complimentary Wi-Fi is included.

Seafood

Serious sushi aficionados might be concerned about eating raw ocean fish so far from the Pacific, but **Off the Hook** (2660 Lake Tahoe Blvd., 530/544-5599, www.offthehooksushi.com, 4:30pm-9:30pm Mon.-Fri., 5pm-9:30pm Sat., 5pm-9pm Sun., $15-28 entrées, $6-16 sushi rolls) offers good rolls and fresh *nigiri* for reasonable prices. Don't expect too much of some of the traditional Japanese dishes and you'll have an enjoyable dining experience.

For an all-around fine dining experience and some of the best fish ever, try **Kalani's** (1001 Heavenly Village Way, South Lake Tahoe, 530/544-6100, www.kalanis.com, 11am-9pm Sun.-Fri., 11am-9:30pm Sat., $31-50). Serving Pacific Rim fusion cuisine, Kalani's offers a luau sampler platter with Dungeness crab cakes and coconut shrimp, mahi mahi, sushi, barbecued ribs, and house specialties like the Miso-Yaki Chilean sea bass and Kona

From top to bottom: Montevina winery; Burger Lounge; Glazed and Confuzed Tahoe Donut.

lobster bisque. The sushi bar is open all day, as is Kalani's Puka Lounge, which serves wine, sake, and cocktails. Kalani's is located in the Shops at Heavenly Village complex.

The **Beacon Bar & Grill** (Camp Richardson, 1900 Jameson Beach Rd., South Lake Tahoe, 530/541-0630, www. camprichardson.com, 11:30am-7:30pm Mon.-Fri., 11am-7:30pm, $24-41) serves excellent food. Enjoy fresh seafood (calamari, clams, shrimp, scallops, sockeye salmon), filet mignon, and a great spinach salad alongside a beachfront patio with live music (1pm-5pm daily) in summer. Their rum runners are famous. If you're driving CA-89 from the north, look for the entrance on the left, 7 miles (11.5 km) south of Emerald Bay State Park.

Vegetarian
For a great combination of delicious healthy food and budget dining, check out **Sprouts Café** (3123 Harrison Ave., South Lake Tahoe, 530/541-6969, www. sproutscafetahoe.com, 8am-8pm daily, $8-11). This cute, casual walk-up eatery offers ultra-healthy dishes made with fresh, mostly organic ingredients. Breakfast is served all day, and the lunch and dinner menus run to several pages. Choose among salads, burritos, rice bowls, smoothies, and tasty vegetarian/vegan desserts.

Simple Bliss Vegan Café (2540 Lake Tahoe Blvd., 530/542-1474, 8am-8pm daily, $6-17) serves a large variety of espresso drinks, chai lattes, smoothies, and juices. All are mostly organic, vegan, and free of soy and/or gluten.

Fine Dining
Ciera at MontBleu (55 US-50, Stateline, NV, 800/648-3353, www.montbleuresort. com, 5:30pm-close Wed.-Sun., $28-68) is a four-diamond steak and chophouse with preparations designed to appeal to visitors. A fixed menu ($50) includes a soup or salad, entrée (Alaskan king

salmon or filet mignon), and dessert. Enjoy it all with a complimentary dish of chocolate-covered strawberries resting atop a frothing container of dry ice.

Accommodations
Under $100
The **Apex Inn** (1171 Emerald Bay Rd., South Lake Tahoe, 800/755-8246, www. apexinntahoe.com, $55-299) offers the winning combination of a good location (close to the Tahoe Keys, the Y, and CA-89) and affordable rates, especially midweek in winter. It has a small outdoor hot tub, free Internet access, and a coffee maker in all of the renovated rooms.

A reasonable option with basic and quiet accommodations is the **High Country Lodge** (1227 Emerald Bay Rd., 530/600-4411, www. highcountrylodgetahoe.com, $35-399). The renovated rooms contain flat-screen TVs, air conditioning, free Wi-Fi, and a mini-fridge. The lodge is within walking distance of several coffee shops and restaurants. Rates vary greatly, with the best deals in spring and fall.

Postmarc Hotel & Spa Suites (3696 Lake Tahoe Blvd., South Lake Tahoe, 530/541-4200, www.postmarchotels.com, $71-239) is within walking distance of the lake, restaurants, and shops. All 52 rooms feature plush mattresses and modern paneling. Some rooms include whirlpool tubs and spacious European showers.

$150-250
One of the best places to stay in the area is ★ **Camp Richardson** (1900 Jameson Beach Rd., South Lake Tahoe, 530/541-1801 or 800/544-1801, www. camprichardson.com, $45-240). This place has it all, including a campground, cabins, lodge rooms ($90-190), and a beachside inn ($145-240). Comfortable hotel rooms have a woodsy feel and come with private baths (one room has a stone fireplace, while another includes a four-poster bed built of polished logs). Individual cabins sleep 2-8 people and

come with full kitchens and linens (but no TVs or phones). The RV and tent village (late May-Oct., $45-135) has more than 100 sites. Accommodations include use of the beach, a lounge, and the marina; facilities include the excellent Beacon Bar & Grill, the Mountain Sports Center, an ice-cream parlor, and a coffee shop. Cross-country ski and snowshoe rentals are available in winter; pedal boats, SUPs, and motorboats are for rent in summer. Dogs are not allowed at the resort or in the camping area.

The **Beach Retreat & Lodge** (3411 Lake Tahoe Blvd., 530/541-6722, www.tahoebeachretreat.com, $139-269) has the advantage of being right on the lake. The more than 200 rooms are accented in soft colors to complement the views of the lake or Heavenly Mountain; most have private balconies and flat-screen TVs. Pets are welcome in non-lakeside rooms for a fee.

Over $250

On the road to Heavenly, the lovely large **Black Bear Lodge** (1202 Ski Run Blvd., South Lake Tahoe, 530/544-4451, www.tahoeblackbear.com, $169-409) features lodgepole pine and river rock, which blend in with the surrounding nature. A giant fireplace dominates the great room, and smaller but equally cozy river-rock fireplaces are in each of the upstairs lodge rooms. The 10 rooms feature king beds, plush private baths, and free Internet access. The interiors are luxurious, with cushy comforters and log beam and stone accents. Take a few moments to stroll along the tree-lined paths and serene green lawns.

Casino Hotels

Tahoe's casino resorts offer upscale attractive hotel rooms, often at lower rates, and are within walking distance of each other and the Heavenly Village.

The most popular casino resort is **Harrah's** (15 US-50, Stateline, NV, 800/427-2177, www.caesars.com/

harrahs-tahoe, $109-609), with upscale accommodations, all the nightlife and entertainment you need, and easy access to Heavenly and the lakeshore in summer. The high-rise hotel has more than 500 upscale rooms; even the lower-end rooms have ample space, a California king or two double beds, two baths, Wi-Fi, cable TV, and minibars. Premium rooms provide excellent views of the lake and the mountains; the premium king room has two full bathrooms. The decor is upscale and contemporary, with sleek furnishings and art. Winter room rates range $109-289, but summer rates are higher, increasing to $529-609 over the July 4 weekend.

Harveys (18 US-50, Stateline, NV, 775/588-6611, www.caesars.com/harveys-tahoe, $65-415) has rooms that tend to be a little less plush and a little less expensive than those at Harrah's, but it brings in great world-class entertainment playing at its outdoor stage in the summer. Midweek off-season rates can run as low as $65 for a value room or as high as $350 during the July 4 weekend. Lake-view balcony suites are around $415 per night in the winter months.

★ **MontBleu Resort Casino & Spa** (55 US-50, Stateline, NV, 775/588-3515 or 800/648-3353, www.montbleuresort.com, $100-280 winter, $350-410 summer) shines with attractive hotel rooms and top amenities. MontBleu's 438 rooms offer a range of affordable choices. Tower rooms come with a comfortable bed, private bath, loud decor, and conveniences such as free Wi-Fi, a flat-screen TV, a spacious desk, and sweeping views of the mountains or lake. The Sierra Suite ($280 winter) is perfect for entertaining and comes with its own wet bar, connected rooms, and even more spectacular views. MontBleu has ample parking and is within walking distance of other casinos.

Cabin and Condo Rentals

The **Condos at Tahoe** (Stateline, NV,

775/586-1587, www.condosattahoe.com) include about 40 condos available for rent, all with full kitchens and easy access to the Heavenly Gondola. Studios run $260-525; the huge three-bedroom units sleep up to 14 people and are $400-675.

Spruce Grove Cabins (3599-3605 Spruce Ave., South Lake Tahoe, 530/802-2343, www.sprucegrovetahoe.com, $99-2,290) offers LGBT- and pet-friendly Tahoe vacation experiences. With 39 rental homes spread over South Lake Tahoe, you can choose your own private abode on the Tahoe Keys, on the edge of a grassy meadow, or a palace in the pines. All one- to five-bedroom cabins have full kitchens, dining rooms, and living rooms. Each cabin has a theme, such as Snowshoe, Steamer, and "Serenity at South Lake." The Spruce Grove collection gets its heaviest traffic in the winter.

For a condo on the South Shore, head over to **The Lodge at Lake Tahoe** (3840 Pioneer Trail, South Lake Tahoe, 530/541-6226 or 800/469-8222, www. lodgeatlaketahoe.com, $135-192 winter, call for summer rates). The one- and two-bedroom suites have homey interiors with log-framed furniture and tasteful Lake Tahoe prints on the walls. The smallest studios have only kitchenettes, but the larger condos offer fully equipped kitchens as well as a nice table and chairs. Complex amenities include a summertime pool and spa, a swing set, a horseshoe pit, and outdoor barbecues near the pool area. Skiers will have easy access to Heavenly, and gamblers can get to the Stateline casinos in Nevada in a few minutes.

Resorts

Zephyr Cove Resort (760 US-50, Zephyr Cove, NV, 775/589-4906 or 800/238-2463, www.zephyrcove.com, $124-344) has it all: lakefront property, lodge rooms and individual cabins, full-service marina, winter snowmobile park, and restaurants. The four lodge rooms all have private baths and attractive modern appointments. For a special treat, ask for the room with the spa tub. The 28 cabins run from cozy studios to multistory chalets that sleep up to 10 people ($319-540, 2-night min. on weekends). Although they look rustic from the outside, inside you'll find modern furniture, phones, TVs, and wireless Internet access. Pets are welcome for an additional fee; when making reservations, let them know which furry friends you'll bring.

Camping

Camping at Lake Tahoe in the summer is so easy and gorgeous that you almost wonder why anyone would sleep indoors. The weather is usually perfect June-August and the prices are reasonable, with campsites just minutes from mountain bike trails or beaches. Make reservations at least six months in advance as campgrounds fill fast.

The two great state parks have gorgeous campgrounds. **Emerald Bay State Park** (Hwy. 89, 800/444-7275, www. reservecalifornia.com, $35) has the 100-site Eagle Point Campground and a boat-in campground (July-Sept.) on the north side of the bay. Campsites include fire rings, and restrooms and showers are available in the park. A mile north of the Emerald Bay Boat Camp is **D. L. Bliss State Park** (Hwy. 89, 800/444-7275, www. parks.ca.gov, May-Sept., $35-45). Of the 150 sites, beachfront campsites have a premium price of $45, and they're worth it. All campsites have picnic tables, bear-proof food lockers, and grills. Hot showers, flush toilets, and potable water are available in the park.

Camp Richardson Resort (530/541-1801 or 800/544-1801, www. camprichardson.com, late May-Oct., $45-135) offers sites for tents, campers, and RVs and sites that sleep up to 12. Amenities include a beach, a group recreation area, and a marina. On-site facilities include the Beacon Bar & Grill and the Mountain Sports Center.

The Lake Tahoe Basin Management

Unit runs 205 sites at **Fallen Leaf Lake Campground** (Fallen Leaf Lake Rd., off Hwy. 89, 530/544-0426 or 877/444-6777, www.recreation.gov, mid-May-early Oct., $35 tents, $86 cabins), including six family-size yurts. RVs are welcome, though there are no hookups or dump stations. Each campsite has a barbecue grill, a picnic table, and a fire ring. Communal restrooms offer flush toilets and coin-operated showers, and you can purchase firewood from the on-site camp store. The campground is a short walk away from Fallen Leaf Lake.

Tucked behind the Tahoe Keys and the Y, **Tahoe Valley RV Resort** (1175 Melba Dr., South Lake Tahoe, 877/570-2267, www.rvonthego.com, year-round, $55 tents, $75-88 RVs; cabins $173-212 winter, $220-241 summer) has 439 sites and three cabins. Sites accommodate small tents and large RVs with water, electric, and cable TV hookups. Tall pines give each site some shade and privacy. Amenities include tennis and pickleball courts, a swimming pool, horseshoe pit, laundry facilities, activities for children and families, and free wireless Internet access. It's located next to a dog park.

Nevada Beach Campground (Elks Point Rd., 2.5 mi/4 km north of Stateline, NV, 2.5 mi/4 km south of Zephyr Cove, 877/444-6777, www.recreation.gov, mid-May-mid-Oct., $35-39) is a U.S. Forest Service campground offering 56 lakefront sites on the Nevada side of Lake Tahoe. RVs up to 45 feet long are welcome, although no hookups are available. Drinking water and flush toilets are available. It's convenient to both Lake Tahoe and South Shore nightlife.

Information and Services

The **Lake Tahoe Visitors Authority** (LTVA) maintains two welcoming and well-staffed visitors centers, one on the California side (4114 Lake Tahoe Blvd., South Lake Tahoe, 530/542-4637, www.tahoesouth.com, 9am-5pm daily) and one in Nevada (169 US-50, Stateline, NV,

775/588-4591, www.tahoesouth.com, 9am-5pm daily).

For medical attention, go to **Barton Memorial Hospital** (2170 South Ave., South Lake Tahoe, 530/541-3420, www.bartonhealth.org, 24-hour emergency) or the **Tahoe Urgent Care Center** (2130 Lake Tahoe Blvd., South Lake Tahoe, 530/541-3277, www.tahoeurgentcare.com, 8am-12:30pm, 1:30pm-5:30pm daily). A local drugstore is **Rite Aid** (1020 Al Tahoe Blvd., South Lake Tahoe, 530/541-2530, www.riteaid.com, 7am-10pm daily).

Getting Around
Car Rentals
Avis (4130 Lake Tahoe Blvd., South Lake Tahoe, 530/544-5289, www.avis.com, 8am-5pm Mon.-Fri., 8am-3pm Sat.-Sun.) and **Budget** (4130 Lake Tahoe Blvd., 530/544-3439, www.budget.com, 8am-5pm Mon.-Fri., 8am-3pm Sat.-Sun.) are next door to the **LTVA Stateline Transit Center** (4114 Lake Tahoe Blvd., 530/541-7149, www.tahoetransportation.org, 9am-5pm daily). You can also try **Enterprise** (2281 Lake Tahoe Blvd., 530/544-8844, www.enterprise.com, 9am-5pm Mon.-Fri., 9am-noon Sat.), which has a full range of cars and small-midsize SUVs.

Public Transportation
In the South Lake Tahoe area, local public transportation is provided by **BlueGo** (530/541-7149, www.tahoetransportation.org, adults $2-5), which runs buses, trolleys, and ski shuttles. The cheerful-looking trolleys and buses can help you get around the South Shore without driving. Routes and schedules vary, so check the Tahoe Transportation District's website for details.

Ski Resort Shuttles
Parking at the ski resorts, especially on weekends, can be a serious hassle. A much better option is to take a ski resort shuttle. Most of the major ski resorts maintain shuttles that bring skiers and their

equipment up to the mountains in the morning and back down to their hotels in the late afternoon. Look for seasonal brochures in major hotels and resorts or check online for the shuttles for Heavenly (www.skiheavenly.com), Kirkwood (www.kirkwood.com), and Sierra-at-Tahoe (www.sierraattahoe.com).

West Shore

The West Shore offers lakeside access and quiet forest. Hidden gems include Chambers Landing (Tahoe's oldest boathouse), Ed Z'berg Sugar Pine Point State Park, and the Homewood Mountain Resort, where the ski trails feel like you'll glide right into the lake. Tahoe City is a hub for both the North and West Shores, with restaurants, cafés, and places to admire the lake.

Getting There

From South Lake Tahoe, drive north on CA-89 for 10 miles (16 km). The small town of Tahoma is considered the center of the West Shore. Tahoe City is 9 miles (14.5 km) north on CA-89.

Sights
Ed Z'berg Sugar Pine Point State Park

The Tahoe area has more than its share of outstanding state parks, and **Ed Z'berg Sugar Pine Point State Park** (Hwy. 89, Tahoma, 530/525-7982, www.parks.ca.gov, $10) is one of the greats. Located on the West Shore, north of Emerald Bay and a few miles south of the town of Homewood, the park features tours of the historical Hellman-Ehrman Mansion, plus cross-country ski trails from the 1960 Winter Olympics.

The park is split into two sections. Sugar Pine Point includes the 175-site General Creek Campground (late May-Aug.), the mansion, a visitors center and gift shop, and buildings that were part of the estate's early years. The smaller

Edwin L. Z'berg Natural Preserve features the former post of the Sugar Pine Point Lighthouse. There is a $10 day-use parking fee ($5 in winter), but it's free if camping overnight.

Hellman-Ehrman Mansion

A fine example of a former home of the wealthy turned tourist attraction, the **Hellman-Ehrman Mansion** (Hwy. 89, 1 mi/1.6 km south of Tahoma, 530/525-7982, www.parks.ca.gov) is located within Ed Z'berg Sugar Pine Point State Park. This beautifully preserved 12,000-square-foot house was built in 1903; the Ehrman family used their Tahoe estate as a summer getaway spot. It was sold to the State of California in the 1960s. Today, visitors can take a **tour** (30 minutes, 10:30am-3:30pm daily mid-June-early Sept.; 10:30am-3:30pm Mon.-Fri., 12:30pm-3:30pm daily late May-mid-June and Sept.; $10 adults, $8 children age 7-17, children 6 and under free) of the home's original redwood trimming, light fixtures set in Spanish hand-hammered metal, and an indoor birdcage elevator.

Sports and Recreation
Ski Resorts
Homewood Mountain Resort

Located in the middle of the West Shore, **Homewood Mountain Resort** (5145 West Lake Blvd., Homewood, 530/525-2992 guest services or 530/525-2900 snow phone, www.skihomewood.com, lifts 9am-4pm daily mid-Dec.-mid-Apr., $49-139 adults, $37-109 ages 13-18 and 62-69, $22-79 ages 5-12 and 70-plus) is one of Tahoe's hidden gems. The spacious mountain offers a variety of terrain on its 1,260 acres, and the best part is that there are incredible views of Lake Tahoe from practically every run. Eight chairlifts service 67 runs; the majority are split between intermediate and advanced/expert terrain. There are two lodges and two parking lots, both right next to the chairlifts.

Stopping in Sacramento

Sacramento makes a convenient stopover to South Lake Tahoe for most San Francisco Bay Area residents.

Sights

The **California State Capitol Building** (10th St. and L St., 916/324-0333, http://capitolmuseum.ca.gov, 7:30am-6pm Mon.-Fri., 9am-5pm Sat.-Sun., hourly tours 9am-4pm daily, free) displays a grandeur befitting the great state, with a magnificent collection of art, artifacts, and antiques. The city's gold rush heritage is celebrated in **Old Sacramento** (1002 2nd St., 916/808-7644, 10am-5:30pm daily, http://oldsacramento.com), with charming cobblestone streets, clattery wooden sidewalks, and old-time shops. Take a cruise on the *Capitol Hornblower* or a brew cruise on the 16-passenger patio boat. Check out the exhibits at the **Wells Fargo History Museum** (1000 2nd St., 916/440-4263, 10am-5pm daily, www.wellsfargohistory.com) and **Old Sacramento Schoolhouse Museum** (1200 Front St., 916/483-8818, www.oldsacschoolhouse.org). Fun **underground tours** (1pm Mon.-Thurs., 1pm and 2:30pm Fri., 11:30am and 1pm Sat.-Sun., www.historicoldsac.org, $12-18 adults, $8-12 youth ages 6-17) depart from the visitors center for an interactive look into gold-rush history. **Sutter's Fort State Historic Park** (2701 L St., 916/445-4422, https://suttersfort.org, 10am-5pm daily, $5 adults, $3 youth 6-17, children free) shows how the early settlers lived.

While you're hopping around downtown Sacramento, try to catch a Sacramento Kings NBA game at the **Golden 1 Center** (500 David J Stern Walk, 888/915-4647, www.golden1center.com). Part of a 16-story entertainment complex, the indoor arena is made of mostly recycled materials. The basketball team's digs seat up to 19,000 spectators and there's a variety of food options on multiple levels.

Food

In Old Sacramento, **Fat City Bar & Cafe** (1001 Front St., 916/446-6768, https://fatcitybarcafe.com, 11:30am-9pm Mon.-Thurs., 11:30am-10pm Fri., 11am-10pm Sat., 11am-9pm Sun., $12-26) is an Old West saloon with an eclectic menu that includes chow mein, tacos, and enormous cheeseburgers. Another option for burgers and nightlife is **Fanny Ann's Saloon** (1023 2nd St., 916/441-0505, www.fannyannsaloon.com, 11:30am-midnight Sun.-Wed., 11:30am-2am Thurs.-Sat., $7-9).

Legendary **Frank Fat's** (806 L St., 916/442-7092, https://frankfats.com, 11am-9:30pm Mon.-Thurs., 11am-10pm Fri., 5pm-10pm Sat., 4pm-9pm Sun., $11-36) has served authentic upscale Chinese food since 1939. For sushi, try **Mikuni Japanese Restaurant and Sushi Bar** (1530 J St., 916/447-2112, www.mikunisushi.com, 11:30am-10pm Mon.-Thurs., 11:30-11pm Fri., noon-11pm Sat., noon-9pm Sun., $6-26) or **Kru** (3135 Folsom Blvd., 916/551-1559, http://krurestaurant.com, 4pm-10pm Mon.-Thurs., 4pm-1am Fri.-Sat., 5pm-10pm Sun., $10-27).

For dessert, hit **Rick's Dessert Diner** (2401 J St., 916/444-0969, http://ricksdessertdiner.com, 10am-11pm Mon., 10am-midnight Tues.-Thurs., 10am-1am Fri.-Sat., noon-11pm Sun., $5-6).

Getting There

I-80 runs roughly east-west through Sacramento; the I-80 Business adjunct enters into downtown on a slightly different route. US-50 runs east to Lake Tahoe, while CA-99 runs north to Chico. To reach downtown Sacramento from I-80, take the US-50/Capital City Freeway toward J Street. Continue on I Street, which leads toward the capitol and the historic part of town. From I-5, take exit 519B onto J Street.

Homewood has the white-canvas **Big Blue View Bar** (11am-3pm daily, $12-14), which serves draft beer, craft cider, hot food, and snacks. Bright blue Adirondack chairs face the lake so you can take in the panoramic views. Take your time sliding down the 2-mile Rainbow Ridge, Homewood's longest run.

Cross-Country Skiing and Snowshoeing

One of the best cross-country ski trails for beginners is the **General Creek Trail,** also known as the 1960 Winter Olympiad X-C Ski Trail. A lot of the Olympic facilities in the area were neglected or forgotten for many years, but some of the ski trails were rediscovered and restored in connection with the 50th anniversary celebration in 2010. The first-ever Olympic biathlon competition was held on this trail, a 20K course designed by the former U.S. Olympian Wendall "Chummy" Broomhall and Allison "Al" Merrill, who was the head coach of the U.S. Ski Team 1963-1968. The trailhead is inside **Ed Z'berg Sugar Pine Point State Park** (Hwy. 89, Tahoma, 530/525-7982, www.parks.ca.gov, $10) just a few miles south of Chambers Landing. On entering the park, drive through the campground to campsite 148. Signs and a trail map are posted and explain a little about the trail's Olympic history. The trail is largely flat, so it's not too challenging for skiers at most levels—it's also amazingly beautiful. It's an out-and-back trip, so you can glide silently through the woods for as long as you like and then turn around before you get too tired. Snowshoers are welcome but must stay out of the ski tracks.

Ed Z'berg Sugar Pine Point State Park (Hwy. 89, Tahoma, 530/525-7982, www.parks.ca.gov, $10) leads **full moon snowshoe tours** (West Shore Sports, reservations 530/525-9920, $35 adults, $25 children ages 12 and under, includes snowshoe rental, parking, and guide) on specific dates in winter; call for details.

Boating and Watersports

High Sierra Waterski Company (Sunnyside Marina, 1850 W. Lake Blvd., Tahoe City, 530/583-7417, www.highsierrawaterskiing.com, 9am-5pm daily summer) rents water-ski and wakeboard boats, Jet Skis, paddleboards, and kayaks, and also gives water-ski, wakesurfing, and wakeboarding lessons. Launching is out of Sunnyside and Homewood marinas.

Hiking

Ed Z'berg Sugar Pine Point State Park (Hwy. 89, Tahoma, 530/525-7982, www. parks.ca.gov, $10) offers trails suitable for all levels of hikers. One simple and pleasant hike is the **Edward F. Dolder Nature Trail** (2.1 mi/3.4 km, 1 hour, easy). To reach the trailhead, enter the northeast section of the park—the Edwin L. Z'Berg Natural Preserve—and begin hiking the paved Rod Beaudry Trail. The Dolder Trail circles the Z'berg Preserve, with views of the subalpine meadow and wildlife habitats. Along the way you'll pass through trees, a sandy beach, and the spot where a small lighthouse used to sit, now marked by a diamond-shaped sign on a steel post.

A good hike in the southwestern section of Sugar Pine Point State Park is along the 1960 Olympic Ski Trails out to **Lily Pond** (3-6 mi/4.8-9.7 km round-trip, 2-3 hours, easy-moderate). Start in General Creek Campground, near site 150, and take the **General Creek Trail,** also known as the 1960 Winter Olympiad X-C Ski Trail. This sunny wooded path is wide enough that it almost feels like an unpaved forest road. After about 1.5 miles (2.4 km), you'll come to a wooden bridge curving off to the left across General Creek. If you're ready to turn around, take the bridge to complete the loop back to the trailhead for a total of 3 miles (4.8 km).

If you're up for a few more miles, bear right; at this point, the path becomes more trail-like, narrow and winding through the woods. In 0.5 mile you'll come to a trail marker directing you to Lily Pond on the right. The next 0.75 mile requires a bit of climbing, but then you're at Lily Pond, a small lake that actually has lily pads. You can walk around the pond or just turn around and head back, rejoining the General Creek Trail for a total of 5-6 miles.

If you like easy terrain and great views, the **Lakeside Trail** (780 N. Lake Blvd., Tahoe City) is a nice paved path right along the water. The easy 1-mile (1.6-km) boardwalk is down by the Tahoe City Marina. This lovely trail is part of a larger 19-mile (31 km) trail network that links the North Shore, West Shore, Truckee River, and Squaw Valley. Access the trail from Heritage Plaza in the center of Tahoe City.

The 165-mile (265-km) **Tahoe Rim Trail** (775/298-4485, www.tahoerimtrail.org) runs along the shore of the entire lake, including the north and west sides. There are two good trailheads where you can gain access and do a segment of the trail. The northern trailhead is at Brockway Summit. To get to the Brockway trailhead, start in Kings Beach at the junction of CA-28 and CA-267. Travel north on CA-267 for 4 miles (6.4 km). Look for a "Tahoe Rim Trail" sign on the right, and then park on the nearby dirt road or on the roadside pullout. This trailhead has no restrooms, water, or other services.

The **Pacific Crest Trail** (916/285-1846, www.pcta.org) joins the Tahoe Rim Trail at Barker Pass and runs concurrent with it for the next 50 miles (80 km) into the Desolation Wilderness. To get to the Barker Pass trailhead from Tahoe City, enter via Blackwood Canyon, 4.5 miles (7.2 km) south on CA-89. Turn right (west) onto Blackwood Canyon Road. When the road splits, take the left fork on Barker Pass Road. Drive 7 miles (11.5 km) to the crest of the hill and then another 0.2 mile on a dirt road. Park at the pullout to the right. Pit toilets are available at this trailhead, but there's no water.

An interesting hike on the West Shore is to **Eagle Rock** (1.5 mi/2.4 km, 20 minutes, easy-moderate), a short hike from the highway to an outcropping overlooking Lake Tahoe. The hike itself is mild and lovely, but the views from the top will take your breath away. The trailhead is at a dirt pullout on CA-89, 1.6 miles (2.6 km) north of Homewood Mountain Resort.

Nightlife

The **Chambers Landing Bar** (6300 Chambers Lodge Rd., Tahoma, 530/525-9190, www.chamberspunch.com, 11:30am-7pm daily late May-early Sept., $5-9) dates from late 19th century, when it used to be a lakefront post office, a market, and a saloon. It also hosted the Gentleman's Races, a classic wooden boat race. Today, it is known for the Chambers Punch, a potent frozen rum runner.

Food

Where We Met (7000 Westlake Blvd., Tahoma, 530/525-1371, 7:30am-7:30pm Sun.-Fri., 7:30am-9pm Sat. summer, $6) is a cute place that serves gelato and coffee drinks. Try the Nutella latte and match it with the mocha gelato for an extra boost of sweetness and caffeine. The tiny space keeps odd hours.

Tahoe House Bakery & Gourmet (625 W. Lake Blvd., Tahoe City, 530/583-1377 or 877/367-8246, www.tahoe-house.com, 6am-4pm daily, $5-10) is a longtime family-owned business that has perfected their baking. Grab a delectable Swiss kiss and enjoy your coffee by the fireplace in the dining area. The back room sells authentic food items, including its branded Tahoe House dressings, marinades, and jams.

Fuel up for a day out on the lake at the **Fire Sign Café** (1785 W. Lake Blvd., Tahoe City, 530/583-0871, www.firesigncafe. com, 7:30am-2:30pm daily, $8-15). This breakfast-and-lunch spot is a local favorite and serves an enormous menu of hearty, house-made fare. Choose from

granola waffles with fruit, a Rubicon scramble, crepes, or baked sweet potato muffins paired with a mimosa. Expect to wait for a table on weekend mornings.

For a light meal and a fabulous sunset view on the water, end your day at the Mountain Grill at the **Sunnyside Restaurant & Lodge** (1850 West Lake Blvd., 530/583-7200, www.sunnysidetahoe.com, 4pm-8:30pm Sun.-Thurs., 4pm-9:30pm Fri.-Sat., $14-28). The patio has an expansive view of the lake and the mountains beyond; it also has plenty of room. The menu is brief—mostly appetizers, tacos, and burgers—and the food is good, though not great. For a relaxing drink and a chance to mellow out by the water, this place is hard to beat. It's 2 miles (3.2 km) south of Tahoe City.

The atmosphere at the **West Shore Café & Inn** (5160 West Lake Blvd., Homewood, 530/525-5200, www.westshorecafe.com, noon-3pm and 5pm-8pm daily, $14-48) is classy, with white tablecloths and well-dressed patrons. On the back patio, watch the sun set over the lake, or grab a table out on the pier, illuminated by strings of lights. The West Shore Burger is the dish you'll be talking about when you get home, and the service is both professional and friendly. Try one of the signature cocktails, such as the Misty Mountain Mule or the White Rabbit. The West Shore Café is across the street from Homewood Mountain Resort. Call before you come as they often close for private events.

Accommodations

★ **Granlibakken** (725 Granlibakken Rd., Tahoe City, 530/583-4242 or 800/543-3221, www.granlibakken.com, $172-205 rooms, $279-418 studios/suites, $473-602 townhomes, 2-night min. stay in summer) has accommodations ranging from standard bedrooms with king,

From top to bottom: Sugar Pine Point State Park; Homewood Mountain; Chambers Landing.

queen, and twin beds to spacious studios, suites, and one- to three-bedroom townhomes. Rustic yet modern furnishings give each unit a mountain-like feel with framed historical photos and artifacts on the walls that pay homage to Tahoe's ski legacy. Some studios and condos come with fireplaces and fully furnished kitchens; all rooms have a hair dryer, telephone, and Wi-Fi. Stays include a hot buffet breakfast, and the Lighthouse Spa offers massage services. Families love Granlibakken for its kid-friendly activities, including a trail system, the Treetop Adventure challenge course, and a sledding hill in winter.

For homey cabin living, you can't beat **The Tahoma Lodge** (7018 Westlake Blvd., Tahoma, 844/755-2226, www.tahomalodge.com, $120-280), a series of seven distinctive lodging varieties with Old Tahoe charm, including two duplexes, an apartment, and four cabins. Each cabin has a furnished kitchen, gas or wood stove, and a heated swimming pool outside. In winter, you'll appreciate the fireplace in each unit and the year-round outdoor hot tub. All accommodations sleep 2-5 people and are dog-friendly. Amenities include HD TVs and hairdryers. A three-night minimum is required on weekends.

For that special vacation when you're willing to spend a little more to make everything perfect, try the **West Shore Inn** (5160 W. Lake Blvd., Homewood, 530/525-5200, www.westshorecafe.com, $169-399). The four suites and two villas exude luxury, with balconies, lake views, leather sofas, fireplaces, and flat-screen TVs. A freshly baked continental breakfast is included with the suites and the two rooms, as is use of the inn's fleet of bicycles, kayaks, and paddleboards.

Camping

Ed Z'berg Sugar Pine Point State Park's **General Creek Campground** (Hwy. 89, Tahoma, 800/444-7275, www.reservecalifornia.com, mid-May-mid-Sept., $35) is a great place to stay on a family vacation or an overnight trip while exploring West Shore attractions. Every campsite in this wooded wildlife-filled park has a picnic table, a charcoal grill, and ample space for a tent or camper. Some sites are ADA compliant. It has clean showers, and you can get a hot five-minute shower ($0.50, bring quarters). The campground can get crowded in midsummer; make reservations at least six months in advance. The campground offers a few sites for off-season camping on a first-come, first-served basis.

Not far from Sugar Pine Point State Park, the Washoe Tribe runs the **Meeks Bay Resort** (7941 Hwy. 89, Meeks Bay, 530/525-6946 or 877/326-3357, www.meeksbayresort.com, mid-May-mid-Oct., $20-30 tents, $30-50 RV sites). The 14 tent sites and 23 RV sites all have a two-night minimum; pets are not allowed. It's 7 miles (11.5 km) north of Emerald Bay.

For great tree-lined campsites with easy beach access, the **William Kent Beach and Campground** (Hwy. 89, 2 mi/3.2 km south of Tahoe City, 877/444-6777, www.recreation.gov, mid-May-mid-Oct., $30) is a good choice. The 80 sites are suitable for tents or campers; none have showers or electrical hookups. There are a few basic yurts ($78) with bunk beds and a futon (no heat or linens). Amenities include restrooms with flush toilets and bear lockers. The facility is operated by the state's Lake Tahoe Basin Management Unit.

If you don't mind giving up a woodsy camping experience, the **Tahoe State Recreation Area** (Hwy. 28, east of Tahoe City, 530/583-3074 or 800/444-7275, www.reservecalifornia.com, late May-early Sept., $35) is a good choice. It has 23 sites, coin-operated showers, and is walking distance to the lake and the shops of Tahoe City. Book early; the campground is usually full by summer.

A utilitarian place to sleep is the **Lake**

Forest Campground (Lake Forest Rd., 1.5 mi/2.4 km east of Tahoe City on Hwy. 28, 530/583-3796, www.tcpud.org, mid-May-early Oct., $20), run by the Tahoe City Public Utilities District. The 20 sites are first-come, first-served; RVs up to 25 feet are welcome, though there are no hookups. Facilities include drinking water and flush toilets but no showers. The campground is next to the public **Lake Forest Boat Ramp** (2500 Lake Forest Rd., 530/583-3796, www.tcpud.org, $15-20 day).

Getting Around

CA-89 provides access along the West Shore and is open year-round; the curvy section around Emerald Bay closes in winter, making a direct route from the South Shore impossible by car.

Tahoe Area Regional Transit (TART, 530/550-1212 or 800/736-6365, www.laketahoetransit.com) is the public bus system. Buses (adults $1.75 one-way, 24-hour pass $3.50) run north around the lake from Tahoma on the West Shore to Incline Village, Nevada, with stops along the way.

North Shore

The quiet and secluded North Shore offers greater access to outdoors with fewer amenities. The North Shore stretches east from Tahoe City to Carnelian Bay and Kings Beach, crossing the California-Nevada state line in Crystal Bay, where casinos such as the Tahoe Biltmore and Crystal Bay Club start to appear. East of Crystal Bay, Incline Village sits on the northeast shore of Lake Tahoe, with restaurants and stores scattered about town.

Getting There

From Tahoe City, follow CA-28 north to reach destinations along the North Shore. Alternatively, from I-80 near Truckee, take CA-89 south for 14 miles (22.5 km) to Tahoe City or CA-267 for 12 miles (19.5 km) into Kings Beach.

From the South Shore, take CA-89 north for 25 miles (40 km) to Tahoe City. Note that this route closes in winter at Emerald Bay.

Sights
Tahoe Maritime Museum

The **Tahoe Maritime Museum** (401 W. Lake Blvd., Tahoe City, 530/583-9283, www.tahoemaritimemuseum.org, 10am-4:30pm Thurs.-Sat., $5 adults, children 12 and under free) illuminates the marine history of Lake Tahoe. Inside, wooden boats, photos, and artifacts showcase the lake's history. Learn about "gentlemen's racing" at the Chambers Landing bar and boathouse and the 1896 steam ferry that used to tour the lake. Young visitors will especially enjoy *The T-Files: The Search for Tessie,* about Tahoe's legendary resident lake monster.

The museum is 0.6 mile southwest of the Gatekeeper's Museum off CA-89, near the Pet Station and Tahoe House Bakery & Gourmet.

Gatekeeper's Museum and Marion Steinbach Indian Basket Museum

The **Gatekeeper's Museum and Marion Steinbach Indian Basket Museum** (130 West Lake Blvd., Tahoe City, 530/583-1762, www.northtahoemuseums.org, 11am-4pm Wed.-Sun., $5) offers an in-depth history of society around the lake. You'll find transcribed oral histories, photographs, dolls, costumes, and many other artifacts displayed in attractive and unusual pine-and-glass cases that match the wooden floors of the galleries. The authentic American Indian artifacts from the Washoe tribe include a large collection of baskets and caps made of willow, tule, and pine needles.

Watson Cabin

Visit an authentic early-20th-century log cabin at **Watson Cabin** (560 North Lake Blvd., Tahoe City, 530/583-1762, www.

northtahoemuseums.org, noon-4pm Thurs.-Sun., by donation). It was built by Robert Watson as a private family residence for his son and daughter-in-law; they moved into the cabin in 1909. In 1990, the North Lake Tahoe Historical Society opened the cabin to the public. Located on the original site, the cabin includes diorama displays of pioneer life in early Lake Tahoe.

The Village at Squaw Valley

You might think of **The Village at Squaw Valley** (1750 Village East Rd., Olympic Valley, 800/403-0206, www.squawalpine.com) as a ski area, but it's actually a small upscale town designed to mimic a European Alpine village. Spend hours rambling around the cobblestone village, cozy up to one of the communal fire pits, or shop, eat, and join the après-ski crowd at one of the restaurants, boutiques, or bars.

Souvenir seekers can go to **Squaw One Logo Company** (530/584-6250, www.squawalpine.com, 10am-5pm Mon.-Fri., 10am-6pm Sat.-Sun.). Those craving outdoor gear and clothing can stop in at **The Ledge Boardshop** (530/452-4477, www.squawalpine.com, 8:30am-6pm Sun.-Thurs., 8:30am-7pm Fri.-Sat.). For fun locally made gifts, visit the aromatic **Lather & Fizz Bath Boutique** (530/584-6001, www.latherandfizz.com, 10am-6pm daily) for soaps, lotions, and face products.

More than half a dozen restaurants, bars, and coffee shops offer sushi, pizza, burgers, and Bloody Marys. For those staying in the village, check out **Le Chamois** (www.squawchamois.com, 11am-7pm daily in winter only), lovingly referred to by locals as "The Chammy." Other options include **The Auld Dubliner** (1850 Village South Rd. #41, Olympic Valley, 530/584-6041, https://aulddublinertahoe.com, 11am-close Mon.-Fri., 9am-close Sat.-Sun., $12-23) or the **Slot Bar** (1pm-9pm Fri.-Sun.), which has a max occupancy of 34.

Recreation options include skiing and snow tubing in winter, hiking in summer, and yoga year-round. The **Aerial Tram** (1990 Squaw Peak Rd., 800/403-0206, www.squawalpine.com, 9am-4pm daily winter and summer, $46 adults, $25 youth ages 5-17, children 4 and under free) transports visitors to **High Camp** (1960 Squaw Valley Rd., Olympic Valley, 530/584-1000, www.squawalpine.com) at 8,200 feet (2,500 m) elevation. At High Camp, go for a swim or soak in a hot tub, or browse the **Olympic Museum** (www.squawalpine.com, free with tram ride), which is open when the tram is running. Outside of ski season, there's often live music and special events.

Northstar California

CA-267 links Truckee to Kings Beach, where **Northstar California** (5001 Northstar Dr., Truckee, 800/466-6784 or 530/562-1010, www.northstarcalifornia.com) offers a mini-village that caters to mountain biking in summer and skiing in winter. It also has shopping, dining, spas, a roller-skating and ice-skating rink, and special events year-round.

Northstar offers **gondola rides** (daily, $39 adults, $24 ages 12 and under) to the other side of the mountain, stopping mid-mountain at **The Lodge at Big Springs** (8am-2:30pm Mon.-Thurs., 8am-3pm Fri.-Sun., $12-18), where you can enjoy an epic burger or a chicken-and-waffles BLT. In the Village, **Tavern 6330'** (8001 North Village Way #8114, www.northstarcalifornia.com, 11am-9pm daily winter, $20-50) serves seasonally inspired and locally sourced cuisine. Northstar's sports bar is **TC's Pub** (2000 N. Village Dr., 530/562-2250, www.northstarcalifornia.com, 2pm-9pm Wed.-Thurs., 11am-9pm Fri.-Sun., $12-18), which serves upscale pub food, but its real treasure is its desserts (try the cookies and milk).

Make your own souvenir at **The Villager Candle Shop** (7001 Northstar Dr., Ste. 7111, 530/562-8884, www.

villagercandles.com, 10am-5pm daily), a candle, pottery, and gift shop. **Village Cinemas** (3001 Northstar Dr., 530/562-8800, www.bloomhufftheatresinc.com/thevillagecinemas, $13 adults, $9 kids and seniors) has two screens that show box-office hits.

Tahoe Gal

The *Tahoe Gal* (952 N. Lake Blvd., Tahoe City, https://tahoegal.com, early May-late Oct., $42-58 adults, $24-28 child) is a large paddle-wheeler that takes up to 120 passengers on a 3.5-hour daily cruise that travels along the West Shore down to Emerald Bay. The boat departs from the Tahoe City Marina daily at noon; passengers are treated to views of the Hellman-Ehrman Mansion, Rubicon Point, Vikingsholm, and Emerald Bay. Lunch is available to purchase. Other options include a 1.5-hour cocktail and brunch cruise ($35-42) and a 2.5-hour sunset dinner cruise ($44).

Sports and Recreation
★ Ski Resorts
Squaw Valley

Squaw Valley (1960 Squaw Valley Rd., Olympic Valley, 800/403-0206, www.squawalpine.com, 9am-4pm daily mid-Nov.-mid-May, $89-169 adults, $72-139 ages 13-17 and 70-plus, $63-109 ages 5-12) was the headquarters for alpine sports during the 1960 Winter Olympics. Today it is one of the most well-known and most-visited ski resorts in California. Squaw Valley has a great ski school with plenty of fun for new skiers and snowboarders, along with a wide selection of intermediate slopes. The Squaw Creek, Red Dog, and Squaw One Express lifts access long slopes perfect for skiers who want to spend more time on the snow. But the jewels of Squaw are the many black-diamond and double-black-diamond slopes and the two terrain parks on the upper mountain. Whether you prefer trees, moguls, narrow ridges, or wide-open

vertical bowls, you'll find your favorite at Squaw. The slopes off KT-22 are legendary. During the day, especially weekends and holidays, expect long lines at the lifts, crowds in the nice big locker rooms, and still more crowds at the numerous restaurants and cafés.

Alpine Meadows

Just one ridge over from Squaw Valley is a local favorite, **Alpine Meadows** (2600 Alpine Meadows Rd., Tahoe City, 800/403-0206, www.squawalpine.com, 9am-4pm daily mid-Nov.-mid-May, $89-169 adults, $72-139 ages 13-17 and 70-plus, $63-109 ages 5-12). This sprawling resort encompasses both sides of its two Sierra peaks, Scott and Ward. With a full range of trails, a daily ski school, and brand-new state-of-the-art rental equipment, Alpine is ideal for all levels of skiers. Beginners will particularly enjoy slashing through powder on "rocker" skis, which make steering easier than ever, and a scenic network of wide green trails. Intermediate skiers and snowboarders prefer Alpine over Squaw, due to the easily accessible Summit Six and Roundhouse Express chairlifts, which lead the way to plenty of blue square and black diamond runs. On the backside, from Scott Peak off the Lakeview Chair, all ski runs are blue. Thirteen lifts serve the mountains, including three high-speed chairs. If you're an expert, take just about any chair up the mountain and you'll find exhilarating ways down. The Scott Chair leads to a bunch of single-black-diamond runs on the front of the mountain, as does the Summit Express six-passenger chair at the back of Ward Peak. You can get to Art's Knob from the Sherwood Express. Alpine has two terrain parks when conditions permit: one off of Meadow Chair in the Subway Beginner Area and one off of the Kangaroo Chair on the other side of Summit Express.

Northstar California
Northstar California Resort (5001 Northstar Dr., Truckee, 800/466-6784 or 530/562-1010, www.northstarcalifornia. com, lifts 8:30am-4pm daily winter, $133-154 adults, $109-126 ages 13-18 and 65 plus, $73-85 ages 5-12) is more of a family resort. Freestyle skiers and riders can use the fast Vista Express quad chair to access terrain park features and find slopes heading gently back to the village. Kids especially love the Pinball run. Lower Main Street and the Village Run provide good spots for those fresh out of ski school. Intermediate runs crisscross the front of the mountain, starting at the peak of Mount Pluto at the top of Comstock and running down the mountain. The Backside, reachable via the Comstock Express quad chair and served by the Backside Express, is reserved for black-diamond skiers and riders, although adventurous intermediates can test their ski legs here. Your Epic daily lift ticket also works at Kirkwood and Heavenly.

Snowmobiling
On the North Shore, check out **Mountain Lake Adventures** (Hwy. 267, 530/546-4280, www.laketahoesnowmobiling.com, $190-330). With the largest fleet of snowmobiles and more than 30 years of guided touring experience, this outfit offers easy two-hour tours with gorgeous lake views as well as three- to four-hour private adventures for expert riders who want to tackle ungroomed backcountry terrain. You'll see sweeping North Shore views and drive through miles of unspoiled forest. Reservations are strongly recommended. Drivers must be age 16 or older and have a valid driver's license; children under age five may not ride.

Sledding and Snow Play
Granlibakken (725 Granlibakken Rd., Tahoe City, 530/583-4242 or 800/543-3221, www.granlibakken.com, 9am-4pm daily, $17-18 per day, resort guests $9) is a great place for sledding down the machine-groomed mountain on saucers (included). Granlibakken also has studios and suites for nightly stays, Saturday yoga classes, a day spa, and a whole slew of activities.

Tahoe City Winter Sports Park (251 N. Lake Blvd., Tahoe City, 530/583-1516, http://wintersportspark.com, 10am-5pm Mon.-Fri., 9am-5pm Sat.-Sun.; 10am-8pm daily for ice-skating, late Nov.-mid-Mar.) is in the center of Tahoe City. In winter, the snowy wonderland offers sledding, ice-skating, cross-country skiing, and fat biking.

Boating and Watersports
Tahoe City Marina (700 N. Lake Blvd., Tahoe City, 530/583-1039, https://tahoecitymarina.com) rents boat slips and buoys, cruisers ($120-156/hr), and a sailboat ($80/hr). It's behind the Safeway in Tahoe City.

Lake Forest Boat Ramp (2500 Lake Forest Rd., Tahoe City, 530/583-3796, www.tcpud.org, 6am-4pm daily Oct.-Apr., 5am-7pm daily May-Aug., 6am-7pm daily Sept., $15-20 daily launch fee) offers a wide, protected boat ramp within an hour's drive of the West Shore's lakefront.

Family-owned and managed by professional paddleboarders, **Waterman's Landing** (5166 N. Lake Blvd., Carnelian Bay, 530/546-3590, www. watermanslanding.com, 7am-6pm daily summer, $25-40/hour) is located on a dog-friendly beach in Carnelian Bay right on the water. It's easy and convenient to get out on the water. A café is attached.

North Tahoe Watersports (8400 N. Lake Blvd., Kings Beach, 530/546-9253, www.parasailtahoe.com, 9am-5pm daily late May-early Sept., $80 per person parasailing) offers parasail adventures and rents Jet Skis ($140/hr) and on-water tricycles ($40/hr).

The **Sierra Boat Company** (5146 N. Lake Blvd., Carnelian Bay, 530/546-2551, 7:30am-5pm daily) sells and restores

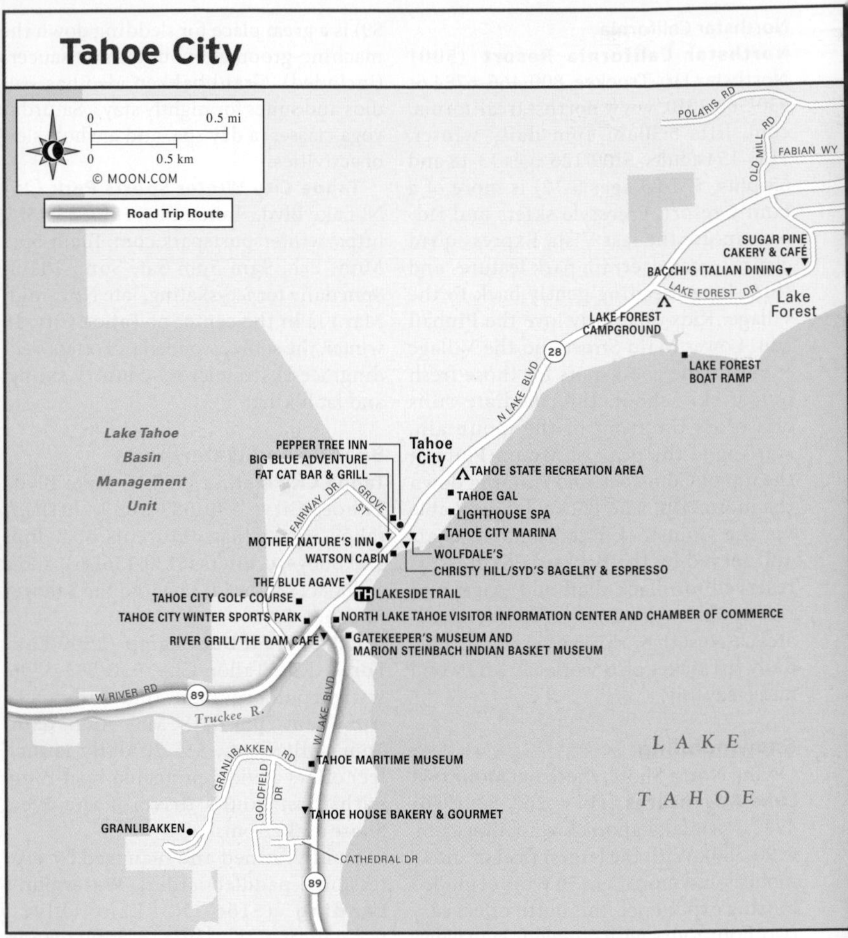

Tahoe City

Map legend/labels:
- 0 — 0.5 mi
- 0 — 0.5 km
- © MOON.COM
- Road Trip Route
- POLARIS RD
- OLD MILL RD
- FABIAN WY
- SUGAR PINE CAKERY & CAFÉ
- BACCHI'S ITALIAN DINING
- LAKE FOREST DR
- Lake Forest
- LAKE FOREST CAMPGROUND
- LAKE FOREST BOAT RAMP
- N LAKE BLVD
- 28
- Lake Tahoe Basin Management Unit
- PEPPER TREE INN
- BIG BLUE ADVENTURE
- FAT CAT BAR & GRILL
- Tahoe City
- TAHOE STATE RECREATION AREA
- TAHOE GAL
- LIGHTHOUSE SPA
- TAHOE CITY MARINA
- FAIRWAY DR
- GROVE ST
- MOTHER NATURE'S INN
- WATSON CABIN
- WOLFDALE'S
- CHRISTY HILL/SYD'S BAGELRY & ESPRESSO
- THE BLUE AGAVE
- TAHOE CITY GOLF COURSE
- LAKESIDE TRAIL
- TAHOE CITY WINTER SPORTS PARK
- NORTH LAKE TAHOE VISITOR INFORMATION CENTER AND CHAMBER OF COMMERCE
- RIVER GRILL/THE DAM CAFÉ
- GATEKEEPER'S MUSEUM AND MARION STEINBACH INDIAN BASKET MUSEUM
- W. RIVER RD
- 89
- Truckee R.
- W LAKE BLVD
- GRANLIBAKKEN RD
- GOLDFIELD DR
- TAHOE MARITIME MUSEUM
- LAKE TAHOE
- TAHOE HOUSE BAKERY & GOURMET
- GRANLIBAKKEN
- CATHEDRAL DR
- 89

wooden boats and also offers boat storage and a gas dock.

Fishing

Mickey's Big Mack Charters (Hwy. 28, Carnelian Bay, 530/546-4444 or 800/877-1462, www.mickeysbigmack.com, 5-hour trip $90 pp, $15 fishing license) operates out of the Sierra Boat Company. The 43-foot fishing boat departs twice daily for cruises that include spectacular views. An onboard restroom adds to the comforts of the trip as you fish for mackinaw, rainbow, and brown trout.

Golf

Tahoe City Golf Course (251 N. Lake Blvd., Tahoe City, 530/583-1516, http://golftahoecity.com, 7am-7pm May-Oct., $60 adults, $50 students 18-23 and seniors, $25 age 17 and under) is a par-66 course behind the main street in Tahoe City. Locals love this course, which was designed by pro golfer May "Queenie" Dunn-Webb.

Old Brockway Golf Course (400 Brassie Ave., Tahoe Vista, 530/546-9909, www.oldbrockway.com, 7am-7pm June-Oct., $40) is a fun 9-hole course in Kings Beach

Basin. Owned by longtime Tahoe locals, the 3,400-yard course winds through pine trees, wildflowers, and quiet neighborhoods.

Spas

One of the most popular day spas on the North Shore is the **Lighthouse Spa** (850 N. Lake Blvd., Suite 20A, Tahoe City, 530/583-8100, www.lighthousespa.com, 9am-6pm by appointment, massage $60-190). Look for it behind the Safeway on the north end of Tahoe City. Once inside, choose a therapeutic, deep tissue, or hot stone massage; expectant moms can get a special prenatal massage. Lighthouse also offers facials, body wraps, luxurious foot treatments, and aesthetic services. This place is perfect for those in desperate need of après-ski TLC. To make its pampering more convenient, Lighthouse Spa has a second location at the **Granlibakken Tahoe** (725 Granlibakken Rd., Tahoe City, 530/583-8111, www.granlibakken. com, 9am-6pm by appointment only). If you're anywhere in the North Shore (California side) or Truckee areas, they'll also come to you for an extra $35 fee.

Festivals and Events

Big Blue Adventure (210 Grove St., Tahoe City, 530/546-1019, https:// bigblueadventure.com, June-early Oct.) holds triathlons, marathons, and bike racing events around the North Shore. Some of the top events include the Squaw Valley Half Marathon, the Lake Tahoe Open Water Swim at Sugar Pine Point, and the Emerald Bay Trail Run.

Yogis and musicians celebrate a weekend of health and well-being at the annual **Wanderlust at Squaw Valley** (1750 Village East Rd., Olympic Valley, https:// wanderlust.com, July). Practice mindfulness and enjoy music set against the backdrop of the beautiful Sierra Nevada.

At the **B4BC Skate the Lake** (310/418-2174, https://b4bc.org, July or Aug.), skateboarders can push their boards 19-22 miles in a group event to raise awareness for breast cancer research. From Sugar Pine State Park, skateboarders ride the bike path through Homewood and along the shoreline through Tahoe City up to the Village at Squaw Valley, before descending back to Tahoe City. Everyone meets at Heritage Plaza (570 N. Lake Blvd., Tahoe City, www.placer. ca.gov) to share stories and award the top fundraisers.

Tahoe Paddle Racing (www. tahoepaddleracing.com, June-mid-Sept., $35-60) is a summer paddleboard race. Paddlers from all over come to train in the lake's water and root on competitors in friendly fun. Most races run 3-6 miles (5-10 km) long and are open to all abilities. The series ends with a Fall Classic/Tahoe Cup lake crossing: paddle 22 miles (35 km) across the entire length of the lake from South Shore to North Shore. Races are held all over Lake Tahoe. Contact **Waterman's Landing** (5166 N. Lake Blvd., Carnelian Bay, 530/546-3590, www.watermanslanding.com) for additional information.

Food

More than half a dozen restaurants, bars, and coffee shops at **The Village at Squaw Valley** (1750 Village East Rd., Olympic Valley, 530/584-1000, www.squawalpine. com) offer sushi, pizza, Irish pub food, and more. Among them are **The Auld Dubliner** (1850 Village South Rd. #41, Olympic Valley, 530/584-6041, https:// aulddublinertahoe.com, 11am-close Mon.-Fri., 9am-close Sat.-Sun., $12-23), **Coffeebar Squaw** (1750 Village East Rd. #61, Olympic Valley, 530/580-4200, www. coffeebar.com, 7am-6pm daily, $6-11), and **Fireside Pizza Co.** (1985 Squaw Valley Rd., 530/584-6150, www.firesidepizza. com, $13-26).

Casual Dining

Relax with some fine caffeine, a local magazine, and your laptop at **Syd's Bagelry & Espresso** (550 N. Lake Blvd., Tahoe City, 7am-3pm Mon.-Thurs.,

7am-4pm Fri.-Sun.). Syd's offers free wireless Internet access, and one of its best features is the location next door to Heritage Plaza, so you can take your latte outdoors while you watch the sunrise over the water.

A good choice for casual, inexpensive dining is **Fat Cat Bar & Grill** (599 N. Lake Blvd., Tahoe City, 530/583-3355, www.tahoefatcat.com, noon-9pm Mon.-Thurs., noon-10pm Fri., 11am-10pm Sat., 11am-9pm Sun., $9-25). The menu includes free-range chicken sandwiches, salads, and grass-fed beef burgers, all of which is locally sourced. The café also has free wireless Internet access. Trivia nights are held once a month on Tuesdays and there is usually live music on Friday and Saturday nights.

Sugar Pine Cakery & Café (2923 Lake Forest Rd., Tahoe City, 530/583-2253, http://sugarpinecakery.com, 7am-3pm Tues.-Thurs., 7am-1pm Sat.-Sun., $4-6) is a lovely bakery serving house-made cookies, pastries, and a variety of delicious espresso drinks. The owners are very nice. It's on the side of Tahoe City toward Kings Beach, tucked into the Lake Forest neighborhood.

The Dam Café (55 W. Lake Blvd., Tahoe City, 530/581-0278, 6am-2:30pm daily, $5-8) is a small coffeehouse perched in a busy spot at the corner of the Y (CA-28 and CA-89). Pop in here to grab a breakfast burrito and an espresso.

The Blue Agave (Tahoe Inn, 425 N. Lake Blvd., Tahoe City, 530/583-8113, www.tahoeblueagave.com, 11:30am-9pm daily, $10-30) is the place to go for Mexican food. The ample and delicious food draws loyal patrons from all over.

Waterman's Landing (5166 N. Lake Blvd., Carnelian Bay, 530/546-3590, www.watermanslanding.com, 7am-6pm daily summer, $4-11) sits perched on a rocky dog-friendly beach in the center of the North Shore and offers organic, delectable dishes and espresso drinks. Pair a house-made scone with the classic Waterman's breakfast burrito, made

paddleboarding on the North Shore

with the signature bacon jam, or order the refreshing house-made granola in an acai bowl.

Fine Dining

Wolfdale's (640 N. Lake Blvd., Tahoe City, 530/583-5700, www.wolfdales.com, 5:30pm-close Wed.-Mon., $11-59) has been serving "cuisine unique" dishes that fuse Asian and Western ingredients since 1978. The small seasonal menu is heavy on seafood but also includes tasty beef and game meats in season. Save room for the delicious desserts, made in a light California style.

An ideal spot for a delicious dinner and some lake-watching is **Christy Hill** (115 Grove St., Tahoe City, 530/583-8551, www.christyhill.com, 5pm-9:30pm daily summer, 5pm-9pm daily winter, $12-55) and its outdoor SandBar (beer and wine only) on the back deck. Entrées range from gnocchi with duck confit to Moroccan-spiced lamb loin.

The **River Grill** (55 West Lake Blvd., Tahoe City, 530/581-2644, www.rivergrilltahoe.com, 5pm-close daily, $18-36) is located where the Truckee River meets Tahoe City. Eat outside on the rustic heated wooden porch, enjoying the river view while listening to live music, or sit indoors in the casually elegant dining room, complete with a fireplace. Happy hour (5pm-6pm daily) features discounted drinks and food in the bar and at the outdoor fire pit.

Established in 1932, ★ **Bacchi's Italian Dining** (2905 Lake Forest Rd., Tahoe City, 530/583-3324, www.bacchistahoe.com, 5:30pm-close daily mid-June-mid-Sept., 5:30pm-close Thurs.-Sun. mid-Sept.-mid-June, bar from 4pm, $22-40) is one of Tahoe's oldest restaurants. Inside the dimly lit restaurant, patrons dine at red-and-white checkered tables and historical photos dot the walls. Authentic Italian dishes come with bread, house-made minestrone soup, and salad with all of the fixings. Save room for the local favorite, spumoni ice cream. (A bear once broke into the restaurant, ate gallons of the spumoni, and then curled up in the freezer to hibernate.)

Accommodations

Mother Nature's Inn (551 N. Lake Blvd., Tahoe City, 530/581-4278, www.mothernaturesinn.com, $79-175) offers a Tahoe camping experience while providing creature comforts. Rooms follow a cozy cabin theme; beds feature polished wood headboards and are draped with warm tartan blankets, nightstands have stand-alone lamps, and there's a small table or desk. All rooms have fridges, ceiling fans, and private baths. Pets are welcome for a small fee. The inn is tucked between the Tahoe City Golf Course and downtown Tahoe City.

If you want to stay in town, the **Pepper Tree Inn** (645 N. Lake Blvd., Tahoe City, 530/583-3711, www.peppertreetahoe.com, $120-180) is a reasonable choice. Pepper Tree is an above-average hotel with whirlpool tubs, free wireless

Internet access, and DirecTV in each room, plus an outdoor seasonal swimming pool, laundry room, and free breakfast. It also has the advantage of a great location across the street from the lake, near the Lakeside Trail and close to the restaurants in Tahoe City. This is a great base for local adventures.

Condo Rentals

For the ultimate convenience in ski vacations, get a condo at **The Village at Squaw Valley** (1750 Village East Rd., Olympic Valley, 866/818-6963, www.squawalpine.com, $199-350 winter) and never leave the vicinity of the lifts. Elegant, modern condos range from compact studios perfect for singles or couples to three-bedroom homes that sleep up to eight. Condos have full kitchens—some even have granite countertops—as well as a living room with a TV. Most units have fireplaces and dining room tables. The skiers' favorite condo has heated tile floors in the kitchen and bath. Included in the price is use of the Village's eight outdoor hot tubs, five saunas, five fitness rooms, and heated underground parking garage. Stay in Building 5; it has the clearest view of the mountain and the most comfortable amenities.

Information and Services

The Lake Tahoe Visitors Bureau maintains the **North Lake Tahoe Visitor Information Center and Chamber of Commerce** (100 N. Lake Blvd., Tahoe City, 530/581-6900, www.gotahoenorth.com, 9am-5pm daily). For medical attention, the **Tahoe Forest Hospital** (10121 Pine Ave., Truckee, 530/587-6011, www.

tfhd.com) and its affiliate, **Incline Village Community Hospital** (880 Alder Ave., Incline Village, NV, 775/833-4100, www.tfhd.com), are the nearest options with full-service emergency rooms.

Getting Around

Tahoe Area Regional Transit (TART, 530/550-1212 or 800/736-6365, www.laketahoetransit.com) is the North Shore's public bus system. Buses (adults $1.75 one-way, 24-hour pass $3.50) run from Tahoma on the West Shore to Incline Village, Nevada, with many stops along the way.

Ski Resort Shuttles

A few ski resort shuttles bring skiers up to the mountains in the morning and back to their hotels in the late afternoon. The **Squaw Valley Express** (www.squawalpine.com, 8:30am-4:30pm daily late Nov.-mid-Apr.), connects Squaw Valley and Alpine Meadows; the **Northstar California** bus (weekends Jan.-early Mar.) runs from Truckee to the ski area as part of the TART Winter Park & Ride program.

The **North Lake Tahoe Express** (866/216-5222, http://northlaketahoeexpress.com, $49 one-way) offers airport shuttles to and from Reno around Truckee and North Lake Tahoe. The red route services Squaw Valley and Tahoe City to Granlibakken; the green route travels between Truckee and Northstar; and the blue route travels around the lake on the North Shore, with stops at Carnelian Bay, Tahoe Vista, Kings Beach, Crystal Bay, and Incline Village.

East Shore

The East Shore straddles the border between California and Nevada from Crystal Bay to Stateline. From Incline Village, NV-28 and US-50 descend almost 30 miles (48 km) south to Stateline and South Lake Tahoe, passing Sand Harbor State Park, Thunderbird Lodge, Spooner Lake, Cave Rock, and Zephyr Cove. Entry into Nevada is usually indicated by the immediate presence of casinos.

Getting There

The fastest way to get from South Lake Tahoe to the East Shore is to take US-50 north for 15 miles, passing Zephyr Cove and Cave Rock en route to Spooner Lake. At Spooner Lake, turn left to continue north on NV-28, reaching the town of Incline Village in 12 miles.

From I-80 and Truckee, take CA-267 south to Kings Beach. Turn east onto CA-28 and drive 1.6 miles (2.6 km) to enter Nevada at Crystal Bay. Continue 4 miles (6.4 km) east toward Incline Village. NV-28 continues south past Sand Harbor, meeting US-50 in the Spooner Lake area. Veer right onto US-50, which reaches Stateline, Nevada, in 13 miles (21 km).

Sights
★ Thunderbird Lodge

The **Thunderbird Lodge** (Hwy. 28, Incline Village, NV, 775/832-8750, www.thunderbirdlodge.org, tours Tues. and Fri.-Sat. late May-late June and late Sept.-mid-Oct.; Tues.-Sat. late June-late Sept., $45 adults, $19 children ages 6-12) was built in 1936 by George Whittell Jr., a playboy who acquired 40,000 acres of land spanning from the lodge to Crystal Bay. Whittell had a zoo with a pet lion, beautiful gardens, and an underground tunnel that led to a boathouse where his wooden yacht was stored, passing an opium den on the way. Today, access to the remaining grounds is available by tour.

Tours depart from the Incline Village/Crystal Bay Visitors Bureau (969 Tahoe Blvd., Incline Village, NV, 775/832-1606, 8:30am-5pm Mon.-Sat., 10am-4pm Sun.). Guests are driven to the lodge for a two-hour walking tour of the grounds and several of the buildings. The 600-foot underground tunnel from the mansion to the boathouse is a tour highlight, especially for kids. The 1930s-era mahogany yacht still sits in the boathouse.

Boat tours (5 hours, Zephyr Cove Marina, 775/230-8907, https://thunderbirdtahoe.org, 9am Tues.-Sat. summer, reservations required, $149 adults, $65 ages 6-12) are also available from Zephyr Cove. The 40-foot *Tahoe* powerboat motors along the eastern shore to dock at the Thunderbird Lodge; the walking tour continues from there. A continental breakfast is served on board, and a buffet lunch at Thunderbird is included. Children under age six are not permitted. Tours operate in summer only; exact dates are set by the lodge.

Cave Rock

Located on US-50 is a short tunnel carved out of rock. **Cave Rock** (US-50, NV, 775/588-7975, http://parks.nv.gov, sunrise-sunset, $10 day-use fee) used to bar travel between the North and South Shores until construction workers blew a hole through the rock in 1931, creating this tunnel. Today, not only can you drive through the tunnel, but also there is a boat ramp and day-use area where you can stop to admire the towering rock.

Cave Rock is 17.5 miles (28 km) south of Incline Village on NV-28/US-50 and 4.5 miles (7.2 km) north of Zephyr Cove.

Sports and Recreation
Ski Resorts
Mt. Rose-Ski Tahoe

Mt. Rose (22222 Mt. Rose Hwy., Reno, NV, 775/849-0704, www.skirose.com, lifts 9am-4pm daily winter, $135 adults,

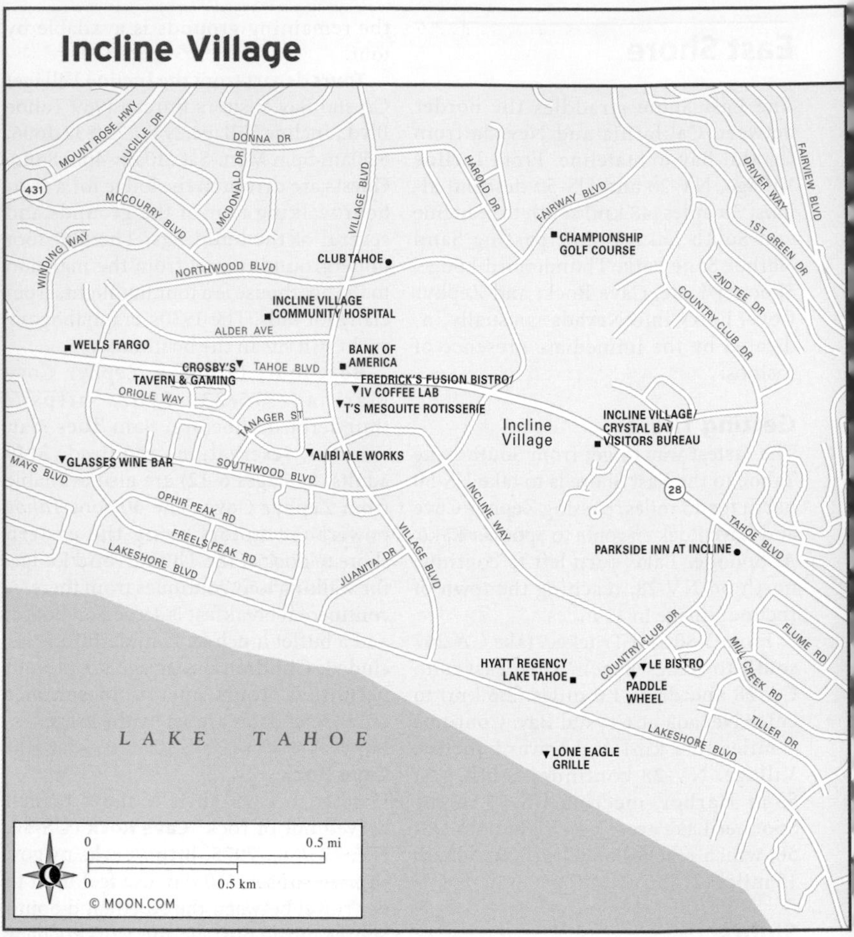

Incline Village

MOUNT ROSE HWY
431
MCCOURRY BLVD
WINDING WAY
LUCILLE DR
MCDONALD DR
DONNA DR
VILLAGE BLVD
HAROLD DR
FAIRWAY BLVD
FAIRWAY BLVD
DRIVER WAY
FAIRVIEW BLVD
1ST GREEN DR
NORTHWOOD BLVD
CLUB TAHOE
■ CHAMPIONSHIP GOLF COURSE
2ND TEE DR
COUNTRY CLUB DR
INCLINE VILLAGE COMMUNITY HOSPITAL
ALDER AVE
■ WELLS FARGO
CROSBY'S ▼ TAHOE BLVD
TAVERN & GAMING
ORIOLE WAY
BANK OF AMERICA
FREDRICK'S FUSION BISTRO
▼ IV COFFEE LAB
▼ T'S MESQUITE ROTISSERIE
Incline Village
INCLINE VILLAGE/ CRYSTAL BAY ■ VISITORS BUREAU
TANAGER ST
▼ ALIBI ALE WORKS
MAYS BLVD
▼ GLASSES WINE BAR
SOUTHWOOD BLVD
INCLINE WAY
28
TAHOE BLVD
OPHIR PEAK RD
FREELS PEAK RD
LAKESHORE BLVD
JUANITA DR
VILLAGE BLVD
PARKSIDE INN AT INCLINE ●
FLUME RD
MILL CREEK RD
HYATT REGENCY LAKE TAHOE ●
COUNTRY CLUB DR
▼ LE BISTRO
▼ PADDLE WHEEL
TILLER DR
LAKESHORE BLVD
LAKE   TAHOE
▼ LONE EAGLE GRILLE

0   0.5 mi
0   0.5 km
© MOON.COM

$75 children ages 6-15, $20 children ages 5 and under; $115 half day after 12:30pm) sits at a base elevation of 8,260 feet (2,520 m), which means it tends to get a lot of snow and stays open longer than other resorts. Mt. Rose offers the most variety of intermediate/advanced and beginner terrain. Ski school packages and private lesson options are also available.

Advanced and expert skiers and riders love The Chutes, 200-acre steeps situated between Mt. Rose and Slide Mountain that have at least 16 black- and double-black-diamond runs accessed through nine gates. Get your adrenaline pumping with chutes named Nightmare and Yellow Jacket, or go for the steepest and longest chute, El Cap. For green runs, ski schools, and rental equipment, park at the Main Lodge and take the Wizard or the Galena chair to beginner territory. For long intermediate tracks, start at Winters Creek Lodge on the Slide side and take the Blazing Zephyr six-pack high-speed chair to the top of the mountain. Enjoy a delicious cider at the Sky Bar within Winters Creek Lodge; lodges on both sides have food courts, bars, and restrooms.

Diamond Peak

Diamond Peak (1210 Ski Way, Incline Village, NV, 775/832-1177, www. diamondpeak.com, lift 9am-4pm daily mid-Dec.-mid-Apr., $89-109 adults, $69-89 ages 65-79 and 13-23, $39-49 ages 7-12, children ages 6 and under and seniors over 80 free) is smaller yet easy to access from Incline Village, with incredible lake views from the top. It's perfect for beginners and families because all runs filter down into a common base area, making it impossible to get lost. Intermediate and advanced skiers and riders will love the views from the top of the Crystal Express quad; the Crystal Ridge run feels like you'll ski right into the lake. Or cut into one of the black-diamond runs that branch off through nicely spaced glades over to the terrain park. Start your day at the Base Lodge, where you can eat, drink, and watch skiers in the beginner area. Then take the Lakeview lift to Snowflake Lodge for an afternoon snack or cocktail.

Beaches

Sand Harbor State Park (Hwy. 28, 3-4 mi/4.8-6.4 km south of Incline Village, NV, 775/831-0494, www.parks.nv.gov, 8am-sunset daily, $10/vehicle, $20/boat launch, $2/walk or bike-in) is East Shore's most accessible park. The sandy, 55-acre beach is one of the most popular places to swim in Lake Tahoe. Big boulders make great destinations to dive off of or perch on top to take in the views. The parking lot fills by 10am on summer weekends.

There's a large picnic area, and the on-site restaurant-snack bar **Sand Harbor Bar and Grill** (530/546-3171, www.charpit. com, 11am-9pm daily summer, $4-23) specializes in burgers and ice cream—the ample barbecue ribs are popular with hungry families.

Sand Harbor Rentals (530/581-4336, www.sandharborrentals.com,

8:30am-6pm daily mid-June-mid-Sept., $25/hour, $80/day single kayak or paddleboard; $40/hour, $100/day double kayak) is the only officially sanctioned boat concessionaire in the park. It's right on the beach next to the boat ramp. Rental reservations are recommended. The company offers a Morning East Shore paddling tour ($95 pp). The "Get Up Stand Up" program (8am-9am daily, $40, 2-person min., summer only) teaches the basics of stand-up paddleboarding to novice paddlers. Book online to ensure a spot.

Hiking and Biking

The Incline Village **Sand Harbor Bike Path** (www.tahoefund.org) is a 4-mile (6.4-km) path perfect for bikers and strollers who want to spend the day at an East Shore beach. The path begins at the Tunnel Creek Café (1115 Tunnel Creek Rd. A, Incline Village) and ends at Sand Harbor State Park.

For a serious lake-to-lake hike, the **Marlette Lake Trail** (10 mi/16 km, 6 hours, moderate) slopes 5 miles (8 km) uphill to the Marlette Dam, but you're on a fire road much of the way. The trail is easy to follow and the terrain never gets too rough. The trailhead is in Lake Tahoe-Nevada State Park (775/831-0494, www.parks.nv.gov, $10) at the junction of US-50 and NV-28.

For a shorter hike with less climbing and more shoreline, hike the **Spooner Lake Trail** (2 mi/3.2 km round-trip, 1 hour, easy) from the Spooner Lake trailhead in Lake Tahoe-Nevada State Park. The level trail features interpretive signage and offers close-up views of birds and wildlife, including—if you're lucky—eagles and ospreys.

Sand Harbor State Park (Hwy. 28, 3-4 mi/4.8-6.4 km south of Incline Village, NV, 775/831-0494, www.parks.nv.gov, 8am-sunset daily, $10/vehicle, $20/boat launch, $2/walk-in or bike-in) has easy and pleasant hiking. The **Sand Point Nature Trail** starts near the visitors center and continues 0.3 mile down a paved boardwalk path, with interpretive signs along the way.

For a quick walk above Crystal Bay in Nevada, head to the **Stateline Fire Lookout** (Reservoir Rd., Crystal Bay, 1 mi/1.6 km round-trip, easy). This is a popular place for local paragliders to launch before landing on Kings Beach.

The spectacular **Tahoe Rim Trail** (www.tahoerimtrail.org) provides mountain bikers access to about half of the 165 miles of rugged and varied terrain. To bike the particularly beautiful section from the Flume Trail to Spooner Lake, contact **Flume Trail Mountain Bikes** (775/298-2501, https://flumetrailtahoe.com, June-Nov.), which offers a private shuttle service. The shuttle leaves from the parking lot at Spooner Lake and delivers you and your bike to the Flume Trail in Incline Village. Signs at the trailhead indicate that the section of the trail between Tahoe Meadows to Spooner Summit is bikable only on even-numbered days of the month.

Flume Trail Mountain Bikes (1115 Tunnel Creek Rd., Incline Village, NV, 775/298-2501, http://flumetrailtahoe.com, 8am-6pm daily May-Oct., $45-130/day) also rents mountain bikes and offers knowledgeable advice about mountain biking in the area. Reservations are recommended and can be made by phone or online.

Fishing

At **Spooner Lake** (US-50 and Hwy. 28, 775/831-0494, www.parks.nv.gov, fishing dawn-sunset, $7-10) you can fish year-round and experience ice fishing in winter, keeping up to five trout per day. A Nevada state fishing license is required (www.ndow.org).

Marlette Lake (10.2 mi/16.4 km one-way, 8 hours, moderate-strenuous) is full of brook, rainbow, and cutthroat trout. Access is from a trailhead at Spooner Lake, and fishing is catch-and-release only. The season runs July 15-September 30. For more information, visit the Nevada Department of Wildlife (www.ndow.org).

Golf

Considered the crème de la crème of Tahoe golf courses, **Edgewood Tahoe** (100 Lake Pkwy. W., Stateline, 775/588-2787, www.edgewoodtahoe.com, $150-300 daily May-Oct.) has holes right on Lake Tahoe's shoreline. Conveniently located on the Nevada side, this iconic 18-hole course is known for its vibrant greens and views of the Sierra Nevada. Its beauty and status are why the Celebrity Golf Tournament returns here year after year.

The **Championship Golf Course** (955 Fairway Blvd., Incline Village, 775/832-1146, www.golfincline.com, sunrise-sunset daily mid-May-early Oct., $100-200) and the **Mountain Course** (690 Wilson Way, Incline Village, www.golfincline.com, sunrise-sunset daily mid-May-early Oct., $50-75) are each distinctly challenging courses in their own way. The Championship Course has long, well-manicured fairways and a few holes with a peek of the lake, ending at a stone and wooden chateau. The Mountain Course is a short executive par-3 course where precision matters more than distance. Both are worth playing if you're spending a few days in Incline Village.

Entertainment and Events
Casinos

Hyatt Regency Lake Tahoe (111 Country Club Dr., Incline Village, NV, 775/832-1234, www.hyatt.com, 24 hours) dazzles with a small casino floor that features table games, a sports book, and slot machines. The casino draws a high-end clientele with roulette, craps, blackjack, and slots. At the bar, a flat-screen TV shows the latest sports. On-site amenities include hotel rooms, a day spa, a gift shop, and Cutthroats restaurant.

A few strides behind the "Welcome to Nevada" sign sits the **Crystal Bay Club** (14 Hwy. 28, Crystal Bay, NV, 775/833-6333,

www.crystalbaycasino.com, 24 hours),
with blackjack tables, roulette, a good
variety of slot machines, and two music
venues and bars. Many bluegrass, classic rock cover bands, country, and reggae
acts play weekends in the Crown Room.
Afterward, head to the other side of the
casino for the after-party in the Red
Room. This is usually the gathering place
for Tahoe locals, especially when Tainted
Love comes to town on Halloween and
New Year's Eve.

Next to the Crystal Bay Club, the **Jim
Kelley's Tahoe Nugget** (20 Hwy. 28,
Crystal Bay) is an average casino with a
couple of hidden gems: the Awful Awful
burger and a bar with 24 craft beers on
tap. The Awful Awful burger, named so
because it is awfully good, gained its no-
toriety from the Nugget casino in downtown Reno, which served the burger any
time day or night. Other Nugget casinos
have adopted the Awful Awful, and it
continues to hit the spot, especially on a
hot summer day.

The **Tahoe Biltmore** (5 Hwy. 28,
Crystal Bay, 775/832-9292, www.
tahoebiltmore.com, 24 hours) has table
games, slots with great payouts, and fun
Football Sunday parties in the Breeze Bar.
The casino is a throwback to 1946, when
it was first built, and has kept its vintage
charm.

Nightlife
Most locals flock to the casinos in Crystal
Bay to catch concerts or gamble a bit, but
there are also bars that stay open past
2am. The **Paddle Wheel** (120 Country
Club Dr., Incline Village, 775/831-2022,
www.paddlewheelsaloon.com, 8am-
5am daily) is Incline's dive bar, across
the street from the Hyatt. The Paddle
Wheel has cheap drinks, salty bartend-
ers, a dartboard, and free popcorn.

One of Incline Village's most popular bars is the **Alibi Ale Works** (204

From top to bottom: the Flume Trail; the
Championship Golf Course; Le Bistro.

E. Enterprise St., 775/298-7001, www.alibialeworks.com, 3pm-9pm Mon.-Wed., 3pm-10pm Thurs., noon-10pm Fri.-Sat., noon-9pm Sun.), with a huge selection. Its handcrafted beers are brewed with Lake Tahoe water.

Festivals and Events

California theater-lovers have been known to drive for hours to see a show at the **Lake Tahoe Shakespeare Festival** (Sand Harbor State Park on Hwy. 28, 3 mi/4.8 km south of Incline Village, 800/747-4697, www.laketahoeshakespeare.com, July-Aug., $35-99 Sat., $30-94 Sun.-Fri.). Built in 1995, the stage offers a memorable backdrop that amplifies performances. Expensive theater sections include reserved seating and chairs; in the cheap seats, bring a chair or blanket to lie in the sand. Gates open at 5pm and performances begin at 7:30pm. Parking can be hectic; come early to enjoy food and drinks from Shakespeare's Kitchen.

Moviegoers come to Lake Tahoe for the **Tahoe Film Fest** (www.tahoefilmfest.org, early Dec., $60 all-access pass). The jam-packed weekend event shows environmental flicks, documentaries, and new releases at **Incline Village Cinema** (901 Tahoe Blvd., Incline Village, 530/546-5951) and **The Village Cinemas** (3001 Northstar Dr., Truckee, 530/562-8800). Directors and actors of big-budget films also drop in.

Support the Diamond Peak Ski Education Foundation at the annual winter **UllrFest** (1210 Ski Way, Incline Village, NV, 775/832-1177, www.diamondpeak.com, end of Jan.-early Feb.), a local event where people dress up in their warmest Scandinavian hats, coats, and horns to gather for a torchlight parade, bonfire, live music, and dancing that celebrates the saint of skiers.

Food

★ **Crosby's Tavern & Gaming** (868 Tahoe Blvd. Ste. 4, Incline Village, NV, 775/833-1030, www.crosbyspub.com, 8am-11pm daily, $10-29) is the place to go for watching football, drinking freshly squeezed mimosas, and diving into a plate of chicken wings amid a crowd of friendly faces. With several big-screen TVs strategically placed around the bar and video poker machines with the double down option, Crosby's is a locals' favorite thanks to its *Cheers*-like atmosphere and delicious food, like the avocado-stuffed gyro and the award-winning pork green chili, a fine selection on a snowy day.

It's not uncommon to see a line out the door of **T's Mesquite Rotisserie** (901 Tahoe Blvd., Incline Village, NV, 775/831-2832, www.tsrotisserie.com, 11am-8pm daily, $7-11 cash only), because their burritos are just that good. Authentic dishes, like chicken slow-cooked to perfection, make this grab-n-go Mexican joint a local favorite. Order a tostada or a chicken burrito with pico de gallo and a Jarritos soft drink to go, or stay and watch the soccer game as you enjoy your meal.

For friendly service and delicious espresso, visit ★ **I.V. Coffee Lab** (907 Tahoe Blvd., Ste. 20a, Incline Village, NV, 775/298-2402, 6am-4pm Mon.-Fri., 7am-3pm Sat., 7am-2pm Sun.), a local coffee joint that's a favorite spot for local university students. This place has lovely decor, and the owners and baristas live in town and are involved in the community.

A former teacher and bookworm with a love for wine opened **Glasses Wine Bar** (760 Mays Blvd., Unit #8, Incline Village, NV, 530/270-9463, http://glasseswinebar.com, 3pm-9pm Tues.-Sat.) to promote good company, fine wine, and a comfortable place to enjoy a good book. Patrons don't need to wait in line at the bar for a refill; just reload a key card and stick it in one of two wine dispensers, which have about 18 different wines on tap.

Owned and managed by Tahoe local chef David Blair, **Le Bistro** (120 Country Club Dr., Ste. 29, Incline Village, NV, 775/831-0800, www.lebistrotahoe.com,

6pm-9pm Tues.-Thurs., 6pm-9:30pm Fri.-Sat., 5-course meal $65 per person) is a fine dining restaurant that utilizes locally sourced seasonal ingredients to create classic French dishes with an Asian flair. The dishes could be considered works of art; however, they taste as good as they look. Choose something off of the unique wine list and stick around for dessert.

If your tastes run to the creative and pleasantly surprising, you'll enjoy **Fredrick's Fusion Bistro** (907 Tahoe Blvd., Incline Village, NV, 775/832-3007, www.fredricksbistro.com, 5pm-9:30pm Tues.-Sat., $11-32), where lobster dogs share a table with surf-and-turf sushi rolls. The fusion is mostly French and Asian, but the seasonal menus have a definite California feeling, as they make good use of fresh and local ingredients.

A good place to splurge on a meal with an exceptional lake view is the **Lone Eagle Grille** (111 Country Club Dr., Incline Village, NV, 775/886-6899, www.loneeaglegrille.com, 11:30am-3pm and 5:30pm-9pm Sun.-Thurs., 11:30am-3pm and 5:30pm-10pm Fri.-Sat., $37-62). Entrées include duck, ahi tuna, and barramundi, plus a lot of vegetarian items such as creative soups, salads, and macaroni and cheese.

Accommodations
Casinos
Built in 1946, the ★ **Tahoe Biltmore** (5 Hwy. 28, Crystal Bay, 775/832-9292, www.tahoebiltmore.com, $89-209) has retained some of its historical charm, back when Frank Sinatra and the Rat Pack ruled Crystal Bay. Comfortable (and affordable) rooms feature plush comforters, flat-screen TVs, air-conditioning, and large closets. The hotel is rumored to be haunted; employees and guests claim to have seen a ghostly woman in a white dress near the stairwells. The Northern Nevada ghost hunters even hold yearly retreats here . . . and they always have odd experiences.

The Biltmore is easy to spot driving into Crystal Bay—just look for the large wagon wheel sign in front.

Considered one of the top hotels in the world, ★ **Hyatt Regency Lake Tahoe** (111 Country Club Dr., 775/832-1234, www.laketahoe.regency.hyatt.com, $162-565) is a destination in itself. The more than 400 rooms are spacious and comfortable and come with superior amenities—plush sitting chairs, gas fireplaces, and luxurious toiletries. Hotel guests have access to a heated swimming pool (year-round), a day spa, a fitness room, shops, and restaurants within the same building. Across the street, the Hyatt keeps a few lakefront cottages ($337-1,140 per night) next to a fine-dining restaurant, the **Lone Eagle Grille.**

Resorts
For a basic Nevada hotel, try the **Parkside Inn at Incline** (1003 Tahoe Blvd., Incline Village, NV, 775/831-1052 or 800/824-6391, www.parksideinnatincline.com, $146-198). The 38 rooms are decked out in wood paneling with 1970s-style quilted comforters, but they are clean and the private baths adequate. Amenities include an indoor pool and a hot tub available year-round, flat-screen TVs, and free wireless Internet access in all rooms.

Condo Rentals
Club Tahoe (914 Northwood Blvd., Incline Village, NV, 775/831-5750, www.clubtahoe.com, $160-200) is a great place to rent a condo on the Nevada shore. These are individually leased timeshare properties. Each three-story unit includes two bedrooms and a loft with twin beds, but the decor varies within an overall theme of wood-paneled walls and vaulted ceilings. The full-size kitchens are stocked with appliances and utensils, and a second bath makes sharing the condo easy. Amenities include an outdoor pool and spa, a tennis court, a racquetball court, an arcade, and a full bar with pool table.

Camping

Within the Spooner Lake area, **Spooner Summit** (US-50 and Hwy. 28, 775/831-0494, http://parks.nv.gov, call for prices and availability) offers two log cabins for foot travelers: the Spooner Lake Cabin (available Apr.-mid-Nov.) and Wildcat Cabin (available May-mid-Oct). Accessible only by snowshoe, cross-country skiing, or hike, these backwoods cabins are basic. The smaller Wildcat Cabin sleeps two, while the Spooner Lake Cabin can sleep up to four guests. Both cabins have a kitchen stove, a wood stove for heat, and compostable toilets, but all food, sleeping bags, and food will have to be carried in. Call for reservations and details.

Information and Services

The **Incline Village Crystal Bay Visitors Bureau** (969 Tahoe Blvd., Incline Village, NV, 775/832-1606, www.gotahoenorth. com, 8:30am-5pm Mon.-Sat., 10am-4pm Sun.) is the best source of information.

To get cash, visit the **Bank of America** (900 Tahoe Blvd., Incline Village, 775/688-8961, www.bankofamerica.com), **US Bank** (923 Tahoe Blvd., 775/831-4780, www.usbank.com) or **Wells Fargo** (776 Tahoe Blvd., Incline Village, 775/885-5500, www.wellsfargo.com). The local bank branches are the best way to save on ATM fees from the machines in the casinos.

Incline Village Community Hospital (880 Alder Ave., Incline Village, NV, 775/833-4100, www.tfhd.com) is the place to go for help on the northeastern corner of the Tahoe Sierra. The hospital has a 24-hour emergency room.

Getting Around

Tahoe Area Regional Transit (TART, 530/550-1212 or 800/736-6365, www. laketahoetransit.com) is the public bus system. Buses (adults $1.75 one-way, 24-hour pass $3.50) run north around the lake from Tahoma on the West Shore to Incline Village, Nevada, with stops along the way.

In the South Lake Tahoe area, local public transportation is provided by **BlueGo** (530/541-7149, www. tahoetransportation.org, adults $2-5), which runs buses, trolleys, and ski shuttles. Routes and schedules vary; check the website for details.

Truckee-Donner

The gateway to Tahoe, Truckee is an Old West town offering ski gear, delicious food, coffee shops, cocktails, and places to stay. Parking can be a little tricky (anywhere close to the main drag costs money), and both the prices and the lines at restaurants can resemble those in San Francisco, but this small mountain town has its charms.

Getting There

Truckee is located on I-80. The drive north from San Francisco to Truckee is 185 miles (300 km) and takes 3.5 hours in good weather. From Sacramento, the trip is about 105 miles (170 km) and 1.5-2 hours. If you're driving to Truckee from Reno, follow I-80 west for 32 miles (52 km, 35 minutes).

Sights
Old Jail Museum

It's hard to believe this cute brick-and-stone building used to be the **Old Jail Museum** (10142 Jibboom St., Truckee, 530/582-0893, www.truckeehistory.org, 10am-4pm Sat.-Sun. late May-early Sept., $2 donation). Built in 1875, it housed prisoners continually until 1964. "Baby Face" Nelson and "Machine Gun" Kelly are among the notorious outlaws believed to have spent time here. Today, it has historical exhibits, cool information, and docents from the local Truckee-Donner Historical Society. In addition to the somewhat erratic weekend schedule, the museum is often open on Thursday evenings (5pm-9pm) in summer during the popular "Truckee Thursdays" farmers market.

Truckee

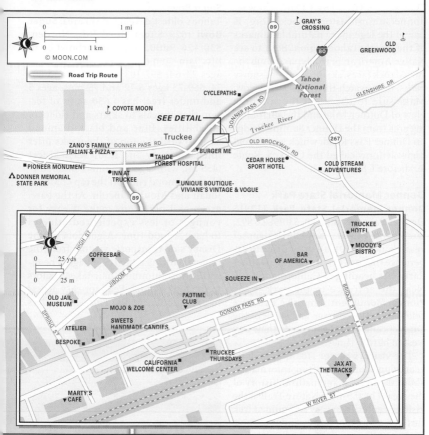

Donner Camp Picnic Ground Historical Site

To learn more about what really happened to the infamous Donner party, visit the **Donner Camp Picnic Ground Historical Site** (1 mi/1.6 km north of Alder Creek Rd. turnoff on Hwy. 89, Truckee, www.fs.usda.gov/tahoe, free). The site is in the Tahoe National Forest, and it's a good place to stop for a picnic, a hike, or to go for a quick mountain bike ride. This is also where 25 members of the Donner party, who had left Springfield,

Illinois, in April 1846 on their way to new lives in California, stopped to repair their wagons in the fall after being slowed down by an ill-fated shortcut through Hastings Cutoff. It was only October when they arrived in the Donner area, but a blizzard hit hard. Some of the party ended up staying the whole winter, and some, as you may know, never left.

The 0.75-mile interpretive **loop trail** is short and pretty flat, with signs along the way that illuminate the Donner Party's history.

Donner Summit

West of Truckee, **Donner Summit** (I-80, 530/426-3376, www.donnersummithistoricalsociety.org) is one of the legendary natural landmarks of the North Tahoe region. Stop to see Native American petroglyphs, climb the varied rock faces, ski the summit's snowy paths, or to watch the trains pass below. Make sure to check out the stunning view of Donner Lake and the surrounding area from the Donner Summit Bridge on Donner Pass Road, which was the old highway (now called the Old U.S. Route 40) before I-80 was built.

Donner Memorial State Park

Donner Memorial State Park (12915 Donner Pass Rd., off I-80, 530/582-7892, www.parks.ca.gov, daily sunrise-sunset year-round, $5-10) is a great place to experience the lush beauty that the Donner Party was heading to California to find. Near the entrance to the park is the **Pioneer Monument,** a massive structure celebrating the courage and spirit of the Donners and others who made their way west in harder times.

The **visitors center** (10am-5pm daily year-round) offers uplifting information about the human and natural history of the area. The 0.5-mile Nature Trail at the visitors center is an easy self-guided trek through a forest of Jeffrey and lodgepole pines past the site of the cabin built by the Murphy family during the Donner party's layover here in the winter of 1846-1847. A moving plaque at the cabin site lists those who perished and those who survived. The trail continues over a creek and through the campground (800/444-7275, www.reservecalifornia.com).

Donner Lake is a paradise for children and adults alike, offering swimming, boating, fishing, and hiking. Walking the **Lakeside Interpretive Trail** along the shore is a great way to enjoy close-up views of the lake.

Sports and Recreation

Ski Resorts

Sugar Bowl

Tahoe's oldest developed ski area, **Sugar Bowl** (629 Sugar Bowl Rd., Norden, 530/426-9000, www.sugarbowl.com, lifts 9am-4pm daily Dec.-Apr., $118-125 ages 23-64, $97-103 ages 13-22 and 65-74, $69-73 ages 6-12 and 75-plus, ages 5 and under free) has 1,650 acres of terrain that appeals to skiers and riders of all abilities. Blue and black-diamond runs toward the top of the peaks offer intense variety and 1,500 vertical feet (455 m), with a good number of double-black-diamond runs off the top of Mount Judah and Mount Lincoln. At the base, green and blue runs make it easy for younger or less experienced athletes to have a good time. A gondola on the Disney side transports visitors from the remote parking lot to the village. The resort's short Summit Chair takes visitors to the top of Judah Peak for easy access to backcountry trails. The resort offers

two base lodges: a day lodge at Judah and the Village Lodge at the base of Nob Hill and Disney Express chairlifts. The on-site **Hotel at Sugar Bowl** (750 Mule Ears Dr., Truckee, 530/426-6742, www.sugarbowl. com, $272-718) allows you to ski right up to your hotel room.

Boreal Mountain Resort

Boreal Mountain Resort (19749 Boreal Ridge Rd., Soda Springs, 530/426-3666, www.rideboreal.com, 9am-9pm daily late Oct.-May, $74 adults, $64 ages 13-17 and 60-69, $44 ages 6-12, $5 ages 5 and under, $34 ages 70-plus) may not feel as fabulous as Squaw or Alpine, but many Californians find their snow legs here. The Accelerator serves Boreal's super pipe, terrain parks, and a night-skiing area; the 49er Chair serves the intermediate and advanced terrain. Even on weekends, the lines at Boreal seem pleasingly short compared to the bigger resorts. The **Woodward Tahoe** (530/426-1114, www. campwoodward.com) offers weeklong summer camps for skiers, snowboarders, bicycle motocross riders, cheerleaders, skateboarders, and gymnasts. Trampolines, foam pits, an indoor skate park, and a digital media learning center make it training heaven. Boreal is very family-friendly, with ski and snowboard lessons for beginners and a lodge with the Boreal Bar on the top floor; a cafeteria (8am-7pm Sat.-Sun., 8am-6pm Mon.-Fri.) offers limited service after 4pm.

Soda Springs

Small **Soda Springs** (10244 Soda Springs Rd., Soda Springs, 530/426-3663, www. skisodasprings.com, 10am-4pm Thurs.-Mon., $50 adults, $45 ages 13-17, $40 ages 6-12, $5 ages 5 and under) is a great family resort. Its claim to fame is tubing ($40 for a tubing-only package). The Planet Kids area for young athletes offers a safe place to practice tubing, skiing, and snowboarding, and there are even two tubing carousels to add to the thrills. Soda Springs has no on-site

Sugar Bowl

lodging but does have an adequate cafeteria. Enrolling your kid in a group lesson is a great way for them to get comfortable sliding on the snow (1 hour, $35-40).

Tahoe Donner Ski Area

Tahoe Donner Ski Area (11603 Snowpeak Way, Truckee, 530/587-9444, www.tahoedonner.com/downhill-ski, 8am-4pm daily Dec.-Apr., $69-89 adults, $59-79 ages 13-17, $39-59 ages 7-12 and 60-plus, $17-22 ages 6 and under) prides itself on being "a great place to begin." With only five lifts, including two conveyor belts and one carpet, 15 runs, and 120 skiable acres, Donner seems tiny compared to Squaw Valley or Northstar. However, it's a great spot to bring your family to get a feel for snowboarding or skiing, take lessons, and enjoy the snow in the beautiful Tahoe forest. To be truly family-friendly, Tahoe Donner offers lessons for children as young as age three, interchangeable lift tickets for parents, and even kid-friendly items on the snack-bar menu.

Cross-Country Skiing and Snowshoeing

The granddaddy of Tahoe cross-country ski areas, the **Royal Gorge Cross Country Ski Resort** (9411 Pahatsi Rd., Soda Springs, 530/426-3871, www.royalgorge.com, 8:30am-4pm daily winter, $35-38 adults, $20 ages 13-22, $30-34 ages 65-74, ages 12 and under and 75 and older free, $5 dog pass) has a truly tremendous chunk of the Sierra—6,000 acres—within its boundaries. Striving to provide a luxurious ski experience comparable to what downhillers expect, the Royal Gorge offers lodging, food, drink, a ski school, equipment rentals, equipment care facilities and services, and much more. With the most miles of groomed trails anywhere in the Tahoe area, Royal Gorge offers two stride tracks and a skate track on every trail to allow easy passing. They even have a surface lift for skiers who want to practice downhill technique or try telemarking. It also hosts nine small warming huts.

Tahoe Donner Cross Country (15275 Alder Creek Rd., Truckee, 530/587-9484, www.tahoedonner.com/cross-country, 8:30am-5pm daily Dec.-mid-Apr., $39-49 adults, $29-39 ages 13-17 and 60-plus, $29-39 ages 7-12, ages 6 and under free) offers more opportunities to slide around in the peaceful trees without the help of a chairlift. Tahoe Donner has 2,800 acres crisscrossed with trails ranging from easy greens up to double-black-diamond trails, with four trails set aside for snowshoers. A cross-country ski school introduces newcomers to the sport and helps more experienced skiers expand their skills. A separate day lodge and a snack bar are halfway up the mountain in Euer Valley. You can even rent a fat tire bike to take on the trails ($33-43/day) or bring your dog with you ($8 daily dog pass). Be sure to start or end your day with a snack or an après ski cocktail at the **Alder Creek Café & Trailside Bar** (15275 Alder Creek Rd., Truckee, 530/587-9484, www.tahoedonner.com, 8:30am-5pm daily, $6-15).

Snowmobiling

Several snowmobile outfits operate west of Truckee along the main roads—you'll see the tracks as you drive in and out of town. **Cold Stream Adventures** (1253 Brockway Rd. 103B., Truckee, 530/582-9090, www.coldstreamadventures.com, hours vary daily, 2-hour tour $175-195) also offers tours into the mountains, promising climbs up to 2,000 feet (600 m) higher than the starting point. These guided tours run through private forest, so you'll see forested landscapes available no other way. Make reservations and be sure to dress warmly and bring sunglasses.

Hiking

The **Donner Camp Picnic Ground Historical Site** (Hwy. 89, 1 mi/1.6 km north of Alder Creek Rd., Truckee, www.ts.usda.gov/tahoe, free) has two hikes, each excellent in its own way. A short 0.75-mile educational interpretive loop trail begins in the picnic-area parking lot. The trail is very well maintained, with raised wooden planks above the grasslands in the sections that occasionally get wet. Six trailside signs explain the history. If you're a fast reader, you can do the whole trail in about 15 minutes.

Follow the shore of Donner Lake for an easy and scenic hike within **Donner Memorial State Park** (12915 Donner Pass Rd., 530/582-7892, www.parks.ca.gov, sunrise-sunset daily year-round, $5-10). Start at the Lagoon parking area near the park entrance and follow the wheelchair-accessible Lakeside Interpretive Trail to China Cove. Turn around and come back the same way for a 3.5-mile (5.6-km) round-trip hike. Note that you can't hike all the way around the lake; some of the shore is on private land outside the park. For a more physically demanding hike, try the excellent **Commemorative Emigrant Trail** (7.5 mi/12 km round-trip, 4 hours, strenuous), also accessible from the parking lot at the Donner Picnic Ground. This mostly flat trail leads to Prosser Creek and the Stampede Reservoir and is popular with mountain bikers and equestrians as well as pedestrians.

An outstanding day trip is the hike from Sugar Bowl to Squaw Valley along the **Pacific Crest Trail** (18 mi/29 km one-way, difficult). To begin, park at **Clair Tappaan Lodge** (19940 Donner Pass Rd., Norden, 530/426-3632, http://clairtappaanlodge.com) and pick up some maps. Look for the Pacific Crest Trail (PCT) trailhead and start walking south behind Mount Lincoln toward Tinker Knob. Snow as late as July is not uncommon. This is a good hike to do with friends and use multiple cars: have someone in your party leave a car at Squaw Valley in the morning to ferry you, or arrange for a ride.

Biking
Cyclepaths (10825 Pioneer Trail, Truckee, 530/582-1890, www.cyclepaths.com, 9am-6pm daily summer, noon-6pm Mon.-Thurs. winter) can hook you up with bike rentals, sales, equipment, and repairs.

Golf
Coyote Moon (10685 Northwoods Blvd., Truckee, 530/587-0886, www.coyotemoongolf.com, daily in summer, $75-150) offers challenging fairways dotted with granite boulders and lined by dense natural forest, a layout that takes advantage of the natural features of this locale.

Gray's Crossing (13051 Fairway Dr., Truckee, 530/550-5804 or 866/703-4653, www.golfintahoe.com/grays-crossing, 8am-sunset daily mid-May-Oct., $60-220) is a beautifully designed 18-hole golf course that has long, manicured fairways set against an incredible mountain backdrop. Named after the man who founded Truckee, this course has many long par-4 and par-5 holes, undulating terrain, and just a smooth, upscale feel. Its sister course, **Old Greenwood** (12915 Fairway Dr., Truckee, 530/550-7024, www.golfintahoe.com/old-greenwood, 8am-sunset daily mid-May-Oct., $60-220) also offers fabulous greens, on 600 acres of beauty designed by renowned golfer Jack Nicklaus.

Entertainment and Events
Nightlife
Truckee's **Pastime Club** (10096 Donner Pass Rd., 530/582-9219, 2pm-2am Mon.-Thurs., noon-2am Fri.-Sun.) is open every night with live music Thursday-Saturday, and occasionally Sunday. There's usually no cover unless it's a special event. The **Bar of America** (10040 Donner Pass Rd., Truckee, 530/587-2626, www.barofamerica.com, 11am-9:30pm Mon.-Thurs., 11:30am-12:30am Fri., 10:30am-12:30am Sat., 10:30am-9:30pm Sun.) offers an upscale atmosphere along with

Exploring Tahoe's Backcountry

West of US-50 near South Lake Tahoe, you'll find beautiful lakes and abundant trails in the **Eldorado National Forest** (www.fs.fed.us). The scenic **Hell Hole Trail** is a popular place to take off-road vehicles. It's accessible off US-50 northwest of Meyers in the wilderness behind Homewood Mountain Resort.

One of the most popular and beautiful places to visit is the 76,000-acre **Loon Lake,** a reservoir created in 1963 with the damming of Gerle Creek. It's a delightful place to camp, swim, SUP, or kayak. It's a long and winding drive north of U.S. 50 between Placerville and Meyers.

Desolation Wilderness

The Desolation Wilderness has 125 alpine lakes and 120 miles of trails, including segments of the Tahoe Rim Trail and the Pacific Crest Trail. Permits are required for day hikers as well as for backpackers. Before venturing into the Desolation Wilderness, stop at the **Taylor Creek Visitors Center** (Hwy. 89, 3 mi/4.8 km north of South Lake Tahoe, 530/543-2674, www.fs.usda.gov, hours vary, late May-Oct.) to get wilderness and campfire permits and up-to-date information on conditions in the Desolation. You can also reserve a permit (877/444-6777, www.recreation.gov, $10) before you arrive. One of the most popular hikes is **Twin Lakes Trail** (7 mi/11.3 km round-trip, 1,200 ft/365 m elevation gain, moderate).

Backcountry camping in the Desolation Wilderness requires a **permit** ($5-10). For information, call the U.S. Forest Service supervisor's office in South Lake Tahoe (530/543-2600) or the Taylor Creek Visitors Center (530/543-2674 in summer); for reservations call 877/444-6777.

Camping

The **Ice House Campground** (9000 Icehouse Rd./Forest Rd. 3, Pollock Pines, 530/293-3321, reservations 877/444-6777, late May-early Oct., $28-56) has 81 tent and RV sites, each with a picnic table, fire pit, and vault toilets close by. A resort with a few rooms and small grocery store is near the campground. It's 37 miles (60 km) east of Placerville and 15 miles (24 km) north of US-50.

More than 60 campgrounds dot Eldorado. One of the most attractive spots is the **Loon Lake Campground** (Ice House Rd./Forest Rd. 3, 877/444-6777, www. recreation.gov, mid-June-early Oct., $28-56). It's 23 miles (37 km) east of Placerville, 15 miles (24 km) north of US-50.

Getting There

To reach Eldorado National Forest and the Desolation Wilderness from the west, travel east on US-50. About 40 miles (64 km) past Placerville, turn left (north) onto Forest Road 3 (Ice House Rd.). Coming from Tahoe, travel west on US-50 and make a right turn onto Ice House Road.

---

local beers, cocktails, food, and music. Bands tend to play Thursday-Saturday, usually without charging a cover.

Festivals and Events

Lake Tahoe hosts festivals every year in both summer and winter, though undoubtedly summer has more. One of the biggest is the **Lake Tahoe Music Festival** (530/583-3101, www.tahoemusic.org, Aug., $30-38). During the weeklong festival, symphony orchestras play all over Truckee, the North Shore, and the West Shore at the **West Shore Café** (5160 W. Lake Blvd., Homewood), PJ's restaurant at **Gray's Crossing** (13051 Fairway Dr., Truckee, 530/550-5804 or 866/703-4653, www.golfintahoe.com/grays-crossing), and the Hellman-Ehrman Mansion at **Ed Z'berg Sugar Pine Point State Park** (Hwy. 89, Tahoma, 530/525-7982, www.parks. ca.gov, year-round, $10 parking).

In summer, the weather starts to warm and local makers come out to showcase unique, handcrafted items at **Truckee Thursdays** (5pm-8:30pm Thurs., www.truckeethursdays.com, mid-June-Aug.). Truckee's main street shuts down as dozens of vendors set up booths portraying artwork, soaps, jewelry, and skateboards. Near the train depot are food trucks and a beer garden, often accompanied by live music. This is a favorite event for locals.

Shopping

Donner Pass Road is the center of Truckee's historical district, and lots of little shops line both sides of the street. For women's clothing, gifts, and handmade jewelry, the woman-run business **Mo Jo & Zoe** (10122 Donner Pass Rd., Truckee, 530/587-3495, www.mojozoe. com, 10am-6pm Sun.-Thurs., 10am-8pm Fri.-Sat.) is a pleasant and friendly spot with reasonably priced goods. If your clothing tastes run to the more dramatic, you will enjoy the **Unique Boutique-Viviane's Vintage & Vogue** (10925 W. River St., Truckee, 530/582-8484, 11am-6pm Mon.-Wed., 11:30am-5:30pm Thurs.-Sun.). Viviane has been dressing partygoers, Burning Man attendees, and anyone else for more than two decades.

Bespoke (10130 Donner Pass Rd., Truckee, 530/582-5500, www. bespoketruckee.com, 10am-6pm Sun.-Thurs., 10am-8pm Fri.-Sat.) sells unique artisanal gifts, greeting cards, and jewelry from independent crafters. Next door is **Atelier** (10128 Donner Pass Rd., Truckee, 530/386-2700, www.ateliertruckee.com, 10am-6pm daily), where people can unleash their creative side by joining a crochet or calligraphy class.

Food
Bakeries and Cafés

For a warm panini and lavender latte, you can't beat the **Coffeebar** (10120 Jibboom St., Truckee, 530/587-2000, www. coffeebartruckee.com, 6am-7pm daily, $5-9), one block from the main drag. Coffeebar feels calm and peaceful with lots of space, free wireless Internet access, captivating art, and good food, including house-made baked pastries, paleo bowls, avocado toast, granola, and burritos.

Breakfast joint **Marty's Café** (10115 Donner Pass Rd., Truckee, 530/550-8208, https://martyscafetruckee.com, 8am-3pm daily, $9-16) is owned and managed by head chef Marty Carlton, and his years of working in eateries on both coasts have really paid off. Order the breakfast burrito filled with green chiles and chorizo or settle for an old fashioned hoagie for lunch.

Squeeze In (10060 Donner Pass Rd., 530/587-9814, www.squeezein.com, 7am-2pm daily, $13-27) has a fun and inviting atmosphere that makes you excited to go to breakfast. There are a lot of options to choose from on the seven-page menu, but it's worth trying the chocolate-covered bacon or the eggs Benedict with a quarter pound of king crab.

American

Jax at the Tracks (10144 W. River St., Truckee, 530/550-7450, www.jaxtruckee. com, 7am-10pm daily, $13-21) looks authentic inside and out. Housed in an actual 1940s diner, it has been thoroughly fixed up to be clean, fresh, and original. Jax has a creative California-style chef who puts his own stamp on comfort food, with homemade English muffins, Kobe beef meatloaf with root-beer raisin glaze, and a mean Cajun blackened burger. This place is also a favorite of celebrity chef Guy Fieri.

Burger Me (10418 Donner Pass Rd., Truckee, 530/587-9814, www. realfreshburger.com, 11am-9pm daily, $7-13) serves unique burgers made with

all-natural beef, bison, ahi tuna, lamb, or cod as the main patty. The burgers are fresh and fast, satisfying all levels of appetites. The turkey burger and blackened chicken burger are notably delicious, especially when paired with thick-cut sweet potato fries.

Italian

Zano's Family Italian & Pizza (11401 Donner Pass Rd., Truckee, 530/587-7411, www.zanos.net, 4pm-9pm Mon.-Wed., 11:30am-9pm Thurs.-Sun., $15-25) serves huge pizzas and tremendous salads in a big casual dining room with sports playing on TV. The full menu includes pastas and Italian entrées; at lunch, the hot crisp panini tastes great. But it's the thin-crust pizzas that rule here; pick one of Zano's interesting combinations or build your own from the list of fresh ingredients.

Fine Dining

One of the best upscale restaurants is **Moody's Bistro** (10007 Bridge St., Truckee, 530/587-8688, www. moodysbistro.com, 11:30am-9pm daily, $17-46). This casual yet elegant eatery adjoins the Truckee Hotel, just off the main drag. A wooden bar and booths give the main lounge an old-time feel, but the white-tablecloth dining room in the back feels more classically elegant. The chef promises ingredients that are "fresh, local, seasonal, and simple" and then jazzes them up with creative preparations. You might find antelope or local fish on the menu. Everything on the dessert menu is made in-house. Make a reservation for weekend evenings.

The food at **Bar of America** (10040 Donner Pass Rd., Truckee, 530/587-2626, www.barofamerica.com, 11am-9:30pm Mon.-Thurs., 11:30am-12:30am Fri., 10:30am-12:30am Sat., 10:30am-9:30pm Sun., $10-47) is worth the extra few bucks. The menu offers fresh organic

From top to bottom: Graeagle Outpost; Gray's Crossing; Burger Me.

ingredients and daily specials, as well as local beers and creative cocktails with professional service; the wood-fired pizzas are especially a hit. Reservations are recommended.

Dessert

Little Truckee Ice Creamery (11620 Donner Pass Rd., Truckee, 530/587-2884, www.truckeeicecream.com, 7am-8pm daily summer, noon-9pm Mon. and Fri., 12:30pm-6pm Tues., 12:30pm-8pm Wed.-Thurs., 7am-9pm Sat.-Sun. spring, noon-6:30pm Fri., 12:30pm-7pm Sat., 12:30pm-6pm Sun. winter) delivers what it promises—lots of ice cream and hot coffee drinks.

At **Sweets Handmade Candies** (10118 Donner Pass Rd., Truckee, 530/587-6556, www.sweetshandmadecandies.com, 10am-9pm Mon.-Thurs., 10am-10pm Fri.-Sat., 10am-6pm Sun.), watch the experts make fudge and then come inside for a free sample or hand-dipped chocolates, honeycomb, and caramel apples.

Accommodations
Under $100

West of Truckee is an unusual lodging option. Since 1934, the Sierra Club has run the **Clair Tappaan Lodge** (19940 Donner Pass Rd., Norden, 530/426-3632, http://clairtappaanlodge.com, $75-80). The lodge is a great starting point for cross-country skiing or hiking day trips. Accommodations are pretty basic: Most travelers sleep in the men's or women's dormitories, though a few small rooms are for couples and larger rooms are for families. Bring your own bedding and expect to share a bathroom. Overnight lodging includes three home-cooked meals. Communal spaces include a toasty library with a wood-burning stove, hot tub, recreation room, and extensive grounds.

$100-150

The **Truckee Hotel** (10007 Bridge St., at Donner Pass Rd., Truckee, 530/587-4444, www.truckeehotel.com, $79-229) offers fabulous period ambiance for reasonable rates. The hotel has welcomed guests to the North Shore since 1873. Rooms show their age with high ceilings, claw-foot tubs, and little Victorian touches. Part of the historical charm includes third- and fourth-floor rooms without an elevator. Most of the 36 rooms have shared baths in the hall that are clean and comfortable, with either a shower or a bathtub and a privacy lock. Breakfast is included, and the hotel also houses Moody's, one of the best restaurants in town.

Low-priced accommodations around Truckee are not easy to come by, especially in ski season. A decent basic hotel with affordable rates is the **Inn at Truckee** (11506 Deerfield Dr., Truckee, 530/587-8888 or 888/773-6888, www.innattruckee.com, $125-205). The renovated rooms feature comfortable mattresses, plush pillows, and headboards. It's also pet-friendly ($25 fee per night) and offers a spa and sauna, free continental breakfast, and free wireless Internet access.

$150-250

If you prefer a longer stay right on the water, call the **Donner Lake Village Resort** (15695 Donner Pass Rd., Truckee, 855/979-0402, www.donnerlakevillage.com, $159-345) on the shores of Donner Lake. Choose from regular motel rooms without kitchens or studio, one-bedroom, and two-bedroom condos with full kitchen facilities. Guest rooms include all the amenities of a nicer motel. Donner Lake Village has its own marina with rental ski boats, fishing boats, and slips if you've brought your own watercraft. A bait and tackle shop is across the street. The nearby Sugar Bowl, Boreal, and Squaw Valley ski resorts are an easy drive. A two-night minimum is sometimes required in summer.

The **Donner Lake Inn** (10070 Gregory Place, Truckee, 530/587-5574, www.donnerlakeinn.com, $189-229) is an intimate five-room B&B offering rustic charm beside Donner Lake. Each room has its own simple homey decorating scheme, private bath with a shower, private entrance, queen bed, large-screen TV with a DVD player, and free wireless Internet access. Each morning, the friendly and hospitable owners serve up a delicious full breakfast in the dining room.

The **Cedar House Sport Hotel** (10918 Brockway Rd., Truckee, 866/582-5655, www.cedarhousesporthotel.com, $180-295) sports an exposed wood exterior and is landscaped with trees, fallen stumps, and a rusty steel girder. The environmentally friendly rooms are all about luxury, with wood platform beds, designer leather chairs and sofas, and shining stainless-steel fixtures in the private baths. Choose comfortable rooms with queen or king beds or fancy suites with flat-screen TVs and every possible amenity. The expert staff can put together guided hikes, bike rides, and rafting or kayaking trips.

Camping

Donner Memorial State Park (12593 Donner Pass Rd., 800/444-7275, www.reservecalifornia.com, reservations late May-mid-Sept., first-come, first-served early Sept.-late May, $35) offers a spacious tree-filled campground with easy access to the lake, the new visitors center, and the trails in the park. It has 152 sites spread across three campgrounds: Ridge Campground (May-Oct.), Creek Campground (June-Sept.), and Splitrock (June-Sept.). Sites include fire rings and picnic tables, and there are restrooms with showers.

The Forest Service (877/444-6777, www.recreation.gov) maintains three campgrounds along CA-89 between Truckee and Tahoe City: **Granite Flat** (74 sites, Hwy. 89, 1.5 mi/2.4 km south of Truckee, late May-mid-Oct., $22-44) and **Goose Meadows** (24 sites, Hwy. 89, 4 mi/6.4 km south of Truckee, late

May-Sept., $22) offer potable water and vault toilets; **Silver Creek** (27 sites, Hwy. 89, 6 mi/9.5 km south of Truckee, late May-Sept., $20) offers potable water and both flush and vault toilets. All three campgrounds get noise from the highway as well as the gentler sounds of the nearby Truckee River.

Information and Services

The comprehensive **California Welcome Center** (10065 Donner Pass Rd., 530/587-2757, www.truckee.com, 9am-6pm daily) features free Internet access on your computer or theirs, huge brochure racks, candy, toys, books, and friendly personal advice. The center is attached to the town's Amtrak station.

If you need medical attention, the **Tahoe Forest Hospital** (10121 Pine Ave., Truckee, 530/587-6011, www.tfhd.com) has a full-service emergency room.

Getting Around

Tahoe Truckee Regional Transportation (TART, 530/550-7451, https://tahoetruckeetransit.com) travels between the Truckee Tahoe Airport, downtown Truckee, and the Donner Memorial State Park and Donner Lake. TART also offers a **Dial-A-Ride service** (8am-5pm Mon.-Fri., 9am-5pm Sat.-Sun., $6 adult one-way, $2 seniors and children 11 and under). Travelers can reserve a time to be picked up from the nearest bus stop and dropped off in another location within town limits.

◈ CA-89 North

Sierraville

From Truckee, the main roads form a loop that roughly surrounds much of the Tahoe National Forest area. CA-89 heads northwest from Truckee toward **Sierraville** (24 mi/39 km).

At **Sierra Hot Springs** (521 Campbell Hot Springs Rd., Sierraville, 530/994-3773, www.sierrahotsprings.org, $20 Mon.-Thurs., $25 Fri.-Sun. and holidays), natural hot springs feed a large outdoor swimming pool and the small Temple Dome Hot Pool. A membership fee ($5/month) is charged at these clothing-optional pools.

Food and Accommodations
Sierra Hot Springs has the **Main Lodge** (521 Campbell Hot Springs Rd., Sierraville, 530/994-3773, www.sierrahotsprings.org, $77-99 private rooms, $55-66 dorm) and the **Globe Hotel** 1 mile (1.6 km) south of the hot springs. Its **Philosophy Café** (521 Campbell Hot Springs Rd., Sierraville, 530/994-3773, www.sierrahotsprings.org, 5pm-8:30pm Fri. and Mon., 12:30pm-3:30pm and 5pm-8pm Sat.-Sun., $7-21) is in the Main Lodge and serves healthy, vegetarian entrées and dessert.

The campgrounds at **Sierra Hot Springs** (521 Campbell Hot Springs Rd., Sierraville, 530/994-3773, www.sierrahotsprings.org, $33-39) have no designated campsites. No campfires are allowed. The nearest U.S. Forest Service campground is **Lower Little Truckee Campground** (Hwy. 89, 11 mi/17.5 km north of Truckee, 877/444-6777, www.recreation.gov or www.fs.usda.gov, May-Oct., $20) with just a handful of sites. For an unusual option, consider the **Calpine Lookout** (3 mi/4.8 km northwest of Calpine, near Hwy. 89, 877/444-6777, www.recreation.gov or www.fs.usda.gov, $45), a former fire lookout available to rent year-round.

Los Dos Hermanos (100 S. Lincoln St., Sierraville, 530/994-1058, 11am-9pm daily, $9-15) serves delicious margaritas and plentiful beans and rice plates with friendly service.

Graegle
Graeagle is 46 miles (74 km) north of Truckee via CA-89. The town offers access into the surrounding **Plumas National Forest** and the **Gold Lakes Basin,** filled with alpine lakes and streams, challenging trails, and memorable vistas.

In the middle of **Plumas-Eureka State Park** (310 Johnsonville Rd., Blairsden, 530/836-2380, www.parks.ca.gov, free) is a **museum** (8:30am-4:30pm daily late May-Sept., donation) in a former bunkhouse for gold miners. Outside is a historic mining area, two old stamp mills, and a blacksmith shop.

Gold Lake Stables (7000 Gold Lake Hwy., Graeagle, 530/836-0430, www.reidhorse.com, June-Sept., $62-160) offers guided trail rides, including overnight trips. Kid-friendly **Graeagle Stables** (7611 Hwy. 89, Graeagle, 530/836-0940, www.reidhorse.com, May-Sept., $22-60) offers private lessons, pony rides, and guided trail rides for adults.

Food and Accommodations
Restaurants are few and far between here, but include the **Grizzly Grill** (250 Bonta St., Blairsden, 530/836-1300, www.grizzlygrill.com, 5pm-9pm daily summer, hours vary fall and spring, $21-30), **Mountain Cuisine** (250 Bonta St., Blairsden, 530/836-4646, www.mountaincuisine.com, 11:30am-3pm Tues.-Sun., $5-11), and **Coffee Tree Express** (196 E. Sierra Ave., Portola, 530/832-4563, 6am-2:30pm Mon.-Sat.). The **Graeagle Outpost** (7358 Hwy. 89, Graeagle, 530/836-5820, 8:30am-3pm Wed.-Sat., $5-7) is a cute coffee shop with a mini library by its patio.

Chalet View Lodge (72056 Hwy. 70, Graeagle, 530/832-5528, www.chaletviewlodge.com, $120-295) is a lovely place to stay in the Plumas area. Tucked into the pines, it has a spa, dining options, and on-site activities.

As many as 50 different campgrounds are scattered throughout Plumas. One of the most scenic and peaceful is **Gold Lake Campground** (9 mi/14.5 km southwest of Graeagle, May-Oct., $10 first-come, first-served). Camp in one of 60 sites at **Upper Jamison Creek Campground** (County Road A-14, Blairsden, 800/444-7275, www.reservecalifornia.com, late May-early Oct., $35). One of the more unusual places to stay is the **Black Mountain Lookout** (Beckwourth Ranger District, 530/836-2575, www.fs.usda.gov, reservations 877/444-6777 or www.recreation.gov, $60).

Reno

Reno, Nevada, is within an hour's drive of Lake Tahoe, home to a major university, two hospitals, and an international airport. What the city is really known for is its casinos and top-notch entertainment, but it also has museums, restaurants, shops, and hotels that are often more convenient and affordable than those in Tahoe.

Getting There

Reno is northeast of Lake Tahoe in the state of Nevada. From Truckee, the drive east on I-80 is the most direct route; plan 30-60 minutes for the 30-mile (48-km) drive. From Incline Village on the East Shore, NV-431 heads northeast for 22 miles (35 km) to meet I-580/US-395 near the southern end of Reno. Continue north on I-580 for 11 miles, then head west on I-80 to reach downtown and the major casinos. Note that this route is not advised in winter.

Sights

Reno Arch

The historic **Reno Arch** (155 N. Virginia St.) sits nestled downtown between the casinos on South Virginia Avenue. Built in 1926, the Reno Arch welcomes visitors to the city with a flashing pink neon sign advertising Reno as the "Biggest Little City in the World." The iconic arch spans South Virginia Avenue and is a worthy photo op.

National Automobile Museum

The **National Automobile Museum** (10 S. Lake St., Reno, 775/333-9300, www.automuseum.org, 9:30am-5:30pm Mon.-Sat., 10am-4pm Sun., $12 adults, $10 seniors, $6 youth 6-18, children 5 and under free) is home to more than 200 classic cars. Highlights include Sammy Davis Jr.'s 1935 Duesenberg roadster and the only 1925 Julian sport coupe ever built. A cozy theater shows a film about the evolution of the automobile.

Nevada Museum of Art

At the south end of downtown, the **Nevada Museum of Art** (160 W Liberty St., 775/329-3333, www.nevadaart.org, 10am-6pm Wed. and Fri.-Sun., 10am-8pm Thurs., $10 adults, $8 students and seniors, $1 children ages 6-12, children age 5 and under free) is an artfully designed multi-level museum housing a captivating display of sculptures, photographs, and paintings by regional and global artists. Modern artworks depict the surrounding natural environment of the nearby Sierra Nevada and Great Basin. This is a must-visit for art lovers, especially when the monthlong Artown festival is on in July.

Parks

Rancho San Rafael Regional Park (1595 N. Sierra St., 775/785-4512) features a rose garden, walking trails, large grassy areas, and picnic tables on 570 acres. **Wingfield Park** (2 S. Arlington Ave., 755/334-2414) is in downtown Reno with a half-dome-shaped stage for live bands. It's a popular place for events like Artown and the Reno River Festival. **Idlewild Park** (1900 Idlewild Dr., 775/827-7600, www.reno.gov) is a spacious park with trees, green grass, a one-acre rose garden, baseball diamonds, and a municipal swimming pool.

Entertainment and Events

Reno hosts themed pub crawls and a myriad of artisan events, and is the gateway to the annual Burning Man festival.

Reno

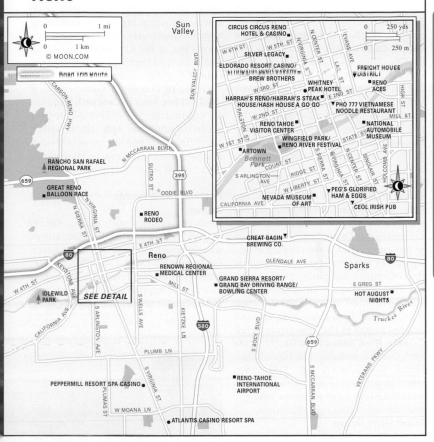

Casinos

Circus Circus

Circus Circus Reno Hotel & Casino (500 N. Sierra St., 775/329-0711, www.circusreno. com) is a great place to stay if you're traveling with kids. Its Midway section features an indoor carnival with games like Whac-a-Mole, a basketball-throwing contest, plus circus acts with live performers. Circus Circus is in the heart of downtown and shares a spa with Silver Legacy.

Silver Legacy

Tucked between Circus Circus and Eldorado, **Silver Legacy** (407 N. Virginia St., 775/325-7401, www.silverlegacyreno. com) is the center point for all the action, with everything from bars and cafés to a gigantic casino floor. On the basement floor, the Grand Ballroom hosts country concerts with top music acts, comedy shows, and MMA fights. It also has a day spa available for guest use. The lobby features a collection of tea kettles encased in glass from the old Silver State mining days. It also has a giant mining machine perched above Rum Bullions whose wheels turn throughout the day, giving kids and visitors a free show.

Eldorado

Next door to the Silver Legacy, **Eldorado Resort Casino** (345 N. Virginia St., 775/786-5700, www.eldoradoreno.com) has slot machines and an array of restaurants. **Brew Brothers** (11:30am-close Mon.-Fri., 11am-close Sat.-Sun.) has fun, easy-to-boogie-to live music. After a night of gaming, it's fun to stop into the **Eldorado Reno Bakery** (775/348-3740, 24 hours) for a big piece of cake.

Harrah's

Harrah's Reno (219 N. Center St., 775/786-3232, www.caesars.com/harrahs-reno) is within walking distance of the major happenings in Reno. The Zone, located on the casino floor, shows the top sporting events in arena-style seating while also offering beer pong, pool tables, and other gaming activities (age 21 and up, free to enter). **Harrah's Steak House** (775/788-2929, 5pm-close daily, $36) put this restaurant in the Fine Dining Hall of Fame. **Hash House A Go Go** (775/788-2895, 6am-10pm Sun., 7am-10pm Mon.-Thurs., 6am-2am Fri.-Sat., $15) serves generous portions of delectable food that is impossible to enjoy all in one sitting.

Grand Sierra Resort

Grand Sierra Resort (2500 2nd St., 775/789-2000, www.grandsierraresort.com) is conveniently located off I-580, close to the Reno Tahoe International Airport. Major acts like Alice Cooper and Death Cab For Cutie perform in the Grand Theatre. Hit a bucket of balls at the **Grand Bay Driving Range** (775/789-2122, 8am-10pm Mon.-Thurs., 8am-midnight Fri.-Sun.) or head downstairs to one of the 50 lanes at the **Bowling Center** (775/789-2296, 8am-3am daily).

Nightlife

The **Freight House District** (250 Evans Ave., 775/334-7094) is an entertainment complex next to the Greater Nevada Field ballpark, where the **Reno Aces** (www.milb.com/reno) play. It's usually open when a game is going on. Get something to drink from Duffy's Ale House, Bugsy's Sports Bar, or the Arroyo Mexican Grill, and enjoy it on the patio overlooking the field.

If you're craving a Guinness in a dimly lit bar, head to **Ceol Irish Pub** (538 S. Virginia St., 775/329-5558, http://ceolirishpub.com, 3pm-close daily). Enjoy free Wi-Fi and live music on Friday and Saturday nights or go on Wednesday for $2 off all whiskey drinks.

Festivals and Events

Artown

Reno comes alive with music, dance, literary, film, and visual performances when it transforms into an artistic haven for **Artown** (528 W. 1st St., 775/322-1538, https://artown.org, July, free). More than 100 events happen all over Reno and nearby Sparks to celebrate local, regional,

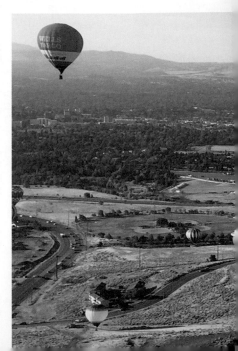

and international creators and entertainers. Catch a live band at Wingfield Park or a synchronized swim show at Idlewild.

★ Hot August Nights

Classic car lovers come to participate in poker runs, drag races, and show 'n' shines, at the annual **Hot August Nights** (775/356-1956, https://hotaugustnights. net, Aug., free). For two weeks in August, hundreds of spectators and vintage car owners cruise the streets of Reno to show off their hot rods. The festivities include classic rock concerts and a Twinkie-eating contest in downtown Reno, as well as drag races at the Nugget Casino Resort in Sparks, Nevada. Parts of South Virginia Street may be blocked off to accommodate the classic cars; check online to confirm road closures.

Reno River Festival

As the snow melts off the Sierra Nevada and into the Truckee River, hard-core kayakers come out to raft its raging waters during the **Reno River Festival** (775/851-4444, https://renoriverfestival. com, May, free). In addition to the white-water event, there's live music all weekend long, a Reno River Roll bike event for families, unique brews in the Craft Beer Village, and carnival-like activities in the pop-up Reno Tahoe Adventure Park.

Burning Man

What began as a few hippies burning a wooden sculpture has become an internationally recognized art and music festival that draws hundreds of thousands of attendees each year. During the annual **Burning Man** festival (Black Rock City, https://burningman.org, late-Aug.-early Sept., costs vary), festivalgoers resembling *Mad Max* film extras come to trade, barter, and ride bikes through the dusty desert and marvel at gigantic art sculptures. Though the Black Rock Desert is 142 miles (229 km) northeast of Reno, everyone gets into the spirit of Burning Man, with local architects, artists, and

Great Reno Balloon Race

engineers displaying what they're going to showcase at Burning Man. Afterward, join in one of the many decompression parties over the Reno area in the days following the festival.

Reno Rodeo

Come all ye cowboys, bucking broncos, cowgirls, and ropers to the annual **Reno Rodeo** (1350 N. Wells Ave., 775/329-3877, www.renorodeo.com, late June, $23-27), held at the rodeo fairgrounds. This week-long event and PRCA bull-riding competition kicks off when the Cattle Drive rolls into town: 60 guests join volunteers to drive 300 steers for five days through the high desert, *City Slickers*-style. Spectators then head to fairgrounds to enjoy carnival-style rides, world-class bull riding, and entertainment by professional horse riders. Be sure to watch the hilarious mutton bustin', where kids try to ride sheep.

Great Reno Balloon Race

Hot-air balloon teams come to Reno to compete in the **Great Reno Balloon Race** (San Rafael Regional Park, 1595 N. Sierra St., 775/384-2554, https://renoballoon. com, Sept., free). Big, bright, and colorful hot-air balloons, some shaped like Smokey the Bear and Darth Vader, fill up the sky over Reno in the early hours. The festival kicks off with an early morning Dawn Patrol, when locals and visitors lie on blankets as balloons light up beneath the dark sky. By 6am, dozens of balloons are floating above Reno.

Food

★ **Pho 777 Vietnamese Noodle Restaurant** (201 E. 2nd St., 775/323-7777, 10am-9pm daily, $9-11) serves the best noodle bowls. Perfectly soaked noodles come in oversized bowls stuffed with veggies and fixings; authentic eggrolls, dumplings, and heaping piles of stir-fried dishes leave little room for dessert. Centrally located downtown, this tiny place only has about a dozen or so tables;

fortunately, the turnover is fast so you won't have to wait long for a seat.

Peg's Glorified Ham & Eggs (420 S. Sierra St., 775/329-2600, http://eatatpegs. com, 6:30am-2pm daily, $8-14) serves hot breakfast dishes in huge skillets, ensuring that you get bang for your buck. This is the perfect place to join friends after a 5K or 10K run; expect a 20-minute wait on the weekends.

Great Basin Brewing Co. (846 Victorian Ave., Sparks, 775/355-7711, 11am-9pm Sun.-Mon., 11am-10pm Tues.-Fri., 11am-11pm Sat., $11-17) is the oldest brewing company in Nevada, owned and managed by former geologist Tom Young. When Young launched his Ichthyosaur IPA (more than 25 years ago), it sold out in two days. It's still one of Northern Nevada's most popular beers. Enjoy an Icky IPA with Willy Dillys deep-fried pickles or the beer cheese soup made with the 39 North blonde beer.

Accommodations

The best and cheapest hotels are within the casinos or close to the airport. However, there can be a serious difference in a "value room" depending on when you travel. Expect to pay triple the rate when traveling in the middle of summer. The best room rates are during ski season.

Under $100

Circus Circus Reno Hotel & Casino (500 N. Sierra St., 775/329-0711, www.circusreno. com, $50-215) is a great place to stay if you're traveling with kids. It is in the heart of downtown and shares a spa with Silver Legacy. The remodeled rooms have clean, modern furnishings. The most expensive rates are over the July 4 weekend.

Silver Legacy (407 N. Virginia St., 775/325-7401, www.silverlegacyreno. com, $55-235) has luxury king and deluxe queen rooms that are the size of a tiny house. Rooms feature plush carpeting and a dresser and desk. Hotel amenities include a salon, fitness center, and indoor access to "The Row," a cluster of restaurants, retail stores, and slot machines that blends into the Eldorado and Circus Circus. Pick the "dealer's choice" for the cheapest rooms.

Next door to the Silver Legacy is **Eldorado Resort Casino** (345 N. Virginia St., 775/786-5700, www.eldoradoreno. com, $55-160). Rooms are more subliminal, with gold accents, and include a desk, an MP3 player, and Wi-Fi.

$100-150

Hotel rooms in the Concierge, Luxury, and Atlantis towers at **Atlantis Casino Resort Spa** (3800 S. Virginia St., 775/825-4700, www.atlantiscasino.com, $131-225) are clean and simply decorated with amenities such as an iPod docking station, marble accents in the bathrooms, and Wi-Fi. Guests enjoy a continental breakfast and complimentary appetizers in the Concierge Lounge. The **Sky Terrace Sushi Bar** (775/824-4434, 11am-11pm daily, $20-27) is a great place for dinner and has some of the best raw fish this side of the Pacific. The Atlantis is 6 miles (9.5 km) south of downtown Reno.

Whitney Peak Hotel (255 N. Virginia St., 775/398-5400, www. whitneypeakhotel.com, $137-350) is possibly the only hotel in Reno without any slot machines. Catering to the young, hip, and environmentally conscious, this 310-room establishment appeals to outdoor adventurers; room decor reflects the nearby Sierras with modern wood furnishings and eco-friendly bath products, as well as flat-screen TVs, Keurig coffee makers, and free Wi-Fi. Facilities include a concert hall as well as the world's tallest climbing wall. Pet- and mountain bike-friendly rooms are available.

Across from the Atlantis, **Peppermill Resort Spa Casino** (2707 S. Virginia St., 866/821-9996, www.peppermillreno. com, $130-440) is one of Reno's nicest hotels and gaming establishments, with a Tuscan-looking interior filled with gold and white stone adornments. Rooms have dark wood furnishings and shiny cream comforters; it feels like sleeping in a fancy European villa.

Information and Services

The **Reno Tahoe Visitor Center** (135 N. Sierra St., 775/682-3800, www. visitrenotahoe.com, 10am-6pm daily) has maps, brochures, and information on what to do in the Reno area.

The nonprofit **Renown Regional Medical Center** (1155 Mill St., 775/982-4100, www.renown.org) has specialized doctors and 24-hour emergency services.

Eastern
Sierra

Eastern Sierra

Humboldt-Toiyabe National Forest

NEVADA
CALIFORNIA

182

Bridgeport Reservoir

★ ⬛ TRAVERTINE HOT SPRINGS

Bridgeport

BRIDGEPORT RANGER STATION

THE VIRGINIA CREEK SETTLEMENT

⬛ BODIE STATE HISTORIC PARK

TWIN LAKES RESORT/ OFF THE HOOK DELI

395

Twin Lakes

ANNETT'S MONO VILLAGE

GLINES CANYON TO VIRGINIA PASS

TH

167

VIRGINIA LAKES RESORT LODGE

LUNDY CANYON CAMPGROUND/ LUNDY CANYON TRAIL

MONO LAKE TUFA STATE NATURAL RESERVE ⬛

Mono Lake

SEE "MONO LAKE" MAP

Hoover Wilderness

LUNDY LAKE RESORT

Saddlebag Lake

SAWMILL WALK-IN

SADDLEBAG LAKE LOOP

TH

GARDISKY LAKE

Lee Vining

BIG BEND CAMPGROUND

120

120

PARKER LAKE

Grant Lake

SEE "JUNE LAKES" MAP

Inyo National Forest

Yosemite National Park

158

June Lake

Gem Lake

395

SEE "MAMMOTH LAKES" MAP

Mammoth Lakes

MAMMOTH YOSEMITE AIRPORT ✈

Crowley Lake

DEVILS POSTPILE NATIONAL MONUMENT ⬛

★

Rainbow Falls

CROWLEY LAKE RV PARK

Crowley Lake

Sierra National Forest

Duck Lake

MCGEE CREEK PACK STATION

━━ Road Trip Route

0 ___ 5 mi
0 ___ 5 km

© MOON.COM

Highlights

★ **Travertine Hot Springs:** The warm sulfuric waters of these natural hot springs are sure to melt your stress away (page 443).

★ **Bodie State Historic Park:** A state of "arrested decay" has preserved this 1877 gold-mining ghost town. Tours of the abandoned mine provide background on the settlement's sordid history (page 448).

★ **Mono Lake Tufa State Natural Reserve:** Freestanding calcite towers, knobs, and spires dot this alien landscape. Several interpretive trails provide history and access to what is undoubtedly the most unusual lake you will ever see (page 451).

★ **June Lake Loop:** This scenic detour winds through sparkling alpine lakes and aspen trees that turn vibrant colors in autumn (page 456).

★ **Devils Postpile National Monument:** One visit to these strange natural rock formations and you'll understand how they got their name. A mix of volcanic heat and pressure straight-sided hexagonal posts that have to be seen to be believed (page 461).

Best Restaurants

★ **Bridgeport Inn, Bridgeport:** This historic inn serves excellent breakfast, lunch, and dinner in a friendly dining room (page 444).

★ **Mono Market, Lee Vining:** You're here for the "Monorito," a tasty burrito that's worth the drive—but get there early (page 453)!

★ **Whoa Nellie Deli, Lee Vining:** Fill both your gas tank and your stomach at this deli/gas station outside Yosemite's eastern entrance (page 454).

★ **Black Velvet Coffee, Mammoth Lakes:** This bright, modern space serves the best cold-brew coffee and locally made snacks around (page 467).

★ **Eatery by Bleu at Mammoth Brewing Company, Mammoth Lakes:** Nosh on inventive pub grub next door to the legendary brewery (page 467).

South of Lake Tahoe, US-395 leads to the east entrance of Yosemite National Park, but there's lots to see and do along the way.

Take a dip in the natural Travertine Hot Springs in Bridgeport, stop and marvel at the tufas in alkaline Mono Lake, and grab a Monorito burrito at Lee Vining before turning east onto CA-120 to enter the national park. Or, continue farther south down US-395 to explore a small town with a big ski resort: Mammoth Mountain. Mammoth caters to the skiers and snowboarders in winter, but there's plenty to do in summer, too—fishing, paddleboarding, backpacking, mountain biking, and skateboarding. Nearby, June Mountain offers snow-oriented activities in winter and scenic lakes in summer.

The towns that dot the Eastern Sierra are pretty sleepy in spring and autumn, but there are incredible sights and great camping opportunities in summer. Hiking, mountain biking, camping, climbing, and dining are main highlights of this region. In winter, snow closes the Tioga Pass Entrance to Yosemite (and most of Lee Vining). Winter sports enthusiasts venture south toward June Lake and Mammoth Lakes to get some powder turns in at the resorts.

The Eastern Sierra embodies a rugged and natural wilderness. Come prepared with the right vehicle (have four-wheel drive or carry chains) in order to best explore the area.

Getting There

Reaching the Eastern Sierra often requires driving mountain passes. From **November to May**, carry tire chains in your vehicle or have a four-wheel-drive vehicle equipped with good snow tires, and consider packing a snow shovel, beanies, gloves, warm clothing, and snacks in case of an emergency.

From Tahoe
135 mi/215 km, 3 hr

From Tahoe, the **Tioga Pass Entrance** (CA-120) offers fairly straightforward access via the park's east side. The scenic drives includes a gradual climb in elevation with quirky ranch towns and cow pastures set between massive glacier-like mountains.

From **South Lake Tahoe,** take US-50 East for about 3 miles (5 km) over the

Best Accommodations

★ **Lundy Canyon Campground, Hoover Wilderness:** Tucked into a grove of aspens, this campground is especially rewarding in fall when the surrounding landscape shimmers with gold leaves (page 447).

★ **Yosemite Gateway Motel, Lee Vining:** Truly a gateway to Yosemite, this rustic motel lies just 14 miles from Tioga Pass (page 455).

★ **Double Eagle Resort and Spa, June Lake:** A luxurious array of accommodations and amenities make this the place to stay in June Lake (page 458).

★ **Tamarack Lodge & Resort, Mammoth Lakes:** In winter, you can cross-country ski right up to the door of your room (page 469).

★ **Juniper Springs Resort, Mammoth Lakes:** For the perfect ski vacation, book a room at this indulgent resort at the base of Mammoth Mountain (page 470).

Nevada-California border. Turn right onto NV-207 East, which follows the Kingsbury Grade into **Gardnerville**. In winter, the pass may close due to snow, or chains may be required. In 10 miles (16 km), NV-207 merges with NV-206 South for 1.3 miles (2.1 km). Turn left onto Centerville Lane (NV-756) and drive 2.8 miles (4.5 km) east to the US-395 junction south of Gardnerville. Turn south on US-395 and continue 88 miles (142 km) to **Lee Vining.** At the junction of US-395 and CA-120, turn right and drive 12 miles (19.5 km) to the **Tioga Pass Entrance.**

Be sure to fill up your gas tank at the Tioga Gas Mart; there are no gas stations until you reach the other side of the park at Crane Flat.

Stopping in Gardnerville

Gardnerville offers a cheap stop to fill your tank. The town has modern casinos with a historical feel. If you have time to spare, pause in Minden to check out the live country acts at the **Carson Valley Inn** (1627 US-395, Minden, 800/321-6983, www.carsonvalleyinn.com) or to gamble at **Sharkey's Casino** (1440 US-395, Gardnerville, 775/782-3133, www.sharkeyscasino.com). Just 21 miles (34 km) south, Topaz Lake is your last stop in Nevada. It has a Chevron gas station,

an RV park, and a casino. From Topaz Lake, continue south for 70 miles (113 km) on US-395 to Lee Vining. At the junction of US-395 and CA-120, turn right and drive 12 miles (19.5 km) to the Tioga Pass Entrance.

From San Francisco
250 mi/400 km, 5 hr

From San Francisco, the **Big Oak Flat Entrance** (Hwy. 120) is the quickest and most direct route into the park. (Time your departure to avoid the weekday rush hours of 6am-10am and 4pm-8pm.) Begin by heading east over the **Bay Bridge** via I-80 and veer right onto I-580 East for 50 miles (80 km) to merge onto I-205 East in Tracy. Stay on I-205 for 15 miles (24 km), before merging onto I-5 for 1 mile (1.6 km). Exit onto CA-120 East toward Manteca. Continue east on CA-120 for almost 90 miles (145 km) to the Big Oak Flat Entrance.

Continuing south now on Big Oak Flat Road (Hwy. 120), drive 4 miles (6.4 km) south to the turnoff for **Tioga Pass Road** (CA-120, summer only) at Crane Flat. Turn left and cross onto Tioga Pass Road, reaching **Lee Vining** and the Eastern Sierra in about 60 miles (97 km).

The best places to fuel up are in Tracy, Manteca, and Oakdale. There is a gas

Eastern Sierra in Three Days

Day 1

From South Lake Tahoe, begin your Eastern Sierra road trip south on US-395. Stop in Gardnerville to fill your gas tank, grab coffee and pick up a snack for the road. Enjoy the easy drive south to Bridgeport, stopping at the historic **Bridgeport Inn** for lunch. Take a scenic detour to **Bodie State Historic Park** for a blast into the past at this rambunctious ghost town. Continue south into Lee Vining for dinner at **Nicely's.** Camp amid the wide array of aspens at **Lundy Lake Campground.**

Day 2

Stop in Lee Vining at the **Mono Basin National Forest Scenic Area Visitors Center** for maps, information, and a glimpse at **Mono Lake.** Get coffee at **Latte Da Coffee Café** or, if it's a hot day, swing by **Mono Cone** for delicious soft-serve ice cream. Spend the morning walking through the **South Tufa** area, where you can admire the flora and fauna.

Drive south and take a detour along the **June Lake Loop.** Stop for a craft brew at **June Lake Brewing** or go for a mountain-bike ride or a hike. Spend the night at one of the many accommodation options in Mammoth Lakes.

Day 3

Wake up with a cold brew at **Black Velvet Coffee,** then board the shuttle to **Devils Postpile National Monument.** It's a short hike to **Rainbow Falls,** where you can look for rainbows shining through the falling cascade.

Exit Mammoth Lakes, returning north on US-395. Stop in to Lee Vining to pick up any last-minute supplies before heading into the park. Get lunch and gas at **Tioga Gas Mart/Whoa Nellie Deli.** Then follow CA-120/Tioga Road west to the Tioga Pass Entrance of **Yosemite National Park.**

station at Crane Flat inside Yosemite National Park and the Tioga Gas Mart on the east end of Tioga Road near Lee Vining.

Winter Option

In winter, Tioga Road (CA-120) is closed. To access the Eastern Sierra, you'll have to go around the Sierras via Tahoe. From San Francisco, cross the **Bay Bridge** and veer left (north) onto I-80 East. Continue north on I-80, crossing the **Carquinez Bridge** ($5 toll) and driving 70 miles (113 km) north to **Sacramento.**

Near Sacramento, turn east onto US-50 for 90 miles (145 km) to **Meyers,** a small town south of Lake Tahoe. In Meyers, turn south on CA-89 for 12 miles (19.5 km). At a junction with CA-88, stay straight on CA-88 for 14 miles (22.5 km). CA-88 will meet US-395 north of Gardnerville, where you can head south on US-395 to **Lee Vining.**

Stops to fuel up include Vacaville, Sacramento, and Gardnerville, but the cheapest options are in Nevada. Plan 6 hours to drive the 300-mile (48-km) trip.

From Yosemite

90 mi/145 km, 1.5 hr

From Yosemite's **Big Oak Flat Entrance** (CA-120, entrance fee required), drive south on Big Oak Flat Road for 4 miles (6.4 km) to the junction with Tioga Road near Crane Flat. Turn left (east) onto **Tioga Road** (CA-120, summer only) and continue 50 miles (80 km) to the **Tioga Pass Entrance Station.** Exit the park and continue east on CA-120, reaching the town of **Lee Vining** in 11 miles (17.5 km).

Bridgeport

This quaint little town is a great place to grab a bite to eat as you're passing through, fill up on gas, get a hot coffee, and plan the next leg of your route.

Getting There
Bridgeport is on US-395, 65 miles (105 km) south of Gardnerville and 45 miles (72 km) south of Topaz Lake, Nevada.

★ Travertine Hot Springs
The **Travertine Hot Springs** (www. monocounty.org) are a naturally occurring series of spring-fed pools hidden in the hills above Bridgeport. If you like to relax outdoors in a peaceful setting, especially under a full moon, you'll find this place memorable. One of the six pools has a concrete bottom, while the rest are the way nature made them, with uneven rocky sides, slippery with moss, and smelly from the sulfur.

Water temperatures vary from warm to extremely hot, so dip a toe in first to find one that's right for you. The population here varies: It's not uncommon to have the whole isolated spot to yourself, but around sunset on a summer weekend you might find the pools crowded with people. And not everyone who visits wears a bathing suit.

Getting There
The pools are accessible by car, though they can be tricky to find. From Bridgeport, drive south on US-395 for 0.8 mile. Look for a ranger station on the side of the road, and then a sign that reads Animal Shelter. At the sign, turn left (east) onto Jack Sawyer Road. In a few hundred yards, turn left onto an unnamed dirt road and drive 1 mile (1.6 km) to the springs. (The road to the springs may close in the winter.)

From top to bottom: Travertine Hot Springs; the Bridgeport Inn; the Three 95 Mexican Café.
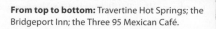

Food

The ★ **Bridgeport Inn** (205 Main St., Bridgeport, 760/932-7380, www. thebridgeportinn.com, 7am-9pm daily mid-Mar.-mid-Nov., $9-30) offers style and class in a historic establishment. Located on the inn's main level is a friendly dining room and bar, where delicious breakfast, lunch, and dinner are served. Popular menu items include prime-rib sandwiches, chicken, and grandma's pot roast. The bar is full of artifacts and photos and has a TV.

Rhino's Bar & Grille (226 Main St., Bridgeport, 760/932-7345, 7am-9pm Sun.-Thurs., 6am-9pm Fri.-Sat. Apr.-Dec., $10-28) is the place to go for something budget-friendly. Rhino's is mainly known for its burgers; try the signature 1/3-pound patty with swiss cheese, bacon, and an onion ring, or the burger topped with a fried egg. The bar is usually open until 2am.

Three 95 Mexican Café (21 Hays St., 760/616-4829, 7am-7pm Tues.-Sat., 7am-2pm Sun. Mar.-Oct., $8-14) serves authentic Mexican comfort food in large portions—try the taco salad or *pozole* (stew). The staff is friendly and the café is a nice place to relax after a day spent exploring Bodie.

Jolly Kone (178 Main St., 760/932-7555, www.jollykone.com, 9am-6pm daily, $4-8) delivers decently priced burgers, ice cream, and Mexican food out of a built-out burger stand. Order at the window and enjoy your meal on the brightly painted deck.

Accommodations

Silver Maple Inn (310 Main St., 760/932-7383, www.silvermapleinn.com, mid-Apr.-Sept., $115-150) caters to weary travelers and Pacific Coast Trail trekkers who are looking for a place to crash (or pick up their resupply) after spending a day outdoors. Spacious rooms have simple, modern furnishings and come with one king or two queen beds. Guests have access to a propane grill and free bicycles. It's also pet-friendly.

A sister property to the Silver Maple Inn, **The Cain House** (340 Main St., 760/932-7383, www.silvermapleinn.com, mid-Apr.-Sept., $150-210) sits in quiet elegance, secluded from the main road by a white picket fence. Two-person suites contain antique furniture and oak dressers, tables, and beds with headboards. The J. S. Cain Suite features a four-poster bed and has a private entrance. Guests enjoy free Wi-Fi, freshly brewed coffee, and a continental breakfast as part of their stay. Reservations are accepted in February at both hotels for the upcoming summer season.

Ruby Inn Bridgeport (333 Main St., 760/932-7241, www.rubyinnbridgeport. com, $125-190) is close to dining and shopping options on the main drag. Rooms come with either a queen or king bed (or two queen beds). A four-queen-bed suite sleeps up to eight people. Amenities include an outdoor swimming pool, gas barbecues, and fast Wi-Fi. Your four-legged friend is welcome.

Information and Services

The best place for information is the **Bridgeport Ranger Station** (US-395, Bridgeport, 760/932-7070, www.fs.usda. gov, 8am-4:30pm daily late May-Sept., 8am-4:30pm Mon.-Fri. winter). The small **Mono County Museum** (129 Emigrant St., 760/932-5281, http://monocomuseum. org, 9am-4pm Tues.-Sat. late May-Sept., adults $2, seniors $1.50, children $1) in Bridgeport is managed by the Mono County Historical Society.

Getting Around

The **Eastern Sierra Transit Authority** bus system (ESTA, 210 Commerce Dr., 760/924-3184 or 800/922-1930, www. estransit.com, $11-13 one-way) carries passengers down US-395 from Reno to Lancaster, stopping in Carson City, Gardnerville, Bridgeport, Lee Vining, and Mammoth Lakes. The Reno to Lone Pine route (the blue line) runs southbound Monday-Friday in winter; call (760/872-1901) with 24 hour notice to stop in Gardnerville or the June Lake Junction.

Hoover Wilderness

The **Hoover Wilderness** (Bridgeport Ranger District, 760/932-7070, www.fs.usda.gov) is a 128,421-acre section of Mono County south of Bridgeport within the Inyo and Humboldt-Toiyabe National Forests. Visitors come here for hiking and camping, with some sweet mountain lakes to help enjoy it all. Enjoy commanding rock formations, gushing waterfalls, scenic canyons, and natural geological formations in this stretch of wilderness that's a bit off the beaten path.

The best time to visit is in summer (Memorial Day-Labor Day), when Tioga Pass (CA-120) and the road to Lundy Lake, Virginia Lakes, and Twin Lakes are open. (Roads close as early as October and won't reopen until early May.) A trip in early autumn offers an opportunity to admire **fall foliage,** hiking and camping amid aspen trees as their leaves turn from emerald green to a glittering and brilliant gold.

Getting There

The main access points into the Hoover Wilderness are Twin Lakes, Virginia Lakes, and Lundy Lake.

From US-395 in Bridgeport, drive 10 miles (16 km) south on Twin Lakes Road to reach **Twin Lakes,** Sawmill Ridge, and Annett's Mono Village.

To reach the **Virginia Lakes,** drive 13 miles (21 km) south on US-395. Turn right onto Virginia Lakes Road and continue 6 miles (9.5 km) to Virginia Lakes Resort.

To reach **Lundy Lake** from Bridgeport, stay on US-395 south for 18 miles (29 km). Turn right onto Lundy Lake Road and drive 3 miles (4.8 km) to the campground.

Hiking
Glines Canyon to Virginia Pass
The hike from **Glines Canyon to Virginia Pass** (10 mi/16.1 km round-trip, 6-8 hours, strenuous) starts from an elevation of more than 8,000 feet (2,400 m) and climbs more than 2,500 vertical feet (760 m), making it a serious workout worth the wildflowers, waterfalls, and mountain lakes. From the trailhead, walk along the western side of Green Creek for 2.5 miles (4 km) to Green Lake. On the north side of the lake, climb Glines Canyon 7.5 miles (12 km) to Virginia Pass (elevation 10,500 ft/3,200 m). From here, views include Twin Peaks, Matterhorn Peak, and Camiaca Peak, the two small Par Value Lakes, and Soldier Lake, all spread out far below.

The trailhead is 5 miles (8 km) south of Bridgeport on Green Creek Road.

Lundy Canyon
The out-and-back **Lundy Canyon Trail** (8 mi/13 km round-trip, 4-6 hours, moderately strenuous) follows the side of Lundy Lake and is beautiful in autumn. The trail gains more than 2,000 feet (600 m) of elevation as it crosses Mill Creek for 1 mile (1.6 km) above Lundy Lake. From the lake, continue 3 miles (4.8 km) along Mill Creek, hiking through brush, granite, and past the waterfall before dropping down into a meadow to reach Oneida Lake (4 mi/6.4 km). Near the end of the trail, look for the remains of the May Lundy Mine; you may also find remnants of railroad ties on the rocky edge.

The trailhead is at the end of Lundy Lake Road. From Bridgeport, drive 18 miles (29 km) south on US-395 and turn right onto Lundy Lake Road. Continue 6.7 miles (10.8 km) to the trailhead at the end of the road.

Gardisky Lake

The trek to **Gardisky Lake** (2 mi/3.2 km round-trip, 1 hour, moderate) offers fit hikers a short yet steep and intensive climb that gains 735 feet (224 m) in a little over a mile to incredible views of eastern Yosemite. Plan this hike after a few days acclimating to the high elevation, and bring lots of water.

The trailhead is on Saddlebag Lake Road. From Lee Vining, drive 12 miles (19.5 km) west on CA-120. Turn left onto Saddlebag Lake Road and drive 1.3 miles (2.1 km) to the trailhead.

Saddlebag Lake

The **Saddlebag Lake Loop** (4 mi/6.4 km round-trip, 1-2 hours, easy) is a great hike with a moderate 300-foot (90-m) elevation gain. The skinny dirt path follows alongside a canyon and yields constant lake views. Come in autumn and you'll have this place to yourself.

A few miles from the west side of Saddlebag Lake, the loop trail continues on the **Twenty Lakes Loop** (7.8 mi/12.5 km round-trip, 8-12 hours, moderate). This graded yet rocky dirt path first leads to Greenstone Lake. Loop around the west side of the lake and continue 0.6 mile to Steelhead Lake. Lake Helen is reachable in another 0.9 mile, hugging the north corner of Shamrock Lake along the way. At Shamrock, the trail splits; turn right and hike 1.5 miles (2.4 km) down to Saddlebag Lake. (If you continue north past Lake Helen, you'll reach Lundy Canyon.)

Food

Virginia Creek Settlement (70847 US-395, Bridgeport, 760/932-7780, http://virginiacreeksettlement.net, 6:30am-9pm daily, $18-42) serves home-style meals in a rustic wooden establishment. Hearty breakfasts include cinnamon rolls and chili-cheese omelets. For lunch, order

From top to bottom: aspens in the Eastern Sierra; Lundy Lake; Saddlebag Lake.

pizza, or wait until dinner to enjoy the 20-ounce signature porterhouse steak ($42). But leave room for dessert (try the homemade apple dumplings) or perk up with a coffee float.

Virginia Lakes Resort Lodge (Little Virginia Lakes Rd., Bridgeport, 760/647-6484, www.virginialakesresort.com, 6:30am-6pm Wed.-Mon. May-Oct., $8-14, cash only) is a good place for a hot meal. In operation since 1923, this diner serves classic eggs and bacon dishes for breakfast and burgers or sandwiches for lunch.

Off the Hook Deli (Twin Lakes Resort, 10316 Twin Lakes Rd., Bridgeport, 760/932-7751, https://twinlakeresort. com, 8am-5pm daily Apr.-Nov., $8-10) is a cute general store with a dialed-in menu that offers breakfast sandwiches, thin-crust pizzas, smoothies, and grab-and-go items.

Accommodations

Accommodations at **Twin Lakes Resort** (10316 Twin Lakes Rd., 760/932-1008, https://twinlakeresort.com, $187-208) include eight cabins and 20 RV sites, plus there's a general store, a gift shop, a deli, boat rentals, and a marina and tackle (summer only). Cabins have one or two bedrooms with queen beds and sleeper sofas. RV sites accommodate vehicles up to 36 feet in length. Equipment rentals include kayaks/SUPs ($20/hour), pontoon boats ($160/half day, $220/full day), and aluminum fishing boats ($50/day). This resort is pet-friendly. Reservations are accepted one year in advance.

Annett's Mono Village (455 Twin Lakes Rd., 760/932-7071, www.monovillage.com, $90 rooms, $25 tents, $35 RVs, $105-225 cabins) is a mini village with motel rooms, tent sites, and RV sites (full hookups), plus coin-operated showers, laundry services, and a small store. Annett's also has a few bare-basic cabins plus modern cabins with upgraded furnishings and cabins on the lake. There is a two-pet maximum at the campsites; pets must be leashed at all times.

Virginia Creek Settlement (70847 US-395, 760/932-7780, http:// virginiacreeksettlement.net, $39 covered wagons, $70-195 motel rooms and cabins) offers the chance to sleep in a covered wagon just like the early pioneers (except with more comfortable bedding). The covered wagon comes with a double bed (linens not included) and a fire ring outside. Guests have use of showers and a shared restroom. In addition to the wagons and tent cabins, the settlement has motel rooms with queen beds; the wood-paneled walls are decorated with pictures of the settlement's past. A family suite features Victorian-style decor and sleeps up to six in a queen bed, two twins, and a double futon.

Camping

Backpacking is allowed throughout the Hoover Wilderness; a wilderness **permit** ($6 reservation fee, www.recreation.gov) is required and is available online or from the Bridgeport Ranger Station (US-395, Bridgeport, 760/932-7070, www.fs.usda. gov, 8am-4:30pm daily summer, 8am-4:30pm Mon.-Fri. winter). For more information, contact the Inyo National Forest (760/873-2483, 8am-4:30pm Mon.-Fri.).

★ **Lundy Canyon Campground** (Lundy Lake Rd., 760/932-5440, www. monocounty.ca.gov, first-come, first-served, mid-Apr.-mid-Nov., $16) offers 37 tent and RV sites tucked into a grove of aspens along Mill Creek. Some sites are bigger than others, and some are secluded and quiet. Each site has a fire ring, picnic table, and food storage locker, and there are vault toilets. Come in early May or October, when it's easier to find a spot and have the place to yourself. The campground is within walking distance of Lundy Lake and the Lundy Canyon trailhead.

Located off CA-120/Tioga Pass, the **Sawmill Walk-In** (Saddlebag Lake Rd., 760/647-3044, www.fs.usda.gov, first-come, first-served, June-mid-Oct., $17) has 12 primitive sites in the Inyo National Forest. Sites have a picnic table, designated fire pit, and bear-proof food lockers. Vault toilets are available, but there is no drinking water; bring your own.

Big Bend Campground (Hwy. 120, 760/873-2400, www.fs.usda.gov, first-come, first-served, May-mid-Sept., $22) has 17 tent sites close to Lee Vining Creek in Inyo National Forest. Sites have a bear box for food storage and can accommodate trailers up to 30 feet. There's one vault toilet and potable water is available.

Ellery Lake Campground (Hwy. 120, 760/873-2400, www.fs.usda.gov, first-come, first-served, May-mid-Sept., $22) has 12 sites in Inyo National Forest close to the Tioga Pass Entrance. The campground sits at 9,500 feet (2,900 m) elevation and fills quickly in summer. Potable water and pit toilets are available.

Tioga Lake Campground (Hwy. 120, 760/873-2400, www.fs.usda.gov, first-come, first-served, May-mid-Sept., $22) has 13 open sites close to the road at an elevation of 9,700 feet (2,960 m) in Inyo National Forest. The campground has potable water, a vault toilet, bear-proof food lockers, and a trail to the historic Bennetville mining remains.

Saddlebag Lake Campground (off Hwy. 120, 760/873-2400, www.fs.usda. gov, first-come, first-served, May-mid-Sept., $22) is at the end of Saddlebag Lake Road in Inyo National Forest at an elevation of 10,000 feet (3,050 m). The 20 sites can accommodate tents and small RVs (no hookups). This is a great place to stay the night, so that you can get up early to hike the Twenty Lakes Loop.

Information and Services

The **Bridgeport Ranger Station** (US-395, Bridgeport, 760/932-7070, www.fs.usda. gov, 8am-4:30pm daily late May-Sept., 8am-4:30pm Mon.-Fri. winter) is the place to go for backcountry permits.

Mono Basin National Forest Scenic Area Visitors Center (US-395, Lee Vining, 760/647-3044, www.monolake. org, 8am-5pm daily summer, 9am-4:30pm Thurs.-Mon. spring-fall) has a museum, information and maps, clean restrooms, and a great view of the lake from the back deck.

For vehicle issues, contact the **California Highway Patrol** (125 Main St., Bridgeport, 760/932-7995, www. chp.ca.gov, 8am-5pm Mon.-Fri.). Call **Caltrans** (800/427-7623) for current road conditions.

★ CA-270: Bodie State Historic Park

Bodie State Historic Park (Hwy. 270, 760/647-6445, www.parks.ca.gov, 9am-6pm daily Apr.-Oct., 9am-4pm daily Nov.-Mar., $8 adults, $5 children 4-17, no credit cards) is the largest ghost town in California. Preserved in a state of "arrested decay," the houses and public buildings remain much the same as when they were suddenly abandoned. In Bodie you see the real thing: peeling wallpaper, uneven wooden floor boards, tempered window panes, rusty tin cans scattered everywhere, and patina-tinted carriages and cars. It would take all day to explore the town on foot, and even then you might not see it all.

The town of Bodie sprang up during the gold rush in 1879 and had a population of 10,000 people—all going toward the gold (considering that nearby Lee Vining has a population of about 200 inhabitants today, Bodie back then was booming). The weather, the work (there were 30 gold mines in the area), the desert scenery, and the sheer number of brothels (65) and saloons attracted the roughest of the Wild West bunch. However, by the 1940s the mining had dried up, a wildfire devastated the area, and everyone left town.

A visit to Bodie takes you back in time to a harsh lifestyle in an extreme climate, miles from the middle of nowhere. Although doors remain locked on many of the falling-apart homes, you can still peer into windows and old outhouses or hike to the cemetery and view the rest of the ghost town. As you stroll down the dusty streets, imagine the whole town blanketed in 20 feet of snow in winter and scorched by soaring temperatures in summer, with precious few trees around to provide shade. In a town filled with hard-core men working the mines, you'd hear the funeral bells tolling at the church every single day—the only honor bestowed on the many murder victims Bodie saw during its existence.

Few families came to Bodie (though a few hardy souls did raise children there, evidenced by a vintage schoolhouse), and most of Bodie's women earned their keep the old-fashioned way—by prostitution. If you take a tour, you can go into the abandoned mine and gain a deeper understanding of the history of the buildings and the town.

Tours

The **Bodie Foundation** (323 Main St., Bridgeport, 760/932-7574, www.bodiefoundation.org, 9am-6pm, late May-Sept.) offers guided and private tours (2 hours, rates vary, reservations required), as well as special tours at certain times of the year. The foundation gives free history talks 10am-4pm daily. To book, visit the office in Bridgeport or inquire directly at the state park entrance booth.

The **Stamp Mill Tour** (50 minutes, 11am, 1pm, and 3pm late May-early Sept., $6) explores the machine shop, electrical room, and mining equipment left onsite. Reservations are required and can be made at the **visitors center** (hours and days vary, mid-May-mid-Oct.).

Ghost Walk Tours (1.5 hours, 6pm, $40) and **Ghost Mill Tours** (8pm, $25) are special events held on select dates in summer and quickly sell out. Call 760/616-5040 for tickets and reservations.

Getting There

From US-395 drive 7 miles (11.5 km) south of Bridgeport, turn east onto CA-270, and drive 13 miles (21 km) to the park. The last 3 miles (4.8 km) are on a rough dirt-and-gravel road. CA-270 closes in winter, due to snow; the road is not plowed. There are no services in the park, other than restrooms at the parking lot.

Lee Vining

Lee Vining sits on the eastern edge of Yosemite and offers a welcoming place for travelers. The small town (pop. 222) is a good stopover for travelers to Mono Lake, the ghost town of Bodie, the Hoover Wilderness, and the recreational paradise of June Lake, Mammoth Lakes, and Bishop. Though many services close in the winter months, folks in Lee Vining are friendly, helpful, and happy to share their favorite hikes, sights, and spots that set this town apart from any other in the Eastern Sierra.

Getting There

Lee Vining is at the junction of CA-120 (Tioga Pass Rd.) and US-395. From Bridgeport (25 mi/40 km) or Mono Lake (2 mi/3.2 km), drive south on US-395. From the south, Lee Vining is 30 miles (48 km) north of Mammoth Lakes on US-395.

In summer, it's possible to reach Lee Vining from the west via Tioga Pass Road. The town is 13 miles (21 km) east of the Tioga Pass Entrance. Note that Tioga Pass Road is closed in winter.

Sights
Mono Lake

Mono Lake, eerie in its stillness and alkalinity content, is the main attraction in the northern part of the Eastern Sierra. This unusual and beautiful lake is 2.5 times as salty as the ocean and is dramatically more alkaline.

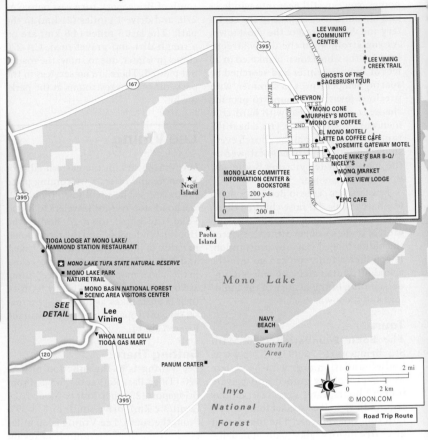

Lee Vining

The reason for Mono Lake's odd appearance? It is fed by only 7 inches of rain and snowfall each year; the rest of the water inflow is from various streams or underground springs. No streams or tributaries flow out of Mono Lake, but it loses about 45 inches of water each year to evaporation. Meanwhile, any salt and minerals that have built up stay in the lake as water evaporates. Over time, the lake has collected huge stores of calcium carbonate, which solidifies into strange-looking tufa (pronounced TOOH-fa) towers.

The lake surrounds two large islands: **Negit Island,** a volcanic cinder cone and nesting area for California gulls, and **Paoha Island,** which was created when volcanic activity pushed sediment from the bottom of the lake up above the surface. Mono Basin, where the lake is located, is part of the Inyo National Forest. In 1984 the U.S. Congress designated Mono Basin a National Forest Scenic Area, which gives it additional protections.

Visitors Center

One of the best viewpoints of the lake is on the grounds of the **Mono Basin National Forest Scenic Area Visitors Center** (US-395, 0.5 mile north of Lee Vining, 760/647-3044, www.monolake. org, 8am 5pm daily summer, 9am-4:30pm Thurs.-Mon. spring-fall). Inside, an interpretive museum details the natural and human history of the tufa towers and the ever-changing conditions of the lake. Original films, interactive exhibits, a bookstore, and a friendly staff can get you up to speed on this beautiful and unusual area. Knowledgeable park rangers are on-site and can share the best hikes and spots to visit. You can also learn about guided walks and hikes at Mono Lake, for a more in-depth look at the wonders of the area.

Exit the back of the building to take one of several brief interpretive walks or to sit on a bench and gaze at the lake.

★ Mono Lake Tufa State Natural Reserve

The tufa formations are freestanding calcite towers, knobs, and spires, which makes Mono Lake one of the most unusual lakes in the state. A boardwalk trail in the **Mono Lake Tufa State Natural Reserve** (US-395, north of Lee Vining, 760/647-6331, www.parks. ca.gov, 24 hours daily, free) provides access to the North Tufa area, where you can wander through the different chunks of this preserve, which line the shore around the lake. Access the reserve on the east side of the lake but be aware that a four-wheel-drive vehicle is required; there are no paved roads that circle Mono Lake.

Free **tours** of the reserve are offered daily (10am, 1pm, and 6pm in summer). Mono Lake is also one of the best places to watch gulls. About 85 percent of California's gulls nest here in the spring. Park rangers host bird walks on Friday and Sunday (8am) in summer.

South Tufa

The **South Tufa area** (Hwy. 120, 760/647-3044 or 760/647 6331, http://monolake. org/visit/southtufa, $3 pp), on the south shore of Mono Lake, is one of the best places to view the spectacular tufa towers. The one-mile **interpretive trail** (southeast of the visitors center, adjacent to Navy Beach) winds through the South Tufa area and describes the natural history of the area and the formations. The area is managed by the U.S. Forest Service, and naturalists lead 1-mile (1.6-km) **walking tours** (1.5 hours, 10am, 1pm, and 6pm daily summer, free) around South Tufa. There's also a **Stars Over Mono** night venture (1.5 hours, start time 7:30pm-8:30pm depending on sunset, Mon., summer, free); dress warmly and bring a blanket.

Old Marina

The stillness of Mono Lake was once broken by boat traffic. The hub of this activity was the marina north of Lee Vining. Private boats and small tour operators still access the lake in the summer, but there is no longer commercial water traffic. Today, the **Old Marina** (US-395, www. monolake.org, $3) is a good spot for a short stroll to the edge of the lake. Enjoy outstanding views of the lake's two large islands and several nearby tufa towers. A 1.5-mile (2.4-km) trail leads from the Mono Basin Scenic Area Visitors Center to the Old Marina; an even shorter boardwalk trail is wheelchair-accessible.

Panum Crater

Even if you aren't a geology buff, the volcanic **Panum Crater** (Hwy. 120, 3 mi/4.8 km east of US-395) is worth a visit. This rhyolite crater is less than 700 years old—a mere baby on geologic time scales. Hike around the rim of the crater, or, if you're feeling up to it, climb the trail to the top of the plug dome. (Slather on the sunscreen and wear a hat; the trails are unshaded and it gets quite warm here.) Check the Mono Lake website (www.

monolake.org) for guided tours of Panum Crater. Access is via a parking area down a short dirt road off CA-120.

Entertainment and Events

Produced by the Mono Basin Historical Society, the annual **Ghosts of the Sagebrush Tour** (129 Mattly Ave., 760/647-6461, www.monobasinhistory.org, late Aug., $25) is a popular event that features guest speakers, raffles, food, and the opportunity to meet the community and learn about the town's past. The two-day event starts with a family-style barbecue dinner on Friday evening, followed by a six-hour tour or hike in the Hoover Wilderness (10am Sat., lunch included). Separate tickets are required for the barbecue, which is limited to 100 people; make reservations by phone or at the museum. The historical society also hosts monthly potluck dinners and meetings at the **Lee Vining Community Center** (296 Mattly Ave., Lee Vining, 760/647-6461, www.monolake.org, 6pm-8pm, free).

Recreation
Hiking

Mono Lake is spread out, and the hiking is quiet and less populated, making it one of the Eastern Sierra's hidden gems. Trails around the Mono Basin National Forest Scenic Area Visitors Center and the South Tufa area are open year-round; bring some snowshoes or cross-country skis in the off-season.

For a quick and informative introduction to the lake's ecosystem, take the **Secrets of Survival Nature Trail** (0.25-mile one-way) located outside the Mono Basin National Forest Scenic Area Visitors Center. The trail offers interpretive signage and long views of the lake.

For an easy walk along the lake, find the **Mono Lake Park Nature Trail** (Cemetery Rd.), 0.5 mile east of Cemetery Road. The boardwalk trail leads 0.25

From top to bottom: Mono Lake; Mono Basin Visitors Center; South Tufa.

mile to the tufa formations. Wandering through the tufa will add distance to your walk, but the ground is flat and the scenery is breathtaking.

The **Lee Vining Creek Trail** (1.6 mi/2.6 km one-way, moderate) is a nature walk that offers both gentle exercise and increased knowledge of the area. The walk stretches from the Mono Basin National Forest Scenic Area Visitors Center to the south end of Lee Vining, following Lee Vining Creek. Pick up a free trail guide at the visitors center. The walk takes an hour or two.

Boating and Swimming

Powerboats are allowed on Mono Lake, but boaters must exercise caution around the highly corrosive tufa towers hidden beneath the water's surface. Kayaks, canoes, and stand-up paddleboards are more popular. Boaters can launch from **Navy Beach** (0.5 mile east of South Tufa); there's no direct access to the water from the parking lot, so carry your kayak or SUP 30 yards to get it into the water. Check the weather forecast at the visitors center before heading out, as frothy whitecaps can occur on windy days, engulfing kayaks and putting them in serious danger.

If you're putting a heavier boat into the lake, check with the **Mono Basin National Forest Scenic Area Visitors Center** (US-395, 760/647-3044, www.monolake.org, 8am-5pm daily summer, 9am-4:30pm Thurs.-Mon. spring-fall) for directions to the launch ramp near Lee Vining Creek. For the protection of nesting California gulls, boaters cannot beach any kind of boat on the islands April 1-August 1. Outside of that time frame, the islands of Mono Lake can be a great destination for boaters.

Swimming is allowed in the lake in summer. Due to the lake's heavy salt content, swimming is more like floating. Access is unrestricted from the shore. There are no lifeguards, so swimming is at your own risk.

Bird-Watching

The birds of the Eastern Sierra are varied and abundant. Three different organizations—the Eastern Sierra Audubon Society (www.esaudubon.org), the Mono Lake Committee (760/647-6595, www.monolake.org), and the Owens Valley Committee (760/876-1845, www. ovcweb.org)—produce the wonderful *Eastern Sierra Birding Trail Map* (http:// easternsierrabirdingtrail.org), which covers 200 miles of territory from **Bridgeport Reservoir** (near the junction of US-395 and CA-182) in the north to **Cactus Flat** and Sage Flat in the south (85 mi/137 km south of Bishop near the junction of US-395 and CA-190). Along the way, 37 stops identify good birding habitats; callouts detail the natural habitat of each area and the species to look out for. For an online map, visit www.easternsierrabirdingtrail. org. To get your own free hard copy, contact the Mono Lake Committee (707/647-6595, birding@monolake.org).

Food

Tioga Pass Resort (85 Hwy. 120 W., Lee Vining, www.tiogapassresort.com) has a historic location and a small café known to serve incredible pie. The staff is friendly, accommodating, and are doing their part to keep this historic site alive. Tioga Pass Resort is under renovation until 2020.

The **Hammond Station Restaurant** (Tioga Lodge, 54411 US-395, Lee Vining, 619/320-8868 or 760/647-6423, www. tiogalodgeatmonolake.com, 7:30am-10:30am and 5:30pm-9:30pm daily mid-June-mid-Oct., $10-25) offers casual California cuisine ranging from wonton soup to shepherd's pie and slow-cooked ribs. Everything is made fresh, including the pasta sauces, and most menu items are dairy-, gluten-, and soy-free. The attached outdoor seating area is a pleasant place to enjoy a meal on a warm summer night.

For breakfast or lunch to go, stop at the ★ **Mono Market** (51303 US-395,

760/647-1010, www.leeviningmarket. com, 7am-10pm daily summer, 7am-8pm daily winter). The breakfast sandwiches and pastries are made fresh daily, as are the sandwiches and wraps, but the market is best known for the Monorito: a chicken, beef, pork, or sautéed vegetable burrito with pinto beans, brown rice, and cheese. Groceries, snacks, souvenirs, and supplies are also available.

Kick off your vacation with a memorable meal (and a tank of gas) at the ★ **Whoa Nellie Deli** (Hwy. 120 and US-395, 760/647-1088, www.whoanelliedeli. com, 6:30am-9pm daily late Apr.-Oct., $8-23) at the Tioga Gas Mart. The deli is near the east entrance to Yosemite, so it's the perfect place to stop when entering or leaving the park. You'll get a hearty meal of fish tacos, buffalo meatloaf, or pizza; a pleasant place to eat it all; and a friendly, festive atmosphere. Expect to wait in line at the counter to order, as Whoa Nellie is popular. Seating is available both inside and out, so there are usually enough tables to go around. There's a well-stocked grocery store and souvenir shop, and the restrooms are large and clean. The place is closed in winter when Tioga Pass closes.

Lee Vining has several charming independent coffee shops. The **Latte Da Coffee Café** (1 3rd St. at US-395, 760/647-6310, http://elmonomotel.com, 7am-7pm daily May-Oct.) uses organic coffee and local water to create delicious coffee drinks at the El Mono Motel. They also make their own whipped cream and serve the best cold brew (get it in the bottle to reuse later).

Over at the Lake View Lodge, enjoy a cup of joe at the **Epic Cafe** (349 Lee Vining Ave., 760/647-6543, www. bwlakeviewlodge.com, 7am-9pm Mon.-Sat., June-Oct.). Get a great start to your day with a smoothie or an all-natural, made-from-scratch pastry, then come back for dinner and a glass of wine.

Mono Cup Coffee (34 2nd St., Lee Vining, 760/616-4771, 6am-6pm daily

May-Oct.) is in the heart of downtown Lee Vining. Enjoy an organic espresso drink on the outdoor patio at this little shop next to Murphey's Motel.

A classic American diner, **Nicely's** (US-395 and 4th St., Lee Vining, 760/647-6477, 7am-9pm daily, $11-30) offers friendly service and familiar food. Inside, you'll find a large dining room with half-circle booths. Order eggs and pancakes in the morning; salads and sandwiches for lunch; and steaks and pasta dishes at dinner. This is a good place for generous portions of hearty comfort food; plus, Nicely's has longer hours (and a longer season) than many places in the area.

For a Wild West atmosphere and a spicy barbecue sauce, dig into the barbecued ribs, chicken, beef, and brisket at **Bodie Mike's Bar B-Q** (51357 US-395 at 4th St., Lee Vining, 760/647-6432, 11:30am-10pm daily late May-Sept.). A rustic atmosphere with unfinished wood, red-checked tablecloths, and local patrons in cowboy boots completes your dining experience, but don't expect the fastest service in the world. At the back of the dining room is the entrance to a small bar populated by locals.

Pop into **Mono Cone** (51508 US-395, 760/647-6606, 11am-6pm daily mid-Apr.-early Oct., $4-17, cash only), where you can get mouthwatering burgers (try the jalapeno cheeseburger), fries, and the best soft-serve ice cream (vanilla, chocolate, or half and half) this side of the Eastern Sierra. Order at the window and then wait outside at one of the picnic tables.

Accommodations

The **Tioga Lodge at Mono Lake** (Hammond Station, 54411 US-395, Lee Vining, 619/320-8868 or 760/647-6423, www.tiogalodgeatmonolake.com, late May-early Oct., $150-209, 2-night min.) promises a view of the lake from every room. Rooms are simply decorated with tile floors and a full private bath (cabin 3 has a vintage clawfoot bathtub), but no

TVs. Some rooms sleep two, while others have room for up to four. There is a bit of noise from the road, so bring earplugs.

For clean, comfortable, affordable lodgings, try **Murphey's Motel** (51493 US-395, 760/647-6316 or 800/334-6316, www.murpheysyosemite.com, year-round, $78-180). The motel provides double-queen and king beds with cozy comforters, TVs, and everything you need for a pleasant stay in the area. The central location in downtown Lee Vining makes dining and shopping convenient.

El Mono Motel (1 3rd St. at US-395, 760/647-6310, www.elmonomotel.com, late May-Oct., $76-103 shared bath, $96-129 private bath) offers comfy beds and clean rooms at very reasonable prices. Enjoy the location in downtown Lee Vining and start each morning with a fresh cup of organic coffee from the onsite **Latte Da Coffee Café** (7am-7pm daily summer).

The comfortable and affordable **Lake View Lodge** (51285 US-395, 760/647-6543 or 800/990-6614, http://lakeviewlodgeyosemite.com, $80-329) offers cottages and glamping trailers (summer only) and motel rooms (year-round). Whether you choose a basic room or a larger one with a kitchen, you'll enjoy the simple country-style decor, outdoor porches, and views of Mono Lake. All rooms have TVs with cable. Internet access is available in the motel rooms but is spotty in the cottages.

Named for its main claim to fame—its proximity to the park, 14 miles (22.5 km) from Yosemite's eastern gate—the ★ **Yosemite Gateway Motel** (51340 US-395, 760/647-6467, www.yosemitegatewaymotel.com, $89-259) offers a charming rustic experience. Outside of the motel, patios, wrap-around decks, and balconies offer great views of Mono Lake. Rooms feature gleaming wood furnishings, clean

From top to bottom: Latte Da Coffee Café; Whoa Nellie Deli; Tioga Lodge at Mono Lake.

baths, TVs, and Internet. The wonderful Eastern Sierra recreation opportunities are just outside the door.

Camping

Inyo National Forest campgrounds line CA-120 en route to Tioga Pass. **Ellery Lake Campground** (Hwy. 120, Upper Lee Vining Canyon, ranger station 760/873-2400, www.fs.fed.us/r5/inyo, June-early Oct., $22) is at an elevation of 9,500 feet (2,900 m) with 12 campsites, drinking water, vault toilets, and garbage cans. Sites are first-come, first-served, so get here at dawn if you want a site on a weekend.

Information and Services

The **Mono Lake Committee Information Center & Bookstore** (US-395, Lee Vining, 760/647-6595, 9am-5pm daily) has a helpful staff and keeps a big selection of free maps and brochures, as well as local souvenirs. The **Mono Basin National Forest Scenic Area Visitors Center** (US-395, 0.5 mile north of Lee Vining, 760/647-3044, www.monolake.org, 8am-5pm daily summer, 9am-4:30pm Thurs.-Mon. spring-fall) is nearby at Mono Lake and is an excellent resource for information about the area.

The nearest medical facility is 30 miles (48 km) south in Mammoth Lakes at **Mammoth Hospital** (85 Sierra Park Rd., Mammoth Lakes, 760/934-3311, http://mammothhospital.org), which has a 24-hour emergency room.

The best place to get gas is at the **Tioga Gas Mart** (Hwy. 120 and US-395, 760/647-1088, www.whoanelliedeli.com), home to the Whoa Nellie Deli. The store sells everything you need to camp in comfort. The **Shell** station (Mattly Ave. and US-395, 760/647-6303, emergency towing 760/647-6444) is across the street from Latte Da Coffee Café. A **Chevron** (1st St. and US-395, 760/647-6330) is in the center of town.

Getting Around

The **Eastern Sierra Transit Authority** bus (ESTA, 210 Commerce Dr., 760/924-3184 or 800/922-1930, www.etransit.com) stops in Lee Vining midweek on the Lone Pine route from Reno to Bishop.

There are plenty of roads in the area worth exploring via dirt bike, jeep, or four-wheel-drive vehicle. Travel is most accessible in the summer. Be sure to have a lunch, plenty of water, and a full tank of gas. Pick up a copy of the latest *Backroad Tours in the Eastern Sierra* guide from the **Mono Basin National Forest Scenic Area Visitors Center** (US-395, 0.5 mile north of Lee Vining, 760/647-3044, www. monocounty.org, 8am-5pm daily summer, 9am-4:30pm Thurs.-Mon. spring-fall) so you know where you're going.

◆ CA-158: June Lakes

The small community of June Lake lies south of Lee Vining. June Lake is a popular ski destination, thanks to June Mountain, which offers everything you need in a ski resort, yet manages to hold on to the feeling of an unspoiled outdoor wonderland. Though the town is named for just one of the alpine lakes nearby, there are actually three others: Gull Lake, Silver Lake, and Grant Lake. Each has its own beauty. If you're short on time, spend it driving the scenic 15-mile (24-km) June Lake Loop.

Getting There

From Lee Vining, drive 14 miles (22.5 km) south on US-395. Turn west onto CA-158 to enter the June Lake Loop.

Sights and Recreation

★ June Lake Loop

The 15-mile (24-km) scenic **June Lake Loop** (Hwy. 158, 760/648-4651, https://junelakeloop.org) is a full-fledged alpine experience. From the junction of US-395 and CA-158 (5 mi/8 km south of Lee Vining), you'll first approach Grant Lake.

June Lakes

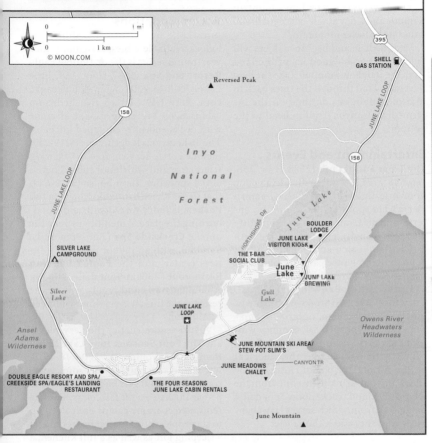

Stop to admire Reversed Peak at 9,481 feet (2,890 m). Continuing south on the loop, Silver Lake is next. About 4 miles (6.4 km) east of Silver Lake, Gull Lake appears to the left with June Mountain Ski Area to the right. June Lake is the last destination before returning to US-395. June Lake offers hiking, fishing, and camping.

Late August, September, and early October offer the best times to see the quaking aspens as they change colors. Note that the June Lake Loop closes in winter after the first snowfall.

June Mountain Ski Resort

In winter, June Lake is a vacation destination for skiing and snowboarding. One of the most popular places to hit the slopes is the **June Mountain Ski Resort** (3819 Hwy. 158, 888/586-3686, www.junemountain.com, lifts 8am-4pm daily mid-Dec.-Apr., $87-139 adults 18-64, $71-114 ages 13-17 and 65-79, children under age 12 free).

June Mountain offers seven lifts (two quads, four doubles, and a carpet) and more than 2,500 feet (760 m) of vertical drop on 1,500 skiable acres. Almost half of its terrain caters to advanced and expert skiers and riders, found on the upper right side of the resort on June Mountain Summit and a few single black-diamond runs on the lower mountain.

Intermediate and beginner skiers will enjoy views and a good lay of the land from the Rainbow Summit. Take the long Silverado Trail through the trees back to mid-mountain or continue on the intermediate Canyon Trail to head to the bottom.

Entertainment and Events

The T-Bar Social Club (2588 Hwy. 158, 760/648-7774, www.tbarsocialclub.com, 4pm-midnight daily) is the Eastern Sierra's hot spot for year-round live entertainment. Grab one of the signature cocktails (usually a classic libation with a twist) and catch an open-mic night, comedy show, dance party, or bluegrass band.

June Lake Brewing (131 S. Crawford Ave., 858/668-6340, www.junelakebrewing.com, noon-8pm Sun.-Thurs., noon-9pm Fri.-Sat. summer, winter hours vary) features 11 handcrafted brews with names like the Buccicat Cream Ale and the potent Hutte Double IPA. Pair your drink with a bite from the Ohanas395 food truck (noon-5pm daily) parked out front, which serves Hawaiian-inspired dishes and Kahuna fries.

Food

At the top of the J1 chair, the **June Meadows Chalet** (June Mountain, 8am-4:30pm daily mid-Dec.-Apr.) serves easy grab-and-go salads, hot dogs, and snacks, including its very own "Mountain Muffin," two fried eggs, cheese, and bacon, ham, or sausage nestled in a housemade bun. It also houses the full-size Antler Bar (11am-close daily).

Located between Rainbow Summit and June Mountain Summit (J4 and J7 chairs), **Stew Pot Slim's** (from 11am when the J7 chair is running) has a nice deck to hang out on. Enjoy a bowl of chili while admiring the skiers and snowboarders brave the chutes off the summit.

Accommodations

June Lake has plenty of cabins and lodges available. One particularly nice year-round resort is the ★ **Double Eagle Resort and Spa** (5587 Hwy. 158, June Lake, 760/648-7004, www.doubleeagle. com, $119-649). Its 15 two-bedroom cabins ($269-349) sleep six, and all come with decks and fully equipped kitchens. The 16 luxurious lodge rooms ($119-249) include coffee service, free Wi-Fi, a refrigerator, and whirlpool tubs. There's also a sprawling guest house ($619-649) that sleeps 12, with three bedrooms, a full kitchen, laundry room, grill, and wood-burning fireplace. Amenities include the on-site **Creekside Spa** (7am-9pm daily, $55-155), with an indoor pool and a fitness center, and the **Eagle's Landing Restaurant** (7:30am-9pm daily, $10-38). Abundant trails and ponds around the resort make this an everything-you-need destination.

A little more rustic, the very pleasant **The Four Seasons June Lake Cabin Rentals** (24 Venice St., 760/648-1919, www.junelakesfourseasons.com, year-round, $189-249) gets busy in autumn as people flock to see the fall colors. The five renovated A-frame cabins each sleep up to six people, with a master bedroom and a sleeping loft as well as a full kitchen, a living room, and a large deck. The resort is 2 miles (3.2 km) from the town of June Lake and 1.5 miles (2.4 km) from the June Mountain Ski Resort.

The inexpensive **Boulder Lodge** (2282 Hwy. 158, 760/648-7533, www.boulderlodgejunelake.com, $135-399) provides an array of options—from simple motel rooms to multiple-bedroom apartments and even a five-bedroom lake house. The simply decorated apartments and suites feature wood furniture and wood-paneled kitchenettes. The rooms could use an upgrade, but the views of June Lake and the surrounding landscape are timeless. An indoor pool, a hot tub, and a game room with a billiard table are available for guest use.

Camping

The U.S. Forest Service maintains several campgrounds near June Lake in the Inyo National Forest. A particularly good one is **Silver Lake Campground** (Hwy. 158, 7 mi/11.5 km west of US-395, www. recreation.gov, mid-Apr.-mid-Nov., $21-23, $7 per each additional vehicle). Each of the 63 sites has a bear-proof food locker, a picnic table, and a fire ring; the campground has flush toilets, drinking water, and even a small store within walking distance. The sites are spread out, with some on the shore of beautiful Silver Lake. This is a good place to fish, watch for wildlife, or just sit and enjoy the view.

Information and Services

The small **June Lake Visitor Kiosk** (US-395 and Hwy. 158, summer only) is staffed by volunteers. There's a café, deli, and a **Shell** gas station (760/648-7509) at the intersection of US-395 and CA-158.

Getting Around

The **Eastern Sierra Transit Authority** (ESTA, 800/922-1930 or 760/872-1901, www.estransit.com) operates local bus routes around Mammoth Lakes. In winter, skiers and snowboarders hop on the June Mountain bus from Mammoth Lakes ($5 one-way). The bus schedule is subject to change; check the ESTA website for current routes.

Mammoth Lakes

The town of Mammoth started out as a gold mining settlement and then shifted toward logging and tourism when the gold ran out. The gorgeous mountain scenery, along with multiple alpine lakes, natural hot springs, and dependable snowfall due to its high elevation, is

the perfect setting for outdoor sports—skiing in winter and mountain biking in summer.

Getting There

The town of Mammoth Lakes is 20 miles (32 km) south of June Lake and about 30 miles (48 km) south of Lee Vining at the junction of US-395 and CA-203. From June Lake Junction, follow US-395 south for 15 miles (24 km) and then turn west onto CA-203, which leads right into town.

In the winter, be prepared with chains, four-wheel drive, and good snow tires and carry extra clothing, food, and a shovel. Even if the weather is predicted to be clear, being prepared can prevent a world of hurt and the need to turn back in a sudden storm. For the latest traffic information, including chain control areas and weather conditions, call Caltrans (800/427-7623).

Sights
The Village at Mammoth Lakes

The Village at Mammoth Lakes (www. villageatmammoth.com) is a hybrid of town, shopping mall, and upscale amusement park. Its central purpose is to provide upscale amenities to complement a day of fun for skiers and snowboarders. The Village offers lodging, eclectic restaurants, shopping, and a good number of bars—all organized around a central pedestrian plaza. In summer, the plaza is sprinkled with outdoor benches, shaded tables, fire pits, and greenery. Concerts and outdoor movies are held in the warmer months. In winter, it's common to see Woolly, Mammoth Mountain's mascot, making the rounds.

Gondola Rides

Mammoth Mountain has plenty of chairlifts, a gondola or two, and plenty of ways to get up to the mountain while relaxing and enjoying the view. **Village Gondola** (7:45am-5pm daily, winter only, free) takes you from the Village at Mammoth Lakes to Canyon Lodge. The other

EASTERN SIERRA

Mammoth Lakes

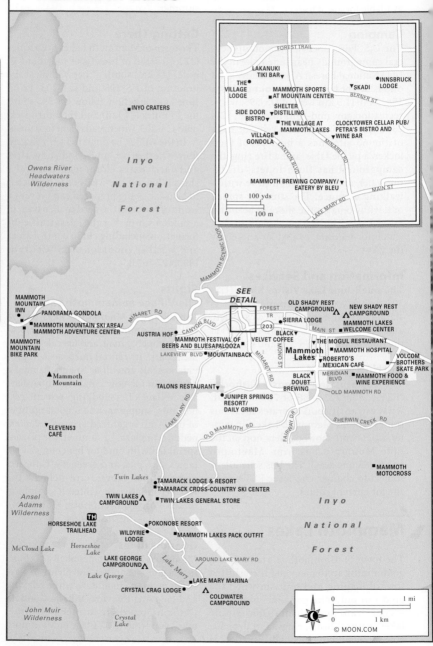

Inyo National Forest

Owens River Headwaters Wilderness

INYO CRATERS

SEE DETAIL

Detail inset:

FOREST TRAIL

LAKANUKI TIKI BAR
THE VILLAGE LODGE
MAMMOTH SPORTS AT MOUNTAIN CENTER
SKADI
INNSBRUCK LODGE
BERNER ST
SIDE DOOR BISTRO
SHELTER DISTILLING
THE VILLAGE AT MAMMOTH LAKES
CLOCKTOWER CELLAR PUB/ PETRA'S BISTRO AND WINE BAR
VILLAGE GONDOLA
CANYON BLVD
MINARET RD
MAMMOTH BREWING COMPANY/ EATERY BY BLEU
MAIN ST
LAKE MARY RD

0   100 yds
0   100 m

MAMMOTH SCENIC LOOP

MINARET RD

FOREST TR
203
MAIN ST

OLD SHADY REST CAMPGROUND
NEW SHADY REST CAMPGROUND
SIERRA LODGE
MAMMOTH LAKES WELCOME CENTER

MAMMOTH MOUNTAIN INN
PANORAMA GONDOLA
MAMMOTH MOUNTAIN SKI AREA/ MAMMOTH ADVENTURE CENTER
MAMMOTH MOUNTAIN BIKE PARK

AUSTRIA HOF
CANYON BLVD
MAMMOTH FESTIVAL OF BEERS AND BLUESAPALOOZA
LAKEVIEW BLVD
MOUNTAINBACK

BLACK VELVET COFFEE
Mammoth Lakes
THE MOGUL RESTAURANT
MAMMOTH HOSPITAL
ROBERTO'S MEXICAN CAFÉ
VOLCOM BROTHERS SKATE PARK
MONO ST
MINARET RD
MERIDIAN BLVD
BLACK DOUBT BREWING
MAMMOTH FOOD & WINE EXPERIENCE
OLD MAMMOTH RD

▲ Mammoth Mountain

TALONS RESTAURANT

LAKE MARY RD

JUNIPER SPRINGS RESORT/ DAILY GRIND

OLD MAMMOTH RD

FAIRWAY DR
SHERWIN CREEK RD

ELEVEN53 CAFÉ

MAMMOTH MOTOCROSS

Twin Lakes
TAMARACK LODGE & RESORT
TAMARACK CROSS-COUNTRY SKI CENTER
TWIN LAKES CAMPGROUND
TWIN LAKES GENERAL STORE

Inyo National Forest

Ansel Adams Wilderness

HORSESHOE LAKE TRAILHEAD
POKONOBE RESORT
WILDYRIE LODGE
MAMMOTH LAKES PACK OUTFIT

McCloud Lake
Horseshoe Lake

LAKE GEORGE CAMPGROUND
Lake Mary
AROUND LAKE MARY RD

Lake George

CRYSTAL CRAG LODGE
LAKE MARY MARINA
COLDWATER CAMPGROUND

John Muir Wilderness
Crystal Lake

0   1 mi
0   1 km

© MOON.COM

gondola, **Panorama Gondola** (8:30am-4pm daily, last ride to top at 3:30pm, summer and winter), sometimes called the Scenic Gondola Ride, runs from the Main Lodge at Mammoth to McCoy Station. After a stop there, it goes all the way to the top of the mountain.

In winter, the gondola is extremely popular with skiers: Intermediate-level skiers get off at McCoy to access the trails there; the top of the mountain is for experts only. In summer, the Panorama Gondola (9am-4:30pm daily June-Sept., adults $40, ages 13-18 $35, 12 and under free with an adult) serves sightseers, mountain bikers, hikers, and anyone else who wants to get to the top of the 11,053-foot mountain. From the top, you can see as far as 400 miles on a clear day.

The ride to the top takes about 20 minutes. Stop for a snack at the **Eleven53 Café** (10:30am-3:30pm daily, $8-20), named for its 11,053 feet (3,369 m) in elevation and open when the gondola is running.

One of the most popular reasons to ride up is to ride down—on your mountain bike. In summer, 70 miles of trails are open for biking and 25 miles of hiking trails are available. You can buy a day pass ($45 adult, $24 children under age 13) to bike the trails, which includes all-day access to both the Panorama Gondola and the shuttle. Hikers only pay to ride the gondola, and then it's free to walk down. If you're not a skier, you can still ride the Panorama Gondola to the top and back in winter ($29 adults, $24 youth).

The Panorama Gondola is usually closed in October for maintenance between the two big seasons. The Village Gondola occasionally operates in summer for special events.

Inyo Craters

California is full of volcanic action, and some of the most interesting results to behold are the three **Inyo Craters** (www.fs.usda.gov). These phreatic craters on and near Deer Mountain were created by explosions of steam. Scientists believe that all three craters came into being at about the same time, around AD 1350. Two of the three craters are about 200 feet deep and large enough that they actually have lakes inside them. The third crater is smaller, but all are worth seeing. If you can, make time for this geologic side trip.

Getting There

To reach Inyo Craters, drive 5 miles (8 km) north of Mammoth Lakes on CA-203. Turn right (east) onto the Mammoth Scenic Route (Dry Creek Rd.) and continue about 3.2 miles (5.2 km) until you see the sign for the Inyo Craters. Turn right at the sign and drive about 1.3 miles (2.1 km) on a dirt road (not plowed or advised in winter). Park in the lot and walk 0.3 mile to the crater site.

Old Mammoth Road

Mammoth Lakes became of interest to miners in the 19th century after the gold rush began—miners got out this far in 1877. Along **Old Mammoth Road** (south off CA-203/Main St.) you'll find a number of old mining sites. At the height of the short-lived boom, about 20 small mines operated in the area. Along this road, you can see the grave of a miner's wife, a stamp mill's flywheel, and then the meager remains of Mammoth City and the nearby Mammoth Mine. The highlight of this summertime half-day trip is the ruins of the Mammoth Consolidated Mine. You can still see some bits of the camp and its housing buildings, the assay office, the mill, and mining equipment. Old mine shafts are extremely dangerous and should not be entered.

★ Devils Postpile National Monument

Devils Postpile National Monument (Minaret Vista Rd./Hwy. 203, 760/934-2289, www.nps.gov/depo, mid-June-mid-Oct., 24 hours daily, ranger station 9am-5pm daily late June-early Sept., $10 per vehicle) is small, but what you'll see is worth a visit. The park is named for the strange natural rock formation called the Devils Postpile. It's hard to fathom that the near-perfect, straight-sided hexagonal posts are a natural phenomenon created by volcanic heat and pressure. Less heavily traveled than many other parks, Devils Postpile has hikes to serene meadows and un-spoiled streams, and you're likely to see the occasional deer or maybe even a bear meandering through the woods. Free guided ranger walks are held daily throughout the summer, starting from the ranger station/bookstore.

Inside the monument is the beauti-ful crystalline **Rainbow Falls.** The thick sheet of water cascades 101 feet down to a pool, throwing up stunning rainbows of mist. For the best rainbows at the water-fall, hike the 3 miles (4.8 km) from Red Meadow near the middle of the day when the sun is high in the sky.

Getting There

A **shuttle** (adults $8, children $4) is man-datory for all visitors during high sea-son (except for vehicles with handicap placards). In summer, the shuttle runs hourly 7am-10am daily from the Village at Mammoth Lakes and every 15-30 minutes 7am-7pm daily (mid-June-early Sept.) from the Mammoth Mountain Adventure Center and Main Lodge area by the gondola and the Mammoth Mountain Inn.

Entertainment and Events
Nightlife

The **Clocktower Cellar Pub** (Alpenhof Lodge, 6080 Minaret Rd., 760/934-2725, www.clocktowercellar.com, 4pm-11pm daily) is a happening nightspot that of-fers a full bar with at least 20 beers on tap and 50 different bottled beers from around the world. The polished wood bar invites patrons to marvel at the more than 160 top-shelf whiskeys. A couple of foosball tables and flat-screen TVs pro-vide entertainment, while a light bar menu (burgers, tacos, nachos) will keep your belly full.

The wine list at the **Side Door Bistro** (100 Canyon Blvd., 760/934-5200, www.sidedoormammoth.com, 11am-9pm Tues.-Thurs., 9am-9pm Fri.-Mon.) is often called the best in the Village. Enjoy an elegant glass of one of California's top vintages, or come in the evening, when you can order a delicious dinner or des-sert crepe to accompany your favorite varietal. Side Door Bistro remains open later in summer and winter and often closes on select weekdays in spring and fall.

The **Lakanuki Tiki Bar** (6201 Minaret Rd., 760/934-7447, www.lakanuki.net, 3pm-2am Mon.-Fri., noon-2am Sat.-Sun. winter, 3pm-10pm Mon.-Fri., noon-2am Sat.-Sun. summer) is a popular tiki bar in the Village, serving fancy mai tais and piña coladas around an island-themed bar. Stop by for happy hour (3pm-6pm Sun.-Fri., 2pm-5pm Sat.) for $4 beers and a tasty bar menu. Hours vary seasonally; the bar is usually closed Monday and Tuesday in fall.

Mammoth Brewing Company (18 Lake Mary Rd., 760/934-7141, www.mammothbrewingco.com, 10am-9:30pm daily) has been brewing craft beer since 1953. The IPA 395 is made with sage-brush and juniper, which brings out the notes of a high-desert rainstorm, while the Wild Sierra saison is brewed with lo-cally harvested piñon-pine needles. The spacious wood-lined bar offers plenty of seating, with an outdoor patio perfect for summer.

Black Doubt Brewing (452 Old Mammoth Rd., 760/484-7845, http://blackdoubtbrewing.com, 2:30pm-9pm Mon. and Wed.-Fri., 11:30am-9pm Sat.-Sun.) was begun by a former Southern Californian who fell into brewing IPAs and Belgian-style beers while in Mammoth. The narrow, industrial space houses 8-13 barrel-aged brews on tap. Bring in your own food to enjoy with their ales.

Shelter Distilling (100 Canyon Blvd., 760/709-2174, http://shelterdistilling. com, 11am-11pm daily) shares the sights, smells, and tastes of the Eastern Sierra through its vodka, whiskey, and gin spirits. Order a cocktail made with one of their in-house spirits, such as the Minaret mule. Pizzas and sandwiches from the on-site kitchen help soak up the alcohol.

Festivals and Events
The classic **Mammoth Motocross** (Mammoth Mountain, 800/626-6684, www.mammothmotocross.com, June, $20) began in 1968 and is the longest-running motocross event in the United States. Famous racers such as Jeremy McGrath and Ricky Carmichael have honed their craft on this track. Bus transportation from the front gate to the racetrack is included in the price of the ticket. Join the after-parties in the Village following the races.

The **Eastern Sierra Symphony** (760/935-3837, www. easternsierrasymphony.org, mid-Aug., free) plays the harmonies of Haydn, Mozart, Brahms, and Vivaldi, performed by local young musicians and seasoned guest performance artists. The free concerts take place at St. Joseph's Catholic Church; a special Thursday benefit concert ($50) kicks off the season at the Edison Theater. Reserve tickets online in advance at the Eastern Sierra Symphony website.

The **Labor Day Festival of the Arts** (760/914-3752, www.monoarts.org, early Sept., free) showcases fine artists and craftspeople. Some of the Eastern Sierra's finest live musicians also perform.

The annual **Mammoth Festival of Beers and Bluespalooza** (888/992-7397, www.mammothbluesbrewsfest.com, $25-99 individual events, $145-160 weekend pass, $180-225 4-day pass, Aug.) gives attendees the chance to sample the work of more than 150 craft breweries and listen to major performers like Ozomatli, Robert Cray, and Blues Traveler.

Local food and wine vendors take over the Village during the **Mammoth Food & Wine Experience** (760/934-3781, http:// mammothfoodandwine.org, July), hosted by the Mammoth Lakes Foundation. For two days, visitors participate in wine seminars, attend grand tastings with more than 30 vintners, and bid at auctions that help support higher education and scholarship funds for Mammoth's youth.

Sports and Recreation
Skiing and Snowboarding
Mammoth Mountain
The premier downhill ski and snowboard mountain is, aptly, **Mammoth Mountain** (10001 Minaret Rd., information 760/934-2571, lodging and lift tickets 800/626-6684, snow report 888/766-9778, www.mammothmountain.com, lifts 8:30am-4pm daily, $149-179 adults, $122-147 ages 65-79 and 13-18, $60-72 ages 5-12). Whether you're completely new to downhill thrills or a seasoned expert looking for different terrain, you'll find something great on Mammoth Mountain. More than two dozen lifts, including three gondolas and 10 express quads, ascend 3,100 vertical feet (945 m) to the 3,500 acres of skiable and boardable terrain; there are also three half-pipes.

The easiest runs on the mountain mostly cluster around the Main Lodge and Mammoth Mountain Inn, easily recognizable by their cute nonthreatening names like Apple Pie and Sesame Street. Another cluster of easy runs is by the Canyon Lodge and includes kid-friendly names like School Yard, Little Bird, and Ginger Bread. There are runs all over the mountain for intermediate skiers. To build your confidence, take the Panorama Gondola to McCoy Station and then ski over to High Five Express. The lift accesses an equal number of intermediate and advanced runs.

Those at an X-Games ability level can take the Panorama Gondola all the way to the Eleven53 Café and drop down into double-black-diamond runs, which contain steep bowls, chutes, and cornices.

Tamarack Cross-Country Ski Center

For a less crowded, human-powered way to enjoy the snow, **Tamarack Cross-Country Ski Center** (163 Twin Lakes Rd., 760/934-2442, www.tamaracklodge.com, 8:30am-4pm Mon.-Thurs., 8:30am-5pm Fri.-Sat. mid-Nov.-Apr., $22-32 adults, $19-25 youth and seniors, $5 children) offers more than 19 miles of groomed cross-country ski tracks, some with groomed skating lanes, for all abilities and levels. This lovely resort also has a restaurant, lounge, and a bar where you can enjoy a nice cup of hot chocolate and good book if you get tired of skiing. And getting here from Mammoth Lakes is free: Just take the ESTA orange shuttle line from the Village, running hourly on the half hour (8:30am-5:15pm daily in winter).

Blue Diamond Trails

The **Blue Diamond Trails** system (www.mammothlakes.us) starts just behind the Mammoth Lakes Welcome Center (2510 Main St., Mammoth Lakes, 760/924-5500, www.visitmammoth.com, 8am-5pm daily), at the entrance to Mammoth Lakes, and winds through 19 miles (31 km) of Inyo National Forest, marked by signs bearing a blue diamond on the trees. Pick up a free trail map in the Welcome Center before you set out. Some trails are not groomed, so be prepared to deal with varying snow conditions and unmarked paths. There's plenty of relatively flat land here for beginners, however.

The Blue Diamond Trails system begins at **Shady Rest Trails** (Hwy. 203, at the Welcome Center/ranger station), which might sound like a cemetery, but is in fact a group of beginner loops with plenty of shade to keep skiers cool. The **Knolls Trail** (Mammoth Scenic Loop, 1.5 mi/2.4 km north of Hwy. 203) makes a good day out for skiers of intermediate

ability, passing through lovely stands of lodgepole and Jeffrey pines. Beginners beware of the deceptively named **Scenic Loop Trail** (Mammoth Scenic Loop, across from Knolls Trail). This reasonably short trail—about 4 miles long (6.4 km)—includes steep descents and some difficult terrain.

Snowshoeing

If you prefer walking to all that sliding around on planks, rent or bring your own snowshoes to Mammoth and enjoy a snowy hike through the mountains and meadows. Check the cross-country ski areas first—many have specifically designated snowshoe trails. Or head out to the backcountry and explore Mammoth Lakes Basin or the Sherwin Range. Groomed trails start right behind the **Mammoth Lakes Welcome Center** (2510 Main St., Mammoth Lakes, 760/924-5500, www.visitmammoth.com, 8am-5pm daily).

Hiking

Hikers will find plenty of worthwhile terrain around Mammoth Lakes for both short day hikes and longer backpacking adventures. The **Mammoth Mountain Bike Park** (10001 Minaret Rd., 800/626-6684, www.mammothmountain.com, 9am-6pm daily summer, $45 adult, $24 ages 12 and under) includes a number of great hiking trails. For an all-downhill walk, take the Panorama Gondola (8:30am-4pm daily June-Sept., last ride to top at 3:30pm, $29 adults, $24 youth) to the Panorama Overlook and hike back down into town. Just be sure to get a trail map at the **Mammoth Adventure Center** (10001 Minaret Rd., 760/934-0706, www.mammothmountain.com, 8:30am-6pm daily June-Sept.) so you can keep to the hiking areas and avoid being flattened by fast-moving mountain bikers.

Mammoth Lakes also acts as a jumping-off point for adventurers who want to take on the **John Muir Wilderness** (south of Mammoth Lakes to Mount

Whitney, www.sierrawild.gov). John Muir pioneered the preservation of the Sierra Nevada, and more than 500,000 acres in the area have been designated national wilderness areas in his honor. Day hikers are welcome, and there's plenty to see. Check with the Inyo and Sierra National Forests (www.fs.usda.gov) for trail maps of the area. The main attractions are the **John Muir Trail** (JMT, 215 mi/345 km Yosemite-Mount Whitney, www.johnmuirtrail.org) and the **Pacific Crest National Scenic Trail** (PCT, 2,650 mi/4,265 km, www.pcta.org), both among the holiest of grails for backpacking enthusiasts from around the world.

Backpacking

If you're planning an overnight camping trip in the John Muir, Ansel Adams, Dinkey Lakes, or Kaiser Wilderness areas of the Sierra National Forest, you must first obtain a permit. You can apply for a **wilderness permit** (559/297-0706, www. fs.usda.gov/sierra, $10 per reservation, 15 people per permit) one year in advance or in person at a ranger station 24 hours before your trip begins. There is no charge for "walk-up" permits, though their availability is limited.

Ranger stations include the **High Sierra Ranger District Office** (29688 Auberry Rd., Prather, 559/855-5355, 8am-4:30pm Mon.-Fri. winter, 8am-5pm daily summer), the **Sierra National Forest Headquarters** (1600 Tollhouse Rd., Clovis, 559/297-0706, 8am-4:30pm Mon.-Fri. winter, 8am-5pm daily summer), and **Bass Lake Ranger District** (57003 Road 225, North Fork, 559/877-2218, 8am-4:30pm Mon.-Fri. winter, 8am-5pm daily summer).

If you're planning an overnight in the Inyo National Forest, apply for a permit in person at the **Mammoth Lakes Welcome Center** (2510 Main St., Mammoth Lakes, 760/924-5500, www. visitmammoth.com, 8am-5pm daily), at the entrance to Mammoth Lakes.

Biking

Come summer, Mammoth Mountain transforms into a mountain-bike mecca. **Mammoth Mountain Bike Park** (10001 Minaret Rd., 800/626-6684, www. mammothmountain.com, 9am-6pm daily, $45 adults, $24 children under age 12, includes gondola and shuttle) spans much of the same terrain as the ski areas, with almost 90 miles of trails that suit all levels of biking ability. The park headquarters is at the **Mammoth Adventure Center** (Main Lodge, 10001 Minaret Rd., 760/934-0706 or 800/626-6684, 8:30am-6pm daily June-Sept.), at the Main Lodge at Mammoth Mountain. You can also buy bike park tickets at the Mountain Center at the Village (60 Canyon Blvd., 760/924-7057).

You can take your bike onto the Panorama Gondola and ride all the way to the top of Mammoth Mountain, then all the way down (3,000-plus vertical ft/900-plus m) on the single tracks. Be sure to pick the trails that best suit your fitness and experience level. Several other major lodges and mountain cafés offer rider services, including the Mountain Center at the Village at Mammoth Lakes and Juniper Springs. If you value scenery as much as extreme adventure, pack your camera and plan to rest at the various scenic overlooks throughout the trail system.

If you need to rent a bike or buy park tickets, go to the **Mammoth Adventure Center** (Main Lodge, 10001 Minaret Rd., 760/934-0706, 8:30am-6pm daily June-Sept.) or to **Mammoth Sports at Mountain Center** (6201 Minaret Rd., next to the Canyon Lodge gondola inside the Village, 760/934-2571, ext. 2078, 8am-8pm Sun.-Thurs., 8am-9pm Fri.-Sat. summer). Both locations offer new high-end bikes for adults and kids. These shops can also help with parts and repairs for bikes you've brought up with you, and they sell accessories.

Horseback Riding

Perhaps the most traditional way to explore the Eastern Sierra is on the back of a horse or mule. Early pioneers to the area came on horseback, and you can follow their example from several locations near Mammoth Lakes. From the **McGee Creek Pack Station** (2990 McGee Creek Rd., Crowley Lake, 760/935-4324 June-Sept., 760/878-2207 Oct.-May for rides in the Alabama Hills, www. mcgeecreekpackstation.com, 11am and 4pm daily June-Sept., $45 per hour, $150 per day), you can ride into McGee Canyon, a little-visited wilderness area. Other day-trip destinations include Baldwin Canyon and Hilton Lakes. Standard rides range from one hour to a full day, but McGee's specialty is multi-day and pack trips that let you really get out beyond the reach of paved roads to camp for a number of days by one of the many pristine lakes dotting the mountains. If you love the outdoors and really want a vacation as far away from it all as you can get, consider a few days of camping in Convict Basin or near Upper Fish Creek in the John Muir Wilderness. The McGee Creek guides will help you pack your gear and guide you through the incredible backcountry of the Eastern Sierra.

McGee Creek Pack Station is 10 miles (16 km) south of Mammoth Lakes on US-395.

Skateboarding

The **Volcom Brothers Skate Park** (1390 Meridian Blvd., 760/965-3690, sunrise-sunset daily, free) is an amazing outdoor 40,000-square-foot space filled with concrete bowls, humps, lumps, and smooth undulations, trannies, and transfers. Located next to Shady Rest Park (off CA-203), the park envelops a modern yet functional architecture and a fun design meant for skaters of all ability levels. It's free to use, but riders must wear a helmet and safety gear.

Lake George in the Mammoth Lakes Basin

Food

Petra's Bistro and Wine Bar (6080 Minaret Rd., 760/934-3500, www. petrasbistro.com, 5pm-9pm Sun. and Tues.-Thurs., 5pm-9:30pm Fri.-Sat.) offers a seasonal menu that's designed to please the palate and a wine list that's worth a visit itself. The by-the-glass offerings change each night, and your server will happily cork your unfinished bottle to take home. Two dining rooms and a wine bar divide the seating, and the atmosphere feels romantic without being too dark. Petra's stays open all year. Reservations are a good idea during ski season.

The popular gourmet establishment **Skadi** (94 Berner St., Ste. A, 760/914-0962, www.skadirestaurant.com, 5pm-close Wed.-Mon., $10-38) serves a menu of "fine alpine cuisine," inspired by Norwegian chef Ian Algeroen's heritage and time spent in the Swiss Alps. This translates into dishes like Canadian duck breast with arctic lingonberries and pan-roasted salmon. Inside, alpine skis and mountain landscapes decorate the walls while the warm lighting illuminates decorative dishes that taste as good as they look.

Roberto's Mexican Café (271 Old Mammoth Rd., 760/934-3667, www. robertoscafe.com, 11am-close daily, $10-16) is special. This casual spot serves classic California-Mexican food in great quantities but includes specialty items like lobster burritos, duck tacos, and "killer" margaritas. It's perfect for skiers and boarders famished after a long day on the slopes. For a quiet meal, stay downstairs in the main dining room. To join a lively younger crowd, head upstairs to the bar, which has tables and serves the full restaurant menu. Roberto's does not accept reservations.

Hopheads will love the ★ **Eatery by Bleu at Mammoth Brewing Company** (18 Lake Mary Rd., 760/934-7141, www. mammothbrewingco.com, 10am-9:30pm daily, $7-18), next to the Mammoth Brewing tasting room. The beer is legendary in these parts, and the restaurant is just as worthy. Standard pub grub gets a new twist with flatbread pizzas, naan tacos, and an Irish Caesar salad. Order a pitcher of the crisp and grassy Golden Trout Kolsch or go for a pint of the hoppy Epic IPA.

The best steaks in town are at **The Mogul Restaurant** (1528 Tavern Rd., 760/934-3039, www.themogul.com, 5:30pm-close daily, $19-60). The menu is full of standard surf-and-turf entrées like sirloin and fresh fish or filet and crab, as well as chicken, pasta, and vegetarian dishes. The house chicken dish is dripping in a marinade of red wine, honey, soy sauce, Worcestershire, brown sugar, and a whole rack of spices. Stop by for happy hour (5:30pm-6:30pm Sun.-Thurs.), when domestic bottled beer starts at $2.75—a steal in this town during the ski season.

★ **Black Velvet Coffee** (3343 Main St., www.blackvelvetcoffee.com, 6:45am-9pm

◈ Side Trip: Mammoth Lakes Basin

Five miles (8 km) south of downtown Mammoth Lakes sits a cluster of small alpine lakes that beckon visitors in summer. From the Village in downtown Mammoth Lakes, follow Lake Mary Road southwest for 3 miles (4.8 km) to Twin Lakes. Note that Lake Mary Road is closed in winter.

Twin Lakes

Twin Lakes is the first of the lakes you'll reach off Lake Mary Road. The popular lake is home to a campground, lodge, and a cross-country ski center. Nearby **Hole in the Wall** is a cool lava-rock tunnel that makes for a scenic hike-to photo-op and a fun destination for backcountry skiers coming off of Mammoth Mountain's Dragon's Tail run.

The **Twin Lakes General Store** (499 Twin Lakes Rd., 760/934-7295, 7am-7pm daily June-mid-Oct.) rents kayaks, canoes, and rowboats and sells camping and fishing gear, firewood, beer, ice, and souvenirs. Showers (7am-6pm daily, $6 pp) are available for campers.

Twin Lakes Campground (499 Twin Lakes Rd., 760/924-5500, www.recreation.gov, $22-24 June-mid-Oct.) has 94 sites perched between two scenic lakes, making it a popular place for stand-up paddleboarding, kayaking, and canoeing.

Lake Mary

From Twin Lakes, continue 0.8 mile south on Lake Mary Road. Turn left onto Around Lake Mary Road to circumnavigate the larger Lake Mary.

Mammoth Lakes Pack Outfit (3244 Lake Mary Rd., 760/934-2434, www.mammothpack.com, 7:30am-5pm daily mid-June-Sept. $350 pp/day, 4-person min.) leads trail rides and multiday trips into the Eastern Sierra backcountry.

The first of the Lake Mary campgrounds is **Pine City** (Lake Mary Rd., 760/873-2400, www.fs.usda.gov, June-mid-Sept., $24), with 10 first-come, first-served campsites. **Coldwater Campground** (Lake Mary/Cold Water Creek Campground Rd., 877/444-6777, www.recreation.gov, June-mid-Sept., $22-24), with 74 sites, appears next at the south corner of the lake.

daily) is a clean and cool modern space with lots of light that exudes productivity. Or maybe that's just a kick of energy from their nutty-tasting cold brew. The baristas take great pride in their grinds and pours—café aficionados will be impressed. Grab a bag of beans to take home or a mix of locally made Giddy Up Nuts, the perfect snack for a hike.

Accommodations
$100-150

Want to ski the slopes of Mammoth, but can't afford the hoity-toity condo resorts? Stay at the **Innsbruck Lodge** (913 Forest Trail, 760/934-3035, www.innsbrucklodge.com, $139-219). Economy rooms offer double, queen, or king beds, a table and chairs, and access to the motel whirlpool tub and lobby. Two-bedroom suites sleep up to six and include kitchenettes. The quiet North Village location is on the ski area shuttle route for easy access to the nearby ski slopes. It's also an easy walk to most restaurants, Village attractions, and the gondola. There's a library, free Wi-Fi in the rooms, and staff that speak Spanish and German.

The **Sierra Lodge** (3540 Main St., 760/934-8881 or 800/356-5711, www.sierralodge.com, $119-139) offers reasonably priced nonsmoking rooms right on the ski shuttle line, and it is 1.5 miles (2.4 km) from the Juniper Ridge chair lift. The simple motel is styled in cool, relaxing colors. All 35 rooms have either a king or two double beds, a kitchenette, and

Crystal Crag Lodge (307 Lake Mary Loop Rd., 760/934-2436, www.crystalcrag.com, late May-early Oct., $169-369) sits near Coldwater with accommodations in cabins that have kitchens, a living room, and bathrooms. Some have fireplaces. Pets are welcome. Crystal Crag also rents small motorboats ($40-60) and pontoon boats ($100-200).

Family-owned **Lake Mary Marina** (Lake Mary Rd., 760/934-5353, www.lakemarymarina.com, 8am-6pm Mon.-Sat. June-Oct.) lies between Coldwater Campground and Crystal Crag Lodge. The marina rents boats by the hour or by the day, including pontoon boats ($90-125 per hour); SUP, canoe, or pedal boats ($28); motorboats ($95 per day); and kayaks ($28-40 per hour), as well as bait and tackle for anglers.

On the northwest edge of the lake lies **Lake Mary Campground** (Lake Mary Loop Dr., 877/444-6777, www.recreation.gov, June-early Sept., $22-24), which has 48 sites.

Lake George

As you're driving the Lake Mary Loop, you'll encounter Lake George, a beautiful blue pond surrounded by trees and granite. It's hidden from the main road, south of Lake Mary. To get there, turn left onto Lake George Road.

Lake George Campground (Lake George Rd., 760/924-5500, www.fs.usda.gov, June-Sept., $24) has 15 first-come, first-served sites nestled between Lakes George and Mary. It's a quiet spot with great views of the lake. Wild animals frequent the area, so bear-proof lockers are provided at campsites.

Lake Mamie

At the junction of Around Mary Lake Road and Lake Mary Road, turn left to continue past Lake Mamie. The **Wildyrie Lodge** (4071 Lake Mary Rd., 760/934-2444, http://wildyrielodge.com, $119-395, June-Oct.) rents cabins and rooms in the main lodge. Across the road, stop for a bird's-eye view of the lake from **Twin Falls Overlook.** Nearby **Pokonobe Resort** (Lake Mary Rd., 760/934-2437, https://pokonobemarina.com, 7am-7pm daily mid-May-Oct.) sells wine and snacks and rents boats.

plenty of space for gear. Breakfast, cable TV, and Internet access are included. The motel's rates are rock-bottom in the off-season and on weekdays in winter.

One of the best things about the ★ **Tamarack Lodge & Resort** (163 Twin Lakes Rd., Mammoth Lakes, 760/626-6684, www.tamaracklodge.com) is that you can cross-country ski right up to your door. The 11 lodge rooms ($93-144) and 35 cabins ($161-552) range from studios to a three-bedroom unit that sleeps up to eight. Lodge rooms are decked out in European flare with knotty pine-wood paneling and patchwork quilt comforters. The rooms are more suited to a romantic getaway and are not recommended for kids. Tamarack prides itself on its rustic atmosphere, so accommodations have fireplaces or wood stoves, but no televisions.

$150-250

From the outside, the ornate, carved-wood, and fringed **Austria Hof** (924 Canyon Blvd., 760/934-2764 or 866/662-6668, www.austriahof.com, $114-225) looks like a ski hotel tucked into a crevice of the Alps. But inside, you'll find the most stylish American adornments. Simple motel rooms, some with king beds and spa tubs, are very relaxing. Also on offer are several lavish condos ($245-274) with 1-3 bedrooms available in winter. In the evening, head downstairs to the Austria Hof Restaurant for some hearty German fare. Austria Hof's location adjacent to the Canyon Lodge makes it a great base for winter skiing or mountain biking in summer. The lodge offers free ski and snowboard storage, Wi-Fi, a continental breakfast, and airport shuttle deals. This is one of the few places where you'll find a better deal on a night's stay in the summer than in the winter.

Located across the street from Mammoth Mountain's Main Lodge, and beside the Panorama Gondola, is the **Mammoth Mountain Inn** (10400 Minaret Rd., Mammoth Lakes, 800/626-6684, www.themammothmountaininn.com). The main building features standard hotel rooms ($139-369). The nearby East-West Building features condos ranging from studios that sleep four ($378) to deluxe two-bedrooms with lofts that can sleep up to 11 ($882/night in ski season). All rooms have flat-screen TVs in addition to upscale amenities. Guests can ride the gondola for free as part of their stay.

Over $250

It's not cheap, but the ★ **Juniper Springs Resort** (4000 Meridian Blvd., 760/934-1102, reservations 800/626-6684, www.juniperspringsmammoth.com, $221-990) has every luxury amenity to make your ski vacation one to remember. Condos come in studios, 1-3 bedrooms, and townhouses with interior furnishings that are the epitome of comfort, from granite-topped kitchen counters to 60-inch flat-screen TVs. Baths include deep soaking tubs and there are incredible mountain views from every room. The resort features heated pools and spas (10am-10pm daily year-round). The **Daily Grind** coffee bar (hotel lobby, 760/924-1102, 7am-11am and 3pm-7pm daily year-round) serves snacks, breakfast, and lunch, while inside the Eagle Lodge is **Talons Restaurant** (760/934-0797 or 760/934-2571, www.mammothmountain.com, 8am-4:30pm daily Dec.-Apr. but hours vary), serving breakfast and lunch. The Eagle Lodge is one of the Mammoth Mountain's base lodges, complete with a six-seat express chairlift to the main ski area.

Part of the Mammoth Lodging Collection, **The Village Lodge** (1111 Forest Trail, 760/934-1982 or 800/626-6684, www.thevillagelodgemammoth.com, $255-850) is a luxury condo complex that's within walking distance to Mammoth's ski slopes.

A fine condo rental option, **Mountainback** (Mammoth Mountain Reservations, 3310 Main St., 888/204-4692, www.mountainbackrentals.com, $520-1,138, 2-night min.) has an array of two-bedroom units close to the center of town; some condos have lofts and full kitchens and sleep up to 10. Most units have an outdoor spa; an outdoor Jacuzzi, swimming pool (summer only), and sauna are available for all guests. Each condo is decorated differently, so look online to find the one that's right for you.

Camping

New Shady Rest Campground (Sawmill Cutoff Rd., 877/444-6777, www.recreation.gov, June-Sept., $20-23) is a pet-friendly campground in Inyo National Forest. The 93 sites are along two large loops nestled in a forest of Jeffrey pines. Each site comes with a picnic table, a fire ring, and a food storage locker. The restrooms have flush toilets, but you'll have to walk to the showers outside of the campground.

Located next to New Shady Rest is **Old Shady Rest Campground** (Sawmill Cutoff Rd., 877/444-6777, www.recreation.gov, June-early Sept., $20-23), with 45 sites and the same amenities as its sister campground. Firewood is available on-site.

Information and Services

The **Mammoth Lakes Welcome Center** (2510 Main St., 760/924-5500 or 888/466-2666, www.visitmammoth.com, 8am-5pm daily) is jointly run by the U.S. Forest Service, Mammoth Lakes Tourism, and the National Parks Service. They can help you with condo rentals, restaurant reservations, and seasonal recreation options.

They're also your best resource for camping information, weather travel advisories, updates on snowmobile trails, and backcountry passes.

Mammoth Hospital (85 Sierra Park Rd., 760/934-3311, http://mammothhospital.org) has a 24-hour emergency room.

Getting Around

Mammoth Yosemite Airport (MMH, 1200 Airport Rd., 760/934-3813, www.townofmammothlakes.ca.gov) receives flights from San Francisco and Los Angeles. There is also seasonal service from Denver, Chicago, New York, and Houston.

The **Eastern Sierra Transit Authority** (ESTA, 210 Commerce Dr., 760/924-3184 or 800/922-1930, www.estransit.com) runs a number of bus lines from Lone Pine through Bishop (the yellow Lone Pine Express), and connecting in Mammoth Lakes via the red line Mammoth Express. Routes continue north to Lee Vining en route to Reno by way of the blue Lone Pine to Reno route.

The **Mountain Shuttle Service** (ESTA, 760/924-3184, www.mammothmountain.com, mid-Dec.-mid-Apr., free) offers complimentary rides around town and between Mammoth Mountain base lodges in the winter. Download the transit map or mobile app (https://transitapp.com) for current schedules.

Yosemite
National
Park

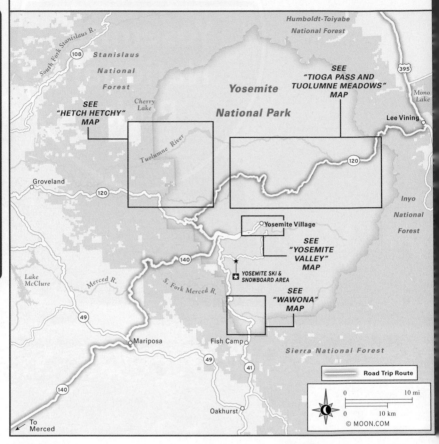

Yosemite National Park

Yosemite is a place of magic, wonder, natural beauty, and grace.

Its majestic granite rocks, towering mountain peaks, impressive waterfalls, and giant sequoias make it a popular destination for rock climbers or families seeking wilderness and solitude.

Half Dome is Yosemite's most popular attraction, a gigantic rock with a sheer granite face at a peak elevation of 8,844 feet (2,696 m). Scaling Half Dome is such a demanding venture that you have to be granted a permit to climb it; serious hikers can put their name in the lottery in March.

No one seems to visit Yosemite without being profoundly affected by it. If this is your first visit, prepare to be overwhelmed. If you're a regular visitor, then you already know you're going to see something new this time that will knock your polar-fleece socks off. Whether you scale a legendary granite precipice, wake at dawn to watch bear cubs frolic in a glistening meadow, hike under a

Highlights

★ **Half Dome:** Even in a park filled with iconic monuments, Half Dome towers over all others. Whether you come to scale its peak or just to see the real-life model for all those wonderful photographs, Half Dome lives up to the hype (page 482).

★ **Bridalveil Fall:** It's the most monumental—and the most accessible—of Yosemite's marvelous collection of waterfalls (page 482).

★ **Mist Trail:** The best way to experience Yosemite Valley's grandeur is on one of its many scenic trails. A hike along the Mist Trail to the top of Vernal Fall brings the valley views alive (page 484).

★ **Yosemite Ski & Snowboard Area:** California's first downhill ski area is as popular as ever, with affordable downhill and cross-country skiing, sledding hills for the kids, and full-moon snowshoe walks (page 493).

★ **Mariposa Grove of Giant Sequoias:** Wander through this impressive grove of giant sequoias and admire natural celebrities such as the Grizzly Giant, Clothespin Tree, and the Faithful Couple (page 496).

★ **Tuolumne Meadows:** Explore the wonders of the park's high elevations at this rare alpine meadow, where numerous hiking trails thread through Yosemite's backcountry (page 502).

Best Restaurants and Accommodations

★ **Yosemite Valley Lodge:** A variety of rooms and dining options makes this the perfect base for exploring the valley (page 490).

★ **Majestic Yosemite Hotel:** Historic luxury is evident in the rooms, cottages, and the grand dining room with soaring 34-foot ceilings (page 491).

★ **Big Trees Lodge Dining Room:** This historic restaurant in Wawona offers friendly, and delicious, dining inside the park (page 500).

★ **Tuolumne Meadows Campground:** The largest campground in Yosemite offers easy access to multiple trailheads (page 505).

★ **High Sierra Camps:** Yosemite's wilderness camps offer a convenient way for backpackers to spend multiple days in the Sierra (page 507).

★ **Groveland Hotel:** This elegant and historic hotel in Groveland makes a great base for trips into the park (page 511).

crashing waterfall, or sit by the fire in one of the park's rustic lodges and watch the snow fall in the moonlight, you'll be different by the time you leave; enjoy the transformation.

Getting There

This road trip enters the park from its east side though **Tioga Pass** (CA-120, summer only), passing Tuolumne Meadows to stop at Tenaya Lake. Wiggle your toes in the sandy lakeshore and take in the views of the towering granite that surrounds this alpine lake. Traveling east to west, CA-120 deposits you in Yosemite Valley, where you should try to spend at least a day. It can take 1-2 hours to drive to other sights within the park, such as Glacier Point (great for snapping a photo of Half Dome) and the towering redwoods in the Mariposa Grove of Giant Sequoias near Wawona.

The **Arch Rock Entrance** (CA-140) accesses the west side of Yosemite and is the closest entrance to Yosemite Valley.

From San Francisco
215 mi/345 km, 4-5 hr

From San Francisco, the **Big Oak Flat Entrance** (CA-120) is the quickest and most direct route into the park. (Time your departure to avoid the weekday rush hours of 6am-10am and 4pm-8pm.) Begin by heading east over the **Bay Bridge** via I-80 and veer right onto I-580 East for 50 miles (80 km) to merge onto I-205 East in Tracy. Stay on I-205 for 15 miles (24 km), before merging onto I-5 for 1 mile (1.6 km). Exit onto CA-120 East toward Manteca. Continue east on CA-120 for almost 90 miles (145 km) to the Big Oak Flat Entrance.

From Shasta and Lassen

There are two routes to Yosemite from either Redding or the city of Mount Shasta; each takes about six hours.

Interior Route: 305 mi/490 km, 6 hr

The **Big Oak Flat Entrance** (CA-120) is the most efficient route from Shasta and Lassen. Start in **Redding,** where you'll take I-5 south for 162 miles (260 km) to Sacramento, a drive of about 2.5 hours. There are plenty of cheap places in Red

Bluff, Corning, and Williams to fill your gas tank. Note that traffic may slow through Sacramento during rush hour.

From **Sacramento,** take CA-99 south for 45 miles (72 km) toward Elk Grove and Lodi. In Stockton, turn east on CA-4 and drive 35 miles (56 km) toward Copperopolis, where you'll head south on Obyrnes Ferry Road for 12 miles (19.5 km). At a T junction with CA-120, turn east and drive 20 miles (32 km) to the Big Oak Flat Entrance.

Scenic Route: 300 mi/485 km, 6 hr

This pretty drive follows the **Volcanic Legacy Scenic Byway** (CA-89) through dense pines and towering mountains into the Eastern Sierra to access the park via the **Tioga Pass Entrance** (CA-120, summer only). Note that this route can only be completed in summer, when Tioga Pass is open.

From the city of **Mount Shasta,** take CA-89 southeast for 79 miles (127 km), passing through **McCloud** and Hat Creek, until the road intersects with CA-44. Take CA-44 east for 45 miles (72 km) toward Susanville, where there are plenty of gas stations and fast-food joints.

From **Susanville,** turn south on US-395 for 86 miles (138 km) to Reno (a cheap overnight option). From Reno, continue south on US-395 for 140 miles (225 km), passing Carson City, Gardnerville, and Bridgeport toward the town of **Lee Vining.** At the junction of US-395 and CA-120, turn right and drive 12 miles (19.5 km) to the **Tioga Pass Entrance.**

Be sure to fill up your gas tank at the Tioga Gas Mart; there are no gas stations until you reach the other side of the park at Crane Flat.

From Tahoe
135 mi/215 km, 2.5-3 hr

From Tahoe, the **Tioga Pass Entrance** (CA-120) offers fairly straightforward access via the park's east side. The scenic drive includes a gradual climb in elevation with quirky ranch towns and cow pastures set between massive glacier-like mountains.

From **South Lake Tahoe,** take US-50 East for about 3 miles (5 km) over the Nevada-California border. Turn right onto NV-207 East, which follows the Kingsbury Grade into **Gardnerville.** In winter, the pass may close due to snow, or chains may be required. In 10 miles (16 km), NV-207 merges with NV-206 south for 1.3 miles (2.1 km). Turn left onto Centerville Lane (Hwy. 756) and drive 2.8 miles (4.5 km) east to the US-395 junction south of Gardnerville. Turn south on US-395 and continue 88 miles (142 km) to **Lee Vining.**

At the junction of US-395 and CA-120, turn right and drive 12 miles (19.5 km) to the Tioga Pass Entrance Station. Be sure to fill up your gas tank at the Tioga Gas Mart; there are no gas stations until you reach the other side of the park at Crane Flat.

Stopping in Gardnerville

Gardnerville offers a cheap stop to fill your tank. The town has modern casinos with a historical feel. If you have time to spare, pause in Minden to check out the live country acts at the **Carson Valley Inn** (1627 US-395, Minden, 800/321-6983, www.carsonvalleyinn.com) or to gamble at **Sharkey's Casino** (1440 US-395, Gardnerville, 775/782-3133, www.sharkeyscasino.com). Just 21 miles (34 km) south, Topaz Lake is your last stop in Nevada. It has a Chevron gas station, an RV park, and a casino. From Topaz Lake, continue south for 70 miles (113 km) on US-395 to Lee Vining. At the junction of US-395 and CA-120, turn right and drive 12 miles (19.5 km) to the Tioga Pass Entrance Station.

From Monterey
200 mi/320 km, 4 hr

From Monterey, the drive to Yosemite National Park is a straight shot through farmland and cow pastures. Start by heading north on CA-1 (Cabrillo Hwy.)

for 13 miles (21 km). Near Salinas, keep right to veer east onto CA-156 before merging onto US-101 North.

At San Juan Bautista, turn east onto CA-156. Drive 45 miles (72 km) northeast, crossing I-5 near Los Banos. Continue east on CA-152 for about 40 miles (64 km) to CA-99. Turn north onto CA-99 and drive 20 miles (32 km) to Merced, where you'll head east on CA-140 for 80 miles (129 km), entering the park at the **Arch Rock Entrance.**

Train and Bus

Amtrak (324 W. 24th St., Merced, 209/722-6862, reservations 800/872-7245, www.amtrak.com) has a station in Merced, an hour away from the park. You can take the train there and then take the **Amtrak Thruway Service bus** ($15 one-way) to locations in Yosemite Valley, including Yosemite Valley Lodge, Majestic Yosemite Hotel, Half Dome Village, Crane Flat, and the Yosemite Visitors Center. The bus schedule changes seasonally but runs all year. It is about a 2.5-hour bus ride from Merced to the park. The bus also goes to White Wolf and Tuolumne Meadows during the summer months (daily service July-Aug., weekends only June and Sept.).

The **Yosemite Area Regional Transit System** (YARTS, 877/989-2787, www.yarts.com, $13) operates daily buses from Merced to Yosemite. They also have seasonal buses taking passengers from towns along CA-120 (Sonora, Jamestown, and Groveland) to the park. In the summer months, an Eastern Sierra service connects Mammoth Lakes, June Lake, and Lee Vining to the park as well. The park entrance fee is included is the price of the ticket.

Starline Tours (800/959-3131, www.starlinetours.com, $119 adult, $79 ages 2-11) offers one-day bus tours of Yosemite. Tours depart from San Francisco at 7am (or 5am) and return late at night. This is a great option if you are staying in the city and don't have transportation.

Visiting the Park

Yosemite National Park (209/372-0200, www.nps.gove/yose) is open daily year-round. Entrance fees are valid for seven days. There are five park entrances, two of which close in winter. The park website provides the best source of comprehensive, well-organized, and seasonal information, along with the downloadable *Yosemite Guide.*

Summer (June-Aug.) is high season and with it comes traffic jams and parking problems—especially in the valley. To avoid the crowds and congestion, park in the lot in the Yosemite Valley visitors center and use the free park shuttles to get around. Tuolumne and Tioga Pass are less congested than the valley, making this a good option in summer.

Come in **spring** (Mar.-May) after the snow melts to see raging waterfalls and wildflowers, or in **autumn** (Sept.-Oct.) when there are fewer crowds.

In **winter** (Nov.-Feb.), park roads may close and crowds are minimal. The valley looks beautiful when blanketed in snow. The Yosemite Ski & Snowboard Area offers a fun and affordable getaway for skiers and snowboarders, or sign up for a full-moon snowshoe hike.

Entrances

The park charges an **entrance fee** (209/372-0200, www.nps.gove/yose, $35 per vehicle, $30 motorcycles, $20 pedestrians/bicycles Apr.-Oct., $20 Nov.-Mar.) at each entrance station; the cost varies depending on season. The Annual Parks Pass ($80, 1 year) is also accepted.

Yosemite National Park is accessible via five park entrances. The westside **Arch Rock** (CA-140) and **Big Oak Flat** (CA-120 West) **Entrance Stations** are usually open year-round. The entrance to **Hetch Hetchy** (off CA-120 West) is only open 8am-7pm. The **South Entrance** (CA-41) near Wawona is open year-round.

One Day in Yosemite Valley

The sights, waterfalls, and hikes here are enough to fill a lifetime, but try to squeeze as much as you can into one day.

Morning

In Yosemite Valley, stop at **Bridalveil Fall** for a photo, then continue to the Valley Visitors Center, where you'll leave your car for the day. At the visitors center, check for any open campsites or tent cabins at Half Dome Village, and confirm your reservations for dinner later at the Majestic Yosemite Hotel. Explore **Yosemite Village,** stopping for picnic supplies and water, then board the Valley Shuttle Bus. The shuttle provides a great free tour of the park, with multiple points to hop on and off.

Afternoon

Choose one of the valley's stellar day hikes (tip: not Half Dome). Take the Valley Shuttle Bus to Happy Isles (shuttle stop 16) and the trailhead for the strenuous **Mist Trail.** This hike is best done in spring when the waterfalls are at their peak, but it's still gorgeous at any time of year. Hike to the Vernal Fall Footbridge (1-2 hours round-trip) and gaze at the Merced River as it spills over Vernal Fall. Hardier souls can continue on the strenuous trail to the top of Vernal Fall (3 hours round-trip) and enjoy a picnic lunch soaking in the stellar views of the valley below. Return via the John Muir Trail back to the Happy Isles trailhead and the Valley Shuttle.

Evening

With all that hiking, you probably built up an appetite. Fortunately, you have reservations at the **Majestic Yosemite Hotel Dining Room.** Change out of your shorts and hiking shoes (and maybe grab a shower at Half Dome Village), and then catch the Valley Shuttle to the Majestic Yosemite Hotel (shuttle stop 3). Grab a drink in the bar and spend some time enjoying the verdant grounds and stellar views of this historic building. After dinner, take the shuttle back to Yosemite Village, where your car awaits, and immediately start planning your return.

Tioga Pass Entrance Station (CA-120 East, summer only) offers seasonal eastern access into Yosemite from US-395 and the Eastern Sierra. Tioga Road closes usually by November, as snow starts to fall, and reopens anywhere from April to June when the road is plowed. Call 209/372-0200 to confirm opening and closing dates.

Yosemite is *very* popular and lines at the entrance stations can be quite long. If you have your heart set on visiting Yosemite Valley, know that parking is extremely limited; it is entirely possible to wait hours to get in only to turn around and exit when there's nowhere to park. If visiting the valley, especially in the height of summer, plan to arrive at the Arch Rock or Big Oak Flat Entrance Station **before 9am** or **after 3pm** for the best chance of securing a spot.

Most of Yosemite's park roads are open in winter, with the exception of Tioga Pass (CA-120) and Glacier Point Road. Chains may be required on park roads at any time.

Visitors Centers

The main visitors center is in Yosemite Valley. The **Valley Visitor Center** (Yosemite Village, off Northside Dr., 209/372-0299, www.nps.gov/yose, 9am-5pm daily) has information, books, maps, films, reservation information, and park rangers who can advise trail conditions.

Reservations

Advance reservations for overnight accommodations are essential. Especially if you are coming from Tuolumne Meadows, it's quite possible to drive a few hours through the park, spend a couple of hours in Yosemite Valley and Mariposa Grove, and then all of the sudden it's dark and you need a place to sleep. Most lodgings, including campsites, fill up quickly—up to months in advance. For reservations and details on lodging within the park, contact Yosemite's concessionaire, **Aramark** (888/413-8869, www.travelyosemite.com, 7am-7pm Mon.-Fri., 8am-7pm Sat.-Sun. MST time). The website allows you to book lodging online, but always confirm prices and other details with a reservation agent.

Yosemite has nine campgrounds managed by **Recreation.gov** (877/444-6777, www.recreation.gov, online reservations available March 15-November), and reservations are absolutely necessary to have during the summer months. Campsite availability is released in one-month blocks, and you can book up to five months in advance. Only two site reservations at a time are permitted per booking. Visit http://go.nps.gov/campground to see a list of all of Yosemite's campgrounds and availability, plus it provides a way to sign up to receive campground updates via email.

When reservations become available in the campgrounds, booking can become competitive. You'll want to be online or start calling first thing in the morning the day that the sites become available. The reservation system works on eastern time.

Information and Services

ATMs are available throughout the park at the Village Store, near the Yosemite Art Center, Degnan's Kitchen, the lobby of Yosemite Valley Lodge, the Half Dome Village, the Big Trees Lodge Store in Wawona, the Crane Flat Store, the Majestic Yosemite Hotel, the Tuolumne Meadows store (seasonal), and the Yosemite Ski & Snowboard Area (seasonal).

Yosemite has several **post offices** ideal for PCT hikers or those staying an extended period of time in the park. These include: Yosemite Village (9017 Village Dr., 800/275-8777, 8:30am-5pm Mon.-Fri., 10am-noon Sat.), inside Yosemite Valley Lodge (12:30pm-2:45pm Mon.-Fri.), in El Portal (5508 Foresta Rd., 800/275-8777, 8:30am-3pm Mon.-Fri.), and in Wawona (Forest Dr., 209/375-6574, 9am-5pm Mon.-Fri.).

Laundry facilities are available at the **Housekeeping Camp** (8am-10pm daily) inside the Half Dome Village complex. Several crowded and limited-stock grocery stores are located in the park: the Yosemite **Village Store** (8am-8pm daily), the **Half Dome Village Gift and Grocery** (8am-8pm daily), the **Yosemite Valley Lodge Gift Shop** (8am-8pm daily), the **Crane Flat Gas Station** (8am-7pm daily May-Oct.), and the **Big Trees Lodge Store** (8am-6pm daily). In summer, you can also get groceries in the **Housekeeping Camp General Store** (8am-6pm daily Apr.-Oct.) and the **Tuolumne Meadows Store** (8am-8pm daily spring-late Sept.).

The **Yosemite Medical Clinic** (9000 Ahwahnee Dr., 209/372-4637, 9am-5pm Mon.-Fri.) in Yosemite Village provides primary and urgent care services.

Getting Around

There are only two gas stations inside Yosemite and they are both on the west side of the park: one in **Crane Flat** and one in **Wawona.** The closest gas station on the east side is in **Lee Vining** at the Mobil/Tioga Gas Mart (summer only) near US-395. On the west side, **El Portal** (CA-140) has gas near the Arch Rock Entrance. There is also a cluster of gas stations in **Mariposa** (CA-140).

There is no gas available within Yosemite Valley. The gas station at Crane Flat is open 24 hours; pay at the pump with a debit or credit card.

If your car breaks down, you can take it to the **Yosemite Village Garage** (9002 Village Dr., off Northside Dr., Yosemite Village, 209/372 1060, 8am-5pm daily, towing 24 hours daily). Because it's the only game in town, expect to pay a high premium for towing and repairs.

Yosemite Valley

Yosemite Valley is usually the first place people go when they visit the park. This 7.5-mile (12 km) scenic valley is the most-visited place in Yosemite, surrounded by granite peaks like El Capitan and Half Dome and with campsites tucked into the dense pines. This is the heart of the park, with a visitors center, theater, art galleries, a museum, several hotels and cafés, and outdoor access to hikes ranging from easy to difficult.

Sights
Valley Visitor Center
After the scenic turnouts through the park, your first stop in Yosemite Valley should be the **Valley Visitor Center** (Yosemite Village, off Northside Dr., 209/372-0299, www.nps.gov/yose, 9am-5pm daily). Here you'll find an interpretive museum describing the geological and human history of Yosemite in addition to information, books, maps, short films in the on-site theater, and park rangers who can advise where to go and what to do. The cluster of buildings includes the **Yosemite Museum** (9am-5pm daily, free) and store, the **Yosemite Theater LIVE,** the **Ansel Adams Gallery** (650/692-3285, www.anseladams.com, 9am-5pm daily), and the all-important public restrooms.

A short, flat walk from the visitors center takes you down to the **Indian Village of Ahwahnee.** Located behind the museum, the village is a reconstructed site

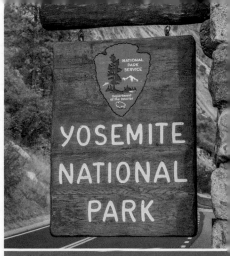

From top to bottom: entrance to Yosemite National Park; El Capitan; Vernal Fall.

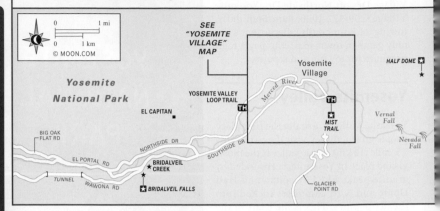

Yosemite Valley

meant to honor the Miwok, the largest Indian tribe in Yosemite Valley. Bark houses, acorn granaries, and ceremonial structures are still intact and are used by descendants of local tribes.

El Capitan

The first natural stone monument you encounter as you enter the valley is **El Capitan** (Northside Rd., west of El Capitan Bridge), a massive hunk of Cretaceous granite that's named for this formation. This craggy rock face rises more than 3,000 feet (900 m) above the valley floor and is accessible two ways: You can take a long hike westward from Upper Yosemite Fall and up the back side of El Capitan, or you can bring your climbing gear and scale the face.

El Cap boasts a reputation as one of the world's seminal big-face **rock climbing** destinations. Scan the rock at night, and you might catch a glimpse of flashlights and lanterns from climbers as they sleep in a nook on the rock's face.

★ Half Dome

One of the most iconic features in Yosemite, and viewable from anywhere in the valley, **Half Dome** (8,844-foot/2,696-meter elevation) rises almost 5,000 feet (1,500 m) above the valley floor. This

natural landmark is easily recognizable from Ansel Adams's many photographs. Half Dome was created by glaciers tens of millions of years ago. Over time, this narrow granite ridge became polished into a smooth dome-like shape, giving it the appearance of half a dome.

Scaling Half Dome is one of Yosemite's most popular activities. A permit (available via lottery) is required for this demanding adventure.

★ Bridalveil Fall

Bridalveil Fall (Southside Dr., past the Hwy. 41 turnoff) is many visitors' first introduction to Yosemite's famed collection of waterfalls. The **Bridalveil Fall Trail** (0.5 mile, 20 minutes, easy) is a pleasant paved walk up to the cascading spray; however, its grade makes it inaccessible to wheelchair users. Although the 620-foot (190 m) waterfall runs year-round, its fine mist sprays most powerfully in the spring, so if you are hiking then expect to get wet!

The trailhead has its own parking area, located west of the main lodge and visitors center complex, so it's one of the first major sights people come to upon entering the park. It's a great first stop as you travel up the valley.

Yosemite Falls

Most of the park's major waterfalls require at least a short hike to the best viewing points. Yosemite Falls, however, is visible from the valley floor near Yosemite Lodge. Three separate waterfalls—Upper Fall, Lower Fall, and middle cascades—work in tandem to create a dramatic formation that, at 2,425 feet (740 m), is considered one of the highest waterfalls in the world.

The **Lower Yosemite Fall Loop** (1 mile, 30 minutes, easy, shuttle stop 6) leads to the base of the fall. Spring and early summer (April-June) are the best times to view the falls; this is when the snow melts and unleashes streams of water down the granite rock faces.

Mirror Lake

Past the end of Southside Drive in Yosemite Valley lies perfectly still **Mirror Lake.** This small pool offers a stunningly clear reflection of the already spectacular views of Tenaya Canyon and surrounding cliffs. A short, level paved **hiking and biking path** circumnavigates the lake (2 mi/3.2 km round-trip, 1 hour, easy). Come in spring or early summer when the lake is more likely to be full, fed by the Tenaya Creek snowmelt. To get there, take the shuttle to stop 17 and the start of the trailhead.

Recreation
Hiking

Yosemite Valley is the perfect place to take a short day hike, with many places to stop and revel in the valley's beauty. Hiking maps are available at the Valley Visitors Center (Yosemite Valley at Valley Village, Northside Dr.). Ask the rangers about trail conditions and be sure to bring your map—and plenty of water—on the trail with you.

In addition to the easy hikes to **Bridalveil Fall** (0.5 mile, 20 minutes) and **Mirror Lake** (2 mi/3.2 km, 1 hour, easy, shuttle stop 17), several other valley hikes provide a good sample of what's available in Yosemite—lots of trails wind through this region. Note that the valley trails are very popular, so it's unlikely you'll be alone.

Cook's Meadow

The **Cook's Meadow Loop** (1 mi/1.6 km, 30 minutes, easy, shuttle stop 5 or 9) offers a short walk through the heart of the valley. Look up to observe Ansel Adams's famous view of Half Dome from **Sentinel Bridge,** where you'll notice the Royal Arches and Glacier Point. You can also extend this hike a bit by doing the whole **Sentinel-Cook's Meadow Loop.** By circling both meadows instead of just one, you'll make the whole trip about 2.5 miles (4 km) and increase the number of angles for your photo ops. Trail signs and plenty of other hikers make it easy to find the turns.

Yosemite Valley Loop

The **Yosemite Valley Loop Trail** (Northside Dr. and Southside Dr.) is a paved path that parallels much of the park road. The moderate **half loop** (7.2 mi/11.6 km, 3 hours, easy, shuttle stop 6) traverses the El Capitan Bridge, following the path of many old wagon roads and historical trails. The **full loop** (11.5 mi/18.5 km, 6 hours, moderate) is a great and moderate day hike. You'll see the most beautiful parts of the valley while escaping the crowded roads. Before hiking any part of the loop, talk to a ranger at the visitors center about the status of the trail; the route is not entirely clear on the map.

Lower Yosemite Fall

If you're staying at Yosemite Valley Lodge and want an easy, gentle walk with a great view, take the **Lower Yosemite Fall Loop** (1 mi/1.6 km, 30 minutes, easy, shuttle stop 6). Enjoy the wondrous views of both Upper and Lower Yosemite Falls, complete with a cooling spray. If you can, hike this trail in the spring or early summer, when the flow of the falls is at its peak.

This easy trail works well for families with children who love the water.

Upper Yosemite Fall

Naturally, some of the more challenging hikes in Yosemite Valley are also the most rewarding. The strenuous trek up to **Upper Yosemite Fall** (7.2 mi/11.6 km, 6-8 hours, strenuous, shuttle stop 7) starts near Camp 4 on the **Valley Loop Trail,** but you can also get there from the Upper Yosemite Fall trailhead or walk from Lower Yosemite Fall. The trail to the falls gets steep right away as you climb 2,700 vertical feet (825 m) in 3 miles (4.8 km), following switchbacks all the way to the top.

In a mile, you'll reach **Columbia Rock,** with spectacular views of Sentinel Rock, Half Dome, and the valley. In another 0.5 mile, the Upper Fall comes into view. At the top of the trail, rewarding views astonish as you gaze down over the falls and across the valley, the distant grassy meadows far below.

Plan all day for this hike and bring plenty of water and snacks to replenish your energy for the tricky climb down. This trail is well marked and well trodden, and the park has done a great job of making the steep parts passable with stone steps, switchbacks, and some railings. But much of the trail tends to be wet and slippery, so take it slow and steady.

★ Mist Trail

Starting at the Happy Isles Nature Center (shuttle stop 16), the moderate-strenuous Mist Trail leads first to **Vernal Fall** (2.4 mi/3.9 km, 3 hours, moderate) over steep, slick granite—including more than 600 stairs. Your reward is the stellar view of the valley below and the chance to relax on the flat granite boulders along the Merced River. This is a good place to stop for lunch before returning the same way.

For acclimated hikers looking for a Stairmaster workout, an option is to follow another steep and strenuous 1.5-2 miles (2.4-3.2 km) of switchbacks to the

Half Dome

top of **Nevada Fall** (5.4 mi/8.7 km, 5-6 hours, difficult) and return via the John Muir Trail. Plan six hours for this hike, with a 2,000-foot (600 m) elevation gain, and consider taking a lightweight rain jacket since this aptly named trail gives hikers a shower in the spring and early summer months.

The Mist Trail is closed in winter due to ice and snow and can be dangerous in the spring months when the river is at its peak; every year, hikers are lost in the waters here. Exercise caution, stay well behind the safety railings, and obey all trail signage.

Half Dome

The most famous climb in Yosemite Valley is to the top of monumental **Half Dome** (14-16 mi/22.5-26 km, 10-12 hours, difficult, May-Oct. by permit only, shuttle stop 16). With a 4,800-foot (1,450 m) elevation gain, this arduous, all-day hike is not for the faint of heart—nor is it for

small children, those with mobility issues, or anyone remotely out of shape.

Plan a sunrise start from Happy Isles (shuttle stop 16) for this all-day hike. Follow the Mist Trail for 2.7 miles (4.3 km) to Nevada Fall, then follow the signs to Half Dome for the next 4.4 miles (7.1 km). The last 400 feet (120 m) climb an almost completely vertical granite face to the top of the dome. Use the cables (in place late May-mid-Oct.) to pull yourself up. Once you stagger to the top, you'll find an expanse of stone on which to rest and enjoy the scenery.

A **permit** (877/444-6777, www.recreation.gov, late May-early Oct., $16) is required when the cables are up, and quotas are strictly enforced. Permits are available via an annual lottery that begins in March. There is a trail quota of 300 hikers per day (255 day hikers, 75 backpackers). Daily lotteries are held for up to 50 day hiking permits (apply two days in advance). The permit rules are complex and must be followed exactly; check the park website (www.nps.gov) for current updates.

Hikers should be mentally and physically prepared for this long and treacherous challenge. Wear hiking shoes that have been broken in and bring a pack with water (1 gallon per person), food, a topo map and compass, a headlamp or flashlight (with batteries), gloves, a hat, and a bag for trash. Check weather conditions and sunrise and sunset times before you hike. The park will post when the trail is closed or unsafe; heed conditions and turn back. Continuing on can result in a life-threatening situation for you and those who have to rescue you. Altitude sickness may affect some hikers; the only way to recover is to hike back down.

For more information, contact the park office (209/372-0826, 9am-noon and 1pm-4:30pm Mon.-Fri., Mar.-early Oct.).

Biking

Biking is a great way to get out of the car, off the crowded roads, and to breathe in

Wilderness Permits

A **wilderness permit** ($10 for fees) allows access to Yosemite's backcountry trails and campsites in the park. Trailhead quotas are enforced, with some permits available in advance and a smaller number of permits available first-come, first-served.

Advance **reservations** (www.nps.gov) for permits are accepted online 24 weeks before the requested hike date. May through October, **first-come, first-served permits** are available at 11am the day prior to your intended hike. November through April, backpackers may self-register for permits at most wilderness centers:

♦ **Yosemite Valley Wilderness Center** (daily May-Oct.) is in Yosemite Village. November to April, pick up permits at the Valley Visitor Center (9am-5pm daily).

♦ **Tuolumne Meadows Wilderness Center** (late May-mid-Oct.) is off Tioga Pass Road. Mid-October to May, self-register at the Tuolumne Meadows Ranger Station.

♦ **Big Oak Flat Information Station** (May-Oct.) is next to the Big Oak Flat Entrance on CA-120. November to April, permits are located on the porch for self-registration.

♦ **Wawona Visitor Center at Hill's Studio** (May-Oct.) is in the south of the park. November to April, permits are located on the porch for self-registration.

♦ **Hetch Hetchy Entrance Station** (8am-5pm daily year-round) issues permits until 5pm daily.

Bear-proof canisters are required in Yosemite's backcountry and are available to rent ($5 for 2 weeks, $95 security deposit required). For more information, contact a **wilderness ranger** (209/372-0826, 9am-noon and 1:30pm-4:30pm Mon.-Fri., Mar.-early Oct.).

the fresh air and explore Yosemite at a quicker-than-walking (and sometimes even quicker than driving) pace. The 12 miles (19.5 km) of paved trails within the valley are mostly flat; you can also ride alongside the main roads.

Bike rentals ($12 per hour, $34 per day, electric scooters $30 per day) are available at Yosemite Valley Lodge (209/372-1208, 10am-4pm, weather dependent, shuttle stop 8) and at the Half Dome Village kiosk (209/372-8323, shuttle stop 13) next to the front office. Helmet rentals are also available.

Ice-Skating

Half Dome Village (end of Southside Dr., 209/372-8333, www.travelyosemite.com, 3:30pm-6pm and 7pm-9:30pm Mon.-Fri., noon-2:30pm, 3:30pm-6pm, and 7pm-9:30pm Sat.-Sun., 8:30am-11am holidays mid-Nov.-Mar.; adults $10, children $9-10, rentals $4) has an ice-skating rink in winter that's been in operation since 1928. Tickets provide up to two hours of rink use, or you can just sit by the warm fire pit and gaze up at Half Dome.

Rock Climbing

The rock climbing at Yosemite is some of the best in the world. **El Capitan,** the face of **Half Dome,** and **Sentinel Dome** in the high country are challenges that draw climbers from all over. If you plan to climb one of these monuments, check with the Yosemite park rangers and the Mountaineering School well in advance for necessary information and permits.

Many of the spectacular ascents are not beginners' climbs. The right place to start climbing in Yosemite is at the **Yosemite**

Yosemite at Night

Yosemite National Park does not roll up its meadows and trails at sunset. In fact, some aspects of the park come alive only at nightfall. Many of the animals that live in the park are crepuscular by nature—they're most active in the twilight hours of dawn and dusk. Take a quiet stroll in the park early in the morning or as nightfall approaches and you're likely to see more wildlife than you'll run into during the day.

If you prefer a guided tour, join the **Night Prowl** (888/413-8869, www.travelyosemite.com, 90 minutes, $10). This guided tour takes you along easy, unpaved trails within the valley where interpretive naturalists share interesting facts about the valley's nocturnal inhabitants. Night Prowl takes place once or twice a week at various times and places, and is fun for both children and adults. Purchase tickets at any activity desk in Yosemite, book your tickets online, or call 888/413-8869 to make reservations. Tours meet at the Majestic Yosemite Hotel back lawn at 8:30pm.

If stargazing is more your thing, budding astronomers should check out **Starry Night Skies** (888/413-8869, www.travelyosemite.com, $10). Equally suited for beginners and experienced stargazers, this one-hour program takes you out to the meadows to view the stars and moon in all of their glory. You'll learn about constellations, comets, and meteors and enjoy the myths and legends about the night sky. Starry Night Skies happens several times weekly and is held in Yosemite Valley.

Yosemite's interpretive naturalists also host evening bus tours to Glacier Point for the four-hour **Glacier Point Starry Night Skies Over Yosemite** (888/413-8869, www.travelyosemite.com, Sun.-Thurs. June-Sept., $64 adults, $55 children 5-12). A bus departs Yosemite Valley at 7pm for the hour-long drive to Glacier Point, where stargazers examine the night sky with bonus views of the valley below.

Relaxing evening programs are also available for families tired after a long day around the park. **Fireside Storytelling** (Majestic Yosemite Hotel, Oct.-Feb., free) invites guests to tell stories around the fireplace inside the Majestic Yosemite Hotel Great Lounge. Take refuge from the cold and listen to great tales in a comfortable environment. Check the *Yosemite Guide* for more information.

In summer, free one-hour evening presentations are held outside at the Yosemite Valley Lodge and Half Dome Village amphitheaters (in winter, they're held in the Yosemite Valley Lodge). The **Yosemite Theater** (Yosemite Valley Visitor Center, 415/434-1782, www.yosemiteconservancy.org, Apr.-Oct., $10 adults, children 12 and under free) hosts entertaining shows about climbing and Yosemite's search and rescue, as well as educational films about Florence Hutchings (the first white woman born in the valley) and the John Muir series starring Yosemite's resident actor Lee Stetson. Check the copy of *Yosemite Guide* for a list of what shows are playing.

Mountaineering School & Guide Service (209/372-8344, www.travelyosemite.com, $172-215 lessons, $360-6,032 per person for guided climbs). The "Welcome to the Rock" classes cater to beginners; future climbers can learn the basics, then rappel 60-foot heights. Guided climbs out of Yosemite Valley are also available, including a guided climb of El Capitan ($6,032) or Half Dome ($4,784). The school offers guided hikes and backpacking trips, cross-country ski lessons, and overnight ski hut trips to Glacier Point in winter. Climbing equipment is also available for rent.

Food
Casual Dining
For casual food options, head to Yosemite Village. **The Loft at Degnan's** (9015 Village Dr., Yosemite Valley, 2pm-8pm Fri.-Sat. summer, $8-11) serves Mexican food, rice bowls, and pizza. **Degnan's Kitchen** (209/372-1002, 7am-6pm daily year-round, $8-11) offers an array of artisan sandwiches, pizzas, and a full-service

bakery, a coffee shop, and a soda fountain. The Grinder sandwich is filled with salami, pepperoni, ham, mixed greens, and cheese with an olive tapenade—it's the perfect meal after a strenuous hike. The **Village Grill** (11am-6pm daily late Mar.-early Oct., $8-15) serves standard burgers and tends to be more crowded than Degnan's.

Half Dome Village is the place to go for relatively cheap fast food (this is also where the hard-core hikers and climbers hang out). The **Half Dome Village Pavilion** (9012 Curry Village Dr., 209/372-8303, 7am-10am and 5:30pm-8pm daily late Mar.-mid-Oct.) serves breakfast ($3-11) and dinner ($10-16). Other options include the **Coffee Corner** (6:30am-11am daily), the **Half Dome Village Bar** (11am-10pm daily late Mar.-mid-Oct.), **Pizza Patio** (11am-10pm daily mid-Mar.-Nov.), and the **Meadow Grill** (11am-8pm daily mid-Apr.-early Sept., $5-7).

The **Base Camp Eatery** (Yosemite Valley Lodge, 6:30am-8pm daily, $8-17) is a food court offering Italian food, classic American fare, and noodle bowls in a cafeteria-style setting. A Starbucks counter (7am-5pm daily) is also available. A casual bar menu is available at the **Mountain Room Lounge** (4:30pm-10pm Mon.-Thurs., 4:30pm-11pm Fri., noon-11pm Sat., noon-10pm Sun., $4-21), immediately across from the Mountain Room Restaurant.

Fine Dining

The ★ **Majestic Yosemite Hotel Dining Room** (9013 Village Dr., 209/372-1489, www.travelyosemite.com, 7am-10am, 11:30am-2pm, 5:30pm-8:30pm Fri.-Sat., 7am-2pm Sun., $29-50) enjoys a reputation for fine cuisine that stretches back to 1927. The grand dining room features expansive 34-foot ceilings with wrought-iron chandeliers while floor-to-ceiling windows frame stellar views. The restaurant serves three meals daily, with an outstanding dinner menu. The California

cuisine mirrors that of top-tier San Francisco restaurants (with a price tag to match). Reservations are recommended for all meals, though it's possible to walk in for breakfast and lunch. A dress code is required for dinner (long pants and a collared shirt for men, a dress, long skirt, or dress pants and blouse for women).

At the other side of the valley, you can enjoy a spectacular view of Yosemite Falls from the **Mountain Room Restaurant** (Yosemite Valley Lodge, 209/372-1499, 5pm-9pm daily year-round, $21-40). The glass atrium lets every table take in the view. Signature entrées include campfire trout, grilled portobello mushroom, and roasted free-range chicken. Several varieties of high-end steaks are also on offer.

Accommodations

All lodgings, including campsites, fill up quickly—up to months in advance. In Yosemite Valley, **Aramark** (888/413-8869, www.travelyosemite.com) handles reservations for most of the lodgings in the park, including Half Dome Village, Housekeeping Camp, Yosemite Valley Lodge, and the Majestic Yosemite Hotel.

Half Dome Village

Half Dome Village (888/413-8869, www.travelyosemite.com, mid-Mar.-Nov. and mid-Dec.-Jan.) offers some of the oldest lodgings in the park. Often referred to as Curry Village, this sprawling array of wood-sided and canvas-tent cabins was originally created in 1899 to provide affordable lodging for visitors. At Half Dome Village, you can rent a tent cabin or a wood cabin, with or without heat and with or without a private bath. You can also reserve a motel room. Half Dome Village has hot water showers (fee) and several eateries. Half Dome Village lodgings have daily housekeeping service, fresh towels and extra blankets (by request), but no TVs or telephones. Accommodations fill quickly in summer; make reservations months in advance if

Yosemite Village

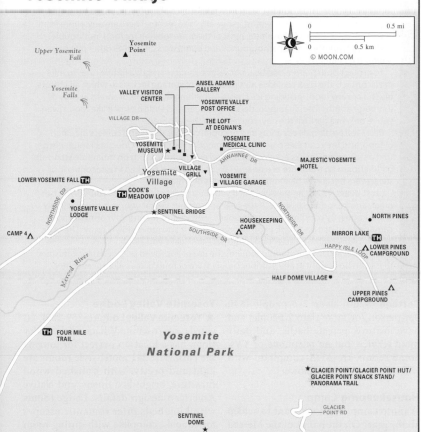

0   0.5 mi
0   0.5 km

© MOON.COM

Upper Yosemite Fall

Yosemite Point

Yosemite Falls

ANSEL ADAMS GALLERY

VALLEY VISITOR CENTER

YOSEMITE VALLEY POST OFFICE

VILLAGE DR

THE LOFT AT DEGNAN'S

YOSEMITE MUSEUM

YOSEMITE MEDICAL CLINIC

AHWAHNEE DR

MAJESTIC YOSEMITE HOTEL

Yosemite Village

VILLAGE GRILL

YOSEMITE VILLAGE GARAGE

LOWER YOSEMITE FALL TH

NORTHSIDE DR

COOK'S MEADOW LOOP TH

YOSEMITE VALLEY LODGE

SENTINEL BRIDGE

HOUSEKEEPING CAMP

NORTH PINES

SOUTHSIDE DR

NORTHSIDE DR

MIRROR LAKE

CAMP 4

Merced River

HAPPY ISLE LOOP

LOWER PINES CAMPGROUND TH

HALF DOME VILLAGE

UPPER PINES CAMPGROUND

FOUR MILE TRAIL TH

Yosemite National Park

GLACIER POINT/GLACIER POINT HUT/ GLACIER POINT SNACK STAND/ PANORAMA TRAIL

GLACIER POINT RD

SENTINEL DOME

you're planning a trip during the busy season.

The 46 **Yosemite cabins** ($218) are hard to come by, and they're usually booked far in advance. These wood structures include one or two double beds (some have a double and a single) that sleep up to four ($14 per person for more than 4 people). Cabins have private baths, electricity, decks or patios, and maid service. There are 14 cabins without private baths; these share a central shower complex instead.

In addition, there are 403 non-heated and heated **canvas tent cabins** ($90-163), which are the most affordable option. These small, wood-frame, canvas-covered structures sleep 2-4 people in a combination of single and double cot beds ($12-17 per person for more than 2 people). Sheets, blankets, and pillows are provided. Bear-proof lockers are available outside each tent cabin. Shared showers and restrooms are found within Half Dome Village. The few **heated tent cabins** (late Sept.-mid-May, $120-163) are available on a limited basis.

The 18 rooms in the **Stoneman**

Bears and Yosemite

Although grizzlies have not been seen in California since 1922, the smaller but still impressive black bears are plentiful, especially in Yosemite. There are anywhere from 300 to 500 black bears in Yosemite; most of them are looking for food, not trouble. This often leads them into campgrounds and dumpsters, as well as other places frequented by humans.

To protect both people and bears, Yosemite rangers strictly enforce rules to minimize contact. The park provides metal bear-proof storage lockers in which all visitors must store any food, including ice chests—anything that looks or smells like food. (Garbage, toothpaste, shampoo, deodorant, beer, and soda *all* smell like food.) Even if you're only in a park for the day, you must use these lockers.

Bears will break open car doors and pry open camper shells and coolers in search of food, and they can cause *significant damage to your vehicle.* One park ranger even told a story of one backpacker who camped overnight, leaving his inflatable stand-up paddleboard on the shore of a nearby lake. It must have smelled like coconut oil or sunscreen, because a bear ripped it to shreds overnight.

Most bears are not aggressive, but if you see a bear stay at least *50 yards away,* be quiet, and keep your distance. If the bear approaches you or your campsite, actively discourage it by banging on pots and pans, yelling, and waving your arms. If you're carrying food or a backpack or other parcel, drop it and move slowly away. The bear will probably switch its attention to the pack and leave you alone.

In the backcountry, Yosemite requires the use of approved bear-resistant canisters; these can be bought at any outdoor supply store or rented at a wilderness center.

Cottage ($260) sleep 2-6 people ($40 per person for more than 2 people) and have heating, private baths, and daily maid service, but no telephone or TVs. Some rooms are ADA-compliant with wheelchair-accessible showers.

Housekeeping Camp

Want to camp, but don't want to schlep all the gear? On the banks of the Merced River, the tent cabins at **Housekeeping Camp** (mid-Apr.-mid-Oct., $120) have their own sandy river beach for playing and sunbathing. Cabins have cement walls, white canvas roofs, and a white canvas curtain that separates the bedroom from the covered patio that doubles as a dining room. Every cabin has a double bed plus two bunks (with room for two additional cots), a bear-proof food container, an outdoor fire ring, two lights, and two electrical outlets. No maid service is provided, but you won't miss it as you sit outside watching the sunset over Yosemite Valley.

Yosemite Valley Lodge

★ **Yosemite Valley Lodge** ($269-289), situated near Yosemite Village on the valley floor, has a location perfect for touring the park. The 241 motel-style rooms are light and pretty, with polished wood furniture, bright bed linens, and Native American design details. Lodge rooms with king beds offer romantic escapes for couples, complete with dining room tables and balconies overlooking the valley. There are also four family rooms with a king bed and a bunk bed for the kids. Enjoy the pool in the summer and use the free shuttle to get around the valley. The amphitheater hosts nature programs and movies. The lodge is central to the Yosemite shuttle system and has a post office, an ATM, the on-site **Mountain Room Restaurant** (209/372-1499, 5pm-9pm daily year-round, $21-40), the **Mountain Room Lounge** (4:30pm-10pm Mon.-Thurs., 4:30pm-11pm Fri., noon-11pm Sat., noon-10pm Sun., $4-21), and the **Base Camp Eatery** (6:30am-8pm daily, $8-17).

Majestic Yosemite Hotel

Built as a luxury hotel in the early 1900s, the ★ **Majestic Yosemite Hotel** ($376-589) lives up to its reputation with a gorgeous stone facade, striking stone fireplaces, and soaring ceilings in the common rooms. The guest rooms feature recycled and repurposed furnishings with modern yet rustic undertones with California Mission influences. The Majestic Yosemite Hotel has about two dozen cottages and close to 100 hotel rooms in the main building. All rooms come with either one king bed or two doubles; rooms in the main hotel may be combined with a parlor to make a suite. The cottages include small stone patios as well as TVs, telephones, small refrigerators, and private baths. An outdoor heated swimming pool is available for guests.

A bonus is the on-site **Majestic Yosemite Hotel Dining Room** (7am-10am, 11:30am-2pm, 5:30pm-8:30pm Mon.-Sat., 7am-2pm, 5:30pm-8:30pm Sun., $29-50), which serves breakfast (including a famous Sunday brunch), lunch, and dinner. Reservations are highly recommended (call 209/372-1489 9am-8pm).

Camping

There are 13 campgrounds in Yosemite National Park and they are all popular. The valley campgrounds include Upper Pines, Lower Pines, and North Pines, all of which require **reservations** (209/372-8502 for campground information, 8:30am-4:30pm daily year-round, 877/444-6777 reservations, www.recreation.gov) up to five months in advance. Campground reservations in Yosemite Valley are very competitive. If you need a reservation for a specific day, get up at 7am (PST) five months before the start date of your trip to attempt booking a reservation.

If you don't have a campsite reservation, call the **campground status line** (209/372-0266) for a recording of what's

From top to bottom: Half Dome Village; the Majestic Yosemite Hotel; Glacier Point.

available that day. Or try one of the first-come, first-served campgrounds, but get there early as they all fill fast.

Showers are available at **Half Dome Village** (24 hours daily year-round, fee) and **Housekeeping Camp** (7am-10pm daily Apr.-Oct., fee).

Leashed pets are permitted in the campgrounds, but not on trails.

Lower Pines

Lower Pines (73 sites, Apr.-Oct., $26-36) sits across from Half Dome Village. Sites accommodate tents and RVs (up to 40 feet) and include fire rings, picnic tables, a bear-proof food locker, water, flush toilets—and very little privacy. Camping supplies and showers (fee) are close by at Half Dome Village. The Mirror Lake and Half Dome trailheads are nearby. Reservations are required and are available up to five months in advance.

Upper Pines

Upper Pines (235 sites, year-round, $26) is the largest campground in the valley. It lies immediately southwest of Lower Pines and is encircled by the park road. Sites accommodate tents and RVs (up to 35 feet, no hookups) and include fire rings, picnic tables, a bear-proof food locker, water, and flush toilets. Supplies and showers (fee) are available in Half Dome Village. Reservations are required and available up to five months in advance.

North Pines

Set along the Merced River and Tenaya Creek, **North Pines** (79 sites, Apr.-early Nov., $26) offers slightly more privacy than its Upper and Lower Pines siblings. Sites accommodate tents and RVs (up to 40 feet) and include fire rings, picnic tables, a bear-proof food locker, water, and flush toilets. Supplies and showers (fee) are available in Half Dome Village.

Camp 4

Camp 4 walk-in tent sites (35 sites, first-come, first-served, year-round, $6 pp) include fire pits, picnic tables, and a shared bear-proof food locker. Each site holds six people, so you may end up sharing with another party. A free parking permit is required. No RVs or trailers are allowed. Restrooms with water and flush toilets are nearby. Showers (fee) are at Half Dome Village and supplies are at Yosemite Valley Lodge.

To grab a site, plan to wait in line at the campground kiosk well before the ranger arrives at 8:30am. Snow camping is permitted in winter with self-registration.

Getting Around

Driving in Yosemite Valley—especially in summer and on weekends—can be slow and stressful. Plan to arrive in the park early (before 9am) and park your car in one of the Village lots, then use the free shuttle buses to get around.

The **Yosemite Valley shuttle** (209/372-0000, 7am-10pm daily year-round, free) runs every 10-20 minutes, stopping near almost all lodging options, stores, the visitors center, campgrounds, and major sights and vistas. Check the map in the *Yosemite Guide* for a list of numbered shuttle stops.

Glacier Point

There's more to Yosemite than what can be seen from the valley floor. For a different perspective of the familiar formations and falls, drive up Glacier Point Road to Glacier Point (16 mi/26 km from Chinquapin junction). At the end of the road is an easy, paved trail (wheelchair accessible) to the actual point—the vista down into Yosemite Valley is stunning. The first part of Glacier Point Road remains open year-round (except when storms make it temporarily impassable) to allow access to the Yosemite Ski & Snowboard Area, but chains may be required.

In summer, park rangers host evening programs at Glacier Point. **Glacier Point Starry Night Skies** (888/413-8869, www.travelyosemite.com, Sun.-Thurs., June-Sept., $64 adults, children 5-12 $55) exposes stargazers to incredible views of Yosemite's magnificent features over a light pollution-free sky. Check the *Yosemite Guide* for details.

Getting There

Glacier Point is in the southwestern quadrant of the park, about an hour's drive from Yosemite Valley. From the Valley Visitor Center, drive 14 miles (22.5 km) south to Chinquapin junction, and then make a left turn onto Glacier Point Road. Drive another 16 miles (26 km) to the end of the road and park in the lot on the left.

Glacier Point Road closes approximately November-May. You can get as far as Yosemite Ski & Snowboard Area (5 mi/8 km) whenever the ski resort is open (usually Dec.-Mar.). Chains or four-wheel drive and snow tires may be required at any time.

Recreation

★ **Yosemite Ski & Snowboard Area**
The **Yosemite Ski & Snowboard Area** (Glacier Point Rd., 5 mi/8 km east of Chinquapin turnoff, 209/372-8430, www.travelyosemite.com, 9am-4pm daily mid-Dec.-mid-Mar.) is a favorite winter destination in Yosemite. This small resort bustles in winter with downhill and cross-country skiers, ice-skaters, and sleds.

Downhill Skiing

The downhill skiing here is perfect for beginner and intermediate levels, with 35 percent beginner terrain and 50 percent intermediate (advanced skiers may be a little bored). There is one triple chair, three double chairlifts, and one tow rope with access to 10 ski runs. **Lift tickets** range $52-59 for adults and $15-34 for children age 7-17.

Downhill ski **lessons** ($70-102) are available and include equipment rental and lift ticket. Ski and snowboard **rentals** ($29-37 adults, children age 12 and under $21-27) are also available.

Cross-Country Skiing

The Yosemite Ski & Snowboard Area offers 25 miles (40 km) of groomed track and 90 miles (145 km) of marked trails for cross-country skiing, but the park has more than 800 miles (1,300 km) of trails, nearly all of which are skiable when the snow is deep.

The **Cross-Country Ski School** (888/413-8869, www.travelyosemite.com, adults $28, under age 13 $21-23) rents telemark skis and camping accessories, and offers guided cross-country ski tours. Groomed trails lead from Yosemite Ski & Snowboard Area to Glacier Point. The wide, flat path is well maintained, accessible to beginners and experts alike.

Cross-country ski **lessons** ($45-55) are available; equipment is included. Guided overnight trips include a stay at **Glacier Point Hut** (888/413-8869, www.travelyosemite.com, $350-550, 3-person min.) and include your guide, all meals, and a roof over your head; bring your own sleeping gear. The 21-mile (34-km) round-trip trek takes 10 hours for experienced cross-country skiers to complete.

Guided Snowshoe Hikes

Yosemite Mountaineering School guides lead the **Adventure Snowshoe Hike to Dewey Point** (6.5 hours, 9am-3pm Sun. and Wed. mid-Dec.-mid-Mar., $50-60), which leads through a winter wonderland past meadows and pines to the valley rim at Dewey Point, where visitors take in the snowcapped views of Half Dome, El Capitan, and the Sierra Nevada. **Reservations** (209/372-1240 or 209/372-8444, www.travelyosemite.com) are required. Children must be at least 12 years old. Trips meet at the Yosemite Ski & Snowboard Area Nordic Center and are limited to groups of 10 people.

The **Full Moon Snowshoe Walk** (7pm-9pm select days Jan.-Feb., $35, snowshoes included) is an adventure to remember. These two-hour treks into the snowy high country are led by expert guides. You'll learn about backpacking in winter, wildlife activity, and the unique environment surrounding the Yosemite Ski & Snowboard Area. **Reservations** (Yosemite Valley Lodge, 209/372-1240) are recommended. Trips meet at the Yosemite Ski & Snowboard Area Nordic Center. Check the *Yosemite Guide* for dates and times.

Hiking

If you love the thrill of heights, head up Glacier Point Road and take a hike up to or along one of the spectacular and slightly scary granite cliffs. Hikes in this area run from quite easy to rigorous, but many of the cliffside trails aren't appropriate for rambunctious children.

Taft Point and the Fissures

Taft Point and The Fissures (2.2 mi/3.5 km round-trip, 2 hours) is a moderate walk past some unusual granite formations (the Fissures) to a magnificent vista at Taft Point. Stay behind the (rickety) guardrails at this precarious precipice to

enjoy the valley views 2,000 feet (600 m) below. The elevation gain from the trailhead to the point is only about 200 feet.

The Sentinel Dome/Taft Point trailhead is just a few miles east of the Bridalveil Creek campground entrance near the end of Glacier Point Road.

Sentinel Dome

The hike to **Sentinel Dome** (1.8 mi/2.9 km round-trip, 2 hours) is a surprisingly easy walk through pines and flower-filled meadows; the only steep part is climbing the dome at the end of the trail. The views at the top are worth the effort. On a clear day, you can see from Yosemite Valley to the High Sierra and even catch a glimpse of Mount Diablo to the west. Exercise caution on the granite dome, as there are no guardrails.

The trailhead is southwest of the end of Glacier Point Road, 6 miles (9.5 km) east of the Bridalveil Creek Campground road.

Four Mile Trail

If you're looking for a challenging hike—and the most spectacular view of Yosemite Falls—take the misnamed **Four Mile Trail** (4.8 mi/7.7 km one-way, 3-4 hours, difficult) from Glacier Point down to Yosemite Village. The steep descent affords a series of views of Yosemite Falls and Yosemite Valley that grow more spectacular with each switchback. Start this hike early (it's unshaded and can get hot), bring plenty of water, and practice careful footing on the path.

One way to enjoy this hike in summer is by reserving a seat on the **Glacier Point Tour** bus (888/413-8869, www.travelyosemite.com, 8:30am-1:30pm daily late May-Oct., adults $26 one-way, children age 5-12 $17 one-way, children under 5 free). Leave your car in Yosemite Valley, take the tour bus to Glacier Point, and then hike back down to the valley. Tours depart from Yosemite Valley Lodge; purchase tickets in advance.

Panorama Trail

If you like a challenge, and the views that go with it, the difficult **Panorama Trail** (8.3 mi/13.4 km one-way, 6-8 hours) runs all the way from Glacier Point to Yosemite Valley with 4,000 feet (1,200 m) of elevation change. The trailhead is located at Glacier Point; the road is usually open late May-September.

From the Panorama Trailhead, the trail travels 2 miles (3.2 km) to a close-up of Illilouette Fall before crossing Illilouette Creek to walk along Panorama Cliff. In about a half mile, an unmarked turnoff leads to Panorama Point. (The sheer drop-off at the point and no guardrails mean this detour is not for everyone!) Those who brave it will be rewarded with views of Half Dome, the Mist Trail, Upper and Lower Yosemite Falls, and a sweeping vista of the eastern side of the valley. Return to the main trail and continue until mile 6, where you turn left to join the Mist Trail. Follow the Mist Trail down past Nevada and Vernal Falls.

In summer, reserve a seat on the **Glacier Point Tour** bus (888/413-8869, www.travelyosemite.com, 8:30am-1:30pm daily late May-Oct., adults $26 one-way, children age 5-12 $17 one-way, children under 5 free). Leave your car in Yosemite Valley, take the tour bus to Glacier Point, and then hike back down to the valley. Tours depart from Yosemite Valley Lodge; purchase tickets in advance.

Ostrander Lake

For a long, high-elevation hike, head to **Ostrander Lake** (11.4 mi/20 km round-trip, 8-10 hours). The lake is a lovely patch of clear, shining water surrounded by granite boulders and picturesque pine trees. This hike can take all day at a relaxed pace, especially June-July when wildflowers bloom along the trail. Start this trail in the morning and pack a picnic lunch to enjoy beside the serene water (bring bug repellent).

A winter option is to cross-country ski to the lake and stay overnight at the **ski hut** (209/379-2317, www.yosemiteconservancy.org, mid-Dec.-Mar., reservations required, $30).

The trailhead is approximately 1.5 miles (2.4 km) past Bridalveil Creek Road on Glacier Point Road.

Food and Accommodations

If you're planning an extended stay at Yosemite, rent a condo or house through the **Yosemite West Condominiums** (7403 Yosemite Park Way, 888/967-3648, $269-625), located off Wawona/Henness Ridge Roads. Studio and loft condos sleep 2-6 and have full kitchens and access to amenities. Luxury suites are one-bedroom apartments with full kitchens, hot tubs, wood-burning fireplaces, and plenty of amenities. The Tioga Logs and Scenic Wonders duplexes sleep up to 16 people, perfect for a family reunion.

The **Glacier Point Snack Stand** (end of Glacier Point Rd., 9am-5pm daily late May-Oct.) sells snacks in summer only.

Camping

Bridalveil Creek (110 sites, first-come, first-served, July-early Sept., $18) is located along Bridalveil Creek, making for an appealing spot. Sites accommodate tents and RVs (up to 35 feet) and include fire pits, picnic tables, and a shared bear-proof food locker. A bathroom with drinking water and flush toilets is nearby.

In addition, there are three equestrian campsites ($30) and two group sites ($50). Reservations (877/444-6777, www.recreation.gov) are required for these sites. RVs and trailers are not permitted.

The campground is midway along Glacier Point Road, 8 miles (13 km) east of Chinquapin junction. It's a 45-minute drive from the valley.

Getting Around

The **Glacier Point Tour** bus (888/413-8869, www.travelyosemite.com, 8:30am-1:30pm daily late May-Oct., adults $26 one-way, children age 5-12 $17 one-way, children under 5 free; round-trip $52 adults, $33 children age 5-12; children under 5 free) operates four-hour trips from Yosemite Valley to Glacier Point and back. Tickets can be purchased by phone or in person at the Yosemite Valley Lodge activity desk.

In winter, **Yosemite Ski & Snowboard Area** (July-early Sept., hours vary seasonally Dec.-Mar., free) offers a morning shuttle bus from Yosemite Valley to the Yosemite Ski & Snowboard Area. Shuttles return to the valley in the afternoon.

Wawona

Wawona is home to the giant sequoias of Mariposa Grove, the historic Big Trees Lodge, which opened in 1879, and the Pioneer Yosemite History Center. The lodge houses a popular restaurant and a store and there's a golf course nearby.

Getting There

From the park's South Entrance, drive 4 miles (6.4 km) north on CA-41 (Wawona Rd.) to Wawona. From Wawona, it's another 1.5 hours to Yosemite Valley.

Sights
Wawona Visitor Center at Hill's Studio

The **Wawona Visitor Center at Hill's Studio** (209/372-0200, 8:30am-5pm daily May-Oct.) is perfect for gathering information and picking up wilderness permits. The on-site gallery features the artwork of Thomas Hill, a famous landscape painter from the 1800s.

Pioneer Yosemite History Center

The **Pioneer Yosemite History Center** (8308 Wawona Rd., 209/372-0200, open daily year-round) is a sprawling outdoor display of the park's relics. Inside a big open barn is an array of vehicles that were used in Yosemite more than a century ago. Cushy carriages once transported wealthy tourists, and oil wagons, used in an ill-conceived attempt to control mosquitoes, now sit abandoned. Walk under the covered bridge to enter the main museum area, a rambling collection of many of the original structures in the park. You'll see military shacks used by soldiers who were the first park rangers, the homes of early settlers, a working blacksmith shop, and even a jail. (Most were moved here from other remote locations.) Self-guided tour brochures are available online.

In summer, sign up for a two-hour horseback-guided tour at **Big Trees Stable** (Pioneer Yosemite History Center, Wawona Rd.) or arrange for a **horse-drawn carriage ride** (adults $5, children ages 3-12 $4). Check the *Yosemite Guide* for living history programs and live demonstrations held in summer.

★ Mariposa Grove of Giant Sequoias

The stunning **Mariposa Grove of Giant Sequoias** (Wawona Rd./Hwy. 41) is the largest of three redwood groves in the park. The grove is divided into three looped trails, ranging from easy to difficult, offering visitors the opportunity to get up close and marvel at these ancient giants.

For a self-guided tour start with the **Big Trees Loop** (0.3 mi, 1 hour, easy). The **Grizzly Giant Loop** (2 mi/3.2 km, 1.5-2 hours, moderate) includes the Bachelor and Three Graces trees and the California Tunnel Tree. On the other side of the Grizzly Giant, look for a historic photo of President Theodore Roosevelt and conservationist John Muir as they stand next to this same tree. The **Guardians Loop Trail** (6.5 mi/10.5 km, 4-6 hours, strenuous) takes hikers on a 1.5-mile (2.4-km) path past the Telescope Tree, Wawona Tunnel Tree, and the Mariposa Grove Cabin.

The **Mariposa Grove Museum** (Upper Mariposa Grove) is housed in a replica of the former cabin of Galen Clark. Inside, exhibits pay homage to the big

Wawona

WAWONA CAMPGROUND

CHILNUALNA FALLS RD

FOREST DR

TH CHILNUALNA FALLS

TH WAWONA SWINGING BRIDGE LOOP

South Fork Merced River

BIG TREES STABLE

PIONEER YOSEMITE HISTORY CENTER

WAWONA POST OFFICE

WAWONA VISITOR CENTER AT HILL'S STUDIO

BIG TREES LODGE/BIG TREES LODGE STORE

TH WAWONA MEADOW LOOP

WAWONA RD

Yosemite National Park

GUARDIANS **TH** LOOP TRAIL

SOUTH ENTRANCE

MARIPOSA GROVE RD

MARIPOSA GROVE TRAIL/ GRIZZLY GIANT LOOP/ **TH** BIG TREES LOOP

MARIPOSA GROVE OF GIANT SEQUOIAS

41

0   1 mi

0   1 km

© MOON.COM

trees; there's even furniture carved from some of the fallen sequoias. Located on the Guardians Loop Trail, the museum is only open in summer when a ranger is present.

A **park shuttle** (8am-5pm daily mid-Mar.-mid-May and mid-Oct.-Nov., 8am-8pm mid-May-mid-Oct., free) transports visitors from the Mariposa Grove Welcome Plaza to the Arrival Area, running about every 10 minutes. Mariposa Grove Road closes at 7:30am while the shuttle is in service. Parking is limited.

Dogs and bicycles are not permitted in the grove.

Mariposa Grove Road closes in winter (Dec.-mid-Mar.), but the grove remains open to snowshoers and cross-country skiers.

Recreation
Hiking

The Wawona area of the park is not as crowded as Yosemite Valley, but the hikes are just as scenic and lovely. The area's giant sequoias and pioneer artifacts offer a different perspective of the park. In addition to the numerous trails throughout the Mariposa Grove of Giant Sequoias, there are easy walks along the **Swinging Bridge Loop** (Big Trees Lodge Store, 4.8 mi/7.7 km round-trip, 2 hours) or the more strenuous **Alder Creek Trail** (12 mi/19.3 km round-trip, 6-8 hours), accessible from the Chilnualna Falls trailhead.

Mariposa Grove of Giant Sequoias

Yosemite's largest grove of giant sequoias, the **Mariposa Grove of Giant Sequoias** (off CA-41 near the South Entrance) invokes a quiet serenity. The easiest way to explore these old-growth redwoods is on the **Big Trees Loop** (0.3 mi, 1 hour, easy). This flat, wheelchair-accessible path starts at the Mariposa Grove Arrival Area and passes a series of interpretive plaques about the grove's ecology en route to the Fallen Monarch. Just standing at the base of this fallen giant will make you feel small.

Walking east past the Fallen Monarch, the trail joins the **Grizzly Giant Loop** (2 mi/3.2 km round-trip, 1.5-2 hours, moderate) for 0.5 mile to approach the Bachelor and Three Graces, a cluster of three redwoods. Continue east to reach the **Grizzly Giant;** this sequoia is thought to be 2,800 years old. Shortly past the Grizzly is the California Tunnel Tree, which you can walk through. In the early 1900s, a large portion of the base was carved out in order to allow vehicles to drive through.

The trail continues north past the Grizzly Giant on the **Mariposa Grove Trail** (7 mi/11.3 km round-trip, 4-6 hours, strenuous), which leads to Wawona Point. Though the trail is wide and smooth, it does climb 1,200 feet (365 m) in elevation. Stop and catch your breath at notable sequoias such as the **Faithful Couple,** the **Clothespin Tree,** and the **Galen Clark Tree.**

En route to Wawona Point, the **Guardians Loop** (6.5 mi/10.5 km round-trip, 4-6 hours, strenuous) leads 0.3 mile south to access the **Mariposa Grove**

Museum and the Columbia Tree. The loop circles east past the **Fallen Wawona Tunnel Tree** to return to the Galen Clark Tree. From here, hike 0.5 mile north to enjoy the sweeping views from **Wawona Point.** Follow the Mariposa Grove Trail back to the trailhead.

To explore the grove, park at the Mariposa Grove Welcome Plaza, which has about 300 parking spots. Plan to arrive early as the lot fills by late morning. A free seasonal **shuttle** (8am-5pm daily mid-Mar.-Nov.) transports visitors from the plaza to the grove. Limited shuttle service is available for overnight guests at Big Trees Lodge in summer. Bikes and pets are not permitted on trails within the grove. Drinking water and restrooms are available at the parking plaza.

Wawona Meadow Loop

From the Big Trees Lodge, cross the road to walk along the **Wawona Meadow Loop** (3.5 mi/5.6 km round-trip, 2 hours, easy), an easy sweep around a lovely meadow

and the Wawona golf course. This wide former fire road has returned to the forest and passes vibrant wildflowers in spring. Leashed pets are allowed on this trail.

Chilnualna Falls

If you're up for a hard-core hike to a series of waterfalls, take the trail to **Chilnualna Falls** (8.2 mi/13.1 km round-trip, 5 hours, strenuous). The trailhead is at the Chilnualna Falls parking lot, 2 miles (3.2 km) along Chilnualna Falls Road. From the parking area, the trail ascends 0.5 mile, following Chilnualna Creek, before switchbacking 2,400 feet (730 m) to the top of the falls. You'll see a few fellow hikers and many tantalizing views of the cascades. Be careful to avoid the stream during spring and summer high flow—it can be dangerous and experienced hikers have been known to slip on the granite rocks. Plan to bring a lot of water, snacks, and a trail map.

Horseback Riding

You'll find more horses than mules at **Big Trees Stable** (Pioneer Yosemite History Center, Wawona Rd., 209/375-6502, www.travelyosemite.com, 7am-5pm daily, late May-Sept., $67-140). The pleasant two-hour trail ride around Wawona's historic wagon trail is great for riders of all ages and abilities, or experienced riders can opt for the challenging all-day trip to the Mariposa Grove of Giant Sequoias (Thurs. only). Reservations are strongly recommended.

Located outside of the park, **Yosemite Trails Saddles and Sleigh Company** (7910 Jackson Rd./Big Sandy, Fish Camp, 559/683-7611, www.yosemitetrails.com, 11am and 2pm daily, mid-May-Oct., $50-185) offers authentic experiences in the spirit of true Yosemite cowboys. In winter, jingling Belgian draft horses pull a **sleigh ride** ($35 adult, $22 ages 4-14, 3 and under free, late Dec.-early Jan.) through the snow to Skidders Camp, where hot apple cider, cowboy coffee, and

Mariposa Grove of Giant Sequoias

roasted marshmallows await. Yosemite Trails Saddles and Sleigh Company is 2 miles (3.2 km) from the South Entrance and Wawona.

Snowshoeing and Cross-Country Skiing

Mariposa Grove maintains winter trails for snowshoeing and cross-country skiing. A popular trail is the **Loop Road** (8 mi/13 km round-trip) from the South Entrance to the Mariposa Grove of Sequoias. Pick up a copy of the *Mariposa Grove Winter Trails* guide ($0.50) at the visitors center, or download a copy from the park's website (www.nps.gov/yose).

Entertainment and Events

Listen to the delightful piano music and singing of the legendary Tom Bopp at the **Big Trees Lodge** lobby (www.yosemitemusic.com, Tues.-Sat. Mar.-Oct.) five nights a week throughout Wawona's season. Visitors love his old-style performance and familiar songs.

In summer, **Evening Ranger Programs** are held at the Yosemite vacation rentals office (Chilnualna Falls Rd., 6:30pm, days vary). The **Pioneer Yosemite History Center** (8308 Wawona Rd., 209/372-0200, daily year-round) hosts three-hour blacksmithing demonstrations. Check the *Yosemite Guide* for information.

Food and Accommodations

The charming **Big Trees Lodge** (888/413-8869, www.travelyosemite.com, late Mar.-Nov. and mid-Dec.-early Jan., $153-216) opened in 1856 and has been a Yosemite mainstay ever since. The hotel's striking Victorian-era architecture brings to mind visions of a 19th-century Mississippi riverboat, with its building-length verandas and tall, white columns. The stylish interior complements the exterior with period wallpaper, antique furniture, and a lack of in-room TVs and telephones. This National Historic Landmark offers 104 rooms, some with shared bath (for a lesser rate).

The ★ **Big Trees Lodge Dining Room** (Big Trees Lodge, 209/375-1425, www.travelyosemite.com, 7:30am-10am, 11:30am-2pm, and 5:30pm-8:30pm daily mid-Mar.-late Nov. and mid-Dec.-early Jan., $22-32) serves a well-rounded selection of American fare in its large white dining room. The menu features lemon-garlic shrimp, fried chicken, and a signature pot roast, as well as soup and salad options for vegetarians. All seating is first-come, first-served and the restaurant is family-friendly. Expect a wait for a table on weekends in high season, and call to confirm hours in the off season (late Oct.-Dec.).

The hotel's large common area offers seating and **drinks** (5pm-9:30pm). Catch a beautiful sunset from the outdoor veranda. Big Trees Lodge also hosts a **barbecue** in summer (5pm-7pm Sat. late May-Aug., $23-29) and during select holidays (noon-3pm), as well as special dinners over the winter holidays.

The **Big Trees Lodge Store** (8am-8pm daily in season) sells camping supplies, wine, snacks, and maps. It's one of your only options to get provisions when the dining room is closed.

Camping

Camp at the lovely and forested **Wawona Campground** (877/444-6777, www.recreation.gov, 96 sites, reservations required Apr.-Sept., $26; first-come, first-served Oct.-Apr., $18), a mile north of Wawona. RVs are welcome, but there are no hookups. There have been increased bear incidents and mountain lion sightings in this area; use the food lockers on-site for safe storage. If you want to camp with your horse, Wawona offers two equestrian sites. A small grocery store near the visitors center can provide a few basics, but most services (including showers) are only in Yosemite Valley.

Getting Around

There is no shuttle in the Wawona region of the park. Guests at the Big Trees Lodge may access a shuttle to Mariposa Grove in summer.

YARTS (877/989-2787, www.yarts.com, daily mid-May-mid-Sept., $18 one-way, $36 round-trip) runs a bus along CA-41 from Fresno to Yosemite Valley, stopping in Wawona. The northbound route starts at 5:30am with stops in Oakhurst, The Pines at Bass Lake, Tenaya Lodge, Mariposa Grove, and the Big Trees Lodge Store. The southbound route from the Yosemite Valley Visitors Center returns to Fresno departing at 9:30am.

Tuolumne Meadows and Tioga Pass

Tioga Road (CA-120, summer only), Yosemite's own "road less traveled," crosses through Yosemite's high country from the west to the Eastern Sierra. Along the way, campgrounds, pristine lakes, and expansive meadows beg further exploration.

The narrow, twisting road reaches an elevation of 9,943 feet (3,031 m) and is open in summer only; the road closes at the first significant snowfall (Oct.-Dec.) and will not reopen until the snow melts (as late as June). Call (209/372-0200) to check road and weather conditions before planning a trip here.

Getting There

Tuolumne Meadows is along Tioga Road (CA-120), which runs all the way across the park to the eastern boundary. Tioga Pass is Yosemite's eastern entrance, accessible from US-395 near Lee Vining.

From the East (US-395)

From the intersection of US-395 and CA-120 at Lee Vining, turn west on CA-120 (it becomes Tioga Pass Road) and continue 11 miles (17.5 km) to the Tioga Pass Entrance. The **Tioga Gas Mart** is the best (and only) place to fill your tank before reaching the other side of the park. (It takes at least 1.5 hours to drive the whole pass.)

From the West (CA-120)

From the west, CA-120 becomes Big Oak Flat Road at the Big Oak Flat Entrance. The **Big Oak Flat Visitor Information Station** (209/379-1899, 8am-5pm daily May-Oct.) is on the right. You can pick up a free wilderness permit here in summer; in winter, self-register outside for a permit.

Drive 9 miles (14.5 km) south, then turn left at the Crane Flat junction onto Tioga Road. **Crane Flat** has a 24-hour gas station and convenience store, and it's the last one you'll see until Lee Vining on the east side of the Sierras.

The **Tuolumne Meadows Visitors Center** is 38 miles (61 km) east along Tioga Road.

Tioga Road is **closed in winter** (Nov.-May). To check weather conditions and road closures, call 209/372-0200.

TOP EXPERIENCE

Tioga Road

Tioga Pass Road (CA-120, summer only) enters the park from the east at the Tioga Pass Entrance and offers a scenic drive through Yosemite's high country. Grassy, alpine **Tuolumne Meadows** is bracketed by **Pothole Dome** on its west end and **Lembert Dome** to the east. Both offer access to myriad trails, plus the opportunity to admire rock climbers. Continuing west on Tioga Road, stop to stroll along the sandy beach at **Tenaya Lake** while staring up toward **Clouds Rest**. In the spring, view the wildflowers around **White Wolf** (turn north on a dirt road to get to the parking lot) and bring your camera to take in the vista at **Olmsted Point**. Tioga Road is a narrow and twisting two-lane road with no shoulders or guardrail. Use the pullouts along the road to take photos and admire the views; watch for stopped cars, pedestrians, and

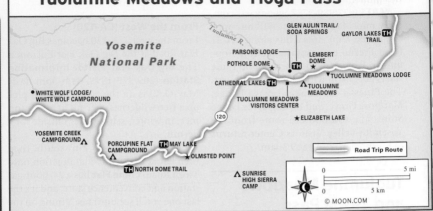

Tuolumne Meadows and Tioga Pass

wildlife along the way. Note that the road is closed in winter.

Sights

★ Tuolumne Meadows

After miles of soaring granite peaks, it's almost surprising to come upon the serene and grassy alpine **Tuolumne Meadows** (Tioga Rd.). In tones of brilliant green or soft maize in the fall, and dotted with wildflowers in spring, the waving grasses support a variety of flora and fauna. Stop the car and get out for a quiet, contemplative view of the meadows and admire the pines as they spring up from the meadow.

The short trail to **Soda Springs** and **Parsons Lodge** (1.5 mi/2.4 km round-trip, 1 hour, easy) leads past a carbonated spring to the historic Parsons Lodge before returning to the Tuolumne Meadows Visitors Center. The trailhead is at Lembert Dome.

Tuolumne Meadows is about 40 miles (64 km) east of the Crane Flat junction.

Tuolumne Meadows Visitors Center

The **Tuolumne Meadows Visitors Center** (209/372-0263, 9am-6pm daily late May-early Sept.) is in a rustic building not far from the campground and the Tuolumne Meadows Store. Come here for books and

maps and to find out the latest trail conditions. Ranger talks are held throughout summer; details on upcoming programs are available in the *Yosemite Guide*.

Tenaya Lake

Tenaya Lake (Tioga Rd., 2 mi/3.2 km east of Olmsted Point) is a natural gem nearly a mile long and framed by granite peaks. The body of water was formed by the action of Tenaya Glacier. Both are named for a local Native American chief. It's a popular place for swimming, fishing, and boating. The northeastern side of the lake has a beach with picnic tables and restrooms.

Tenaya Lake is 12 miles (19.5 km) west of the east entrance on Tioga Road.

Olmsted Point

Olmsted Point (Tioga Rd., west of Tenaya Lake) offers sweeping views of Tenaya Canyon, the mass of granite known as Clouds Rest, and the northern side of Half Dome, which, from this vantage point, looks like a giant helmet. Seeing them requires little effort. Turn your vehicle off Tioga Road into the parking area and then climb onto the large rock formation to the south. This spot is named after landscape architect Frederick Law

Olmsted Jr., who worked as a planner in Yosemite National Park.

Olmsted Point is 30 miles (48 km) east of the Crane Flat turnoff.

Recreation
Hiking

For smaller crowds along the trails, take one or more of the many scenic hikes along Tioga Road. Just be aware that they don't call it "high country" for nothing; the elevation starts at 8,500 feet (2,600 m) and goes higher on many trails. Take the elevation into account when deciding which trails to explore. If you experience symptoms of altitude sickness, you'll need to return to the trailhead.

Tuolumne Meadows serves as a good base for a high-country backpacking trip. The **Tuolumne Meadows Wilderness Center** (8am-5pm daily May-mid-Oct.) issues backcountry wilderness permits and rents bear canisters. The wilderness center is along Tioga Road, on the road to Tuolumne Meadows Lodge.

Hikes below are listed east to west along Tioga Road.

Gaylor Lakes

Hikers willing to tackle somewhat longer, steeper treks will find an amazing array of small scenic lakes within reach of Tioga Road. The crowd-averse will enjoy the trek to **Gaylor Lakes Trail** (2 mi/3.2 km round-trip, 2 hours, moderate), which is one of Yosemite's less-populated scenic hikes. From the trailhead at almost 10,000 feet (3,000 m), the trail climbs a steep 600 vertical feet (185 m) to the pass to the Gaylor Lakes valley. Once in the valley, you can wander around the lovely lakes, stopping to admire the views out to the mountains surrounding Tuolumne Meadows or visiting the 1860 abandoned Sheepherder lode mine site above Upper Gaylor Lake.

Elizabeth Lake

The trail to **Elizabeth Lake** (4.8 mi/7.7 km round-trip, 4-5 hours, moderate) begins from Tuolumne Campground to climb almost 1,000 vertical feet (300 m) to the lake; most of the climb occurs during the first mile of trip. Evergreens ring the lake, and the steep granite Unicorn Peak rises high above it. This stunning little lake makes a perfect photo op that's not necessarily recognizable as Yosemite.

Glen Aulin Trail

The **Glen Aulin Trail** (11 mi/17.7 km round-trip, 6-8 hours, strenuous) follows the Tuolumne River as it ascends into the high country before descending into the Grand Canyon of the Tuolumne. From the Soda Springs/Lembert Dome parking area, the trail heads west past cascading pools and granite domes to reach Tuolumne Fall and White Cascade in 4 miles (6.4 km). There are plenty of pretty little lakes, as well as some steep and rocky areas, and you'll be rewarded with fabulous views. This hike may get a bit crowded in the high season, when backpackers hike the trail to the High Sierra Camp at Glen Aulin. Farther downstream of Glen Aulin lie **California Fall** (13 mi/21 km round-trip), **LeConte Fall** (15 mi/24 km round-trip), and **Waterwheel Fall** (18 mi/29 km round trip).

Cathedral Lakes

If you can't get enough of Yosemite's granite-framed glassy alpine lakes, take the long hike out to the **Cathedral Lakes** (7 mi/11.3 km round-trip, 4-6 hours, moderate). From the trailhead (0.5 mile west of Tuolumne Meadows Visitors Center), the trail climbs about 1,000 feet (300 m) over 3.5 miles (5.6 km) to a pair of picture-perfect lakes surrounded by dramatic alpine peaks, lodgepole pines, and crystalline waters. This is a very popular trail and the small parking area fills quickly.

May Lake and Mount Hoffman

May Lake (2.4 mi/3.9 km round-trip, 1-2 hours, moderate) sits peacefully at the base of the sloping granite of Mount

Hoffman. Although the hike to May Lake is short, the elevation gain is a steep 485 feet (150 m). The more difficult trail to the top of **Mount Hoffman** (2 mi/3.2 km one-way) rises 2,000 feet (600 m) along granite slabs and rocky trails, with clear views of Cathedral Peak, Mount Clark, Half Dome, and Clouds Rest along the way. As you pass May Lake, look for May Lake High Sierra Camp (one of Yosemite's High Sierra camps) at the lake's southeast corner. The final climb to Mount Hoffman's summit, at 10,850 feet (3,305 m), is very rocky, with a narrow trail through boulders. On top is a flat plateau where you can relax and enjoy the outstanding vistas.

The May Lake Trailhead is 1 mile (1.6 km) southwest of Tenaya Lake on Tioga Road, via a partly paved, one-lane road. There are clean vault toilets at the trailhead.

North Dome

For an unusual look at a classic Yosemite landmark, hike the trail to **North Dome** (10.4 mi/16.7 km round-trip, 5-8 hours, strenuous). The path leads through woods and out to the dome, which is right across the valley from Half Dome. There are a few steep, granite climbs thrown in along the way, but getting to stare at the face of Half Dome from eye level makes the effort worth it. Don't miss the side trip to **Indian Rock** (0.3 mi).

The Porcupine Creek trailhead is on Tioga Road (east of Porcupine Campground). Parking is limited. There is a vault toilet near the trailhead.

Tuolumne Grove

The trail into **Tuolumne Grove** (2.5 mi/4 km round-trip, 1-2 hours, moderate) descends about 500 vertical feet (150 m) into a grove with more than 24 mature

From top to bottom: Tioga Pass Road; Tuolumne Meadows; pond at the May Lake trailhead.

giant sequoias. (You do have to climb back up the hill to get to your car.)

The trailhead and parking lot are at the junction of Tioga Road and Old Big Oak Flat Road, near Crane Flat. There are only about 30 parking spots, so get there early. Restrooms are at the trailhead.

Snowshoeing and Cross-Country Skiing

Crane Flat (Tioga Rd. and Big Oak Flat Rd.) has a variety of short, ungroomed winter trails at relatively low elevations (5,200-7,200 ft/1,600-2,200 m) that are perfect for snowshoeing and cross-country skiing. Pick up a copy of the *Crane Flat Winter Trails* guide at the visitors center or download a copy online (www.nps.gov/yose).

Food and Accommodations

Tuolumne Meadows Lodge (888/413-8869, www.travelyosemite.com, early June-mid-Sept., $144) offers rustic lodging and good food in a gorgeous subalpine setting. There is no electricity, no private baths, and no plush amenities in the 69 canvas-covered cabins. You'll find small, charming wood-frame tents that sleep up to four, with wood stoves for heat and candles for light. Central facilities include restrooms, hot showers, and a dining room. The location is perfect for starting or finishing a backcountry trip through the high-elevation areas of the park.

The **Tuolumne Meadows Lodge Restaurant** (209/372-8413, 7am-9am and 5:30pm-8pm daily early June-mid-Sept., $14-29) serves breakfast and dinner in a rustic central building near the tent cabins. The quality of the food is superior to the mess hall setting, with grilled flatiron steak, shrimp linguine, and warm apple pie for dessert. A children's menu ($7-9) is also available. Reservations are required.

Located near Tuolumne Meadows campground, **Tuolumne Meadows Grill** (209/372-8426, 8am-6pm daily June-Sept., $4-11) offers classic American fare

for hungry campers. Breakfast sandwiches, buckwheat pancakes, and a breakfast bundle (eggs, meat, and a biscuit) are served 8am-11am. Lunch follows with hamburgers, hot dogs, and a vegetarian chili. Eat outside on the accompanying picnic benches with views of Tuolumne Meadows across the road.

A rustic high-country lodging option, **White Wolf Lodge** (9211 White Wolf Rd., 888/413-8869, www.travelyosemite.com, mid-June-early Sept., $135-165) sits back in the trees off Tioga Road. Accommodations are in either 24 tent cabins (set on wood platforms with a wood stove and use of a central restroom with shower facilities) or 4 solid-wall cabins (with a private bath, limited electricity, and daily maid service). All cabins include linens and towels. A buffet-style breakfast is served 7:30am-10am. Dinner (6pm-7:45pm, reservations required) is served family style in the White Wolf dining room. Purchase a sack lunch to take with you on your day hikes. Amenities are few, but the scenery is breathtaking.

Camping

Yosemite visitors who favor the high country tend to prefer to camp rather than to stay in a lodge (it's more affordable and farther from crowds and noise). Fortunately, Yosemite has many places to pitch a tent with an unspoken camaraderie between hikers and campers.

Tuolumne Meadows

★ **Tuolumne Meadows** (Tioga Rd. at Tuolumne Meadows, 209/372-4025 or 877/444-6777, www.recreation.gov, 304 sites, July-late Sept., reservations strongly advised, tents and RVs $26) has one of the largest campgrounds in the park, with more than 300 sites. Half of the sites are available by reservation; the remaining half are first-come, first-served. Sites are assigned upon arrival and include fire rings, picnic tables, and bear-proof food lockers, with water and restrooms with flush toilets located nearby. Leashed pets are permitted in the campground. Food is available at Tuolumne Meadows Lodge and the Tuolumne Grill. The closest showers are in Yosemite Valley.

Tuolumne Meadows is at 8,600 feet elevation (2,600 m), so nights can get chilly even in summer. The campground is crowded in summer and tends to fill every night, so make reservations online in advance. Sites accommodate RVs (up to 35 feet, no hookups). There are also four equestrian sites ($30).

Crane Flat

Crane Flat (Big Oak Flat Rd. and Tioga Rd., 877/444-6777, www.recreation.gov, 162 sites, reservations mid-July-Oct., $26) is at 6,200 feet (1,900 m) elevation north of Yosemite Valley. Sites accommodate tents and RVs (up to 35 feet, no hookups) and include fire pits, picnic tables, bear-proof food lockers, water, and flush toilets. Leashed pets are permitted in the campground. Crane Flat is 17 miles (27 km) from Yosemite Valley. A small grocery store is down the road at Crane Flat gas station; the closest showers are in Yosemite Valley.

Hodgdon Meadow

If you're entering the park from the west end on CA-120, the first campground you'll come to is **Hodgdon Meadow** (877/444-6777, www.recreation.gov, 103 sites, reservations mid-Apr.-mid-Oct., $26; first-come, first-served late Oct.-early Apr., $18). This can be an excellent choice for people who drive up Friday night, since you can set up camp right after entering the park and won't have to drive in the dark. At 4,900 feet (1,500 m), Hodgdon Meadow can accommodate tents or RVs, though it has no hookups. Sites include fire rings and picnic tables, and there are bear-proof food lockers, water, and flush toilets. Supplies are available at Crane Flat, and the closest showers are in Yosemite Valley. Pets are permitted.

First-Come, First-Served Campgrounds

Those without reservations can try their luck at snagging one of the first-come, first-served sites at Tuolumne Meadows, but several other campgrounds along Tioga Road also offer last-minute options.

West of Tenaya Lake and Tuolumne Meadows, **Porcupine Flat** (Tioga Rd., 52 sites, first-come, first-served, July-Oct. 15, $12) sits at 8,100 feet (2,500 m). Closely packed sites accommodate tents, but the rough and bumpy camp road is not recommended for RVs. There are fire pits, picnic tables, bear-proof food lockers, and vault toilets, but no water. Leashed pets are permitted in the campground.

Ditch the traffic and the crowded central visitor areas and head for **Yosemite Creek** (Tioga Rd., 75 sites, first-come, first-served, July-mid-early Sept., $12). Yosemite Creek flows right through this tent-only campground, a perfect spot for cooling off on a hot day. There are few amenities—fire pits, picnic tables, vault toilets, and bear-proof food lockers—and no groceries, showers, or water (filter or boil creek water or bring your own). Turn off west of Porcupine Flat onto the rough dirt road to the campground.

Serene **White Wolf** (White Wolf Rd., 74 sites, first-come, first-served, July-early Sept., $18) is at 8,000 feet (2,400 m) elevation. Sites accommodate tents and RVs (up to 27 feet, no hookups) and include fire pits and picnic tables. Bear-proof food lockers, drinking water, and flush toilets are available, and leashed pets are permitted in the campground. Crane Flat is the closest place for supplies. To get there from Tioga Road, look for White Wolf Road and turn north on the narrow road.

Tamarack Flat (Tioga Rd., 52 sites, first-come, first-served, late May-mid-Oct., $12) is at 6,300 feet (1,900 m) elevation and is reasonably close to Yosemite Valley, but still in a fairly primitive environment. Sites at this tent-only campground have picnic tables and bear-proof food lockers, but there are no restrooms (pit toilets only) and you must bring your own water. RVs are not recommended.

High Sierra Camps

Yosemite's five ★ **High Sierra Camps** (888/413-8869, www.travelyosemite.com, June-early Sept., adults $152-160, children age 7-12 $80-85) offer far more than your average backcountry campground. Accommodations are in tent cabins and include breakfast and dinner in camp, plus a sack lunch for purchase. Choose from Merced Lake, Vogelsang, Glen Aulin, May Lake, and Sunrise Camp—or hike from one to another if you're lucky enough to get a spot. Starting October 1, a lottery takes place for spots at High Sierra Camps for the following summer. You must submit an application to join the lottery; even if you get a spot, there's no guarantee you'll get your preferred dates. The general booking period opens mid-March; check the website to see if any dates are available.

Getting Around

In summer, the **Tuolumne Meadows shuttle** (see *Yosemite Guide* for operating schedule) runs along Tioga Road between Olmsted Point and the Tuolumne Meadows Lodge. Usually trips begin early in the morning (7am or so) at Tuolumne Meadows Lodge and run every half hour, stopping at the Dog Lake Parking area, the Tuolumne Meadows Wilderness Center, Lembert Dome, Tuolumne Meadows Campground and Store, Tuolumne Meadows Visitors Center, Cathedral Lakes Trailhead, Pothole Dome, the east end of Tenaya Lake, Sunrise Lakes Trailhead at the west end of Tenaya Lake, May Lake Trailhead, and Olmsted Point.

YARTS (877/989-2787, www.yarts.com; Sat.-Sun. late May, June, and Sept.; daily July-Aug.; $18 one-way, $36 round-trip) runs a shuttle between Yosemite Valley and Mammoth along Tioga Pass Road in summer. It travels through Tuolumne Meadows; let the bus driver know when you board if you want to get off at a particular stop in that area.

A **guided bus tour** (209/372-1240, www.travelyosemite.com, June-mid-Sept., adults $5-14.50 one-way, $9.50-23 round-trip, children age 5-12 half-price) is offered seasonally between Yosemite Valley and Tuolumne Meadows. The coach makes multiple stops, starting from Half Dome Village (8am) and ending at Tuolumne Meadows Lodge (arriving at 10:35am). It departs Tuolumne Meadows again at 2:05pm for the return trip, ending at Half Dome Village at 4:15pm.

Hetch Hetchy

Hetch Hetchy Reservoir supplies clean water (plus some hydroelectric power) to the city of San Francisco and other parts of the Bay Area. With 1,972 acres of surface area, a maximum depth of 312 feet, and a capacity of 117 billion gallons, the water is deep and blue. Trees surround its perimeter, casting stunning reflections in its calm surface, and the gushing waterfalls along its sides are some of the loveliest in the park. Hiking in Hetch Hetchy usually offers a more peaceful experience because it isn't as crowded as the rest of the park.

Named for Michael M. O'Shaughnessy, the original chief engineer of the Hetch Hetchy Project, **O'Shaughnessy Dam** is a massive curved gravity dam that turns part of the Tuolumne River into Hetch Hetchy Reservoir. Completed in 1938, the dam stands more than 300 feet tall and 900 feet long. The reservoir provides water to San Francisco via the Hetch Hetchy Aqueduct.

Getting There

Hetch Hetchy (Hetch Hetchy Rd. past the Hetch Hetchy Entrance) is in the

Hetch Hetchy

Tueeulala Fall

Wapama Fall

Hetch Hetchy Reservoir

RANCHERIA FALLS CAMP TRAIL **TH**

O'SHAUGHNESSY DAM

HETCH HETCHY BACKPACKERS CAMPGROUND

POOPENAUT TRAIL **TH**

TH SMITH PEAK

HETCH HETCHY ENTRANCE

Tuolumne River

Middle Tuolumne River

EVERGREEN LODGE

Stanislaus

National

Forest

Yosemite

National

Park

South Fork Tuolumne River

RUSH CREEK LODGE

120

TH CARLON FALLS

YURTS AT YOSEMITE

SUNSET INN YOSEMITE CABINS

BIG OAK FLAT ENTRANCE

HODGDON MEADOW CAMPGROUND

0   2 mi

0   2 km

© MOON.COM

northwest corner of Yosemite National Park, about 30 miles (48 km) north of Big Oak Flat on CA-120. The road to Hetch Hetchy is open year-round, but the park gate is only open during daylight hours.

Recreation
Hiking
At less than 4,000 feet (1,200 m) in elevation, Hetch Hetchy is one of the lowest parts of Yosemite; it receives less snow and has a longer hiking season than other areas of the park. It's pretty warm here in summer, so plan a spring or fall visit for cooler temps. The relative warmth, combined with the abundance of water, may be one reason rattlers and poison oak seem particularly common in this area, but don't let that deter you from exploring this scenic area.

Popular hikes are listed below, but there are many more in the area. Trails to **Lookout Point** (2.8 mi/4.5 km, 1 hour, easy), **Smith Peak** (13-16 mi/21-26 km, 6-8 hours, difficult), and **Poopenaut Trail** (2.5 mi/4 km, 2 hours, moderate) all start from the Hetch Hetchy Entrance Station.

Wapama Fall

If you like waterfalls, you'll love the hike to **Wapama Fall** (5 mi/8 km round-trip, 2 hours, moderate). Begin by crossing O'Shaughnessy Dam, and then follow the **Wapama Falls Trail** (also known as Rancheria Falls Camp Trail) through the tunnel and along the shore of the reservoir. Along the way, you'll also see close-up views of the spectacular **Tueeulala Fall.** Tueeulala is set back in the hillside a little, so you can get some great photos of it. Wapama Fall comes splashing down right onto the trail, so you'll experience it in a whole different way—and you'll probably want to keep your camera safely packed away. For a longer hike, bring a large poncho or rain gear to protect yourself and your pack before stepping onto the wooden bridge that crosses under these falls. On a hot day, the shower could be a very welcome treat.

A word of warning: The amount of water flowing over Tueeulala and Wapama Falls varies greatly with the season and recent precipitation in the park. In spring, water can be especially abundant and powerful—and quite dangerous at times. Follow any posted restrictions to stay safe.

Rancheria Falls

A longer day hike (and a recommended backpacking trip), **Rancheria Falls Trail** (13.4 mi/21.4 km round-trip, 6-8 hours, moderate) begins at O'Shaughnessy Dam and continues past Wapama Fall along the shore of Hetch Hetchy Reservoir. The terrain is rolling, with some up and some down each way, and the total elevation gain is less than 700 feet (215 m). Along the way, you'll enjoy beautiful views of Hetch Hetchy Reservoir, pass Tueeulala Fall, and become one with Wapama Fall (bring rain gear). The path continues through pine forests, on stone stairs, across creeks, and past sunny overlooks to Rancheria Falls, a wide expanse with water flowing gradually over massive rocks. Large and flat granite slabs make a great stop for lunch before turning around to return the same way.

Carlon Falls

For a short hike that still includes a nice waterfall at the end, try **Carlon Falls** (2.8 mi/4.5 km round-trip, 1-2 hours, easy). The trail follows the South Fork of the Tuolumne River and blooms with wildflowers in the spring. The payoff at the end, after one brief uphill climb, is the lovely Carlon Falls. This year-round waterfall is much smaller than dazzling superstars like Bridalveil Fall, but it's no less attractive and much more approachable. You may even want to play in the river nearby or have a picnic on the rocks.

To get to the trailhead from the Big Oak Flat Entrance, drive north on CA-120 for 1 mile (1.6 km). Bear right onto Evergreen Road toward Mather and Hetch Hetchy, and continue another mile. Just past the Carlon Day Use Area is a pullout on the right with room for a few cars. The trail begins outside the Yosemite park boundaries, in the Stanislaus National Forest, but enters the park soon after.

Backpacking

Rancheria Falls makes a great backpacking destination in Hetch Hetchy. The trek along the **Rancheria Falls Trail** (13.4 mi/21.4 km round-trip, 6-8 hours, moderate) begins at O'Shaughnessy Dam and continues past Wapama Fall along the shore of Hetch Hetchy Reservoir. The rolling terrain results in an elevation gain of less than 700 feet (215 m). When you get to Rancheria Falls, you'll find a beautiful woodsy area with plenty of space for tents. The sense of privacy and seclusion here is enhanced by the sound of the nearby falls, which muffles the noise of human activity. This area makes a good base camp for challenging day hikes. A backpacking permit is required (apply online).

Food and Accommodations

Although most visitors come to **Evergreen Lodge** (33160 Evergreen Rd., Groveland, 209/379-2606, www.evergreenlodge.com, Feb.-Dec., $160-495) for the easy access to Yosemite, it is almost a destination in itself. Organized activities—painting, yoga, wine-tasting, white-water rafting, and guided hikes—lend the place a summer camp atmosphere while a children's play area includes a bocce ball court, an oversize Connect Four, and ziplines. The 88 cabins come in a variety of styles and sizes. The largest is the 2,500-square-foot John Muir House ($850-1,350 per night), which sleeps 10 in three bedrooms and includes a loft, a private deck, and a hot tub. The **custom camping** option ($115-150, sleeps up to 4) supplies a fully furnished tent site for guests. On-site dining options include the main restaurant (7am-10:30am, noon-3pm, 5pm-9pm daily), a tavern (noon-close daily), and a poolside bar (hours vary seasonally).

The Evergreen Lodge accepts reservations up to one year in advance. The location on Evergreen Road is only 1 mile (1.6 km) from the Hetch Hetchy Entrance and 7 miles (11.5 km) from the Big Oak Flat Entrance.

There are no developed campgrounds in the Hetch Hetchy region of the park. The **Hetch Hetchy Backpackers Campground,** located next to the overnight parking lot, offers a one-night option for wilderness permit holders exploring Hetch Hetchy's backcountry.

A wilderness **permit** ($5 per reservation, $5 per person) and a bear canister are required for overnight trips. To request a permit, contact the **Hetch Hetchy Entrance Station** (209/372-0200, 8am-5pm daily Apr. and mid-Sept.-Mar., 7am-5pm daily May-early Sept.) during daylight hours. The entrance station does not issue wilderness permits after 5pm.

Wapama Falls Trail

Gateways to Yosemite

Several small towns on the outskirts of Yosemite offer convenient alternatives to the few, and often crowded, options in the park—all while maintaining remnants of their rustic, historic heritage.

Highway 120
Groveland

The town of Groveland is 24 miles (39 km) west of the **Big Oak Flat Entrance** on CA-120. It's the perfect place to stop for gas, food, coffee, and anything else you need before entering the park. To get a jump on your weekend trip to Yosemite, consider spending the night in Groveland and entering the park early the next morning.

Food

Established in 1852, the **Iron Door Saloon** (18761 Main St., 209/962-8904, www.irondoorsaloon.com, 7am-10pm, $12-27) claims to be the oldest bar in California. It served gold prospectors in the 1850s and was the saloon of choice for the O'Shaughnessy Dam engineers. It's still arguably the center of nightlife for miles around, with live music on summer weekends and holidays. The food is average, but the drinks are strong. The bar stays open until 2am but may close earlier in the off-season.

Six generations of the Priest-Anker family have operated the **Priest Station Café** (16756 Old Priest Grade, Big Oak Flat, 209/962-1888, http://prieststation.com, 8am-8pm daily Apr.-Oct., 11am-3pm Mon.-Thurs., 8am-8pm Fri.-Sun. Nov.-Mar., $11-25) since the 1850s. This tiny roadside eatery serves hearty dishes: rib eye steak sandwiches, roasted turkey, and a sassy brisket, along with vegan and vegetarian items. But nothing tops the stellar views from the outdoor seating area. The station also rents two cabins ($149) from the 1940s for families or couples seeking cozy confines.

Groveland Provisions (18767 Main St., 209/962-4000, www.groveland.com, 7am-9pm daily, $19-39) is a grab-and-go bistro selling snacks, mimosas, wine, and souvenirs. Inside, grab a seat at one of the tall tables and admire the repurposed window frames that now hold historic photos of the Groveland Hotel. In summer, enjoy your meal on the outdoor patio.

Accommodations

Built in 1849, the ★ **Groveland Hotel** (18767 Main St., 209/962-4000, www.groveland.com, $104-162 winter, $200-325 summer 2-night min.) is the most elegant option in Groveland. This character-filled hotel brims with intrigue and has hosted gold miners, gamblers, and even ghosts (most notably Lyle, a gambler who still haunts the room he passed away in). Each of the 18 rooms features modern comforts such as hypoallergenic bedding and large flat-screen HDTVs. The charming establishment

also has an open-door pet policy. The proprietors, Doug and Jenn Edwards, also own the **Hotel Charlotte** (18736 Main St., 209/962-6455, www.hotelcharlotte.com, $95-139 winter, $179-275 summer) across the street.

The best feature of the **Yosemite Riverside Inn** (11399 Cherry Lake Rd., 209/962-7408 or 800/626-7408, www.yosemiteriversideinn.com, $69-295) is its proximity to Yosemite—it's 11 miles (17.5 km) west of the Big Oak Flat Entrance. Rooms range from simple ($129-215) to deluxe ($99-275), with kitchenettes and river or courtyard views. One- and two-bedroom suites ($235-355) and cabins with full kitchens ($135-245) are also available. A free continental breakfast (mid-Apr.-mid-Sept.) includes juice, coffee, oatmeal, cereal, bagels, toast, yogurt, and fruit. Wireless Internet is available ($10).

The modern **Yosemite Westgate Lodge** (7633 Hwy. 120, 800/253-9673 or 209/962-5281, www.yosemitewestgate.com, $185-235) is a convenient overnight spot 12 miles (19.5 km) from the Big Oak Flat Entrance. This independently owned lodge features 45 rooms that are all non-smoking and pet-free. A heated pool, spa, laundry facilities, and playground are some of the notable amenities. It also has a sister restaurant and accommodations at the **Buck Meadows Lodge** (7649 Hwy. 120, Groveland, 800/253-9673 or 209/962-5281, www.buckmeadowslodge.com, $89-229).

A sister resort of the Evergreen Lodge, **Rush Creek Lodge** (34001 Hwy. 120, Groveland, 209/379-2373, www.rushcreeklodge.com) offers a combination of 143 hotel rooms ($255-415), suites ($290-475), and villas ($330-565) tucked away on a hillside. Rooms feature modern amenities like Wi-Fi, a Keurig coffee maker, air-conditioning and heating, and streamed entertainment. Guests have access to a tavern and games like foosball, Ping-Pong, and bumper pool.

The history of the **Sunset Inn Yosemite Cabins** (33569 Hardin Flat Rd., Groveland, 888/962-4360, www.sunsetinn-yosemitecabins.com, $295-345) includes the Miwok Indians, a brothel, and a hunting lodge before it became the Crocker Station homestead in the late 1800s. Today, it offers three vacation properties: the Meadow Lark Cabin and two vacation rentals nearby. Sleeping configurations and amenities vary. Pets are not allowed. A three-night minimum stay is required.

For roomy and affordable accommodations that offer modern amenities, spend the night at the **Yurts at Yosemite** (31191 Hardin Flat Rd., Groveland, 888/535-2151, http://yurtsatyosemite.com, $143-305). These round, canvas-sided structures feature satellite TV, a full kitchen with a refrigerator, bathrooms, and deck with a gas barbecue.

Located 5 miles (8 km) from the Big Oak Flat Entrance is the 400-acre **Yosemite Lakes RV Resort** (Hwy. 120, 877/570-2267, https://rvonthego.com, $58-96). This RV park has 285 sites, including 130 tent sites ($41-68), four canvas-covered cabins, three cottages, and a nine-room hostel ($39-89). Some yurts are pet-friendly and sleep 2-6 people.

Highway 140
Mariposa and Midpines
Mariposa lies 30 miles (48 km) southwest of the **Arch Rock Entrance** to Yosemite Valley. The tiny enclave of Midpines is 6.5 miles (10.5 km) north of Mariposa. Both towns are along CA-140.

Food and Accommodations
You can't miss the **River Rock Inn and Deli Garden Café** (4993 7th St., Mariposa, 209/966-5793, http://riverrockncafe.com, $89-189), with its vivid orange-and-purple exterior. This quirky, whimsical motel features nine uniquely decorated rooms. Three suites, built in 1891, include two queen beds and enough space for families. A free continental breakfast is included and Wi-Fi is available. The

on-site **Deli Garden Café** (6am-10pm daily summer, 8am-5pm daily winter) sells freshly baked breads, desserts, and homemade organic food.

For cozy seclusion, stay at the **Highland House** (3125 Wild Dove Ln., Mariposa, 559/696-3341, www.highlandhouseinn.com, $139-169). The house is set deep in the forest far from town, providing endless peace and quiet away from civilization. This tiny B&B has only three rooms, each decorated in soft colors and warm, inviting styles. All rooms have down comforters, sparkling clean bathtubs and showers, free wireless Internet access, and TVs.

A small and lovely B&B, **Poppy Hill Bed and Breakfast** (5218 Crystal Aire Dr., Mariposa, 209/742-6273 or 800/587-6779, www.poppyhill.com, $150-160) is a cute country-style home an hour's drive away from the Arch Rock Entrance. Four airy rooms are done in bright white linens with white walls, lacy curtains, and antique furniture. No TVs mar the sounds of birds from the expansive gardens surrounding the old farmhouse, but you can take a dip in the patio hot tub any time. The complimentary gourmet breakfast includes Mary Ellen's special puffed apple pancakes.

The **Yosemite Bug Rustic Mountain Resort** (6979 Hwy. 140, Midpines, 209/966-6666 or 866/826-7108, www.yosemitebug.com, dorm $28-38, tent cabin $40-90, private room $85-175, private cabin $65-135) is part hostel, part rustic lodge. This facility includes five hostel dormitories, attractively appointed tent cabins with real beds, and a few cabins with private rooms (some with private baths). Solo travelers and families on tight budgets favor Yosemite Bug for its comfortable and cheap accommodations. The Bug is part of the Hostelling International network; HI members receive discounted rates on dorm rooms.

For a contemporary glamping experience, spend the night at **AutoCamp** (6323 Hwy. 140, Midpines, 888/405-7553, https://autocamp.com, $200-450). Tucked into the woods are 102 shiny silver Airstream trailers with 31 feet of sleeping area. These vintage abodes are decked out with 21st-century amenities, such as flat-screen TVs, queen beds with memory-foam mattresses (plus a sofa bed), a shower, a mini-fridge, and Wi-Fi. AutoCamp also has small private cabins and tent cabins with similar amenities.

El Portal

El Portal is less than 4 miles (6.4 km) west of the **Arch Rock Entrance** and only 15 miles (24 km) from Yosemite Valley, making it one of the closest places for a final overnight before entering the park.

Accommodations

Indian Flat RV Park (9988 Hwy. 140, 209/379-2339, www.indianflatrvpark.com, tents $20-30, RVs $37-48, tent cabins $59-139, cottages $85-289, pet fee $5) is an affordable, full-service resort, with 25 RV sites (water and electricity; some with sewer hookups), 25 tent sites, and 2 cabins. Showers are available ($3), even if you're not spending the night. The Yosemite Cedar Lodge next door has a gift shop and permits campers use of their outdoor pool. Reservations are strongly recommended May-September and are accepted up to one year in advance.

Yosemite Cedar Lodge (9966 Hwy. 140, 209/379-2612, www.yosemiteresorts.us, $79-99 rooms, $119-440 suites winter; $189-199 rooms, $199-450 suites summer) is 8 miles (13 km) from the park. Rooms, suites, and apartments come with cable TV; some also have coffee makers and mini-fridges. Accommodations cater to families, as 130 rooms have two queen beds. Guests also have access to indoor and outdoor pools, a convenience store, an on-site restaurant, and a sports bar.

Highway 41
Oakhurst

Oakhurst lies less than 15 miles (24 km)

from the **South Entrance** of Yosemite National Park along CA-41.

Food

Attached to the elegant Chateau du Sureau, **The Elderberry House Restaurant** (48688 Victoria Ln., Oakhurst, 559/683-6800, www.elderberryhouse.com, 5:30pm-8:30pm daily, $112) is an astonishingly chic establishment serving classical French cuisine with a farm-to-table sensibility. The five-course prix fixe dinner features a different menu nightly. The five-course Sunday brunch (11am-1pm, $68) includes a glass of its signature Ceroux with elderberry essence or a mimosa. Diners should dress in classic casual wear: suit, tie, and jacket for men; dress or slacks for women; and closed-toe shoes for all.

Accommodations

The **Best Western Plus Yosemite Gateway Inn** (40530 Hwy. 41, www.yosemitegatewayinn.com, 559/683-2378, $190-209) offers better-than-your-average-chain rooms, both indoor and outdoor pools and spas, and free wireless Internet. Groups should consider reserving the two-room "family suites," which features four queen beds ($210/night in summer), or the three-bedroom, two-bath cottage ($245). The complimentary breakfast is incredible. The on-site **Oakhurst Grill & Whiskey 41 Lounge** (6:30am-3pm and 5pm-10pm daily, $13-36) serves breakfast, lunch, and dinner daily with brunch on Sunday.

The independently owned **Oakhurst Lodge** (40302 Hwy. 41, 559/683-4417, www.theoakhurstlodge.com, $59-300) has 33 rooms within walking distance of Oakhurst's shops and restaurants. Wi-Fi and a continental breakfast are included. The unheated outdoor pool is open during summer.

Queen's Inn By the River (41139 Hwy. 41, 559/683-4354, www.queensinn.com, $99-239) offers affordable and contemporary accommodations with the added perk of a wine bar and beer garden right next door at the Idle Hour. Accommodations are in queen ($99-109) or king rooms ($189-209). The king suite ($129-239) is equipped with a mini-fridge, microwave, and a patio with incredible views of the valley. Enjoy a complimentary wine-tasting as part of your stay.

Far Meadow (42727 Old Yosemite Rd., https://farmeadow.com, $75-260) offers a variety of homey cabins, tepees, and trailers in the woods. The three A-frame or log cabins are set in a grove of oak trees; each has either an extra loft, a sofa bed, or a sleeping nook to accompany the bedrooms. There is a three-night minimum stay; reservations are accepted online. Pets are permitted for a fee ($25 per night).

Built in 1991, **Chateau du Sureau** (48688 Victoria Ln., Oakhurst, 559/683-6860, www.chateausureau.com, $385-585) is a nine-acre estate with a breathtakingly beautiful lodge. Each of the 10 rooms is spectacularly appointed and is named after a flower or herb. Request a canopy bed, a French balcony, a Jacuzzi tub, a garden view—whatever your idea of luxury, you can probably find it in this five-star European-style hotel. A charming Parisian manor (2-bed, 2-bath, $3,000 per night) is also available. Rates include an elegant European-style breakfast served in the dining room, plus free wireless Internet. A two-night minimum is required for Friday and Saturday arrivals.

Fish Camp

Fish Camp is 3 miles (4.8 km) south of Yosemite's **South Entrance** on CA-41.

Yosemite Mountain Sugar Pine Railroad (56001 Hwy. 41, Fish Camp, http://ymsprr.com, Apr.-Oct., $24 adults, $12 ages 3-12 for the Logger Steam Train, $19 adults, $9.50 ages 3-12 for the Jenny Railcars) offers a unique experience for the whole family, with activities such as gold panning, a history museum to wander through, a gift shop, and the main attraction—the scenic train rides through the Sierra National Forest. The Logger Steam Train holds up to 200 passengers on a one-hour trip, and the two trains weighing 59-82 tons power along the Sugar Pine Railroad, while the small 8- to 10-passenger Jenny Railcars take passengers on a 30-minute route around the property. Train tickets are available to purchase on-site but may sell out in the summer; fortunately, you can buy your tickets online in advance.

Food and Accommodations

The **Narrow Gauge Inn** (48571 Hwy. 41, 559/683-7720, www.narrowgaugeinn. com, $79-229) has 27 one- and two-bed nonsmoking rooms done in wood paneling, light colors, white linens, and vintage-style quilts. Each room has its own outdoor table and chairs to encourage relaxing on gorgeous summer days. The restaurant and common rooms feature antique oil lamps, stonework, and crackling fireplaces. Step outside your door and you're in a magnificent pine forest. Pets are welcome for an additional fee. Request the "Romance Package" ($80) and receive chocolates, flowers, and a bottle of wine for you and your sweetie.

For inexpensive lodge-style accommodations, check into the **White Chief Mountain Lodge** (7776 White Chief Mountain Rd., 559/683-5444, www. whitechiefmountainlodge.com, $70-220). The 26 rooms feature light wood paneling and furniture, framed photos of Yosemite on the walls, flat-screen HDTVs, and Wi-Fi access.

The **Tenaya Lodge** (1122 Hwy. 41, 559/683-6555 or 888/514-2167, www. tenayalodge.com, $169-409) offers plush lodge-style accommodations. Lodge rooms are styled with rich fabrics in bright colors; the three dozen cottages exude a Native American decor. The modern wall art evokes the woods and vistas of Yosemite. The beds are comfortable, the baths attractive, and the views forest-filled. Tenaya Lodge focuses on guest care, offering five dining venues on-site, from pizza and deli to fine dining; a full-service spa; a lobby featuring an expansive stone fireplace; an outdoor swimming pool; and plenty of outdoor activities for families.

The **Pines Resort** (54432 Rd. 432, Bass Lake, 559/642-3121 or 800/350-7463, www.basslake.com, $89-399) is perfectly located on the shores of Bass Lake. Choose from one of 20 suites ($139-450); each features a split-level king room with dark floors, light walls, and a fireplace; some have spa tubs. The Pines also has a chalet ($89-399) and a lake house ($800) that sleeps 12-15. Facilities include a tennis court, a swimming pool, a hot tub, and complimentary Wi-Fi. The Pines is a full-service resort with a lake-view restaurant, **Ducey's on the Lake** (7am-11am and 4pm-8pm Mon.-Thurs., 7am-11am and 4pm-9pm Fri., 7am-noon and 4pm-9pm Sat., 7am-noon and 4pm-8pm Sun.), and a market (7am-9pm Sun.-Thurs., 7am-10pm Fri.-Sat. summer; 7am-8pm Sun.-Thurs., 7am-9pm Fri.-Sat. winter).

A mile south of the South Entrance is the small, attractive **Summerdale Campground** (Hwy. 41, Fish Camp, 877/444-6777, www.recreation.gov, May-Sept., $32-34). This lovely spot on the cusp of the Sierra National Forest has just 32 campsites and a strict limit on RV size (25 feet), making it a bit quieter and less city-like than the mega-campgrounds. You'll have a fire ring and a grill at your site, plenty of room under mature shade trees close to giant sequoias, and potable water.

Monterey
and Big
Sur

Monterey and Big Sur

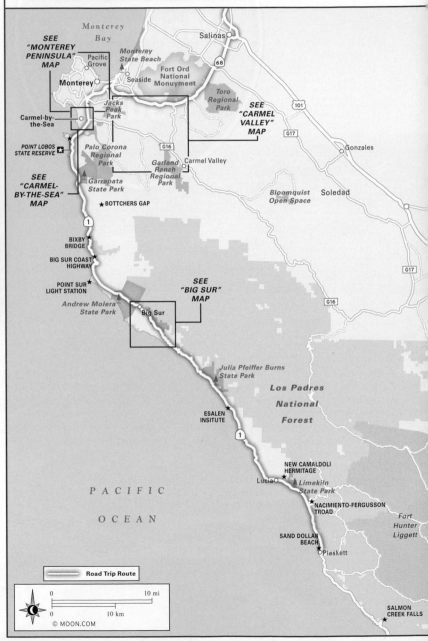

SEE "MONTEREY PENINSULA" MAP

Monterey Bay

Salinas

Pacific Grove

Monterey State Beach

Seaside

Fort Ord National Monument

68

Monterey

Jacks Peak Park

Toro Regional Park

SEE "CARMEL VALLEY" MAP

101

Carmel-by-the-Sea

POINT LOBOS STATE RESERVE

Palo Corona Regional Park

G16

Carmel Valley

Garland Ranch Regional Park

Gonzales

G17

SEE "CARMEL-BY-THE-SEA" MAP

Garrapata State Park

Bloomquist Open Space

Soledad

★ BOTTCHERS GAP

1

BIXBY BRIDGE

BIG SUR COAST HIGHWAY

POINT SUR LIGHT STATION

Andrew Molera State Park

Big Sur

SEE "BIG SUR" MAP

G16

G17

Julia Pfeiffer Burns State Park

Los Padres

National

Forest

ESALEN INSTITUTE

1

NEW CAMALDOLI HERMITAGE

Lucia

Limekiln State Park

PACIFIC

NACIMIENTO-FERGUSSON TROAD

Fort Hunter Liggett

OCEAN

SAND DOLLAR BEACH

Plaskett

Road Trip Route

0   10 mi

0   10 km

© MOON.COM

SALMON CREEK FALLS

Highlights

★ **Monterey Bay Aquarium:** This mammoth aquarium astonishes with a vast array of sealife and exhibits on the local ecosystem (page 524).

★ **Scuba Diving, Kayaking, and Stand-Up Paddleboarding:** Experience Monterey Bay's calm water and unique wildlife by getting into the water (page 532).

★ **Carmel Beach:** A great place for a stroll, a surf, or a picnic, this is one of the finest beaches on Monterey Bay (page 545).

★ **Point Lobos State Natural Reserve:** The crown jewel of California's impressive state park system has pocket coves, tidepools, forests of Monterey cypress, and diverse marine and terrestrial wildlife (page 547).

★ **Big Sur Coast Highway:** This scenic drive on CA-1 stars California's most stunning coastal scenery (page 557).

★ **Hiking in Big Sur:** To truly experience Big Sur, get out of your car and hit the trail (page 559).

Best Restaurants

★ **Montrio Bistro, Monterey:** Montrio satiates diners with an expansive appetizer menu and filling entrées (page 535).

★ **The Sandbar & Grill, Monterey:** This intimate local favorite on the Municipal Wharf has the best calamari in town (page 535).

★ **Hula's Island Grill & Tiki Room, Monterey:** Potent tropical cocktails, a menu with South Pacific flair, and a lively atmosphere make Hula's one of Monterey's best good-time restaurants (page 535).

★ **Crema, Pacific Grove:** Housed in a cozy cottage, Crema serves hearty and creative comfort food, like their popular chicken and waffles (page 540).

★ **Passionfish, Pacific Grove:** A local leader in sustainable seafood, Passionfish offers an upscale atmosphere for the bounty of Monterey Bay (page 542).

★ **Carmel Belle, Carmel:** The menu at this casual eatery highlights quality California ingredients in its sandwiches, salads, and comfort-food classics (page 550).

★ **Akaoni, Carmel:** Carmel's best seafood is at this hole-in-the-wall sushi joint that features items flown in from Japan (page 552).

★ **Café Rustica, Carmel Valley:** Soak up the Carmel Valley sun while enjoying wood-fired pizzas, salads, and entrées (page 556).

★ **Nepenthe, Big Sur:** A sweeping view of the Big Sur coast enhances a menu of casual yet satisfying food that includes the outstanding Ambrosia burger (page 566).

★ **Deetjen's, Big Sur:** Morning in Big Sur is enhanced by breakfast at Deetjen's, known for its superb eggs Benedict (page 567).

The Monterey and Big Sur area is a favorite getaway for locals as much as visitors.

The wild and rugged coastline provides ample opportunities to explore marine ecosystems, historic sights, and charming small towns.

Monterey Bay is the largest marine sanctuary in the country. Dive into its pristine waters to explore the bay's swaying kelp forests, or visit the Monterey Bay Aquarium for close-up views of local sea creatures. Victorian architecture and butterfly migrations are the draws at Pacific Grove. Exclusive Pebble Beach offers some of the most-photographed scenery in the state. Artsy Carmel-by-the-Sea is an idyllic village gently descending to a white-sand beach. Inland Carmel Valley offers a burgeoning wine industry with enough tasting rooms to fill a long, relaxing afternoon.

Big Sur's 90 miles (145 km) of rugged coastline begin just south of Carmel on the Monterey Peninsula and stretch south to San Simeon. Here, the mountains rise up suddenly and drop just as dramatically into the sea. CA-1 twists and turns like a two-lane snake, trying to keep up with the land- and seascape.

Best Accommodations

★ **Monterey Hostel, Monterey:** Budget travelers can stay within walking distance of Cannery Row and the famous aquarium without the boutique hotel prices (page 536).

★ **Portola Hotel & Spa, Monterey:** A convenient downtown location makes this a great base for exploring the Monterey Bay area (page 537).

★ **Spindrift Inn, Monterey:** Rooms at this small Cannery Row hotel feature wood-burning fireplaces, canopy beds, and bay views (page 538).

★ **Gosby House Inn, Pacific Grove:** This yellow and white Queen Anne-style Victorian is right on the main drag (page 542).

★ **Asilomar Conference Grounds, Pacific Grove:** Stay a block from the beach at this scenic lodge designed by Julia Morgan (page 542).

★ **La Playa Carmel, Carmel:** Carmel-by-the-Sea is a place for indulgence, and La Playa fits the bill with beautiful grounds and a champagne breakfast (page 552).

★ **Carmel Valley Ranch, Carmel Valley:** This upscale version of a summer camp offers daily activities and posh amenities on 500 park-like acres (page 557).

★ **Deetjen's Big Sur Inn, Big Sur:** Rustic Deetjen's offers a unique stay at a good price in Big Sur (page 567).

★ **Glen Oaks Big Sur, Big Sur:** Choices here range from elegant motor lodge rooms to quiet riverside cabins (page 570).

★ **Pfeiffer Big Sur State Park:** Sleep under redwoods and along the Big Sur River at this popular campground (page 570).

Planning Your Time

Many people drive through Big Sur in one day, taking CA-1 south from Carmel and pulling off at the road's many turnouts. Outdoors enthusiasts who want to *really* experience Big Sur will need at least a **couple of days.** Big Sur (26 mi/42 km south of Carmel) is a good place to stay for a great outdoors experience, plus amenities such as restaurants and lodging. Big Sur is also home to Pfeiffer Big Sur State Park, which has more than 200 campsites. The coast south toward San Simeon has fewer options.

Summer is the busy season; reservations are essential for hotels and campsites. Monterey Bay's summer fog catches a lot of visitors off guard. If you crave sun, spend an afternoon in Carmel Valley, which is inland enough to dodge the coastal fog. **Fall** is the ideal time for a trip to the area, with warmer temperatures and fewer crowds (and less fog).

Getting There

A trip to Big Sur involves planning—secure supplies and get gas in advance. Big Sur does have a few markets and gas stations, but you will pay a premium for both. Landslides, bridge failures, and wildfires can all close CA-1 through Big Sur at any time. Check road and weather conditions.

From Yosemite
200 mi/320 km, 4.5 hr

From **Yosemite Valley,** head west on CA-140 for 70 miles (113 km) to Merced. Hop onto CA-140 West/CA 99 North for 1.5 miles (2.4 km), returning to CA-140 West for 36 miles (58 km). CA-140 meets a T junction with I-5, where you'll turn south and drive 17 miles (27 km) toward Los Banos. Turn west on CA-152 and continue 40 miles (64 km) to Gilroy and US-101. (As CA-152 West passes the San Luis Reservoir, the road becomes windy and curvy in sections.)

Turn south on US-101 and drive 20 miles (32 km) to Prunedale, where you'll veer right onto CA-156. Continue west on CA-156 for 7 miles (11.5 km). Just south of Castroville, US-101 merges with CA-1 South for 15 miles (24 km) to **Monterey.**

Stopping at Casa de Fruta
On CA-152, 27 miles (43 km) west of I-5 is **Casa de Fruta** (10021 Pacheco Pass Hwy., Hollister, 408/842-7282, www.casadefruta.com, 7am-8pm Mon. and Thurs., 7am-7pm Tues.-Wed., 7am-9pm Fri.-Sun.), a fruit stand from the 1940s that has since blossomed into a roadside attraction, complete with an inn, an RV park, a 24-hour restaurant, a gas station, and a gourmet grocery store.

From San Francisco
120 mi/195 km, 2-2.5 hr

From San Francisco, take US-101 south for almost 100 miles (160 km) to Gilroy. In Gilroy, hop onto CA-156 West for 6 miles (9.5 km). CA-156 ends at CA-1; continue south on CA-1 for 14 miles (22.5 km) to **Monterey.**

US-101 in San Jose can become jammed during rush hour (7am-9am and 4pm-6pm). The sections of US-101 and CA-156 near Gilroy can also become bottlenecked on summer weekends and holidays.

Coastal Route
If you have time, the drive on **CA-1** (120 mi/195 km, 2-2.5 hours) from San Francisco to Monterey is a treat. The route follows a coastal terrace with views of the Pacific Ocean and agricultural fields, making for a nice country drive. From San Francisco, CA-1 heads south past the scenic communities of **Half Moon Bay** (19 mi/31 km), **Pescadero** (36 mi/58 km), and **Davenport** (56 mi/90 km). As CA-1 nears **Santa Cruz** (67 mi/108 km), rush hour traffic may become problematic, and the two-lane section of road into **Moss Landing** (95 mi/153 km) can also be slow.

From Shasta and Lassen
315 mi/505 km, 5 hr

In the Shasta and Lassen region, the gateway town of **Redding** offers the easiest starting point for this drive. From Redding, take I-5 south for 127 miles (204 km) past the town of **Williams.** Hop onto I-505 south for 35 miles (56 km) through Winters to meet I-80 in Vacaville.

From Vacaville and I-505, continue on I-80 West toward San Francisco for 15 miles (24 km). Veer left to take I-680 south for 70 miles (113 km) into San Jose. I-680 merges onto US-101 south and continues 30 miles (48 km) to Gilroy. Stay on US-101 south through Gilroy for 20 miles (32 km) before turning west onto CA-156 West toward the coast. Continue west on CA-156 for 7 miles (11.5 km). Just south of Castroville, US-101 merges with CA-1 South for 15 miles (24 km) to **Monterey.**

Monterey and Big Sur in Three Days

Day 1: Monterey

Start your day in Monterey with a coffee and pastry at **Café Lumiere,** then spend the afternoon on the bay on a **kayak, stand-up paddleboard,** or **whale-watching trip.** After working up an appetite, grab a seafood lunch (the Dungeness crab club sandwich and calamari are recommended) at **The Sandbar & Grill.** Now that you've seen the surface of the bay, dive beneath it at the **Monterey Bay Aquarium.** End the afternoon with a drink downtown at Monterey's **Alvarado Street Brewery & Grill** before walking to nearby **Montrio Bistro** for dinner.

Day 2: Carmel

Fuel up with a coffee and a gourmet breakfast sandwich at **Carmel Belle** before heading to nearby **Carmel Beach** for a stroll on one of the Central Coast's nicest beaches. Stop in to admire the **Carmel Mission,** then continue on to **Point Lobos State Natural Reserve.** Walk along the headlands, passing wind-sculpted cypress trees perched above the crashing sea. After your stroll, return to downtown Carmel for some wine-tasting followed by sushi at **Akaoni** or upscale Mexican cuisine at **Cultura Comida y Bebida.**

Day 3: Big Sur

Spend this morning on a scenic drive down the **Big Sur Coast Highway** (CA-1). Give yourself enough time to pull over and stop to admire the stunning coastal vistas. Lunch is at the **Big Sur River Inn & Restaurant;** enjoy a drink while sitting in the giant chairs plopped in the river behind the restaurant. Leave enough time for a hike, whether it's the **Ridge and Panorama Trail Loop** in Andrew Molera State Park or the **Partington Cove Trail** in Julia Pfeiffer Burns State Park. End the day with an Ambrosia burger at **Nepenthe,** where you can also take in the great coastal views, or soak up the romantic ambiance at **Deetjen's** restaurant.

Stopping in Williams

Williams is midway between Redding and Santa Rosa, so it is a good place for a pit stop. **Granzella's Restaurant & Deli** (451 6th St., 530/473-5496, www.granzellas.com, 6am-9pm daily, $8-10) is a popular deli, restaurant, and sports bar. Try the New Orleans muffuletta, the meatball sandwich, or create your own sandwich.

Cramped and exhausted from hours on the road? A soak in the hot, natural mineral springs at **Wilbur Hot Springs** (3375 Wilbur Springs Rd., 530/473-2306, https://wilburhotsprings.com, 10am-5pm daily, Mon.-Fri. $59, Sat.-Sun. $65) will cure what ails you. It's 23 miles (37 km) west of Williams on CA-20.

Train

Amtrak trains (800/872-7245, www.amtrak.com) stop in Salinas, a 20-mile (32-km) drive west of Monterey. The Coast Starlight route stops in Redding, Sacramento, Emeryville, and San Jose before passing through Salinas. Use a ride-sharing app (Uber, Lyft) to continue into Monterey.

Monterey

Monterey has roots as a fishing town. Native Americans were the first to ply the bay's waters, and fishing became an economic driver with the arrival of European settlers in the 19th century. Author John Steinbeck immortalized this unglamorous industry in his novel *Cannery Row*. Monterey's blue-collar past is still evident in its architecture, even though the cannery workers have been replaced by visiting tourists.

There are two main sections of Monterey: the old downtown area and "New Monterey," which includes Cannery Row and the Monterey Bay Aquarium. The old downtown is situated around Alvarado Street and includes the historic adobes that make up Monterey State Historic Park. New Monterey bustles with tourists during the summer. The six blocks of Cannery Row are packed with businesses, including the must-see Monterey Bay Aquarium, seafood restaurants, shops, galleries, and wine-tasting rooms. One way to get from one section to the other is to walk the Monterey Bay Coastal Recreation Trail, a paved path that runs right along a stretch of coastline.

Getting There

Most visitors drive into Monterey via scenic CA-1. Inland, US-101 allows access into Salinas from the north and south. From Salinas, CA-68 travels west into Monterey.

Sights
Cannery Row

Cannery Row (www.canneryrow.com) did once look and feel as John Steinbeck described it in his famed novel of the same name. In the 1930s and 1940s, fishing boats docked here and offloaded their catches straight into the huge, warehouse-like cannery buildings. But overfishing took its toll, and by the late 1950s Cannery Row was deserted. A slow renaissance began in the 1960s, driven by new interest in preserving the historical integrity of the area, as well as by a few savvy entrepreneurs who understood the value of beachfront property. Today, what was once a worker's wharf is now an enclave of boutique hotels, big seafood restaurants, and souvenir stores selling T-shirts adorned with sea otters. Cannery Row is anchored at one end by the aquarium and runs for several blocks that include a beach; it then leads into the Monterey Harbor area.

Thankfully, a few remnants of Cannery Row's past remain. Of greatest interest is a battered little shack located between the Monterey Bay Aquarium and the InterContinental hotel. **Pacific Biological Laboratories** (800 Cannery Row, 831/646-5640, www.monterey.org) was the workplace and home of famed marine biologist Ed Ricketts, a good friend of the author John Steinbeck. Ricketts appeared as "Doc" in Steinbeck's classic novel *Cannery Row*. The lab is now owned by the city and is open for free tours one day a month and for group tours by reservation.

★ Monterey Bay Aquarium

The **Monterey Bay Aquarium** (886 Cannery Row, 831/648-4800, www.montereybayaquarium.org, 9:30am-6pm daily, adults $50, seniors and students $40, children 3-12 $30) displays a dazzling array of local sealife. First-class exhibits include the Kelp Forest, which mimics the environment just outside; the Open Sea exhibit, with its deepwater tank that's home to giant bluefin tuna and hammerhead sharks; Wild About Otters, which gives an up-close view of rescued otters; and the Jellies Experience, which illuminates the delicate creatures. Check the feeding schedules when you arrive, and show up in advance to get a good spot near the critters for the show. The aquarium is wildly popular, and in the summer, the crowds can be forbidding. Weekdays

Monterey Peninsula

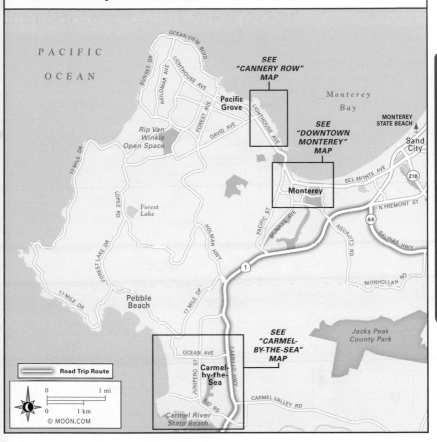

PACIFIC OCEAN

OCEAN VIEW BLVD

SUNSET DR

ASILOMAR AVE

LIGHTHOUSE AVE

FOREST AVE

Pacific Grove

DAVID AVE

LIGHTHOUSE AVE

SEE "CANNERY ROW" MAP

Monterey Bay

MONTEREY STATE BEACH

Sand City

SEE "DOWNTOWN MONTEREY" MAP

DEL MONTE AVE

218

Monterey

N FREMONT ST

68

PACIFIC ST

MUNRAS AVE

AGUAJITO RD

SALINAS HWY

Rip Van Winkle Open Space

17 MILE DR

LOPEZ RD

Forest Lake

FOREST LAKE DR

HOLMAN HWY

1

MONHOLLAN RD

Pebble Beach

17 MILE DR

17-MILE DR

SEE "CARMEL-BY-THE-SEA" MAP

Jacks Peak County Park

OCEAN AVE

JUNIPERO ST

Carmel-by-the-Sea

CABRILLO HWY

RIO RD

CARMEL VALLEY RD

Carmel River State Beach

Road Trip Route

0   1 mi

0   1 km

© MOON.COM

can be less crushing (though you'll run into school groups much of the year), and the off-season is always a better time to visit. Most exhibits at the aquarium are wheelchair-accessible.

Monterey State Historic Park

Monterey State Historic Park (20 Custom House Plaza, 831/649-2907, www.parks. ca.gov, 9am-5pm daily May-Sept., 10am-4pm daily Oct.-Apr., free) pays homage to the long and colorful history of the city of Monterey. This busy port town acted as the capital of California when it was under Spanish and Mexican rule. Today, the park is a collection of old buildings scattered about downtown Monterey, and it provides a peek into the city as it was in the mid-19th century.

Built in 1827, the **Custom House** (east of Fisherman's Wharf, 10am-4pm daily, $5) is the oldest government building still standing in the state. Wander the adobe building and check out the artifacts on display, meant to resemble the building's goods when it was under Mexican rule. On the nearby plaza, enter the first floor of the **Pacific House Museum** (hours

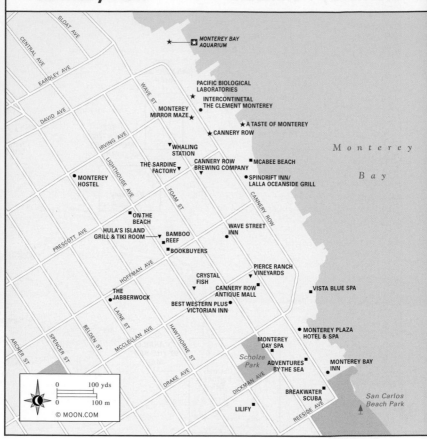

Cannery Row

and days vary seasonally) to see a range of Monterey's history from the Native Californians to the American Period. The second floor has a plethora of Native American artifacts.

The other buildings that compose the park were built mostly with adobe and/ or brick between 1834 and 1847. These include the **Casa del Oro** (210 Oliver St., 831/649-3364, 11am-3pm Thurs.-Sun.); the **First Brick House** (10am-4pm daily); the **Larkin House** (464 Calle Principal, 831/649-7172, private tours $75 for up to 12 people); the **Old Whaling Station**

(391 Decatur St., 831/375-5356, 10am-2pm Tues.-Fri.); the **Sherman Quarters** (closed to the public); and the **Stevenson House** (530 Houston St., hours and days vary seasonally), once a temporary residence of Robert Louis Stevenson.

For an introduction to the park and its history, take a **guided tour** (Custom House, hours and days vary, $10). The one-hour walk includes the Pacific House, the Custom House, the First Brick House, the Old Whaling Station (with its whalebone sidewalk out front), California's First Theatre, Casa del Oro,

Steinbeck

John Ernst Steinbeck was born in Salinas, California, in 1902 and grew up in its tiny, isolated agricultural community. He somehow managed to escape life as a farmer, a sardine fisherman, or a fish canner, and ended up living the glamorous life of a writer for his too-short 66 years.

Steinbeck's experiences in the Salinas Valley farming community and in the fishing town of Monterey informed many of his novels. The best known of these is *Cannery Row*, but *Tortilla Flat* is also set in working-class Monterey (though no one knows exactly where the fictional "Tortilla Flat" neighborhood was supposed to be). The Pulitzer Prize-winning novel *The Grapes of Wrath* takes more of its inspiration from the Salinas Valley. Steinbeck used the valley as a model for farming in the Dust Bowl during the Great Depression.

Steinbeck was fascinated by the plight of workingmen and -women; his novels and stories generally depict ordinary folks going through tough and terrible times. Steinbeck lived and worked through the Great Depression, thus it's not surprising that many of his stories do *not* feature happy Hollywood endings. Steinbeck was a realist in almost all of his novels, portraying the good, the bad, and the ugly of human life and society. His work gained almost immediate respect: In addition to his Pulitzer, Steinbeck also won the Nobel Prize for Literature in 1962. Almost every American high school student from the 1950s onward has read at least one of Steinbeck's novels or short stories; his body of work forms part of the enduring American literary canon.

As the birthplace of California's most illustrious literary son in the 20th century, Salinas became equally famous for spawning the author and inspiring his work. You'll find a variety of Steinbeck maps online (www.mtycounty.com) that offer self-guided tours of the regions made famous by his various novels. Poor Steinbeck's name is taken in vain all over now-commercial Cannery Row, where even the cheesy wax museum tries to draw customers in by claiming kinship with the legendary author.

Serious scholars of Steinbeck prefer the **National Steinbeck Center** (1 Main St., Salinas, 831/796-3833, www.steinbeck.org, 10am-5pm daily, adults $13, seniors and students $10, children 6-17 $7, children 5 and under free) and the **Steinbeck House** (132 Central Ave., Salinas, 831/424-2735, www.steinbeckhouse.com, restaurant 11:30am-2pm Tues.-Sat., $12-30, gift shop 11am-3pm Tues.-Sat.), both in the still-agricultural town of Salinas. In June, the Steinbeck Center hosts the annual **Steinbeck Festival** (www.steinbeck.org), a big shindig that celebrates the great man's life and works in fine style.

and the Memory Garden. A **cell phone tour** (831/998-9458) offers a two-minute rundown on each building.

Cooper-Molera Adobe

The **Cooper-Molera Adobe** (525 Polk St., 831/223-0171, https://savingplaces. org, 11am-4pm Tues.-Sat., 11am-2:30pm Sun., free) is a complex of historic buildings and gardens consisting of the **Cooper Molera Adobe Museum, Cella Restaurant, Alta Bakery & Café,** a day-use garden, and the **Barns at Cooper-Molera,** an event space. The adobe buildings were built in 1827 and initially included two homes, one of which housed early American resident John Bautista Rogers Cooper (Cooper came to live in Monterey when it was under Mexican rule). The interactive museum contains rooms decorated with Victorian-era decor, exhibits about the adobe's residents and visitors, and a rotating collection of local art.

The on-site restaurant, **Cella,** serves fresh California fare both indoors and in an outdoor garden. Surrounded by a historic adobe wall, the 2.5-acre facility is an oasis for contemplating Monterey's rich history.

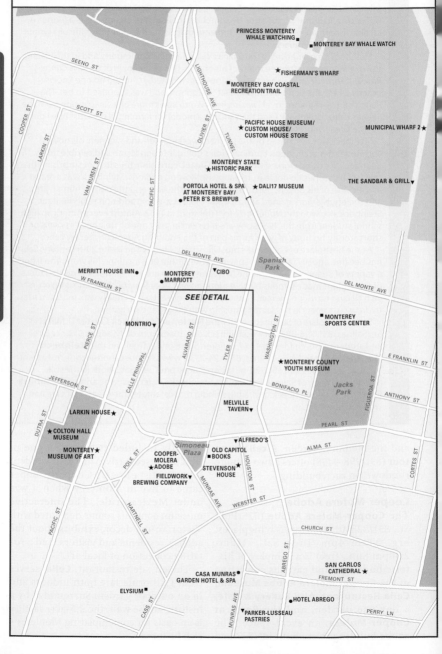

Downtown Monterey

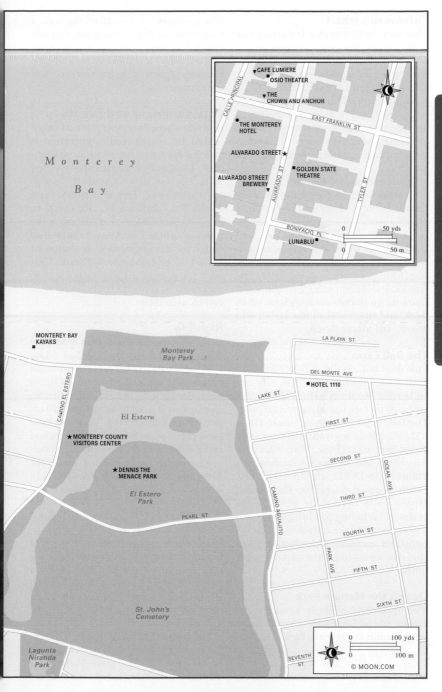

CAFE LUMIERE
OSIO THEATER
THE CROWN AND ANCHOR
CALLE PRINCIPAL
EAST FRANKLIN ST
THE MONTEREY HOTEL
ALVARADO STREET
ALVARADO ST
GOLDEN STATE THEATRE
ALVARADO STREET BREWERY
TYLER ST
BONIFACIO PL
0   50 yds
0   50 m
LUNABLU

Monterey
Bay

MONTEREY BAY KAYAKS

Monterey Bay Park
LA PLAYA ST

DEL MONTE AVE
HOTEL 1110
LAKE ST

CAMINO EL ESTERO
El Estero
FIRST ST

MONTEREY COUNTY VISITORS CENTER
SECOND ST
OCEAN AVE

DENNIS THE MENACE PARK
CAMINO AGUAJITO
THIRD ST

El Estero Park
PEARL ST
FOURTH ST

PARK AVE
FIFTH ST

St. John's Cemetery
SIXTH ST

Lagunta Niranda Park
SEVENTH ST
0   100 yds
0   100 m
© MOON.COM

Fisherman's Wharf

Monterey's scenic harbor is a great place to stroll along the shore, spot marine life, and explore the area's three wharves. Most popular is **Fisherman's Wharf** (1 Old Fisherman's Wharf, 831/238-0777, www.montereywharf.com, hours vary daily, free), which hosts a collection of seafood restaurants, touristy gift shops, and whale-watching boats. It has also been featured in the HBO series *Big Little Lies*.

The **Coast Guard Pier,** a 1,700-foot-long breakwater on the north end of the harbor, is one of Monterey's best wildlife-viewing areas. Look for sea lions and harbor seals as you walk out on the structure.

Municipal Wharf II is on the eastern edge of the harbor. It still has working fishing operations along with a few wholesale fish companies, a couple of restaurants, an abalone farm underneath its deck, and fine views of the harbor and nearby Del Monte Beach.

The Dalí Expo

One does not usually associate Salvador Dalí with Monterey. In 1941, the artist lived at Monterey's Hotel Del Monte, where he threw a legendary, surreal party. **The Dalí Expo** (5 Custom House Plaza, 831/372-2608, www.thedaliexpo.com, 10am-5pm Sun.-Thurs., 10am-6pm Fri.-Sat., adults $20, seniors $18, students $15, children 13-17 $12, children 6-12 $10, children under 6 free) has the second-largest collection of his works in the country, including 557 lithographs and 230 originals. Take a stroll through the two-floor museum, which portrays well this one-of-a-kind artist and his many quirks.

Dennis the Menace Park

The brainchild of Hank Ketcham, the creator of the *Dennis the Menace* comic strip, **Dennis the Menace Park** (777 Pearl St., 831/646-3860, www.monterey.org, 10am-dusk daily May-Sept., 10am-dusk Wed.-Mon. Sept.-May) opened in 1956. The park has a 9-foot climbing wall, a suspension bridge, curvy slides, brightly colored jungle gyms, and a (fenced-in, nonworking) locomotive, as well as a bronze sculpture of the little menace near the entrance.

Entertainment and Events

In days where everything seems dominated by social media, everyone is looking for a striking photo to post online. Monterey's **Selfieville** (Golden State Theatre, 417 Alvarado St., www.selfieville.com, days and times vary, adults $25, children $12.50) offers to help you post images that will make the Internet jealous. Check out the light show and short film (included with admission) in the historic Golden State Theatre, then pose for photos with oversized candy, unicorns, or butterflies at this unique, artistic attraction.

Nightlife

Descending into **The Crown & Anchor** (150 W. Franklin St., 831/649-6496, www.crownandanchor.net, 11am-1:30am daily) feels a bit like entering a ship's hold. Along with the maritime theme, The Crown & Anchor serves up to 20 international beers on tap. They also have good pub fare, including cottage pies and curries; the curry fries are a local favorite.

Microbrew fans should make for **Alvarado Street Brewery & Grill** (426 Alvarado St., 831/655-2337, www.alvaradostreetbrewery.com, 11:30am-10pm Sun.-Thurs., 11:30am-11pm Fri.-Sat.), a popular brewery and hot spot downtown. The big, boisterous modern space has more than 20 beers on tap, including their own sours, ales, and Mai Tai PA, a Great American Beer Festival gold-medal winner. Enjoy sipping the tasty brews out front on their sidewalk patio or in the beer garden in back.

Fieldwork (560 Munras Ave., 831/324-0658, https://fieldworkbrewing.com, noon-11pm Fri.-Sat., noon-11pm Sun.-Thurs.) is a Berkeley-based craft brewery with a satellite taproom in Monterey. This stripped-down operation has taps (and bathrooms) housed in shipping containers. Seating is outdoors in a beer garden. People come here for the creative brews, including a Churro Cream Ale, inspired by the Mexican dessert, and Galaxy Juice, a hazy IPA.

A distinct stone building just a couple of blocks off Alvarado Street, **Alfredo's Cantina** (266 Pearl St., 831/375-0655, 10am-midnight Sun.-Thurs., 10am-2am Fri.-Sat., cash only) is a cozy dive bar. This comfortable drinking establishment has dim lighting, a gas fireplace, cheap drinks, and a good jukebox.

Live Music

Downtown Monterey's historic **Golden State Theatre** (417 Alvarado St., 831/649-1070, www.goldenstatetheatre.com) hosts live music, movies, and events. The theater dates to 1926 and was designed to resemble a Moorish castle. Performers have included music legends like Patti Smith, Willie Nelson, and "Weird Al" Yankovic.

Festivals and Events

The annual **Monterey Wine Festival** (Custom House Plaza, 360/693-6023, http://montereywine.com, June) celebrates wine with a generous helping of food on the side. The outdoor festival is the perfect introduction to Monterey and Carmel wineries, many of which have not yet hit the "big time" in major wine magazines. It is also, incongruously, home to the West Coast Chowder Competition.

One of the biggest music festivals in California is the **Monterey Jazz Festival** (Monterey County Fairgrounds, 2004 Fairground Rd., 831/373-3366, www. montereyjazzfestival.org, Sept.). As the site of the longest-running jazz festival on earth (since 1958), Monterey attracts 500 artists from around the world to the fest's eight stages. Past acts to grace the

From top to bottom: the Custom House; the Monterey Bay Aquarium; Cannery Row.

Sea Sanctuary

Monterey Bay is in a federally protected marine area known as the **Monterey Bay National Marine Sanctuary** (MBNMS). Designated a sanctuary in 1992, the protected waters stretch far past the confines of Monterey Bay to a northern boundary 7 miles (11.5 km) north of the Golden Gate Bridge and a southern boundary at Cambria in San Luis Obispo. The sanctuary was created for resource protection, education, public use, and research. The MBNMS is the reason so many marine research facilities, including the Long Marine Laboratory, the Monterey Bay Marine Laboratory, and the Moss Landing Marine Laboratories, dot the Monterey Bay shoreline.

Among the many marine treasures of the MBNMS is the Monterey Bay Submarine Canyon, which is right offshore of the fishing village of Moss Landing. The canyon is similar in size to the Grand Canyon and has a rim-to-floor depth of 5,577 feet (1,700 m). In 2009, the MBNMS expanded to include another fascinating underwater geographical feature: the Davidson Seamount. Located 80 miles (129 km) southwest of Monterey, the undersea mountain rises an impressive 7,480 feet (2,280 m), yet its summit is still 4,101 feet (1,250 m) below the ocean's surface.

stage include Herbie Hancock, Booker T. Jones, and The Roots.

Monterey Car Week (www.seemonterey.com, Aug.) lures car enthusiasts to the Monterey Peninsula for seven days of car shows, races, and high-end automobile auctions. An event with a big sense of humor, the **Concours d'Lemons** (Seaside City Hall, 440 Harcourt Ave., Seaside, https://24hoursoflemons.com, Aug.) showcases clunkers, junkers, and automotive oddities.

Get into the holiday spirit by securing a ticket to **Christmas in the Adobes** (downtown Monterey, www.mshpa.org, Dec.). This popular event permits ticketholders to explore Monterey's oldest buildings, including those in Monterey State Historic Park as well as other private adobes that are open to the public only for this event. You'll find people in period dress, dancers, and music performances.

Sports and Recreation
★ Scuba Diving

There's one great place to get certified in scuba diving: Monterey Bay. Accordingly, dozens of dive schools cluster in and around the city of Monterey. Locals' favorite **Bamboo Reef** (614 Lighthouse Ave., 831/372-1685, www.bambooreef.com, 9am-6pm Mon.-Fri., 7am-6pm Sat.-Sun.)

offers scuba lessons and rents equipment just a few blocks from popular dive spots, including Breakwater Cove. The aquamarine storefront has been helping people get underwater since 1980.

Aquarius Dive Shop (2040 Del Monte Ave., 831/375-1933, www.aquariusdivers.com, 9am-6pm Mon.-Thurs., 9am-7pm Fri., 7am-7pm Sat., 7am-6pm Sun.) offers air and nitrox fills, equipment rental, and certification courses, and can help book a trip on a local dive boat. Aquarius works with five boats to create great trips for divers of all interests and ability levels. Call 831/657-1020 for local dive conditions.

Breakwater Scuba (225 Cannery Row, Ste. M, 831/717-4546, http://breakwaterscuba.com, 9am-6pm Mon.-Fri., 7am-6pm Sat.-Sun. summer, 9am-6pm Mon.-Tues. and Thurs.-Fri., 7am-6pm Sat.-Sun. winter) occupies an enviable spot close to Breakwater Cove. They rent equipment, teach classes, and conduct tours of the Breakwater Cove diving area.

★ Kayaking and Stand-Up Paddleboarding

The coast off Monterey is an ideal place for paddling: It is less exposed than other spots along the coast, and if the swells are big, you can duck into Monterey Harbor and paddle past moored boats and harbor seals. When the surf is manageable, the paddle from San Carlos Beach to the aquarium and back (1.5 mi/2.4 km round-trip) guarantees you will see an otter or a harbor seal. Note that Monterey Bay National Marine Sanctuary regulations require all paddlers to stay 150 feet (45 m) from all sea otters, sea lions, and harbor seals.

Adventures by the Sea (299 Cannery Row, 831/372-1807, www.adventures-bythesea.com, 9am-sunset daily, kayak tours $60-85 pp, kayak rentals $35/day, SUP rentals $50/day) rents kayaks and SUPs and lets you choose your own route around the Monterey Bay kelp forest. Adventures also offers tours (2.5 hours, 10am and 2pm daily in summer) from Cannery Row. Guides can tell you all about the wildlife you'll see: harbor seals, sea otters, pelicans, gulls, and maybe even a whale in the winter. The tandem sit-on-top kayaks make it a great experience for children. They also run a tour of Stillwater Cove at Pebble Beach. Reservations are recommended for all tours. The company has other locations in Monterey (685 Cannery Row, 32 Cannery Row, and 210 Alvarado St.).

Rent a kayak or SUP from **Monterey Bay Kayaks** (693 Del Monte Ave., 831/373-5357, www.montereybaykayaks.com, 9am-7pm daily summer, 9am-6pm daily spring, 9am-5pm daily fall/winter; kayak tours $45-100, kayak rentals $30-50 pp, SUP rentals $35 pp) and paddle into the bay from the beach just south of the Municipal Wharf. Tours include kayak fishing, Sunday sunrise excursions, and a Point Lobos paddle.

Whale-Watching

Whales pass quite near the shores of Monterey year-round. Although you can sometimes even see them from the beach, boats can take you out for a closer look. The area hosts many humpbacks, blue whales, and gray whales, plus the occasional killer whale, minke whale, fin whale, and pod of dolphins. Bring your own binoculars for a better view, but the experienced boat captains will do all they can to get you as close as possible to the whales and dolphins. Most tours last 2-3 hours and leave from Fisherman's Wharf.

Monterey Bay Whale Watch (84 Fisherman's Wharf, 831/375-4658, www.montereybaywhalewatch.com, adults $47-155, children 4-12 $36-39, children under 4 $15) leaves from an easy-to-find red building on Fisherman's Wharf and runs tours in every season. You must make a reservation in advance, even for regularly scheduled tours. Afternoon tours are available.

Princess Monterey **Whale Watching** (96 Fisherman's Wharf, 831/372-2203, www.montereywhalewatching.com, adults $50-70, children 3-11 $35-55) prides itself on its knowledgeable guides and its comfortable, spacious cruising vessels. It costs a bit extra to secure a space on the ship's upper deck. The *Princess Monterey* offers morning and afternoon tours, and you can buy tickets online or by phone.

Fast Raft Ocean Safaris (Monterey Harbor and Moss Landing Harbor, 408/659-3900, www.fastraft.com, $165-175 pp) offers an intimate way to explore the coast and wildlife. The "fast raft" is a 33-foot-long inflatable boat with a rigid hull that accommodates six passengers. The outfit does whale-watching trips out of Moss Landing and coastal safaris that depart from Monterey and head south to Pebble Beach's Stillwater Cove and Point Lobos. Note that the fast raft does not have a restroom.

Fishing

J&M Sport Fishing (66 Fisherman's Wharf, 831/372-7440 or 800/251-7440, https://jmsportfishing.com, $80-90) took over the longtime Randy's Fishing fleet. The new operation leaves shore for salmon, rock cod, and a fishing/crabbing combo trip.

To catch your own seafood, head out with **Westwind Charter Sport Fishing & Excursions** (66 Fisherman's Wharf, 831/392-7867, http://montereysportfishing.com). Depending on what's in season, you can catch salmon ($675/up to four people), rock cod, lingcod, or halibut ($575/up to four people).

Chris' Fishing and Whale Watching trips (48 Fisherman's Wharf, 831/375-5951, https://chrissfishing.com, adults $85-90, children $55) go out for rock cod, salmon, and a crab-sand dab combo on a three-boat fleet.

Hiking

The 18-mile (29-km) paved **Monterey Bay Coastal Recreation Trail** (831/646-3866, https://monterey.org) stretches from Pacific Grove north to the town of Castroville. The most scenic section is from Monterey Harbor down to Pacific Grove's Lovers Point Park. It's a great way to take in Monterey's coastline, sea otters, and harbor seals.

Jack's Peak County Park (25020 Jacks Peak Park Rd., 831/775-4895, www.co.monterey.ca.us, 8am-dusk daily, $4-5) is home to the highest point on the Monterey Peninsula. The park has picnic sites and 8.5 miles (13.5 km) of walking paths, including the 0.8-mile-long **Skyline Trail.** The trail passes through a rare Monterey pine forest and offers glimpses of fossils from the Miocene epoch before reaching the summit, which offers an overview of the whole peninsula.

Fort Ord Dunes State Park was home to a U.S. Army post from 1917 to 1994 (831/649-2836, www.parks.ca.gov, 8am-sunset daily, free). Across the park, paths lead to remnants of the military past plus miles of beach access. To get there from Monterey, head north on CA-1 and take the Lightfighter Drive exit. Turn left onto 2nd Avenue and then take a left on Divarty Street. Turn right on 1st Avenue and follow the signs to the park entrance at the 8th Street Bridge over CA-1.

Biking

Rent a bike at **Adventures by the Sea** (299 Cannery Row, 831/372-1807, www.adventuresbythesea.com, 9am-sunset daily, bike rentals $35-60/day, surrey rentals $150-210/day) and bike along the 18-mile (29-km) **Monterey Bay Coastal Recreation Trail.** Their surreys are fun, pedal-driven carriages that carry 2-6 people. The company has other locations in Monterey (685 Cannery Row, 32 Cannery Row, and 210 Alvarado St.).

Golf

The **Monterey Pines Golf Course** (Fairground Rd. and Garden Rd., 831/656-2167, www.montereypeninsulagolf.com, Mon.-Fri. $18-34, Sat.-Sun. $20-37) is a beginner-friendly 18 holes next to the Monterey County Fairgrounds. The Pebble Beach Company manages the **Del Monte Golf Course** (1300 Sylvan Rd., 800/877-0597, www.montereypeninsulagolf.com, $110), an 18-hole course that claims to be the oldest continuously operating course west of the Mississippi.

Motor Sports

The **WeatherTech Raceway Laguna Seca** (1021 Monterey-Salinas Hwy., 831/242-8201, www.weathertechraceway.com, May-Oct.) is one of the country's premier road-racing venues. You can see historic auto races, superbikes, speed festivals, and an array of Grand Prix events. Laguna Seca also hosts innumerable auto clubs and small sports car and stock car races. You can also camp here, and you'll find plenty of concessions during big races.

Food

The Monterey Bay Seafood Watch program (www.seafoodwatch.org) is the definitive resource for sustainable seafood, while the Salinas Valley inland hosts a number of organic farms. The primary farmers market in the county, the **Monterey Farmers Market** (Alvarado

St. between Del Monte Ave. and Pearl St., 831/655-2607, www.oldmonterey.org, 4pm-7pm Tues. Oct.-Apr., 4pm-8pm Tues. May-Sept.) takes over downtown Monterey with fresh-produce vendors, restaurant stalls, jewelry booths, and live music.

Cafés

Connected to the Osio Cinemas, Monterey's art-house movie theater, **Café Lumiere** (365 Calle Principal, 831/920-2451, http://cafelumieremonterey.com, 7am-8pm daily), is where Monterey's old Sicilian anglers hang out in the morning while sipping coffee drinks and munching on pastries. There are a lot of tempting options behind the counter's glass case, but the café also offers breakfast, lunch, and Sunday brunch dishes. In addition, the café has weekday lunch specials including a very popular giant bowl of pho (Vietnamese noodle soup) on Thursday. The tasty coffee is from Acme Coffee Roasting Company, a local favorite.

American

Inside an old brick firehouse, ★ **Montrio Bistro** (414 Calle Principal, 831/648-8880, www.montrio.com, 4:30pm-close daily, $19-46) is an elegantly casual Monterey eatery. The ever-changing menu includes meat and seafood entrées, but Montrio is also an ideal place for a lighter dinner. Dine inside under ceilings decorated with art that resembles clouds, or out front on the patio. Executive chef Tony Baker is known for his dry-cured bacon. Happy hour (4:30pm-6:30pm daily, $6.50) is worth a visit for cocktails and well-priced snacks.

A cozy locals' spot in a brick building a block off Alvarado Street, **Melville Tavern** (484 Washington St., 831/643-9525, www.melilletav.com, 11am-9pm Mon.-Fri., 10am-9pm Sat.-Sun., $12-26) does a bit less damage on the wallet. The straightforward but well-executed menu of sandwiches, salads, tacos, and a green chile cheeseburger will hit the spot. There's a nicely curated mix of beers on tap and wine by the glass or the bottle (look for the $3 beer of the week and the $6 wine of the week).

Seafood

On weekends, there is typically a line out the door at **Monterey's Fish House** (2114 Del Monte Ave., 831/373-4647, http://montereyfishhouse.com, 11:30am-2:30pm and 5pm-9:30pm Mon.-Fri., 5pm-9:30pm Sat.-Sun., $12-25), one of the peninsula's most popular seafood restaurants. It has a fun, old-school Italian vibe. Inside, expect attentive service and fresh seafood including snapper, albacore tuna, and calamari fished right out of the bay.

★ **The Sandbar & Grill** (Municipal Wharf II, 831/373-2818, www.sandbarandgrillmonterey.com, 11am-9pm Mon.-Sat., 10:30am-9pm Sun., $18-33) has the best fried calamari around. The strips are pounded thin and then deep-fried a golden hue. The Sandbar is also known for their fresh sand dabs and the Dungeness crab sandwich with bacon. The restaurant sits on the Municipal Wharf over Monterey Harbor.

For a South Pacific spin on seafood, head to ★ **Hula's Island Grill & Tiki Room** (622 Lighthouse Ave., 831/655-4852, www.hulastiki.com, 4pm-9:30pm Sun.-Mon., 11:30am-9:30pm Tues.-Thurs., 11:30am-10pm Fri.-Sat., $12-23). Hula's is a fun and casual place serving tasty, and sometimes, imaginative food. The menu features fresh fish, a range of tacos, and land-based fare like Jamaican-jerk chicken. Happy hour (4pm-6pm Sun.-Mon., 2pm-9:30pm Tues., 2pm-6pm Wed.-Sat.) features tiki drinks and pupus (appetizers) for just six bucks a pop.

The Sardine Factory (701 Wave St., 831/373-3775, http://sardinefactory.com, 5pm-10:30pm Sun.-Thurs., 5pm-11pm Fri.-Sat., $26-59) is the area's iconic seafood and steak house. Its abalone bisque was served at one of President Ronald Reagan's inaugural dinners, and part of

Clint Eastwood's directorial debut *Play Misty for Me* was filmed in the restaurant. This place oozes old-school cool, complete with a piano player in the lounge (Tues.-Sat.). The menu includes pasta, steak, and wild abalone medallions. Ask for a tour of the building, which has a glass-domed conservatory and an exclusive wine cellar that feels transported from a European castle.

Steak

The Whaling Station (763 Wave St., 831/373-3778, www.whalingstation.net, 5pm-9pm Sun.-Thurs., 5pm-10:30pm Fri.-Sat., $26-64) has been a local institution since 1970. Waiters present different cuts of meat on a tray and answer questions about the best qualities of each piece. Options include a New York steak, beef Wellington, and red-wine-braised beef short ribs. Non-beef items include rack of lamb, seafood, and pasta. The moderately priced bar menu includes a burger made with ground filet mignon and some filet-mignon medallions with garlic mashed potatoes.

Sushi

Fresh seafood and creative rolls make **Crystal Fish** (514 Lighthouse Ave., 831/649-3474, http://crystalfishmonterey.com, 11:30am-2pm and 5pm-9:30pm Mon.-Thurs., 11:30am-2pm and 5pm-10pm Fri., 1pm-10pm Sat., 1pm-9:30pm Sun., $14-35) the Monterey go-to for sushi. There's not a lot of ambiance, but there are a lot of rolls, including fresh salmon, tuna, eel, octopus, calamari, and unusual ingredients like asparagus and eggplant.

Accommodations
Under $150
The ★ **Monterey Hostel** (778 Hawthorne St., 831/649-0375, http://montereyhostel.

From top to bottom: kayaking off Monterey's Municipal Wharf; whale-watching in Monterey Bay; the Monterey Bay Inn.

org, dorm bed $45-55, private room $169-209) offers inexpensive accommodations within walking distance of the major attractions of Monterey. Accommodations include a men's dorm room, women's dorm room, private rooms, a five-person family room, and a coed dorm room with 16 beds; linens are included. A self-service laundry is within walking distance. Common areas include a large, fully stocked kitchen and spaces with couches and a piano. The kitchen serves a free pancake breakfast every morning.

$150-250

Jabberwock Inn (598 Laine St., 831/372-4777, www.jabberwockinn.com, $209-599) is named after a nonsense poem written by Lewis Carroll as part of his novel *Through the Looking Glass*. Despite its name, the amenities of this comfortable former convent turned eight-room bed-and-breakfast are no-nonsense. The common area has a covered wraparound sun porch with views of Monterey Bay and two fireplaces. There are no TVs or telephones. Breakfasts are tasty and filling, while the innkeepers are warm and knowledgeable. Perks include free parking and late-afternoon wine and appetizers, along with evening milk and cookies. The B&B is just a short walk to Cannery Row, the aquarium, and Lighthouse Avenue.

The ★ **Portola Hotel & Spa** (2 Portola Plaza, 800/342-4295, 888/222-5851 reservations, www.portolahotel.com, $229-600) occupies a prime piece of real estate between Alvarado Street and the Custom House Plaza. Portola is a large hotel complex with 379 rooms connected to the Monterey Conference Center. Comfortable rooms are decorated with a red and blue motif, and many have full or Juliet balconies and patios to take in views of the harbor. On-site amenities include Jack's restaurant, a spa, a large fitness center, a pool, a hot tub, and the brewery Peter B's.

The greatest asset of **Monterey Tides** (2600 Sand Dunes Rd., 831/394-3321 or 800/242-8627, www.jdvhotels.com, $200-400) is its proximity to the sand and surf. The four-story building sits right over Monterey State Beach; 102 of its 196 rooms face Monterey Bay. At night, take in the tapered triangle of lights on the Monterey peninsula from the wooden patios off the hotel's lobby. There's a heated pool (year-round) alongside a spa, and bikes and stand-up paddleboards are available for rent. The lobby bar, Bar Sebastian, and the top-floor Vizcaino restaurant have stellar views to accompany meals and drinks. The hotel also offers something most don't: fires on the beach (firewood $25; bonfire kit with s'mores $30).

Over $250

Luxury hotel **InterContinental The Clement Monterey** (750 Cannery Row, 831/375-4500, www.ictheclementmonterey.com, $250-850) has a can't-be-beat location just a splash away from the bay and aquarium. The hotel has 208 rooms and 12 luxury suites decorated with tasteful Asian elements such as a bonsai tree, a tiny Zen garden, and live orchids. Most of the bathrooms have a separate soaking tub and walk-in shower. Oceanside rooms have views of the bay, while units on the other side of Cannery Row have fireplaces. There are a lot of amenities, including a fitness room, an outdoor whirlpool, **The Spa, The C Restaurant & Bar,** a sliver of an outdoor pool to swim laps in, and an artsy, jellyfish-inspired staircase connecting the first and second floors.

Located between San Carlos Beach and Cannery Row, the **Monterey Bay Inn** (242 Cannery Row, 831/373-6242 or 800/424-6242, www.montereybayinn.com, $309-600) has oceanfront rooms with private balconies that overlook Monterey Bay and in-room binoculars for spotting wildlife. The hotel's rooftop hot tub offers another vantage point to take in the action offshore. Enjoy a continental breakfast delivered to your room in the morning and cookies in the evening.

The ★ **Spindrift Inn** (652 Cannery Row, 831/646-8900, www.spindriftinn. com, $309-689) is a boutique hotel towering above the golden sand and clear green waters of scenic McAbee Beach. This 45-room establishment has been called the country's most romantic hotel. Most of the hardwood-floored rooms have wood-burning fireplaces and full or half canopy beds. The very friendly staff serves a wine and cheese reception daily (4:30pm-6pm) and delivers a complimentary continental breakfast to your room.

Camping
A mile up a hill from downtown Monterey, the 50-acre **Veterans Memorial Park** (Via Del Rey and Veterans Dr., 831/646-3865, www.monterey.org, $30/single vehicle, $38/two vehicles) has 40 first-come, first-served campsites with views of Monterey Bay.

Information and Services
For medical needs, the **Community Hospital of the Monterey Peninsula** (23625 Holman Hwy., 831/624-5311 or 888/452-4667, www.chomp.org) provides emergency services to the area.

Getting Around
For a leisurely ride, **Amtrak**'s Coast Starlight (11 Station Pl., Salinas, 10am-2pm and 3pm-8pm daily) travels through Salinas.

The **Greyhound** bus station (3 Station Pl., Salinas, 831/424-4418, www.grey-hound.com, 9am-noon and 1pm-4pm Mon.-Fri., 9am-3pm Sat.-Sun.) is 19 miles (31 km) east of Monterey. To get to Monterey, walk two blocks to the **Salinas Transit Center** (110 Salinas St., 888/678-2871, https://mst.org) and hop on a Monterey-Salinas Transit bus to the coast.

In Monterey, take advantage of the free **Monterey Trolley** (Waterfront Area Visitor Express, 888/678-2871, https:// mst.org, hours vary daily late May-early Sept., 10am-7pm Sat.-Sun. early Sept.-late May), which loops between downtown Monterey and the aquarium. **Monterey-Salinas Transit** (888/678-2871, www.mst. org, $1.50-3.50) has routes throughout Monterey.

Pacific Grove

Sandwiched between historic Monterey and exclusive Pebble Beach, Pacific Grove makes a fine base for exploring the peninsula. It's also worth a visit for its colorful turn-of-the-20th-century Victorian homes and its striking strand of coastline. Founded in 1875 as a Methodist summer retreat, this quiet city is perfect for a relaxing afternoon of strolling among the yellow, purple, and green Victorian homes and cottages on Lighthouse Avenue. (There's a different Lighthouse Avenue in adjacent Monterey.)

Pacific Grove's "Poor Man's 17-Mile Drive" winds around a piece of coastal real estate between Lovers Point Park and Asilomar Beach that's almost as striking as Pebble Beach's 17-Mile Drive. Start on Ocean View Boulevard by Lovers Point and continue onto Sunset Drive to get the full experience. In the spring, flowering ice plant right along the road adds a riot of color to the landscape.

Getting There
Most visitors drive into the area via scenic CA-1. From CA-1, take the CA-68 West exit to reach downtown Pacific Grove.

Sights
Lovers Point Park
Aptly named **Lovers Point Park** (Ocean View Blvd. and 17th St., 831/648-3100, www.cityofpacificgrove.org) is one of the area's most popular wedding sites. A finger of land with a jumble of rocks at its northernmost point, Lovers Point offers expansive views of the interior

section of Monterey Bay. The park also has a sheltered pocket beach that is ideal for a dip. A kelp forest right offshore offers a superb spot for snorkelers to get a feel for Monterey Bay's impressive underwater ecosystem. During summer, an old-fashioned hamburger stand operates above the beach, and a vendor rents kayaks, bikes, and snorkeling equipment.

Point Pinos Lighthouse

Surrounded by a golf course, **Point Pinos Lighthouse** (80 Asilomar Ave. between Lighthouse Ave. and Del Monte Ave., 831/648-3176, www.pointpinoslighthouse.org, 1pm-4pm Thurs.-Mon., adults $4, children $2) is the oldest continuously operating lighthouse on the West Coast, in service since 1855. Point Pinos is also notable for the two female lighthouse keepers who served there during its long history. The light was automated in 1975, but it is still an active aid to local marine navigation. Lighthouse lovers will enjoy walking through the building's two floors and cellar.

Monarch Grove Sanctuary

Pacific Grove is also known as "Butterfly Town U.S.A." An impressive migration of monarch butterflies descends on the town each year. The small **Monarch Grove Sanctuary** (Ridge Rd. between Lighthouse Ave. and Short St., 831/648-5716, www.cityofpacificgrove.org, free) offers stands of eucalyptus and pine trees that are cloaked with colorful insects during the migration period (Oct.-Feb.). The best time to visit is in the early afternoon, when sunlight illuminates the butterflies and docents can answer your questions.

Asilomar State Beach

One of the Monterey Peninsula's most popular beaches, **Asilomar State Beach** (Sunset Dr., 831/646-6440, www.parks. ca.gov) draws beachgoers, walkers, and surfers. The beach is a narrow, mile-long strip of coastline with a boardwalk trail on the dunes behind it. Keep walking on the trail to get to nearby Pebble Beach.

Right across Sunset Drive visitors can explore the **Asilomar Dunes Natural Preserve** and the **Asilomar Conference Grounds** (800 Asilomar Ave., 888/635-5310, www.visitasilomar.com). The dunes preserve is 25 acres of restored sand dune ecosystem that can be accessed via a 0.25-mile boardwalk. The conference grounds are shaded by Monterey pines and studded with Arts and Crafts-style structures designed by Hearst Castle architect Julia Morgan. Enjoy the facilities, including the Phoebe A. Hearst Social Hall, which has pool tables, a fireplace, and some comfy seats. One-hour **ranger-guided tours** of the grounds (831/646-6443) focus on the architecture, the dunes, the forest, and the coast.

To reach Asilomar, take the CA-68 West exit off CA-1 and turn left onto Sunset Drive.

Pacific Grove Museum of Natural History

Stop into the **Pacific Grove Museum of Natural History** (165 Forest Ave., 831/648-5716, www.pgmuseum.org, 3pm-7pm Mon., 10am-5pm Tues.-Sun. summer, 10am-5pm Tues.-Sun. winter, adults $9, military, students, and children $6) and learn how to identify the animal and plant species of the Monterey Peninsula. The museum provides a fairly comprehensive overview of the region's biodiversity. One room is dedicated to feathered friends and includes 300 mounted birds found around the county, among them the gigantic California condor. Other rooms highlight large terrestrial mammals (mountain lions, bears) and whales. There's also a space devoted to the monarch butterfly. Out front is a life-size gray whale statue, while out back is a native plant garden.

Entertainment and Events

A couple of family-friendly annual events occur in "America's Last Hometown."

Recalling another era, Pacific Grove's **Good Old Days** (831/373-3304, www.pacificgrove.org, Apr.) is a weekend of good clean fun that includes a parade, a quilt show, pony rides, and live entertainment. For more than 70 years, kids have been getting dressed up like butterflies at the **Butterfly Parade and Bazaar** (831/373-3304, www.pacificgrove.org, first Sat. of Oct.), which welcomes the wintering monarch butterflies to the area every fall.

Sports and Recreation
Scuba Diving and Snorkeling
Some of the best scuba diving and snorkeling spots lie off Pacific Grove. **Lovers Point Park** (Ocean View Blvd. and 17th St., novice to advanced, 10-40 ft/3-12 m) has a protected cove and kelp forest right off its shores. The cove's protected, sandy beach makes an easy entry point for scuba divers and snorkelers. A few blocks away, **Otter Cove** (Ocean View Blvd. and Sea Palm Ave., novice to advanced, 10-60 ft/3-18 m) is a dive spot best explored during days of calm seas. One of the highlights is an underwater pinnacle that rises from 50 feet (15 m) to just 18 feet (5.5 m) below the surface. Nearby **Coral Street Cove** (Coral St. and Ocean View Blvd., advanced, 20-50 ft/6-15 m) is known for its fish population.

For equipment, visit **Bamboo Reef** (614 Lighthouse Ave., 831/372-1685, www.bambooreef.com, 9am-6pm Mon.-Fri., 7am-6pm Sat.-Sun.), **Aquarius Dive Shop** (2040 Del Monte Ave., 831/375-1933, www.aquariusdivers.com, 9am-6pm Mon.-Thurs., 9am-7pm Fri., 7am-7pm Sat., 7am-6pm Sun.), or **Breakwater Scuba** (225 Cannery Row, Ste. M, 831/717-4546, http://breakwaterscuba.com, 9am-6pm Mon.-Fri., 7am-6pm Sat.-Sun. summer, 9am-6pm Mon.-Tues. and Thurs.-Fri., 7am-6pm Sat.-Sun. winter).

Surfing
During the summer and fall, clean swells produce fun waves at **Asilomar State Beach** (Sunset Dr., 831/646-6440, www.

parks.ca.gov), making it one of the peninsula's most popular surf spots. Winter produces big, often dangerous swells, so stay out of the water during that time of the year. To get there, take the CA-68 West exit off CA-1 and turn left onto Sunset Drive.

During big swells, **Lovers Point** (Ocean View Blvd. and 17th St.) turns into a nice left. There are some rocks in the lineup, so it is probably best that first-timers go out with someone who knows the break.

On the Beach (693 Lighthouse Ave., 831/646-9283, http://onthebeachsurfshop.com, 10am-6pm Sun.-Thurs., 10am-7pm Fri.-Sat., surfboard rental $30-35/day, wetsuit rental $20/day) rents surfboards and wetsuits.

Golf
The **Pacific Grove Golf Links** (77 Asilomar Blvd., 831/648-5775, www.playpacificgrove.com, daily sunrise-sunset, Mon.-Thurs. $48, Fri.-Sun. and holidays $73) doesn't have the acclaim of the nearby Pebble Beach courses, but it's on a similarly gorgeous length of coastline just a few miles away.

Food
American
★ **Crema** (481 Lighthouse Ave., 831/324-0347, http://cremapg.com, 7am-3pm daily, $8-18) is a gourmet comfort food restaurant located in a multilevel building that feels like someone's home. Dine on the locally renowned chicken-and-waffles or their popular bacon-cheddar biscuits with spicy-sausage gravy. They also serve a stout beer float (stout beer, ice cream, and espresso) and bottomless mimosas, as well as coffee in their downstairs espresso bar.

In the cavernous American Tin Cannery shopping mall, **First Awakenings** (125 Oceanview Blvd., 831/372-1125, www.firstawakenings.net, 7am-2pm Mon.-Fri., 7am-2:30pm Sat.-Sun., $6-12) serves oversize versions of classic breakfast fare including huevos rancheros, eggs Benedict, crepes, and omelets. Locals frequently vote this place the county's top breakfast spot. On sunny days, dine outside on the large patio while surrounded by the sounds of nearby Monterey Bay.

Italian
Il Vecchio (110 Central Ave., 831/324-4282, www.ilvecchiorestaurant.com, noon-1:30pm and 5pm-9pm Mon.-Thurs., noon-1:30pm and 5pm-9:30pm Fri., 5pm-9:30pm Sat., 5pm-9pm Sun., $17-26) is a Pacific Grove favorite. The phrase *il vecchio* means "the old" and refers to traditional Italian fare like gnocchi with pesto. They make their pasta daily and offer traditional Italian takes on meats and seafood. They also have a good lunch special (noon-1:30pm Mon.-Fri., $11.50) serving a salad and a pasta.

Mediterranean
The **Jeninni Kitchen & Wine Bar** (542 Lighthouse Ave., 831/920-2662, www.jeninni.com, 4pm-close Thurs.-Tues., $18-30) has elevated Pacific Grove's dining scene. The Mediterranean-inspired menu changes frequently, but the eggplant fries are favorites. Sit in the dining area in the front of the building or walk up a few stairs to the bar area for small plates, wine, and craft beers.

Mexican
For a healthy, California-style take on Mexican food, visit popular **Michael's Grill & Taqueria** (1126 Forest Ave., 831/647-8654, www.michaelsgrillandtaqueria.com, 10am-9pm daily, $11-30), uphill from downtown Pacific Grove. There are shades of Cajun cooking in the blackened chicken and shrimp used to fill their burritos and tostadas. Whether you order a fajita platter, a burrito, or a fajita salad, you will get a tasty, filling meal.

From top to bottom: Asilomar State Beach; the Gosby House Inn; 17-Mile Drive.

Seafood

One of the Monterey Peninsula's most lauded seafood restaurants is ★ **Passionfish** (701 Lighthouse Ave., 831/655-3311, www.passionfish.net, 5pm-9pm Sun.-Thurs., 5pm-10pm Fri.-Sat., $16-36), which is on a mission to spread the gospel about sustainable seafood. Passionfish does great food, especially creative and flavorful sustainable seafood. The menu starts with a nice scallop appetizer and features a list of seafood-heavy entrées. They are also known for their extensive, yet moderately priced, wine list. The knowledgeable waitstaff could teach a course on seafood.

Accommodations

Pacific Grove is known for bed-and-breakfasts in nice Victorian buildings.

Under $150

The ★ **Gosby House Inn** (643 Lighthouse Ave., 800/527-8828, www.gosbyhouseinn. com, $125-280) has been taking care of visitors since the 1880s. The white-and-yellow Queen Anne-style Victorian, which sits on downtown Pacific Grove's main street, is a welcome cross between a boutique hotel and a B&B. Amenities include free Wi-Fi, flat-screen TVs in most rooms, and a complimentary breakfast. The photo- and antique-heavy main house has 22 rooms, some with gas fireplaces. The two deluxe rooms in the adjacent Carriage House have a balcony, a gas fireplace, a roomy bathroom, and a nice-size soaking tub.

$150-250

Staying overnight at the ★ **Asilomar Conference Grounds** (804 Crocker Ave., 831/372-8016, www.visitasilomar.com, $190-335) can feel like going back to summer camp. Common areas on the 107 acres include the Phoebe Apperson Hearst Social Hall, where visitors can relax by a roaring fire or play pool at one of two billiards tables. Accommodations range from historical rooms to family cottages to modern rooms with a view of nearby Asilomar Beach, but they purposefully lack TVs and telephones. Rooms with an ocean view and a fireplace are definitely recommended. The lodging hosts a multitude of conferences, so expect to see corporate types walking through the forests of Monterey pine, Monterey cypress, and coast live oaks.

The **Old St. Angela Inn** (321 Central Ave., 831/372-3246, www.oldstangelainn. com, $165-290) spoils with cozy accommodations, a friendly staff, and terrific food. The nine homey rooms have pine antiques, live plants, and comfortable beds. Comfy common areas are downstairs, while out back is a brick patio area with a fire pit and a waterfall fountain. One of the best features of The Old St. Angela Inn is its house-made food. Afternoon teatime offers wine, a dessert, and an appetizer. The scrumptious breakfast includes yogurt, granola, muffins, and a hot sweet or savory item.

One of the finest and most notable Queen Anne Victorian buildings is the dark green and white **Green Gables Inn** (301 Ocean View Blvd., 831/375-2095 or 800/722-1774, www.greengablesin-npg.com, $169-359). The main building, which was built in 1888, has a downstairs common area with ocean views—it's the place to stay, with a throwback feel and antique furnishings. Behind the main inn, the Carriage House has five spacious rooms, each with a gas fireplace, a jetted tub, and ocean views. The inn offers afternoon wine and appetizers, a morning breakfast buffet, and a few bikes that can be borrowed for a spin on the nearby Monterey Bay Coastal Recreation Trail.

Over $250

The most striking bed-and-breakfast on the Pacific Grove coast, the **Seven Gables Inn** (555 Ocean View Blvd., 831/372-4341, www.sevengablesinn.com, $329-469) is perched just feet away from Lovers Point. Every room has superb ocean views. Decorated with antique furniture and artwork, the inn is for those who want to step back in time and experience ornate Victorian- and Edwardian-style lodging.

Information and Services

For medical needs, the **Community Hospital of the Monterey Peninsula** (CHOMP, 23625 Holman Hwy., 831/624-5311 or 888/452-4667, www.chomp.org) in Monterey provides emergency services to the area.

Pebble Beach

Between Pacific Grove and Carmel, the gated community of Pebble Beach lays claim to some of the Monterey Peninsula's best and highest-priced real estate. Pebble Beach is famous for the scenic 17-Mile Drive and its collection of high-end resorts, restaurants, spas, and golf courses, owned by the Pebble Beach Company, a partnership that included golf legend Arnold Palmer and film legend Clint Eastwood. Pebble Beach also hosts the annual **AT&T Pebble Beach National Pro-Am** (831/649-1533, www.attpbgolf.com, Feb., event prices vary), a charity golf tournament that pairs professional golfers with celebrities.

Getting There

Pebble Beach is a gated community and entry requires a **fee** ($10.25). There are several gates to get into Pebble Beach, including three in Pacific Grove and one in Carmel. You can get the fee waived if you are dining at a Pebble Beach restaurant. Just make a reservation and tell the guard at the entry gate.

Sights

17-Mile Drive

The best way to take in the stunning scenery of Pebble Beach is the **17-Mile Drive** (27 km, $10.25/vehicle). Pay the fee at the gatehouse and receive a map of the drive that describes the parks and sights you'll pass along the winding

coastal road: the much-photographed Lone Cypress, the beaches of Spanish Bay, and Pebble Beach's golf course, resort, and housing complex. If you're in a hurry, you can get from one end of the 17-Mile Drive to the other in 20 minutes. But go slowly and stop often to enjoy the natural beauty of the area. Plenty of turnouts let you stop to take photos, and you can picnic at many of the beaches; most have basic restroom facilities and ample parking lots. The only food and gas are at the Inn at Spanish Bay and the Lodge at Pebble Beach.

Sports and Recreation

Spa at Pebble Beach (1518 Cypress Dr., 831/649-7615 or 800/877-0597, www.pebblebeach.com, 8:30am-7:30pm daily, $165-470) has specialty massages for golfers before or after a day on the greens.

Biking

Traveling the **17-Mile Drive** by bike means you don't have to pay the vehicle admission fee. It's also a great bike route. Expect fairly flat terrain with lots of twists and turns, and a ride that runs ... about 17 miles (27 km). Foggy conditions can make this ride a bit slick in the summer, but spring and fall weather are perfect for pedaling.

Adventures by the Sea (831/372-1807, www.adventuresbythesea.com, 9am-sunset daily) rents bikes ($35-60/day) and surreys ($150-210/day) from locations all over Monterey (299 Cannery Row, 685 Cannery Row, 32 Cannery Row, and 210 Alvarado St.).

Golf

Golf has been a major pastime here since the late 19th century; today avid golfers come from around the world to tee off (and pay $200 or more for a single round of golf). The 18-hole, par-72 **Spyglass Hill** (1700 17-Mile Dr., 800/877-0597, www.pebblebeach.com, $395) gets its name from the Robert Louis Stevenson Novel *Treasure Island*. Spyglass Hill boasts some of the most challenging play in this golf course-laden region. Expect a few bogeys, and tee off from the championship level at your own (ego's) risk.

A favorite with the Pebble Beach crowd is the famed 18-hole, par-72 **Poppy Hills Golf Course** (3200 Lopez Rd., 831/622-8239, www.poppyhillsgolf.com, $250). Poppy Hills shares amenities with the other Pebble Beach golf courses. Expect the same level of care and devotion to the maintenance of the course and your experience as a player.

Pebble Beach Golf Links (1700 17-Mile Dr., 800/877-0597, www.pebblebeach. com, $550) has been called the nation's best golf course by *Golf Digest*. The high ranking might have something to do with the fact that some of the fairways are perched above the Pacific Ocean. The course will host its sixth men's U.S. Open championship in 2019 and is one of three courses utilized during the popular AT&T Pro-Am.

Less pricey than the Pebble Beach Golf Links, **The Links at Spanish Bay** course (2700 17-Mile Dr., 800/877-0597, $290) is on native sand dune habitat. Due to the environmental sensitivity of the grounds, the course caps the number of players and spectators on the greens.

Food and Accommodations

You need to drop some serious money to stay in Pebble Beach. To experience the luxury of Pebble Beach without spending your savings, consider having lunch, dinner, or a drink and then heading back to a less expensive lodging in nearby Pacific Grove or Monterey.

The Hawaiian fusion cuisine of celebrity chef Roy Yamaguchi takes center stage at **Roy's at Pebble Beach** (The Inn at Spanish Bay, 2700 17-Mile Dr., 800/877-0597, www.pebblebeach.com, 6:30am-10pm daily, $27-50). Island-inspired dishes include seafood and sushi, all with an Asian flair.

Head to **Peppoli** (The Inn at Spanish Bay, 2700 17-Mile Dr., 831/647-7433,

www.pebblebeach.com, 6pm-10pm daily, $25-110) for a hearty Italian dinner of gnocchi with black truffle cream sauce or seared local halibut.

The Bench Restaurant (The Lodge at Pebble Beach, 1700 17-Mile Dr., 800/877-0597, 11am-10pm daily, $25-36) overlooks the famed 18th hole of the Pebble Beach Golf Links. The chef employs wood-roasting and open-flame cooking techniques to create wood-fired Brussels sprouts and grilled steaks.

The Tap Room (The Lodge at Pebble Beach, 1700 17-Mile Dr., 831/625-8535, 11am-midnight daily, $22-79) serves burgers, bratwurst, Wagyu-beef filet mignon, fresh Maine lobster, and prime-rib chili that is worth your time. All of this with 14 beers on tap (at an inflated price of $10.75). It's still a nice spot to soak up the Pebble Beach ambiance without totally emptying your wallet. Bill Murray is an occasional customer.

Located beside the Poppy Hills Golf Course, **Porter's in the Forest** (3200 Lopez Rd., 831/622-8240, http://poppyhillsgolf.com/porters, 6am-6pm Mon.-Tues., 6am-6:30pm Wed.-Thurs. and Sun., 6am-7pm Fri.-Sat., $13-25) serves ingenious twists on clubhouse fare like Korean Philly cheesesteak and carne asada fries. Breakfast, lunch, and a twilight menu are also available.

Expect luxury amenities at **The Lodge at Pebble Beach** (1700 17-Mile Dr., 831/647-7500 or 800/654-9300, www.pebblebeach.com, $900-4,400), near the 18th hole of the Pebble Beach Golf Links. Most rooms and suites have wood-burning fireplaces as well as private patios or balconies. Some high-end rooms have their own spas. A stay includes access to The Beach & Tennis Club, which has a heated outdoor pool, a whirlpool spa, and a tennis pavilion. **The Inn at Spanish Bay** (2700 17-Mile Dr., 831/647-7500 or 800/654-9300, www.pebblebeach.com, $790-4,450) has rooms with fireplaces and decks or patios, along with a fitness center and tennis pavilion on-site.

Carmel-by-the-Sea

Formerly a Bohemian enclave where local poets George Sterling and Robinson Jeffers hung out with literary heavyweights including Jack London and Mary Austin, Carmel-by-the-Sea is now a popular vacation spot for the moneyed, the artistic, and the romantic. People come to enjoy the small coastal town's almost European appeal. They stroll its sidewalks, peering into the windows of upscale shops and art galleries that showcase the work of sculptors, plein air painters, and photographers. Between the galleries are some of the region's most revered restaurants. The main thoroughfare, Ocean Avenue, slopes down to Carmel Beach, one of the finest on the Monterey Peninsula.

The old-world charms of Carmel can make it a little confusing for drivers. Because there are no addresses, locations are sometimes given via directions, for example: on 7th Avenue between San Carlos and Dolores Streets; on the northwest corner of Ocean Avenue. The town is compact, laid out on a plain grid system, so you're better off getting out of your car and walking anyway. Expect to share everything from Carmel's sidewalks to its restaurants with our canine friends. Carmel is very pro-pup.

Getting There

The quick way to get to Carmel from the north or the south is via CA-1. From CA-1, take Ocean Avenue into the middle of downtown Carmel.

There are **no street addresses** in Carmel-by-the-Sea, so pay close attention to the street names and the block you're on. To make things even more fun, street signs can be difficult to see in the mature foliage, and a dearth of streetlights can make signs nearly impossible to find at night. Show up during the day to get the lay of the land before trying to navigate after dark.

Sights

★ Carmel Beach

Carmel Beach (Ocean Ave., 831/624-4909, http://ci.carmel.ca.us/carmel, 6am-10pm daily) is one of the Monterey Bay region's best beaches. Under a bluff dotted with twisted, skeletal cypress trees, it's a long, white, sandy beach that borders a usually clear blue-green Pacific. In the distance to the south, Point Lobos juts out from the land like a pointing finger, while just north of the beach, the green-as-billiard-table-felt golf courses cloak the grounds of nearby Pebble Beach. Like most of Carmel, Carmel Beach is very dog-friendly. On any given day, all sorts of canines fetch, sniff, and run on the white sand.

One unique aspect of Carmel Beach is that it is one of a handful of California beaches that permit fires. Fires in the designated pits are allowed 4pm-10pm daily. Interested parties should secure a fire pit south of 10th Avenue. For more information, call 831/620-2020.

One of the best places to access the beach is at the west end of Ocean Avenue. There's a parking lot here, along with four beach volleyball courts, a wooden observation deck, and restrooms.

Carmel Mission

San Carlos Borromeo de Carmelo Mission (3080 Rio Rd., 831/624-1271, www.carmelmission.org, mission and museum store 9:30am-5pm daily, adults $9.50, seniors $7, children $5) was Father Junípero Serra's favorite among his California mission churches. He lived, worked, and died here; visitors can see a replica of his cell. An active Catholic parish remains part of the complex, so please be respectful when taking the self-guided tour. The rambling buildings and courtyard gardens show some wear, but restoration work makes them attractive and eminently visitor-friendly.

The Carmel Mission has a small memorial museum in a building off the second courtyard that shows a slice of the

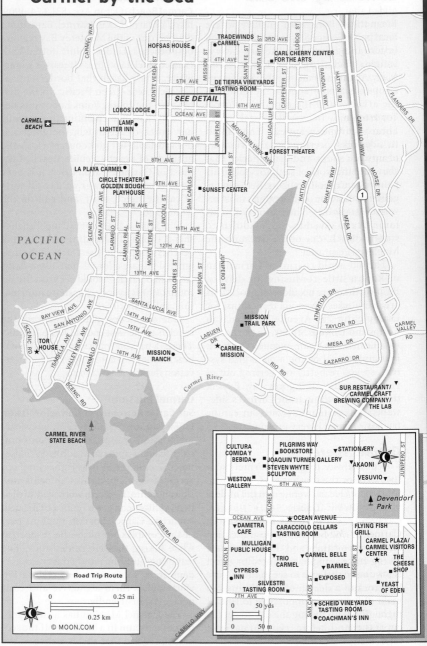

Carmel-by-the-Sea

TRADEWINDS CARMEL

HOFSAS HOUSE

CARL CHERRY CENTER FOR THE ARTS

DE TIERRA VINEYARDS TASTING ROOM

SEE DETAIL

LOBOS LODGE

LAMP LIGHTER INN

CARMEL BEACH

PACIFIC OCEAN

FOREST THEATER

LA PLAYA CARMEL

CIRCLE THEATER/ GOLDEN BOUGH PLAYHOUSE

SUNSET CENTER

MISSION TRAIL PARK

TOR HOUSE

MISSION RANCH

CARMEL MISSION

CARMEL RIVER STATE BEACH

Carmel River

SUR RESTAURANT/ CARMEL CRAFT BREWING COMPANY/ THE LAB

CARMEL WAY, MONTE VERDE ST, SANTA FE ST, SANTA RITA ST, 3RD AVE, LOBOS ST, 4TH AVE, 5TH AVE, OCEAN AVE, 6TH AVE, 7TH AVE, 8TH AVE, 9TH AVE, 10TH AVE, 11TH AVE, 12TH AVE, 13TH AVE, SANTA LUCIA AVE, 14TH AVE, 15TH AVE, 16TH AVE

MISSION ST, JUNIPERO ST, CARPENTER ST, GUADALUPE ST, MOUNTAIN VIEW AVE, RANDALL WAY, HATTON RD, FLANDERS DR, CABRILLO HWY, MORSE DR, SHAFTER WAY, MESA DR, ATHERTON DR, TAYLOR RD, MESA DR, LAZARRO DR, RIO RD, CARMEL VALLEY RD

SCENIC RD, SAN ANTONIO ST, CARMELO ST, CAMINO REAL, CASANOVA ST, MONTE VERDE ST, LINCOLN ST, DOLORES ST, SAN CARLOS ST, TORRES ST, JUNIPERO ST, LASUEN DR

BAY VIEW AVE, SAN ANTONIO AVE, SCENIC RD, ISABELLA AVE, VALLEY VIEW AVE, CARMELO ST, SCENIC RD, RIBERA RD, CABRILLO HWY

Road Trip Route

0   0.25 mi
0   0.25 km
© MOON.COM

SEE DETAIL

CULTURA COMIDA Y BEBIDA

PILGRIMS WAY BOOKSTORE

STATIONÆRY

JOAQUIN TURNER GALLERY

STEVEN WHYTE SCULPTOR

AKAONI

VESUVIO

WESTON GALLERY

6TH AVE

Devendorf Park

OCEAN AVE

OCEAN AVENUE

DAMETRA CAFE

CARACCIOLO CELLARS TASTING ROOM

FLYING FISH GRILL

CARMEL PLAZA/ CARMEL VISITORS CENTER

MULLIGAN PUBLIC HOUSE

TRIO CARMEL

CARMEL BELLE

THE CHEESE SHOP

CYPRESS INN

BARMEL

EXPOSED

YEAST OF EDEN

SILVESTRI TASTING ROOM

7TH AVE

SCHEID VINEYARDS TASTING ROOM

COACHMAN'S INN

LINCOLN ST, DOLORES ST, SAN CARLOS ST, MISSION ST, JUNIPERO ST

0   50 yds
0   50 m

lives of the 18th- and 19th-century friars. The highlight is the church with its gilded altar front, its shrine to the Virgin Mary, the grave of Junipero Serra, and an ancillary chapel dedicated to his memory. Round out your visit by walking the gardens to admire the flowers and fountains and to read the grave markers in the small cemetery.

Tor House

Local poet Robinson Jeffers penned nature poems to the uncompromising beauty of Carmel Point and nearby Big Sur. He built this rugged-looking castle on the Carmel coast in 1919. Jeffers named it **Tor House** (26304 Ocean View Ave., 831/624-1813, www.torhouse.org, tours 10am-3pm Fri.-Sat., adults $12, students $7) after its rocky setting, and he added the majestic Hawk Tower a year later.

Volunteer docents offer tours of the property that include a walk through the original home, which was hand built by Jeffers with giant stones. The poet once hosted luminaries like Ansel Adams, Charlie Chaplin, Edna St. Vincent Millay, and Dylan Thomas within the dining room, which offers fine views of Carmel Point and Point Lobos. The highlight of the tour is a visit to **Hawk Tower,** a four-story stone structure crowned with an open-air turret.

★ Point Lobos State Natural Reserve

Said to be the inspiration behind the setting of Robert Louis Stevenson's *Treasure Island,* **Point Lobos State Natural Reserve** (Hwy. 1, 3 mi/4.8 km south of Carmel, 831/624-4909, www.parks.ca.gov and www.pointlobos.org, 8am-7pm daily spring-fall, 8am-sunset daily winter, $10) is a wonderland of coves, hills, and jumbled rocks. The reserve's Cypress Grove Trail (0.8 mile round-trip, easy) winds through a forest of antler-like Monterey cypress trees that are cloaked in striking red algae. Point Lobos offers a lesson

on the region's fishing history in the **Whaler's Cabin** (9am-5pm daily, staff permitting), a small wooden structure that was built by Chinese fishermen in the 1850s. Half of the reserve is underwater, open for scuba divers who want to explore the 70-foot-high kelp forests just offshore.

The parking lots in Point Lobos tend to fill on crowded weekends; park on nearby CA-1 and walk in to the park during these times. The reserve plans to implement a parking reservation system during peak times.

Wineries

The town of Carmel (www.carmelcalifornia.org) has wine-tasting rooms in its downtown area.

Inside dark, sleek **Caraccioli Cellars Tasting Room** (Dolores St. between Ocean Ave. and 7th Ave., 831/622-7722, www.caracciolicellars.com, 2pm-7pm Mon.-Thurs., 11am-10pm Fri.-Sat., 11am-7pm Sun., tasting $20), a sophisticated atmosphere reflects the upscale wines served; most start at more than $50 a bottle. Caraccioli's most popular pours include a brut and a brut rosé best enjoyed at the wooden slab bar. They also have a small selection of snacks, from locally spiced nuts to caviar.

The family-owned **De Tierra Vineyards Tasting Room** (Mission St. and 5th Ave., 831/622-9704, www.detierra.com, 2pm-8pm Mon.-Thurs., noon-8pm Fri.-Sun. summer; 2pm-6pm Mon.-Thurs., noon-8pm Fri.-Sun. winter, $10-15) has a rosé, syrah, merlot, chardonnay, red blend, riesling, and a pinot noir. A chalkboard lists a cheese and chocolate plate menu.

Grammy Award-winning composer Alan Silvestri makes wines in Carmel Valley. They can be sampled in the **Silvestri Tasting Room** (7th Ave. between Dolores St. and San Carlos St., 831/625-0111, www.silvestrivineyards.com, noon-6pm Sun.-Thurs., noon-7pm Fri.-Sat., $10-15).

Al Scheid and his employees take

winemaking seriously. The estate utilizes 10 vineyards in inland Monterey County to produce 38 varietals of grapes. They keep the best grapes for themselves to make their popular claret and 50/50, a cabernet sauvignon-syrah mix that starts peppery before smoothing out. Sample their wares at the clean and friendly **Scheid Vineyards Carmel-by-the-Sea Tasting Room** (San Carlos St. and 9th Ave., 831/626-9463, www.scheidvineyards.com, noon-7pm Sun.-Thurs., noon-8pm Fri.-Sat., tasting $10-20). A large map behind the counter shows where all of the Scheid vineyards are located, while photographs on the wall document the winemaking process.

Entertainment and Events
Nightlife
Barmel (San Carlos St. between Ocean Ave. and 7th Ave., 831/626-2095, 3pm-2am Mon.-Sat., 3pm-midnight Sun.) has given Carmel's nightlife a youthful kick. It is the only bar in Carmel with live music (Thurs.-Sat. 7pm-9pm). On weekends, follow up the bands with a DJ party starting at 9:30pm on Fridays and Saturdays hosted by local favorite DJ Hanif Wondir.

One of downtown Carmel-by-the-Sea's more unassuming establishments for food and drink is **Mulligan Public House** (Dolores and Ocean, 831/250-5910, http://mulliganspublichouse.com, 11am-midnight Mon.-Fri., 9am-midnight Sat.-Sun.). Decorated like an Irish golf bar, there's a narrow indoor dining and drinking area along with a heated, dog-friendly patio. The most popular pub grub items are the wings, the Kobe beef sliders, and the burgers.

Carmel has two breweries. **Carmel Craft Brewing Company** (3777 The Barnyard, 831/776-3379, www.carmelcraft.com, 3pm-8pm Mon. and Wed.-Thurs., 2pm-8pm Fri., noon-8pm Sat.-Sun.) is from the same people behind Mad Otter Ale, available in town before the brewery opened. They also serve blondes, IPAs, porters, ambers, and a roster of rotating brews.

The terrifically named **Yeast of Eden** (Carmel Plaza, Mission St. and Ocean Ave., Ste. 112, 831/293-8621, https://yoebeer.com, 11:30am-11pm Sun.-Thurs., 11:30am-midnight Fri.-Sat.) is an offspring of the very popular Alvarado Street Brewery with only sour beers. There are more than 20 beers on tap, including their very own Skeptics & Believers Blend, an award-winning golden sour ale. They also serve a menu of global street food in this upscale establishment in tony downtown Carmel.

Live Music
The **Chamber Music Monterey Bay** society (831/625-2212, www.chambermusicmontereybay.org) brings talented ensembles and soloists from around the world to perform on the lovely Central Coast. String quartets rule the small stage. Shows are performed at the **Sunset Cultural Center** (San Carlos St. at 9th Ave., 831/620-2048, www.sunsetcenter.org), a state-of-the-art performing center with more than 700 seats. Chamber Music Monterey Bay reserves up-front seats for children and their adult companions.

The **Sunset Cultural Center** (San Carlos St. at 9th Ave., 831/620-2048, www.sunsetcenter.org) also snags some big-time music acts occasionally, including Willie Nelson and Buddy Guy.

The Lab (3728 The Barnyard, Ste. G-23) hosts occasional art, film, and live performances by great local and touring acts. Email for information about upcoming events (info@thelabarts.com).

The Arts
The **Pacific Repertory Theater** (831/622-0100, www.pacrep.org, prices vary) is the only professional theater company on the Monterey Peninsula. Shows travel the region, but most are in the **Golden Bough Playhouse** (Monte Verde St. and 8th Ave.), the company's home theater.

Other venues include **The Forest Theater** (Mountain View St. and Santa Rita St.) and the **Circle Theater** (Casanova St. between 8th Ave. and 9th Ave.) within the Golden Bough complex. The company puts on dramas, comedies, and musicals both new and classic. Buy tickets online or by phone to guarantee a seat.

Festivals and Events

One of the biggest events of the year is the **Carmel Art Festival** (Devendorf Park at Mission St., www.carmelartfestivalcalifornia.com, May). This three-day event celebrates visual arts in all media with shows by internationally acclaimed artists at galleries, parks, and other venues all across town. This wonderful festival also sponsors here-and-now contests, including the prestigious plein air (outdoor painting) competition. A wealth of children's activities help even the youngest festivalgoers become budding artists.

One of the most prestigious festivals in Northern California is the **Carmel Bach Festival** (831/624-1521, www.bachfestival.org, July). For 15 days each July, Carmel-by-the-Sea and its surrounding towns host dozens of classical concerts. You can also hear Mozart, Vivaldi, Handel, and other heavyweights of Bach's era. Concerts and recitals take place every day of the week.

Shopping

It is easy to spend an afternoon poking into Carmel's many art galleries. Sample Carmel's art scene at the monthly **Carmel Art Walk** (www.carmelartwalk.com, 5pm-8pm second Sat. of the month), a self-guided tour of the town's art galleries. Talk to the artists, sip wine, and listen to live music.

The paintings at the **Joaquin Turner Gallery** (Dolores St. between 5th Ave. and 6th Ave., 831/869-5564, www.joaquinturner.com, 11am-5pm

From top to bottom: Carmel Beach; Carmel Mission; Point Lobos State Natural Reserve.

Thurs.-Mon., by appointment Tues.-Wed.) are a nod to the works of early-20th-century Monterey Peninsula artists.

At the **Steven Whyte Sculpture Gallery** (Dolores St. between 5th Ave. and 6th Ave., 831/620-1917, www.stevenwhytesculptor.com, 9am-5pm Mon. and Thurs., 9am-4:30pm Wed., 9am-6pm Fri., 10am-6pm Sat., 10am-4pm Sun.), you can watch the artist create amazing life-size sculptures in this open studio.

One of the best galleries in town is the **Weston Gallery** (6th Ave., 831/624-4453, www.westongallery.com, 11am-5pm Tues.-Sun.), which highlights the photographic work of 20th-century masters including Ansel Adams, Diane Arbus, Robert Mapplethorpe, and Edward Weston.

A tiny art gallery owned by two local photographers, **Exposed** (Carmel Sq., San Carlos St. and 7th Ave., 831/238-0127, http://galleryexposed.blogspot.com, 1pm-3pm Sat., 5pm-8pm first Fri. of the month) is worth a peek.

Carmel Plaza (Ocean Ave. and Mission St., 831/624-0138, www.carmelplaza.com, 10am-6pm Mon.-Sat., 11am-5pm Sun.) is an outdoor mall with luxury fashion shops like Tiffany & Co. as well as the hip clothing chain Anthropologie. Don't miss locally owned establishment **The Cheese Shop** (800/828-9463, www.thecheeseshopinc.com, 10am-6pm Mon.-Sat., 11am-5:30pm Sun.), which sells delicacies like cave-aged gruyère cheese.

Sports and Recreation

Devendorf Park (Ocean Ave. and Junipero Ave., 831/624-3543, https://ci.carmel.ca.us) is downtown Carmel-by-the-Sea's best public place. This block-long park features a grassy lawn rimmed by live oaks, benches, and monuments honoring U.S. service people. It's the site of many Carmel-by-the-Sea events, including a Fourth of July celebration, a Halloween parade, and an annual tree-lighting ceremony. It is also home to one of downtown's only public restrooms.

Carmel Beach (Ocean Ave., 831/624-4909, 6am-10pm daily) has some of the area's most consistent beach breaks. Being a beach break, the sandbars shift, so the best spot on the beach frequently changes. The waves are usually at their finest from spring to late summer. The winds blow out a lot of area breaks in the spring, but Carmel Beach really comes alive during this time of year.

Carmel Surf Lessons (831/915-4065, www.carmelsurflessons.com) can teach you to surf at Carmel Beach. **On the Beach** (693 Lighthouse Ave., 831/646-9283, http://onthebeachsurfshop.com, 10am-6pm Sun.-Thurs., 10am-7pm Fri.-Sat., surfboard rental $30-35/day, wetsuit rental $20/day) rents surfboards and wetsuits.

Food
American

★ **Carmel Belle** (Doud Craft Studios, Ocean Ave. and San Carlos St., 831/624-1600, www.carmelbelle.com, 8am-6pm daily, $6-15) is a little eatery with big attention to detail. The superb breakfast menu includes an open-face breakfast sandwich featuring a slab of toasted bread topped with a poached egg, strips of thick bacon, a bed of arugula, and wedges of fresh avocado. Its slow-cooked Berkshire pork sandwich with red onion-currant chutney is a perfect example of what can happen when savory meets sweet.

Tucked into San Carlos Square, **Stationæry** (San Carlos and Mission St., www.thestationaery.com, 8am-2pm Mon.-Fri., 8am-3pm Sat.-Sun., $10-16) is worth seeking out. The intimate eatery seats just 34 and serves a changing breakfast and lunch menu. The coffee is great and their *chilaquiles* with chorizo are superb.

Sur Restaurant (3601 The Barnyard, 831/250-7188, www.surcarmel.com, 11:30am-9pm Tues.-Sun., $19-35) is the latest creation by well-known area restaurateur Billy Quon. The food menu accommodate most appetites with meal-size appetizers, salads, seafood, and a popular fried-chicken-and-waffles dish. The ambiance, along with fine cocktails, craft beers, and wines by the bottle **and** glass, makes this a worthwhile destination.

Italian

On paper, **Vesuvio** (6th Ave. and Junipero St., 831/625-1766, http://chefpepe.com, 4pm-11pm daily, $16-32) dishes out cannelloni, gnocchi, and wood-oven pizzas, but there's a lot more going on. Popular items include a spicy cioppino and a tricolored cannelloni dish topped with marina, alfredo, and pesto sauces. The popular rooftop bar has fire pits, heat lamps, and love seats.

Mediterranean

Dametra Café (Ocean Ave. at Lincoln St., 831/622-7766, www.dametracafe. com, 11am-11pm daily, $11-27) has a wide-ranging international menu that includes the all-American cheeseburger and Italian dishes like spaghetti *alla Bolognese*. Still, it's best to go with the lively restaurant's signature Mediterranean food. The Greek chicken kebab is a revelation with two chicken-and-vegetable kebabs drizzled with aioli sauce over yellow rice and a Greek salad. The owner and his staff have been known to serenade evening diners.

Mexican

Cultura Comida y Bebida (Dolores St. between 5th Ave. and 6th Ave., 831/250-7005, www.culturacarmel.com, 5:30pm-midnight Mon.-Fri., 10:30am-midnight Sat.-Sun., $18-28) satisfies adventurous diners with superb upscale Mexican cuisine. Try the *chapulines* (toasted grasshoppers) appetizer or skip ahead to the relleno-style abalone. The restaurant's large mescal menu offers the smoky spirit in cocktails or one-ounce pours. The

From top to bottom: the Cypress Inn; Carmel Belle; Carmel Valley Ranch.

late-night menu (10pm-midnight daily) includes $2 street tacos.

Seafood

The **Flying Fish Grill** (Mission St. between Ocean Ave. and 7th Ave., 831/625-1962, http://flyingfishgrill.com, 5pm-10pm daily, $21-36) serves Japanese-style seafood with a California twist. Entrées include rare, peppered ahi and black bean halibut. You might even be able to score a market-price meal of Monterey abalone. Relax over your meal in the dimly lit, wood-walled establishment.

Sushi

★ **Akaoni** (Mission St. and 6th Ave., 831/620-1516, 5:30pm-9pm Wed.-Thurs., 11:30am-1pm and 5:30pm-9pm Fri.-Sat., 11:30am-1pm Sun., $7-40) is a superb hole-in-the-wall sushi restaurant. Sit at the bar (or one of the few tables) and order tempura-fried oysters, softshell crab rolls, and an *unagi donburi* (eel bowl). Daily specials showcase the freshest seafood, including items flown in from Japan. Adventurous diners can opt for the live Monterey spot prawn.

Accommodations
$150-250

Just two blocks from the beach, the **Lamp Lighter Inn** (Ocean Ave. and Camino Real, 831/624-7372 or 888/375-0770, www.carmellamplighter.com, $225-425) has 11 rooms in five cottages with a comfortable, beachy decor. The cottages encircle a courtyard area that has two fire pits. Guests are treated to an afternoon wine and cheese reception and a morning continental breakfast. This is a pet-friendly property; two of the units have fenced-in backyards.

Outside of downtown Carmel, **Mission Ranch** (26270 Dolores St., 831/624-6436, www.missionranchcarmel.com, $125-320) is a sprawling old ranch complex with views of sheep-filled pastures and Point Lobos in the distance. If you get a glimpse of Mission Ranch's owner,

it might just make your day: It's none other than Hollywood icon and former Carmel-by-the-Sea mayor Clint Eastwood. On the grounds is a restaurant with a nightly sing-along piano bar.

Over $250

Touted by *Architectural Digest,* **Tradewinds Carmel** (Mission St. and 3rd Ave., 831/624-2776, www.tradewinds-carmel.com, $255-575) brings a touch of the Far East to California. The 28 serene hotel rooms are decorated with Asian antiquities and live orchids. Outside, the grounds have a water fountain that passes through bamboo shoots and horsetails, along with a meditation garden, where an oversize Buddha head overlooks a trio of cascading pools. A continental breakfast includes French pastries and fruit.

Coachman's Inn (San Carlos St. and 8th Ave., 831/624-6421, www.coachmansinn.com, $249-329) is a small downtown motel with 30 clean, well-appointed rooms. The rooms have large flat screens, mini-fridges, microwaves, and Keurig coffee makers. Some also have gas fireplaces and jetted spa tubs. A stay includes access to a hot tub, sauna, and exercise bike. Enjoy a hot breakfast buffet in the morning.

The initial structure at ★ **La Playa Carmel** (Camino Real at 8th Ave., 831/293-6100 or 800/582-8900, www.laplayahotel.com, $599-899) was a mansion built for a member of the Ghirardelli family. It still has many features from an earlier era, including the dark, wood-walled bar, stained-glass windows, and a tiled staircase. Half of the 75 rooms at La Playa look out onto nearby Carmel Beach, only two blocks away. Wander the grounds and stop by the library, the heated outdoor pool, and the courtyard with its oversize chessboard. The staff will treat you to an afternoon wine reception, a dessert of freshly baked cookies, and a champagne breakfast with made-to-order omelets and waffles.

The landmark **Cypress Inn** (Lincoln St.

and 7th Ave., 831/624-3871 or 800/443-7443, www.cypress-inn.com, $279-699) welcomes human and canine guests in a white, ornate Mediterranean-inspired building. This is one of the most pro-pup hotels in the state. They have dog cookies at the desk, water bowls are situated around the hotel, and they provide dog beds and dog towels by request. The rooms come with complimentary cream sherry, fruit, and snacks for guests, while some also have fireplaces and/or jetted tubs. Human visitors are treated to a breakfast that includes several hot items.

Information and Services

The nearest major medical center is in Monterey at the **Community Hospital of the Monterey Peninsula** (23625 Holman Hwy., Monterey, 831/624-5311, www.chomp.org).

◆ Carmel Valley

The landscape changes quickly as you leave the coast. You'll see the mountains rising above you, as well as farms, ranches, and orchards. East of CA-1 is the unincorporated Carmel Valley Village. In the small strip of businesses hugging Carmel Valley Road is a collection of wineries, tasting rooms, restaurants, and even an Old West saloon.

Getting There

From CA-1 south of Monterey, take Carmel Valley Road east for 13 miles (21 km) to Carmel Valley Village, where most of the area's restaurants and wineries are.

Sights

One of the largest purveyors of organic produce in the United States, Earthbound Farm began at **Earthbound Farm's Farm Stand** (7250 Carmel Valley Rd., 831/625-6219, www.earthboundfarm.com, 8am-5pm Mon.-Sat., 9am-5pm Sun.). This 2.5-acre farm and roadside stand offers visitors easy access to the company's smallish facility in the Carmel Valley. Browse organic fruits, veggies, and flowers or ramble the fields, checking out the chamomile labyrinth and the kids' garden (yes, your kids can look *and* touch). Select and harvest your own fresh herbs from the cut-your-own-herb garden, or purchase delicious prepared organic dishes at the farm stand. Scheduled walks offer a guided tour of the fields.

Wineries

The Carmel Valley's tiny size limits the number of vineyards and wineries that set up shop here, but this small, charming wine region still makes for a perfect wine-tasting day trip from Monterey. Expect small crowds, light traffic, and meaningful tasting experiences at family-owned wineries. Seven of the best wineries are clustered on the East End Wine Row (https://eastendwinerow.wordpress.com), where you'll enjoy personal attention and delicious wines, all in a gorgeous green setting.

The **Bernardus Winery** (5 W. Carmel Valley Rd., 831/298-8021 or 800/223-2533, www.bernardus.com, 11am-5pm daily, tasting $12-20) sits on a vineyard estate that hosts a luxurious lodge and gourmet restaurant. The surrounding grapes are the pride of the winery, which creates a small list of wines that include the Bordeaux-style blended red Marinus Vineyard wine. Other varietals (chardonnay, pinot noir, and sauvignon blanc) originate from coastal vineyards. If you're lucky, you might get to sip a small-batch vintage of single-vineyard wines, available only in the tasting room.

Chesebro Wines (19 E. Carmel Valley Rd., Ste. D, 831/659-2125, www.chesebrowines.com, noon-5pm Thurs.-Sun., tasting $10). Former Bernardus Winery employee Mark Chesebro makes chardonnays, pinot noirs, Grenache rosés, vermentino, and a signature white wine, all of which are smart and affordable.

Located in the same strip of wineries,

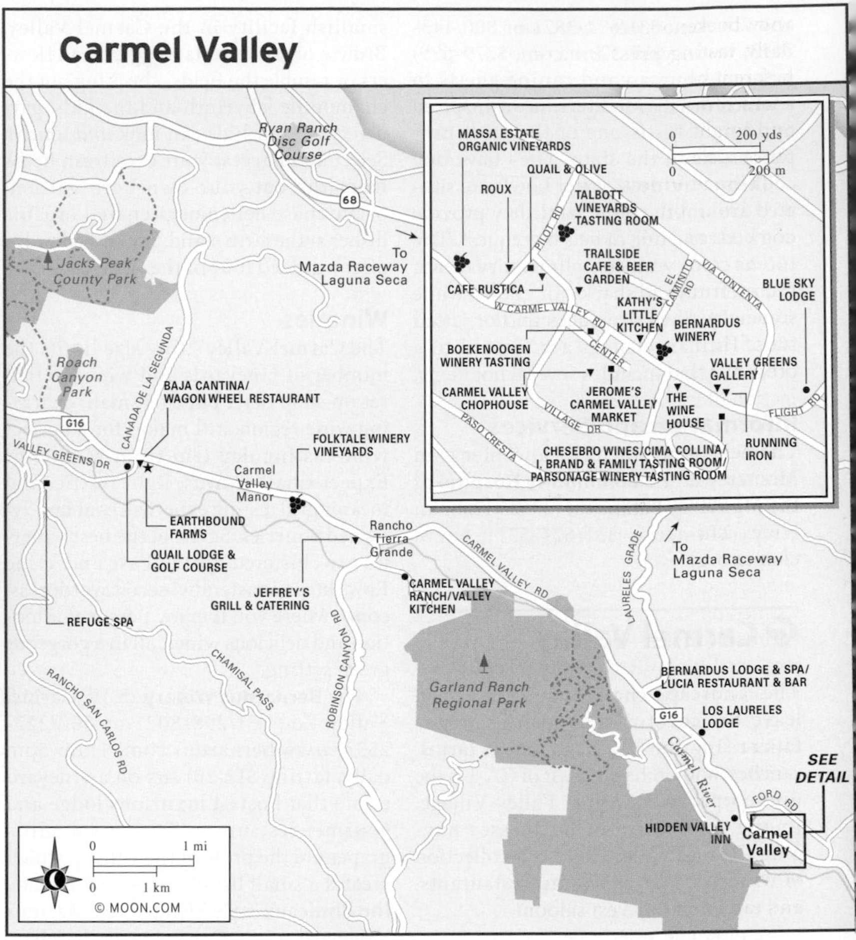

Carmel Valley

[Map of Carmel Valley with the following labels:]

Ryan Ranch Disc Golf Course

MASSA ESTATE ORGANIC VINEYARDS

QUAIL & OLIVE

ROUX

TALBOTT VINEYARDS TASTING ROOM

68

To Mazda Raceway Laguna Seca

TRAILSIDE CAFE & BEER GARDEN

CAFE RUSTICA

PILOT RD

EL CAMINITO

VIA CONTENTA

BLUE SKY LODGE

KATHY'S LITTLE KITCHEN

Jacks Peak County Park

W CARMEL VALLEY RD

BERNARDUS WINERY

BOEKENOOGEN WINERY TASTING

CENTER

VALLEY GREENS GALLERY

Roach Canyon Park

CANADA DE LA SEGUNDA

CARMEL VALLEY CHOPHOUSE

JEROME'S CARMEL VALLEY MARKET

THE WINE HOUSE

FLIGHT RD

VILLAGE DR

BAJA CANTINA/ WAGON WHEEL RESTAURANT

G16

VALLEY GREENS DR

PASO CRESTA

CHESEBRO WINES/CIMA COLLINA/ I. BRAND & FAMILY TASTING ROOM/ PARSONAGE WINERY TASTING ROOM

RUNNING IRON

FOLKTALE WINERY VINEYARDS

Carmel Valley Manor

EARTHBOUND FARMS

Rancho Tierra Grande

CARMEL VALLEY RD

QUAIL LODGE & GOLF COURSE

JEFFREY'S GRILL & CATERING

CARMEL VALLEY RANCH/VALLEY KITCHEN

To Mazda Raceway Laguna Seca

LAURELES GRADE

REFUGE SPA

ROBINSON CANYON RD

Garland Ranch Regional Park

BERNARDUS LODGE & SPA/ LUCIA RESTAURANT & BAR

CHAMISAL PASS

G16

LOS LAURELES LODGE

RANCHO SAN CARLOS RD

Carmel River

FORD RD

SEE DETAIL

0   1 mi
0   1 km

HIDDEN VALLEY INN

Carmel Valley

© MOON.COM

200 yds
200 m

Cima Collina (19 E. Carmel Valley Rd., Ste. A, 831/620-0645, http://cimacollina. com, noon-6pm Sun.-Tues., noon-7pm Wed.-Sat. summer, noon-6pm Thurs.-Mon. winter, tasting $5) has a tasting room that resembles a farmhouse with a front porch. Inside, enjoy pinot noir, chardonnay, sauvignon blanc, pinot blanc, and Cima Collina wines that are available only in the tasting room, like the Howlin' Good Red.

I Brand & Family Winery (19 E. Carmel Valley Rd., 831/298-7227, http://lppwines. com, noon-6pm Wed.-Sun., tasting $18) is a small family operation with three labels (Le P'Tit Paysan, La Marea, I Brand) that appeal to three different price points. Winemaker Ian Brand gravitates toward uncommon varietals with grapes sourced from small growers. Enjoy the fruits of his labor in the cozy, casual tasting room adorned with the works of local photographer Nic Coury. Vintage vinyl plays on an in-house record player. In 2018, Brand was awarded the Winemaker of the Year from the *San Francisco Chronicle*.

Boekenoogen Vineyard & Winery (24 W. Carmel Valley Rd., 831/659-4215, www.boekenoogenwines.com, 11am-5pm daily, tasting $15-20) was a cattle ranch before it became a winery. Their tasting room offers pinot noirs, chardonnays, and syrahs, as well as a garden patio for those sunny Carmel Valley afternoons.

Talbott Vineyards (25 Pilot Rd., 831/659-3500, www.talbottvineyards. com, 11am-5pm daily, tasting $20-30) utilizes two vineyards to produce their chardonnays and pinot noirs. At the Carmel Valley tasting room, they pour six of their chardonnays and six of their pinot noirs alongside an impressive collection of vintage motorcycles.

Folktale Winery and Vineyards (8940 Carmel Valley Rd., 831/293-7500, www. folktalewinery.com, 11am-8pm daily, tasting $20) promises to liven up the local wine scene, aiming to become "an extension of your backyard" with bocce, horseshoes, and cornhole. The winery has even teamed up with local radio station KRML to host concerts in their barrel room. Acts such as Lukas Nelson, G. Love, and Matt Costa have performed here.

After the wineries close, **The Wine House** (1 E. Carmel Valley Rd., 831/298-7438, www.thewinehousecv.com, 2pm-9pm Thurs., 2pm-10pm Fri.-Sat., 2pm-8pm Sun. summer, 3pm-9pm Wed.-Fri., 1pm-9pm Sat., 1pm-8pm Sun. winter) becomes the place for the area's tasting room servers and visitors to hang out. The interior has an old farmhouse feel and serves a list of 50 local and European wines and six rotating craft beer taps. The large outdoor area has fire pits, a bocce ball court, and cornhole. There's a real youthful energy here.

Tours
Get around the Carmel Valley Village's wineries by hitching a ride on the **Happy Trails Wagon Tour** (831/970-8198, noon-dusk daily, adults $25, children $10). Cowboy Pete pulls a 10-passenger wagon behind an antique tractor to wineries and restaurants in the area.

Or hop on the **Wine Trolley** (pick up at 209 Figueroa St., Monterey, 831/624-1700, www.toursmonterey.com, $119-169), which picks up in downtown Monterey for a five-hour tour of the Carmel Valley. The trip includes 3-5 winery stops and lunch at Roux.

DreamTours By the Sea (831/888-7555, https://dreamcastersvoyage.com, $120) offers Carmel Valley wine-tasting tours with visits to four wineries.

Sports and Recreation
Hiking
The 4,462-acre **Garland Ranch Regional Park** (700 W. Carmel Valley Rd., 831/372-3196, www.mprpd.org, sunrise sunset daily, free) boasts the best hiking trails in Carmel Valley. The **Lupine Loop** (1.4 mi/2.3 km round-trip, 45 minutes, easy) is a level, dog-friendly trail that circles a flat part of the park, while **Snively's Ridge Trail-Sky Loop** (6 mi/9.7 km round-trip, 4 hours, difficult) involves a very steep hike to a ridge that offers views of the ocean and mountains. The **Mesa Trail** (1.6 mi/2.6 km one-way, 2 hours, moderately strenuous) climbs to a saddle with valley views and a small pond.

Golf
The **Quail Lodge Golf Club** (8505 Valley Greens Dr., 831/620-8808, www.quail-lodge.com, $125-185) has an 18-hole course with 10 lakes, as well as an academy to improve your game.

Spas
Sprawled over two acres in the shadow of the Santa Lucia Mountains, **Refuge Spa** (27300 Rancho Carlos Rd., 831/620-7360, www.refuge.com, 10am-10pm daily, admission $52, treatments $86-292) features warm waterfalls tumbling into soaking pools and two kinds of cold plunge pools. Don't miss the eucalyptus steam room, where a potent cloud of steam will purge all of your body's impurities.

Food

Lucia Restaurant & Bar (Bernardus Lodge & Spa, 415 W. Carmel Valley Rd., 831/658-3400, www.bernarduslodge. com, 7am-11am, 11:30am-2:30pm, and 5pm-9pm daily, $25-53, chef's tasting menu $125) opened in 2015, taking the place of the Bernardus Lodge's Marinus and Wicket's Bistro. Led by revered local chef Cal Stamenov, Lucia serves a menu of high-end seafood and meat entrées that uses herbs from the garden in front. Oenophiles can consider wine pairings likes the superb Bernardus Pisoni pinot noir and the Bernardus Ingrid's Vineyard chardonnay, or ask the knowledgeable and friendly staff to properly guide you. The dining room faces the vineyards and there's also an outdoor terrace. This is a great place to get a feel for what makes Carmel Valley special.

★ **Café Rustica** (10 Del Fino Pl., 831/659-4444, www.caferusticavillage. com, 11am-2:30pm and 5pm-9pm Tues.-Sun., $15-35) offers some of the valley's best food for the best value. Specialties include the nightly fish specials (the petrale sole is superb), Hungarian goulash, sausages, and creative pizzas. The outdoor patio is perfect for the valley's frequent sunny afternoons, while the interior offers a rustic, faux-alpine vibe with stone walls. Wine is served by the bottle and by quarter liters (about 1/3 of a bottle) rather than by the glass.

Sip a wide range of tasty, intoxicating margaritas on the large wooden deck at **Baja Cantina** (7156 Carmel Valley Rd., 831/625-2252, www.carmelcantina.com, 11:30am-11pm Mon.-Fri., 10am-midnight Sat.-Sun., $13-20). The menu includes hearty Americanized Mexican cuisine, like rosemary chicken burritos and wild mushroom and spinach enchiladas. Even the nachos are worthwhile—they have so much baked cheese that they resemble a casserole. Catch a sports game on one of the big-screen TVs and enjoy the car memorabilia covering the walls.

Carmel Valley has two great breakfast joints. **Jeffrey's Grill & Catering** (112 Mid Valley Center, 831/624-2029, www. jeffreysgrillandcatering.com, 7am-3pm Tues.-Sat., 7am-2:30pm Sun., $7-15) is the more gourmet choice, serving creative breakfasts in an inconspicuous space in a Carmel Valley strip mall. The menu includes sausages with apple fritters and an omelet with sweet pasilla peppers countered by salty ham. The weekend specials are outside the box with smoked-turkey hash and grilled lamb with eggs.

The **Wagon Wheel Restaurant** (7156 Carmel Valley Rd., 831/624-8878, 6:30am-2pm daily, $7-15) is a classic Western-style diner decorated with horseshoes, ropes, and other knick-knacks. The menu includes hearty three-egg dishes, oatmeal pancakes, and biscuits drenched in sausage gravy.

The **Running Iron Restaurant and Saloon** (24 E. Carmel Valley Rd., 831/659-4633, www. runningironrestaurantandsaloon.com, 11am-2am Mon.-Fri., 10am-2am Sat., 9am-2am Sun.) keeps the region's cowboy past alive. This watering hole has an Old West style that includes branding irons and cowboy paraphernalia on the ceiling and walls. The Running Iron serves beer, wine, and liquor, and offers an extensive menu with seafood, burgers, steaks, and ribs.

Accommodations

There's plenty of space to absorb Carmel Valley's sunshine at the **Blue Sky Lodge** (10 Flight Rd., 831/659-2256, www. blueskylodge.com, $119-413). Units are a bit dated, but in a charming, retro-chic way, and come with a private patio or sundeck; six rooms have kitchens. The lodge courtyard has a pool, a lawn, a multi-person hot tub, table tennis, and lots of lounge chairs. Behind the pool is a comfy common room with a fireplace, an extensive library, a piano, tons of houseplants, and a computer for guest use. The location can't be beat—it's just a few hundred feet from Carmel Valley Village and its many tasting rooms.

To truly spread out and relax, book a stay at ★ **Carmel Valley Ranch** (1 Old Ranch Rd., 855/687-7262, www.carmelvalleyranch.com, $600-1,100). The spacious suites include fireplaces and decks to take in the valley views. With rooms this nice you may be tempted to stay inside, but the ranch has so much to do that it feels like an upscale summer camp. The activity calendar includes everything from a beekeeping class to horseback riding to nightly s'mores. Wild turkeys often wander through the grounds.

Locally owned **Carmel Valley Lodge** (8 Ford Rd., 831/659-2261, www.valleylodge.com, $299-500) is just a one-block walk from the village, which is ideal for winetasting. The property has 12 remodeled rooms along with 19 renovated one- and two-bedroom bungalows. The grounds include a garden, an Olympic-size pool, and a yoga pavilion. A complimentary breakfast is served.

Big Sur

The 90 miles (145 km) of coastline that run from Carmel to San Simeon comprise Big Sur, one of the most stunning coastal regions in the world. Big Sur is known for its seaside cliffs, redwood forests, abundant waterfalls, and natural wonders. Nature lovers come to camp and hike the pristine wilderness areas, don thick wetsuits and surf the oft-deserted beaches, or even hunt for jade in rocky coves.

Others come to relax at unbelievably posh hotels and spas with dazzling views of the ocean. Whether you prefer a low-cost camping trip or a luxury resort, Big Sur offers beauty and charm to all. Part of that charm is Big Sur's determination to remain peacefully apart from the information age, which means that cell phone reception is nonexistent.

Getting There

Big Sur can only be reached via CA-1, which can have one or both lanes closed at times, especially in the winter months when rockslides occur. Big Sur's CA-1 also gets very crowded on summer weekends and holidays. Check the **Caltrans** website (www.dot.ca.gov) or the **Big Sur California Blog** (www.thebigsurblog.com) for current road conditions.

Big Sur Kate (https://bigsurkate.blog) is an informative blog written by a local that features up-to-date information on road closures, wildfires, and mudslides.

TOP EXPERIENCE

★ Big Sur Coast Highway

Even if you're not up to tackling the endless hiking trails and deep wilderness backcountry of Big Sur, you can still get a good sense of the glory of this region just by driving through it. The **Big Sur Coast Highway** (CA 1) is quite simply one of the most picturesque roads in the country. A two-lane road, CA-1 twists and turns with Big Sur's jagged coastline, running along precipitous cliffs and rocky beaches, through dense redwood forests, over historic bridges, and past innumerable parks. In winter, you might spot migrating whales offshore spouting fountains of air and water, while spring finds yucca plants feathering the hillsides and wildflowers coloring the landscape. Construction on this stretch of road was completed in the 1930s, connecting Cambria to Carmel.

Start out at either town and spend a whole day making your way to the other end of the road. The road has plenty of wide turnouts set into picturesque cliffs to make it easy to stop to admire the glittering ocean and stunning wooded cliffs running right out to the water. (Please use the turnouts to park, rather than looking away from the road.) Bring a camera as you'll want to take photos every mile for hours on end. Be aware that there can

Big Sur

Andrew Molera State Park

Los Padres National Forest

BIG SUR RIVER INN RESTAURANT/RIVER INN BIG SUR GENERAL STORE — **Big Sur**

GLEN OAKS BIG SUR/ RIPPLEWOOD CAFE

BIG SUR ROADHOUSE

GRANGE RD

FERNWOOD RESORT

BIG SUR COAST HIGHWAY

PFEIFFER RIDGE RD

MIDDLE RD

CLEAR RIDGE RD

BIG SUR LODGE

PFEIFFER BIG SUR

MANUEL PEAK TRAIL

BIG SUR STATION

Pfeiffer Big Sur State Park

SYCAMORE CANYON RD

PFEIFFER BEACH

COAST RIDGE RD

BIG SUR TAPHOUSE/ BIG SUR DELI

BIG SUR BAKERY

POST RANCH INN/ SIERRA MAR RESTAURANT

VENTANA INN & SPA

THE SUR HOUSE

NEPENTHE

HENRY MILLER MEMORIAL LIBRARY

DEETJEN'S BIG SUR INN

RANCHO GRANDE RD

P A C I F I C

O C E A N

0   0.5 mi

0   0.5 km

© MOON.COM

Road Trip Route

---

be frequent highway delays due to road construction.

Garrapata State Park

Garrapata State Park (Hwy. 1, 6.7 mi/10.8 km south of Carmel, 831/624-4909, www. parks.ca.gov, 8am-sunset daily, free) has most of the features that make Big Sur such a famed destination for outdoor enthusiasts: redwood trees, rocky headlands, pocket beaches, and ocean vistas from steep hills and mountains. **Garrapata Beach** is northern Big Sur's finest, with 2 miles of coastline.

Hiking

The **Soberanes Point Trail** (2 mi/3.2 km round-trip, 1 hour, easy) is a mild hike up and around the park's rocky headlands. Stroll along the beach, scramble up the cliffs for a better view of the ocean, or check out the seals, sea otters, and sea lions near Soberanes Point. In winter, grab a pair of binoculars to look for migrating gray whales passing close to shore.

An inland option is the **Soberanes Canyon Trail** (2.5 mi/4 km round-trip, 1.5 hours, easy). It begins in an exposed section of the canyon dotted with cacti and enters a redwood forest as you follow the creek 1.25 miles (2 km). Hike back out the way you came.

Bixby Bridge

Bixby Bridge (Hwy. 1, 15 mi/24 km south of Carmel) is one of the most-photographed bridges in the nation. The picturesque, open-spandrel arched cement bridge was built in the early 1930s as part of the massive government works project that completed CA-1 through Big Sur. Pull out north of the bridge to take photos or just look out at the attractive span and Bixby Creek flowing into the Pacific far below. Get another great view of the bridge by driving a few hundred feet down the dirt Old Coast Road, which is on the bridge's northeast side.

Exercise caution when stopping to view Bixby Bridge. The turnout is quite small, and cars sometimes stop in the middle of the highway for a photo (not a good idea!).

Point Sur Light Station

Sitting lonely and isolated out on its cliff, the **Point Sur Light Station** (Hwy. 1, 19 mi/31 km south of Carmel, 831/625-4419, www.pointsur.org, tours 1pm Wed., 10am Sat.-Sun. Oct.-Mar.; 10am and 2pm Wed. and Sat., 10am Sun. Apr.-Sept., adults $15, children $5) crowns the 361-foot-high volcanic rock Point Sur. It's the only complete 19th-century light station in California that you can visit, and even here access is severely limited. First lit in 1889, this now fully automated light station still provides navigational aid to ships off the coast.

Tours

Take one of the **moonlight tours** (call 831/625-4419 for information) to learn about the haunted history of the light station buildings.

You can't make a reservation for a Point Sur tour, so just show up and park your car off CA-1 on the west side by the farm gate. Your guide will meet you there

and lead you up the paved road 0.5 mile to the light station. Once there, you'll climb the stairs up to the light, explore the restored keepers' homes and service buildings, and walk out to the cliff edge. Expect to see a great variety of flora and fauna, from brilliant wildflowers in the spring to gray whales in the winter to flocks of pelicans flying in formation at any time of year. Dress in layers; it can be sunny and hot or foggy and cold, winter or summer, and sometimes both on the same tour! Tours last three hours and require more than a mile of walking, with a bit of slope, and more than 100 stairs.

If you need special assistance for your tour or have questions about accessibility, call 831/649-2836 as far in advance as possible of your visit to make arrangements.

Andrew Molera State Park

Andrew Molera State Park (Hwy. 1, 21 mi/34 km south of Carmel, 831/667-1112, www.parks.ca.gov, half hour before sunrise-half hour after sunset daily, $10/vehicle) has several hiking trails that run down to the beach and up into the forest along the river.

At the park entrance, you'll find bathrooms but no drinking water or food concessions.

★ Hiking

The **Creamery Meadow Trail** (2 mi/3 km round-trip, 1 hour, easy) is a flat trail on the edge of a meadow that leads from the parking lot to the beach. Hikers must cross the Big Sur River; a footbridge is in place July 15-October 31. For a better look at the river, take the flat, moderate **Bobcat Trail** (5.5 mi/8.9 km round-trip, 3 hours, easy) and perhaps a few of its ancillary loops. You'll walk right along the riverbank, enjoying the local microhabitats.

For a longer and more difficult trek up the mountains and down to the beach, the **Ridge Trail and Panorama Trail Loop** (8 mi/12.9 km round-trip, 5 hours, moderate) is one of the best coastal hikes in

Big Sur. Start at the parking lot on the **Creamery Meadow Beach Trail,** then make a left onto the long and fairly steep **Ridge Trail** to get a sense of the local ecosystem. Then turn right onto the **Panorama Trail,** which has sweeping views of the coast, including Molera Point and Point Sur, as it runs down to the coastal scrublands. Take the small **Spring Trail** (0.2 mile round-trip, easy) down a driftwood-littered gully to a scenic stretch of beach. Hike back out and take a left connecting to the **Bluffs Trail,** which takes you back to Creamery Meadow along the top of a marine terrace.

The only trail that explores the park's east side is the **East Molera Trail** (5 mi/8.1 km round-trip, 3 hours, strenuous), which switchbacks up a steep hillside to a ridgeline dotted with redwoods. The saddle at the top provides fine views of Point Sur to the north and Pico Blanco (the large white triangular mountain) to the east.

Pfeiffer Big Sur State Park

The most developed park in Big Sur, **Pfeiffer Big Sur State Park** (Hwy. 1, 26 mi/42 km south of Carmel, 831/667-1112, www.parks.ca.gov, sunrise-sunset daily, $10/vehicle) is home to a lodge, a restaurant and café, hiking trails, and lovely redwood-shaded **campsites.** This is one of the best parks in the area to see Big Sur's redwoods and a great place to dip into the cool Big Sur River.

Hiking

Pfeiffer Big Sur has the tiny **Ernst Ewoldsen Memorial Nature Center** (open seasonally), which features taxidermy examples of local wildlife. The historic **Homestead Cabin,** off the Big Sur Gorge Trail, was once the home of part of the Pfeiffer family, who were the first European immigrants to settle in Big Sur.

On a hot summer day, a dip in the cool waters of the Big Sur River couldn't feel better. On the **Gorge Trail** (0.5 mile round-trip, easy) rock-hop and wade to a deep, clear pool hemmed in by two steep canyon walls. The path can be accessed from the east end of the campground (between sites 111 and 112). Wear river shoes or sandals.

The **Nature Trail** (0.7 mile round-trip, easy) leaves from Big Sur Lodge and provides an introduction to the park's natural assets. No bikes or horses are allowed on trails in this park, which makes it quite peaceful for hikers.

The **Buzzard's Roost Trail** (3 mi/4.8 km round-trip, 2 hours, moderate) explores the park's west side. Climb from the river's edge through redwoods and oak trees on the way up to the summit of Pfeiffer Ridge, where you'll have a view of the coastline.

The most challenging hike is the **Mount Manuel Trail** (8 mi/12.9 km round-trip, 5-6 hours, strenuous), a 3,000-foot (900-m) climb to the top of this large mountain that towers over the park. The unshaded trail is not recommended on hot days.

Big Sur Station

The ranger station at **Big Sur Station** (Hwy. 1, 27 mi/43 km south of Carmel, 831/667-2315, 9am-4pm daily) offers maps and brochures for all the major parks and trails of Big Sur, plus a minimal bookshop. This is where the trailhead for the popular backcountry **Pine Ridge Trail** is located. Get a free backcountry fire permit as well as pay for Pine Ridge Trailhead parking. This is also one of the only places on CA-1 with public restrooms.

Pfeiffer Beach

Pfeiffer Beach (end of Sycamore Canyon Rd., http://campone.com, 9am-8pm daily, $10/vehicle) is one of the coastline's most picturesque spots. This frequently windswept beach has two looming rock formations right where the beach meets the surf, and both of these rocks have holes that look like doorways, allowing waves and sunlight to pass through. Occasionally, purple sand colors the beach; it is eroded manganese garnet from the bluffs above. It can be incredibly windy here some days.

Getting There
Getting to Pfeiffer Beach is a bit tricky. It is at the end of the second paved right south of the Big Sur Station. Motorists (no motor homes) must then travel down a narrow, windy road before reaching the entrance booth and the beach's parking lot. It's part of the adventure. This road gets very busy during the summer and on weekends. Plan a trip to Pfeiffer Beach when it's less busy. Otherwise, the 2-mile (3.2-km) drive might take a lot longer than expected.

Henry Miller Memorial Library
Henry Miller lived and wrote in Big Sur for 18 years, and his 1957 novel *Big Sur and the Oranges of Hieronymus Bosch* describes his time here. Today, the **Henry Miller Memorial Library** (Hwy. 1, 31 mi/50 km south of Carmel, 831/667-2574, www.henrymiller.org, 11am-5pm Wed.-Sun. though hours vary, free) celebrates the life and work of Miller and his brethren in this quirky community center, museum, coffee shop, and gathering place. Inside is a well-curated bookstore featuring the works of Miller as well as other authors like Jack Kerouac and Richard Brautigan. There's coffee and tea, but it's also a great spot to do nothing and just take in Big Sur. The small redwood-shaded lawn also hosts concerts, including impressive national touring acts and literary events.

Julia Pfeiffer Burns State Park
One of Big Sur's best postcard-perfect views can be attained at **Julia Pfeiffer Burns State Park** (Hwy. 1, 37 mi/60 km

From top to bottom: Garrapata State Park; Bixby Bridge; McWay Falls in Julia Pfeiffer Burns State Park.

south of Carmel, 831/667-1112, www. parks.ca.gov, sunrise-sunset daily, $10/ vehicle)—the scenic, if crowded, walk to McWay Falls. To get to the stunning view of **McWay Falls,** follow a section of the **Overlook Trail** (0.3 mile round-trip; partially closed) to the lookout. The 80-foot-high waterfall cascades year-round off a cliff and onto the beach of a remote cove, where the water wets the sand and trickles out into the sea. You'll look down on a pristine and empty stretch of sand—there's no way down to the cove that is even remotely safe.

★ Hiking

The west side of the road is where you pick up the **Partington Cove Trail** (1 mi/2 km round-trip, 1 hour, easy), an underrated walk that goes to a striking, narrow coastal inlet. It begins as a steep dirt road and continues through a 60-foot-long tunnel blasted into the rock. The trail arrives at a cove where John Partington used to ship out the tanbark trees that he had harvested in the canyon above. There is a bench at the end of the trail with views of the cove and the coastline to the south. To reach the trailhead from the north, drive 9 miles (14.5 km) south of Pfeiffer Big Sur State Park on CA-1. Look for a big bend in the road to the east with dirt pullouts on either side. Park here and then begin your hike where the gated road departs from the west side.

The **Tanbark Trail and Tin House Loop** (5.6 mi/9 km round-trip, hours, strenuous) begins on the east side of Highway 1 across from the Partington Cove Trail pullout. The hike begins in a redwood forest along Partington Creek and climbs 1,600 feet to an oak forest. At the top is the Tin House, an abandoned building known for its tin exterior. To turn this hike into a loop, descend the steep fire road and cross the highway to the scenic overlook. It's about a 1-mile (2 km) walk north on Highway 1 back to the trailhead.

Limekiln State Park

The 716-acre **Limekiln State Park** (Hwy. 1, 56 mi/90 km south of Carmel, 805/434-1996, www.parks.ca.gov, 8am-sunset daily, $10/vehicle) is home to redwoods, an impressive waterfall, a campground, ruins from the region's rugged past, and a nice beach on the stunning coastline. The park is named for four large, rusted limekilns accessed via the **Limekiln Trail.** From 1887 to 1890, the Rockland Lime and Lumber Company extracted and processed the land's limestone rock deposits in kilns, which used hot wood fires to purify the stones.

It's worth hiking the trail to **Limekiln Falls,** a 100-foot-high waterfall that splashes down a rock face in two distinct prongs. A sandy stretch of beach is littered with boulders, with the Limekiln Creek Bridge as a backdrop. A single picnic table plopped in the sand provides a terrific place for lunch. The park also has a **campground** with 32 sites.

Nacimiento-Fergusson Road

The only road that traverses Big Sur's Santa Lucia Mountains, the **Nacimiento-Fergusson Road** (58 mi/93 km south of Carmel) offers spectacular coastal views to those who are willing to wind their way up this twisty, paved, 1.5-lane road. Simply drive a few miles up to get an eyeful of the expansive Pacific Ocean or to climb above Big Sur's summer fog. It also heads in and out of infrequent redwood forests on the way up. The high point of the road is 2,780 feet (847 m). The road connects CA-1 to US-101, passing through Fort Hunter Liggett army base on its journey.

The road is frequently closed during the winter months. It is not recommended for those who get carsick.

Sand Dollar Beach

Sand Dollar Beach (60 mi/97 km south of Carmel, www.fs.usda.gov, 10am-6pm daily, $10/vehicle) is one of Big Sur's biggest and best beaches. This half-moon-shaped beach is tucked under cliffs that keep the wind down. Though frequently strewn with rocks, the beach is a great place to plop down for a picnic or an afternoon in the sun. From the beach, enjoy a striking view of Big Sur's south coast mountains, including Cone Peak, rising like a jagged fang from a long ridgeline. A series of uncrowded beach breaks offer waves for surfers even during the flatter summer months.

The area around the parking lot has picnic tables with raised grills, pit toilets, and a pay phone. If the parking lot is full, park on the dirt pullout to the south of the entrance.

Jade Cove Recreation Area
It's easy to miss **Jade Cove Recreation Area** (Hwy. 1, 61 mi/98 km south of Carmel). A road sign marks the area, but there's not much in the way of a formal parking lot or anything else to denote the treasures of this jagged, rough part of the Big Sur coastline. Park in the dirt/gravel strip off the road and head past the fence. It's fun to read the unusual signs along the narrow, beaten path that seems to lead to the edge of a cliff. Once you get to the edge of the cliff, the short trail gets rough. It's only 0.25 mile, but it's almost straight down a rocky, slippery cliff. Don't try to climb down if you're not in reasonable physical condition, and even if you are, don't be afraid to use your hands to steady yourself. At the bottom, you'll find huge boulders and smaller rocks and very little sand. But most of all, you'll find the most amazing minerals in the boulders and rocks. Search the smaller rocks beneath your feet for chunks of sea-polished jade. If you're a hard-core rock nut, join the locals in scuba diving for jewelry-quality jade. As long as you find it in the water or below the high-tide line, it's legal for you to take whatever you find here.

Jade Cove has no water, no restrooms, no visitors center, and no services of any kind.

Salmon Creek Falls
One of the best natural attractions is **Salmon Creek Falls** (Hwy. 1, 71 mi/114 km south of Carmel). A pair of waterfalls flow year-round down rocks more than 100 feet (30 m) high, their streams joining halfway down. For a great perspective of the falls, take an easy 10-minute walk over a primitive trail littered with rocks fallen from the highway. The unmarked parking area is a pullout in the middle of a hairpin turn on CA-1.

Sports and Recreation
Backpacking
If you long for the lonely peace of backcountry camping, the **Ventana Wilderness** (www.ventanawild.org) area is ideal for you. This area comprises the peaks of the Santa Lucia Mountains and the dense growth of the northern reaches of the Los Padres National Forest. It has 167,323 acres of steep, V-shaped canyons and mountains that rise to more than 5,000 feet (1,500 m). You'll find many trails beyond the popular day hikes of the state parks, especially as Big Sur stretches down to the south.

The Pine Ridge Trail travels to **Sykes Hot Springs** from Big Sur Station; however, the trail is closed for the foreseeable future. Farther south, the **Vicente Flat Trail** (4 mi/6.4 km south of Lucia on Hwy. 1, across from the Kirk Creek Campground, 10 mi/16 km round-trip) heads up toward Cone Peak, the jagged mountain rising in the distance, while gaining sweeping views of the coast. Do this one as a grueling up-and-back day hike to the Vicente Flat Camp or backpack it. Check the Ventana Wilderness Alliance website (www.ventanawild.org) in advance to find reports on the conditions of the trails you've decided to tackle, and stop in at Big Sur Station to get the latest news on the backcountry areas.

Fishing
The region offers your choice of shore or river fishing. Steelhead run up the Big Sur

River to spawn each year, and a limited fishing season follows them up the river into **Pfeiffer Big Sur State Park** and other accessible areas. Check with Fernwood Resort (831/667-2422, www.fernwoodbigsur.com) and the lodges around CA-1 for the best spots this season.

The numerous creeks that feed into and out of the Big Sur River also play home to their fair share of fish. The California Department of Fish and Game (831/649-2870, www.wildlife.ca.gov) can give you specific locations for legal fishing, season information, and rules and regulations.

If you prefer the fish from the ocean, cast off several of the beaches for the rockfish that scurry about in the nearshore reefs. **Garrapata State Beach** has a good fishing area, as do the beaches at **Sand Dollar.**

Scuba Diving

There's not much for beginner divers in Big Sur. Expect cold water and an exposure to the ocean's swells and surges. Temperatures are in the mid-50s in the shallows, dipping into the 40s as you dive deeper down. Visibility is 20-30 feet (6-9 m), though rough conditions can diminish this significantly; the best season for clear water is September-November.

The biggest and most interesting dive locale here is **Julia Pfeiffer Burns State Park** (Hwy. 1, 37 mi/60 km south of Carmel, 831/667-1112, www.parks.ca.gov, sunrise-sunset, $10/vehicle). You'll need to acquire a special permit at Big Sur Station and prove your experience to dive at this protected underwater park. You enter the water from the shore, which gives you the chance to check out all the ecosystems, beginning with the busy life of the beach sands before heading out to the rocky reefs and then into the lush green kelp forests.

Divers at access-hostile **Jade Cove** (Hwy. 1, 61 mi/98 km south of Carmel) come to stalk the wily jade pebbles and rocks that cluster in this special spot. The

semiprecious stone striates the coastline right here, and storms tear clumps of jade out of the cliffs and into the sea. Much of it settles just off the shore of the tiny cove, and divers hope to find jewelry-quality stones to sell for a huge profit.

Bird-Watching

The Big Sur coast is home to innumerable species, from the tiniest bushtits up to grand pelicans and beyond. The most famous avian residents of this area are the rare and endangered California condors. Once upon a time, condors were all but extinct, with only a few left alive in captivity and conservationists struggling to help them breed. Today, around 70 of these birds soar above the trails and beaches of Big Sur. You might even see one swooping down low over your car as you drive down the highway!

The **Ventana Wildlife Society** (VWS, www.ventanaws.org) watches over many of the endangered and protected avian species in Big Sur. As part of their mission to raise awareness of the condors and many other birds, the VWS offers bird-watching expeditions.

Spas

Spa Alila at Ventana Big Sur (Ventana Big Sur, 48123 Hwy. 1, 28 mi/45 km south of Carmel, 800/628-6500, www.ventanabigsur.com, massages $175-615) offers a large menu of spa treatments to both hotel guests and visitors. Indulge in a soothing massage, purifying body treatment, or rejuvenating or beautifying facial. Take your spa experience a step further in true Big Sur fashion with an astrological reading, essence portrait, or a jade stone massage. Hotel guests can choose to have a spa treatment in the comfort of their own room or out on a private deck.

Across the highway from the Ventana, the **Post Ranch Inn's spa** (Post Ranch Inn, 47900 Hwy. 1, 30 mi/48 km south of Carmel, 831/667-2200, www.postranchinn.com, 5am-6pm Mon.-Fri.,

California Condors

With wings spanning 10 feet (3 m) from tip to tip, the California condors soaring over the Big Sur coastline are some of the area's most impressive natural treasures. But, in 1987, there was only one bird left in the wild, and it was taken into captivity as part of a captive breeding program. The condors' population had plummeted due to their susceptibility to lead poisoning, along with deaths caused by electric power lines, habitat loss, and being shot by indiscriminate humans.

Today the reintroduction of the high-flying California condor, the largest flying bird in North America, to Big Sur and the Central Coast is truly one of conservation's greatest success stories. In 1997, the Monterey County-based nonprofit Ventana Wildlife Society (VWS) began releasing the giant birds back into the wild. Currently, almost 100 wild condors soar above Big Sur and the surrounding area, and in 2006, a pair of condors were found nesting in the hollowed-out section of a redwood tree.

The species' recovery in the Big Sur area means that you may be able to spot a California condor flying overhead while visiting the rugged coastal region. Look for a tracking tag on the condor's wing to determine that you are actually looking at a California condor and not just a big turkey vulture. Or take a two-hour tour with the **Ventana Wildlife Society** (831/455-9514, $75/person), which uses radio telemetry to track the released birds. You can also visit the **VWS Discovery Center** (Andrew Molera State Park, Hwy. 1, 22 mi/35 km south of Carmel, 831/624-1202, www.ventanaws. org, 10am-4pm Sat.-Sun. Memorial Day-Labor Day), where an exhibit details the near extinction of the condor and the attempts to restore its population.

10am-6pm Sat.-Sun., massages $175-260) is an ultra-high-end resort spa open only to those spending the evening at the luxurious resort. Shaded by redwoods, the relaxing spa offers massages and facials along with more unique treatments, including Big Sur jade stone therapy and craniosacral therapy. They also offer sessions inspired by Native American shamanism ($315-365), including a shamanic session, a fire ceremony, and a drum journey.

Entertainment and Events
Nightlife

Fernwood Tavern (Fernwood Resort, 47200 Hwy. 1, 27 mi/43 km south of Carmel, 831/667-2422, www.fernwood-bigsur.com, 11am-11pm Sun.-Thurs., 11am-1am Fri.-Sat.) is a classic watering hole with redwood timbers and a fireplace that warms the rooms in the chilly months. It's a great place to watch a sporting event or listen to a live band, especially on Saturday nights. Outside, there is a large deck under the redwoods with heat lamps, fire tables, and a Ping-Pong table. The bar serves nine beers on tap, along with a full bar of options including handmade Bloody Marys and margaritas. Fernwood can be an intriguing mix of longtime locals, international tourists, and everyone in between. The bar also has free Internet, a prized commodity in Big Sur.

The **Big Sur Taphouse** (47250 Hwy. 1, 29 mi/47 km south of Carmel, 831/667-2197, www.bigsurtaphouse.com, noon-10pm daily) has 10 rotating beers on tap, with a heavy emphasis on West Coast microbrews. The cozy interior has wood tables, a gas fireplace, and board games. With two big-screen TVs, the Taphouse is also a good place to catch your favorite sports team in action. Out back is a large patio with picnic tables and plenty of sun. They serve better-than-average bar food, including tacos and pork sliders.

The **Big Sur River Inn & Restaurant** (46840 Hwy. 1, 831/667-2700, www.big-surriverinn.com, 8am-11am, 11:30am-4:30pm, and 5pm-9pm daily) is a fine place for a cocktail or beer and is known for spicy Bloody Marys. In the late afternoon and early evening, the intimate bar area fills with a fun local crowd. On summer weekends, order your drink in a plastic cup and go out back to sip it in one of a few giant chairs plopped in the middle of the Big Sur River.

Live Music

Big Sur has become an unexpected hotbed of concerts. More than just a place to down a beer and observe the local characters, **Fernwood Tavern** (Fernwood Resort, 47200 Hwy. 1, 27 mi/43 km south of Carmel, 831/667-2422, www.fernwoodbigsur.com, 11am-11pm Sun.-Thurs., 11am-1am Fri.-Sat.) also has live music. Most of the big-name acts (Mac DeMarco, Kurt Vile, Chris Robinson) swing through in the summer and fall, but a wide range of regional acts perform on Saturday night starting at 10pm.

Down the road, the **Henry Miller Memorial Library** (48603 Hwy. 1, 31 mi/50 km south of Carmel, 831/667-2574, www.henrymiller.org) hosts even bigger concerts, book readings, and film screenings.

Big Sur River Inn & Restaurant (46480 Hwy. 1, 25 mi/40 km south of Carmel, 831/667-2700, www.bigsurriverinn.com, 1pm-5pm Sun. late Apr.-early Oct.) hosts Sunday afternoon concerts on the back deck in summer and fall. The live music tradition began in the 1960s with famed local act Jack Stock and the Abalone Stompers. Today, mostly local jazz bands play on the restaurant's sunny deck, while a barbecue is set up on the large green lawn.

Festivals and Events

The **Big Sur International Marathon** (831/625-6226, www.bsim.org, $175-200, Apr.) is one of the most popular marathons in the world, due in no small part to the scenery. Begin at the Big Sur Station and then wind, climb, and descend again on the way to Carmel's Rio Road.

The **Jade Festival** (Pacific Valley School, 69325 CA-1, 60 mi/97 km south of Carmel, 805/924-1725, https://bigsurjadefestival.com, Oct.) is a three-day festival that celebrates the sea green gemstone found on southern Big Sur's beaches. Expect amazing pieces of jade, jade carvings, and live music.

The **Big Sur Food & Wine Festival** (831/596-8105, www.bigsurfoodandwine.org, Nov.) celebrates cuisine and vino in stunning settings. Events include live music, dinner, and hiking with stemware.

Food

In Big Sur, a ready meal isn't something to take for granted. Pick up supplies in Carmel before you enter the area to avoid paying premiums at the few mini-marts.

Casual Dining

The **Fernwood Bar & Grill** (Fernwood Resort, 47200 Hwy. 1, 27 mi/43 km south of Carmel, 831/667-2129, www.fernwoodbigsur.com, 11am-10pm daily, $15-29) looks and feels like a grill in the woods ought to. Even in the middle of the afternoon, the aging, wood-paneled interior is dimly lit and strewn with casual tables and chairs. The menu includes a range of burgers, including a vegan option, along with 16-inch pizzas.

One of Big Sur's most popular attractions is ★ **Nepenthe** (48510 Hwy. 1, 29 mi/47 km south of Carmel, 831/667-2345, www.nepenthebigsur.com, 11:30am-10pm daily, $18-50), a restaurant built on the site where Rita Hayworth and Orson Welles owned a cabin until 1947. The deck offers stellar views. Sit under multicolored umbrellas on long, bar-like tables with stunning south-facing views. Order a basket of fries with Nepenthe's signature Ambrosia dipping sauce and wash them down with a potent South Coast margarita. The restaurant's most popular item is the Ambrosia burger, a ground steak burger on a French roll drenched in their tasty Ambrosia sauce.

If there's a line, consider dining at **Café Kevah** (weather permitting, 9am-4pm daily mid-Feb.-Jan.1, $9-16), an outdoor deck below the main restaurant that serves brunch, salads, and paninis.

The **Big Sur Bakery** (47540 Hwy. 1, 29 mi/47 km south of Carmel, 831/667-0520, www.bigsurbakery.com, bakery 8am daily; restaurant 5:30pm-8:30pm Wed.-Sun., $18-32) might sound like a casual establishment, and the bakery part is. Stop in beginning at 8am for a fresh scone, a homemade jelly doughnut, or a flaky croissant sandwich. On the dining room side, an elegant surprise awaits. Make reservations or you might miss out on the creative wood-fired pizzas, wood-grilled meats, and seafood. At brunch, they serve their unique wood-fired bacon and three-egg breakfast pizza.

The locals know ★ **Deetjen's** (48865 Hwy. 1, 31 mi/50 km south of Carmel, 831/667-2378, www.deetjens.com, 8am-noon and 6pm-9pm daily, $10-42) for its breakfast—an almost required experience for visitors to the area. Among fanciful knickknacks and framed photos of inn founder "Grandpa" Deetjen, diners can fill up on Deetjen's popular eggs Benedict dishes or the equally worthy Deetjen's dip, a turkey and avocado sandwich with hollandaise dipping sauce. In the evening, things get darker and more romantic as entrées, including the spicy seafood paella and an oven-roasted rack of lamb, are served at your candlelit table.

If it's a warm afternoon, get a table on the sunny back deck of the **Big Sur River Inn & Restaurant** (46840 Hwy. 1, 25 mi/40 km south of Carmel, 831/667-2700, http://bigsurriverinn.com, 8am-11am, 11:30am-4:30pm, and 5pm-9pm daily, $15-40). On summer Sundays, bands perform on the crowded deck, and you can take your libation to one of the chairs situated right in the middle of the cool Big Sur River. If it's chilly out, eat in the wood-beamed main dining room. The restaurant serves sandwiches, burgers, and salads for lunch along with steak, ribs, seafood, and the recommended Noelle's salad at dinner. For dessert, they still do the famous apple pie that put them on the map back in the 1930s. The bar is known for its popular spicy Bloody Mary cocktails.

The unassuming **Ripplewood Café** (47047 Hwy. 1, 26 mi/42 km south of Carmel, 831/667-2242, www.ripplewood-resort.com, 8am-2pm daily, $9-16) may save the day on summer weekends when Deetjen's is flooded. Dine inside at the classic breakfast counter or on the outside brick patio among flowering plants. The breakfast menu includes pancakes, three-egg omelets, and a worthwhile chorizo and eggs. The grilled potato gratin is a highlight. Ripplewood shifts to lunch at 11:30am; offerings include sandwiches, Mexican food items, and salads.

The Big Sur Roadhouse (47080 Hwy. 1, 26 mi/42 km south of Carmel, 831/667-2370, www.glenoaksbigsur.com, 8am-2:30pm daily, $7-16) is one of the best bets for affordable, creative California dining in Big Sur for breakfast and lunch. The decor is homegrown modernism, with contemporary art hanging on the walls. The outdoor seating area has heating lamps and two fire pits. The menu skews toward Mexican items, including huevos rancheros and *chilaquiles.*

Oceanview Sushi Bar (Treebones Resort, 71895 Hwy. 1, 64 mi/103 km south of Carmel, 805/927-2390, 4:30pm-8pm Wed.-Sun. Mar.-Nov., $8-19) offers an intimate place to eat artfully prepared sushi. Just 10 seats are available at a redwood sushi bar within a tent-like structure. The menu includes simple rolls, garden rolls, specialty rolls, and hearty rolls designed to resemble burritos. There are two beers on tap along with sake, Japanese beer, and California wine. Seating priority is given to Treebones' guests, though nonguests can make same-day reservations.

Fine Dining

The Sur House (48123 CA-1, Ventana Big Sur, 29 mi/47 km south of Carmel, 4 mi/6.4 km south of Pfeiffer Big Sur State Park, 831/667-4242, www.ventanabigsur.

com, 7:30am-10:30am, 11:30am-4pm, and 6pm-9pm daily, lunch $15-30, dinner $20-50, tasting menu $90) has a spacious dining room that boasts wooden beams, a wood fire, and an open kitchen. Dinner showcases the chef's skills with a four-course tasting menu. The outdoor deck has views of the coast that rival nearby Nepenthe. A bar menu (4pm-9pm) offers the same ambiance with a lighter fare at a more affordable price.

The **Sierra Mar** restaurant (Post Ranch Inn, 47900 Hwy. 1, 28 mi/45 km south of Carmel, 831/667-2800, www.post-ranchinn.com, noon-2pm and 5:30pm-9pm daily) offers a decadent four-course prix-fixe dinner menu ($125) every night and a less formal three-course lunch ($75) every day. With floor-to-ceiling glass windows that overlook the plunging ridgeline and the Pacific below, this is a good place for a sunset dinner. The daily menu rotates but is always a memorable meal.

Markets

The best of the local markets is the **Big Sur Deli** (47520 Hwy. 1, 29 mi/47 km south of Carmel, 831/667-2225, www.bigsurdeli.com, 7am-8pm daily). Very popular with locals, the deli has large, made-to-order sandwiches, burritos, tamales, tacos, and pasta salads. If the line is long at the counter, opt for a premade sandwich for a quicker exit. They also have cold drinks, wine, beer, and some basic supplies.

River Inn Big Sur General Store (46840 Hwy. 1, 25 mi/40 km south of Carmel, 831/667-2700, 11am-7pm daily) has basic supplies, along with beer and a nice selection of California wines. Even better, it has a wonderful burrito bar and smoothie counter in the back. There are also simple premade turkey and ham sandwiches in a nearby fridge for taking out on a hike or picnic.

From top to bottom: Nepenthe; the Big Sur Deli; Deetjen's Big Sur Inn.

Accommodations
$100-150
New Camaldoli Hermitage (Hwy. 1, 51 mi/82 km south of Carmel, 831/667-2456, www.contemplation.com, $135-325) offers a quiet stay in the mountains above Lucia. The hermitage is home to Roman Catholic monks who offer overnight accommodations for people of any or no religious denomination. The five private hermitages are basically trailers decorated with religious iconography and outfitted with a bed, desk, bathroom, and kitchen with a gas stove. There are also nine private rooms with a half bath and garden. Male guests can stay overnight in a monk's cell within the monastic enclosure; there are also a few units outside the enclosure for groups of two guests. Meals from the monastery's kitchen are included in the price. In addition to being a unique experience, staying at the Hermitage is one of the region's best deals. The accommodations can be rustic, but they are worth it if it's solitude you're after. Radios, musical instruments, and children under 16 are not permitted.

Each guest room at ★ **Deetjen's Big Sur Inn** (CA-1, 5 mi/8 km south of Pfeiffer Big Sur State Park, 831/667-2377, www.deetjens.com, $115-290) is unique, still decorated with the art and collectibles chosen and arranged by Grandpa Deetjen. The historic inn prides itself on its rustic construction, so expect thin, weathered walls, funky cabin construction, and no outdoor locks on the doors. Five rooms have shared baths, but you can request a room with private bath when you make reservations. Deetjen's prefers a serene environment; children under eight are not permitted unless renting both rooms of a two-room building. Deetjen's has no TVs or stereos, no phones in rooms, and no cell phone service, but you can have a night's worth of entertainment and reflection by reading a book from the on-site library or your room's guest journals, which have been written about in *The New York*

Times. Deetjen's is a nonprofit, thus the prices here are not as high as other area accommodations.

$150-250
Budget travelers should be thankful a place like **Fernwood Resort** (47200 CA-1, 25.5 mi/41 km south Carmel, 831/667-2422, www.fernwoodbigsur.com, motel rooms $170-215, cabins $270) still exists in Big Sur. The motel rooms are flanked on either side of the bar and are basic; rates increase for amenities like gas fireplaces and hot tubs. Located near the Big Sur River, cabins have fully equipped kitchens and a refrigerator and are a good deal for groups of 2-6 people. Fernwood offers coin-operated washers and dryers in the campground.

Over $250
The best part about staying at the **Big Sur Lodge** (Pfeiffer Big Sur State Park, 47225 CA-1, 27 mi/43 km south of Carmel, 855/238-6950, www.bigsurlodge.com, $309-479) is that you can leave your room and hit the trail. In the early 1900s, the park was a former resort owned by the pioneering Pfeiffer family. Though the amenities have been somewhat updated, the Big Sur Lodge still evokes the classic woodsy vacation cabin. Set on a sunny knoll, the lodge has 62 units; many are family-friendly and accommodate groups. Twelve units come with kitchenettes. Though a bit dated, each room has a front or back deck, but no TV. Internet access is available for a fee. Stays include a pass that allows entrance to all of Big Sur's state parks. In summer, guests can take advantage of the lodge's pool (9am-9pm daily late May-early Sept.).

The **Big Sur River Inn & Restaurant** (46480 Hwy. 1, 25 mi/40 km south of Carmel, 831/667-2700, www.bigsurriverinn.com, $260-425) has 14 rooms on the east side of CA-1 and six suites on the west side of the road. The east-side rooms are cozy, with knotty pine walls and small porches. The west-side suites each have two rooms, one with a king bed and the other with a trundle bed, which is good for families and small groups. The suites have decks overlooking the Big Sur River. Also, on-site is a seasonally heated outdoor pool.

Filled with creative touches and thoughtful amenities, ★ **Glen Oaks Big Sur** (47080 Hwy. 1, 26 mi/42 km south of Carmel, 831/667-2105, www.glenoaksbigsur.com, $300-800) offers the region's best lodging for the price. Its 16 units bring the motor lodge into the new millennium with heated stone bathroom floors, in-room yoga mats, spacious showers, and elegant gas fireplaces. Glen Oaks also has two cottages and eight cabins by the Big Sur River. The cabins are clean, with a modern rustic feel, and have kitchenettes along with outdoor fire pits. Guests have access to two on-site beaches on scenic sections of the Big Sur River.

Ventana Big Sur (48123 CA-1, 4 mi/6.4 km south of Pfeiffer Big Sur State Park, 831/667-2331, www.ventanabigsur.com, $750-3,000) has a rustic design in its 59 rooms, each of which comes with a private balcony or patio. Don your plush spa robe and rubber slippers and head for the Japanese bathhouses (clothing-optional and gender segregated); there's one at each end of the property. The upper house has glass and open-air windows that look out onto the ocean. Two swimming pools offer a cool respite; the Mountain Pool is clothing-optional, while the Meadow Pool perches on a high spot for enthralling views. Daily complimentary yoga classes are yours for the asking. The Social House includes a communal space with a stone fireplace, record player, pool table, and coffee lounge.

A night at **Post Ranch Inn** (47900 Hwy. 1, 28 mi/45 km south of Carmel, 831/667-2200 or 888/524-4787, www.postranchinn.com, $995-4,350), staring at the stars over the Pacific from one of the stainless-steel hot soaking tubs, can temporarily cause all life's worries to ebb away though it costs as much as a month's rent in most major cities. Situated on a 1,200-foot-high ridgeline, the rooms at this luxury resort have striking views of the ocean or the jagged peaks of the nearby Ventana Wilderness. The units blend in with the natural environment, including the seven tree houses, which are perched 10 feet (3 m) off the ground. Each one has a king bed, an old-fashioned wood-burning fireplace, a spa tub, and a private deck. Take advantage of complimentary activities including yoga classes, nature hikes, garden tours, and stargazing. Breakfast includes made-to-order omelets and French toast as well as a spread of pastries, fruit, and yogurt served in the Sierra Mar restaurant with its stellar ocean views.

Camping

The **Fernwood Resort** (47200 Hwy. 1, 25 mi/40 km south of Carmel, 831/667-2422, www.fernwoodbigsur.com, tent site $65, campsite with electrical hookup $85, tent cabin $130, adventure tent $170) offers a range of options. There are 66 campsites around the Big Sur River, some with electrical hookups for RVs. Fernwood also has tent cabins with room for four in a double and two twins. Bring your own linens or sleeping bags, pillows, and towels. The rustic Adventure Tents are canvas tents draped over a solid floor with fully made queen beds and electricity courtesy of an extension cord. All camping options have easy access to the river. Hot showers and restrooms are a short walk away. The **Fernwood General Store** (Fernwood Resort, 47200 Hwy. 1, 27 mi/43 km south of Carmel, 831/667-2129, www.fernwoodbigsur.com, 8am-10pm daily) sells tents, sleeping bags, air mattresses, and groceries.

The biggest and most developed campground in Big Sur is at ★ **Pfeiffer Big Sur State Park** (Hwy. 1, 26 mi/42 km south of Carmel, 800/444-7275, www.parks.ca.gov, www.reservecalifornia.com, $35-50), with more than 150 sites, each of

Esalen: An Advanced California Experience

The **Esalen Institute** is known throughout California as the home of Esalen massage technique, a forerunner and cutting-edge player in ecological living, and a space to retreat from the world and build a new and better sense of self. Visitors journey from all over the state and beyond to sink into the haven that is sometimes called "The New Age Harvard."

One of the institute's biggest draws, the bathhouse, sits down a rocky path right on the edge of the cliffs overlooking the ocean. The bathhouse includes a motley collection of mineral-fed hot tubs with ocean views—choose the open-air Quiet Side or the indoor Silent Side, and then sink into the water and contemplate the Pacific Ocean's limitless expanse, meditate on a perfect sunset or arrangement of stars, or (on the Quiet Side) get to know your fellow bathers—who will be naked. Regardless of gender, marital status, or the presence of others, Esalen's bathhouse area is "clothing optional"; its philosophy puts the essence of nature above the sovereignty of humanity, and it encourages openness and sharing among its guests—to the point of chatting nude with total strangers in a smallish hot tub.

You'll also find a distinct lack of attendants to help you find your way around. Once you've parked and been given directions, it's up to you to find your way down to the cliffs. You'll have to find your own towel, ferret out a cubby for your clothes in the changing rooms, grab a shower, and then wander out to find your favorite of the hot tubs. Be sure you go all the way outside past the individual claw-foot tubs to the glorious shallow cement tubs that sit right out on the edge of the cliff with the surf crashing just below.

In addition to the nudity and new-age culture of Esalen, you'll learn that this isn't a day spa. You'll need to make an appointment for a massage (831/667-3002, $155-195), which grants you access to the hot tubs for an hour before and an hour after your 75-minute treatment session. If you just want to sit in the mineral water, you'll need to stay up late. Very late. Esalen allows **Night Bathing** ($35, reserve at https://nightbaths.esalen.org) in the tubs from 1am to 3am on certain evenings. Many locals consider the sleep deprivation well worth it to get the chance to enjoy the healing mineral waters and the stunning astronomical shows.

If you're not comfortable with your own nudity or that of others, you don't approve of the all-inclusive spiritual philosophy, or you find it impossible to lower your voice or stop talking for more than 10 minutes, Esalen is not for you. If you've never done anything like this before, think hard about how you'll really feel once you're in the changing area with its naked hippies wandering about. But if this description of a California experience sounds just fabulous to you, make your reservations now! **The Esalen Institute** (55000 Hwy. 1, 41 mil/66 km south of Carmel, 831/667-3000, www.esalen.org) accepts reservations by phone if necessary. Go to the website for more information.

which can handle two vehicles and eight people or an RV (max. 32 feet, trailers max. 27 feet, dump station on-site). A grocery store and laundry facility operate within the campground, and plenty of flush toilets and hot showers are scattered throughout. In the evenings, walk down to the Campfire Center for entertaining and educational programs. Pfeiffer Big Sur fills up fast in the summer,

especially on weekends. Reservations are recommended.

Julia Pfeiffer Burns State Park (Hwy. 1, 37 mi/60 km south of Carmel, 831/667-2315 or 800/444-7275, www.parks.ca.gov, www.reservecalifornia.com, $30) has two walk-in environmental campsites perched over the ocean behind McWay Falls. It's a 0.3-mile walk to these two sites, which have fire pits, picnic tables, and a shared pit toilet, but no running water. More importantly, they have some of the best views of the California coast that you can find in a developed state park campground. Fall asleep to the sound of waves crashing into the rocks below. Saddle Rock is the better of the two, but you can't go wrong with either. The sites book far in advance, particularly in summer. Reservations can be made seven months in advance.

A popular U.S. Forest Service campground on the south coast of Big Sur, **Kirk Creek Campground** (Hwy. 1, 58 mi/93 km south of Carmel, 877/444-6777, www.recreation.gov, $35) has a great location on a bluff above the ocean. Right across the highway is the trailhead for the Vicente Flat Trail and the scenic Nacimiento-Fergusson Road. The sites have picnic tables and campfire rings with grills, while the grounds have toilets and drinking water.

Plaskett Creek Campground (Hwy. 1, 63 mi/101 km south of Carmel, 877/444-6777, www.recreation.gov, $35) is right across the highway from Sand Dollar Beach. The sites are in a grassy area under Monterey pine and cypress trees. There are picnic tables and a campfire ring with a grill at every site, along with a flush toilet and drinking water in the campground.

Camping on the Big Sur coast is very popular during the summer. If you haven't made campsite reservations months in advance, it's going to be difficult to find a place to pitch your tent. **Nacimiento Campground** (Nacimiento-Fergusson Rd., 11 mi/17.5 km east of CA-1, 831/385-5434, www.fs.usda.gov, first-come, first-served, $20) is 10 miles inland but does offer a possible place to stay. There are eight here, all located by the Nacimiento River.

Two miles east of Nacimiento Campground, and far more spacious, **Ponderosa Campground** (Nacimiento-Fergusson Rd., 13 mi/21 km east of CA-1, reservations 877/444-6777, www.

recreation.gov, $25) has 23 sites along the Nacimiento River. All sites have picnic tables, fire pits, and raised grills. Reservations must be made more than eight days in advance. Or, try to secure a site in person. Be aware that it will be hot and bug-filled in summer.

For the ultimate high-end California green lodging-cum-camping experience, book a yurt (a circular structure made with a wood frame covered by cloth) at the **Treebones Resort** (71895 Hwy. 1, 64 mi/103 km south of Carmel, 877/424-4787, www.treebonesresort.com, $310-420). The yurts tend to be spacious and charming, with polished wood floors, queen beds, seating areas, and outdoor decks for lounging, but they are not soundproof. There are also five walk-in campsites ($98 for two people, breakfast and use of the facilities included). For a truly different experience, camp in the human nest ($175), a bundle of wood off the ground outfitted with a futon mattress, or a hand-woven twig hut ($218). Any stay includes a complimentary breakfast with make-your-own waffles. In the central lodge, you'll find nice hot showers and clean restroom facilities. There is also a heated pool with an ocean view and a hot tub on the grounds. Treebones has a couple of on-site dining options: the **Wild Coast Restaurant** and the **Oceanview Sushi Bar.**

Information and Services
Big Sur Station (Hwy. 1, 27 mi/43 km south of Carmel, 831/667-2315, 9am-4pm daily) is the closest thing to a visitors center. The staffed building offers maps and brochures for all the major parks and trails of Big Sur, plus a bookshop and public bathrooms. Get a **free backcountry fire permit** as well.

Your **cell phone** may not work anywhere in Big Sur. The best places to get cell service are around Andrew Molera State Park and Point Sur, along with the large dirt pullout 0.25 mile south of Big Sur Station on CA-1. Likewise, GPS units may struggle in this region. It's best to have a map in your vehicle, or pick up a free *Big Sur Guide,* which has a general map of the region.

The **Big Sur Health Center** (Hwy. 1, 24 mi/39 km south of Carmel, Big Sur, 831/667-2580, http://bigsurhealthcenter. org, 10am-1pm and 2pm-5pm Mon.-Fri.) can take care of minor medical needs, and it provides an ambulance service and limited emergency care. The nearest full-service hospital is the **Community Hospital of the Monterey Peninsula** (23625 Holman Hwy., Monterey, 831/624-5311 or 888/452-4667, www. chomp.org).

Getting There

Getting to San Francisco

Air

San Francisco's major airport is **San Francisco International Airport** (SFO, US-101, 650/821-8211 or 800/435-9736, www.flysfo.com), located approximately 13 miles (21 km) south of the city center, near the town of Millbrae. Plan to arrive at the airport up to three hours before your flight leaves. Airport lines, especially on weekends and holidays, are notoriously long, and planes can be grounded due to fog.

To avoid the SFO crowds, consider booking a flight into one of the Bay Area's less crowded airports. **Oakland International Airport** (OAK, 1 Airport Dr., Oakland, 510/563-3300, www. oaklandairport.com) serves the East Bay with access to San Francisco via the Bay Bridge and commuter trains. **Mineta San José Airport** (SJC, 1701 Airport Blvd., San Jose, 408/392-3600, www.flysanjose. com) is 45 miles (72 km) south of San Francisco. These airports are quite a bit smaller than SFO, but service is frequent from many U.S. destinations.

Airport Transportation

Several public and private transportation options can get you into San Francisco. **Bay Area Rapid Transit** (BART, 415/989-2278, www.bart.gov, one-way ticket to any downtown station $9.65) connects directly with SFO's international terminal, providing a simple and relatively fast (under one hour) trip to downtown San Francisco. The BART station is an easy walk or a free shuttle ride from any point in the airport. BART trains also connect Oakland Airport to the city of San Francisco. Both BART and **Caltrain** (800/660-4287, www.caltrain. com, tickets $3.75) connect Mineta San José Airport to San Francisco. To access Caltrain from the airport, you must first take BART to the Millbrae stop, where the two lines meet. This station is designed for folks jumping from one line to the other. Caltrain tickets vary in price depending on your destination.

Shuttle vans are another cost-effective option for door-to-door service, although these make several stops along the way. The average one-way fare from the airport to downtown San Francisco starts at about $20 per person. Shuttle vans congregate on the second level of SFO above the baggage claim area for domestic flights, and on the third level for international flights. Advance reservations guarantee a seat, but these aren't required and don't necessarily speed the process. Some companies to try include **Quake City Shuttle** (415/255-4899, www.quakecityshuttle. com) and **SuperShuttle** (800/258-3826, www.supershuttle.com).

For **taxis,** the average fare to downtown San Francisco is around $40. Use your cell phone to access ride-sharing services **Lyft** (www.lyft.com) or **Uber** (www.uber.com), which charge $30-113 for a ride from the airport to downtown.

Train

Several long-distance **Amtrak** (800/872-7245, www.amtrak.com) trains rumble through California daily. Eight train routes serve the region: The *California Zephyr* runs from Chicago and Denver to Emeryville; the *Coast Starlight* travels down the West Coast from Seattle and Portland as far as Los Angeles; the *Pacific Surfliner* will get you to the Central Coast. There is no train depot in San Francisco; the closest station is in Emeryville (5885 Horton St.) in the East Bay. Fortunately, comfortable coach buses ferry travelers to and from the Emeryville Amtrak station with many stops in downtown San Francisco.

Bus

An affordable way to get around California is on **Greyhound** (800/231-2222, www.greyhound.com). The San

Francisco Station (200 Folsom St., 415/495-1569) is a hub for Greyhound bus lines. There are also stations along the coast from Crescent City to San Diego. Greyhound routes generally follow the major highways, traveling US-101. Most counties and municipalities have bus service with routes to outlying areas.

Megabus (http://us.megabus.com) offers affordable bus service to San Francisco and San Jose.

Getting to Sacramento
Air
The **Sacramento International Airport** (SMF, 6900 Airport Blvd., 916/929-5411, https://sacramento.aero/smf) is serviced by American Airlines, Air Canada, Delta, and United Airlines, among others. Car rentals are available at the airport.

Train
Amtrak (800/872-7245, www.amtrak. com) travels to Sacramento via two routes. The train's classic *Coast Starlight* runs from Seattle to Los Angeles and includes stops in Northern California (Dunsmuir, Redding, Chico) and in the Bay Area (Emeryville, Oakland). The *California Zephyr* heads from Chicago to end in Emeryville east of San Francisco, stopping in Reno and Truckee. Both routes stop at Sacramento's **Sacramento Valley Station** (401 I St., 4am-11:59pm daily).

Bus
Greyhound (800/231-2222, www. greyhound.com) provides affordable bus transportation to San Francisco, Redding, and Reno, Nevada. Purchase tickets online or at the **Sacramento Greyhound Station** (420 Richards Blvd., 916/444-6858, www.greyhound.com, 6:30am-3am daily).

Megabus (http://us.megabus.com) provides inexpensive bus service to San Francisco and Oakland.

Getting to Reno, Nevada
Air
The **Reno-Tahoe International Airport** (RNO, 2001 E. Plumb Ln., 775/328-6400, www.renoairport.com) is serviced by nine airlines, including Alaska, American, Delta, JetBlue, Southwest, and United. Car rentals are available at the airport.

Train
Amtrak's (800/872-7245, www.amtrak. com) *California Zephyr* train travels between Chicago and the San Francisco Bay Area, stopping at the **Reno, Nevada station** (280 N. Center St., 7:15am-4:45pm daily).

Bus
There's a **Greyhound** station (1421 Victorian Ave., Sparks, 775/322-2970, www.greyhound.com, 5am-10am, 12:30pm-2:30pm, and 5pm-midnight daily) in nearby Sparks, Nevada.

Road Rules

In California, scenic coastal routes such as CA-1 and US-101 are often destinations in themselves. **CA-1**, also known as the Pacific Coast Highway, follows the North Coast from Leggett to San Luis Obispo on the Central Coast and points south. Running parallel and intertwining with CA-1 for much of its length, **US-101** stretches north-south from Crescent City on the North Coast through the Central Coast, meeting CA-1 in San Luis Obispo.

CA-120 from San Francisco to Yosemite National Park starts off going through nondescript Central Valley towns, but the road really becomes scenic as it climbs up into the foothills of the Sierra Nevada. From the town of Groveland to the entrance to the park, it is a nice drive with occasional mountain vistas and worthwhile stops like Rainbow Pool on the Tuolumne River. If it's summer or fall, you can take CA-120 across the park and over Tioga Pass. It is one of California's best mountain drives.

I-80 stretches from the San Francisco Bay Area north to Tahoe, rising to 7,239 feet across Donner Pass before dropping down into Nevada. In winter, I-80 is subject to snow. Though the highway is frequently plowed, vehicles may be required to use tire chains during heavy snow, and traffic congestion is common.

I-5 is a major north-south highway through inland California and into Oregon.

US-395 runs along the Eastern Sierra between Yosemite National Park and Las Vegas, Nevada. The desert highways of **I-95** and **I-40** connect California with neighboring Nevada and Arizona, respectively.

Car and RV Rental

Most car-rental companies are located at each of the major California airports. To reserve a car in advance, contact **Budget Rent A Car** (U.S. 800/218-7992, outside U.S. 800/472-3325, www.budget.com), **Dollar Rent A Car** (800/800-5252, www.dollar.com), **Enterprise** (855/266-9289, www.enterprise.com), or **Hertz** (U.S. and Canada 800/654-3131, international 800/654-3001, www.hertz.com).

To rent a car, drivers in California must be at least 21 years of age and have a valid driver's license. California law also requires that all vehicles carry liability insurance. You can purchase insurance with your rental car, but it generally costs an additional $10 per day, which can add up quickly. Most private auto insurance will also cover rental cars. Before buying rental insurance, check your car insurance policy to see if rental-car coverage is included.

The **average cost** of a rental car is $50 per day or $210 per week; however, rates vary greatly based on the time of year and distance traveled. Weekend and summer rentals cost significantly more. Generally, it is more expensive to rent from car rental agencies at an airport. To avoid excessive rates, first plan travel to areas where a car is not required, then rent a car from an agency branch in town to further explore more rural areas. Rental agencies occasionally allow vehicle drop-off at a different location from where it was picked up for an additional fee.

Another option is to rent an **RV.** You won't have to worry about camping or lodging options, and many facilities, particularly farther north, accommodate RVs. However, RVs are difficult to maneuver and park, limiting your access to metropolitan areas. They are also expensive, both in terms of gas and the rental rates. Rates during the summer average $1,300 per week and $570 for three days, the standard minimal rental. **Cruise America** (800/671-8042, www.cruiseamerica.com) has branches in the San Francisco Airport, San Mateo, Sacramento, and Santa Rosa. **El Monte RV** (800/337-2214, www.elmonterv.com) operates out of San Francisco, Santa Cruz, and Sacramento.

Jucy Rentals (800/650-4180, www.jucyrentals.com) rents minivans with pop-up tops. These colorful vehicles are smaller and easier to manage than large RVs, but still come equipped with a fridge, a gas cooker, a sink, a DVD player, and two double beds. A rental location is in San Francisco.

Road Conditions

Road closures are not uncommon in winter. CA-1 along the coast can shut down due to flooding or landslides. I-5 through the Central Valley can close or be subject to hazardous driving conditions resulting from tule fog, which can reduce visibility to only a few feet.

In addition, many mountain roads close in winter due to snow. CA-120 (Tioga Pass) through Yosemite closes from fall to late spring, as does the main road through Lassen National Park. The roads and freeways around Lake Tahoe are subject to winter conditions; tire chains may be required at any time.

Traffic jams, accidents, mudslides, fires, and snow can affect interstates and local highways at any time. Before heading out on your adventure, check road conditions online with the state highways department, **Caltrans** (www.dot.ca.gov).

Roadside Assistance

In an emergency, **dial 911** from any phone. The American Automobile Association, better known as **AAA** (800/222-4357, www.aaa.com), offers roadside assistance that is free to members; others pay a fee.

Be aware of your car's maintenance needs while on the road. The most frequent maintenance needs result from **summer heat.** If the car gets hot or overheats, stop for a while to cool it off. Never open the radiator cap if the engine is steaming. After the engine cools, squeeze the top radiator hose to see if there's any pressure in it; if there isn't, it's safe to open. Never pour water into a hot radiator because it could crack the engine block. If you start to smell rubber, your tires are overheating, and that's a good way to have a blowout. Stop and let them cool off. During **winter** in the high country around Yosemite, a can of silicone lubricant such as WD-40 will unfreeze door locks, dry off humid wiring, and keep your hinges in shape.

Parking

Parking is at a premium in big cities. Most hotels within San Francisco will charge guests $50 or more per night for parking. Remove any valuables from your vehicle for the evening, because some hotel valets just park your car in an adjacent public parking deck.

Parking is strictly regulated at the national parks. At Yosemite, **park entrance fees** include entry and parking for up to seven days. Visitors are encouraged to park their cars at the outer edges of the parks and use the extensive network of **free shuttles** to get around the parks.

International Driver's Licenses

If you are visiting the United States from another country, you need to secure an International Driving Permit from your home country before coming to the United States. It can't be obtained once you're here. You must also bring your government-issued driving permit.

Visitors from outside the United States should check the driving rules of the states they will visit at www.usa.gov/Topics/Motor-Vehicles.shtml. Among the most important rules is that traffic runs on the right side of the road in the United States. Note that California bans using handheld cell phones while driving. If you get caught, expect to pay a hefty fine.

Maps and Visitor Information

When visiting **California,** rely on **local, regional,** and **national park visitors centers,** which are usually staffed by rangers or volunteers who feel passion and pride for their locale. The **Golden State Welcome Centers** (www.visitcalifornia.com) scattered throughout the state are less useful but can be a good place to pick up maps and brochures. The state's **California Travel and Tourism Commission** (916/444-4429, www.visitcalifornia.com) also provides helpful and free tips, information, and downloadable maps and guides.

The American Automobile Association, better known as **AAA** (www.aaa.com), offers free maps to its members. The **Thomas Guide Road Atlas** (866/896-6277, www.mapbooks4u.com) is a reliable and detailed map and road guide and a great insurance policy against getting lost. Almost all gas stations and drugstores sell maps.

California is in the Pacific time zone (PST and PDT) and observes daylight saving time March-November.

Visas and Officialdom

Passports and Visas

Visiting from another country, you must have a **valid passport** and a **visa** to enter the United States. If you hold a current passport from one of the following countries, you may qualify for the **Visa Waiver Program:** Andorra, Australia, Austria, Belgium, Brunei, Chile, Czech Republic, Denmark, Estonia, Finland, France, Germany, Greece, Hungary, Iceland, Ireland, Italy, Japan, Latvia, Liechtenstein, Lithuania, Luxembourg, Malta, Monaco, the Netherlands, New Zealand, Norway, Portugal, San Marino, Singapore, Slovakia, Slovenia, South Korea, Spain, Sweden, Switzerland, Taiwan, and the United Kingdom. To qualify, you must apply online with the Electronic System for Travel Authorization at www.cbp.gov and hold a **return plane or cruise ticket** to your country of origin dated less than **90 days** from your date of entry. Holders of Canadian passports don't need visas or visa waivers.

In most other countries, the local U.S. embassy should be able to provide a **tourist visa.** The application fee for a visa is US$160, although you will have to pay an issuance fee as well. While a visa may be processed in as little as 24 hours on request, plan for at least a couple of weeks, as there can be unexpected delays, particularly during the busy summer season (June-Aug.). For information, visit http://travel.state.gov.

Consulates

San Francisco is home to consulates from many countries around the globe. If you should lose your passport or find yourself in some other trouble while visiting California, contact your country's offices for assistance. The website of the **U.S. State Department** (www.state.gov) lists the websites for all foreign embassies and consulates in the United States. A representative will be able to direct you to the nearest embassy or consulate.

The **British Consulate** (www.gov.uk) has California offices in **San Francisco** (1 Sansome St., Ste. 850, 415/617-1300).

The **Australian Consulate** has offices in **San Francisco** (575 Market St., Ste. 1800, 415/644-3260, www.usa.embassy.gov.au).

The **Consulate General of Canada** has an office in **San Francisco** (580 California St., 14th Fl., 415/834-3180).

Customs

Before you enter the United States from another country by sea or by air, you'll be required to fill out a customs form. Check with the U.S. embassy in your country or the **Customs and Border Protection** website (www.cbp.gov) for an updated list of items you must declare.

If you require medication administered by injection, you must pack your syringes in a checked bag; syringes are not permitted in carry-ons coming into the United States. Also, pack documentation describing your need for any narcotic medications you've brought with you. Failure to produce documentation for narcotics on request can result in severe penalties in the United States.

If you're driving into California along I-5 or another major highway, prepare to stop at **Agricultural Inspection Stations** a few miles inside the state line. You don't need to present a passport, a visa, or even a driver's license; instead, you must be prepared to present all your fruits and vegetables. California's largest economic sector is agriculture, and a number of the major crops grown here are sensitive to pests and diseases. In an effort to prevent known pests from entering the state and endangering crops, travelers are asked to identify all produce they're carrying in from other states or from Mexico. If you've got produce, especially homegrown or from a farm stand, it could be infected by a known problem pest or disease. Expect it to be confiscated on the spot.

You'll also be asked about fruits and veggies on your U.S. Customs form, which you'll be asked to fill out on the airplane or ship before you reach the United States.

Travel Tips

Conduct and Customs

The legal **drinking age** everywhere in the United States is 21. Expect to have your ID checked if you look under age 30, especially in bars and clubs, but also in restaurants and wineries. California bars and clubs that serve alcohol close at 2am; you'll find the occasional after-hours nightspot in San Francisco.

Smoking has been banned in many places throughout California. Don't expect to find a smoking section in any restaurant or an ashtray in any bar. Smoking is illegal in all bars and clubs, but your new favorite watering hole might have an outdoor patio where smokers can huddle. Taking the ban one step further, many hotels, motels, and inns throughout California are strictly nonsmoking, and you'll be subject to fees of hundreds of dollars if your room smells of smoke when you leave. There's no smoking in any public building, and even some parks don't allow cigarettes. There's often good reason for this; the fire danger is extreme in the summer, and one carelessly thrown butt can cause a catastrophe.

In 2016, the state of California officially legalized **recreational marijuana.** Visit https://potguide.com to find a list of recreational dispensaries.

Money

California uses the **U.S. dollar ($).** Most businesses also accept the **major credit cards** Visa, MasterCard, Discover, and American Express. ATM and debit cards work at many stores and restaurants, and ATMs are available throughout the region.

You can **change currency** at any international airport in California. Currency exchange points also crop up in downtown San Francisco and at some of the major business hotels in urban areas.

Banks and ATMs

As with anywhere, traveling with a huge amount of cash is not recommended, which may make frequent trips to the bank necessary. Fortunately, most destinations have at least one major bank. Bank of America and Wells Fargo have a large presence throughout California. **Banking hours** tend to be 8am-5pm Monday-Friday, 9am-noon Saturday. Never count on a bank being open on Sunday or on federal holidays. If you need cash when the banks are closed, there is generally a **24-hour ATM** available. Furthermore, many cash-only businesses have an ATM on-site for those who don't have enough cash ready in their wallets. The unfortunate downside to this convenience is a fee of $2-4 per transaction. This also applies to ATMs at banks at which you don't have an account.

Tax

California sales tax varies by city and county, but the base rate is 7.25 percent. All goods are taxable with the exception of food not eaten on the premises. For example, your bill at a restaurant will include tax, but your bill at a grocery store will not. The hotel tax is another unexpected added expense to traveling in California. Most cities have enacted a **hotel room tax** largely to make up for budget shortfalls. As you would expect, these taxes are higher in areas more popular with visitors.

Tipping

Tipping is expected and appreciated, and a **15 percent tip** for **restaurants** is the norm. When ordering in bars, tip the bartender or waitstaff $1 per drink. Cafés and coffee shops often have tip jars out. There is no consensus on what is appropriate when purchasing a $5 beverage.

Often $0.50 is enough, depending on the quality and service. For **taxis,** plan to tip **15-20 percent** of the fare or, for short rides, simply round up the cost to the nearest dollar.

Traveling Without Reservations

During the busy summer months, accommodations can be hard to come by. If you find yourself without reservations in one of the major cities, many online travel services (including www. hotels.com) can set you up with a last-minute room. Download the superb **HotelTonight** (www.hoteltonight.com) app on your smartphone for great last-minute deals on hotel stays.

It's not unusual for national park lodgings and campgrounds to fill during high season (usually summer). However, it may be possible to find a last-minute campsite at one of the nearby national forests. The **Stanislaus National Forest** (www.fs.usda.gov/stanislaus) and the **Sierra National Forest** (www.fs.usda.gov/sierra) both surround Yosemite and provide viable options for last-minute sites.

Communications and Media

Cell phone reception is good in most major cities. However, there are many places in Northern California where you will be unable to get a signal. Make any important calls in the bigger cities before heading into the more remote areas.

Internet access is available in most communities. The bigger cities are well wired; in small towns, you can log on either at a library or in a café with a computer in the back. Be prepared to pay a per-minute usage fee or purchase a drink.

The main newspapers in Northern California are the *San Francisco Chronicle* (www.sfchronicle.com), the *Sacramento Bee* (www.sacbee.com), and the *Santa Rosa Press Democrat* (www. pressdemocrat.com). Other regional papers may offer international news in addition to local color.

There are some news stations on the FM radio dial. In most regions, you can count on finding a **National Public Radio** (NPR, www.npr.org) affiliate. While they will all offer some NPR news coverage, some will be more geared toward music and local concerns.

Because of the area's size both geographically and in terms of population, you will have to contend with multiple **telephone area codes.** Any time you are dialing out of the area, you must dial a 1 plus the area code followed by the seven-digit number. The 800, 833, 844, 855, 866, 877, and 888 area codes are **toll-free numbers.**

To **mail** a letter, look for blue post office boxes, which are found on the main streets of any town, or a post office. Postage rates vary by destination. You can purchase stamps at the local post office, where you can also mail packages. Stamps can also be bought at some ATMs and online at www.usps.com, which can also give you the location and hours of the nearest post office. Post offices are generally open Monday-Friday, with limited hours on Saturday. They are always closed on Sunday and federal holidays.

Accessibility

Most California attractions, hotels, and restaurants are accessible for **travelers with disabilities.** State law requires that public transportation must accommodate travelers with disabilities. Public spaces and businesses must have adequate facilities with equal access. This includes national parks and historic structures, many of which have been refitted with ramps and wider doors. Many hiking trails are also accessible to wheelchairs, and most campgrounds designate specific campsites that meet the Americans with Disabilities Act standards. The state of California also provides a free telephone TDD-to-voice relay service; just dial 711.

If you are traveling with a disability, there are many resources to help you plan your trip. **Access Northern**

California (http://accessnca.org) is a nonprofit organization that offers general travel tips, including recommendations on accommodations, parks and trails, transportation, and travel equipment. **Gimp-on-the-Go** (www.gimponthego. com) is another travel resource. The message board on the **American Foundation for the Blind** (www.afb.org) website is a good forum to discuss travel strategies for the visually impaired. For a comprehensive guide to wheelchair-accessible beaches, rivers, and shorelines, contact the **California Coastal Conservancy** (510/286-1015, www.scc. ca.gov), which publishes a free and downloadable guide. **Accessible Vans** (708/536-1842, www.accessiblevans. com) in San Francisco (800/638-1912) rents wheelchair-accessible vans and offers pickup and drop-off service from airports ($100-300).

Traveling with Children

Many spots make ideal destinations for families with children. Amusement parks, interactive museums, zoos, parks, beaches, and playgrounds all make for family-friendly fun. On the other hand, there are a few spots in the Golden State that beckon more to adults than to children. Frankly, there aren't many family activities in Wine Country. This adult playground is all about alcoholic beverages and high-end dining. In fact, before you book a room at a B&B that you expect to share with your kids, check to be sure that the inn can accommodate extra people in the guest rooms and whether they allow guests under age 16.

Senior Travelers

Senior discounts are available nearly every place you go, including restaurants, golf courses, major attractions, and even some hotels. The minimum age ranges 50-65. Ask about discounts and be prepared to produce ID if you look younger than your years. You can often get additional discounts on rental cars, hotels, and tour packages as a member of **AARP** (888/687-2277, www.aarp.org). If you're not a member, its website can also offer helpful travel tips and advice.

Road Scholar (800/454-5768, www. roadscholar.org) is another great resource for senior travelers. Dedicated to providing educational opportunities for older travelers, Road Scholar (formerly Elderhostel) provides package trips to beautiful and interesting destinations. Called "Educational Adventures," these trips are generally 3-9 days long and emphasize nature, history, art, and music.

Gay and Lesbian Travelers

The Golden State is a golden place for gay travel. As with much of the country, the farther you venture into rural and agricultural regions, the less likely you are to experience liberal attitudes and acceptance. The **International Gay and Lesbian Travel Association** (www.iglta.org) has a directory of gay- and lesbian-friendly tour operators, accommodations, and destinations.

San Francisco has the biggest and arguably best **Gay Pride Festival** (www. sfpride.org) in the nation, usually held on the last weekend in June. Year-round, the **Castro District** offers fun of all kinds, from theater to clubs to shopping, mostly targeted at gay men but with a few places sprinkled in for lesbians. If the Castro is your primary destination, you can even find a place to stay in the middle of the action. Guerneville in the Russian River area of Sonoma County is a popular LGBT destination.

Health and Safety

Medical Services

For an emergency, **dial 911.** Inside hotels and resorts, check your emergency number as soon as you get to your guest room. In urban and suburban areas, full-service hospitals and medical centers abound, but in more remote regions, help can be more than an hour away.

Wilderness Safety

If you're planning a **backcountry expedition,** follow all rules and guidelines for obtaining **wilderness permits** and for self-registration at trailheads. These are for your safety, letting the rangers know roughly where you plan to be and when to expect you back. National park and state park visitors centers can advise in more detail on any health or wilderness alerts in the area. It is also advisable to let someone outside your party know your route and expected date of return.

Being out in the elements can present its own set of challenges. Despite California's relatively mild climate, **heat exhaustion** and **heatstroke** can affect anyone during the hot summer months, particularly during a long strenuous hike in the sun. Common symptoms include nausea, lightheadedness, headache, or muscle cramps. **Dehydration** and loss of electrolytes are the common causes of heat exhaustion. If you or anyone in your group develops any of these symptoms, get out of the sun immediately, stop all physical activity, and drink plenty of water. Heat exhaustion can be severe, and if untreated can lead to heatstroke, in which the body's core temperature reaches 105°F (40°C). Fainting, seizures, confusion, and rapid heartbeat and breathing can indicate the situation has moved beyond heat exhaustion. If you suspect this, call 911 immediately.

Similar precautions hold true for **hypothermia,** which is caused by prolonged exposure to cold water or weather. For many in California, this can happen on a hike or backpacking trip without sufficient rain gear, or by staying too long in the ocean or another cold body of water without a wetsuit. Symptoms include shivering, weak pulse, drowsiness, confusion, slurred speech, or stumbling. To treat hypothermia, immediately remove wet clothing, cover the person with blankets, and feed him or her hot liquids. If symptoms don't improve, call 911.

Ticks live in many of the forests and grasslands throughout California, except at higher elevations. Tick season generally runs late fall-early summer. If you are hiking through brushy areas, wear pants and long-sleeve shirts. Ticks like to crawl to warm moist places (armpits are a favorite) on their host. If a tick is engorged, it can be difficult to remove. There are two main types of ticks found in California: dog ticks and deer ticks. Dog ticks are larger, brown, and have a gold spot on their backs, while deer ticks are small, tear-shaped, and black. Deer ticks are known to carry Lyme disease. While Lyme disease is relatively rare in California, it is very serious. If you get bitten by a deer tick and the bite leaves a red ring, seek medical attention. Lyme disease can be successfully treated with early rounds of antibiotics.

There is only one major variety of plant in California that can cause an adverse reaction in humans if you touch the leaves or stems: **poison oak,** a common shrub that inhabits forests throughout the state. Poison oak has a characteristic three-leaf configuration, with scalloped leaves that are shiny green in the spring and then turn yellow, orange, and red in late summer-fall. In fall, the leaves drop, leaving a cluster of innocuous-looking branches. The oil in poison oak is present year-round in both the leaves and branches. Your best protection is to wear long sleeves and long pants when hiking, no matter how hot it is. A product called

Tecnu is available at most California drugstores; slather it on before you go hiking to protect yourself from poison oak. If your skin comes into contact with poison oak, expect a nasty rash known for its itchiness and irritation. Poison oak is also extremely transferable, so avoid touching your eyes, face, or other parts of your body to prevent spreading the rash. Calamine lotion can help, and in extreme cases a doctor can administer cortisone to help decrease the inflammation.

Wildlife

Many places are still wild in California, making it important to use precautions with regard to wildlife. While California no longer has any grizzly bears, **black bears** thrive and are often seen in the mountains foraging for food in the spring, summer, and fall. Black bears certainly don't have the size or reputation of grizzlies, but there is good reason to exercise caution. Never get between a bear and her cub, and if a bear sees you, identify yourself as human by waving your hands above your head, speaking in a calm voice, and backing away slowly. If a bear charges, do not run. One of the best precautions against an unwanted bear encounter is to keep a clean camp; store all food in airtight, bear-proof containers, and strictly follow any guidelines given by the park or rangers.

Even more common than bears are **mountain lions,** which can be found in the Coast Range as well as in grasslands and forests. Because of their solitary nature, it is unlikely you will see one, even on long trips in the backcountry. Still, there are a couple things to remember. If you come across a kill, probably a large partly eaten deer, leave immediately. And if you see a mountain lion and it sees you, identify yourself as human, making your body appear as big as possible, just as with a bear. And remember: Never run. As with any cat, large or small, running

triggers its hunting instincts. If a mountain lion should attack, fight back; cats don't like to get hurt.

The other treacherous critter in the backcountry is the **rattlesnake.** They can be found in summer in generally hot and dry areas from the coast to the Sierra Nevada. When hiking in this type of terrain (many parks will indicate if rattlesnakes are a problem in the area), keep your eyes on the ground and an ear out for the telltale rattle. Snakes like to warn you to keep away. The only time this is not the case is with baby rattlesnakes that have not yet developed their rattles. Unfortunately, they have developed their fangs and venom, which is particularly potent. Should you get bitten, get immediate medical help.

Crime

In both rural and urban areas, **theft** can be a problem. Don't leave any valuables in the car. If you must, place them out of sight, either in a locked glove box or in the trunk. Don't leave your wallet, camera, or other expensive items accessible to others, for example, in a backpack or purse. Keep them on your person at all times if possible.

Take some **basic precautions** and pay attention to your surroundings, just as you would in any unfamiliar place. Carry your car keys in your hand when walking out to your car. Don't sit in your parked car in a lonely parking lot at night; just get in, turn on the engine, and drive away. When you're walking down a city street, be alert and keep an eye on your surroundings and on anyone who might be following you. Certain **urban neighborhoods** are best avoided at night. If you find yourself in these areas after dark, call a taxi to avoid walking blocks and blocks to get to your car or waiting for public transportation. In case of a theft or any other emergency, **call 911.**

Resources

California Outdoor and Recreational Information

www.caoutdoors.com

This recreation-focused website includes links to maps, local newspapers, festivals, and events as well as a wide variety of recreational activities throughout the state.

California State Parks

www.parks.ca.gov

The official website lists hours, accessibility, activities, camping areas, fees, and more information for all parks in the state system.

Caltrans (California Department of Transportation)

www.dot.ca.gov

Check Caltrans for state map and highway information before planning a coastal road trip.

National Parks

www.nps.gov

The national park's website has lots of great information for trip planning, including an overview of park features, a write-up on trails, and the latest road conditions.

SFGate

www.sfgate.com

This website affiliated with the *San Francisco Chronicle* offers information on activities, festivals, and events.

SF Weekly

www.sfweekly.com

This website for one of San Francisco's weekly alternative papers has a strong arts and entertainment emphasis.

Visit California

www.visitcalifornia.com

Before your trip, visit the official tourism site of the state of California.

Wine Country

www.winecountry.com

This tourism website offers information on all of California's wine regions, including Napa and Sonoma.

INDEX

LIST OF MAPS

PHOTO CREDITS

Craft a personalized journey through the top national parks in the U.S. and Canada with Moon Travel Guides.

ACADIA
NATIONAL PARK

HILARY NANGLE

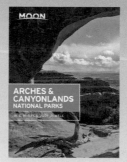

**ARCHES &
CANYONLANDS**
NATIONAL PARKS

W. C. MCRAE & JUDY JEWELL

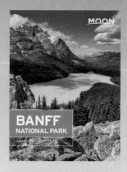

BANFF
NATIONAL PARK

ANDREW HEMPSTEAD

DEATH VALLEY
NATIONAL PARK

JENNA BLOUGH

GLACIER
NATIONAL PARK

BECKY LOMAX

**GRAND
CANYON**

KATHLEEN BRYANT

**GREAT SMOKY
MOUNTAINS**
NATIONAL PARK

JASON FRYE

**MOUNT RUSHMORE
& THE BLACK HILLS**

Including the Badlands

LAURAL A. BIDWELL

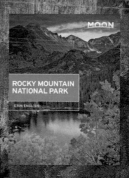

ROCKY MOUNTAIN
NATIONAL PARK

ERIN ENGLISH

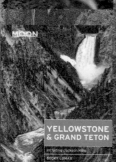

**YELLOWSTONE
& GRAND TETON**

Including Jackson Hole

BECKY LOMAX

YOSEMITE
SEQUOIA &
KINGS CANYON

ANN MARIE BROWN

**ZION &
BRYCE**

Including Arches, Canyonlands,
Capitol Reef, Grand Staircase-
Escalante & Moab

W. C. MCRAE & JUDY JEWELL

MAP SYMBOLS

≡≡≡	Expressway	○	City/Town	✈	Airport	⌊ Golf Course
≡≡	Primary Road	◉	State Capital	✗	Airfield	▣ Parking Area
—	Secondary Road	⊛	National Capital	▲	Mountain	≜ Archaeological Site
------	Unpaved Road	★	Point of Interest	✦	Unique Natural Feature	⌂ Church
—	Feature Trail	•	Accommodation			⌂ Gas Station
------	Other Trail	▼	Restaurant/Bar	⌇	Waterfall	Glacier
··········	Ferry	■	Other Location	▲	Park	Mangrove
≡≡	Pedestrian Walkway			▯	Trailhead	Reef
▥▥▥	Stairs	Λ	Campground	✗	Skiing Area	Swamp

CONVERSION TABLES

$°C = (°F - 32) / 1.8$
$°F = (°C \times 1.8) + 32$
1 inch = 2.54 centimeters (cm)
1 foot = 0.304 meters (m)
1 yard = 0.914 meters
1 mile = 1.6093 kilometers (km)
1 km = 0.6214 miles
1 fathom = 1.8288 m
1 chain = 20.1168 m
1 furlong = 201.168 m
1 acre = 0.4047 hectares
1 sq km = 100 hectares
1 sq mile = 2.59 square km
1 ounce = 28.35 grams
1 pound = 0.4536 kilograms
1 short ton = 0.90718 metric ton
1 short ton = 2,000 pounds
1 long ton = 1.016 metric tons
1 long ton = 2,240 pounds
1 metric ton = 1,000 kilograms
1 quart = 0.94635 liters
1 US gallon = 3.7854 liters
1 Imperial gallon = 4.5459 liters
1 nautical mile = 1.852 km

MOON NORTHERN CALIFORNIA ROAD TRIPS

Avalon Travel
Hachette Book Group
1700 Fourth Street
Berkeley, CA 94710, USA
www.moon.com

Editor and Series Manager: Sabrina Young
Acquiring Editor: Nikki Ioakimedes
Copy Editor: Deana Shields
Production and Graphics Coordinator:
  Suzanne Albertson
Cover Design: Erin Seaward-Hiatt
Interior Design: Darren Alessi
Moon Logo: Tim McGrath
Map Editor: Albert Angulo
Cartographers: John Culp, Andrew Dolan
  and Albert Angulo
Proofreader: Alissa Cyphers
Indexer: Greg Jewett

ISBN-13: 978-1-64049-150-2
Printing History
1st Edition — December 2019
5 4 3 2 1

Front cover photo: coastal highway view © Derek
  Gardner /Getty Images

Printed in China by RR Donnelley
Avalon Travel is a division of Hachette Book Group,
Inc. Moon and the Moon logo are trademarks of
Hachette Book Group, Inc. All other marks and
logos depicted are the property of the original
owners.